MINISTRY OF EDUCATION

15 to 18

A report of the Central Advisory Council for Education (England)

VOLUME I. REPORT

LONDON
HER MAJESTY'S STATIONERY OFFICE
1959

FOREWORD

This report deals with a reference which was given to the Central Advisory Council for Education (England) by my predecessor, Sir David Eccles, in March, 1956.

I have arranged for its immediate publication because the Council's recommendations, which cover a wide field, are of great importance and will need to be studied very carefully not only by the Government but also by the many other interests concerned, including parents.

Whatever the decisions eventually reached, I am sure that we owe a great debt of gratitude to Sir Geoffrey Crowther and his colleagues on the Council. They have dealt with a reference which raised many difficult and complicated issues with great thoroughness and they have presented their findings in a very readable and interesting report. It will, I believe, come to be accepted as well worthy to take its place in the line of distinguished reports which have had so much influence on the development of education in England and Wales.

GEOFFREY LLOYD

August, 1959.

MINISTRY OF EDUCATION

15 to 18

24th July, 1959

Dear Minister,

Your predecessor, Sir David Eccles, asked the Central Advisory Council for Education (England) in March, 1956 to advise him on the education of boys and girls between the ages of 15 and 18.

I have much pleasure in submitting our report on this subject.

Yours sincerely,

GEOFFREY CROWTHER,

(*Chairman*).

The Rt. Hon. Geoffrey Lloyd, M.P., Minister of Education

MEMBERSHIP OF THE CENTRAL ADVISORY COUNCIL

Sir Geoffrey Crowther (Chairman), Deputy Chairman, The Economist Newspaper, Ltd.

Mr. G. S. Bosworth, Chief Technical Personnel Administrator, English Electric Company, Ltd.

Mr. M. H. Brown, Headmaster, Nelson Grammar School, Lancashire.

Mr. M. H. Cadbury, Director, Cadbury Brothers, Ltd.

Alderman S. M. Caffyn, C.B.E., Former Chairman, County Borough of Eastbourne Education Committee; Joint Managing Director, Caffyns Ltd.

Mr. A. B. Clegg, Chief Education Officer, West Riding of Yorkshire.

Dr. H. Frazer, Headmaster, Gateway Boys' School, Leicester.

Mr. T. F. Gilbert, Headmaster, Ashford North Modern Boys' School, Kent.

Miss B. A. Godwin, O.B.E., Member, General Council of the Trades Union Congress, and Member of the Education Committee of the T.U.C.

Miss M. G. Green, Headmistress, Kidbrooke School, London.

Dr. V. M. Grubb, Principal, Salisbury Training College for Teachers; formerly Headmistress, Westonbirt School, Gloucestershire.

Dr. R. Holroyd, Deputy Chairman, Imperial Chemical Industries, Ltd.

Miss E. M. Huxstep, Headmistress, The County Grammar School for Girls, Chislehurst, Kent.

Lord James of Rusholme, High Master, Manchester Grammar School.

Miss A. P. Jephcott, Senior Research Officer, Social Science, London School of Economics and Political Science.

Professor A. V. Judges, Professor of the History of Education, University of London.

Mr. B. G. Lampard-Vachell, C.B.E., J.P., Chairman, Education Committee, Devon County Council; President of the Association of Education Committees, 1956–57.

Sir Patrick Linstead, C.B.E., F.R.S., Rector, Imperial College of Science and Technology, University of London.

Professor N. F. Mott, F.R.S., Master, Gonville and Caius College, and Cavendish Professor of Experimental Physics, University of Cambridge.

Mr. W. F. Oakeshott, Rector, Lincoln College, Oxford; formerly High Master, St. Paul's School, and Head Master, Winchester College.

Mr. S. H. Porter, Headmaster, Rotheram County Secondary School, Luton, Bedfordshire.

Professor S. G. Raybould, Professor of Adult Education and Director of Extra-Mural Studies, University of Leeds.

Dr. M. E. Reeves, Vice-Principal, St. Anne's College, Oxford.

Professor T. S. Simey, Charles Booth Professor of Social Science, University of Liverpool.

Mr. G. H. Sylvester, Chief Education Officer, Bristol.

Dr. P. F. R. Venables, Principal, College of Advanced Technology, Birmingham.

Mr. H. A. Warren, Principal, South-East London Technical College.

Miss E. M. Wedekind, Headmistress, Sir Humphrey Gilbert Secondary School, London.

Mr. J. V. C. Wray, formerly Education Department, Trades Union Congress.

Mr. B. W. M. Young, Head Master of Charterhouse.

Mr. D. G. O. Ayerst, H.M. Inspector of Schools (Assessor)
Mr. J. A. Humphreys (Secretary)
Miss M. L. Smith (Clerk)
} Ministry of Education

Miss C. Avent, Careers Advisory Officer, London County Council Youth Employment Service, was co-opted by the Council.

Lieutenant-General Sir Kenneth McLean, K.C.B., K.B.E. (who resigned for domestic reasons), Mr. O. W. Mitchell (who resigned for reasons of health) and the late Dr. J. Macalister Brew (who died in May, 1957), were also members during the consideration of the present terms of reference.

Note: The estimated gross cost of the preparation of Volume I is £10,654 of which £5,294 represents the estimated cost of printing and publication.

Table of Contents

Page

Part Two

The Development of the Modern School

Part Three

"Secondary Education for All"

PART FOUR

THE WAY TO COUNTY COLLEGES

PART SEVEN

INSTITUTIONS AND TEACHERS

APPENDICES

List of Tables

No. *Page*

List of Charts

Preface

1. In March, 1956, the Minister of Education asked the Council "to consider, in relation to the changing social and industrial needs of our society, and the needs of its individual citizens, the education of boys and girls between 15 and 18, and in particular to consider the balance at various levels of general and specialised studies between these ages and to examine the inter-relationship of the various stages of education".

2. In the following year we were asked by the Minister to include in this report our views on the place of examinations below the level of that for the General Certificate of Education in the education of boys and girls between 15 and 18. The correspondence between the Minister and the Chairman of the Council is given in Appendix II. The Minister's reference of this matter to this Council, and to its sister body for Wales, was made known in Circular 326.

3. Early in our deliberations it became apparent that the main obstacle to educational progress was the shortage of teachers and that the possibility of carrying out the recommendations we were likely to make would depend on a considerable expansion of the provision for training teachers. Accordingly the Chairman wrote to the Minister in February, 1958, to draw his attention to the way in which our thoughts were taking shape and to its consequences for the Ministry's training policy. This letter, with the Minister's reply, was published under the title of "The Future Demand for Teachers". At the same time the Minister was advised by the National Advisory Council on the Training and Supply of Teachers that the number of training college places was insufficient even to meet the schools' existing commitments, without any addition for further steps in policy. They proposed an addition of 16,000 places; approval was given for 12,000 in 1958, and for a further 4,000 places in June, 1959.

4. During the three years in which we have been concerned with this report other committees have been at work on tasks which have overlapped our own. Their work has materially assisted us. In particular, there has been the report on "Training for Skill" of the Sub-Committee of the Minister of Labour's National Joint Advisory Council under the Chairmanship of Mr. Robert Carr, M.P., published in 1958. This report dealt specifically with the problem of apprenticeship during the period when there is a large temporary increase in the size of the age-groups entering employment. It has resulted in the establishment of the Industrial Training Council. At the end of the same year came the report of the Committee on

Further Education for Agriculture Provided by Local Education Authorities under Lord De La Warr which recommended substantial changes in the position of Farm Institutes and the transfer of the Minister of Agriculture's responsibilities for them to the Minister of Education. Early this year an Advisory Committee of the National Advisory Council on Education for Industry and Commerce, under the Chairmanship of Mr. J. G. McMeeking, reported on further education for commerce. The Minister has also recently appointed a National Advisory Council on Art Education whose first Chairman is Sir William Coldstream. We have therefore not thought it necessary to go at all deeply into the last three subjects. In 1958 the Minister appointed a special committee under Lady Albemarle to consider priorities in the Youth Service. Its report is expected shortly, and we have devoted less attention to this aspect of the problem than we would otherwise have done. A special committee under Sir Colin Anderson is reviewing the system of grants to university students; we have accordingly only touched in passing on this aspect of the relation of the universities to the schools. In addition, the Secondary School Examinations Council appointed in 1958 a sub-committee to consider the question of examinations other than for the General Certificate of Education, which is discussed in Chapter 8 of this report. It has not yet reported.

5. The years covered in the Council's terms of reference are those which immediately follow the end of compulsory school life. We are concerned quite as much with the needs of those who at that point lose all contact with the educational services as with the different problems of those who are still at school or receiving some form of part-time education. This alone would have made it necessary to seek information from sources other than the official statistics of public education. The Council, therefore, decided to invite the co-operation of other bodies in three fact-finding investigations. These are fully described in the second volume of the report, and it will be sufficient here to describe their main characteristics. The first investigation was undertaken by the Social Survey Division of the Central Office of Information. Interviews were held in the spring of 1957 with a representative cross-section of boys and girls who had left school about two years earlier, and with their parents. This was the only one of the three enquiries which covered any substantial number of girls—indeed, it provided virtually the only statistical information available to us about girls after they had left school. It is referred to throughout our report as the Social Survey. A second investigation was carried out by interview of a representative cross-section of recruits joining the Army in 1956–57 and the Royal Air Force in 1957–58. We are deeply indebted to the War Office and the

Air Ministry for making these enquiries possible. They covered a good deal of the same ground as the Social Survey, but, alone among the sources available to us, they provided an ability assessment in the form of intelligence tests for each man interviewed. The third investigation, based on a representative cross-section of students following certain courses in technical colleges in 1956 and 1958 was designed to elicit the facts about success and failure rates in National Certificate courses and in certain City and Guilds of London Institute courses. (The former deal with qualifications mainly for technicians or, in the later stages, for technologists; the latter for craftsmen.) The National Certificate students completed a questionnaire giving a great deal of background information, which has thrown much light on factors associated with success and failure. The information about the students in the City and Guilds courses was derived solely from the college records. It establishes what happens to them in the examinations, but it does not give much background information. We wish to record our gratitude to the principals and staffs of technical colleges for all the trouble they have taken.

6. The Council is concerned with England only—it is perhaps the only secular statutory body which is based on a recognition of the separate national entity of England—and the three investigations referred to in the last paragraph dealt mainly with this country. In our use of public statistics, however, we have usually given figures which refer to England and Wales; exceptions are noted as they occur. There are two other ambiguities which it may be well to refer to here. First, it is sometimes important to discuss boys and girls separately, but there are many occasions on which we are concerned equally with both. Here we have usually used a neutral noun—such as pupil or student—but a masculine pronoun. The context should make it clear whether the reference is to boys or to both sexes. Secondly the phrase "15 to 18" can be read as meaning either three or four age-groups, and is used in this report sometimes in one sense, sometimes in the other. We hope that the context will make it clear which is intended, but in general our concern is with young people up to the end of the year in which they are 18—that is, for four full years after the 15th birthday. We have not thought it necessary to make any review of the provision for "educationally sub-normal" boys and girls and for others requiring special treatment.

7. We have taken as our main task an appreciation of the needs and possibilities of the educational system in the ten years after 1965. We have, however, made a number of specific suggestions about the next five years. Our report is divided into seven parts. In Part One

we are concerned to paint the broad educational picture, and to give the background to what follows. We are dealing here with the "changing social and industrial needs" of our terms of reference. The next three parts are all concerned with different aspects of the educational provision made for the great majority of English children who do not go to selective schools. Part Two is entitled "The Development of the Modern School" and is chiefly concerned with the development in recent years of "extended courses", beyond the statutory leaving age, in these schools. In this context we make certain recommendations about external examinations. Part Three, entitled "Secondary Education for All", is concerned with those who leave school at 15 or thereabouts, and sets out at length the case for extending the period of compulsory full-time attendance to 16. We propose that this should be done somewhere between 1966 and 1968. Part Four turns to the other suspended provision of the Act of 1944, that there should be compulsory part-time attendance at county colleges up to the age of 18 for all who have left school before then. We recommend a progressive sequence of development, which would reach its final stage of compulsory part-time day education at some time in the 1970's.

8. Part Five is called "The Sixth Form". It contains an assessment of the forces which are causing the remarkable development of Sixth Forms since the war and a consideration of the closely interwoven problems of specialisation and university entrance. We are anxious to see both a retention of the English system of education in depth (specialisation), and also a much greater attention paid to the use of that time in school which is devoted to other than specialist subjects. The unsatisfactory elements in the present situation seem to us to arise fundamentally from one cause: the fact that the demand for education after 18 (and especially the competition for places at the universities of Oxford, Cambridge and London) exceeds the supply. While we make suggestions for easing the pressures in the schools, we do not believe that they can be removed until there is a better balance between the supply of places in higher education and the demand for them.

9. Part Six has a double purpose. In so far as it is descriptive, it is concerned very largely with that section of boys (there are very few girls) who, having left school and entered a career, pursue a part-time education designed in close relation to the needs of their employment. A number of matters are discussed which might improve the working of this system and extend its application. We also suggest certain principles that should guide the future development of this section of the nation's educational provision.

10. Part Seven deals with two topics which, we have found, run right through all our deliberations. One of these is the institutional framework, the organisation and pattern of schools and other places where education is carried on. The other is the vital question of the number and quality of the teachers who staff these institutions. Special aspects of these two questions are dealt with as they arise in Parts Two to Six, but they are both too pervasive to be confined within any one of these parts.

11. In attempting to deal with so vast a field we have had to exclude much that is of importance. We have confined ourselves very largely to such broad questions as the balance of the curriculum and the degree of specialisation without going into problems of teaching method or of the claims of individual subjects for inclusion. We have not indeed been able to discuss any one subject of the curriculum in detail. If we had felt able to make any exceptions to this it would have been in favour of some discussion of the teaching of English and of Mathematics, which seem to us to be the key subjects. We cannot help but be disturbed both by the mediocre standards of spoken and written English among children leaving our schools and by the low standards in the field of mathematics which are (so it seems to us) wrongly accepted as inevitable for far too many pupils.

12. We have attempted throughout the report to write for the general public, whose rising interest in all educational matters is one of the most encouraging developments of recent years. Education, however, like all other subjects, is full of special terms, and many ordinary words are defined by educational experts in ways peculiar to themselves. To have attempted to avoid all these special words and meanings would have forced us into many circumlocutions. We have therefore not made any such attempt. Indeed, we may have invented one or two special words of our own. To assist the reader, we have therefore appended a glossary.

Part One

Education in a Changing World

CHAPTER 1

Sixty Years of Growth

13. This report is about the education of English boys and girls aged from 15 to 18. Most of them are not being educated. But they are all at a highly impressionable age, with their characters still being formed and, except in rare instances, with their minds still capable of considerable development. It seems to us clear—to anticipate our conclusions—that it is both necessary and practicable greatly to extend in the next few years the provision made for the education of boys and girls in their later teens. Looked at from where we are now, the prospect may seem daunting—there is so much to be done. Looked at, however, in the light of the distance that we as a nation have come in the last hundred years, the prospect is surely encouraging. Each step forward, which seemed so difficult at the time and to many so intolerably expensive, has quickly been found to have justified itself and indeed to have paid for itself. We could not as a nation enjoy the standard of living we have today on the education we gave our children a hundred or even fifty years ago. If we are to build a higher standard of living—and, what is more important, if we are to have higher standards in life—we shall need a firmer educational base than we have today. Materially and morally, we are compelled to go forward.

THE NUMBERS OF PUPILS

14. In this report we shall often be concerned with percentages. It is well to start with actual numbers. This year (1959) there are in England and Wales 1,771,000 boys and girls who have passed their 15th birthday but not yet reached their 18th, and another 547,000 aged 18. In the total of 2,318,000 (for the four age-groups), the boys outnumber the girls by 44,000. The last decade has been a period of relative stability, between a sustained fall in the numbers in the 1930's and the early 1940's and a rise that is already beginning. In 1965, the peak year, there will be about 700,000 more boys and girls aged 15 to 18 inclusive than there are now, bringing the number to over 3,000,000. The position is shown in Chart 1. This remarkable prospective increase of 30 per cent in the four age-groups combined, or of 35 per cent if we compare the 17 year-olds of this year (1959) with the 17 year-olds of 1965, is, of course, the result of the large

CHART NO. 1

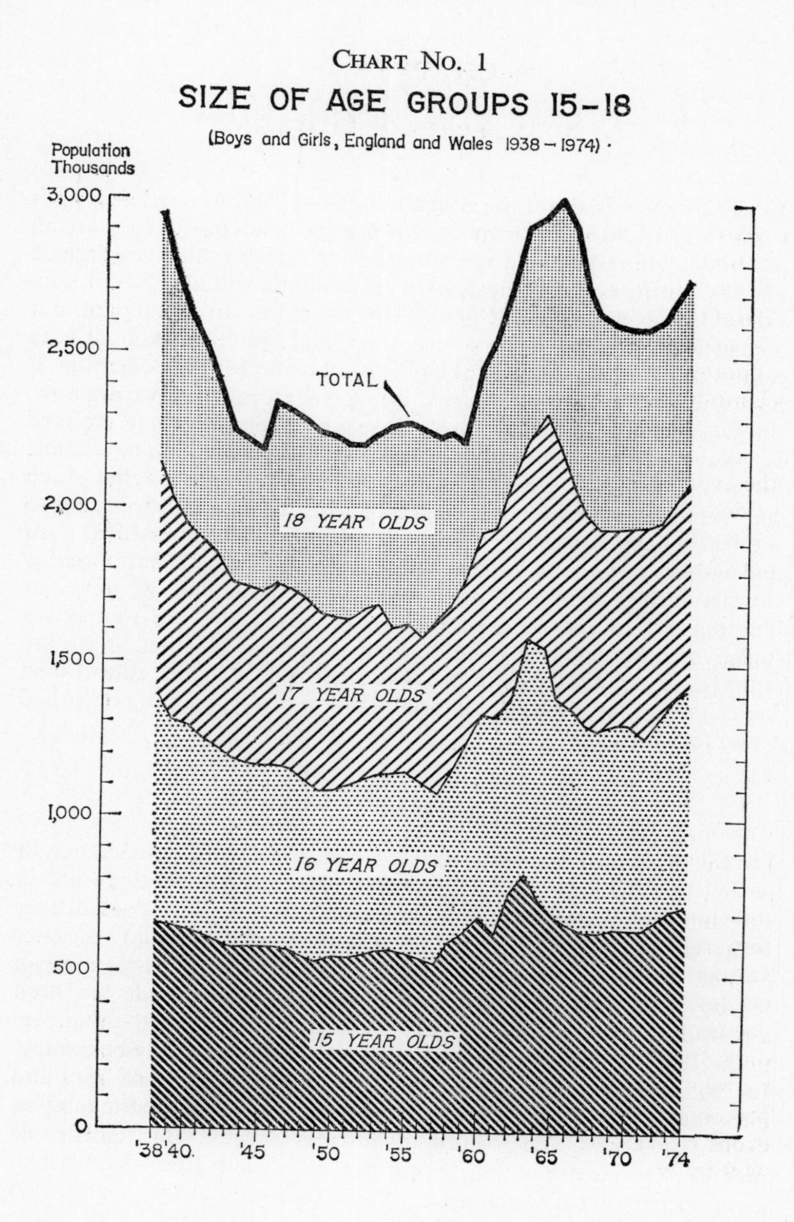
SIZE OF AGE GROUPS 15-18
(Boys and Girls, England and Wales 1938 – 1974)
Population Thousands
3,000
2,500
2,000
1,500
1,000
500
0
TOTAL
18 YEAR OLDS
17 YEAR OLDS
16 YEAR OLDS
15 YEAR OLDS
'38
'40
'45
'50
'55
'60
'65
'70
'74

rise in the birth-rate in the years immediately after the war. Educationalists and parents have long worried over the "bulge", as it has come to be called. The passage of this tidal wave through the primary schools has been marked by protests against over-large classes; its course through the narrows of the "11-plus" has largely increased public clamour against a competitive element in grammar school selection, which seems to parents to be contrary to the promise of secondary education according only to "age, aptitude and ability". By the time the wave reaches and passes through the juvenile employment market, it would be rash to believe that its force will have become exhausted. There are, indeed, already in some parts complaints of a lack of apprenticeships and of other opportunities for training, which are the successors of the earlier clamour against the lack of grammar school places. We write our report, then, in a moment of relative calm—when, for instance, there are fewer 17 year-olds than at any time since the war—but on the eve of a great flood. When it is past there will be another easier period, but it too will not endure. The number of children born in 1958 was greater than in any year since 1948, and has been exceeded only three times in two decades. There will be another bulge of 17 year-olds in the middle 1970's.

15. The one and three-quarter million boys and girls aged 15–17 inclusive would all be receiving either full-time or part-time day education if the Act of 1944 had been fully put into effect by raising the school-leaving age and introducing county colleges. How many of them are getting one or the other? The position is shown in Table 1. In the latest year for which complete figures are available (1957-58) some 674,000, about two-fifths, got either full-time or part-time day education at these ages. In full-time education there is virtually no difference in number between boys and girls—a quarter of each (25·5 and 24·7 per cent respectively) are either at school or full-time students in colleges of further education. But when we turn to part-time day education, the picture is entirely different for boys and girls. There are very nearly as many boys in part-time day classes as in full-time education during these years, but only 5 to 6 per cent of the girls get part-time day release. In total, therefore, only 31 per cent of all girls are accounted for during these years. If we separate the three years, we find, naturally enough, that the percentage receiving part-time day education or full-time education drops year by year—for boys from 56 to 46·6 to 37·6; for girls from 44·9 to 29·1 to 16·8.

16. In our report we shall be concerned in turn with three groups—those who are getting full-time education (25 per cent of the boys and girls in the three age-groups), those who are getting part-time

Table 1. Proportion of Total Age Groups in Different Kinds of Education, 1957–58 (England and Wales)

Education	BOYS 15	16	17	15–17	18	GIRLS 15	16	17	15–17	18
	per cent	per cent	per cent	per cent	per cent	per cent	per cent	per cent	per cent	per cent
Full-time at school	*37·4*	*20·0*	*11·1*	*23·4*	*4·5*	*35·7*	*18·5*	*8·8*	*21·5*	*2·3*
Full-time in further education	*2·4*	*2·1*	*1·9*	*2·1*	*3·3*	*4·0*	*3·5*	*2·0*	*3·2*	*3·1*
All full-time education	*39·8*	*22·1*	*13·0*	*25·5*	*7·8*	*39·7*	*22·0*	*10·8*	*24·7*	*5·4*
Part-time day	*16·2*	*24·5*	*24·6*	*21·6*	*18·1*	*5·2*	*7·1*	*6·0*	*6·0*	*2·2*
Full-time and part-time day	*56·0*	*46·6*	*37·6*	*47·1*	*25·9*	*44·9*	*29·1*	*16·8*	*30·7*	*7·6*
Evening	*24·5*	*25·3*	*23·8*	*24·5*	*17·8*	*23·1*	*23·7*	*20·3*	*22·4*	*14·9*
None	*19·5*	*28·1*	*38·6*	*28·4*	*56·3*	*32·0*	*47·2*	*62·9*	*46·9*	*77·5*
Total (thousands) = 100 per cent	309	272	277	858	289	295	263	269	827	283

NOTES: 1. 1957/58 figures are not yet available for universities and the 1956/57 figures have been used. This affects only those aged 18 and the appropriate percentage should not differ by more than 0·1 per cent.
2. No figures are available for those in attendance at private commercial establishments.

day education (22 per cent of the boys and 6 per cent of the girls) and those without either. The third group may be sub-divided into those who are pursuing a serious educational course by evening classes or through correspondence colleges, and those who take little or no part in any educational activity. The position is shown in Chart 2. We shall not only be concerned with the internal characteristics of each group, for our object is to find ways of increasing the size of the first and reducing the number in the third.

WHO GETS FULL-TIME EDUCATION?

17. This all-important group of full-time pupils has four characteristics which are worth bearing in mind. The first is the fact that, as far as numbers go, there is no distinction to be drawn between boys and girls—the proportions of each in full-time education between 15 and 18 are very nearly the same. Moreover, if the individual years are examined separately, the record for the first two years is closely similar; it is not until 17 and 18 that the boys begin materially to outnumber the girls.

18. The second characteristic is the extent to which social background enters into the decision about which boys and girls will continue in full-time education beyond the minimum leaving age. This was

CHART No. 2

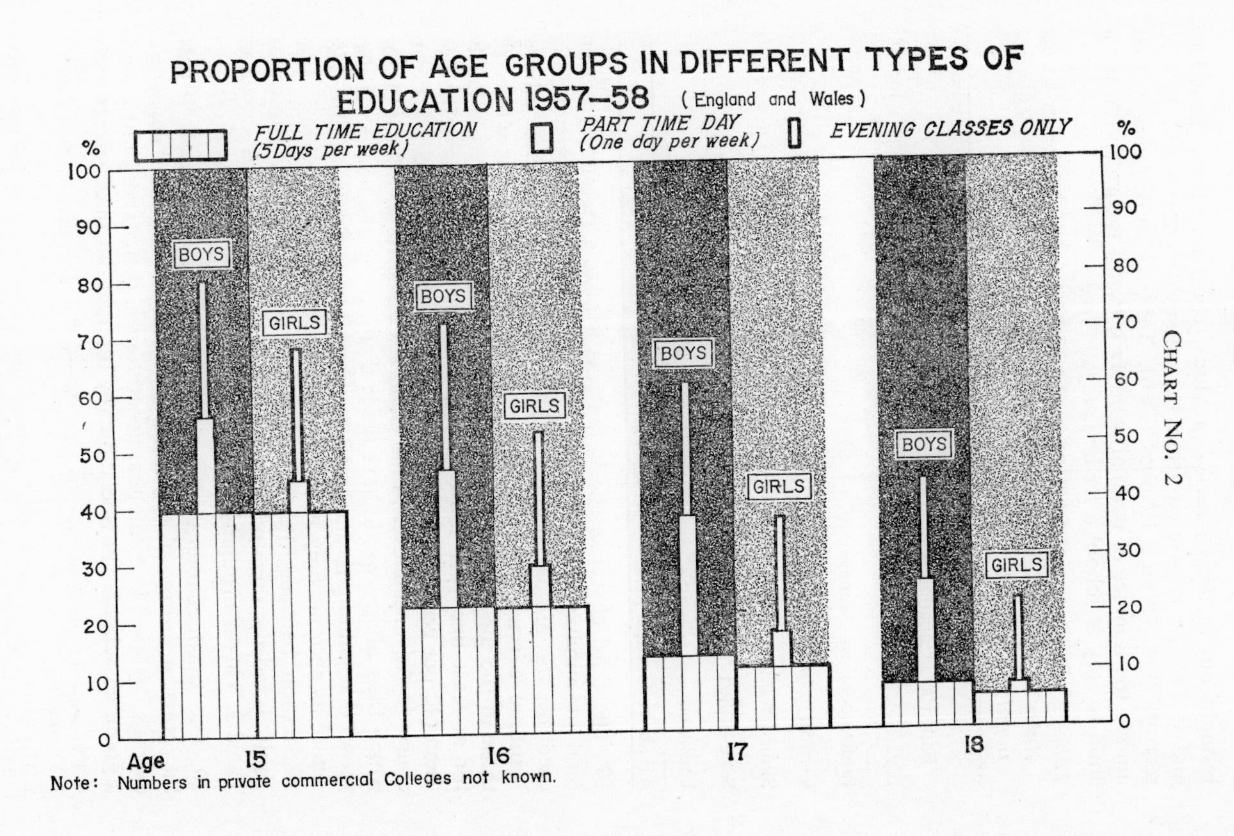
PROPORTION OF AGE GROUPS IN DIFFERENT TYPES OF EDUCATION 1957–58
(England and Wales)
FULL TIME EDUCATION (5 Days per week)
PART TIME DAY (One day per week)
EVENING CLASSES ONLY
BOYS
GIRLS
%
100
90
80
70
60
50
40
30
20
10
0
Age
15
16
17
18
Note: Numbers in private commercial Colleges not known.

brought out in the Council's previous report on "Early Leaving" and is further illustrated from the survey of Army and R.A.F. recruits (see Volume II, Part Two). Table 2 shows clearly that among the families of manual workers it is still the exception for a child to stay at school after he is legally free to go.

Table 2. Percentage Distribution of National Service Recruits to the Army and R.A.F. by Age on Leaving School and Father's Occupational Background.

Father's Occupation	Number = 100 per cent	Recruit's age on leaving school			
		15 or less	16	17	18 or more
		per cent	per cent	per cent	per cent
Professional or Managerial	929	*25*	*24*	*17*	*34*
Clerical or other non-manual	882	*59*	*22*	*9*	*10*
Skilled Workers	3,666	*78*	*15*	*3*	*4*
Semi-skilled	946	*85*	*11*	*2*	*2*
Unskilled	852	*92*	*6*	*1*	*1*
All above Groups	7,275	*72*	*15*	*5*	*8*

19. The third characteristic is that the available resources of men (and presumably also of women) of high "ability"* are not fully used by the present system. Table 3 makes it clear that, among National Service men entering the Army, while nine-tenths of those in the top 10 per cent in ability† stayed at school voluntarily for at least one year more than they had to, over four-tenths of them (42 per cent) left by 16 and did not attempt the Sixth Form course to Advanced level in the General Certificate of Education for which their ability would have made them strong candidates. It also shows that, among the next ability group very nearly two-thirds left school as soon as they were allowed to. Of course, there is a close association between the facts of under-utilised ability shown in Table 3 and the facts of under-represented social groups shown in Table 2. This is brought out in Table 4.

20. The fourth characteristic, at least in maintained schools, is that the great majority of boys and girls whose full-time education extends beyond 15 are the first generation in their families to attend a grammar school. The Social Survey brought out the fact that both

* The sense in which we use the term "ability" is discussed in Part Two of Volume II.

† The Army measure of "ability" groups is based on a battery of five tests given to recruits on joining for duty, and expressed in terms of percentage groups. Ideally 1 and 6 each represent a tenth, and the remainder each a fifth, of the army population. Group 1 is the most intelligent tenth.

Table 3. Percentage Distribution of "Ability" among 5,940 National Service Recruits to the Army who left School at various Ages.

Ability Groups	Number = 100 per cent	School-leaving age 15 or less	16	17	18 or more
		per cent	per cent	per cent	per cent
1 (highest)	681	*9*	*33*	*17*	*41*
2	1,824	*65*	*22*	*6*	*7*
3	1,014	*94*	*4*	*1*	*1*
4	1,184	*98*	*2*	*Tce*	*Tce*
5	863	*98*	*1*	—	*1*
6 (lowest)	374	*97*	*3*	*Tce*	*Tce*
All Groups	5,940	*77*	*12*	*4*	*7*

Tce=trace, less than 0·5 per cent.

Table 4. School-leaving Age for (*a*) *All Men in Ability Groups 1 and 2 and* (*b*) *Sons of Manual Workers* (*except in Agriculture*).

	Number = 100 per cent	School-leaving age 15 or earlier	16	17	18 or later
		per cent	per cent	per cent	per cent
All men in Ability Group 1	681	*9*	*33*	*17*	*41*
Manual Workers' sons in Ability Group 1	295	*19*	44	*13*	24
All men in Ability Group 2	1,824	*65*	22	*6*	7
Manual Workers' sons in Ability Group 2	1,286	*75*	20	*3*	2

parents of two-thirds of the boys and girls who attended selective schools (grammar schools and technical schools) themselves left school at 14, which was in their day the legal minimum leaving-age. Only 12 per cent of the boys and girls came from homes where both parents had had a longer education than the legal minimum. This is a measure both of the task that confronts English schools at the present, and of the promise that lies ahead of them. The Social Survey results confirm the natural expectation that parents who have had more than the minimum education rarely allow their children to do with less than they themselves had. Only 8 per cent of the fathers who had themselves stayed at school after 14 allowed their sons or daughters to leave as soon as they were legally free to do so; no less than 40 per cent of them kept their children at school until the age of 18. When, therefore, the schools receive a large influx of second-generation grammar pupils in the later 1960's and early 1970's, it may be expected that the proportion staying on beyond the statutory minimum age will sharply rise.

21. It is, of course, the national picture that we have been drawing. To some it will seem too bright, to others unduly pessimistic, for there are considerable regional variations as well as sharper local ones. In the north-east, for example, voluntary staying on in full-time education for an extra year is in the neighbourhood of 16 or 17 per cent of the age-group and in East Anglia 18 per cent; but in large parts of the south it is about 25 per cent and of the south-west 28 per cent.* These variations reflect, we believe, the local employment pattern and the scale of educational provision, but not the needs of the children.

22. A word should be added on some of the characteristics of the part-time day system which it is well to keep in mind. First, it is almost entirely a privilege granted by employers to their employees. There is little part-time day education for young people that does not come out of paid working hours. Secondly, a day off a week to attend a technical college is granted in the main, but not exclusively, to skilled workers in training—it is granted because there is an economic advantage to the employers as well as to the employee; the general purposes of education play a relatively small part. Thirdly, not only is it given almost exclusively to boys and not to girls, but to boys only in a restricted range of industries.

HISTORICAL RETROSPECT

23. This, then, in briefest outline, is the picture in the middle of the twentieth century. Schools and the opportunities of attending them, are, however, changing so rapidly that it is necessary to form some idea of the rate and direction of development if a study of the present is to help us to shape the future. It may be helpful to look back on what has happened in the life-time of a man who is now about to retire at the age of 65. When he was born, there were two main ways by which a boy was likely to get to a university. One was through one of the independent public schools which the Victorians had either created—like Clifton or Cheltenham—or adapted out of older foundations originally designed to serve rather different ends, like Rugby or Harrow. The other way was by one of the endowed grammar schools which had remained day schools, usually serving a local community. The Bryce Commission on Secondary Education found that over half of the 4,200 undergraduates of Oxford and Cambridge in 1894 came from the 89 schools represented on the

* The calculation is made by taking the 15 and 16 year-olds in school or full-time further education as a percentage of the 13 and 14 year-olds who had been in school two years before.

Headmasters' Conference, but 17 per cent came from other schools in England and nearly as many from private study or home tuition. Two per cent only came from the ranks of pupil teachers, teachers' training colleges or public elementary schools. The door was not closed on a poor boy of talent, but it was not open very far. Jude was still likely to remain obscure.

24. How much better were the chances in 1894 of getting a secondary education than a university education? It would be wrong to picture the endowed grammar schools of England at that time as upper class or middle class preserves to which a mere handful of elementary school boys were admitted. The Bryce Commission had careful surveys made in 1894 of the whole extent of secondary provision in seven counties which between them contained 30 per cent of the population. A quarter of the pupils in all the secondary schools (excluding only those schools in which the headmaster was the proprietor) had formerly attended elementary schools. The range of variation, of course, was very wide—some schools admitted none, while in others "about all," or 75 or 80 per cent, came from elementary schools. When the endowed grammar schools were taken as a class, the justifiable complaint was not that they were socially exclusive, but that there were not nearly enough of them, so that only about 4 or 5 pupils per 1,000 in the elementary schools were able to pass to the grammar schools, a figure which may be contrasted with the 200 per 1,000 for whom there are grammar school places to-day. To some extent this shortage was offset by the growth of "higher grade" elementary schools, whose work may be very roughly compared with the "extended courses" in secondary modern schools with which we shall be much concerned in Part Two of our report. They provided a way to secondary, and sometimes to higher, education for boys and girls who would otherwise have been deprived of it. (At least one Nobel Prizewinner was a pupil in a higher grade elementary school). In the seven counties, 4 per cent of all boys and girls aged 14 or 15 were in school and 1 per cent of those aged 16 and 17. It is only necessary to remember that among the professional classes it was already the practice for boys and girls to stay at school at least until 16, and often to 18, to realise how small was the chance of a working man's child, especially a daughter, learning at school more than the traditional 3 R's. It would appear that less than one-third of all pupils aged 14 or over were girls; by 1921 the numbers were equal.

25. This was the position when a man now retiring at 65 was born. The years of his boyhood were years of great advance in secondary education under the Act of 1902, which virtually created out of the old endowed schools and the new municipal secondary schools the

grammar school element in the present national system of secondary education. By 1911, when the generation of 1894 was aged 17, the proportion of the population which was receiving full-time education between 14 and 18 was certainly twice what it had been at the time of their birth. The 1911 census and enquiries made then by the Board of Education* show that about 8 per cent of the 14 and 15 year-olds and 2 per cent of the 16 and 17 year-olds were receiving education in institutions either publicly provided or recognised by the Board of Education (see Chart 3). This was the extent to which the generation which fought the first world war had received an education extending beyond the minimum age of 14. The sons of the generation of 1894—the young men of the second world war—had a much better chance of a longer education. By 1938 there were roughly six times as many pupils over the age of 14 as there had been in 1894. It was the development of the new secondary schools of the 1902 Act which had made it possible for England to keep pace with the growing technical demands of our civilisation. Extensions of secondary education were paralleled, and to some extent made possible, by extensions of elementary education, both on a compulsory and on a voluntary basis. The nominal school-leaving age had been 14 ever since 1876, but a system of exemptions during the latter years of school life made this largely ineffective. It was not until 1918 that full-time education until 14 became binding on everybody. Extensions of compulsion were preceded by greater voluntary use of the schools. Thus in 1895 a third of the children aged 12 were still in school. In 1911 it is probable that about half the children stayed at school until they were actually 14—that at least was the view of the Departmental Committee of 1916. But many elementary school pupils' desire for education extended beyond 14. It was soon clear that the 1902 Act with its secondary schools could not meet the full demand, and by 1911 new central schools, part of the elementary provision, had been established to take up the work of the higher grade schools. These two processes—the extension of compulsion to round off a practice already well established, and the reflection of a higher compulsory age in an increased voluntary attendance over the age of compulsion—have been characteristic of English education throughout the century and a quarter in which it has been a national concern, and especially of the 90 years since the Forster Act. We believe that they are still operative and mark out the way for the further progress in education to which the bulk of our report is directed.

26. How new is the system of part-time day education—that is, the release of boys and girls by their employers for one day's instruction

* Quoted in the report of the Departmental Committee on "Juvenile Education in Relation to Employment after the war" (1916).

CHART No. 3

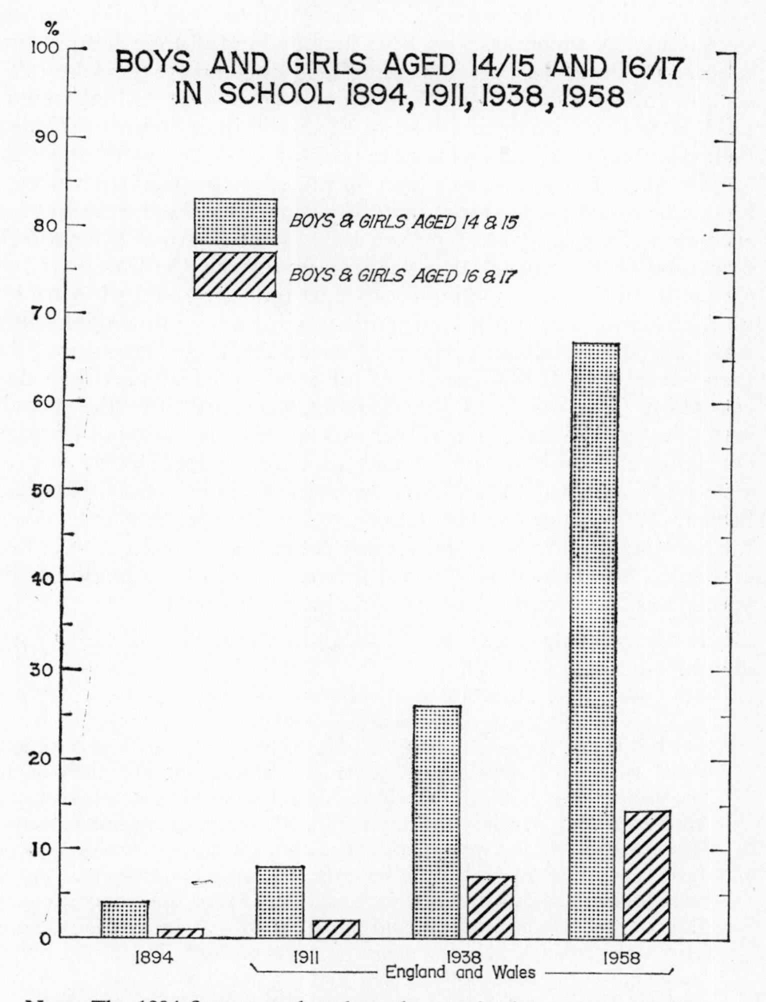

NOTE: The 1894 figures are based on the enquiry into seven counties made for the Bryce Commission: those for 1911 on the estimate of the Departmental Committee of 1916. The figures for 1938 and 1958 are drawn from the Annual Report of the Ministry of Education. The figures for different years are not therefore strictly comparable, but the general picture will not be affected.

a week? The Factory Bills and Acts of the 1840's contained clauses providing for some education to be given to children employed in industry, but they were largely ineffective and the children concerned were of an age which has long been included in full-time compulsory education. The earliest known examples in England are the Admiralty schools for dockyard apprentices which were started as long ago as 1843. A few private firms (some of them still in existence) provided their own technical schools for the training of skilled workers in the 1870's, and day release has been given even to unskilled workers by one or two firms for more than fifty years. But these were and are exceptions. In spite of the report in 1909 by the Board of Education's Consultative Committee, the predecessor of the Central Advisory Councils, in favour of compulsory part-time day education to 17, on the basis of local option, progress was for a long time deplorably slow. Part-time education virtually meant evening classes—in 1911 there were only 45,000 people of all ages who had part-time day education. This remained substantially true until after the second war—the provisions of the Fisher Act of 1918 for compulsory day continuation schools soon became in effect a dead letter, and in 1938 there were only 6,000 more day release students than there had been in 1911. Since the last war there has been a great expansion, but very largely for boys and almost entirely for training for skilled craftsmen or technicians. No real impression has been made on the young unskilled workers or on girls in employment.

27. It seems fitting in conclusion to quote the report of the Departmental Committee of 1916:

> "No doubt . . . education and, still more, industrial training, are not confined within the four walls of a school; there is a discipline of the workshop and the office as well as of the classroom. Can it be assumed, then, that the conditions of juvenile employment are such as in themselves, and without the aid of formal schooling, to establish the character and develop the industrial efficiency of young citizens? The question is one we cannot ask without a sense of irony, and its answer is written large in the records of former enquiries and in the sociological literature of the last decade. More than once already the country has gaped at it and passed it by . . . In a sense there is only one remedy . . . *porro unum est necessarium**. But it is a pretty thorough-going one, nothing less than a complete change of temper and outlook on the part of the people of this country as to what they mean, through the forces of industry and society, to make of their boys and girls. Can the age of adolescence be brought out of the purview of exploitation and into that of the social conscience? Can the conception of the juvenile as primarily a little wage-earner be replaced by the conception of the juvenile as primarily the workman and the citizen in training? Can it be established that the educational purpose is to be the dominating one, without as well as within the

*S. Luke X. 42.

school doors, during those formative years between 12 and 18? If not, clearly no remedies at all are possible in the absence of the will by which alone they could be rendered effective."

Between 12 and 18 there are six years. Since 1916 society has used its will to halve the problem by removing 12, 13 and 14-year olds entirely from the labour market. It has only nibbled at the other half of the problem. What should be done to solve it is the theme of Parts Two, Three and Four of our report.

CHAPTER 2

The Pattern of Secondary Education

28. Our terms of reference allow us the same sort of partial view of secondary education as the mariner gets of an iceberg. Most of the iceberg is hidden under the sea; most of secondary education has taken place before boys and girls reach 15. There are over 2,550,000 boys and girls in maintained secondary schools; about 320,000 of them are aged 15 or above. A boy's or a girl's place in secondary education is determined (with relatively few exceptions) by a decision taken when he or she is 11. We are not in this report concerned either with the general pattern of secondary education, or with the problems of allocation; but it is necessary to be aware of what has occurred before 15 if one is to understand what happens afterwards. Equally, what we have found out about boys and girls of 15 and over throws a good deal of light on the kind of provision that ought to be made for them in earlier years if a great deal of good human material is not to be wasted. The purpose of this chapter is to describe the general public provision for educating boys and girls from the age of 11 onwards as it existed before the war and to describe the revolutionary changes in it that have been made during this generation's lifetime.

1938 AND 1958

29. The first step is to set out the main types of publicly maintained school in 1938 and 1958 and the numbers in each type at both dates. Names have changed, but in Table 5, as nearly as possible, like is matched with like. The 1958 position is set out in Chart No. 4.

Table 5. Organisation of Maintained Secondary Education, 1938 and 1958 (England and Wales).*

1938

Type of School	Number of Schools	Number of Pupils	
		11–14	15–18
1. All-age or all-standard	12,778	737,121	1,976
2. Senior Elementary†	3,074	804,580	14,157
3. Secondary schools on Grant List	1,398	294,788	145,332
4. Junior Technical etc. schools	271	18,601	12,915
	17,521	1,855,090	174,380
		2,029,470	

For Notes to the Table see next page.

Table 5 (continued)
1958

Type of School	Number of Schools	Number of Pupils	
		11–14	15–18
1. All-age	2,297	120,189††	723
2. Secondary modern and other secondary†	3,890	1,499,183	49,800
3. Grammar including Direct Grant	1,414	452,652	229,324
4. Secondary Technical	279	67,681	27,513
5. Comprehensive**	86	63,666	11,384
6. Bilateral and Multilateral	54	29,614	3,133
	8,020	2,232,985	321,877
		2,554,862	

NOTES TO TABLE 5.

* The table omits independent schools, owing to lack of information for 1938, when there were far fewer "recognised efficient" schools, and no information about unrecognised schools. Special schools are also omitted.

** The figure for comprehensive schools is misleading for England, because they play a far more than arithmetically proportionate part in Wales, where there are 25 schools and 13,000 pupils.

† These headings include a number of "selective central" or "intermediate" schools, for which entry is selective. In 1958, there were rather under 200 of these schools, accounting for about 23 per cent of the total of pupils aged 15 or over in secondary modern schools.

†† This figure is for ages 12–14 inclusive; the 52,679 11 year-olds in all-age schools cannot be accurately apportioned between junior and senior.

It is at once apparent that there are two types of school today that had no pre-war counterpart. Bilateral and comprehensive schools are described in paragraphs 36–38. The other four main types were already in existence before the war, but they did not then form one system as they do today. The predecessors of the present all-age and modern schools were administered under the Elementary Code, many of them in the smaller boroughs and the urban districts by local education authorities which had no responsibility for secondary education. The predecessors of the present grammar schools were administered under the grant regulations for secondary schools by the county councils and county borough councils as the local education authorities for higher education. The predecessors of the present technical schools were administered under the regulations for further education. There is today only one type of local education authority, and there is no distinction in the regulations under which modern, grammar and technical schools are administered. All-age schools, which contain pupils from 5 or 8 up to the end of compulsory school life, are officially classified as primary schools.

CHART NO. 4

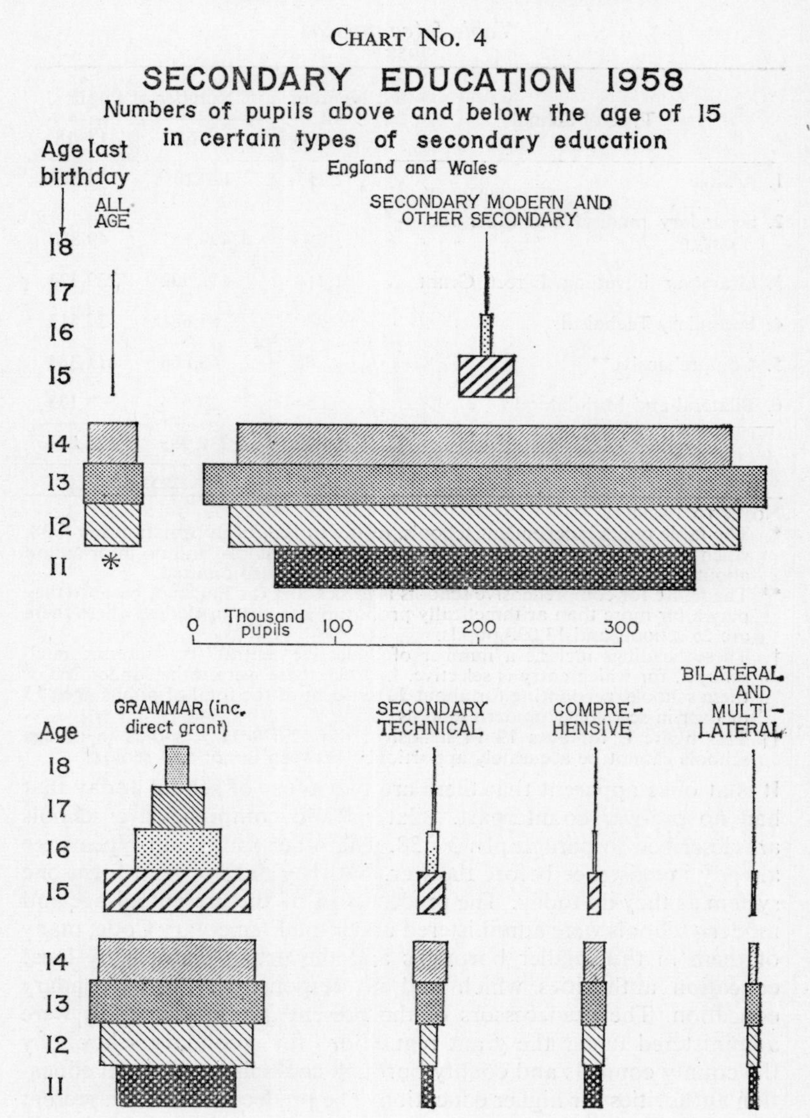

NOTE: Comprehensive, Bilateral and Multilateral Schools are designed to serve the whole age range 15–18, but few of them have been in existence long enough to have many pupils over the age of 15.

* The eleven year olds in All Age Schools are excluded since they include a proportion who are not senior pupils.

30. All-age schools, which, it is hoped, will have very largely disappeared by the mid 1960's, are the vestigial remains of the pre-Hadow system of organisation of elementary education. The Hadow report on the Education of the Adolescent, issued in 1926, recommended the establishment of separate senior elementary schools for children over the age of 11. Authorities differed greatly in the rate at which they reorganised their elementary schools. Where this had been accomplished before 1944, the senior elementary school changed its name, but at first little else, when it became a secondary modern school. In other areas, secondary modern schools have been new creations, and their pupils have benefited in improved conditions from the previous backwardness of their Authority as much as their elder brothers and sisters had suffered from it. The addition of an extra year to the course in 1947 by the raising of the minimum leaving age from 14 to 15 has been more important than the change in status, the better buildings and accommodation to which this entitled the schools. If four years or less still seems to us too short, it is at least one-third longer than the ridiculously short period which was all the senior elementary school could count on.

31. There is another important change that is coming over the secondary modern schools—more of them than of the old senior elementary schools take boys and girls. Before the war about 38 per cent of them were co-educational; today about 53 per cent are. On the other hand there is no appreciable change in the proportion of grammar schools which are co-educational; it remains under 30 per cent. Most of the newer types of schools are co-educational—for example, 63 per cent of comprehensive and bilateral schools. This question, which is obviously of increasing importance as secondary education extends upwards in age and outwards from the classroom to out-of-school activities, is further discussed in Chapter 36. Here it is only necessary to show that a varied national provision does not ensure varied local opportunities. In country districts, variety is often impossible, and it is not surprising to find that 90 per cent of the pupils of secondary modern schools situated in rural areas are in co-educational schools. There is, however, opportunity for greater variety in towns, and normally, but by no means always, this is provided. Table 6 sets out the position in 178 urban areas, the smallest units to which the national statistics can conveniently be broken down. These urban areas should not be confused with the local education authorities. They consist of the urban parts of county authorities (that is to say, their schools situated in towns), the excepted districts (43 of those towns which were formerly their own elementary education authorities), the 79 county boroughs, and the 9 divisions of the County of London.

Table 6. Percentage of Modern and Grammar School Pupils in Co-educational Schools in Towns (England).

Modern Schools		Grammar Schools	
Percentage in Co-educational schools	Number of Areas	Percentage in Co-educational schools	Number of Areas
None	16	None	87
1–25%	32	1–25%	21
26–50%	45	26–50%	29
51–75%	52	51–75%	14
76–99%	19	76–99%	6
All	14	All	19

NOTE: One county and one excepted district have no grammar schools. Fourteen areas have no modern or grammar co-educational schools; three have only co-educational schools. In roughly half the areas there is a fairly evenly balanced provision for modern school pupils, but in only about a quarter for grammar school pupils.

32. A change so great as to seem revolutionary came over the grammar schools ("secondary schools on the grant list" in the phraseology of pre-war days) when the payment of fees was abolished by the Education Act of 1944; but this reform, like so much in English social legislation, was the completion of a process already far advanced. By 1938 the majority (53 per cent) of pupils admitted to secondary schools paid no fees at all; 31 per cent were ordinary fee-payers, while 16 per cent had won special places but, under the local education authority's regulations, were either not exempt or only partially exempt from fees. In 21 per cent of the grant-earning secondary schools in England the only way to secure admission was by winning a free, or special, place through the equivalent of the present "11 plus examination", and in a further 7 per cent of schools at least three-quarters of the places were awarded in this way. Of the 773 council secondary schools, which contained 57 per cent of the secondary school pupils in England and Wales, 29 per cent were entirely free or "special place" in their entry by 1938. Another change in the nature of the grammar schools has been the development of their Sixth Forms from, in many cases, a handful of boys and girls in 1938 to the large numbers of today. This is treated at length in Part Five of the report; it is reflected in the steeper rise between 1938 and 1958 in the number of pupils aged 15 and over in Table 5 compared with that in the numbers under 15.

33. In 1938 nearly all of what are now called secondary technical schools were included in the buildings of technical colleges and shared to a considerable extent a common staff with them. They were described as Junior Technical or Commercial Schools, Junior Housewifery Schools, Schools of Nautical Training or Junior Art Departments. The Board of Education's annual report gave a fairly detailed list of occupations for which the schools prepared their pupils. These schools admitted pupils at 13 for a course lasting to 16. Few boys or girls who had been admitted to a secondary school at 11 were willing to transfer their allegiance two years later; few pupils in elementary schools were willing to forgo their chance of a "special place" at 11 in order to hold themselves in reserve for a Junior Technical school at 13. The Spens report published in 1938 advocated the establishment of separate Technical High Schools with the age of entry at 11 so that they might recruit on equal terms with the secondary schools. The Technical High School was envisaged as providing a suitable form of education for boys and girls of high intelligence, and it is in this direction that the secondary technical schools of the post-war era are developing. Since 1944 the majority of them have moved into buildings of their own,* and with this move there has come a broadening of their curriculum and outlook so that the majority now provide integrated academic and technical courses leading on to all forms of higher education (by no means only in technological faculties) as well as directly into industry and commerce. Not only has the age of entry been lowered, but the age of leaving has been raised to allow of the growth of Sixth Forms. While the grammar schools ultimately derive their pattern of education from literary traditions profoundly modified by the development of the natural sciences, the technical schools are following a new and complementary approach, congenial to this century, which would reach many of the same goals from a different starting point. If its aims could be compressed into a single phrase, we would say that it starts where its pupils' interests are, but that (as a former Minister of Education said) its sights are set "as high educationally as sights can be set".

THE "TRIPARTITE SYSTEM"

34. We have, then, good examples of modern, grammar and technical schools; but we do not now have, and never have had, a tripartite system. Individual technical schools have been developed to a pitch where they can stand comparison with any other schools, but technical schools as a group are slightly less numerous today than they were in 1947. To justify us in talking of a tripartite system, we

* The process had started as early as 1928 when one now existing school moved to buildings of its own.

should need as many technical schools as grammar schools. In fact we have four grammar schools to every technical school and six grammar school pupils to every technical school pupil. Over 40 per cent of the local education authorities do not provide technical schools. Instead of a tripartite system we have (if we may generalise about England as a whole) a two-sided system, based on the assumption, where maintained schools are concerned, that all boys and girls alike go to undifferentiated primary schools, and that from the age of 11 onwards all go to a modern school unless they can show cause to the contrary and there is a place for them in a school giving a different kind of education. The secondary modern school is the school for the great majority of the population from the age of 11.

35. We have been writing as if schools could be adequately described by the labels they bear. In fact, that is impossible. The proportion of grammar school places to the total population varies so greatly from one part of England to another, and bears so varying a relation both to the social background and the distribution of ability in particular communities, that about the only thing one can safely say is that the grammar school will contain the ablest, and the modern school the least able, of the boys and girls in its catchment area (excluding the educationally sub-normal). There is a considerable intermediate group of boys and girls whose abilities would in one place give them a grammar school education and in another a modern school one. There are also everywhere large numbers of boys and girls whose performance falls well short of their early promise, and others (probably quite as numerous) whose development exceeds anticipation. Chapter 30 of this report shows the large extent to which grammar and modern school pupils are intermingled in the employment they take up and the further education they get. Part Two of the report is largely concerned with the consequences of the discovery that a fair number of the pupils in modern schools are capable of reaching academic standards that have in the past been confined to grammar schools. Overlaps will occur wherever the line of division is drawn between grammar and modern schools; but the general level of ability of the pupils in the floating or borderline group will differ according to the percentage who are admitted to grammar schools. This implies that there will be differences in the level and character of the overlapping courses that will have to be provided. There is, of course, nothing new in the realisation that any system of allocation at 11 needs some correction at a later date. Until recently, however, the extent of the overlap has been underestimated, and individual transfers were the solution which was favoured. It is now becoming increasingly apparent that the numbers involved are such as to make the provision of overlapping courses, at least up to

16, a more practicable solution than any system of individual transfers. It is fair to say that more satisfactory progress has been made with the provision of modern school courses which overlap the grammar school curriculum than with grammar school courses designed for pupils who turn out not to respond readily or effectively to an academic approach.

NEW TYPES OF SCHOOL

36. The two-sided system is unlikely to survive in the form in which it existed five or six years ago, or to be replaced by a tripartite system of the kind which used to be suggested. Once it is agreed, as more and more people are coming to believe, that it is wrong to label children for all time at 11, the attempt to give mutually exclusive labels to the schools to which they go at that age will have to be abandoned. All over the country changes are being made that profoundly modify the previous pattern of education, and in certain areas, the system is not being modified so much as replaced by a different form of organisation. There are many variants, and no doubt there will be many more. We distinguish three for particular mention because of the contrast of their approach. They are the comprehensive school, the bilateral school and the two-tier organisation of secondary education. All aim at reducing the waste of talent which arises from the overlap in ability which we have just been discussing, or—to put it in another way—all aim at giving each individual pupil a better chance of an education suited to his needs. All have two points of internal organisation in common. The first is that all levels of ability are represented in the same school; the second is that all levels of ability are not represented in every class. All the variants try to provide a common social life; none tries to provide a uniform curriculum. There are not yet many schools of these new kinds, and many of those that exist are still in their early stages, but they are spread throughout the country and are being tried in a very great variety of circumstances. Details of the distribution of comprehensive and bilateral schools are given in Table 7 overleaf. A single age-group rather than the total size of the school has been chosen as the basis for this table because it gives a more accurate estimate of the position in the early days of a school when it has not yet developed a full age-range. Percentages of the total population in each authority's area who attend the comprehensive or bilateral schools have not been given because they would be seriously misleading in the county districts, where the new form of organisation may form the main provision for a self-contained area, but a very small part of the county's total provision. This objection does not

Table 7. Comprehensive and Bilateral Schools 1957–58 (England).

Comprehensive Schools Number of Schools	Comprehensive Schools Number of Pupils aged 13	Ministry of Education Division	Bilateral Schools Number of Schools	Bilateral Schools Number of Pupils aged 13
2	142	Northern	3	416
6	1,279	East and West Ridings	—	—
1	191	North Midland	2	325
1	373	Eastern	11	2,303
30	8,513	Metropolitan (London and Middlesex)	—	—
—	—	South-Eastern	2	222
3	412	Southern	3	509
—	—	South-Western	10	1,685
15	3,645	Midland	10	1,542
3	472	North-Western	4	421
61	15,027		45	7,423

TOTALS

Pupils aged 13: In comprehensive or bilateral schools 22,450
In England 658,000

Local Education Authorities: With comprehensive or bilateral schools 33
(Counties 18; County Boroughs 15)
Without comprehensive or bilateral schools 96
(Counties 32; County Boroughs 64)

apply in the same way to cities, and it is worth noting that 22 per cent of London's 13 year-olds and 31 per cent of Coventry's were in comprehensive schools last year, while 28 per cent of Bristol's were in bilateral schools.

37. The best known, the most discussed and the most controversial of the variants is the comprehensive school. A comprehensive secondary school is one which at the age of 11 takes in pupils of all ranges of ability. Once inside the school, however, there is no attempt (as there is in the typical American High School, on which the English comprehensive school is often mistakenly said to be modelled) to teach all grades of ability together. The pupils are placed in forms or sets according to their abilities—a typical comprehensive school will start with eight to fifteen forms in a single year—and those who can move ahead fast are not held back by the others. It

is in social matters, in games and in extra-curricular activities that the ability ranges are grouped together; not in their studies. Over the age of 15 or 16, comprehensive schools provide Sixth Form courses not only of the grammar school type but of other types catering for a wide range of interests and abilities. If its grammar school component is to be of an efficient size, a comprehensive school cannot have a smaller catchment area than a grammar school; and if it is to take in at 11 not only the children of grammar school ability but all the children in that area, it will need to be a large school. As can be seen from Table 7, the average size of an age-group in a comprehensive school was about 250, which would give a fully developed school of about 1,500 pupils, but those in large towns will often be a good deal bigger. In some cases, a comprehensive school, while catering for all the pupils in its immediate neighbourhood, also takes in a selection of pupils (either the ablest or those requiring special courses) from a wider area; in these cases the efficient size for a comprehensive school will be smaller. This variant is, perhaps, more likely than the former to suit sparsely populated districts, which would then be served by two secondary schools—a local one offering a restricted range of courses and a more distant one offering a wider range. The existing English comprehensive schools have been formed in two main ways. Some have been new schools in new districts, or in districts where greatly increased grammar school provision was needed. Others have been formed by accretion round an existing grammar school. No English comprehensive school is old enough to have completed Sixth Form courses with pupils who, joining at 11, have spent the whole of their secondary school life in a comprehensive school, and few of the schools have yet completed a fifth year on this basis. It is impossible, therefore, as yet to form a valid opinion about the effect that comprehensive schools will have on the education of their pupils in the ages covered by our terms of reference. For this reason they can figure only slightly in our report, though they have never been far from our thinking and discussions.

38. A bilateral school differs from a comprehensive school in that the pupils are clearly assigned to grammar, technical or modern streams, though easy transfer from one to another is possible. The task of deciding whether a particular school should be classified as comprehensive or bilateral is sometimes very easy, sometimes so difficult as to defy accuracy. Table 7 is based on the Ministry's classification; another interpreter of the same data might have made a number of different dispositions. The important thing is that both types differ from the traditional system much more sharply than from one another. This does not, however, apply to the nature of the

courses the pupils take, which is much the same as in the traditional schools. Thus, whether they are grouped in comprehensive and bilateral schools, or separated between modern and grammar schools, it still remains true that two-thirds of the pupils are following courses of a modern school type and one-fifth courses of a grammar school type.

39. The schools that we have been describing, however revolutionary in other ways, all accept the traditional view that pupils should stay at the same school from the age of 11 to the end of the secondary course. One authority is already trying a different age structure for its secondary education; several others have similar plans in active preparation. In Leicestershire in two areas (more are to follow) secondary education is being divided into two stages. The first stage from 11 to 14 (or 10 to 13 for some children) is accommodated in what are called, misleadingly enough, high schools, where the course also extends to 15 for those who do not wish to commit themselves to the second stage. The second stage is from 14 to 18 and is open to all those who will undertake to stay at school at least until the age of 16. This second stage is accommodated in what is called the grammar school (with even less reason than the usual use of the term in England). Thus there is a number of middle-sized schools for the three years of secondary education up to 14—with which we are not concerned in this report—leading on to another school, providing a full range of academic and non-academic subjects, to which anybody may go provided that he undertakes to stay there at least two years. It is too early, as with the comprehensive schools, to form any judgement of the effects of this new pattern of organisation on English education. Indeed assessment will have to wait even longer in the case of this newest variant. Once again, we can only welcome an ingenious and interesting experiment in a field where much remains to be done if we are really to educate our teen-agers.

40. How fast is the rate of change in organisation? Any answer to this question must be open to a great deal of qualification because of difficulties of classification, which bedevil attempts to measure what has already happened, and because of uncertainties about what may happen in the future. Table 8, which presents data covering virtually the whole of England supplied to us by the Association of Chief Education Officers, shows, however, both a remarkable growth in recent years and a remarkable extension of it to come in the next few years if the authorities' present intentions are realised. The figures given in Table 8 cannot be reconciled with those in Table 7 partly because of the differences in classification and partly because Table 8 refers to June, 1959 while Table 7 refers to January, 1958.

Table 8. Growth of Secondary Schools providing for All Levels of Ability (England).

This table relates to:

(1) schools which provide for all the children over the age of 11 in a given area; or

(2) schools which provide for all children over the age of 11 in a limited area but which may also recruit some selected children from a wider area.

	A. Total No. of Secondary Schools	B. No. of pupils in (A)	C. No. of schools as defined in (1) and (2) above	D. No. of pupils in (C)	D expressed as a percentage of B.
1956	4,393	1,783,374	52	38,926	*2·18*
1959	4,809	2,228,793	127	122,872	*5·51*
Estimate for 1965	4,993	2,248,930	227	254,371	*11·31*

NOTE: It should be emphasised that the estimated figures for 1965 are subject to a variety of conditions and reservations but by and large they express the intentions of the L.E.A. at the time the information was asked for.

It is clear, therefore, that the shape of the English school system in 1978 will differ from that of 1958—perhaps almost as much as that of 1958 did from 1938.

CHAPTER 3

Population Changes and their Educational Consequences

41. Men and women live longer and marry earlier than they used to, but they have smaller families. More married women have paid employment. All this is, of course, a matter of general knowledge: the purpose of this chapter is to give some indication of what the consequences of these facts have been, and ought to be, for education. What is taught in schools cannot, at least directly or quickly, influence these general social changes; but they profoundly affect what can and needs to be done in schools. It is in their context that we must plan.

EARLIER MARRIAGE AND SMALLER FAMILIES

42. People live longer. A hundred years ago only about one-third of the children born could expect to live to 65, while less than half of those who reached the age of 15 were still alive at 65. Now two-thirds of the children born, and three-quarters of those reaching the age of 15, may expect to be alive at 65. The improvement has been continuous. In the last half-century, between 1906 and 1956, the expectation of life at birth for men has risen from 48·5 years to 67·8 and for women from 52·4 years to 73·3. But beyond 65 there has been little change for over a century in the expectation of life. A man reaching 65 today may expect to live only one year longer than his great-grandfather a hundred years ago (for women the comparative figure is 3 years). The contemporary problem of old age is caused not by the elderly living longer, but by more people surviving to become elderly. Men and women aged 65 and over were only 5 per cent of the population in 1871 and 1901, by 1931 they had become 7 per cent and by 1951, 11 per cent. The proportion is still rising.

43. Men and women marry earlier—women markedly so. Unlike the increasing expectation of life, this has not been a continuous process, but a swinging pendulum. From 1871 to 1911 the proportions of men and women marrying early steadily dropped. From 1911 to 1951 they have risen, slowly at first but latterly with a velocity that has carried them well above the 1871 level. This is shown in Table 9. The changes are much more marked for women than for men. Today half the women in the country (and a quarter of the men) are married

Table 9. Proportions per Thousand Men and Women of Age-groups 15–19 and 20–24 who were or had been Married (Census Dates; England and Wales).

Age-Group		1851	1861	1871	1881	1891
15–19	Men	4	5	5	5	4
	Women	25	30	32	25	19
20–24	Men	200	223	230	221	193
	Women	308	331	343	331	296

Age-Group		1901	1911	1921	1931	1941	1951
15–19	Men	3	2	4	3		5
	Women	15	12	18	18	No Census	44
20–24	Men	173	143	178	139		238
	Women	272	243	274	258		482

before they are 25. This compares with a third (and nearly a quarter of the men) at the previous peak ninety years ago. The trend towards early marriage has continued since the 1951 census. Over 4 per cent of the girls with whom this report is concerned are married women.

44. Families are smaller. The decline in the number of births per family has been a continuous process for over a hundred years. The average number of children born to a woman marrying in mid-Victorian times has been estimated to have been 5·8; for women married in 1925 it was 2·2. The Royal Commission on Population estimated that about 9 per cent of marriages taking place about 1860 were childless compared with 17 per cent of those taking place in 1925. Of the 1860 marriages, 5 per cent produced one child only; 6 per cent, two; 8 per cent, three; and 72 per cent, more than three children. The corresponding figures for the 1925 marriages were 25 per cent with one child, 25 per cent with two, 14 per cent with three children and 19 per cent with more than three. At first the fall in size of families was much more marked in the professional classes, but this contrast has grown less, primarily through a reduction in the size of families of manual workers, but to some extent also by a tendency to slightly larger families than a generation ago in the professional classes. We have no firm data of recent years about the distribution of family size, but the 1951 census provides details for each social class of the size of private households and of the number of children under 16 that they contained, which is close enough to the same thing to serve as a rough guide. (It should be explained

that a retired person living alone, and an establishment in which parents and children, relations and domestic staff live together, both equally constitute a single household). The remarkable thing is that the size of households, and the number of children under 16 they contain, vary very little class by class from the average of all classes, though social classes 4 and 5* still contain a rather higher proportion of households with 3 or more children. Broadly speaking, however, we may say that, in every class, over half the households had no children at home on the day the 1951 census was taken, that getting on for a quarter had one child, about one-seventh had two children and one-twelfth had three or more.

45. More married women are engaged in paid work. The 1901 census classified just under one-third of all women (32 per cent) as 'gainfully occupied'; the 1951 census just over one-third (35 per cent). The proportion of married women who were 'gainfully occupied' rose from 13 per cent in 1901 to 23 per cent in 1951. In 1901 22 per cent of the women who were 'gainfully occupied' were married; in 1951 the percentage was 40. Quite as significant is the change in the nature of women's occupations. In 1901 four of every five women employed were either in domestic service occupations (including laundry work), or in the manufacture and sale either of textile fabrics and dresses or of food, drink and tobacco. Even so, the range of occupations followed by women was considerably more diversified then than it had been twenty years before. The process of diversification has gone steadily on, and there have been large increases in the last twenty years in the numbers and proportion following occupations which require some education above the minimum. The greatest single increase, both proportionately (122 per cent) and absolutely (700,000), was among clerks and typists. The increase in the professional and technical occupations (which include nursing and all the medical services, as well as teaching and social work) was 35 per cent; but even so the ratio of women to men in this whole group was lower in 1951 than in 1931.

SMALLER FAMILIES, LONGER EDUCATION

46. These radical changes in the structure and way of life of the population have had, and will continue to have, many repercussions on the educational system. We choose six which seem to us of special consequence in their bearing on our terms of reference. Three of these have a direct connection with the organisation and content of education. They are: the greater ability of the individual family to support a lengthy education for its children; the greater freedom of the married woman to take up paid employment; the fact that, for

* The Registrar General defines five social classes.

an increasing number of girls, marriage now follows hard on, or even precedes, the end of education. The other three are more concerned with the nature of the society in which children grow up. They are: the larger proportion of old people which society as a whole has to support; the fact that the family group covers a much smaller age-range than previously, thus limiting a boy's or girl's intimate circle (apart from parents) to his or her own precise contemporaries; and the fact that both births and deaths are now rare events in most children's lives.

47. It seems clear that most families can now support a longer school education for their children than used to be the case. Families are, as we have seen, smaller in all social groups. They are started earlier in life; and, as the Royal Commission on Population pointed out, about four-fifths of all the children who will be born to a group of married couples are born in the first ten years of married life. These facts taken together seem to us significant. Lack of money used to make it necessary in the days of large families for manual workers to put their children to work as early as possible. The father reached his peak earning capacity in early manhood; each additional child meant an increased cost on a fixed income until the older children could go to work to relieve, and contribute to, the family exchequer. The younger children in a large family, moreover, might still be dependent as the parents approached the time when their earning capacity would grow less or disappear. To this economic force working against any longer education than the unavoidable minimum may probably be added a psychological one. Young children obviously need attention, and nearly always receive it. Older children may need it just as much, but their need is not so apparent. They are more likely to get it when there are no younger ones to distract the parents' notice. It is a tribute to the courage and the conviction of their parents that many boys and girls from the homes of manual workers did in the past get a secondary education or better; but the number of them was necessarily small. It was not until the days of generally small families that manual workers and their wives could reasonably be expected to look at education for their children in the same sort of perspective as non-manual workers. The manual worker of today normally has a family whose numbers do not constitute an excessive burden on his income, and whose members may all be expected to be grown up and independent, however long the education he gives them, before he retires on pension. Moreover his wife is very likely to be able to supplement the family income when the children are older. This diagnosis is corroborated by the fact that children in large families tend to have a shorter education than those in small families. Among National Service recruits to the Army and the R.A.F. the proportion who

had left school at 15 rises with each additional member of the family from which they come, from 58 per cent among only children, to 61, 71, 80, 86 and 92 per cent in families with six or more children. And this pattern is repeated in each occupation group. (Further statistics on this are contained in Part Two of Volume II). With the exception of these large families, then, we can today for the first time say that the family situation of all classes is such as to put no barriers in the way of longer education. But the exception remains. In recent years, society has made some provision towards the cost of supporting a large family through family allowances, income tax allowances and, for those with really low incomes, through maintenance allowances, but the provision is hardly sufficient as yet to give equality of opportunity to members of large families.

WOMEN'S EDUCATION FOR MARRIAGE AND EMPLOYMENT

48. The reduction in family size, the earlier age of marriage, the earlier incidence of child-bearing inside marriage, longer life and better health—all these are making it increasingly possible for marriage to mark not the end, but simply a break in a woman's career. Indeed it is no longer marriage itself, but child-bearing and child-care which today signal a withdrawal from outside employment. How long a withdrawal? There is a period when part-time employment is possible, but not full-time. But when full allowance has been made for this, for any slight increase in family size, and for the years of retirement, it remains true that the wife of today has a large number of years which she can devote to activities outside her home (whether "gainful" or voluntary), and that the changed outlook of today makes her want to use them in this way. This desire is in line with the economic and social needs of the community; it does not, however, fit in well either with the organisation and conditions of employment, or, in some respects, with the education provided for girls in secondary schools. The Royal Commission on Population pointed out that

> "there is often a real conflict between motherhood and a whole-time 'career'. Part of this conflict is inherent in the biological function of women, but part of it is artificial and the persistence of this artificial element tends to depress the status of motherhood into that of an inferior alternative to outside employment or public life. We therefore welcome the removal of the marriage bar in such employment as teaching and the civil service and we think that a deliberate effort should be made to devise adjustments that would render it easier for women to combine motherhood and the care of a home with outside activities."*

*(Cmd. 7695 pp. 159–60).

49. The conclusion to which this leads is twofold. In the first place, attention must be paid (as the Royal Commission suggested) to the re-organisation of those professions and occupations which do (or might) employ women so as to enable married women to play their part in them, or to resume it when the period of pregnancy and infant care is over. Education authorities are in an especially responsible position in this regard in so far as married women are urgently needed as teachers, and teaching is a profession in which women are employed alongside men. It is increasingly important to solve the problem of the exodus of married women from teaching. Secondly, girls should be encouraged to qualify before marriage in a greater number of professions or occupations which will provide opportunities for them in later years. Teaching, social work, the health services, the clothing trades and commerce are the occupations usually thought of when the school curriculum is planned, but experience in this and other countries suggests that there are other occupations which can be combined with marriage or in which a married woman can bring herself up to date after a few years' absence from work by a relatively brief refresher course.

50. The earlier age at which women now marry has serious consequences for the education of adolescent girls. It hardly leaves time for a girl to become fully qualified professionally, and to gain experience in the exercise of her skill, before marriage and childbirth interrupt her career. It will, we think, be generally agreed that some period of independence, of being out in the world, before marriage is highly desirable. It is increasingly difficult to reconcile this with the demands of school life. Certainly it points to a radically new conception of the way in which girls of 17 and 18 should be treated. If they are to remain in full-time education, it will, we think, be necessary to treat them far more as students than as schoolgirls. Some schools are, we know, aware of the problem, but they are not yet the majority. It is not only, though this is important, that girls will not stay at school if they feel that they are being treated as children and are identifiable by the general public as schoolgirls on irrelevant occasions. We are even more concerned that they should learn to behave and to react as adults. It is not calf love, but the love which leads to marriage that they feel. Where the intellectually abler girls are concerned, it is difficult for the schools to adjust to this sharpening contrast between career interests and personal demands, for most of what they learn in school is related to their professional training and to entrance into the universities and other institutions where it is pursued. There is not much scope—in school hours, at least—for giving them any education specifically related to their special interests as women.

51. With the less able girls, however, we think that the schools can and should make more adjustments (more than all but a handful have yet done) to the fact that marriage now looms much larger and nearer in the pupils' eyes than it has ever done before. Their needs are much more sharply differentiated from those of boys of the same age than is true of the academically abler groups. Nearly nine times as many girls as boys get married before they are 19. This is reflected in the immediate interests of the boys and girls in the last year or two of the school course. There can be no doubt that at this stage boys' thoughts turn most often to a career, and only secondly to marriage and the family; and that the converse obtains with girls. It is plain, then, that, if it is sound educational policy to take account of natural interests, there is a clear case for a curriculum which respects the different roles they play. While the ultimate objective should be to help both boys and girls to grow up as intelligent and responsible citizens, the proximate objective should take the interests they display during this phase of their lives into consideration.

52. At this time, therefore, the prospect of courtship and marriage should rightly influence the education of the adolescent girl. Though the general objectives of secondary education remain unchanged, her direct interest in dress, personal appearance and in problems of human relations should be given a central place in her education. The greater psychological and social maturity of girls makes such subjects acceptable—and socially necessary. Girls must be treated, even more completely than adolescent boys, as young adults. It is the extension of education to older pupils, as well as the increasingly early sophistication of girls which have not only made this differentiation necessary, but have also given the subjects we have mentioned their strong emotional charge. The increase in the number of early marriages is, in any case, creating a problem for the schools; it will be more serious when the school-leaving age is raised.

THE OLD AND THE YOUNG

53. The fact that the elderly and retired now form a higher proportion of the whole population than in the past, and that the proportion is still rising, has important educational consequences. It is certain that we can support them and increase the standard of living of the whole community only if there is increased efficiency in production and distribution at all levels. And increased efficiency means both better education and longer education. But there is another educational consequence, quite as serious in its implications, of the ageing population. Are the old to be regarded as a burden—an unwelcome bye-product of the efficiency of the welfare state—or are they to

have a highly regarded place in society? The problem is not only an economic one, but a moral one—in both aspects it has a bearing on education.

54. There remain the two less tangible, but no less important, influences of population changes on education—the disappearance of death, and indeed of birth, as a common incident of growing up in a family, and the disappearance of the "all-through" family which bridged the generations, to borrow a metaphor from the title of those older schools which cater for all ages from 5 to 15. Death, in fact, in the experience of most children is limited to the death of the old, whereas not so long ago it was realised as something that might strike anyone at any time. Throughout the whole of the last half of the nineteenth century the infant mortality rate was of the order of 150 per thousand live births; in this century it has steadily and dramatically fallen—to 63 in the period 1930–1932 and to 30 in 1951. Ninety years ago half the male deaths were those of boys and men under 20; by 1951 the proportion had dropped to 6 per cent. The great majority were of men over 45. Fifty to a hundred years ago boys and girls were frequently reminded that they were, so to speak, tenants-at-will of life, not freeholders. Today they have—mercifully—a much greater sense of personal security, but this may well make the shock of corporate insecurity all the greater when in their teens they first become consciously aware of the fundamental political anxieties of our time. The old 'all-through' family, though it had its disadvantages, especially in curtailing education, acted as a school for personal responsibility and informal social education. No one child could long hold the centre of the stage. Parents had younger children to occupy their attention as the older ones grew up. There was a constant succession of new roles to be played by the various members of the family circle as its numbers grew and its composition gradually changed. The generations merged into one another. In the characteristic household of today there is no change in the composition of the family, once established, until it suddenly disrupts some sixteen to twenty years later. The new family pattern, and it is new not only in relation to the recent past but to all recorded history, tends to emphasise and increase the inherent isolation and self-centredness of the adolescent. But this takes us to the changing social world which is the subject of the next chapter.

CHAPTER 4

Changing Social Needs

55. Our terms of reference require us to consider changing social needs. In every aspect of education and at every stage of our thinking we have been keenly aware of the way in which social conditions, attitudes and habits affect what education can achieve. In this chapter we select two main directions of change which seem especially important for their impact on teen-agers and for the way in which they define some of the objectives of educational policy. The first is the emancipation, or isolation, of the individual (it can be looked at in both ways) and the rejection of traditional authority; the second, the conquest of the field of communications by the mass production techniques which were first applied to the manufacture of goods.

EMANCIPATION AND THE MORAL CODE

56. In Chapter 3 we approached the first of these directions of change through our consideration of the dwindling of the family to a small unit, in which the mother is increasingly likely to be employed outside the family as well as in her essential role at home. In the next chapter we shall be dealing with the growing financial independence of the children, with the result that today by the later teens they are no longer beholden to their parents for their pleasures. A generation ago "a room of one's own," and the spiritual independence for which it stood, was often something to be fought for and attained only with difficulty. Today it is taken for granted, at least in its metaphorical sense, by young people. The family group, of course, survives as the unit of living for nearly all boys and girls of the ages with which we are concerned, but it does not dominate or direct the way they spend their time. Less than 8 per cent of the boys and girls who had left modern schools two years before were not still living at home at the time of our Social Survey (when they were, presumably, about 17) but 36 per cent of the boys and 32 per cent of the girls had only spent one or two evenings at home out of the previous seven. A further 28 per cent of the boys and 6 per cent of the girls had been out every evening. The survival of the family is based on consent; it is not now thought to be guaranteed by the nature of things.

57. It is not only that the children know (as children have always known) that when they grow up most of them will leave home and set up families of their own; increasing numbers of them are also

aware that the continuation of the family into which they were born is not to be taken for granted. Divorce and remarriage are matters with which they have become familiar as an element in the lives of prominent and admired people, and are no longer unknown within their own circle. The Registrar General estimated in his Statistical Review for 1946–50 that "about 1 in 4 of the women marrying now at ages 16–18, 1 in 10 of those marrying at ages 19–22, and 1 in 16 of those marrying at ages 23–27 will have been divorced by the twentieth anniversary of their marriage." It is true that there has been a slight, but welcome, decline in the divorce rate since then, but the general picture remains true. It is with this situation around them that the teen-agers with whom we are concerned approach their own courtship and marriage. The durability of the family (its tyranny, as it seemed to many a generation ago) can no longer be taken for granted. If a secure home is to be achieved (and what couple approaching marriage does not desire one?), it has to be worked for. The transition from discipline by order and convention to self-discipline is not easy in any field; it is especially difficult where sex is concerned because of the force of the instinctive desires. If the family is to be as secure in the future as it has been in the past (and we can be content with nothing less), there will have to be a conscious effort to prepare the way for it through the educational system on a much greater scale than has yet been envisaged. Rightly or wrongly, divorce is not only legally recognised; in growing sectors of the community it is socially accepted. It is with this knowledge and within this context that those concerned with the upbringing of teen-agers must strive to produce those attitudes and actions which in the fulness of time help to make the marriage of a man and a woman an effective instrument both for the nurture of children and for "the mutual society, help and comfort that the one ought to have of the other, both in prosperity and adversity."

58. The problem of sexual ethics is, of course, far wider than marriage. Indeed in the years from 15 to 18 it is not mainly a marriage problem. It seems beyond question that behaviour which would have been rejected a generation ago as improper and anti-social—most people would simply have said wrong—is today tolerated or endorsed by adult public opinion. Young people enjoy a much greater freedom to live their own lives without adult supervision, and to meet and spend their time together as they like without censure and without restraints other than those which their own individual taste or conviction imposes. In this change there has been both gain and loss. It is surely gain that boys and girls, young men and young women, should have the opportunity, which earlier generations often lacked, to get to know one another really well before committing themselves

to the choice of a mate. It is surely loss that new guiding rules of behaviour in the changed situation have not been sufficiently developed to replace the old customs which nearly everybody has to some extent abandoned and which some have altogether thrown overboard. Clearly it is not possible for an educational service, which is designed to prepare the young for adult life, to establish by itself such a code. This is the concern of society as a whole, young and old alike. Education can only function within the broad directives of right and wrong which society gives. Teachers and youth leaders are, however, well placed to bring to attention the personal bewilderment and disaster to which this public indecision over moral issues often leads the young. There can be no doubt of the disaster. On 1956 figures, one girl in fifty might expect to give birth to a child conceived before she was 17. It is important to disentangle the two strands—the rise in unsupervised association between teen-age boys and girls; and the virtual disappearance of many of the old rules of right and wrong which were formerly accepted even when they were not obeyed. These two changes have happened at the same time, but they are not necessary consequences of one another. It seems to us quite possible to imagine a society in which teen-agers had their present freedom to live their own lives; but in which they were not deprived of the security which comes from a well understood knowledge of what is right and what is wrong. After all, it was the adults and not the teen-agers who first cast doubt on the rules.

JUVENILE DELINQUENCY

59. In writing of the climate of opinion, as it affects marriage and the relation of the sexes, we have been dealing with something which touches society as a whole, though there are certain geographical and religious groups which to some extent stand apart from contemporary changes. We must still bear this general climate of opinion in mind in turning to juvenile delinquency. In its conventional meaning of getting into trouble with the law this is still largely a male prerogative. It is, however, at its worst in specific neighbourhoods which are marked by a high concentration of almost every social problem, and where the local climate of opinion is, to quote a phrase from Mr. J. B. Mays, often not only "deviant but defiant." Typical of such areas are the inner, declining rings of impoverished districts near the centre of the great cities, where resident populations, without the initiative to follow their abler and more industrious neighbours to the suburbs, are often intermixed with immigrants from other districts and other cultures. The special, and depressing, characteristics of such areas have been the theme of many important social studies from the time of Sir Cyril Burt's classic "Young

Delinquents" to the work now being done in Liverpool. But they are not the only areas where the risk of contamination is especially high. A new housing estate, if left without appropriate provision for communal life and adequate social leadership, can be as deadly as any decaying slum.

60. These districts provide many posts of educational honour. It is sad and serious that this is not more widely recognised. The qualities they call for are not extraordinary—they are the ordinary human virtues of courage, sympathy, affection and firmness. It is the degree to which they are needed that is exceptional. Some at least of those who teach in schools or run youth clubs in such areas ought to be men and women who are prepared to find their life-work in the neighbourhood—one of the best qualifications for teaching a class in this sort of district is to have taught their parents before them. None should be transients on their way from college to a good job nearer home; the reserve of occasional teachers intended to meet such emergencies as illness ought not to be relied on to fill gaps which exist because no regular teacher can be found. A quick turnover of teachers is, however, too often the distinguishing mark of these schools. It is our contention that teaching is always allied to other forms of social work, but the terms of the alliance certainly differ greatly from one area to another. In these specially difficult districts the teacher must be more of the social worker than in other places. Indeed with some of his pupils that role must come first. And, of course, he needs far closer contacts with other social workers than are needed elsewhere. We have not made any special studies which enable us to say what proportion of the whole population live in these areas, but we do not believe that it can be so large as to make special provision impossible. Neither are we able to estimate exactly what proportion of juvenile delinquency is located in these places, but we believe it to be very high. The job to be tackled, therefore, though difficult, is both limited and extremely important—well worth the difference in cost between "getting-by" and making an all-out effort. Incidentally, the gain to the public reputation of the educational system as a whole would be almost as great as the contribution to social welfare. It is these areas which have provided the setting for most of the popular books which have fiercely portrayed the difficulties and deficiencies of the secondary modern school. They have, quite unjustly, been taken by readers without first-hand experience as typical of modern schools as a whole. It is just because they are not typical that we can hope for a quick improvement.

61. It is, perhaps, almost as difficult to estimate the incidence of juvenile delinquency in general as to gauge how much of it lies within

the special areas we have just been discussing. The trouble is that the criminal statistics are statistics of action taken by the authorities, which is by no means the same thing as statistics of action taken by those who break the law. At one time, or in one town, there may be more policemen to enforce the law than in another; similarly there will be differences in the completeness with which crimes are reported to the police, and variations in the way in which the police deal with offenders, especially juvenile offenders. Still, in spite of these important reservations, an attempt must be made to set out the position. In 1958 the Christian Economic and Social Research Foundation published a pamphlet called "Trends in Teenage Delinquency" which, on the basis of the Annual Report on Criminal Statistics, set out the convictions per 10,000 civilian males resident in England and Wales for various groups of offences. The result is summarised in Table 10.

Table 10. Convictions per 10,000 Civilian Males at two Dates for five Groups of Offences.

Type of Offence	Males 14–16 (3 age-groups) 1947	1956	Males 17–20 (4 age-groups less Forces) 1947	1956
Theft	165	174	181	260
Violence	3·7	9·2	12·8	40
Sexual	5·5	10·8	6·9	15·9
Drink	1·2	8	17·8	94
Disorder*	43	49	66	141

It is important neither to overlook the exceedingly heavy increase in crimes associated with violence, sex and drunkenness, nor to exaggerate the total number of boys and young men affected. If one could aggregate the five types of offence, the overall rate would still only be 5·5 per cent. for the older age-group and 2·5 per cent for the younger.

62. Mr. Leslie T. Wilkins of the Home Office Research Unit has recently drawn attention to the different degrees of delinquency which various generations have shown. His thesis may briefly be summarised in two statements. The first is that it is the war-time infants, and not the war-time babies, who as a generation have given most trouble in each year of their growth from 8, when criminal responsibility begins, to 20. They are, of course, the generation whose

* Disorder—a miscellaneous group which includes riding a bicycle without lights and playing football in the street.

CHART NO. 5

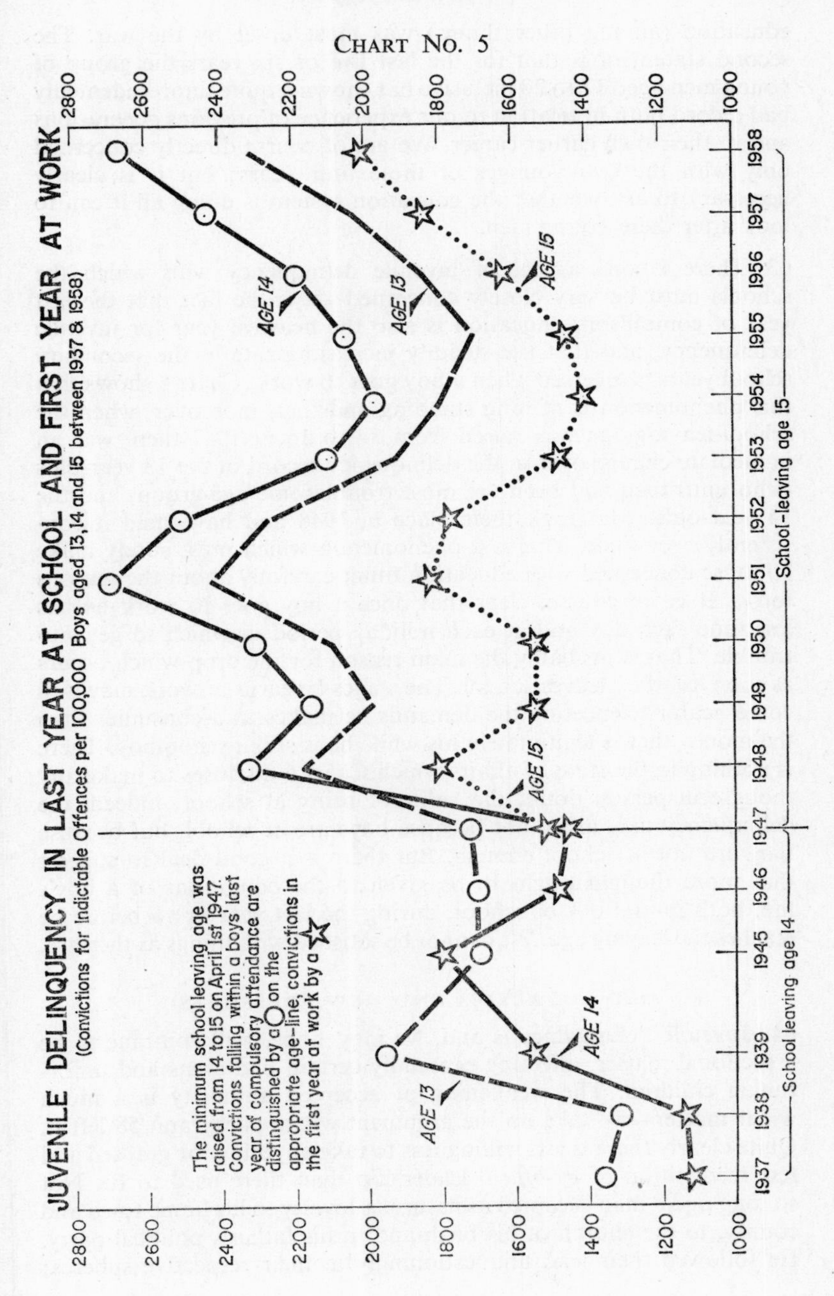
JUVENILE DELINQUENCY IN LAST YEAR AT SCHOOL AND FIRST YEAR AT WORK
(Convictions for Indictable Offences per 100,000 Boys aged 13, 14 and 15 between 1937 & 1958)
The minimum school leaving age was raised from 14 to 15 on April 1st 1947. Convictions falling within a boys' last year of compulsory attendance are distinguished by a ○ on the appropriate age-line, convictions in the first year at work by a ☆
AGE 13
AGE 14
AGE 15
AGE 13
AGE 14
AGE 15
2800
2600
2400
2200
2000
1800
1600
1400
1200
1000
1937
1938
1939
1945
1946
1947
1948
1949
1950
1951
1952
1953
1954
1955
1956
1957
1958
School leaving age 14
School-leaving age 15

education (among other things) was most upset by the war. The second statement is that for the last five or six years the group of young men aged 17 to 20 inclusive has shown a quite unprecedentedly bad record both in relation to our experience of previous generations and to their own earlier career. We are of course directly concerned only with the two younger of these four years; but it is clearly necessary to ask whether the education system is doing all it can to look after these young men.

63. There is one aspect of juvenile delinquency with which the schools must be very closely concerned—it is the fact that the last year of compulsory education is also the heaviest year for juvenile delinquency, and that the steadily increasing rate in the secondary school years is reversed when a boy goes to work. Chart 5 shows that this phenomenon is of long standing and that, moreover, when the school-leaving age was raised from 14 to 15 in 1947 there was an immediate change over in the delinquency record of the 13 year-olds (who until then had been the most troublesome age-group) and the 14 year-olds, who took their place in 1948 and have held it consistently ever since. This is a phenomenon which must surely make all those concerned with education think carefully about the reasons for it. It is, of course, clear that once a boy goes to work he has less time each day and at each holiday period in which to get into trouble. That is probably the main reason for the drop which occurs as soon as a boy leaves school. The wages he earns at work may well come nearer to meeting the demands he makes as a consumer than the money that is legitimately his while he is still a schoolboy. There is nothing in the state of affairs which Chart 5 discloses to make any thoughtful person doubt the value of being at school; indeed, the delinquency may arise, not because boys are at school, but because they are not at school enough. But there is a good deal to suggest that more thought ought to be given to the conditions of a boy's life, both in and out of school, during the last year or so before he reaches the leaving age. We cannot be satisfied with things as they are.

OLD LOYALTIES AND NEW PRESSURES

64. Juvenile delinquency is and, we may hope, will continue to be a sectional matter, affecting especially certain bad areas and unfortunate children. The weakening of accepted authority is a much wider matter—we take up the argument where paragraph 58 left it. Quite clearly there is less willingness to take anything for granted and less recognition of *ex-officio* leadership than there used to be. Not so long ago a man accepted as natural a loyalty to his home town and county, to the church of his birth and to his father's political party. He followed their lead unquestioningly in their respective spheres;

they in turn gave him significance. To change sides, to abandon an old loyalty, was something only to be done for grave cause and sometimes with serious misgiving. Those who did so were for this very reason likely to be serious men and, often, the salt of the earth. No doubt in practice many men sat very lightly to these loyalties, though they continued to acknowledge them. The important thing in both cases was that this permanent connection was the norm to which it was assumed that behaviour ought to conform. In so far as these old loyalties were local, no doubt their weakening has come from the greater mobility of the population. In 1901, out of England's forty counties, in only three were the natives less than 60 per cent of the population; by 1931 there were twelve counties in that position; by 1951 the number had risen to twenty. And one can change one's environment without changing one's county. How many people today are born and die in the same district, let alone the same street? In so far as these loyalties were intellectual or spiritual, their decline has no doubt been caused partly by the unprecedented rate at which knowledge has grown, a rate which has often far outstripped the capacity of the old institutions to adapt themselves, and partly by the role of education itself as a solvent of untried assumptions. Many loyalties, too, were part local, part mental—often a move to a new home has broken an old connection, which had come to rest more on custom or sentiment than on conviction.

65. Whatever the reasons, neither adults nor teen-agers are willing nowadays to take very much on authority—that is to say as far as their conscious minds are concerned. Indeed if young people's insistence on questioning all received authority meant that they were determined to think for themselves, there would be more room for surprise than for alarm. But in fact all that has happened is the substitution of the public opinion of their peers for the wisdom of the ages. Teen-age opinion is often badly informed, fickle and superficial. How should it be otherwise? Of all age-groups, the teen-agers are most exposed to the impact of the "mass media" of communication. At school, they had the help of educated adults to enable them to distinguish and to criticise; to master the suggestive and imaginative material put before them in a never-ending stream, and not to be mastered by it. As adults, they can hope to acquire a sufficient knowledge of life, a certain mastery in the art of running a home and earning a living, which will give them a touchstone for the vicarious experiences they get from screen or printed page. Most teen-agers have neither the one safeguard nor the other. They know they are not important as producers or as citizens. But their money is as good as anybody's. In their capacity as consumers, they get their fair share, and perhaps more than their fair share, of the

attention of those who have goods or entertainment to sell; and though many of them are cynical enough about the reason for the attention they receive, who does not like being flattered? It needs, moreover, a very wise head to resist the suggestions of those who have to make their living by the correctness of their applied psychology—a science which does not rest on the art of intellectual conviction. But the welfare of the democratic state rests precisely on that.

66. Once again it is important to remember the strictly limited field in which education can operate. It could not, if it would, destroy the "mass media" of communications. It ought not to want to do so. The high standard of technical efficiency that modern methods have developed has brought experiences of the greatest value to many whose lives were often pitifully empty of anything but the daily task of keeping alive. They have enlarged the imagination and widened the horizons of millions. They have quickened many who were intellectually dead. They give education new possibilities. But just because they are so powerful, they need to be treated with the discrimination that only education can give. There is undoubtedly a duty on those who wield such great power to use it responsibly. That is a matter for the whole community, and not especially for educationalists. There is also in our view a duty on those who are charged with the responsibility for education to see that teen-agers, who are at the most insecure and suggestible stage of their lives, are not suddenly exposed to the full force of the "mass media" without some counter-balancing assistance. The tremendous power of these methods of communication makes it important not to cut short the educational period. Surely society ought not to withdraw from the young worker the help it gave the schoolboy. Nor is this help of which we have been writing merely a defensive armour of criticism. Something more is needed. The Education Act of 1944 imposes on local education authorities the obligation to "contribute towards the spiritual, moral, mental and physical development of the community." The teen-agers with whom we are concerned need, perhaps before all else, to find a faith to live by. They will not all find precisely the same faith and some will not find any. Education can and should play some part in their search. It can assure them that there is something to search for and it can show them where to look and what other men have found.

CHAPTER 5

The Pressure of Economic Change

67. Of all the driving forces of change in the present day, among the strongest are those that show up in economic form, those that bear upon the amount of money and of other resources that is made available for the educational system, or upon the living the pupils in the schools are looking forward to being able to earn. The essential verities of a sound education are, no doubt, the same from generation to generation. But the particular form that the education takes, the number of pupils who receive it, the number and nature of the schools they attend and the length of time they stay there—all these things are influenced by economic circumstances. We leave aside until the next chapter the question of the economic and financial relationships between the state and the schools. The present chapter is concerned with the impact on the individual of economic changes and the consequences that they can be expected to have for the schools.

THE ADVANCE FROM POVERTY

68. It has hardly yet been generally realised how sharply the average standard of living has risen in the fourteen years since the end of the war. It is useless to quote money figures because of the great rise in prices in the past two decades. But in the broadest of terms, it can be said that the total real output of the United Kingdom (it is impracticable to give figures for England alone) in 1958 was about one-third greater than it had been twenty years earlier. Even after more had been set aside for the needs of the government (especially for defence), for additions to productive and other capital and for exports, there was still enough left over to sustain an increase in consumption. An index number of all forms of consumption by individuals—the best statistical measure of the standard of living of the people—shows an increase of about 10 per cent per head from 1938 to 1958. This great increase in wealth-producing capacity cannot be left out of any consideration of educational policy. As compared, for example, with our predecessors of the Consultative Committee who produced, in 1938, the Spens Report on Secondary Education, we are prescribing for a community that is one-third richer in material wealth. This has a double implication: there should be more real resources available for education; and, since a high level of national productivity can only be sustained by brains and skill, the schools have a higher challenge to meet.

69. The basis of the great improvement in the standard of living of the average family has, of course, been the full employment that has prevailed for two decades. But it has not been full employment alone, for the combined effect of inflation, of progressive taxation and of the social security schemes of the welfare state has been to divert the larger part of the rise in the national standard of consumption to the lower income groups. They have, therefore, gained proportionately even more than the population as a whole. Those who knew the schools twenty years ago can see the revolution in the faces of the children. The Chief Medical Officer of the Ministry has recently reported that obesity in children is now attracting at least as much attention as under-nutrition. Whether the economic security and prosperity of the 1950's will last through the 1960's, no one can say, and it is certainly no part of the task of this report to venture into economic prophecy. We have, however, based our recommendations on the assumptions, which we trust are reasonable, that at least there will be no sharp and complete reversal; and that, though employment may perhaps from time to time be somewhat less full than it has been in recent years, there will be no relapse into the conditions of the twenty years between the wars. We are thinking here of the state of employment in general and of its effect on the prosperity of the community as a whole. Where the employment of young people is concerned, there is an important reservation to be made, to which we return in paragraph 74.

70. The transformation in the economic conditions of the people, and particularly of the families in which the great mass of school children are to be found, has had several effects on education, not all of them pointing in the same direction. In the first place, more wealth has meant that more education can be afforded. So far as this relates to public expenditure, it will be dealt with in the next chapter. But even in these days of universal free education, there is still something that a family has to "afford" when it sends its children to school, especially when the legal compulsion to do so has expired and the cost of clothes and meals has to be weighed against the money that might come in from wages. With greater affluence in the family, there is at least less economic compulsion on the sons and daughters to leave school on the earliest day that the law permits. But, secondly, if the father (and mother) can earn better wages, so can the son and daughter. Indeed, in proportion, it is the earnings of young people that have risen most. While the average weekly earnings of adult men in 1958 had risen to 372 per cent of the 1938 figure, and of adult women to 412 per cent, those of boys and girls rose to 429 per cent and 469 per cent respectively. Thus while the economic compulsion to leave school as early as possible has

diminished, the economic attraction of doing so has increased. Moreover, not only has the boy or girl who stays on at school after 15 had to resist the lure of an easy job at good wages, he has had to suffer a handicap in his income that lasts for several years. Two of the enquiries made for us have shown, as have many other pieces of evidence, that it is not until the early twenties, and sometimes even later, that the boy who has stayed on at school catches up in earning capacity the boy who left at 15. But, thirdly, it is now much more evident than it has ever been before that he does catch up in the end, and go well ahead. (So does his sister, if she continues in employment). Not only in the highest grade in intelligence, where the grammar school boy has always been able to look forward to a "career," but well down into the modern schools, it is now (or should be) apparent to all that education pays, always in the long run, and often quite quickly. This also is something new; for in the old days it was never certain, if a boy stayed at school to increase his intellectual attainments, that he would be able to find a job, either at once or for many years, that would match up to the additional qualifications he would obtain. In recent years there has been no such doubt. Not only have there been plenty of jobs for the qualified, there has been a steadily growing list of desirable callings that cannot be entered without a qualification. If, then, there are greater attractions in leaving school early, there are also, for the longer sighted, more prizes to be won by staying on.

71. On balance—but only on balance—these various effects of prosperity have been favourable to education. The sharp, the almost startling, rise in the numbers of 15 year-old boys and girls staying on to 16 in full-time education, and of 16 year-olds staying on to 18, is the most potent encouragement to further educational progress that can well be imagined. But every headmaster and headmistress can also tell of many promising young people whose development is interrupted by the lure of immediate high wages. The social changes described in the last chapter combine with high juvenile wages to give the young people of today infinitely more independence of their elders than they ever had before. Both in spirit and in purse, they are ready to support themselves. If, therefore, there is a greater demand for education, it is a conditional demand—it is for an education that seems to the boys and girls themselves to be meeting their needs.

THE IMPORTANCE OF BEING QUALIFIED

72. The other great force, in addition to growing material wealth, that is transforming the role of education is the rising importance of being properly qualified, to which some reference was made in

the last paragraph. To the grammar school boy and girl, this is of course nothing new: qualifications have always been required for the professions. What has been happening in the last twenty years is that the same requirement has been spreading over a much larger field of employment. Not so long ago, there were very few qualifications below those of the professions, save those that could be secured by merely serving in a given status for a stated length of time, as in many apprenticeships. Now there are scores of thousands of boys, and a smaller but steadily growing number of girls, in every type of school, who have a specific qualification of one kind or another in view. Two separate trends have combined to produce the same result. In the first place, there has been a rapid rise in the number of jobs that cannot be performed without some special knowledge or experience. It is difficult to quantify the trend by statistics; it is perhaps most clearly apparent in manufacturing industry, where the onrush of modern technology is yearly creating new jobs that never existed before, each with its special expertise. But it exists also in other technical employments and in commerce, where the old simple broad categories are steadily being split up into more specialised callings, for each of which some qualification is necessary.

73. In addition to this, however, there is a growing tendency for many occupations, which do not absolutely require a specific expertise for their performance, nevertheless to demand an attested standard of general education for entrance. This tendency is not perhaps to be endorsed without reservation. Admirable though any incentive to continued education is, it is sometimes applied too rigidly, and works harshly on individuals, who are debarred from entering a calling in which they could give good service for lack of some examination result which is not, when isolated by itself, of apparent relevance. But whether because they are really necessary or because they are required by regulation, qualifications are clearly here to stay. We shall have a great deal to say in this report, especially in Part Five, about the principle of specialisation in secondary education. Here it is enough to observe that the qualifications now sought in such large numbers, though they may be specific, are not by any means always specialised. Perhaps the largest aspect of the general phenomenon is the extent to which the General Certificate of Education at Ordinary level is being used as a means of selection for many particular forms of employment and training which did not demand the old School Certificate.

74. The tendency to seek special qualifications may be reinforced in the years immediately ahead by a special influence. We have been living through a period when juvenile labour has been unusually

scarce, and when young people have accordingly found it unusually easy to get jobs. There is at any one time a certain natural shape to the labour market and the number of openings for which boys and girls are sought will tend to be proportional to the size of the whole population of working age. But the numbers of boys and girls available (or potentially available) for the jobs, expressed as a proportion of the total working population, can vary quite considerably. This is shown in Table 11.

Table 11. Persons aged 15–19 as a Proportion of Total Population of Working Age (England and Wales).

Year	Persons Aged 15–19	Persons Aged 15–64	Column (1) as percentage of Column (2)
	(1) (000)	(2) (000)	(3) (%)
1901	3,247	20,463	*15·9*
1911	3,337	23,141	*14·4*
1921	3,503	25,095	*14·0*
1931	3,435	27,467	*12·5*
1951	2,704	29,242	*9·2*
1956	2,755	29,330	*9·4*
1958	2,840	29,465	*9·6*
1963	3,600	30,315	*11·9*
1968*	3,331	30,515	*10·9*
1973*	3,361	30,569	*11·0*
1978*	3,518	30,783	*11·4*

* Figures for these years are based on the Registrar General's projections, and assume nil net migration.

In the post-war years the ratio of young people to the total population of working age has been abnormally low, and barely more than two-thirds of what it was only a generation ago. But as the "bulge" moves into the population of working age, the ratio is going to rise quite sharply. This means, in all probability, that the supply of young workers is going to rise relatively to the demand for them. The 15 year-olds may be withdrawn from the labour market by a higher school-leaving age, but there will still be relatively more 16 year-olds, 17 year-olds and 18 year-olds seeking employment than there were. And whether or not the country as a whole continues to enjoy full employment, this is likely to mean that jobs for young people are going to be somewhat harder to find than they would otherwise have been. This will have several consequences for education, with some of which we shall be concerned later. The point to be made here is that it can hardly fail to increase the premium on being qualified.

THE IMPACT OF TECHNOLOGY

75. This growth in the importance of qualification is the latest manifestation of the principle of the division of labour, on which the whole of industrial civilisation has been erected. And though, as we have said, it is visible in every part of the field of employment, there can be no doubt that the biggest driving force behind it is that of technology. It is difficult for people whose outlook on the world took shape more than twenty years ago to realise how much the speed of change has increased since then. It is still more difficult to grasp the exciting challenge that it presents for those whose working lives will extend into the twenty-first century. Three brief examples may assist. The population of the world is at present increasing at the rate of at least 130,000 a day, so that in terms of population a new town the size of Derby comes into being every day. Even at present, about half the world's inhabitants are at starvation levels and all man's ingenuity will be needed to meet the challenge posed by his own fertility. The dimensions of another of the problems of the future are given by the comparison between the energy consumed in the United States, which is the equivalent of nine tons of coal per person each year, and the figure for India and great tracts of Africa and Asia, where it is less than five hundredweight. The world's annual demand for energy was 3,200 million tons of coal equivalent in 1950; it may be 7,000 in 1975 and 20,000 by the end of the century. The scientists and the technologists have little more than a generation to develop new sources of energy to meet these needs. Or, finally, there is the problem of endemic and epidemic disease, which there is now, for the first time in the world's history, reason to hope can be brought under control. These are only some of the problems with which the generation now at school will be faced.

76. To say that the world is living through a scientific revolution has become a truism. For all that, we are not sure that its consequences for education are always rightly drawn. The most obvious and familiar of them is, of course, the need to produce an adequate number of qualified scientists, technologists and technicians. This has been much emphasised in recent years, and we would not wish to say anything that would detract from its imperative character. It is not for us to express any opinion on the numbers of scientists and technologists that should be aimed at. Our concern is with the schools and we wonder whether it is generally realised how sharp has been, and still more will be, the increase in the numbers of boys and girls leaving school and seeking further scientific and higher technological training. There are three forces at work, which have come to be known in educational slang as the "Bulge," the "Trend" and the "Swing"—the increase in the numbers of young people,

the crest of which will not reach the age of 18 until 1965; the tendency to stay longer at school—specifically, in this connection, to enter the Sixth Form; and the growing preference for science and mathematics as subjects for specialisation. If all three continue for another few years as they have been going recently, their combined effect will be to produce by the middle of the next decade so many young people qualified to enter upon higher scientific and technological courses that it will be difficult to accuse the schools of not playing their part. The criticism may rather come from the young people themselves, who may find a lack of opportunities in higher education for pursuing the careers they have chosen. When, however, we turn to the technicians—the next grade down*—we have considerably more apprehension both about the numbers of boys and girls between the ages of 15 and 18 who are putting their feet on the lower rungs of the ladder and about the treatment they receive as they climb up it. This is the subject to which Part Six of the report is largely devoted.

77. Even when the technicians are added to the scientists and the technologists, even when the numbers of all three are made adequate, they will still remain a fraction, and a relatively small fraction, of the total working population. If the first impact of the technological age upon education is to create a need for large numbers of specially trained persons, this is not the way in which the great majority will be affected. In addition to the duty of setting increasing numbers of young people on the road to becoming scientists, technologists and technicians, the schools must also consider what needs to be done to the education of those who are not going to earn their living in these ways, in order to adapt it to the nature of the age in which they will spend their lives. There seem to be three main needs which can be identified. First, there is a need to ensure that the generality of educated men and women can comprehend the impact of technology upon society and to demolish the barrier of language and of modes of thought that tends to separate those who have been trained in the scientific discipline from those who know nothing of it. There is a danger in a further division of society, and in our opinion the community ought to insist that no man or woman should in future complete his or her education in such ignorance both of the dialect and of the philosophy of science as has been customary for so many in this country. To this proposition there is the natural corollary that greater efforts should also be made to see that the scientists and technicians should be exposed to the radiation of humane letters. We have a great deal to say both about the proposition and about its corollary in Chapter 25.

* For definitions of these terms, see Appendix A to Chapter 29.

78. If this first requirement is chiefly (but by no means entirely) a matter for abler boys and girls, the second affects all alike. This is that every citizen should be able to use the fruits of technology and to do so intelligently. Not all of our children will be scientists or technicians or even mechanics; but all of them will increasingly use machinery and scientific equipment of all kinds. It is not necessary to know how to make a motor car, or even to be able to repair it, in order to drive it; but to use a machine with intelligence and economy, it is desirable to have some conception of the principles on which it is designed and the limits of its capacities. Just as it is necessary for a craftsman to understand his materials, so it is necessary for every one in the second half of the twentieth century to have a modicum of mechanical common sense. For some, this can be made the foundation on which a sound course can be built; but for all, it needs to be part of the background to their education.

79. The third aspect of the impact of technology on general education—and, in the long run, undoubtedly the most potent—is the emphasis that it places on the rapidity of change, particularly in the conditions of work. A boy who enters industry today will not retire until well into the next century. In that time, the odds are that he will see at least one complete technological revolution in his industry. The job he will hold when he becomes a grandfather may not exist at all today; it will be concerned with processes not yet invented, using machines still to be designed. This is true not only of the "progressive" industries such as chemicals and electronics. It is probably just as true of agriculture, of older industries such as printing and of services such as transport. It may even be true of large sectors of the retail distributive trades. Clearly, the first quality that is needed to cope with such a world is adaptability.

80. This need for adaptability exposes an ambiguity in the word "skill," which could otherwise be used to sum up the whole argument. For many centuries, a skilled worker has meant one who in his early years acquired proficiency in a particular specialised form of craftsmanship and spent the rest of his life applying the skill thus acquired. Admittedly, the meaning of the word has been broadening out in recent decades, particularly in the engineering industry. But if one were to say, without further explanation, that what was needed today was an ever larger supply of skilled craftsmen, there is a risk that the conclusion drawn by many people would be that the need could be met by exposing a larger number of boys to the traditional methods of acquiring skill by watching and doing. Watching and doing will always be indispensable, but clearly they are not all that is needed when what the boy will in fact be doing in a few years' time is not now here to be watched. Skill has been thrown back from

the actual manufacturing process to the preparatory stages. The transition has been well put by Dr. Kate Liepmann in the report* of her enquiry into the present adequacy of the apprenticeship system:

> "Fifty or sixty years ago there was, in most industries, a clear-cut distinction between skilled and unskilled jobs. The former required considerable (though not, as a rule, outstanding) intelligence, a very high degree of trained sensitivity of certain senses, highly efficient eye-hand co-ordination, an intuitive knowledge of the properties and behaviour of a limited number of types of fundamentally simple machines, together with literacy and an acquaintance with simple arithmetic . . . Nowadays, the situation is very different . . . the locus of the skill which goes into a product has shifted from the shop-floor to the preparatory stages: to work done by technicians (draughtsmen, production, planning and development engineers), by designers and metallurgists, by works managers, estimating clerks, quantity surveyors and so forth. These are the real skilled occupations in modern industry."

It may be that there will even be a reduced need in the future for "skill" in the old-fashioned sense of the term; what will be needed in ever growing volume will be the quality that can perhaps best be described as "general mechanical intelligence." To say this is not, of course, to assert that training on the job must in future be replaced by an instruction based entirely on books. That would be absurd. But it is to assert that training in the new kind of skill will require an active collaboration between the workshop and the school or college, in which the relative participation of each and the methods they use will need to be kept under the most constant review.

81. The task of education in the technological age is thus a double one. On the one hand, there is a duty to set young people on the road to acquiring the bewildering variety of qualifications they will need to earn their living. On the other hand, running through and across these vocational purposes, there is also a duty to remember those other objectives of any education, which have little or nothing to do with vocation, but are concerned with the development of human personality and with teaching the individual to see himself in due proportion to the world in which he has been set. In the chapters that follow, we have tried not to lose sight of the economic and vocational purposes that an effective educational system should serve. But children are not the "supply" that meets any "demand" however urgent. They are individual human beings, and the primary concern of the schools should not be with the living they will earn but with the life they will lead.

* Apprenticeship—An Enquiry into its Adequacy under Modern Conditions. Pages 19–20 Kegan & Paul, 1960.

CHAPTER 6

Burdens and Benefits

82. The visitor to an old parish church will often see on the walls a list of parish charities and among them, often enough, gifts for the education of the children of the poor or for enabling orphans or poor boys to be apprenticed to a good trade. Entangled here, as always, are the twin conceptions of education. Look at it one way and the gifts are designed as a form of social service—to provide for the children of the poor something of what the benefactor acknowledged to be his duty to provide for his own children. But from another point of view, he was indirectly providing for a supply of craftsmen to maintain the wealth of the community—his gift was a form of capital investment. The community needed (and, of course, still needs) men who could read and write, conduct complicated business, sing elaborate music, build cathedrals, lead armies, frame and administer laws. To meet this need there were founded schools so that "there may never be wanting a succession of persons duly qualified to serve God in church and state." And so, today, as the methods by which wealth is produced become ever more complicated, new colleges are founded that the supply of men trained in their operation and development may not fail. But, equally, those who are educated in them may find in that training their personal fulfilment—their education is at one and the same time both a basic human right and a necessary individual contribution to society.

HUMAN RIGHTS AND NATIONAL INVESTMENT

83. These are still the two purposes that education serves in the vastly different circumstances of today. Both, however, have been transmuted. To the father's duty to his son and the rich man's charity to his neighbours has been added the state's duty to its future citizens; it is now considered to be the right of every boy and girl to be educated; and the right exists regardless of whether, in each individual case, there will be any return. From this point of view, education is one of the social services of the welfare state. The "service of God in church and state" has also been expanded (and has lost something in the process) into the need of the community to provide an adequate supply of brains and skill to sustain its economic productivity. From this point of view, education is a national investment.

84. These two purposes have been present throughout the development of public education in England described in Chapter 1. The relative emphasis has shifted from time to time. In the 1870's, for example, though the economic advantages of universal literacy were not ignored, it would be wrong to suppose that Gladstone and Forster were chiefly moved by considerations of this sort. They saw their Education Act as part of the great movement of reform, undertaken for its own sake, which was the special glory of Victorian liberalism. At the next great step forward, in 1902, the motives were more mixed; one historian has expressed the view that "no statesman less dominated than Balfour was by the concept of national efficiency would have taken [the Bill] up and carried it through."* But this was hardly the general attitude in the period when the foundations of the welfare state were being laid. Until very recently, education has been treated statistically, and, one may guess, generally regarded, as one of the social services—that is, as one of the burdens that the state lays on its taxpayers for the benefit of its citizens.

85. More recently, however, the emphasis has come back to education as an investment. There are perhaps two special reasons for this. The first is the new doctrine (how new few people now remember) that the nation can control its own economic development. And secondly, there is the new emphasis placed upon the belief that the prosperity, and even the safety, of the nation depend on "keeping up in the economic race." The consequential need to invest in education has been seen most clearly in the technological field; but it does not require much imagination for the argument to be extended to other educational spheres. Today, it seems to us that education is generally thought to be a "nation-building" investment fully as much as part of the welfare state.

86. In this report, we have made no attempt to disentangle these two purposes of education. Both are worthy and compelling, and we accept them both. Primacy must be given to the human rights of the individual boy or girl. But we do not believe that the pursuit of national efficiency can be ranked much lower—not least because without it the human rights themselves will not be secure. And in any event, the two purposes could not be disentangled even if it were desirable to do so. The education of the Nobel prizewinner is, by any test, a profitable investment for the community; there are many persons the justification for whose education must be sought almost entirely in what it does for them as individuals. But it is hard to tell which is which at the start, and not always easy later on. There are indeed parts of everybody's education which have no economic value, and there is nobody whose education is entirely without it.

* R.C.K. Ensor, *England, 1870–1914*, page 355.

THE COST OF EDUCATION

87. It is in the light of this dual objective that the "cost" of education should be considered. It is partly a burden on the national income, partly a means of sustaining it, and there is no way of distinguishing the parts. Expressed in money terms, the cost of education has been going steadily up. But so has everything else, and it serves little purpose to quote ever mounting figures in pounds sterling. The only way to arrive at a true measure of the cost of education is to estimate what proportion of the total national income is represented by education—that is, what proportion of each year's total national output of goods and services is devoted to the educational system. This is not an easy statistical problem. A statement by the Minister of Education in answer to a parliamentary question on the 11th March, 1958 referred to the expenditure of local education authorities out of public funds and showed the expenditure to have stood at 2·04 per cent of the national income in 1947 and at 2·88 per cent in 1957. A more comprehensive recent attempt to establish the position in percentages of the national income has been made by Mr. John Vaizey* using statistics for the whole area of the United Kingdom and for a wider range of publicly supported institutions than those referred to by the Minister. If all forms of expenditure that might be classified as coming under the head of education are included, Mr. Vaizey finds that the total rose from about 2·7 per cent of the national income in 1938 to about 3·4 per cent in 1955. A large part of this increase, however, was due to the great rise in expenditure on school meals, milk in schools and the school health service. Valuable as these things are, they do not form part of "education" as we use the term in this report. When they are excluded, both in the earlier year and the later, and also expenditure on universities and other forms of higher education, the percentage figures are, of course, reduced; and it appears to be demonstrable that the total cost of education in schools in 1955, expressed as a proportion of the total real national income, did not substantially exceed the real cost in 1938. We are fully aware that comparative exercises in showing overall percentages can be unprofitable even in social accounting. Our purpose in referring to these estimates is the wide-spread belief that education is now imposing a much greater burden on the economy of the nation than it did in the years before the war. So far as the position can be estimated, it would appear that, in the last twenty years, expenditure on the central purposes of education in schools, as distinct from health services on the one side and higher education on the other, has been doing little more than keep up with

* John Vaizey, *The Costs of Education*, George Allen & Unwin, 1958, to which reference should be made for the definitions and assumptions underlying the calculation and the qualifications to which the results are subject.

the general expansion of the national income. Moreover, this includes one more year of compulsory schooling.

88. Our concern in this report is not with education as a whole but with the education of boys and girls between the ages of 15 and 18. We make a number of recommendations in the following pages for extensions and improvements in the educational facilities that are at present available for young people of these ages. In some of these recommendations, we have had most clearly in mind what is due to these future citizens as a matter of equity; in others we have sought, in the national interest, to avoid any preventable waste of talent. And in almost every chapter we have found ourselves faced with the double need for larger numbers of teachers, instructors and tutors and for maintaining the standards of intellectual quality and personal character among them. Whatever their nature and whatever their purpose, all these things will cost money. We have not thought it appropriate, or even possible, to attach a price tag to each recommendation as we put it forward. But we do feel it incumbent upon us, before we begin to expound the programme for the teen-agers that has emerged from our enquiries and discussions, to establish that it is not beyond the country's means.

89. The most "costly" single recommendation we make is that the statutory leaving age should be raised to 16 in the second half of the next decade. What its cost will then be will depend on the circumstances of the time, but we can get some idea of it by considering what the cost would have been if the school-leaving age had been raised in a recent year. In 1957 about 420,000 15 year-old boys and girls (in Great Britain) entered employment. If the school leaving age had been 16, they would have remained at school. The real cost of raising it is therefore represented by the value of their work that would be lost *plus* the cost of providing schools and teachers to continue their education. The value of their work can be roughly measured by the wages paid to them.* If we assume (generously) that the average earnings of these boys and girls were £220 a year, that gives a total of £92 million, which compares with a national total of income from work of all kinds of £14,700 million, which would, therefore, have been reduced by about two-thirds of 1 per cent if the higher leaving age had been in force in

* The value of output is, of course, normally greater than the total of wages paid out. But these 15 year-olds are all beginners and many of them are in training. In view of this we do not think that the value of their output is underrated by being equated with the wages paid to them.

1957*. The average cost per place in secondary schools in 1957–58 was £77. For these older pupils the cost would be above the average, so let us take it at £100 a year. Thus to the cost of keeping these 420,000 boys and girls out of employment has to be added £42 million as the cost of keeping them in school. The total real cost of a further year of compulsory school would therefore in 1957 have been something of the order of £134 million—the financial cost to the Exchequer would, of course, have been much less. To this the costs of our other recommendations have to be added. By a similar calculation it can be shown that the annual real cost—in production lost and in expense incurred—of providing one day's release per week for the 16 and 17 year-olds (after the initial expense of providing the county colleges) might be in the region of £55–60 million. But even if the total direct and indirect effect of all our recommendations were to add something of the order of £200–250 million a year to the present cost of education, the addition to be gradually built up over a period of seven to ten years from now, it is still small in the context of social accounting. If it be regarded as an investment in national efficiency (as some parts of it assuredly are), it should be set alongside such annual investment items as £583 million (in 1958) for dwellings, £1,319 million for plant and machinery, £578 million for vehicles, ships and aircraft, or a total national annual outlay for fixed capital formation of £3,514 million.† Even if it be regarded as wholly "social service" expenditure with no economic yield at all (as all of it assuredly is not), it does not look very large alongside the *increase* of £228 million (from £1,575 million to £1,803 million) that occurred in the nation's annual outlay (at 1954 prices) on alcohol and tobacco in the seven years from 1950 to 1957.

90. One final comparison may not be out of place. Not so long ago the Chancellor of the Exchequer of the time set before the nation the objective of doubling the national income in twenty-five years.

* The main constituents of the gross national product in 1957 were as follows:

	(£ million)
Income from Employment	14,729
Gross profits from public and private enterprise	3,729
Rent	862
Net income from abroad	226
	19,546
Adjustments for stock appreciation and for residual errors	— 168
Gross National Product	19,378

† All these figures, of course, are of the *additions* made in a year to the total stock of the respective forms of capital and therefore properly (though roughly) comparable to the *additional* cost of education, if it is regarded as an investment.

The achievement of this would imply an average annual rate of increase of the resources available to the nation for all purposes of about 2·8 per cent compound. In eight years' time (which is roughly the time for which we are prescribing), that rate of increase (starting from the present gross national product of about £20,000 million) would have cumulated to something like £5,000 million *extra* resources available each year. What proportion of this additional national income will it be possible to give to education? Some will be needed in any event to meet the rising cost of the existing services. What we are suggesting is that, in addition, a volume of resources equal to less than one-twentieth of the national increase should, by that time, be devoted to improving and extending education between 15 and 18. This is not negligible. But it does not seem to us to be extravagant, particularly since it will help to bring about that increase in productive capacity on which the whole calculation depends. Nor must it be supposed that longer schooldays necessarily mean a shorter working life. Improvements in health (themselves in part the product of educational progress) are steadily lengthening the period over which the average man is gainfully occupied—gainfully both to himself and to the community. That statistical abstraction, the average male, leaving school at the statutory age, was one year older in 1955 than in 1931, but he could nevertheless look forward to one more year of working life and two more years of retirement. The nation had gained four more years of potential productive work for its average male citizen and had given one of them back for longer schooling and two for longer retirement.*

91. These calculations of "social cost" are one thing. Finding the money is likely to seem to a harassed Chancellor of the Exchequer to be quite another. We have no wish to underrate the practical difficulties of financing educational expansion. Nor is it for us to set the relative priorities of education and of the many other claims upon the national resources. But we have no doubt in our minds that the time is ripe for another step forward—indeed, for a series of co-ordinated steps forward—in the progressive development of English education. If it be regarded as a social service, as part of the "condition of the people," there seems to us to be no social injustice in our community at the present time more loudly crying out for reform than the condition in which scores of thousands of our children are released into the labour market. If it be regarded as

* The actual figures are that, in 1931, a boy leaving school at 14 had an average expectation of 47·5 years at work followed by 4·5 years in retirement. In 1955 a boy leaving school at 15 had an average expectation of 48·4 years at work followed by 6·5 years in retirement. If reckoned not from the statutory leaving age but from birth, the increase in the expectation has been much greater—from 40·6 years of working life starting at 14 to 45·6 years starting at 15. See *The Length of Working Life of Males in Great Britain*. H.M.S.O., 1959

an investment in national efficiency, we find it difficult to conceive that there could be any other application of money giving a larger or more certain return in the quickening of enterprise, in the stimulation of invention or in the general sharpening of those wits by which alone a trading nation in a crowded island can hope to make its living.

Part Two

The Development of the Modern School

CHAPTER 7

The Demand for a Longer School Life

92. Our terms of reference cover the period from 15 to 18, the years that lie between the end of compulsory school life and the time at which for many generations professional and middle class parents have thought it right that their own children, almost irrespective of ability, should leave school and go out into the world. Other social groups have been content, and even anxious, that their children should start to earn a living as early as possible, unless perhaps a particular boy or girl was clearly marked out by ability to rise to a higher position in the world than his parents occupied. It is on this basis that our educational institutions have been moulded: the majority of schools have not the means to carry the education of more than a handful of their pupils much beyond the compulsory age of attendance.

PARENTS' AND PUPILS' WISHES

93. There are still those who believe that education is an expensive luxury forced on a reluctant people. Is it lack of opportunity or lack of desire which decides that more than four-fifths of the boys and girls in England should have left school before they are 16? One of the main limiting factors in educational advance has been the belief that education resembled an unpleasant medicine of which parents, who are also electors, could not be expected to swallow more than a small dose at a time. This may well have been true in the past—we have no means of knowing—but we believe that it is far from the truth at present. Old opinions, however, die hard, and it is important to look carefully at the evidence.

94. What, to begin with, do parents now make of the raising of the school-leaving age to 15 which happened in 1947? Of the parents of children in modern and all-age schools questioned in the Social Survey, over four-fifths have now apparently accepted 15 as the right age for leaving school. Ten per cent would have liked their children to have stayed longer at school, but only 4·5 per cent thought they should have left earlier. This is surely a remarkable degree of acquiescence in a reform which was certainly controversial, and of which the first effects came in for a good deal of criticism on the grounds of the waste of public money and of pupils' time which was felt to be involved. Moreover the parents of 48 per cent of the boys and of 42 per cent of the girls who left at Christmas or Easter said

they would have been willing for them to stay on to the summer to complete the school year. In the grammar and technical schools, where there is provision for courses extending to the age of 18, the proportion of parents who would have liked their children to have made longer use of the facilities than they had done rose to over one-fifth, and only 3 per cent regretted that they had not left earlier. Before the war it was not uncommon for the parents of a child who had won a 'special place' at a secondary school, as grammar schools were then called, to refuse to allow him to take it up because of the longer school life which it would have involved. Those who have been responsible for interviewing candidates for the state scholarships to universities given to mature students have told us how often in their experience they have encountered men and women in their thirties who lost the chance of a secondary education in this way. We believe that this reluctance to allow a child to have his chance is now uncommon except in a few places. Indeed the burden of the complaints which become increasingly numerous from parents in every kind of neighbourhood and occupation is that their children, through failure to secure admission to a grammar school, have been condemned to an abbreviated schooling.

95. It is encouraging to find that the demand for a longer education is greater among the boys and girls than among their parents. We have seen that about 10 per cent of the parents of boys and girls who had been educated in secondary modern schools would have liked a longer school life for their children. Sixteen per cent of the boys and 23 per cent of the girls who had been brought up in modern or all-age schools, when they were asked the same questions, said that they would have liked at least a year longer at school—they were not asked about shorter periods. Six per cent of the boys, and 8 per cent of the girls, not necessarily those who wanted to stay longer at school, claimed to have had some full-time education or training afterwards elsewhere than at school, though we are doubtful whether a good deal of it was of a kind that could be considered the equivalent of a longer school life. Four or five years ago, when these boys and girls in the Social Survey sample left school, there were relatively few fifth-year courses in modern schools. They lived in all parts of England and the answers they gave seem to us to support the view that the encouraging experience of those areas which have subsequently made generous provision is not caused by some peculiar local circumstances, but could be reproduced generally almost wherever an authority made the necessary provision.

96. How justified is the complaint that two-thirds of the population go to "blind alley" schools? It will, we think, be generally conceded that a pupil in an all-age school, that is to say a school taking pupils

of all ages from 5 or 7 to 15, is genuinely penalised. He will not get more than the minimum educational provision without a special effort to seek it elsewhere. The all-age schools are not the only ones that cannot cater satisfactorily for the needs of those who want to carry their education on beyond the statutory leaving age. A small school has much to commend it, but a small secondary modern school is unlikely in existing circumstances to provide a sufficiently large number of candidates for a complete fifth-year course to make it economic to provide one. A school receiving only one new form of thirty pupils a year is certainly too small for this purpose, and only in favourable conditions is it likely that a two-form entry school will be big enough. It is difficult to make any accurate estimate of the proportion of pupils who are in secondary modern schools too small ever to be able to offer attractive and economic facilities for extended courses,* but it is probably in the neighbourhood of 17 per cent of the number in modern schools, or about 10 per cent of the secondary school population of school age. We conclude that at least 15 per cent of the whole age-group are pupils in schools which by reason of their size or organisation are not in a position to provide extended courses of their own. And geography, not ability, decides which children shall go to these schools. Authorities, then, will have to take special steps to see that these boys and girls have opportunities to carry further their full-time education, whether by transfer to another school or to a college of further education.

97. It must not be thought that all large secondary modern schools offer extended courses. Those that do, indeed, are still a minority, though a rapidly growing one. In 1954, for example, in one of the largest cities, extended courses were available in only 12 out of 101 modern schools; by 1957 the number was 17, and last year it was 37. But although the courses were open to pupils in all the hundred schools, four-fifths of those taking them in 1957 came from the 17 schools where the courses were held. There is nothing unusual in this experience. It takes a very strong desire for education to overcome inertia and the discomfort of settling in for a short time to a new school with strange companions. Very few authorities, if any, provide extended courses in all their secondary modern schools, and some do so in none. For three reasons then—the survival of all-age schools, the existence of large numbers of small secondary modern schools, the embryonic stage of provision even in large secondary modern schools—the present numbers of extended courses are very inadequate evidence of the strength of the desire among modern school parents and pupils to stay longer than they need at school.

* By an extended course we mean a fifth-year course given in a school where not all are expected to make use of it. Thus a fifth-year course in a grammar school is not an extended course; in a modern school it is.

The most that the national figures show is that about 4 per cent of those who leave modern schools each year have stayed there until they are 16 compared with only 0·3 per cent of pupils in all-age schools. But if the absolute numbers are small, the rate of growth is healthy.

98. Because the possibility of a longer school life is so new—few of the existing extended courses are more than five years old—it is only by looking at the position in those areas and those schools which have made effective provision that the strength of the potential demand can be effectively seen. In some of the schools in the city we have been considering, half the age-group are now enrolling for extended courses. The numbers enrolled for a fifth-year course have risen from 331 in 1956 to 1,188 in 1958. In a large southern county borough, where for some years now there has been fairly wide provision of extended courses in modern schools, parents are asked at the end of the primary school course how much secondary education they want their children to receive. The answer for last year (1958) was that 27 per cent of the girls and 28 per cent of the boys were put down for seven years, the full grammar school course to 18, and that a further 30 per cent of the boys and 40 per cent of the girls were entered for a five-year course. The parents, then, of two-thirds of the whole age group wanted their children to stay at school at least one year more than they need by law.

99. It may be argued that it is one thing for parents of an 11 year-old child to say that they want him to stay at school until he is 16 or 18 (especially when they may think that this will help to determine the school to which he is sent) and quite another thing to see that he does so. The past history of early leaving from grammar schools suggests that a good many who undertook to complete a five-year course failed to do so. No doubt there will always be some wastage—some inescapable, some not—in any voluntary enrolment for education; and no doubt the longer ahead the commitment has to be made, the greater will be the wastage to be expected. For this reason it is important to set beside the two-thirds figure given by the southern county borough other proportionate figures taken when the children are older and more able to take a hand in the decision—it is noteworthy how often the final decision is left by the parents to the child. A middle-sized county borough in the North of England has long made provision in its technical college for full-time courses for boys and girls leaving secondary modern schools, which up to the present have not had extended courses of their own. About a quarter of the age-group apply, and as another fifth are already in grammar schools, this means that at 15 rather over 45 per cent of the boys and girls are seeking full-time education; the proportion

has been rising steadily. Lack of room prevents some getting what they want. In Leicestershire where, in two areas, the entry to the grammar school is now delayed until 14 and is then open to all who agree to stay at school at least until 16, the provision of grammar school places was made on the assumption that 40 per cent of the parents would opt for the full course to 16; that proportion was reached in the first year. The whole experience of the comprehensive schools shows a much greater willingness to stay on than had ever been expected by those who argued from the experience of the working of the tripartite system as it was a very few years ago.

THE PROVISION OF EXTENDED COURSES

100. We can now answer the question that was asked in paragraph 93. The evidence seems to us to establish that it is insufficient opportunity, at least for a very large number of children, and not lack of desire for more education, that makes them leave school at 15. Given the chance, it looks as if parents would soon see to it that the proportion of 15 year-olds at school was doubled. The evidence goes to show that good educational facilities, once provided, are not left unused; they discover or create a demand that public opinion in the past has been slow to believe existed. If this is so, then it follows that many boys and girls are at present deprived of educational facilities which they would use well and which they are legally entitled to receive. The translation of this great potential demand into effective demand, by the provision of extended courses manifestly within the reach of every secondary school boy or girl who wants them, seems to us to be an immediate task for the educational system.

101. In the White Paper on Secondary Education, published in December, 1958, the government has asked local education authorities to take the necessary steps to bring this about, and has promised them its financial support. The way forward lies through the abolition of all-age schools and the provision of the necessary specialist facilities for five-year courses in secondary schools of all types—though the material facilities will not be of much avail without an increased supply of teachers, particularly of specialists. On what scale should this provision be? In previous paragraphs we have shown that in small pockets there is already an effective demand for five-year courses for 40 per cent of the pupils. There is nothing exceptional about these areas except in the generosity of the provision. In our opinion they could be reproduced in most, if not in all, parts of the country. If this is to be done, however, it will require a big effort wherever it is undertaken, and a very big one indeed in many areas. Table 12 shows what would be involved both in the country

as a whole and also in certain areas, chosen because they are virtually self-contained, and between them comprising about 13 per cent of the total.

Table 12. Estimated Proportion of all pupils who have 5 years full-time education in maintained schools or colleges of further education (England).

Area	Location of Area	15 and 16 year-olds as percentage of 13 and 14 year-olds two years earlier		Average annual increase
		1950–51 percentage	1956–57 percentage	percentage
A	South-West	*21*	*28*	*1·1*
B	South-West	*20*	*28*	*1·3*
C	South	*19*	*25*	*1·0*
D	East Anglia	*15*	*18*	*0·5*
E	East Anglia	*14*	*19*	*0·8*
F	North-West	*20*	*23*	*0·5*
G	North-West	*29*	*32*	*0·5*
H	North-East	*12*	*17*	*0·8*
I	North-East	*12*	*15*	*0·5*
England and Wales		*19*	*25*	*1·0*

NOTE: A–I are each self-contained units so far as education of 13 to 16 year-olds is concerned.

It is clear that we should not get very far by 1965 towards a target that we could regard as acceptable if we could only count on the continuation of the recent rate of increase. But whereas when we speak of the 'trend' towards a longer Sixth Form life in Part Five we shall primarily be thinking of a movement to make fuller use of existing facilities, at this earlier age we are more concerned with the creation of facilities which in most secondary schools did not exist a few years ago. A sudden growth is to be expected in each school that becomes equipped to meet, and to create, the demand for five years of secondary education. Even on the voluntary system, most authorities, in our view, ought to provide for nearly half the 15 year-olds to be in school by 1965, and some authorities will need to find places for more. To do less would be to deprive boys and girls, who could easily have been persuaded to stay on, of the chance of a real secondary education promised them in the 1944 Act.

102. There does not seem to be much doubt that the form in which provision is made for the years after the end of compulsory school life does have a bearing on the proportion who will make use of it. Maximum yield is not, of course, the only criterion to be considered, but it is an important one for a country which is short of educated manpower, and a serious one for those boys and girls whose effective chance of carrying their education further may depend on the way in which the opportunity is presented to them. An "escape clause" attitude of mind—"there was a perfectly good opening, if he'd had the sense to see it and take it"—will not do. This said, however, it is clear that different methods of provision will be followed in different parts of the country, and that in some areas make-shift arrangements will have to be made for the next few years if there is to be any possibility of extended courses at all. In the main, the form of provision for those who want to carry their full-time education on to the age of 16 will depend upon the general form of provision for secondary education adopted by the local education authority. We do not propose in this chapter to discuss the merits of the various methods of organising secondary education except to insist that any satisfactory system must allow for a substantial overlap between various kinds of courses. There are no natural frontiers which isolate one group of pupils from another, so that one passes from one mental climate to another as one moves from one intelligence quotient or examination mark to the next. There are, however, some general matters affecting organisation to which we feel that attention should be directed.

103. First, then, voluntary continuation of full-time education, apart from pupils following a grammar school curriculum, usually means staying at school to 16, not to 17 or 18; 16 is, on the one hand, the age of apprenticeship, and, on the other, the customary age at which boys and girls first tackle an external examination (if the 11-plus test is excluded). Twelve years ago there was a gap of two years or more between the end of the modern school and the end of the first stage of the grammar school, at which most pupils left. Today that gap has been halved. We are thus concerned in general only with one additional whole year of school life—the question of the fractional parts of a school year caused by leaving at Christmas or Easter is considered in Chapter 13.

104. Side by side with this, we put as the second general consideration the fact that we are not dealing with especially able boys and girls. It is true that most of the pupils in extended courses are drawn from the 'A' streams in modern schools, but they are not necessarily those boys and girls who just failed to secure admission to a grammar school at 11. We know that modern schools do in fact recruit a

substantial proportion of their boys and girls for extended courses from their 'B' streams, and a few from even lower down. Comprehensive schools have a corresponding experience. It follows that neither transfer to a grammar school at 12 or 13, nor the equally early identification of candidates for an extended course, will catch all those who, when the time comes, will be able and willing to undertake one. On the other hand, it is almost equally inappropriate to plan an extended course simply as a one-year pendant to a normal modern school course complete in itself. The most widely adopted and easiest solution seems to be to make up the membership of the extended course at the end of the third year, when the thoughts of pupils as well as of parents turn seriously to preparation for careers, and to provide a continuous two-year programme of work lasting through the fourth and fifth years.

105. The third point is that the fifth year of secondary education, with which extended courses are now concerned, will lie almost entirely within the period of compulsory school life as soon as the leaving age is raised to 16. Every modern school will then provide a fifth year course.

106. These three considerations, taken together, suggest strongly that the right place for an extended course is in the school in which a boy or girl is at the moment he decides to take one. These boys and girls are only going to stay one year beyond the minimum leaving age in full-time education so there is hardly time both for settling in to a new institution and learning its ways and for covering the new work. Too many of them only discover the desire for a course too late to make transfer to a grammar school at 12 or 13 possible, and too few have the capacity really to stand the grammar school pace, or the accelerated pace necessary to catch up. All are still at an age when the general aspects of education are as important as any vocational aims or material. It seems to us to follow that the provision for extended courses should wherever possible avoid the necessity for transfer to another institution for the last year, though in certain areas, until all-age schools can be eradicated and where modern schools are small or especially overcrowded, it may be necessary temporarily to provide a specially designed course in the local technical college. It follows, too, that as many secondary schools as possible should have extended courses. It would be folly to expect every secondary school to provide every sort of extended course, and provision may have to be made for transfer between schools and courses; but we expect that on the whole the pull of familiar surroundings and companions will be stronger than the vocational pull of a particular type of extended course. Once again it follows that, if secondary schools generally are to have extended

courses, there is a minimum size below which they would be highly uneconomical to staff. A school with an intake of 90 boys and girls a year (a three-form entry) can usually support with reasonable economy extended courses for both boys and girls, even though their interests rapidly diverge at this stage, but we should be happier if co-educational schools had an intake of 120 boys and girls (a four-form entry). In single sex schools, as far as the economical provision of extended courses is concerned, a rather smaller size is practicable.

CHAPTER 8

The Nature of Extended Courses and the Place of External Examinations

107. Perhaps the major impulse which leads to the establishment of extended courses in modern schools comes from a recognition that any system of selection of pupils, however accurate a classification it may have provided at the time it was made, becomes to some extent inaccurate with the passage of time. It is also one of the principal reasons why in some areas comprehensive and bilateral schools are being introduced. The longer the period for which a system of selection is asked to predict, the greater the subsequent need for redistribution. Much careful research work has shown pretty clearly that a fresh classification after four years, i.e. about the age of 15, would have redistributed between selective and non-selective schools about 14 per cent of the pupils. By the time they join up for National Service this 14 per cent has become 22 per cent among Army recruits and 29 per cent among the more homogeneous group of R.A.F. recruits, according to the evidence of the National Service Survey. This is what we should expect from the changes and chances of mortal life, and it seems increasingly clear that we cannot hope to avoid error by further refinements in the process of selection. The problem is not confined to selection for secondary schools. It occurs whenever it is necessary to select candidates—for employment quite as much as for education. With human beings, no selection can be regarded as final.

WHO TAKES EXTENDED COURSES?

108. The fallibility of selective systems is not, however, the only reason for the provision of extended courses. Vocational education for the learned professions, the education of the grammar school, was always necessary and has always been respectable. Other forms of vocational education have in the past been looked at a little askance by most schools. But today an increasing number of secondary schools of various kinds have extended courses in such varied subjects as agriculture, building or engineering; or related to commerce, nursing and the needle trades. They have become respectable as they have become more necessary, and most of them have in the process been discovered to be exceedingly good educational instruments, even for those who may not in the end follow the

occupation to which they are allied. They can serve, too, the wider social purpose of enabling pupils to see that one reason for their education is to enable them to make a contribution to the wealth of the community. Those vocational courses which have not these general educational qualities have no right in our view to a place in the school curriculum.

109. In the same way, if we look at what lies behind the individual decisions to enrol for an extended course, we shall find that the prevailing reason is concerned with the pupil's career. Boys and girls, and their parents, rightly have an eye on what they are to do with their life. They decide to stay longer at school because doing so will enable them to take up careers which would not otherwise be open to them—more interesting or secure jobs, jobs which in the end will be better paid. A longer school life is not only absolutely an advantage to them (though this is certainly the case), but relatively so as well. By taking an extended course they get something that others have not got. These are not the only reasons which influence individual boys and girls, and certainly the benefit they get from the decision, once it is made, is not limited to a vocational advantage; but, again, it is the strength of this career ambition which provides the bulk of the demand for a longer school life.

110. It is not surprising, therefore, to find that it is on the whole the abler pupils in modern schools who provide the majority of those who at present demand a longer school education. It is more important to realise that the demand is by no means confined to them. This is most clearly visible in the experience of the comprehensive schools. In one girls' comprehensive school, for instance, two-thirds of the girls at present decide to take a full two-year course from 14 to 16, and this is fairly general experience in other comprehensive schools. Those who stay on in this school are drawn from every one of the 15 forms in an age-group in gradually decreasing numbers ranging from the whole of the top two ability streams and all but two girls in the third stream to 3 out of 30 in the fifteenth. The fact that there are substantial numbers of boys and girls, with intelligence quotients not above 90, who wish, given a suitable opportunity, to stay at school until they are 16 gives those schools which have courses for them a great responsibility. They have the opportunity of discovering what all schools will need to know when the school-leaving age is raised to 16—what is best for those of well below average ability. More commonly, however, the result of an extended course is confined to showing how much pupils of average ability can achieve in an academic course, given the chance and the desire—and it is far more than we used to think possible. In one four-form entry girls' school, in a district where there are grammar

school places for about 17 per cent of the intake, about 85 per cent of the girls in the 'A' stream of the modern school and between 13 and 20 per cent of the 'B' stream girls enter the G.C.E. form.

111. The pupils taking extended courses come from very varied backgrounds. We noted in Chapter 2 that the modern schools as a whole are the most homogeneous element among English schools—the children of non-manual workers are much under-represented, and the children of semi-skilled workers over-represented. This is much less true of their extended courses, where there is a substantial contribution from most social groups. No systematic information is available, but the records of a number of individual schools show among the parents a fair proportion of officers from the Services, farmers, professional men and managers as well as larger numbers of manual workers of all kinds. If it is important in the grammar schools to make sure that there is, especially in the Sixth Form, a good representation of boys from working class homes, it is just as important that middle class families should be well represented at the top of modern schools. What becomes of the boys and girls who have been on extended courses? Very few indeed become unskilled workers—well under 1 per cent, if the experience of a big midlands city is anything to go by. The majority of the boys are probably looking for skilled manual work or hoping to become technicians. Apprenticeships in electrical and aeronautical engineering or Service apprenticeships are very common among the jobs which are taken by boys. The girls go mainly into clerical work, but a considerable number have nursing in view. There is a small but steady stream of transfers from extended courses in modern schools to grammar school Sixth Forms. From no school are they likely to be numerous in any one year, but the yield over a period is often considerable. One school, where extended courses are of long standing, has provided in nine years 19 students for training colleges and 7 for universities. A group of schools with a combined intake of about 650 boys and girls recently sent on 15 pupils in one year to a grammar school Sixth Form.

THE GROWTH OF EXTERNAL EXAMINATIONS

112. The first ten years, or a little less, of the history of the modern school was a period largely free of external examinations. School life had not lengthened to the stage at which the School Certificate or its successor was a possibility, and there was neither the will nor the means to introduce anything else in its place. The last few years, however, have seen a remarkable change. The growth of extended courses and the growth of external examinations have gone hand in hand. This is a matter on which the Minister has specially asked us

to advise him.* There are probably few schools with extended courses whose pupils do not sit for one or other of the available examinations. And, since some external examinations can be taken successfully after a four-year secondary course, pupils are entered for them from some schools which do not have an extended course in the sense which we have given the term.** The number of secondary schools that use one external examination or another is approaching, and may very possibly already have passed, half the total number; but the number of candidates they put forward, though increasing rapidly, is very much less than half the age-group (except, of course, in selective schools).

113. It may seem strange that, on this important matter, no precise statistics should be available and that we should be able to go no further than the rough proportions given in the last paragraph. The reason is not far to seek. The General Certificate of Education awarded by one or other of the nine authorised examining bodies is the only officially recognised public examination, and it has hitherto been the policy of the Ministry of Education to discourage, if not actually to prohibit, the taking of any other public examinations by the schools. A special sub-committee of the Secondary School Examinations Council is at present undertaking a detailed enquiry into the facts, which will in due course throw a great deal of badly needed light on the present state of affairs. We were given the opportunity, for which we are grateful, to appoint one of our members to sit with this sub-committee as an observer. For this reason, we have made no enquiries of our own. But there are certain broad considerations which do not rest upon detailed information. It has seemed to us that we can best answer the Minister's request by attempting to explain how we think external examinations would (or would not) fit into the general picture of the educational system as we see it. There can be no doubt that the taking of external public examinations in modern schools is growing very rapidly, in respect both of the number of schools taking part and the proportion of pupils becoming candidates. There is little reason to doubt that it will continue to grow—and not necessarily out of conviction but by the sheer difficulty from a public relations point of view of being the odd school, or the odd pupil, out. We think that this is already becoming the case, and that an attempt must now be made to work out arrangements that will both meet the genuine needs of individuals for some certification of their standard of knowledge and also safeguard the real educational interests of the whole body of pupils, both those who can achieve a certificate and those who cannot.

* See Appendix II.

** See the footnote to paragraph 96.

THE GENERAL CERTIFICATE OF EDUCATION IN THE MODERN SCHOOL

114. One aim of extended courses, in the eyes of both parents and authorities, is to provide opportunities for boys and girls who were not selected for grammar schools at 11, but who subsequently show themselves capable of reaching the same educational standards as many of those who were. For this group there is no adequate substitute for the General Certificate of Education. It alone is universally acceptable to universities and professional bodies as exempting candidates from their own entrance examinations, and in some areas at least it is being prescribed by employers as a necessary qualification for certain engineering apprenticeships—in the aircraft industry, for example. In the last five years the number of G.C.E. candidates from modern schools has more than doubled, although the size of the 15 year-old and 16 year-old age-groups as a whole has declined. It looks, moreover, as if the G.C.E. is coming to play an increasing part in the curriculum of extended courses, as Table 13 suggests.

Table 13. G.C.E. Candidates from Modern Schools compared with the number of 15 year-olds in Modern Schools in the preceding January (England and Wales).

(1) Year	(2) 15 year-old Age Group	(3) Pupils Aged 15 in January	(4) G.C.E. Candidates in July	Col. 4 as percentage of Col. 3
1953	571,000	19,363	4,068	*21*
1954	578,000	21,283	5,585	*26*
1955	568,000	23,412	7,334	*31*
1956	545,000	24,329	8,571	*35*
1957	537,000	29,428	11,266	*38*
1958	604,000	33,984	16,787	*50*

NOTE: The number of pupils aged 15 in January is taken as the best available indication of the size of the group starting an extended course. All but a handful could have left school at the end of the Christmas term; but by no means all will complete the fifth year, or even the full four years.

115. The General Certificate of Education, unlike its predecessors the School and Higher School Certificates, is an examination in which no minimum number or special combination of subjects is laid down by the examining boards, though of course stipulations of this kind are made by most of the professional and other bodies which allow it to count towards exemption from their own requirements. How many subjects does the typical candidate take? In 1954,

the last year for which a full analysis was given in the Ministry's annual report, 68 per cent of all Ordinary level candidates under 17 were entered for 6, 7 or 8 subjects. In 1958 the average number of subjects for which candidates from modern schools were entered was 4. The over-all pass rate for all subjects at Ordinary level in 1958 was 59 per cent; for candidates from modern schools it was 52 per cent. Results of this order certainly justify, as far as over-all figures can, the existence of extended courses and the policy of entering at least their more promising members for the G.C.E.

116. It is not, however, sufficient to ask how many subjects a candidate took. It is necessary to consider what combinations of subjects are most commonly selected before coming to any conclusion about the place of G.C.E. in modern schools. Once again there are, no doubt, very wide variations in practice, and so there should be; but it seems worth while to compare in broad terms what happens in modern and grammar schools. English language and other English subjects—English literature, history and geography—are common to all types of school, but foreign languages are a relatively much more common element in grammar school G.C.E. courses, while the so-called "practical" subjects—art, handicraft, technical drawing, domestic subjects, and commercial subjects—play a relatively very much greater part in modern schools than in grammar schools. It is probable that most candidates from a modern school Fifth Form offer at least one of these subjects. Of the total number of subjects entered for by boys 28 per cent are mathematics and science subjects—the impetus no doubt comes from the exemptions which they confer in the National Certificate series of examinations at technical colleges and because they are asked for by employers. Only 13 per cent of the girls' entries are in this category, and four-fifths of their science entries are for biology, which is closely linked with nursing as a career. It is reasonable to conclude that where three or four subjects are offered in the G.C.E. by modern school boys, they reflect a curriculum which has at least a sensibly balanced core. We have more reserve about the suitability of the curriculum of the girls' G.C.E. courses, where commercial subjects form a large part of it. It is fair to add that the pattern of G.C.E. courses in modern schools is a reflection of the strength and weaknesses of their staffing. Art and crafts rank high because (with some exceptions) they are subjects with an ample supply of well qualified teachers. Mathematics, science and foreign languages would have more candidates if more suitably qualified teachers were available.

117. Although two or three G.C.E. subjects will, we believe, prove to be within the reach of more modern school pupils than would have been thought possible a few years ago, these pupils are never

likely to be more than a small fraction of the total. In the last few years there has been a vocal demand for a new examination at a lower level than G.C.E. to be made available for boys and girls at the age of 16. This demand is now being met by some of the various examining bodies which have previously been concerned almost wholly with the vocational field and with part-time students but which now have "School Certificates" intended to be taken at the end of the fifth year. They resemble the old School Certificate, which was the predecessor of the G.C.E., in that they are examinations in which a minimum number and a particular combination of subjects are required, but they are designed to examine work at a considerably lower level.* These examinations are only at the beginning of their development and the number of candidates is still small, but it is likely to grow rapidly.

118. It is, therefore, important to consider their relation to the position of G.C.E. in modern schools. The importance of G.C.E. is that it provides the same qualification (subject to the right combination of subjects) that a grammar school gives. It opens the same doors to the same careers. Given the certificate, the school at which it was won is irrelevant from the point of view of admission to further education. A lower level qualification is no substitute. Where a boy can get a G.C.E. with a sufficient range of subjects from a modern school, the late-developer has the opportunity and incentive he needs; in schools where this is not possible, his original handicap remains. A G.C.E. form** in a modern school, then, is a sensible recognition that, however careful the selection at 11, there will be a substantial overlap by 15 between grammar and modern schools.

119. But the G.C.E. candidates are a small minority in the modern schools. Is it right that extended courses should be virtually confined to G.C.E. courses, at least as far as the possibility of getting some sort of external certificate is concerned? Is there a group of boys and girls of lower ability, whose achievements will never reach G.C.E. level, but who could work for some kind of external examinations whose certificate would be worth having? If so, can we expect both groups to be provided for in the same school? To answer this it is necessary to go back to the variable factors which govern what can

* There are in addition a number of examinations designed to be taken at the age of 15 instead of 16. These are referred to in paragraph 134.

**The term is ambiguous. It may mean an opportunity to take one subject, perhaps a 'non-academic' one, often in conjunction with other subjects in some lower-level examination. It may also mean a form preparing for a sufficiently wide range of "academic" subjects to secure transfer to a grammar school Sixth Form or exemption from some of the requirements of a professional body. It is in the latter sense we use it here.

be done in a modern school, of which the most important are the actual size of the school itself and the extent to which the brightest boys and girls in its neighbourhood have been diverted to selective schools. A large modern school in an area where the selective school provision is not markedly above the national average can probably provide courses both for the G.C.E. and for other examinations. A smaller school in the same conditions would probably have to choose between them—we do not believe that it is practicable to teach for both types of examination in the same class, except where staffing is so generous as to make individual tutorial work possible. Where the selective provision is markedly above the national average, unless social conditions are especially favourable, it is probable that only big modern schools would at present have enough pupils capable of taking a balanced set of G.C.E. subjects to make a form, though middle-sized schools could hope to provide lower-level examination groups.

120. It is clear that there cannot be equality of educational opportunity unless G.C.E. courses are made available to all boys and girls who have the ability to take them. By "made available" we do not necessarily mean that they should be able to take a G.C.E. course in their own school. Great though the difficulties of transfer to another school in mid-course are, that will often be the only possibility. Only a minority of modern schools, as we have just seen, are likely to have enough candidates to make a G.C.E. form. Moreover, there are disadvantages in taking two examinations in the same school, even where numbers permit.

THE CASE FOR A LOWER-LEVEL EXAMINATION

121. But it would obviously be wrong to let the desirability of G.C.E. courses for the brightest pupils of the modern schools stand in the way of a lower-level examination for a much greater number—if there is a good purpose to be served by one. Is there? This is a question which cannot be decided without some consideration of the role of examinations in school life. In a schoolboy's education they certainly play a useful part in assessing progress and in stimulating effort. All English secondary schools, with very few exceptions, use examinations for these two purposes; they are used at least once a year and, of course, most of them are not external. Even in a grammar school, for example, where external examinations traditionally bulk large, five of the seven annual full-scale examinations which pupils face are internal. In the later stages of education, however, when the attention of pupils is already fixed on what lies beyond school, it is probable that internal examinations depend for some of heir efficacy on the relation they bear to forthcoming external ones, for which they are regarded as a preparation.

122. A second reason for examinations is that they give a particular school and its staff the opportunity to assess their results against the general experience of all schools. For this purpose a purely internal examination is useless, a purely external examination the easiest to administer. The latter is not, however, the only method by which this safeguarding of standards can be achieved through examinations, while it has dangers to which we shall return. An alternative method is that of an internal examination externally assessed by the addition to the school's panel of examiners of one or more strangers with experience of other schools. This is, of course, the method by which universities conduct their degree examinations, and it is one which is widely used in a slightly different form by secondary schools on the continent.

123. A third function of examinations is to act as an encouragement to stay longer at school. This, clearly, is a useful function—until it is carried so far as to make success in an examination a condition for staying on, which would, in our opinion, be quite wrong in a non-selective school. An internal examination at 15 may fulfil this purpose if all that is required is some reassurance of capacity to profit by the particular extended course under consideration or help in choosing the right one out of several possibilities. But more commonly the encouragement looked for is the prospect of receiving at the end of the extended course some certificate which could not otherwise be obtained and which has, or is thought to have, some validity beyond the school. Once again the easiest way administratively to provide this is by some form of external examination, but it is not the only way. There is little doubt that the prospect of some external certificate has played a very large part in the great growth of extended courses during recent years. It is easy to argue that if external certificates were within the reach of a higher proportion of modern school pupils the growth of extended courses would be still more rapid.

124. The fourth function of examinations is to act as a credential to employers and educational institutions which have never heard of the applicant or his school, and have no idea what weight to attach to any school report or testimonial he may bring with him. In the case of the grammar schools, so many of their pupils go into professions which lay down uniform national standards for admission that a national currency for a school leaving certificate is essential for them. Moreover, many of the careers they take up involve advanced further education for which it is important to get as accurate an assessment as possible of the candidate's present standard of knowledge. It is on these grounds that the case for an external examination like the G.C.E. rests. It seems clear to us that boys and

girls who have not the ability to pass G.C.E. are not likely to seek or secure openings which require a nationally valid school qualification. Their employers are more likely to be interested in their character and temperament than in the precise level of their educational attainments, subject by subject, (though knowledge of their ability to perform simple arithmetical calculations and to understand written instructions may be important). There is, no doubt, a middle group which falls below the level of ability required of a likely G.C.E. candidate, but which will enter occupations requiring some quite serious further education. It is, we agree, of the first importance that the college of further education to which they will go should know what they can do when they leave school; but we do not believe that a national examination is the only, or the best, way of transmitting this information. With few exceptions, the boys and girls will not leave home when they leave school, nor for some years thereafter. The qualification with a national character which these boys and girls need is the one that comes at the end of apprenticeship or its equivalent. What is needed at the beginning of apprenticeship could probably be met equally well either by a local examination or by an agreed and detailed form of school record of attainments which would enable the college of further education to know at what point it takes over responsibility for teaching. We think much more thought should be given to the desirability of organising the transmission of information of this sort by leaving certificates. It is a problem that needs to be studied in relation to the number of colleges and schools which form an inter-connected group; and the answer may differ from district to district.

125. We conclude that examinations are a valuable and necessary part of the school system as a means of showing pupils where they stand, of providing them with an incentive to continue, and of raising habits of work and standards of attainment. We agree that for a proportion of the pupils some form of external assessment is desirable both to enable individual schools to measure themselves against general standards, and to enable those who have to deal with the products of various schools to assess accurately the pupils' knowledge and to make reasonable comparisons between them. We agree, too, that external examinations are an obvious and reasonable way of doing these things, as well as the traditional one; but they are not the only way. They have certain quite marked dangers and these must now be discussed.

THE DANGERS OF EXTERNAL EXAMINATIONS

126. The greatest contrast between internal examinations and external examinations as we usually think of them is that internal

examinations follow the syllabus and examine what has in fact been taught, while external examinations tend to prescribe the syllabus so that what is taught is what is most likely to be examined. External examinations, then, tend to stabilise and make uniform patterns of teaching and the content of a subject syllabus. Once laid down, they take a deal of altering. Such examinations may raise low standards, but they may also discourage experiment and encourage teachers to play for safety. The success which often attends getting up prepared answers to expected examination questions can soon depreciate the educational currency.

127. In some subjects a good modern school education seems to us very difficult to reconcile with an external examination. If it is right, and we believe it is, that the approach to knowledge should be as little abstract as possible for boys and girls of ordinary ability; if full use is to be made of their environment, then a good deal of the approach to history and the social sciences, to geography and to biology will be dictated by the character of the place in which the school is. In practical subjects, also, the right teaching approach does not lie through a series of graduated exercises standing by themselves, which is what a large-scale examination tends to encourage, however much the examiners may wish to discourage it. In language teaching too,—and while we are thinking mainly of foreign languages, we would not exclude the teaching of the mother tongue—we believe that for modern school pupils more attention than is customary should be paid to speech. But speech does not lend itself as well to external examination as does written work. On the other hand, mathematics and physics seem well fitted to external examination.

128. The trouble with any large-scale examination is that it must be remote from the individual classrooms in which boys and girls are taught. If there were a system of nationally integrated lower-level examinations to be taken at 16, designed to be within the reach of the top third of the modern school, the possible field, as far as ability is concerned, would be 165,000 pupils by 1960; if they were designed for the top half of the modern school, the field would be over 240,000—95 per cent of all the Ordinary level G.C.E. candidates in 1958 and twice as many as all candidates for the examinations of the City and Guilds of London Institute in that year. Of course, for some years to come the actual field would be very much smaller because most modern school pupils still leave at 15; but we believe that it would grow step by step with the growth of extended courses. And it would be larger still when the school-leaving age is raised. We are afraid that neither schools nor parents would be able to resist the pressure to give border-line candidates a chance, and that in consequence the border-line itself would be pushed further down

year by year. An examination for the top third might soon find its fringe candidates drawn from the half-way mark: an examination designed for the top half might find itself serving all but the bottom quarter. Two factors would make it difficult to halt this progression. The first is the uncertainty about what a modern school is. In some areas it contains 90 per cent of the 12 year olds; in some 70 per cent or less. The top half or third of a particular modern school bears no fixed relation to the top half or third of the whole modern school population. Secondly, the minor examinations in question are thought of as general examinations, good for all who can pass them, and not as special examinations with a particular defined purpose such as securing admission to this or that institution or profession. There is little temptation to inflate the numbers taking the latter sort of examination; there is nothing to limit the numbers taking the former. We think, then, that a nationally integrated system of minor examinations would before long become a major undertaking. There would be great difficulty in finding sufficient competent and willing examiners, and in keeping standards level. It might be that the only solution in the long run would be by a system of standardised attainment tests. If this were so, it ought not to be embarked on without careful study. Many of these dangers and difficulties are not apparent at the start, when the numbers are still small. The present experience of the schools, and of the examining bodies, throws no light on what the situation would be if these minor examinations were nationally recognised, especially when the school-leaving age is raised to 16.

129. The teaching objections which lurk in the large-scale external examination need not apply with anything like the same force to a small local examination, provided that it does not slavishly copy the techniques of a large-scale one. We would define a local examination as one that can really be under the control of those who are actually teaching the subject, and where the examination papers can be devised to fit what the schools teach. Of course, teachers are associated in an advisory capacity with the large-scale examining bodies, but in this respect, teachers' representatives are not the same thing as the teachers themselves. In a local examination committee it is the men and women who have done the teaching who set the questions, which can be set to suit individual school syllabuses. Answers can be not only read but heard. Moreover, it seems to us quite possible to include within the arrangements for granting a local certificate a careful assessment of what is called course work—all the work done by a pupil in a subject over a term or a year, and not only of what can be reproduced within the space of two hours in an examination room. The more "practical" and "non-academic" the subjects, the more important this is.

130. There is a further point that should be considered—the relative advantages of a subject and of a group examination. A subject examination, like the G.C.E., has certain obvious advantages for the modern school. It enables a pupil to limit his field of intensive examination preparation—and the capacity for juggling with many balls at the same time is not characteristic of modern school pupils. But it throws the onus of maintaining a generally balanced education back on the school; and, though we accept that this is where it rightly belongs, this freedom can be abused. Moreover a subject examination provides no evidence to employers or technical colleges about anything except the subjects examined. A group examination no doubt gives a better guarantee of width of academic education, but it may in practice exclude certain aspects of education, to which we attach importance, even more successfully than a subject examination; because so much is to be examined there is felt to be no time for anything else. But a good deal of what ought to be taught does not lend itself to examination, and even when it can be examined, to do so would defeat the purpose for which it ought to be included in the supporting subjects of an extended course. What can happen with group examinations may be illustrated from the curriculum of pupils taking extended courses in one city in 1957. In none of the technical courses for boys was there any opportunity for music; while art and the crafts, other than woodwork and metalwork, were usually omitted as were history, geography, current affairs and sometimes religious instruction. In the commercial courses for girls, only one school included art; while music, history, geography and current affairs appeared in only about half the time-tables. Moreover the conditions of a group examination are such as to cut off from any hope of a certificate a good many boys and girls who have some real capacity in certain directions, but a marked incompetence in other required subjects.

131. All extended courses should attempt to combine a well-balanced curriculum with the opportunity to devote a more than strictly proportionate amount of time to the pupil's main interest. The school's great problem is how to secure, both inside the school and beyond it, adequate regard for the rest of the work, which is not only bound to occupy less of the time, but is also quite likely to be in some respects and for some pupils really poor. There is no easy answer, but we believe that the right one is more likely to be found within the compass of a strictly local organisation than by a nation-wide minor examination.

132. It is impossible, however, not to recognise the strength of the pressures, coming from the pupils themselves and their parents, for examinations that result in the award of a certificate of some public

validity. We do not think it is any longer possible to maintain an attitude of complete negation or of blanket discouragement. To do so would be to lose all chance of asserting control over a movement that will clearly develop in unofficial forms if it is not given an official framework. We think that the policy hitherto pursued by the Ministry of Education therefore requires some modification. But we would strongly urge that to set about the construction of a national system of minor examinations would be to rush to the other extreme. The right course, in our view, for the next five years or so is to watch very closely the development of regional and local examinations and to postpone any question of a national system until the experience of these years is available to be assessed. We should hope, in particular, that it will then be easier than it is now to form a judgement on the relative advantage, in this field, of subject and group examinations.

133. There is one form of external examination in modern schools which we have no hesitation in condemning—the use of examinations devised for part-time students. The conditions under which evening institute and day release courses are held have quite naturally, if wrongly, been reflected in unavoidably limited syllabuses, especially in certain subjects. To make these part-time syllabuses the basis of a year's whole-time school work is indefensible. This is, however, happening to a considerable extent; and, where no alternative is provided, it will, we think, continue. It gives the promise of an easy success,* which may be doubly misleading. On the one hand it seriously underestimates what some candidates could successfully tackle. On the other hand, through the advantages of full-time education, it gives an unduly flattering picture of what a less able pupil can be expected to do when he comes on to the less favourable conditions of part-time courses.

134. Up to this point we have been considering examinations at the end of an extended course lasting for at least a year after the end of compulsory school. There are also external examinations designed to be taken at the end of the fourth year—that is, at the age of 15. They present a temporary problem which should disappear when the school-leaving age is raised. A good many of the candidates have, it is true, stayed at school one or two terms longer than they must, but to call this completion of the fourth year an extended course is, we think, a misnomer. The ground covered is only that of the school's normal syllabus. The majority of these fourth-year examinations are local, but at least two of the professional examining bodies have now entered this field. Three arguments are produced for

* The results of 9 modern schools in one city taking the Preliminary Technical Examination of the Union of Educational Institutions, showed over three years a 90 per cent success rate

examinations at this stage. One is that they induce boys and girls who would otherwise leave to complete a fourth year, and persuade some of the successful candidates to undertake a fifth year on top of it. Secondly, it is said that the incentive to hard work provided by an external examination should be available to pupils in schools which do not offer fifth-year courses, to boys entering apprenticeships at or before 16, and indeed to all boys and girls who exercise their admitted right to leave at the minimum legal age, whatever it may be. The third argument is that an examination of this kind gives employers and those concerned with further education much needed information. We are not greatly impressed by these arguments. Nor should we wish to see this examination used as an excuse for not providing fifth-year courses—we are clear that boys and girls of the ability to take any external examination worth organising ought to be at school until they are 16. Increasingly they themselves are of the same opinion, and we note with interest that in at least one county borough, which has instituted a fourth-year examination, it looks as if the examination may, so to speak, be marooned by the tide of pupils seeking fifth-year courses. We should not wish immediately to kill by prohibition such examinations, because we recognise that there are areas in which they are useful since fifth-year courses are not immediately practicable owing to shortage of buildings and staff. We would not, however, "strive officiously to keep alive" something in our opinion better dead, or at least superseded as soon as possible. In any event fourth-year examinations should not be more than local; there is in our view no place for regional or national examinations at this age.

PUPILS WHO SHOULD NOT BE EXAMINED

135. External examinations not only tend to direct attention, and attach value, to the subjects which are examined at the expense of those which are not (and within the examined subjects only to their examinable aspects); they also focus attention on pupils who are examined at the expense of those who are not. It is important here to notice the difference between grammar schools and modern schools. The theory behind the grammar school is that it serves a relatively homogeneous group of pupils in terms of ability. An external examination system may therefore provide, up to a point and with many qualifications, a valid basis of comparison between pupil and pupil inside a grammar school, and also between one grammar school and another. It cannot in the same way serve such a purpose for modern schools. All modern schools have a much wider range of ability among their pupils than any grammar school has; and, since grammar schools as a group are designed to be relatively homogeneous, the great differences that exist between one neighbourhood and another are as far as possible excluded from the

grammar schools which only admit children above a certain level of ability. But these differences come out all the more in the modern schools. Broadly speaking, there are no pupils in the grammar schools who should not be externally examined. But there are many such in the modern schools. None of the advocates of external examinations for modern schools, so far as we know, contemplates their going more than one-third, or one-half at the furthest, down the scale of intellectual ability. We should enter a vigorous protest if they did. The majority ought not to be subjected to an external examination, and their interest must be protected. They are, after all, the main concern of the modern schools. There is a tendency of long historical standing in English educational thought (it is not nearly so visible in some other countries) to concentrate too much on the interests of the abler pupils in any group that is being considered and to forget about the rest. It is a tendency which, in this instance at least, should be resisted. The problem of the modern schools is not the same as the problem of the grammar schools, and it would be wrong, just because the grammar school system makes such constant use of external public examinations, to wish the same thing on to the modern schools as part of a programme of "parity of esteem". External examinations have a role to perform in modern schools, and it is a larger part than they have hitherto played. What is all-important, in our view, is that it should be the role of a helpful servant, not that of a dominating master.

136. There are, then, three important groups among those four-fifths of the nation's children who do not get into grammar schools or streams at the age of 11 or 12. The first, a small group, will develop along the lines which properly permit of their being assessed by a written examination at the age of 16 or 17 and whose knowledge, comparable to that of many grammar school pupils, makes it worth while to do this. They are the modern school's potential G.C.E. candidates and must not be robbed of their chance. There is a second group, larger than the first, for whom an external test is both possible and sensible—provided that it has a well defined objective. Few of them require to take at 16 a nationally recognised examination; but many of them will be carrying their education further in ways that should and do lead to their getting a nationally valid qualification later on. The disadvantages of really large-scale external examinations are such that we do not think that they ought to be used except where they are necessary.* The third group, which

* It has been suggested that our first and second groups could be amalgamated if a slightly lower pass mark (with or without a credit standard above it) were introduced into the Ordinary level of the G.C.E. The question of pass marks is a technical matter, and one so clearly within the sphere of the Secondary School Examinations Council that we have not discussed it; but it seems improbable that a change of this kind would bring into the first group all those whom we now regard as falling into our second group

is certainly larger than either of the others and probably as big as both together, consists of those for whom an external examination at the age of 16 is an absurdity, and whose education ought to be developed on quite different lines. All three groups are of equal importance. It is not practicable to segregate them into different types of school; nor, if it were, would it be desirable. But since they are all in the same schools there is a risk (and we think it is a real one) that the interests of the third group may suffer from the attention given to the first two. There is also a risk that because external examinations are manifestly good for some, they will be thought to be good for all—or too many—so that the size of the first group may be exaggerated at the expense of the second, and of the second at the expense of the third. There is, finally, the risk, well known though not always avoided in grammar schools, that only the examined subjects and aspects of education will be felt to have real importance. These are the risks and it is essential that they should be clearly observed. Nevertheless, the interests of the first and second groups must not be sacrificed; boys and girls in both these groups respond to a challenge which comes from outside the schools and can gain much from it.

SUMMARY

137. Our views about examinations in modern schools can be summed up as follows:

(*a*) Many, probably more than half, of the pupils of the modern schools would have their education deflected from its proper lines by being prepared for an external examination. It is important that attention to the needs of the minority should not be allowed to lead to neglect of the interests of these boys and girls, who are and will remain by far the largest single group in the modern schools. All our other recommendations are subject to this.

(*b*) In the examinable minority, two groups can be distinguished. One of these consists of those pupils who have the ability to attempt some of the subjects in the G.C.E. at Ordinary level. It is important that none of them should be denied the opportunity to do so.

(*c*) There remains another group—consisting of about one-third or rather more of the pupils in modern schools—for whom external examinations below the level of the G.C.E. may serve a useful purpose, and official policy should be modified to recognise this.

(*d*) We are, however, impressed with the dangers of large-scale external examinations, which a national system could not avoid. External examinations should therefore develop on a regional, or preferably a local, basis. Experiments on these lines should continue for a period of about five years, and a further enquiry should be held into their results, before any decision is taken concerning the creation of a national system.

(*e*) There is also need for further experience and enquiry before a judgement can be expressed on the relative advantages of subject examinations and group examinations.

(*f*) Some of the purposes served by an external examination can also be met by a formal assessment by the school, at the time of leaving, of a pupil's performance and attainments during his whole time at the school. Irrespective of the growth of external examinations, we recommend that thought should be given to the development of a system of leaving certificates on these lines. This also, in our view, can best be organised locally, or at most regionally, certainly not nationally.

(*g*) There is no case, except as a temporary measure in a few localities, for an external examination at the end of the fourth year—that is, at the age of 15. Where such examinations exist, they should be purely local.

(*h*) Examinations designed for part-time students should not be taken in secondary schools.

CHAPTER 9

The Consequences of Extended Courses for the Modern School

138. Nobody who has had personal experience of an established five-year course in a modern school has any doubt that it has far-reaching effects on the school as a whole. In what way does this influence make itself felt?

THE SHAPE OF THE SCHOOL

139. The first and most obvious difference is in what may be called the "shape" of the school. The characteristic modern school has hitherto had the same number of forms in the Christmas term in each of its four years; in the succeeding two terms, the fourth-year class gradually diminishes in size so that the numbers in the summer term are about a third of the numbers at the beginning of the year. The major selective principle at work, however, is only the accident of the time of year at which the pupils were born. Those who complete the year are not, as a group, more industrious, or more intelligent than those who fall out. They are not better qualified to give leadership to the school as a whole. On the contrary, the distracting nature of bye-term leaving tends to take the eyes of the remaining pupils off their school life, and to fix their attention on the fact that their old class-mates who came up the school with them now have more money and more independence. An extended course, on the other hand, provides a small group of boys and girls who have made up their minds to stay at school for five whole years—at least a year longer than they must. They are there by deliberate choice and not by accident. They are older, and they are on the whole drawn from the abler pupils. Very likely they will also come from more careful homes. They are likely to be more responsible.

140. The attitude and behaviour of the oldest pupils in a school is naturally reflected by their juniors. The top of the school cannot help setting the pace for the main body. On this basis it is clear that anything which tends to exercise a steady influence on the later years of school life is of great importance. The presence at the very top of the modern school of a group of older boys and girls is an advantage to the school as a whole which no headmaster who has experienced it would willingly forgo. There is, however, another

way of looking at the matter. Does the existence of a Fifth Form rob boys and girls who leave as soon as they are 15 of an opportunity which they would otherwise have had of occupying positions of responsibility and trust? In reproducing the "shape" of the grammar school, with its relatively small Sixth Form heading a large main school, are we cutting off natural leaders, perhaps among those gifted at games, from positions of leadership? Are these offices going instead to boys and girls whose merits at 15 are more likely to be recognised by their teachers than by their peers? The question is asked, and should be answered. There is no evidence that this is happening or is likely to happen. The withdrawn intellectual is not very common even among the most intelligent modern school pupils, and headmasters are well aware of the dangers. But the whole fear seems to rest on a misconception of what is significant in the organisation of most day schools. In their social life the horizontal is quite as important as the vertical. It is not usually the 'house' but the form which is the real focus of life and games and friendship as well as of work. Most of the learning to live together, to shoulder responsibility for oneself and on behalf of others, comes to a boy or girl in this way with his contemporaries. Where the value of the top of the school comes in most clearly is in setting relatively mature and responsible standards of behaviour which are taken up and copied by younger boys and girls. We cannot see, then, that extended courses are 'unfair' to the majority of modern school pupils or prejudice their chances. Indeed we think they should now be taken for granted and that the life of secondary modern schools should be planned on a five-year basis. This would involve some consequential changes in the customs affecting various inter-school arrangements. Boys and girls over 15 are, apparently, sometimes now excluded by regulation from the competitive games and athletics in which their schools normally take part.

141. The influence of an extended course on the whole school is not confined to the social influence of its members. It soon affects the general attitude to work of all the four previous years, in the ablest stream at least, and frequently also in all forms. There is a new seriousness about work because there is a recognisable purpose to it; recognisable, that is, to pupils and parents as well as to teachers. The outward and visible sign of this new attitude is the introduction of homework, often enough at the request of parents. At first homework and hard work may be confined to the last year or two, but it does not take long to realise that a G.C.E. course, for instance, cannot be improvised on top of three years of very much less arduous work than the abler grammar school boy or girl has had to put in. There seems to be no doubt that the introduction of an extended

course soon raises the sights of the majority of boys and girls who are in any way near the intellectual level it requires. *Possunt quia posse videntur*: they can because they think they can.

"THE ORDINARY CHILD"

142. But wherever the margin of examinable candidates is finally set there will always be a large proportion of pupils who will not be included. In the last chapter we referred to the risk that their interests might suffer from the expansion of examination work. We must now discuss their position in rather more detail. Will the best teachers tend to be assigned to the examination classes? In appointing new masters and mistresses will heads tend to look first for men and women who are capable of tackling examination work? Will the forms which contain the probable examination candidates tend to be smaller than the other forms, and the others therefore larger than they should be?

143. There is evidence that in some instances this is happening, and we fear that it may increase as the number of schools with extended courses grows. Once there is some quantitative, and apparently just, criterion by which one modern school can be compared with another, there is a risk that the schools will turn too much of their energies towards success in that measurable respect. Some of the best things in the old elementary and new modern school tradition will help to keep the scales even. Many of the best teachers have made their mark and taken especial pride in their handling of backward boys and girls. They have felt that it is here that their skill is most needed; and, besides skill, devotion. They have found it the most satisfying form of work, and have been more than content to leave the teaching of brighter boys and girls to other hands. But we shall not be able to rely on a succession of equally gifted men and women to take up this exacting but peculiarly rewarding work unless the authorities and governing bodies do their part. By this we mean, on the positive side, that a due proportion of special responsibility allowances should be assigned to those whose work lies with below-average pupils, that opportunities of promotion should come their way, that the size of the classes they are asked to teach should be kept as low as they can be and that the accommodation and special equipment necessary for their work should not be neglected. And, on the negative side, it is essential that authorities and governing bodies should not judge their modern schools by public examination results, comparing one school unfavourably with another on this basis and forgetting how entirely different are the communities served by different modern schools.

144. Among these backward boys and girls there are some who are patently too immature to go out into the world at 15. They are physically and emotionally, as well as mentally, below average. In a real sense they can still be described as children. Very often a close link is established between the teachers and the parents of these boys and girls, and an increasing number of schools find that there is a demand that they should have a fifth year at school, although the numbers seeking it are far less than those who want the ordinary sort of extended course. Unfortunately in the modern school there may often be nothing suitable to offer them, so that they must either leave or stay longer in a fourth-year form. If, however, they had been in a special school (as some might very well have been), their education would have been planned from the beginning on the basis of a leaving age of 16. We regard the early development of suitable courses for these immature boys and girls as important, because their need is clearly great. It is important also because of the light it will throw on what will have to be provided when the general school-leaving age is raised to 16. There is no escape from the fact that below-average children make above-average demands on the educational system; and, just as we think it right that the classes in the lowest streams should generally be smaller than the rest, so we recognise that extended courses for these boys and girls will be smaller and more expensive to staff than the examination courses. Their development will, we think, require close co-operation between the schools and the youth employment service.

145. We are not, of course, arguing that all relatively dull children fall into this immature group. There is another, and probably a larger group, who are physically quite as developed as any boys and girls of their age, and who are straining at the leash to get out into the world. They are most unlikely to be attracted by any voluntary extended courses. Some people indeed doubt whether there is very much that the schools could do for them between 15 and 16 which could not be better done elsewhere. These boys and girls will present the main educational difficulty that the schools will have to face when the minimum school-leaving age is raised. Certainly it seems clear that schools which have been able to gain experience of the education of 15 year-olds on both wings—the bright and examinable and the backward and immature—will be better able to tackle, when it comes, the education of these reluctant pupils.

146. The great challenge to the modern school lies in this middle group. Above them there are the extended courses for the abler pupils, which will require at least in the later years a large part of the attention of the academically better qualified teachers. Below them there are the lowest streams with their specially difficult and

interesting teaching problems, and the occasional possibility of an extended course, which call for and elicit teaching skill of a very high order. There is at least a risk that the forms just below the examination stream or streams may be left to follow a humdrum syllabus with the dullest teachers. Is this inevitable? It is probably unavoidable that for a time at least the boys and girls in the ablest stream will be taught as nearly as possible in the same way as grammar school pupils, since some of them will be sitting for the same examination, and a few will be transferring to a grammar school Sixth Form. This will often mean that their education will be highly verbalised, and abstract in its approach even to practical subjects—almost the opposite to the way in which they set about learning for themselves in their spare-time occupations. The boys and girls in the lower streams, on the other hand, will be taught by methods which are much less formal and much more closely related to exploration than to exposition. We think that a little more of the latter methods, and a little less of the former, would be a good prescription for the streams in the middle, who are neither the brightest nor the dullest. It was not for nothing that Mr. John Duncan called the book in which he drew on his experience with educationally sub-normal pupils 'The Education of the Ordinary Child'. The most promising part of the educational system for experiments in new methods of teaching relatively difficult things will be the middle streams of modern schools—but only if they are left free from the cramping effect of a large-scale external examination. On the one hand, the teachers can draw on the expertise of teachers of backward children; on the other, they can use the stimulus of a "man-sized" job which the technical schools have found so valuable. These too long neglected middle streams have a future, and an exciting one, if they can attract teachers who will take at face value the fact that their pupils will nearly always prefer 'I see' to 'I understand'.

TEACHERS FOR EXTENDED COURSES

147. Whether they will be able to get the right teachers, however, seems to us a doubtful matter. Some modern schools and some comprehensive schools are exciting places to work in. They have all the compelling power of being in the van. There is evidence that many schools with flourishing extended courses can secure a good choice of teachers, while schools which everybody leaves as soon as they can are beginning in some areas to find that this is true of staff as well as pupils. The success of extended courses has taken place in the face of a nationally static and, in some respects, slightly worsening staff position in modern schools as a whole. It is only if

this tendency is now to be reversed that our hopes for the middle streams of modern schools can be fulfilled. What is the present position? We can apply two quantitative tests. The first is that of the ratio of teachers to pupils. Table 14 sets out the position for secondary modern schools for each year from 1949 to 1958. (The overall staff ratio is not, of course, the same thing as the average size of classes, which is much larger).

Table 14. Number of pupils in Secondary Modern Schools per full-time teacher 1949 to 1958 (England)

1949	24·1
1950	23·4
1951	22·8
1952	22·4
1953	21·9
1954	21·9
1955	22·2
1956	22·9
1957	22·9
1958	22·9

NOTE: If part-time teachers are included the ratio is improved by about 0·5

The picture shown by these figures is disappointing in two ways. First, the steady improvement recorded until 1953 has not been maintained. Secondly, the years in which secondary modern schools have been developing extended courses, and in which, therefore, we would have hoped to see improved staffing ratios, have in fact shown a deterioration. Extended courses have been developed in spite of, not because of, the staffing position.

148. The second quantitative test is that of the supply of graduate teachers to secondary modern schools. It would be ludicrously untrue to suggest that all graduates are more valuable teachers than any two-year trained teacher. It would be equally false to say that of two teachers of equal ability, the graduate was automatically to be preferred in a secondary modern school to the training college man or women. But it may confidently be said that, as extended courses are developed, the proportion of graduates ought to rise, and that any reduction in the proportion of graduates would be a danger signal. Table 15 shows what has happened in each year since 1947.

Table 15. Graduates in Secondary Modern Schools 1947–1958 (England).

	1 All Men Teachers	2 Graduate Men Teachers	3 Col. 2 as percentage of Col. 1	4 All Women Teachers	5 Graduate Women Teachers	6 Col. 5 as percentage of Col. 4
1947	14,599	2,736	*18·7*	13,654	1,644	*12·0*
1948	18,294	3,089	*16·9*	16,005	1,982	*12·4*
1949	20,892	3,247	*15·5*	17,812	2,149	*12·1*
1950	22,205	3,285	*14·8*	18,222	2,127	*11·7*
1951	23,879	3,505	*14·7*	18,964	2,230	*11·7*
1952	24,762	3,773	*15·2*	19,775	2,391	*12·1*
1953	25,424	4,136	*16·3*	20,421	2,527	*12·4*
1954	26,456	4,635	*17·5*	21,171	2,661	*12·6*
1955	27,356	4,996	*18·3*	22,265	2,911	*13·1*
1956	28,258	5,221	*18·5*	23,699	3,204	*13·5*
1957	30,120	5,675	*18·8*	25,361	3,504	*13·8*
1958	32,075	6,196	*19·3*	26,374	3,663	*13·9*

149. It will be noted that the sudden drop in the percentage, but not in the number, of men graduates in the early years of the period under review, caused by the entry of emergency training college students, has now been made good. There are now more than twice as many graduate men teachers in secondary modern schools as in 1947, but they still represent only one-fifth of all men teachers. On the other hand, there has been a decline in the proportion of men graduates in modern schools whose main field of study was in mathematics or science, from 33 per cent in 1947 to 21 per cent in 1958.

150. The number of women graduates in secondary modern schools, like that of men graduates, is a little more than twice what it was in 1947—3,663 instead of 1,644 and the proportion has actually risen from 12·0 per cent to 13·7 per cent. There was, however, no decline like that among the men in the early post-war years. Among the women graduates the number who include mathematics or science in their degree has nearly doubled, but they form a much lower proportion of the total than the corresponding figure for the

men—13·7 per cent compared with 20·6 per cent. Moreover this 13·7 is 2 per cent *less* than the highest point reached in post-war years in 1953. The actual number is depressingly small—502 in 1958. In broad terms, then, we may say that the supply of graduates to modern schools is not discouraging, but that there is a marked deficiency on the mathematics and science side—an average of half a graduate per modern school is surely insufficient. This deficiency is greater for women teachers than for men, and also more serious because of the considerable number of training college students, especially in the women's colleges, who have done virtually no mathematics for three or four years before admission, and had been unable to secure a pass in Ordinary level in that subject.

THE SIZE OF THE SCHOOL

151. Extended courses demand a reasonably large school if they are to be run both efficiently and economically. Since there is a growing demand for extended courses, it seems clear that there will be a tendency to bring rather larger modern schools into existence. This is something which is, we believe, as much in the interest of the average and below-average pupils as it is of the abler ones who at present provide most of the candidates for extended courses. They require quite as much specialist teaching as more gifted boys and girls; they need a full range of crafts; they need a choice among the arts. Indeed, just because of their limitations, they cannot so easily adjust themselves to whatever is put in front of them as their abler brothers and sisters often can. It is necessary to find the few things, sometimes the one thing, which lies within a particular boy's capacity or which kindles a response within him. Only a relatively large school will have the varied equipment and the diversely qualified staff. But, of course, a large school will always have many boys and girls of greater ability than those whose interests we are considering. Especial care then needs to be taken in the organisation of the school's activities to see that no boy or girl is deprived of the chance of developing whatever talents he has—social as well as intellectual—merely because there is somebody else available who would obviously do it better. No clearer example could be found of the difference between a school and the world, between the responsibilities of a teacher and an employer.

152. How big must a relatively big school be? When everybody is at school to 16 we think it should be possible for an annual intake of about 100 to 120 pupils to support economically a sufficiently wide variety of fourth-year and fifth-year courses to cater for most of the needs of the modern school population. But in the intervening

years before the school-leaving age is raised, the numbers who will stay on into the fifth year will only be a fraction, rarely more than half, of the original entry, and will often be too small for really effective extended courses. This creates a dilemma. It would obviously be wrong to start on a campaign for still larger schools if the 100–120 entry school will before long be large enough to support with economy a broad range of options at the top. But nearly a third of the modern schools are small communities with an annual intake of 75 or less. They will clearly be too small, even when the school-leaving age is raised, to provide adequately for the needs of all their older pupils. We do not think they have a useful future except in those parts of the country where the pattern of settlement is such that larger schools are out of the question. There is no solution for them except by the provision of staff on a more generous scale than normal. Sometimes this may best be accomplished by the establishment of 'village colleges' which, by adding responsibility for further education to the role of the school, make possible a more generous provision. But three-quarters of these small modern schools are in towns. In the long run they will, we think, have to be replaced if they cannot be enlarged. In the meantime some temporary arrangements are needed.

PROGRESS IN FACE OF DIFFICULTY

153. Are modern schools as a whole too weak to bear the extra load which extended courses impose? Are they in the main making sure that all their pupils are decently literate before they take their better ones on to G.C.E.? These are questions which deserve an answer, however difficult it may be to satisfy a questioner who often has in the back of his mind a comparison, blurred through time, of things as they were in 1939 or in the old days before then. There are two very important misconceptions to be cleared away before an answer can be attempted. Except in a few areas, there was less chance then than now for a poor boy to proceed from a primary to a grammar school. The modern school is therefore liable to have fewer able pupils than its predecessor, the senior elementary school. This is the first point that is often forgotten. We forget, too, that it has to produce far more boys and girls capable of filling positions which require a sound basic education of an academic kind. We have already noted that between 1931 and 1951 the number of women engaged in commerce increased by 122 per cent and that the rise continues. There has also been an increase in the number of men in commerce. In industry, too, a far greater number of apprentices need a reasonable working knowledge of mathematics than ever

before. Boys and girls, who in the past would have gone into jobs where their formal education was immaterial, now enter employment which demands a standard which they find it difficult to attain. In fact, though with difficulty, they reach a standard of education they would not previously have attempted. Unless the change in circumstances since the war is realised, there can be no fruitful discussion of the work done in modern schools.

154. Nevertheless what matters is what the schools are doing now. In 1954 and 1955 reports were written by H.M. Inspectors on about one-eighth of the modern schools in England and Wales. They give between them a comprehensive picture of the condition of modern schools on the eve of the serious development of extended courses. It is, naturally enough, a chequered picture. There are accounts of a great many exciting and valuable developments. We are not concerned with them at this point in the argument. Our present desire is to hear the worst that can be said. Poor buildings and constant changes of staff are recurrent themes. Often the two are found together. The following examples may be taken as typical of many schools:

(*a*) 375 pupils—19 staff changes between 1952 and 1955; only 4 teachers with continuous service since 1952. Physical education mistress and handicraft master about to leave for schools with better facilities.

(*b*) 372 pupils—14 staff changes between 1951 and 1954; 2 vacancies. Situation partly attributable to premises and to housing shortage.

(*c*) 394 pupils—73 staff changes in 10 years; school half-way between district with acute housing shortage and one in which additional allowance payable.

(*d*) 283 pupils—at no time in last six years fully staffed; constant changes among younger teachers. A small mining village with no easily accessible town.

Nevertheless, in spite of all these handicaps, a close and ruthless study of all these reports, made with a view to determining the incidence of weakness in the basic subjects of reading, writing and arithmetic, led in the end to what we accept as a reassuring verdict. On the evidence available (and admittedly the reports were not written for this purpose), it appears that about three-quarters of the schools were doing consistently sound and successful work in these subjects with all their pupils, many of them of poor ability and from discouraging surroundings.

155. This judgement is necessarily impressionistic, but there is fortunately no need to rely entirely on subjective assessments. The over-all favourable view can be confirmed by objective measurements of attainments. The Ministry's pamphlet, "Standards of Reading 1948–1956," should certainly be read by all who are concerned to know what the schools are doing. A similar yard-stick to measure gain or loss in mathematics has now been established, but the base line is 1955 and we do not yet know what the results of the first follow-up survey will show. "Standards of Reading" compares the results of applying the same thorough test to a nationally representative sample of boys and girls aged 11 and 15 in 1948, 1952 and 1956. The results showed that in 1956 the average 15 year-old pupil was four months ahead of his predecessor of 1948, while the still greater gain of nine months in the primary schools suggests that by 1960 there should be a further marked improvement in the secondary schools. The proportion of pupils aged 15 scoring 20 points or more in the test rose from 59 per cent in 1948 to 61 per cent in 1952 and 66 per cent in 1956, and this improvement was almost entirely in the unselective schools. It is an encouraging picture.

156. It may be well before leaving this chapter to take stock of the magnitude and rapidity of the changes which have overtaken the modern school in its short life. For its first two years (1945–47) it carried on the organisation of the old senior elementary school, where the oldest pupils were only just turning 14. It provided a two-year course for all, with a third year which only one-third of the pupils completed. There followed the period when the "extra year" dominated the thought of the teachers. By the "extra year" they normally meant the fourth year, but of course for some time that was always as fractional as the third year had been before 1947. Essentially the course was "three years plus," and the oldest pupil had barely turned 15. We have now moved into a period when schools in a good many places can plan their programme with a fair degree of realism either as a four-year course with some pupils dropping out at Christmas and Easter, or even as a four-year course with an additional year for a good many. In these schools the oldest pupil will often have turned 16½ before he leaves. Present developments suggest that it may not be long before some heads can reasonably regard their schools as providing a five-year course for most, while recognising that some will leave before the end and making provision for them. This changing view of organisation has been accompanied by a growing realisation of what the ordinary boy and girl can achieve, a knowledge that was previously obscured by the fact that he nearly always left school before his potentialities had become apparent. These great changes, crowded into about a third of a teacher's

professional lifetime, have called for a much greater flexibility of mind, inventiveness and imagination than would normally be necessary. Where these have been found—and it is in more places than we had any right to expect—schools are beginning to look like the first blue-prints of what secondary education for all should be.

Part Three

"Secondary Education for All"

CHAPTER 10

The Act of 1944

157. Fifteen years ago Mr. Butler's Education Act gave all children for the first time the right to free secondary education. Twelve years ago the minimum school-leaving age was raised from 14 to 15. Two further provisions of the Act affecting older children remain to be brought into force. One would add another year to compulsory school life, extending it to 16; the other would provide compulsory part-time day education until 18 for those who leave school before that age. Any review, such as ours, of the educational provision for boys and girls between 15 and 18 must almost of necessity start from these remaining provisions of the 1944 Act. When will it be possible to take these promised further steps forward? Which foot should be advanced first—the extension of compulsory full-time education, or the introduction of compulsory part-time day education? Before these can be answered, there is a preliminary question. Is it wise to go forward with any extensions of compulsion at school beyond the age when, at home, parental orders are gradually replaced by parental requests? The 1944 Act was inevitably a bold act of faith. Was it misjudged? We have now had half a generation's knowledge of keeping at school until 15 boys and girls who would not have stayed if left to themselves. Has it been a good thing? Is there anything in our experience since the war to suggest that the two further extensions of compulsion provided for by the 1944 Act were ill-conceived, and should not be brought into force? We shall later examine each measure separately. But at the outset we must state our belief that both should be confirmed in their position on the agenda of educational advance. They are important and complementary reforms, which are necessary if we are to have a satisfactory educational system for the teen-agers. It is not a matter of one or the other, though it must be one before the other. Both are necessary. Had we had any hesitation in coming to this conclusion it would have been removed by the weight of the evidence we received from the leading educational associations of the country and from other public bodies with a concern for education. Some of our witnesses would give part-time education up to 18 a priority in time over full-time schooling to 16; others put the emphasis the other way round. But there was hardly one of these bodies which did not want to see both steps taken as soon as they practicably could be.

We have been greatly impressed by this evidence of public opinion, which is clearly not content to leave the Act of 1944 in its present state of incomplete fulfilment. But, though there would thus be plenty of support for a policy of further advance, it would obviously be foolish to move forward without preparation. We must make sure that the schools and the colleges of further education are themselves ready to undertake the advance when the time comes. This is more than a question of logistics or material readiness, and we shall have a great deal to say about it. It is after an examination of what still remains to be done that we arrive at the conclusion that it will be possible to raise the school-leaving age before we are ready to introduce compulsory part-time day education.

158. This recommendation is based on the encouraging experience of what has been achieved in secondary education since the war. The first of the three instalments of compulsion has been very generally accepted, and is now taken for granted; indeed, as we have seen, wherever the opportunity has been provided, a growing number of ordinary boys and girls who were, at 11, below the normal grammar school standard of admission have stayed on beyond the statutory school-leaving age to take fifth-year courses. Schools which have provided these extended courses are united in their judgement that those who stay at school until 16 not only know much more than they did at 15, but are far more ready to take their place in the world as responsible and balanced people. There is now sufficient experience to justify us in saying that the ordinary boy or girl can benefit by staying at school until 16.

159. There are, however, many schools in which he cannot stay until he is 16—more, in fact, than there are schools with suitable provision. The picture of secondary education since the war is not all sunlight. There is the uncompleted plan of re-organisation—the survival of all-age schools and of very small secondary schools. In December, 1958, the White Paper on Secondary Education (Cmnd 604) announced a building programme, dealing with this problem, to be completed by 1964–65, but that will still be twenty years after the Act. There is the more intractable problem of the supply, and, above all, of the distribution of teachers. It is the most difficult areas which are shortest of specialist teachers, and which even have to fall back in considerable numbers on unqualified men and women, many of whom are waiting to get into a training college. These are matters in which real progress must be made before it will be safe to raise the school-leaving age. They are not a substitute for it, but the first step in what should be planned as a single operation to secure a full secondary education for all.

160. It is perhaps right to ask whether example and imitation will not effectively raise the normal school-leaving age, once the facilities are provided, without resort to compulsion. These are certainly powerful influences, and in the United States they have operated to secure an effective school-leaving age above the legal minimum (which in most states is still 16). They will carry us a good long way, and in the years immediately ahead we should exploit them for all they are worth; but will they carry us far enough? There are, for instance, areas in which the prevailing type of employment makes relatively little demand for better educated employees; and in which, therefore, we shall not be able to rely much on the well-tried English incentive to a longer school life—the hope of securing the better position which a better education commands. Moreover, voluntary staying-on seems both too haphazard and too precarious to be depended on as the basis of a national system. A change in the general employment situation might cause a major set-back, just as a change in a family's position often sends a boy or a girl out prematurely to work. Or it might select in a negative fashion in the modern school: the better pupils might leave to get the jobs which their records procured them, while the poorer pupils stayed on because they could find no work to do. At all times, too, there are many boys and girls who will not take the positive step of staying longer at school on their own responsibility, though they will cheerfully acquiesce in it, and benefit from it, once the decision is taken off their shoulders and their parents'. That at least has been the experience with the raising of the minimum leaving age to 15.

161. If, as we believe, secondary education for all is really necessary in the general interest, and if, as we also believe, it cannot from its nature often be completed before 16, then it follows that compulsory school life should extend to 16. Such is the theme of this part of our report. In Chapters 11 and 12 we argue the case, as we see it, for raising the school-leaving age as soon as it proves to be practicable to do so. In Chapter 13 we turn aside to consider whether there should be one, two or (as at present) three leaving dates in the year. In Chapter 14 we state our reasons for giving the school-leaving age a priority in time over the introduction of compulsory county colleges. And, finally, in Chapter 15 we tackle the difficult question of when the further year should be added, and make a recommendation.

CHAPTER 11

Why the School-Leaving Age should be Raised:

(1) The Benefit to the Individual

162. "In this Act the expression 'compulsory school age' means any age between five years and fifteen years . . . provided that, as soon as the Minister is satisfied that it has become practicable to raise to sixteen the upper limit of the compulsory school age, he shall lay before Parliament the draft of an Order in Council" to bring this into force. This was not enacted in 1944 in a fit of war-time exuberance. It was in 1938, after its five-year study of secondary education, that the Consultative Committee of the Board of Education under the chairmanship of Sir Will Spens reported that "the adoption of a minimum leaving age of 16 years . . . may not be immediately practicable, but in our judgement must even now be envisaged as inevitable". In Chapter 3 we discussed the change in the age of marriage and family size, and saw reason to believe that the structure of the typical English family was now such that it could reasonably be asked to support compulsory education to 16. In Chapter 6 we discussed whether the national productivity is great enough to allow this expansion of the educational services and decided that it was. In this and the following chapters we take up the question at that point and discuss whether it is in the national interest that secondary education to 16 should now be made compulsory for all. By 'now' in this context we mean that a definite phased programme to bring it about at a named date should now be put in hand.

163. There are two main arguments for raising the school-leaving age. One starts from the social and personal needs of 15 year-olds, and regards education as one of the basic rights of the citizen; the other is concerned with education as a vital part of the nation's capital investment. As far as the former argument is concerned, nothing has happened in the last twenty years, or could happen, which would weaken our agreement with the view of John Dewey that what the best and wisest parent wants for his own child the community must want for all its children. A boy or girl of 15 is not sufficiently mature to be exposed to the pressures of the world of industry or commerce. He needs an environment designed specifically to develop his powers, and not one in which he finds a

place only, or mainly, in so far as an employer can make use of him. Our reasons for believing that the promise of secondary education for all, made in the Act, cannot be redeemed without education for all to the age of 16 are set out at length in this chapter. The second argument, that educational advance is a form of capital investment that serves the national interest, is the concern of Chapter 12.

164. What ought to fix the end of compulsory school life? Presumably nobody now wants to reduce the age to 12, as it was not so long ago; and few would want to keep everybody at school until 18. Compulsion should, therefore, presumably stop at some point between 12 and 18. But where? There can, of course, be no universally right age since boys and girls vary widely in their rate of physical, emotional and intellectual growth. The most and the best that Parliament can do is to fix the age which will be right for most people. Should it be 15 or 16? That, in broad terms, is the decision that faces the country; though, as we shall see in Chapter 13, there are a number of different ways in which the definition can be framed. We are, of course, discussing only the minimum leaving age. Clearly the abler boys and girls should continue their full-time education for a number of years beyond that point. But what about the rest? Is there reason to believe that by leaving school at 15 they are leaving with an essential job unfinished? We have already given that as our opinion. In this chapter we attempt to set out why we think so.

THE YEARS OF ADOLESCENCE

165. A change in vocabulary can be significant. The primary school teacher thinks and speaks naturally and appropriately of children; the secondary school teacher does so at his peril well before the school-leaving age is reached. By about 13, pupils have reached the stage of growth when any word that harks back to childhood is misleading and resented. They think and speak of themselves as 'teen-agers' and the word, though not yet standard English, is descriptive enough of the troubled and exciting time of adolescence which lies half within and half beyond the school life of most English boys and girls. Not long ago it lay almost entirely beyond. As late as 1917 a Departmental Committee reported that "in many localities . . . the effective leaving age approximates rather to 13 than to 14"; while in the old senior elementary school of the inter-war years only one of the three years lay in the teens. Not only has school life been extended upwards, but the onset of puberty is earlier than it used to be. Medical evidence given to us made it clear that menstruation in girls has over a long period of years gradually been beginning earlier in most western countries, and there is no doubt that boys also

mature earlier. Of course, the physical changes are spread over a wide belt of years with great individual variations, but for most children they are nearly complete by the time of leaving school.

166. But this is not true of the emotional and social consequences of puberty. The problems they raise are made more difficult by the earlier emotional development of girls. Few girls leave school before they are conscious of the attraction of the opposite sex. But, on the whole, the boys in whom they are interested are not those of their own age, although 44 per cent of all pupils in secondary schools are in mixed forms. For boys, a personal interest in girls is usually still in the future when they leave school, though only just over the horizon. Another year at school would pretty certainly bring it within the term of school life. But boys and girls alike are already, while still at school, subject to the frequent mood swings, and mingled brashness and tenderness, assertiveness and deep uncertainty—all that April weather of the soul which marks the time of adolescence. Coming to terms with one's new self is a difficult and lengthy process, complicated by the fact that sexual maturity precedes by several years emotional and social maturity.

167. This is surely the period in which the welfare of the individual ought to come before any marginal contribution he or she could make to the national income. Going to work may be the right thing for the adolescent; but, if so, it should be justified on this ground and not by any reference to industry's need of juvenile labour or to the family's need of additional income. A sympathetic employer and a wise foreman may provide just the unsentimental guiding hand a teen-ager needs, but there can be no guarantee that he will find them, since industry does not exist for the sake of the teen-ager. His main need at this age is not of course to be protected, still less to have everything his own way, but he does still need an environment that is designed for him. School is such a world, but is it the right world for the ordinary boy or girl who is rising 16? Can it provide for him, and not only for his abler brothers and sisters, a sufficiently progressive and demanding programme to feed his mind, hold his interest, develop his sense of responsibility and provide him with growing independence, including the opportunity to make and profit by mistakes? We think it can, and in some instances does. We are very far, however, from asserting that this is yet generally the case.

THE ADOLESCENT'S NEEDS

168. One of the marks of the secondary school period is the greater physical skill and control which come to boys and girls in their teens.

This is one reason for the specialist teaching,* and specialist rooms, in secondary schools—the gymnasium, the stage, the craft shops, the housecraft rooms, the laboratory and the art room. Many boys begin to be able to work to fine limits in the woodwork and metalwork shop; in the art room they are not satisfied unless they can attain a conscious mastery of technique. Some will soon exhaust their interest or competence in one or more directions, but few in all. Most specialist teachers of these subjects will agree that a gratifyingly large proportion of their pupils are not only still learning at the end of the course, but really beginning to go rapidly ahead. They leave school at a time when the law of increasing returns is operating. They are not only gaining skill, but insight. Many teachers of these specialist subjects would cheerfully give up the first year, or possibly even two years, of the secondary course if they could be allowed one more at the end. The course is over too soon. Not only does it finish when there is still more to be learned—that would be true whenever it occurred—but too often it really is an end. Seed has been sown but the crop will not ripen.

169. Side by side with this growing physical competence, this approach to adult standards of performance, goes an intensified interest in the "real" world. For boys especially this is apt to be the world of machines. For thousands of years the tools were simple enough—the skill lay in the hands which used them. Now it lies as much in the mind—the mind of the mechanic who looks after the machines as well as the mind of the designer. It is fostered by the delight that so many boys experience in tinkering with a motor-cycle or in constructing a radio set. This mechanical ability is far more widespread than would have seemed credible a generation ago. Every man needs, for himself and for society, as much of this scientific or, more properly, technological knowledge as he can master. Essentially it is a secondary, not a primary school subject, and it is not one in which many boys and girls will have begun to reach the limit of their competence by the age of 15. It is probably true, also, that many boys find technological subjects their easiest and most natural approach to science both as a body of knowledge and as a method of acquiring it. By cutting off compulsory education at 15 we lose the opportunity fully to exploit this mechanical interest in the service of scientific understanding.

170. Inevitably there is a strong vocational flavour to what boys and girls value most in secondary education. Before the end of the present

* Specialist teaching (i.e. teaching by a master or a mistress who teaches virtually only the one subject he has been specially trained to teach) should not be confused with Specialisation in Sixth Forms (i.e. the system by which a pupil spends the greater part of his time on a few closely related subjects).

secondary course they have reached the stage when they desire to see the relevance of what they are doing in school to what they will be doing when they leave school. They are anxious to see a purpose in education, and this anxiety seems to us wholly natural. It should be neither ignored nor played down, but used to enlist their co-operation. There is, of course, a great deal more to life than earning a living, and it is natural that the strength of the vocational test of relevance will vary a good deal between individuals, and that it should be more frequent in boys than in girls, for a good many of whom wage-earning is likely to seem a more temporary preoccupation. Teachers have always been conscious that education has a value in the world to which their pupils are looking forward, but they have not perhaps always been sufficiently concerned to make what they teach manifestly relevant to it. This need has become more apparent now that the senior pupils are older. But our belief that what is taught should be, and appear to be, relevant to the world outside school does not imply that every skill which an employer would like a worker to possess should be taught in school. There are many tricks of the trade which are best learned in the trade, and many skills which are insufficiently educational to be worth a place in the curriculum, at any rate before the minimum leaving age.

171. The passionate interest that many girls feel in living things can be as strong an educational incentive as the love of machines. It is not for nothing that biology is the main science taught to girls, as physics and chemistry are to boys. The same forces, whether innate or social does not matter, probably determine the fact that girls show a more conscious and avowed interest in personal relations than boys do. To the primary school child, characters in fiction and history alike are either black or white, heroes or villains for his admiration or his hate. He plays at being them. To the secondary school girl, imaginary characters are like real characters, like herself. The interaction between her real character and their imagined characters is subtle and two-sided. This analytical and introspective interest in literature in the widest sense—in everything that tells a human story—is not found in most girls at the beginning of the secondary course; it is there before the end; but, once again it needs to be, and could be, developed much further than is possible by the age of 15. Too many girls' reading interests are needlessly left fixed for life within the covers of a hopelessly unreal romantic love novel. Often enough reading in any serious sense soon disappears. Over half the modern school boys and girls interviewed for us by the Social Survey had at one time belonged to a public library; only 16 per cent still belonged two years after leaving school.

172. It is true that there is a broad distinction between boys' and girls' interests which is rightly reflected in curriculum planning, but the point should not be over-stressed. It is sometimes almost implied that no girl is interested in physics or mathematics, and no boy in biology or English literature. This is, of course, nonsense; and, even if true, it would be something to be corrected, not accepted. It should not be accentuated, as we think it sometimes is in co-educational schools, by the tendency for mathematics, physics and chemistry to be taught by men, and therefore to be regarded as boys' subjects, and for English, history and kindred subjects to be taught by women and to be looked on as more suitable for girls. Of course this is bound up with the shortage of women science and mathematics graduates and with the relatively greater difficulty of finding women teachers for co-educational than for girls' schools. It may, therefore, often be unavoidable at present.

173. Another subject or group of subjects, which is characteristic of the secondary stage, is foreign languages. It may be only tradition and the lack of qualified staff which prevents their being started in the primary school; but they are now wholly, and would always be mainly, a matter for the secondary school. We are not concerned to argue that all boys and girls should study a foreign language; but we note that a good many modern schools, especially girls' schools, are teaching one with success. It is important that the numbers should grow. Teaching a foreign language is one of the surest ways of awakening a sensitivity to the use of words. It is not only through the discipline of vocabularies and translation that learning a foreign language improves a pupil's knowledge of English, but also in a more general way through arousing an awareness of words and their meaning, and of the structure of sentences. Once reading has been mastered, far too many pupils, especially boys, take English for granted and regard it as a something which comes by nature, which it is fussy to try consciously to improve; communication in a foreign language can never be taken for granted. There are also, of course, strong social reasons for teaching a foreign language, especially now that foreign travel is within the reach of so many. But these are not, in our view, the main reasons for the place of languages in the curriculum. They have a strictly educational task to perform—and it can be much more fully performed by 16 than by 15.

STANDARDS OF LIFE

174. We turn to another aspect of education. If primary and secondary schools have been doing their job properly, boys and girls

will have grown up in a society which has without fuss or preaching taught them to respect and practise a way of living which is certainly higher than much of that with which they are familiar through the world of entertainment; and, unfortunately, in many instances also better than a good deal of what they meet in the streets and even at home. There is no cause for complacency—indeed we are clear that much more thought needs to be given to what can be done in the secondary years—but at least this rather negative praise of what the schools accomplish can, we think, be substantiated. If children have learned to treat one another with consideration and respect, they have a good foundation on which as teen-agers they can build when the strong winds of sexual attraction begin to ruffle the relatively placid waters of pre-adolescent companionship. A boy or girl, chameleon-like, is quick to take on the moral characteristics of the environment in which he finds himself. He finds one way of living appropriate at school, another in the streets. If the schools are to do their duty of moral education efficiently—and one strong strand in the tradition of English education even sees this as their main duty—they must come into the open with full and frank treatment of ethical problems, so that boys and girls may perceive that the way of living they have been taught to respect at school is not only appropriate there, but relevant everywhere. This is a task which cannot be hurried; it also is not one of the things that can be finished at 15.

175. It is not only about right and wrong that boys and girls need explicit and frank discussion in which all points of view can be expressed. Adolescence is a period of uncertainty, unwelcome uncertainty, about life as a whole and about man's place in the universe, about what is real, what is true, what is the purpose of it all, and what matters. The adolescent is just as conscious of the different metaphysical assumptions that are made in different circles as he is of different ethical assumptions. He knows, though he could not explain it, that philosophy, religion and behaviour are related to one another. The adolescent needs help to see where he stands, but it must be given with discretion and restraint. He does not want to be 'told', but he wants a guide, and a guide who will be honest in not over-stating a case. There is no period of life when people more need what the Education Act means when it refers, perhaps rather unhappily, to "religious instruction", and no period when it is more difficult to give. What is true of ethics and philosophy is true also of politics. The fact that politics are controversial—that honest men disagree—makes preparation for citizenship a difficult matter for schools. But it ought to be tackled, and not least for the ordinary boys and girls who now leave school at 15 and often do not find it easy to see any argument except in personal terms.

THE ASSERTION OF INDEPENDENCE

176. One of the main problems raised at the beginning of this chapter was whether a school can provide for the gradual increase of independence which is necessary to adolescent boys and girls, or rather whether it can carry the process far enough to give them some real experience of standing on their own feet at a time when the friendly support of the school is still there to see that the conditions are favourable and that no serious harm occurs. Certainly there is a demand for the independence which money can buy. Boys, and to a less extent girls, are prepared to work for it. Over half the boys in the Social Survey had held paid jobs while still at school—and this was true alike of modern, technical and grammar school pupils. Do the schools accept this fact and draw the necessary conclusions from it in the way in which they treat senior boys and girls at school? Some schools are much more successful than others in this respect, but the interviews carried out by the Social Survey showed that one-fifth of the boys and one-quarter of the girls who left school as soon as they could gave as their main reason for leaving the fact that they disliked school or some aspect of it. Do they feel that school is holding them down, instead of bringing them up? They are not likely to tolerate a situation in which they are treated nearly as adults at home and nearly as children at school.

177. The Social Survey showed that 46 per cent of the boys and 60 per cent of the girls who left modern or all-age schools had no further full-time or part-time education. But it would be quite wrong to suppose that education could do nothing more for these boys and girls. To realise how much undeveloped talent there is in quite ordinary people one has only to look at the experience of the armed forces. The job of the present-day infantryman, for instance, calls for an adaptability and resource which would have surprised the army of a hundred or even fifty years ago. The challenge produces the response. Indeed it was always so. Those occupations, such as the fisherman's, which have called for more than the average capability, have found it. The experience of the test expedition in the Duke of Edinburgh's Award has shown that some boys whose official intelligence rating is very low have been able successfully to meet the considerable demands it makes on what would normally, and rightly, be regarded as intelligence. Why has this talent been left undeveloped? It is partly caused by the fact that until recently boys and girls left school while they were mere children, and so yesterday's late-developers rarely got a chance; partly because the scope of education was often defined in too narrow and abstract terms to

elicit the qualities of practical wisdom, and partly because of the very large classes which were normal until recently, and are not yet by any means things of the past. But where schools have developed fifth-year courses, they have found that their pupils, so far from marking time, have advanced with an unexpected rapidity.

178. Secondary education is, then, in our view essentially the education of the adolescent. And adolescence coincides much better physically than it does psychologically with the present length of the compulsory secondary course. Until they are 16, boys and girls need an environment designed for their needs. Each extension of the school-leaving age obviously brings the schools increasingly difficult emotional and social problems, especially perhaps with the education of girls. But the difficulty of the problems is no reason for refusing to face them, though it is a reason for considering very carefully what qualities are needed in the teachers who will have to deal with them. We may hide, but we do not solve, teen-age problems simply by letting boys and girls leave school. Indeed, we condemn many of them to do without the help they need. It is true that the protective side of education is likely to be quite ineffective if the educational side is unsatisfying, but we are convinced that there are sufficient important, fresh educational interests which can be aroused in boys and girls during their teens which are today often left only half-exploited, or barely touched upon, when they leave school.

179. We conclude that the promise of secondary education for all cannot be redeemed unless it is continued for all to 16. This does not, of course, mean that simply keeping all boys and girls at school until they are 16 will automatically provide them with a secondary education worthy of the name. We recognise that some schools are already discovering how to provide it for completely unacademic pupils, but we know how few they are, though their number is growing. There is much to be done if the schools are to be ready for a higher school-leaving age by the date we recommend.

CHAPTER 12

Why the School-Leaving Age should be Raised: (2) The National Interest

180. In the previous chapter we were concerned with the benefits to the individual boy and girl which, in our view, justify an extra year of full-time schooling. The benefit to the individual is important. But it is not the only argument; there is also the national interest to consider. In one important respect the last ten years or so may be thought to have altered this argument. It is now apparent, as it has never been before, that it is possible to attract a sizeable proportion of each age-group into staying on voluntarily at school after the compulsion of the law has expired. If the current trend continues at the present rate, before long nearly half the boys and girls in this country, including nearly one-third of those in modern schools, will be staying at school until they are 16. It is clear that this half who undertake a voluntary extension of full-time education will include most, but certainly not all, of those whom the schools regard as academically promising pupils. Provide the opportunity, it may be argued, and those who can make best use of it can be relied on to take it. If for the moment we set aside the argument from human rights, and look on an extra year of schooling as a form of national capital investment, will not this voluntary investment give the country all it needs?

THE LIMITS OF VOLUNTARY STAYING-ON

181. The argument is attractive, but not convincing. There are two main forces which decide that a boy or girl should have a longer education than is enforceable by law. One is the expectation that this will give him better prospects in life than he would otherwise have; the other is that it would be unthinkable within the social group to which his parents belong to cut short his education before whatever age is the norm for that particular section of the community. The two forces are not entirely independent of one another. The children of the better-off on the whole enter, or are expected to enter, careers for which education at least beyond the age of 15 is a necessity. But, even if that expectation is not realised, the educational battle is won. Once a family has established itself inside a group with a conventionally high school-leaving age, its children,

almost irrespective of ability, will be given that full secondary education at least until 16 which we earlier gave reasons to think was desirable for all children.

182. We are much more concerned with the children of parents who themselves left school at 14, as did their neighbours, and who feel that a positive case of personal economic advantage should be established before their own children are kept at school longer than the law insists. This feeling that a case ought to be made out is a prudent and in its way a sensible one; but, as we think, it concentrates too closely on the economic advantages of education. Moreover, the parents are often in no position to judge for themselves. Their knowledge of what is valuable above their own economic level is necessarily limited. Will a longer time at school make it more likely that their boy or girl will get a job with better prospects than if he left now and relied on part-time education? In such points they must take advice without much possibility of checking it. They can only trust, or distrust, the teacher who advises them. If his advice, or the youth employment officer's, is couched, as it must in honesty often be, in the conditional tense, it is not altogether easy for the parents to decide on what must often seem to them a gamble. An additional year or so more of education must often seem to them like a football pool in which you lose your stake unless you win a cash prize; and not, as it should, like a premium bond in which your capital is safe whether you win an additional cash prize or not. Against the decision to leave a boy another year at school there must be set not only the tradition of the elders, but the practice of his contemporaries and the solid satisfaction, spiritual as well as financial, that bread-winning will give him. If we can only reasonably expect to reach within ten years a position where half the nation's children are at school until 16, we must realise that we shall have made but a relatively slight impression on the traditions governing the majority of our fellow-citizens. We shall still be at the stage when the battle for a longer school life must be fought individually for each boy and girl—and lost in many instances where losing will mean a clear waste of talent. Some indication of the odds that have to be considered is given by the classification of Army recruits. Half of all those in the two highest ability groups left school at 15; the country's economic welfare demands, at the very least, that the whole of the first group and a substantial section of the second should have had a secondary education until 16.

183. It does not seem likely that we shall achieve our object quickly if we limit ourselves to voluntary persuasion. Table 16 shows clearly enough how hard that road would be. It would mean a reversal of the present outlook of the manual workers of the country as a whole.

Table 16. Proportion of Army National Service men who left school at the minimum age (15 or below) falling into the highest two ability groups in the army tests, analysed by occupational background of the father.

	Leavers at 15 or below	
	Ability Group 1	Ability Group 2
	per cent	per cent
Professional and Managerial	*1*	*27*
Clerical and other non-manual	*5*	*58*
Skilled manual workers	*19*	*73*
Semi-skilled manual workers	*16*	*77*
Unskilled manual workers	*28*	*86*
Whole sample	*9*	*65*
Total Numbers	681	1,824

One of the factors which contributes to this pattern of early leaving is the size of family. This was mentioned in Chapter 3, and Table 17 repeats the figures that were given there.

Table 17. National Service Recruits (Army and R.A.F.) Age of leaving school by number of children in family.

Number of Children in Recruit's Family (including himself)	Percentage of Recruits who left school at 15 or before
1	*58*
2	*61*
3	*71*
4	*80*
5	*86*
6+	*92*
Whole sample (7,253 persons)	*72*

In families of any considerable size the odds seem to be so heavily weighted against taking an extended course, that in most instances the decision is virtually taken before the discussion begins. In these circumstances it does not seem that voluntary persuasion is likely to be very effective as a means of attaining our object. If the abler children of the lower social groups, and if members of large families from all but the highest groups are to receive a full secondary education, it does not look as if it can be achieved without increasing the length of compulsory school life.

THE PART-TIME ALTERNATIVE

184. One factor which perhaps tells against voluntary persuasion may be the extensive provision of part-time education as a method by which those who have been denied the normal full-time route, or have rejected it, can yet reach the same goal. This is a real contribution towards equality of opportunity, an invaluable piece of corrective mechanism. But it can easily become a dangerous deception when individual parents are considering whether to leave a boy or girl a year longer at school. They hear that he can become an engineer or an architect either by continuing his full-time education and receiving at best a small maintenance allowance, or by part-time study while he is earning reasonable wages or salary. 'Earn while you learn' has an attractive sound; but what if you don't learn so much, or enough? In Chapter 31 of this report we examine in some detail the wastage rates in several forms of part-time education for which the evidence is given in full in Volume II. Here it is sufficient to point out that the part-time route is an arduous one and that success on it is a good deal easier if a solid foundation has been laid in full-time education beyond 15. This is becoming more so every year as the complexity of modern technology increases. It is very difficult to climb the part-time ladder to the top, and will soon be impossible, without at least the additional full-time grounding that another year at school provides. This is very different from the picture parents have in mind when they decide that their sons and daughters might just as well leave school and continue their education part-time.

185. It is, of course, common sense that full-time study, given similar incentives, should be more effective than part-time—not only is the time given to it more, but the distractions fewer, the intervals less, the mind and body less fatigued. It is the reverse of common sense that it should be, all too often, the less favourably placed candidates who have to rely on part-time education. They come, as we have seen, from homes where full-time education in the mid-teens is not accepted as a matter of course. Relatively few of them will have been outstanding pupils, virtually all of whom nowadays get their chance of a longer full-time education. It is the marginal candidates, those who

most need the best conditions, who are perhaps least likely to get them—boys and girls about whom their teachers are not quite sure enough to put up a strenuous fight; boys and girls who look less like certain winners in that calculus of individual advantage which we have pictured taking place in the anxious family council—those of whom it is easy to say "we'd better play safe and get him a good job now". A decision to leave school, especially in these marginal cases, may look like prudence in the individual family situation but may be folly in the national perspective. We need to make the best we can of marginal talent. This means compulsion. The words which Lord Attlee used in the House of Commons in 1946 are still substantially true: "We are straitened in our manpower. We must make up in quality what we lack in quantity. We are, therefore, raising the school-leaving age".

THE JUVENILE LABOUR MARKET

186. Those words, of course, were spoken at a time of general full employment and of a particular shortage of juvenile labour. These words are written after a winter when there has been more unemployment than for some time past. For a short time in the winter of 1958–59, the number of boys and girls under the age of 18 registered as unemployed was more than twice the figure of a year earlier. This spurt of unemployment has fortunately proved to be short-lived and by the summer of 1959 the number of young people out of work was little greater than in 1958. In a few years' time, when the bulge reaches the juvenile labour market, the position is likely to be a good deal worse than it was last winter. As we pointed out in Chapter 5, the proportion of persons in the early working years to the total labour force of the country is beginning to rise and will go on rising for some time to come. After many years when juvenile labour has been relatively scarce, we are moving into a period when it will be relatively plentiful.

187. This is a most important fact whose implications have not, we think, been generally grasped. Plainly we cannot assume that all of the favourable economic conditions under which the great voluntary expansion of education since the war has taken place will continue unchanged. These years of full employment for young workers and adults alike have been invaluable in paving the way by voluntary action for a general increase in the length of school life. They have made it possible to demonstrate both to educationists and to employers and to many parents that another year at school is worth while. They have shown beyond a doubt that we are not 'scraping the bottom of the barrel'; that the old pre-war scale of provision for

secondary education over the age of 15 fell far short of the numbers who could use it to their own and the country's advantage. The ground thus won must not be lost. A boy or girl once taken away from school has the whole of the rest of his or her life affected. Except for a few with above-average tenacity, ambition and ability, the age at which a boy or girl leaves school, and the kind of employment then taken up, largely determine between them the pattern of his whole working life. A decision to leave school, taken in the light of what may be only a passing employment opportunity or difficulty, can impose a quite disproportionate penalty on those at whose expense it is made. It is not only the unschooled pupil who suffers; the community has lost for good the skill it needs and might have enjoyed.

188. If in the years immediately ahead juvenile employment is going to be a little less full than it has been in the immediate past, what will be the effect on voluntary staying-on at school? In the 1930's, when juvenile unemployment was a little less bad than adult unemployment, the result (so far as it can be traced in the statistics) was to encourage the earliest possible school-leaving; and the son, who could get a job, had to help his father who could not. If, in the 1960's, we are going to experience the opposite conditions, and the juvenile labour market is going to be rather more difficult than the adult labour market (which may not, of course, mean that it will be at all bad in absolute terms), we may get the opposite result, and there may be a positive stimulus to voluntary staying-on at school. Many of those who cannot find satisfactory jobs may, as a newspaper put it in a recent survey of juvenile employment, "go back to school and wait in the classroom for better things". But we cannot be sure that this would happen. Nor is education pursued in such a spirit, and liable to interruption the moment a job comes along, likely to give a good yield. In such circumstances, the brighter boys and girls, who will be able to get the best jobs, will leave promptly to make sure of them, and though the size of the fifth year in the schools might rise, its quality might decline. Furthermore, it might be that in times when employers do not have to compete for a scarce supply of able boys, some of them might be less willing to grant part-time day release, a tendency of which the first signs can perhaps already be glimpsed. If the best pupils of the modern schools were leaving earlier, and getting less education after they left school, there would be little comfort to be found in the return to the schools of greater numbers of disappointed job-seekers. And if the major assumption—that *general* employment continues good and the country prosperous—proved to be wrong, all these tendencies would be affected for the worse.

189. All in all, it seems most unwise to rely on the unassisted effects of economic conditions to continue to produce advances in education of the kind that have been seen in the past decade. It is unlikely that, without compulsion, it will become the accepted thing in all classes of society for boys and girls of average intelligence to stay at school until 16. In the majority of neighbourhoods, the question of whether to stay on at school will still have to be individually debated, the presumption being that it is better to leave unless there is a strong reason to the contrary. In such a situation we believe the odds are weighted against the national interest. If there is going to be less pressure from industry for juvenile labour, then the real cost to the country of taking a whole age-group out of the labour market will also be less, especially if this results in their being better equipped when eventually they come into it. It is by no means so clear that, in default of collective action, it will be to the economic advantage of an individual boy or girl to stay longer than he must at school, especially if his ability is marginal to the occupation he desires. Without a rise in the statutory leaving age, the opportunity may be missed.

UPGRADING OF JOBS

190. That the average worker in industry and commerce requires much more education than was needed only a short time ago is the result of two separate tendencies that have combined to produce the same effect. On the one hand, the people of superior intelligence who used to spend their lives in middling jobs because they were denied educational opportunities in their youth, now pass into the grammar schools and the universities or colleges of advanced technology and finish up in the professions. On the other hand, there has been a great increase in the number of skilled and professional jobs, which have sucked up into higher ranks many whose abilities would never in the past have got them so high. The result has been to create a universal upgrading of the sort of post that is filled by a given level of intelligence. This, it seems to us, is one explanation of the phenomenon, so often remarked upon, that "standards are not what they were". Employers, and others, blame the schools. But they are not comparing like with like. The job they are thinking of may be the same—though even this is doubtful—but certainly the boy or girl who does it is a different person from his predecessor of twenty years ago. The great increase in higher positions, and the much wider access to higher education, have between them deprived the middling jobs in industry and business of the level of ability they formerly attracted and retained because of lack of prospects of promotion. But the jobs have to be done, and call for very much the same level

of attainments as of old. If they are not to be done by people of superior ability, more time and care must be spent on education and training. The growth in the proportion of highly skilled jobs, and the decline in the proportion of unskilled jobs, imply a re-assessment of what must be attempted by people of only average intelligence. That re-assessment carries with it a fresh estimate of the length of time their education should last. It is not only at the top but almost to the bottom of the pyramid that the scientific revolution of our times needs to be reflected in a longer educational process.

191. The case for raising the minimum leaving age is further strengthened by the lack of opportunities for part-time day education for girls. Boys have been more fortunate in securing the help of part-time day release. Roughly a third of all boys in employment under 18 now get it. Few girls have this opportunity—only 8 per cent. This is not unnatural, because the early age of marriage makes it unlikely that the original employer can look forward to a sufficiently long period of assistance to justify him in providing day release. Moreover, the bulk of women's employment is not in fields where considerable technical knowledge is required—and it is this need which has been the principal factor in securing day release for boys. There does not seem, then, to be much prospect of any change, short of compulsion, which would make day release much more widely available to girls. We shall later discuss the possibility of making part-time day education compulsory, but we may here anticipate the argument to say that we do not think this is the right form of statutory provision for 15 year-olds. Full-time education is, therefore, even more important for girls than for boys. It is true that more girls than boys follow extended courses in secondary modern schools and full-time courses in colleges of further education, but the difference is not great. In 1958, taking these two types of course together, girls exceeded boys by roughly 3,000 at the age of 15 and half that figure at 16. Moreover, most of this difference can be explained by the popularity of courses in shorthand and typewriting, of which the educational value, though by no means non-existent, is distinctly limited. If we are to make the best use of the ability of girls, it seems clear that we shall have to raise the school-leaving age.

192. We have no thought of recommending the raising of the school-leaving age—that is, the age to which all boys and girls are kept compulsorily at school—beyond 16 or thereabouts. But we are equally convinced that full-time education to 17 or 18 is right for many more boys and girls than now get it. If we are right in our belief that one of the strongest forces leading to a longer school life on a voluntary basis is a desire by parents to put their children in a

stronger economic bargaining position than they would otherwise command, to give them something that others have not got, and, often enough, as it is put, "a better chance than I (the parent) ever had", it follows that the raising of the school-leaving age to 16 is likely to lead to more people seeking an education to 17 or 18 for their children. As long as the ordinary grammar school course to 16 was two years above the ordinary end of school life, it gave a marked advantage to grammar school pupils. The raising of the school-leaving age to 15 reduced the margin, but still left it substantial, especially since for the first six or seven years after 1945 extended courses were rarely available in the modern school. Their introduction has further narrowed the gap. Raising the minimum leaving age to 16 would close it. We should expect this to be followed by a growing wish for an education to 17 or 18 by grammar school parents and pupils and by others too.

193. Are there, in the final analysis, some boys and girls for whom an extra year at school is not necessary? If we restrict the argument strictly to the economic side, to the educational demands of the job to be done, there are certainly some. We do not think they are very many. The Registrar General's classification places 16 per cent of the working population in semi-skilled occupations, but in a good many of these there is a strong case to be made out for a good education for at least many of the workers. Agricultural labourers, for instance, are classified as semi-skilled; but few would deny the advantage of education in their work. Only 12 per cent of the working population are classified as unskilled workers. It is probably true that no one individual employed in this way needs more education than can be given by 15—needs for his work, that is; let us never forget his leisure. But it is important that there should be among them sufficient men and women to provide leadership, and this leadership cannot be provided by importation from above. In the past the country could count on a fair scatter of ability, if not of education, among the unskilled workers just because for so many men anything more than the minimum education was quite out of reach. In this state of affairs the provision of junior leadership looked after itself. It no longer does so. Every advance in the availability of education has (quite rightly) reduced the number of able men and women left in the unskilled occupations. Their loss can only be made good by better education so that responsibility may not fall into irresponsible hands. Unskilled employment often brings men and women together in large groups where difficult problems of human relations arise. The sort of education, and it is a long process, which develops the qualities of the good citizen, develops also the qualities of the good fellow-worker. This is something

which industry needs at every level, but certainly not least among its unskilled workers.

THE FIFTH YEAR AS A TRANSITION

194. The economic argument for another year of compulsory schooling—the argument from what the public interest demands—therefore seems to us to be a very strong one. There is, however, one condition in it which has been implicit in much that we have written but should now be made explicit. If there is to be a fifth year of secondary education for all, it should not be simply one more year such as the other four have been. When boys and girls left school at 12 to go to work, it would have been nonsense to talk of the last year at school as a transitional year. They were children right up to the time they left school, and beyond. But by 15, and still more by 16, they have already acquired a good deal of independence. There is still an abrupt transition from school to work, but there is no sharp break in the way they spend their spare time—many of them have begun before they leave school to adopt in their leisure hours the patterns of the late teens. This imposes a serious responsibility on the schools, of which they are aware. We single out two aspects from many for comment. The first concerns working hours. It is natural that as boys and girls grow older their waking day and their working day should grow longer. When they pass from the infant school to the junior school, half-an-hour a day is added to the length of lessons. But no further addition is made to official school hours whether a boy is 8 or 18, and he continues to go to school only on about half the days in the year. As soon as he leaves school, however, his hours of work become much longer and his holidays much shorter. Which is right? If the school-leaving age were still 14, nearly everybody would agree, we think, that the school day and year were much closer than industry's to what boys and girls ought to be putting in at the end of their school life. Now that the leaving age is 15, a good many people have doubts whether school conditions should not be brought for everybody (as they already are for a good many) a little nearer to subsequent working conditions. When the school-leaving age is raised to 16 these doubts will, we think rightly, become virtual certainties. They apply, however, only where the actual hours spent in school are the sum total of work done by the pupils. Wherever homework is set, and conscientiously done, the balance is substantially redressed. The experience of comprehensive and modern schools is showing that homework can profitably form part of the education of far more boys and girls than used to be believed, but it cannot be anything like the whole solution for pupils who are markedly below average. Allowance must also be made for

other forms of work quite unconnected with school. Half the boys add such paid work as paper rounds to their school day, and most girls have home duties—for these the disparity between school hours and industrial hours is probably reduced as far as it should be. Moreover, many country children, and some town children, have long and tiring journeys to and from school.

195. But when all these allowances have been made, it is still true that many boys and girls have too little to do during their last year at school, and that these are precisely the boys and girls who will stay at school until they are 16 only when they are compelled to do so. We can, therefore, get no advance experience from those 15 year-olds who now take extended courses to help us in meeting the challenge that the abundant and, in a sense, enforced leisure of the unacademically minded majority will present. It will be a far more serious challenge than we have grown accustomed to from the same sort of boys and girls at 14. Their home circumstances, and their lack of ability and purpose, make it almost certain that for them the solution does not lie in homework so much as in some form of directed activities out of school hours. The solution we have in mind is likely to be possible only where staffing ratios are generous enough to allow for some adult leadership out of school hours (and ultimately out of school terms as well) in addition to work in the classroom in the ordinary way. There is a precedent in the staffing arrangements of technical colleges.

196. The second point concerns the feeling of growing independence and usefulness that 15 year-old boys and girls ought to have, which is often closely connected with the amount of money they have to command. There is no doubt that the world as it has grown to be offers them tempting opportunities for spending considerable sums of money on clothes, sport and entertainment, and that these luxuries have become virtual necessities to many. An older generation looks askance, but is powerless to reverse the trend; nor, in fact, is it all to the bad. Spending wisely is something that has to be learned, and is perhaps best learned where there is interest in the spending. But the money has to come from somewhere, and some at least of us feel that the raising of the minimum leaving age to 16 may increase the frustration of prolonged dependence on parents for every penny of spending money. It seems to us important that boys and girls who want to stand on their own feet financially should not be prevented from doing so; but there is a vital responsibility laid on the local authorities, within the statutory powers they already possess, to see that the conditions under which pupils can earn money are reasonable and do not stand in the way of their education and their healthy physical growth. There is an obvious difference, for

instance, between work during term and work in the holidays. We have no ready-made solution, but we are convinced that the point is an important one. If the desire of a teen-ager to get more independence can be linked with a realisation that this is something that has to be paid for and worked for—in fact that work is worth doing—a valuable moral lesson has been learnt.

197. In what we have said about leisure and about paid work we have suggested that the schools should bear in mind that the teen-ager has a world other than school and home, and it is for school and home to help him to gain the benefits and avoid the dangers of this private world. In both these matters it seems to us that (not least for the less able pupils, who are often the most early to mature) the last year at school should take full account of their interest in the world of employment, which they are soon going to enter, and in their leisure hours, of which they are already in full control with money to spend as they like. There is a duty to those older pupils, who are already half independent in their activities and behaviour, to assist them to fit in to life as it is generally lived by adults. Abundant experiment will be necessary; and, because this is a no man's land between school and work, it is pretty certain that some of the experiments which ought to be tried will be difficult to carry out because they will not easily be kept within the bounds set by school regulations, trade union rules, labour legislation, insurance requirements and, no doubt, many other accidental impediments. Those concerned with young people both before and after they leave school should discuss together what experiments would be worth trying, and then see that the way is smoothed for those responsible to go ahead.

SHOULD THERE BE EXCEPTIONS?

198. Boys and girls in their 16th year, then, may require significantly different treatment, if they are to be kept at school, than boys and girls in their 15th year. Are there any for whom the appropriate treatment would be so different that it should not be attempted at all at school? Are there any boys or girls whose lives would be happier, richer and more useful if they had left school at 15 instead of 16? In schools, handicapped as many are today by inadequate premises, poor equipment and an insufficiency of teachers, the answer must be that there are some boys and girls who will get more from spending their 16th year at work, if it is well chosen, than at school. The argument turns not on the inherent incapacity of certain pupils to benefit from another year at school, but on the accidental incapacity of certain schools to provide the right education for them. This is not something which springs from the nature of things; but

something which is remediable, and is being remedied. The schools will not be perfect by the later 1960's (or at any time), but we believe that they can be so much improved by then that this argument will lose most of the force which it has today.

199. But let us assume that the schools are as ready as can be expected before the school-leaving age is raised. Will there still be boys and girls who would be better out in the world? Certainly, if they exist, they do not form a group which can be identified by their intelligence or attainment level. They are not, for instance, those of lowest intelligence. Boys and girls who are admitted to special schools for the educationally sub-normal do not leave until they are 16. They are better, not worse, citizens as the result. But if there is no homogeneous group, are there not perhaps many individual boys and girls who would be better out of school? Admittedly chronological age is only a rough way of reckoning physical and emotional growth, and few parents would blindly rely on it in bringing up their families. It is, however, the most practicable way of defining the law of school attendance, though it would not be surprising if it gave rise to hard cases. At 12, school is clearly the right place for everybody, and at 20 for nobody. Somewhere between these ages it becomes the wrong place for some people, and at each succeeding point in the scale the number for whom it is the wrong place will tend to grow. Has school begun to be the wrong place for any by 15 or 16? We are agreed that, if the alternative to school for all is work for all, we would choose school for all. We agree, too, that school is, or can be made, the right environment for nearly all boys and girls of 15. It must, however be socially acceptable to them as well as intellectually suitable; and we think that English education may have to consider considerable changes both in organisation and in attitude if it is to deal with pupils who—at least in their own opinion—put on and off childish things as they enter and leave the school buildings. But, even given fairly radical changes to meet the needs of older boys and girls, we accept the view that there will be a few whose development has carried them by 15 to a point where what is right for their contemporaries is not right for them. An obvious illustration is the girl who is either a mother or pregnant before she is 16. There are other less obvious, and less unfortunate, examples.

200. What is to be done, then, about the few? It is on the local education authority that the duty falls of enforcing school attendance, if necessary by bringing a case before the magistrates. Before doing so, the authority will naturally satisfy itself that it will be able to win its case, which it will not be able to do if the parents are able to convince the court that their child is in fact receiving efficient

education; and this can, of course, be given in other places and by other means than at school. There is in our view sufficient elasticity in the present law to deal sensibly with the few exceptions we are concerned about. Authorities do not need, and certainly do not want, to be invested with a dispensing power to exempt certain boys and girls from fulfilling their legal obligations. Such dispensing power would also, we believe, be against the interests of other children, and might seriously prejudice the effective raising of the leaving age. To allow some children to go to work, or to stay at home, because they were "difficult" to deal with in school, would be to put a premium on insubordination; and experience has abundantly shown that any scheme of exemptions which would be of financial advantage to the children exempted, or to their parents, would be exceedingly difficult to administer justly, and would result in such pressure on teachers and members of authorities to extend its operation that in many cases the advantages of a longer school life would be lost. At the same time we are very much concerned with the welfare of this small minority of boys and girls, and we believe that, when the school leaving age is raised, local education authorities may need to exercise more freely and flexibly the discretionary power they already possess to vary the ordinary provision where that is clearly necessary. The Chief Medical Officer of the Ministry of Education pointed out in his report for 1956 and 1957 that nursery school arrangements have been greatly modified as the needs of small children have been increasingly recognised, and went on to suggest that similar flexibility might with advantage be introduced into arrangements for the education of adolescents. In some cases of the sort we are considering, transfer from school to a college of further education would doubtless suffice. In others something more radical would be required; and as an example of what can be done we may cite the provision by at least one authority of a "Home Tuition Unit", off school premises, for particularly difficult and backward boys nearing school-leaving age who had been disturbing influences in ordinary schools. The teacher in charge of the unit had a completely free hand to plan the boys' environment and work, and achieved conspicuous success. Freedom of this kind is essential in such cases, constituting as they do a series of individual problems which defy classification and general prescriptions. The only criterion to be applied is that whatever is provided for a particular boy or girl should be designed to make him or her a better person and a more useful member of society. The principle warranting the provision is that although the child is not attending school in the normal sense the education authority continues to have a direct and continuing responsibility for his or her education until the age up to which other children must remain at school. Obviously such a principle is incompatible with the withdrawal of any child from the effective charge of the education service before the school-leaving age, and we accordingly think that its application must stop short of arrangements which would have the practical effect of removing boys or girls, not simply from school, but from the care of the education service altogether, as would happen if they were allowed to take up full-time employment or to stay at home.*

CONCLUSION

201. There is, then, a strong case on economic grounds for raising the school-leaving age; but, if this were the only reason for doing so, it might not be a sufficient reason. It is true, of course, that the country cannot afford to let so much talent go unutilised at a time when industry demands greatly increased skill and knowledge, and especially in the face of the tremendous efforts being made by other countries to develop all their human resources. There might, however, be other measures which could be taken to see that this kind of human waste was avoided. It is possible to imagine, for instance, though it would not be easy to produce, a system of financial incentives which made it so clearly worth while for a relatively able boy to carry his education to a later age than he does now, that it would, perhaps, in the end hardly be necessary to raise the school-leaving age. After all, the present encouraging growth of extended courses has taken place in spite of a wages structure which certainly does not encourage a boy to stay longer at school unless he is prepared to look very far ahead. The economic argument alone, in fact, stops a little way short of being finally conclusive. We come back, therefore, to clinch the matter, to the point from which this chapter started. Our main case is not economic at all. It rests on the conviction that all boys and girls of 15 have much to learn, and that school (in the broadest sense) and not work is the place for this. "Secondary Education for All" will not be a reality until it is provided for all up to the age of 16. We believe that this is a duty which society owes all its young citizens just as we individually recognise it as an obligation in our own families.

202. We summarise the case for raising the school-leaving age in six points:

(*a*) The country is a long way from tapping all the available supply of talent by present methods. Half of the National Service recruits to the Army who were rated in the two highest ability groups had left school at 15.

* A Reservation to this paragraph, signed by some members of the Council, is printed at the end of this chapter.

(*b*) It is most unlikely that this waste of talent can be remedied within a reasonable period without compulsion, because leaving at 15 is so deeply embedded in certain parts of the social structure—among National Service recruits to the Army coming from families of manual workers two-thirds of those in the two highest ability groups had left school at 15.

(*c*) The part-time route even with day release is not an efficient substitute for longer full-time education.

(*d*) While the number staying on at school voluntarily is increasing, this trend provides only a precarious basis for a national system, and may depend to a considerable extent on the continuation of general prosperity and in particular of a plentiful supply of jobs for young workers.

(*e*) The demand both for more educated workers and for more deeply educated workers is growing at almost all levels in industry —raising the school-leaving age to 16 would give those near the bottom a better foundation, and would be reflected in larger numbers receiving full-time education to 18 or beyond.

(*f*) The strongest part of the case is the general need for secondary education for all to 16 extending through the difficult and important period of adolescence.

Note of Reservation to Paragraph 200 *by some Members of the Council.*

We do not think paragraph 200 goes far enough. In our view, the boys and girls for whom exceptional provision should be made, though they are doubtless a small minority in the age-group, are nevertheless never likely to be so few that the law need not take note of them. We do not regard them as being limited to "particularly difficult and backward" boys and girls. These do exist, and will exist in much larger numbers when the school-leaving age is raised. But there are also frustrated and unhappy young adults who, without being in any way disturbing influences in their schools, nevertheless cannot develop in a soil which, for one reason or another, has become sterile for them. Very often this is a matter of early physical development, as witness the six-foot boy who, through nobody's fault (least of all his own), has become increasingly inhibited by the stark comparison between his classroom inadequacies and his man's physique.

We do not think that there is "sufficient elasticity in the present law", certainly as it is at present interpreted, to "deal sensibly" with all these cases. We should like, for example, to see considerable freedom of transfer, at or even before the statutory leaving age, from school to other full-time educational institutions of several different varieties, existing and to be created. If this is permitted under the present law, the permission is not effective. We think it should be made clear that transfers of this kind are not merely permissible but, in many cases, desirable.

But even this does not go far enough. We think there are a few young people, mainly boys, whose further development after the age of 15 or thereabouts can best be served, not by full-time attendance at any educational institution, but by hard work in an adult but understanding environment. We think there are some young people—and we are thinking chiefly of girls who become pregnant—who can best be saved for society and for themselves by being allowed to leave school and perhaps be set to work in a babies' home, day nursery or similar institution. We do not think that any of these young people should be released from the care of the local education authority. But it is the core of our case that there is no monopoly of educational influences in educational institutions, and where the authority decides that something other than full-time formal education would be the best thing for a boy or girl, in his or her own interest, it should not be prevented by the law from putting its decision into effect.

The difficulty in this line of thought, as we freely recognise, is whether or not wage-earning employment should be permitted. On the one hand, to encourage boys and girls to think that, by being troublesome, they can get permission to leave school and earn large wages would be dangerous. On the other hand, to ban all wage-earning employment would be to close the door to many things that might serve very well the purposes we have in mind. In our view, then, the local education authority should have power to allow a young person to engage in employment before the school-leaving age, but only subject to four safeguards: first, that the initiative should remain wholly with the authority and not with the boy or girl or the parents; secondly, that the authority should continue to have a responsibility for oversight; thirdly, that there should be power to withdraw the permission; and, finally, that the authority should be empowered to make the condition that part, or the whole, of the earnings should be placed in trust or dealt with in some other manner for the young person's benefit. We believe that these safeguards would prevent a recurrence of what happened with the "beneficial employment" exemptions of the past, which virtually became, in some areas, open general licences to leave at will.

To avoid any possibility of misunderstanding, we want to make it clear that this note does not imply any dissent on our part from the major recommendation that the school-leaving age should be raised. On the contrary, we feel confident that provision on the lines we have suggested for a small minority would be held in public opinion to reinforce the case for keeping the great majority in school for another year. We certainly so regard it ourselves.

GEOFFREY CROWTHER	M. H. CADBURY	T. S. SIMEY
G. S. BOSWORTH	V. M. GRUBB	H. A. WARREN
S. M. CAFFYN	M. E. REEVES	B. W. M. YOUNG

CHAPTER 13

The Duration of Secondary School Life

203. We have recommended that the minimum school-leaving age should be raised to 16. If this meant what it says, boys and girls would be free to leave school on their 16th birthdays. But since 1918 a child's age has been given an artificial or conventional definition for the purposes of school attendance, and there are now, so to speak, only three legal birthdays in the year. Boys and girls are now free to leave school at the end of the term in which they become 15, and there are thus three possible leaving dates in the year.

204. The word "term" is also given an artificial or conventional meaning. For the purpose of compulsory attendance the whole calendar year is divided into three terms, and holidays are counted as part of the preceding term, so that a boy or girl reaching the age of 15 during the holidays is not required to return to school for the next term. The dates on which the three terms begin and end are fixed by local education authorities and there is some variation. Subject to this, the age at which a boy actually attends his last compulsory lesson will vary in completed months from 14 years and 11 months to 15 years and 3 months.

THE DISADVANTAGES OF THREE LEAVING DATES

205. All boys and girls start their secondary school life in the autumn—there is only one beginning date in any authority's area though there are always three permissible ends. We talk of the secondary school course as lasting four years, but that is careless and misleading talk. It makes us feel better than we are. It is in fact the maximum, not even the average, period of compulsory secondary education. In practice, rather less than one-third are required to attend for four complete school years. Others are free to leave after three years and two terms, three years and one term and a few after only three years. If the school-leaving age were raised to 16 by Order in Council under the Act of 1944, these periods would vary from five years to four years, but the jagged end would remain.

206. It is clear that nobody would now wish to go back to the old strict definition of age by the actual date of birth. Once, however, a conventional definition is adopted, it is clearly permissible to consider whether the existing convention is the one that makes best sense. When the present system was adopted it was felt to be a great step

forward because it did away with the unsettling process of attrition which wore away the top class day by day within each term. It became possible to plan the school's work term by term. In fact two alternative patterns of organisation grew up in the old senior elementary school and have persisted into the new secondary modern school. Some headmasters prefer to "stream" their pupils, dividing them in a three-form entry school, for instance, into A, B and C streams according to ability. Others, who may well have followed this practice in the earlier part of the course, choose to re-group their pupils for the last year into Christmas, Easter and summer leavers. The existence of these two patterns, for both of which convincing arguments can be put forward, indicates the dilemma with which the existing convention confronts schools. Those which continue throughout the course to organise their forms according to ability point to the fact that they have to cater for the enormous range of intelligence which is represented in their schools, schools which serve three-quarters of the whole population. Those which re-group by expected date of leaving point to two other important factors. There is the difficulty of planning a year's work not only to give good value as a whole, but so that each term's instalment is complete in itself and a suitable stopping point for those who are going to leave. There is the even greater difficulty of overcoming the restlessness which settles on a group of boys or girls who have come up the school together but who are now to be broken up by the accident of a few months' or weeks' difference in age, a difference which has never counted in their experience until now. They become eager for the new experience of the adult world of work. They have travelled so far together; why should they not go on together?

LEAVING AT THE END OF THE YEAR: PROS AND CONS

207. It is clear, then, that there is a good deal to be said against the present convention. Would any other be more satisfactory? There is no question of the educational advantages of a common ending to a course begun by all at the same time. The junior school with its orderly four-year programme from 7+ to 11+ knows where it stands, and plans accordingly. The grammar school with its five, six and seven year courses, and the university with its three or four years of undergraduate study have the same advantages. Only the modern school with its three different lengths of course, decided neither by mind nor maturity but solely by accident of birth, is left to do the best it can with our educationally indefensible upper end to the course. As far as the work of the school is concerned, there

can be little doubt that the convention ought to be amended so that compulsory attendance would stop at the end of the school year, not term, in which the pupil attained the stated age.

208. What should the stated age be—15, 16 or even 15½? If 15 were selected, the age on leaving would then range from 14 years 11 months for those with birthdays in August to 15 years 11 months for those with birthdays in September, and the secondary school course would be four years for all.* One-third of the age-group would be getting no more secondary education than a third do now—though they are the third who now get the full four years. None would have reached, and only a few would have nearly reached, the age of 16 which, as we said in Chapter 11, is in our view psychologically a better age than 15 for the end of secondary education. It is, perhaps, well to repeat the caveat that there is a wide range in the chronological age at which boys and girls emerge from adolescence, but to add the rider that there is no reason whatever to suppose that the one-third who would be free to leave school at or about 15 would be likely to contain more than a strictly proportionate share of those maturing early. The definition of compulsory school life as extending to the end of the school year in which the pupil becomes 15 would, it seems to us, not only be educationally valuable but also a useful tidying up of the present system. But it would hardly be by itself a sufficient change to constitute the major advance which we believe to be both practicable and necessary. Indeed it might even stand in the way of such an advance, since there would be little sense, when the age was raised to 16, in going back to the present system of termly leaving.

209. In the same way, a definition that extended compulsory school life to the July following the 16th birthday might be thought to go too far. It would mean that one-half of the age-group would be nearer 17 than 16 before they were free to leave and, again, there is absolutely no reason to suppose that this half would contain more than its proportionate share of especially slow developers. While our belief that far more boys and girls than now ought to be at school to 17 is, we hope, abundantly clear, we do not believe that this is true of all boys and girls. Many of us would have grave reservations about approaching so nearly to that position as would be involved by defining the end of compulsory school life as the end of the school year in which the pupil became 16.

210. Attendance at school until the end of the year in which the pupil became 15½ would be the nearest approach to combining com-

* Different authorities have different transfer dates, but the months quoted in the text give a sufficiently true general picture.

pulsory education to 16, but not substantially beyond it, with a secondary course which had as orderly an end as it already has an orderly beginning. The average age of leaving would then be 16. This definition, however, would seem to entail major consequential changes in the structure of primary education, because an alteration of this kind in the end of the secondary course would almost certainly necessitate alterations in the age of transfer from primary to secondary education, and possibly also of admission to primary education. We do not, therefore, pursue this interesting idea.

211. Moreover, there are other reasons for suggesting a different form of definition. It is clear that the point of transition from school to employment cannot be defined exclusively in terms of educational convenience, or even of solid educational advantage, without regard to other factors, which we must now consider.

212. It is of over-riding importance that boys and girls leaving school should be able to find employment—and it is as well to remember once again that this may be more difficult in the years ahead than in recent experience. Would those who employ boys and girls be able to accommodate themselves to an annual instead of a termly intake from the schools? Other countries do. In Western Germany, for instance, compulsory education extends to the close of the school year, ending at Easter. In the greater part of the United States custom, though not law, has produced much the same result—the great majority of boys and girls do not leave until the end of the school year. In both countries, however, the school year ends rather earlier in the calendar year than in England; and this may be a help in placing leavers in employment. It is clear, however, that in England employers who want recruits with an external examination qualification have had to accustom themselves to waiting until after the summer examinations, and have found little difficulty in doing so. We feel justified in saying that recruitment to jobs where an initial qualification is desired, or a long process of training is involved, is well served by an annual output from the schools. But where the skill needed, or to be acquired, is small there is no attraction to the employer in an annual school output over a termly one; and indeed there must be considerable disadvantages for small firms.

213. Any proposal to substitute annual for termly school-leaving would be bound to have important consequences affecting the entry of young people into employment. Two in particular seem to us to need careful consideration. In the first place, there might be difficulty in quickly securing employment for the least employable school leavers if all left at once. The second is that the interviewing of leavers by the youth employment officers would have to be spread over

the last three terms of their school life instead of being concentrated into their final term. Would this make the whole year one of unsettlement? There is a risk of it, but only in our view if the situation were mishandled. Properly planned, the last year might in this way be given a transitional and forward-looking character which would give a new reality to school work.

214. There is another consideration which many would feel cuts across the otherwise overwhelming case for fixing secondary school life by completed school years. The difference of one day in date of birth might make a difference of one year in being allowed to leave school. This is, of course, true; but how serious an objection is it—how many, in other words, would experience a real grievance as a result of defining compulsory school life in this way? In the Social Survey investigation it was found that the parents of 48 per cent of the boys and 42 per cent of the girls who actually left modern schools at Easter or Christmas said they would have been willing for their children to have stayed until July. There might at first be some discontent among the remainder, especially no doubt in certain areas; but it is to be expected that this, like other educational reforms, would soon come to be taken for granted. This would, we think, happen the more readily because the school year has been the unit of life and companionship from the time a boy or girl entered the junior school. The boy who leaves school a year earlier because he was born a day earlier than the boy next door would probably never have been in the same form or class with him. On the other hand, the present system of termly leaving does disrupt the well-established school social group, and cause that sense of unfairness and unsettlement to which we have referred.

215. It may be helpful at this point to summarise the considerations which must be taken into account in defining the legal obligation. They are:

(*a*) The upper age limit should not be fixed below 16.

(*b*) The definition of secondary school life in terms of the school year instead of the school term has, from the educational point of view, overwhelming advantages.

(*c*) But, if the school year chosen is to be that in which pupils become 15, too many adolescents will be excluded; and, if it is to be that in which pupils become 16, some who will be nearly 17 will be included.

(d) The definition of school life in terms of the school year instead of the school term would mean that about one-third of an age group would be retained in school two terms longer than at present.

A further third would be retained one term, and for a further third the reform would make no difference in length of school life. (These figures do not, of course, take account of voluntary staying on beyond the minimum age; in fact, the number retained against their wishes would be little more than half the above figures.)

(*e*) One leaving date a year would not seem likely to produce serious difficulties in securing jobs for boys and girls capable of skilled employment; it might, however, lead to considerable delays in placing the least employable school leavers.

A SUGGESTED COMPROMISE: TWO LEAVING DATES

216. These considerations lead us to propose a system by which two instead of three permissible leaving dates would be established in the school year—at Easter and in July. The simplest way of doing this would be simply to abolish Christmas leaving, but this would mean that the majority would leave at Easter, whereas our intention is that the great majority should complete the year. We, therefore, propose that only the oldest group—those with birthdays in September to January inclusive—would be eligible to leave at Easter, and that most of the present Easter leavers would not be allowed to leave until the end of the summer term. It would follow that, when the school-leaving age was raised, no boy or girl would be allowed to leave before he or she was 16 years old or compelled to stay at school after he was 16 years and 7 months old. Any change in the method of defining the ages between which education is compulsory would require legislation. The opportunity might well be taken to introduce a nationally uniform system of dates for the beginning and end of compulsory attendance, and for transfers from primary to secondary education. There are anomalies under the present system of local arrangements which can cause serious difficulties.

217. The effect of a change of this kind in secondary school organisation would be to establish two lengths of secondary course (apart from Sixth Form courses)—one of four years and two terms and one of five years. The latter is clearly preferable on educational grounds, and we hope would become the normal one. This purpose would clearly be defeated if external examinations were allowed in the Easter term and we expect, as we have stated in Chapter 10, that a fair proportion of secondary school pupils will wish to take some such examination before leaving. It is impossible at this stage to say what that proportion will be, but we should expect it to be half and possibly more. These pupils, whatever their birthday, would stay on until the end of the summer term. The Easter leavers would be largely confined to those, eligible by age, who had neither ability nor inclination to try their hand at an external examination The Youth

Employment Service would have an opportunity to place some of these boys and girls, who are often among the more difficult to place in employment, before the others were available. The objections to one leaving date from the side of finding employment would, we think, be very largely met by such an arrangement. From the educational point of view this plan is not as good as a straight five-year course for all; but it is, we think, a useful compromise which is much to be preferred to the present system of termly leaving.

218. A school year with two leaving dates would probably mean that the work of the school would be planned on a basis of $4\frac{2}{3}$ years—that is to say that the syllabus would be completed by Easter in the fifth year. This would leave the summer term free for two purposes. Those who were candidates for an external examination—all those in the selective schools and a substantial proportion of those in other schools—would do what they do now, revise and polish up work already tackled. The last term in the fifth year, the term that would be optional as far as the law is concerned for five-twelfths of the pupils, would be the summer term. There are few subjects in the curriculum (though there are certainly some) which do not lend themselves to an extension out of school through application or illustration of work that has been prepared by classroom studies. Field work is a vital part of educational experience, not least for the less academic type of mind. Indeed, if in earlier years it has played a regular part in the rhythm of the school year, we believe that there will be a good many non-examination candidates, legally free to leave at Easter, who will prefer to come back for the summer term.

219. It is important to be clear about just how much or how little this suggested procedure would help the schools. To raise the school-leaving age to 16 will for the first time confront the schools with the need to provide a fifth-year course for pupils some of whom are educationally uninterested and allergic to classroom work. This is a new task irrespective of whether one of the three leaving dates is abolished then or in the interval. There is no direct help to be got from abolishing Christmas leaving at an earlier date; but it would be a good deal easier to plan a successful fifth year if in the meantime the fourth year work could be put on a more satisfactory basis than it is at present. As things stand, the choice, as we saw in paragraph 206, is often between "streaming" on grounds of academic ability and "batching" by date of leaving. This does not leave much room for the development of options to meet the varying needs and tastes of the older pupils. It would be a good deal easier to arrange this if no leaving took place until the end of the Easter term of the fourth year. It must not be forgotten, however, that when the school-

leaving age is raised to 16 there would still be another twelve months to add. Abolition of Christmas leaving would only take us a small part of the way we shall have to go in experience of handling boys and girls who are not very intelligent and not at all scholastically inclined.

220. When we come to consider the date at which the leaving age should be raised to 16, one of the factors to be weighed is the fact that, while secondary schools are getting good experience through extended courses in educating their more intelligent boys and girls up to the age of 16, there is relatively little experience available about the less able and less interested boys and girls, who do not stay on at school for extended courses. The raising of the school-leaving age will be much easier, and much more immediately beneficial, if the schools are able during the next few years to get some practical experience of handling and teaching boys and girls of this kind in their 16th year. Fortunately, to a limited extent, this is possible, and we can in effect raise the school-leaving age in two instalments. We recommend that the amending legislation to fix two leaving dates in the year should be introduced now, to come into effect as soon as possible—that is, with the present leaving age of 15. The Order in Council substituting 16 for 15 as the upper age limit could later be introduced independently of the amending legislation. The abolition of Christmas leaving by itself makes no extra demands on accommodation because it does not add another year or age-group to school life. It only carries on until Easter the fourth-year pupils who would have left at Christmas. The places they occupied in the winter term are still there for them to occupy. It would make only a fractionally greater demand on staff. It therefore seems to us to be a useful instalment of reform which need not wait, as so much else inevitably must, for the passing of the "bulge".

CHAPTER 14

School-Leaving Age or County College: The Problem of Priority

221. Before we go on to discuss when the minimum school-leaving age should be raised to 16 it is necessary to consider the relation of this reform to the introduction of compulsory part-time education to 18, the other major portion of the 1944 Act within our terms of reference which has not yet been implemented. Too often county colleges and a longer school life are presented as if they were alternatives. "If you choose to raise the school-leaving age", it is suggested, "you will not be able to introduce compulsory part-time education. One major educational reform is about all that can be expected in a generation, and unused powers, even under an Act of Parliament, soon become unusable through atrophy. As it was with the day continuation schools of the Fisher Act, so it will be with the county colleges of the Butler Act." That is the suggestion; but it is not our view. Of course, it would be an unbearable strain on resources if the government decided to introduce at the same moment both another year at school and compulsory attendance at county colleges. Both will require large building programmes, and both will require many teachers. But they are not the same buildings and, for the most part, the men and women required for the additional year in the schools and for county colleges should come from different backgrounds and will need a different training. Provided that the country can afford both extensions of the national system of education—and we have seen in Chapter 6 that it ought to be able to do so—there is no reason in our view why one should not follow the other in fairly close succession.

222. In what order? As far as cost is concerned, the various estimates that have been made for us, on slightly different assumptions, agree in indicating that there is likely to be insufficient difference to justify us in preferring one to the other on financial grounds. Both reforms are so important and so overdue that, if one could be adequately prepared earlier than the other, it ought to be preferred. We have studied the state of preparedness for both operations, and we have tried independently to set a target date for each. The result of this exploration is to suggest that the raising of the school-leaving age can, and therefore should, be accomplished first.

223. The argument turns largely on the position of the 15 year-olds, who occupy, as it were, debatable ground between the county college and the school. All those who accept the desirability of both reforms must automatically hold that the right place for 15 year-old boys and girls is in full-time education. To introduce compulsory part-time education before raising the school-leaving age would put them temporarily in the wrong place, for nobody suggests leaving a gap of twelve months between the end of compulsory school life and the beginning of the compulsory part-time obligation. It would be necessary, therefore, if the school-leaving age were not first raised, to provide part-time education for all 15 year-olds as a temporary measure. We take it as axiomatic that it would be disastrous to launch a completely new educational venture like county colleges in discarded schools or makeshift accommodation. A very considerable building programme would, therefore, be necessary before part-time education could be made compulsory. It would be wasteful to provide for three age-groups—15 to 17 inclusive—when ultimately only two would be available because the 15 year-olds would be in school.

224. It seems probable, too, that the raising of the minimum leaving-age to 16 would lead to a considerable increase in voluntary staying on until 17 or 18. It would be our hope that, if the introduction of compulsory part-time education took place five or six years after the raising of the school-leaving age, it would only be necessary to provide for about one-and-a-half age-groups instead of the two-and-a-half for whom room would have to be found if it were introduced while the minimum school-leaving age was still 15. While it is true that in recent buildings for further education some provision has been made for the wide range of activities which county colleges presuppose, it is clear that we are a good deal nearer to having the buildings ready for raising the school-leaving age than for county colleges. Not only is the type of accommodation required known with a precision which we believe to be lacking on the county college front, but all secondary schools built since the war either have themselves already the right balance of facilities to provide a full five-year course, or have been planned as instalments of a programme designed for that purpose and awaiting completion.

225. To introduce county colleges while the leaving age is still 15 would, then, be to do something which would later have to be undone, and to gain experience which would subsequently be irrelevant. It might be misleading as well as irrelevant. It would be necessary to recruit a high proportion of staff suitable for dealing with 15 year-olds. They would not automatically be well fitted to deal with 17 year-olds. The outlook of the staff and the character of the institution would be adjusted to a younger age than it would ultimately have

to serve; and, among teen-agers, a relatively small difference in age makes a very great difference in behaviour and interests. Moreover, we may hope that a 16 year-old who has had five full years in a secondary school will be educationally more than twelve months in advance of the 15 year-olds of today. To start compulsory part-time education at 15 as an interim measure would have the unfortunate effect of launching county colleges with their sights fixed on too low as well as on too young a target.

226. In Part Six of our report we examine the present working of the part-time system in vocational education especially in its higher branches. The conclusion is irresistible—that those who enter upon it after only four years of full-time education do so under a severe handicap. To make the fifth year universal is the most obvious single step to improve the chances of the abler boys who get part-time release from their employers to take National Certificates and City and Guilds courses. Of course, the proportion of them who already voluntarily stay at school to 16 is rising, but in Chapter 12 we saw reason to believe that many who most need the extra year will only get it through compulsion. The introduction of compulsory part-time release would do relatively little for this group.

227. If this is true of the apprentices and the other abler boys and girls—who, after all, should be learning all the time, whether in class or at the bench—it is even more true of the less able young workers. The boy or girl engaged in simple repetitive work is in a different position from the apprentice. His work does not sharpen his mind; it may even dull it. Normally he is less intelligent than the apprentice; and his general education is often in a sadly unfinished state when he leaves school. There is a great deal that he can and ought to learn between 15 and 16. He is much more likely to learn it at school than during one day a week at a county college where what he does must, from the nature of his employment, be completely divorced from his duties during the other four days of the week.

228. The reason for his need of a longer school life needs a little more explanation. In almost every way he will be a slower and less competent performer than his more intelligent neighbour—not only in book work, but in hand work. The case for the crafts as the backbone of his education does not rest on the false idea that he is especially good at them, or better at them than a brighter boy is. It rests on the fact that it is through making things, and through doing things, that his interest is best aroused and his capacity to reason trained. Progress is not quick, and it takes just as long (or longer) to acquire skill in a craft which is being taught as an instrument of general education as in one which is being taught for vocational reasons. We saw reason in Chapter 11 to believe that at

present his school life ends when the law of increasing returns is still in full operation. We do not believe that within the compass of one day a week that momentum can be retained. Moreover, what we hope to see happening between 15 and 16 in the practical subjects is the culmination of a continuous process of learning begun some four years before. The individual processes painfully mastered one by one can now be brought together into "man-sized", or "woman-sized", projects that take time and give the satisfaction of an almost adult mastery. This is something worth waiting at school for.

229. The case for full-time education for the less able does not rest alone on the needs and possibilities of the practical subjects, though it is they that make it palatable. No teacher has ever had any doubt about the importance of daily practice in the basic skills of reading, writing and speaking English and in arithmetical manipulation and reasoning if the facility slowly being gained is not to be lost. We think that part-time education has a much better chance of accomplishing something really worth while for the less able if it can be superimposed on a full-time education to 16 than on one ending at 15.

CHART NO. 6

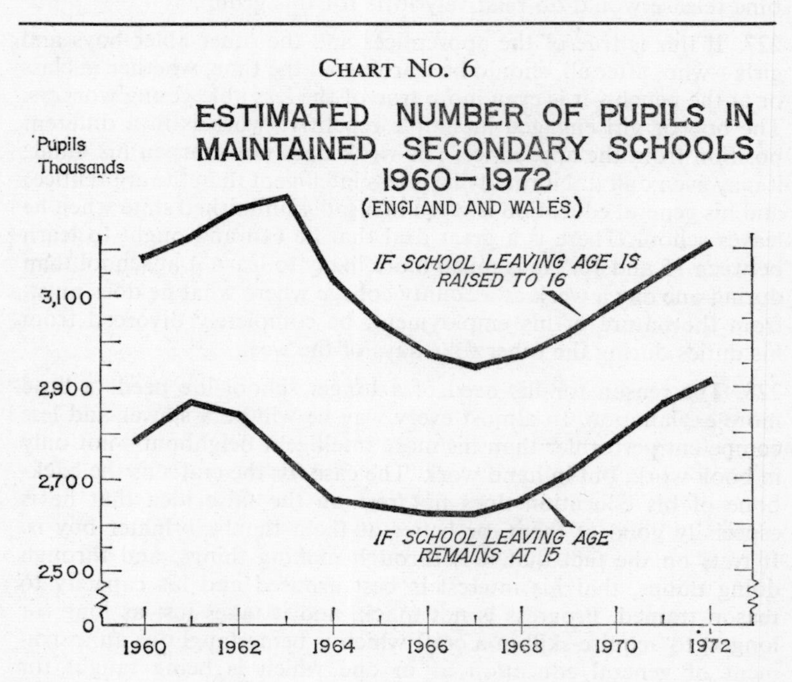

CHAPTER 15

When the School-Leaving Age should be Raised

230. In Chapters 11 and 12 we made clear our opinion that the school-leaving age should be raised. By this we mean that the Government should now announce its intention to make the necessary Order in Council at a certain specified date. It is the purpose of this chapter to consider what advice we should give the Minister about the most suitable date to choose.

231. There are any number of matters that properly come into consideration in fixing a date—the quality of teaching in the present schools, the prospective attitude of pupils and their parents, the extent of agreement about what would be done with them in an additional year, the availability of buildings and, not least, the financial cost. But the biggest element in deciding the timing must inevitably be the supply of secondary school teachers and the demand for secondary school places. The former, as recent events have shown, is difficult to forecast at all accurately even a few years ahead. The latter can be known with a considerable degree of precision. We know five years in advance how many primary school children there will be; we have eleven years' notice of any change in the numbers entering secondary schools. Allowance has, of course, to be made for those who voluntarily stay longer than they must; while, if we attempt forecasts more than fifteen years ahead, we are entirely dependent on intelligent guessing about the size of the age-groups the secondary schools will have to accommodate. But even then, with these reservations, pretty precise forward planning is possible. Chart 6 opposite sets out in broad terms the numbers expected at various dates to be attending maintained secondary schools of all descriptions (including the senior classes of all-age schools) on two alternative assumptions: first, that the minimum leaving-age remains at 15 and that the recent trend towards longer school life on a voluntary basis continues; or, secondly, that the school-leaving age is raised to 16, and that the trend to a longer voluntary school life among pupils over the age of 16 continues as at present.

THE VALLEY OF THE LATER SIXTIES

232. If we consider the total load that the secondary schools will have to bear in the near future, it is clear that the easiest period in sight is the years from 1965 to 1969, which lie in the valley between two

peaks. Other things being equal, it seems clear that the right moment to raise the school-leaving age would be somewhere inside this relatively easy period.

233. There is another point to be considered—the actual number of boys and girls who will reach the age of 15 in any given year. This year (1959) there are 633,000. Their numbers will rise steadily to a peak of 829,000 in 1963 after which they will fall continuously, and at first sharply, for four or five years. The point here is one of psychology rather than of logistics. Those who become 15 in the year selected for raising the minimum leaving age will have to stay at school for another whole year. Should the first age-group to have this experience be large or small? From the year above them at least half will have left by the end of the fourth year in the secondary school; from the non-selective schools, which are the ones mainly concerned, the proportion will in all probability be at least five-eighths. We are convinced that the first age-group to be affected by a higher leaving age will get something well worth having, and that before long a leaving-age of 16 will seem as natural as 15 does now. But can we be sure that the first age-group to receive what it would not have chosen will come to share our opinion before leaving? In so far as there is any doubt about this, it would point to making the change in a year when there are relatively few boys and girls aged 15. Moreover it will be easier for the schools to make a success of new fifth-year courses if the numbers involved are not at first too great. Chart 7 shows, on an exaggerated scale, the numbers of additional pupils who would be in the schools in the different years if the leaving age were raised. It is clear that to make the change before 1966 would impose a very heavy burden. For some years after that, however, the variations in numbers are small.

HOW MANY TEACHERS?

234. The next task is to calculate how many additional teachers would be needed if the school-leaving age were raised in the period 1965 to 1970. But this is a problem that cannot be isolated from the general question of teacher supply; even if there were no question of raising the school-leaving age, the numbers of teachers required in the next decade or so would vary considerably. The numbers of pupils in the schools up to the age of 15 will change from year to year. Moreover, the years after the "bulge" have been looked forward to as the time when real progress will be possible with the reduction in the average size of classes; urgent though the raising of the school-leaving age is, we would not want it unduly to obstruct this very long delayed reform. Finally, though teachers are not interchangeable, and a

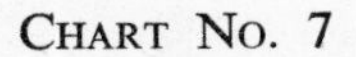

CHART No. 7

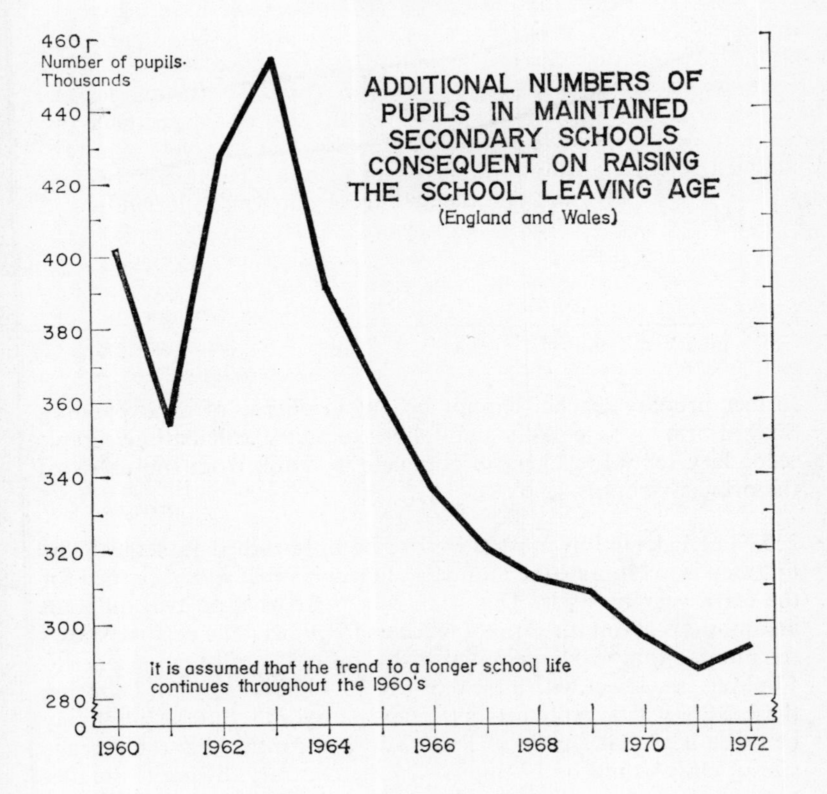
ADDITIONAL NUMBERS OF PUPILS IN MAINTAINED SECONDARY SCHOOLS CONSEQUENT ON RAISING THE SCHOOL LEAVING AGE
(England and Wales)
Number of pupils· Thousands
460
440
420
400
380
360
340
320
300
280
0
1960
1962
1964
1966
1968
1970
1972
It is assumed that the trend to a longer school life continues throughout the 1960's

CHART No. 8

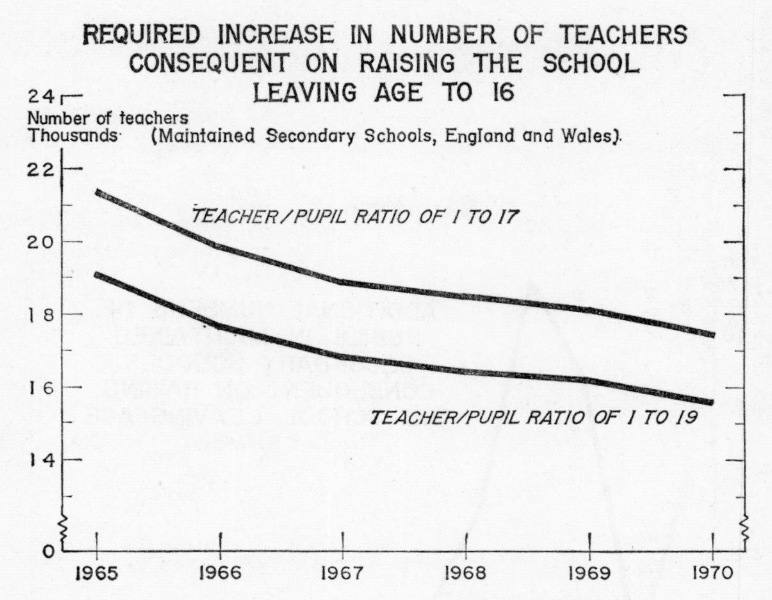

former primary teacher cannot be put in charge of an expanding Sixth Form, it is equally impossible to make calculations about secondary school teachers in complete isolation from the needs of the primary schools.

235. The calculation must therefore be approached in stages. The first step is to estimate the numbers of teachers that will be needed for the extra year by itself. This is shown in Chart 8 on two different assumptions about the ratio of teachers to pupils—the top line shows the number that will be required with a ratio of 1 full-time teacher to 17 pupils, the lower with a ratio of 1 to 19. (The reasons for choosing these ratios will be explained in the next paragraph. But the point may be made here that a ratio of 1 to 17 does not mean that the average size of class would be 17 pupils. On the contrary, owing to smaller teaching groups for certain subjects, and in the higher stages of the course, the average size of classes would be much larger.) It will be seen that the number of additional teachers required lies somewhere between 15,600 and 21,300. These are not overwhelmingly large figures; they represent no more than 5 to 7 per cent of the present total number of teachers. Moreover, this would be in the nature of a once-for-all provision. Once it was made, the addition to the annual maintenance requirement would be no more than a thousand or so.

236. The second step in the calculation is to add on to these figures the numbers of additional teachers that will be needed in the secondary schools, even if there is to be no raising of the school-leaving age, in order to reduce the number of over-large classes. Table 18 gives the total numbers of additional teachers (i.e. including those that would be required for the additional year) on the two alternative assumptions about the teacher-pupil ratio, and the figures are also shown in Chart 9 on the next page.

Table 18. Additional Teachers required for Maintained Secondary Schools, assuming a School-Leaving age of 16 (England and Wales). (Additional over estimate of 124,600 for 1959).

	Teacher-Pupil Ratio of	
	1 to 19	1 to 17
1965	33,400	52,000
1966	31,300	49,600
1967	30,300	48,600
1968	31,500	49,900
1969	34,300	53,000
1970	37,500	56,600

The 1958 ratio in the secondary schools was one full-time teacher to 21·2 pupils. The target of official policy is to reduce the *maximum* permitted size of classes in secondary schools to 30, and it has been calculated that to prevent any class from exceeding this size would require an over-all ratio of about 1 to 16. The two alternative ratios we have employed in our calculations thus lie between the present state of affairs, which is admittedly most imperfect, and the officially acknowledged target, which can hardly be said to be extravagant. We have chosen the ratios of 1 to 17 and 1 to 19 to represent what we think to be the upper and lower limits of practicable action in the next decade or so. A ratio of 1 to 17 is an ambitious one, but still short of the target. A ratio of 1 to 19 would still leave far too many large classes, though it would mark a substantial improvement on the present state of affairs. We do not think that many people, even those who are most impatient for the leaving age to be put up, would wish thereby to push the staff-pupil ratio, after a few years of improvement, back to a worse figure than 1 to 19. Nor, we think, would those who are most anxious to see a real improvement in staffing before the extra burden of another full year is placed on the schools, hold out for a better ratio than 1 to 17.

CHART NO. 9

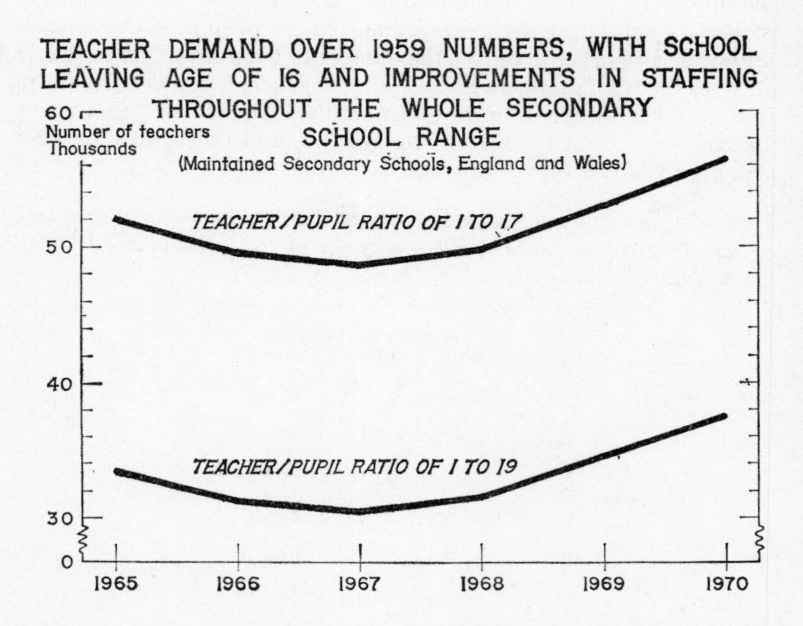

237. There remains to be added the third element in the calculation, the needs of the primary schools. For about three years from now the number of pupils in primary schools will be decreasing from roughly 4,400,000 to about 4,000,000. Thereafter it will rise again, though the highest figure within sight—which will not be reached until 1968—is not much over 4,250,000. It is the declared intention to use the easier years immediately ahead to reduce the size of classes in the primary schools. If this is done, and the average size of primary classes is reduced to 30 (which, it is calculated, would be necessary to ensure that there were no classes of more than 40), and held at that figure, then, clearly, increased numbers of teachers will be needed for these schools, as well as for the needs of the secondary schools which we have hitherto been considering.

238. We can now put the total picture together. This is done in Chart 10, and in Table 19. There are two main conclusions to be drawn from these figures. The first is that the problem of teacher supply in the next decade is a formidable one, if all the objectives (none of which is unreasonably large) are to be attained. The second is that, of the total requirement, the need arising directly out of the proposal to raise the school-leaving age forms a relatively small part.

CHART No. 10

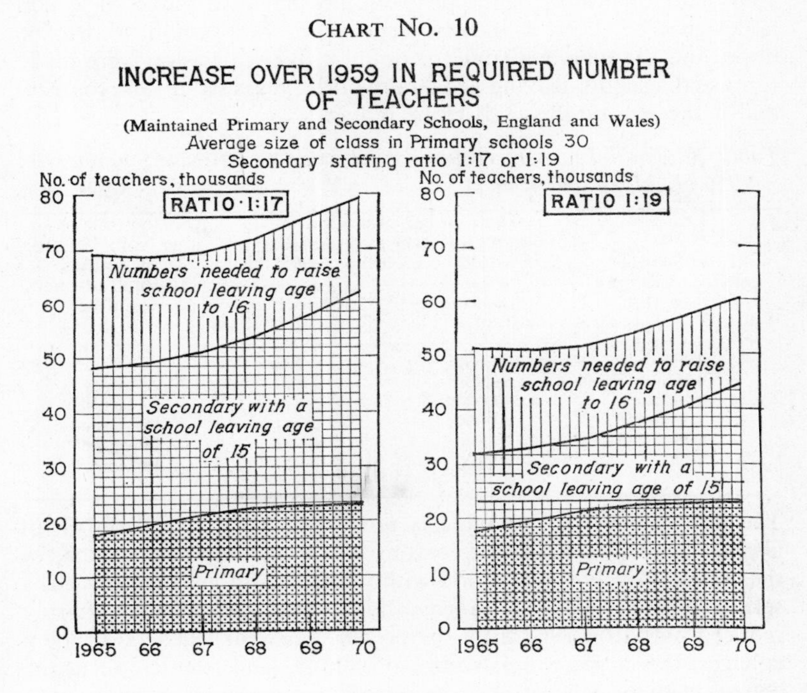

Table 19. Additional Teachers required to reduce the size of classes and to raise the school-leaving age (Maintained Secondary and Primary Schools, England and Wales).

	Primary Average class size of 30 (additional over estimate of 139,000 in 1959)	*Secondary* Ratio of full-time teachers to senior pupils of 1 : 17 (additional over estimate of 124,600 in 1959)		*Secondary* Ratio of full-time teachers to senior pupils of 1 : 19 (additional over estimate of 124,600 in 1959)		Aggregate additional demand	
	A	To raise school-leaving age B	To reduce size of classes C	To raise school-leaving age D	To reduce size of classes E	A+B +C F	A+D +E G
1965	17,600	21,300	30,700	19,100	14,300	69,600	51,000
1966	19,300	19,800	29,800	17,700	13,600	68,900	50,600
1967	21,000	18,800	29,800	16,800	13,500	69,600	51,300
1968	22,100	18,400	31,500	16,400	15,100	72,000	53,600
1969	22,500	18,100	34,900	16,200	18,100	75,500	56,800
1970	22,600	17,400	39,200	15,600	21,900	79,200	60,100

239. The dimensions of the problem are shown in Table 20, which is designed to show, as clearly as possible, what would need to be done, and the time available for doing it, if the decision were made to raise the school-leaving age in any of the years from 1965 to 1970, and if the size of classes is to be reduced.

Table 20. Total Teachers required additional to estimated numbers in 1959 (England and Wales).

If the School-Leaving Age were raised to 16 in:	The number of additional teachers, primary and secondary, that would be required, would be:		And the time available from 1959 to provide these additional teachers would be:
	With Secondary Ratio of 1: 17	With Secondary Ratio of 1: 19	
1965	69,600	51,000	7 years*
1966	68,900	50,600	8 years
1967	69,600	51,300	9 years
1968	72,000	53,600	10 years
1969	75,500	56,800	11 years
1970	79,200	60,100	12 years

The last column of this table is not expressed in the form of an average annual increase for reasons which are important. First, in the comparatively short period with which this table is concerned, a serious difficulty would arise from the fact that there will be a sharply reduced output in 1962 from the present two year teachers' training colleges, the largest single source of supply, since the length of the course in these colleges is to be raised to three years, starting with those enrolling in 1960. Secondly, it is misleading to think of the growth in the number of teachers taking place at a uniform rate. The present expansion in the number of training college places, designed partly to offset reduced output from the longer course, can hardly begin to relieve the situation in the schools before 1963. At the best, the further expansion of training college places which we believe to be necessary can only follow hard on its heels. On the face of it, then, we have to expect a lean season followed by a bountiful one—there is no way of eliminating the trying period which separates sowing from harvest.

THE SUPPLY OF TEACHERS

240. But, although we feel that it would be misleading to express our future task in terms of an average annual increase, it is certainly worth while to look back in this light at the experience of recent years. The years up to 1956 gave grounds for the belief that a steady net increase in the teaching force of some 6,000 to 7,000 teachers a year

* The full demand for additional teachers would not be felt until the second year of the higher school-leaving age.

could be counted on. The experience of the last two years has disappointed this expectation; the net increase was 4,400 in 1957 and 5,200 in 1958. The low net gain in these years has not been due to a fall in the numbers of teachers entering the profession, but to an increase in the numbers leaving it, especially in the number of young married women teachers. In considering the probable supply of teachers in the years to come to meet existing and additional commitments, it is therefore difficult at the moment to know what the datum line is from which any calculation must start.

241. The numbers of teachers required, if the 1960's are to be a period of real educational progress and not once again of frustrated hopes, are formidable. It will now, we think, be apparent why our Chairman wrote to the Minister of Education on our behalf in February 1958 to ask that, in planning the future supply of teachers, the needs of future educational advances should be taken into account and not simply the maintenance of the present state of affairs in the schools. It is now our recommendation that the National Advisory Council on the Training and Supply of Teachers should be asked as a matter of urgency to consider the supply problem that would be caused by raising the school-leaving age and to make the necessary recommendations for dealing with it.

242. The next few years are in our view an especially propitious time for recruiting teachers. In a later part of this report we draw attention to the continued rapid growth in the size of Sixth Forms, and the less rapid increase in the provision of university places. Here, then, is a potential source of supply for teachers if the facilities for training them are available. This applies equally, of course, to both men and women, but the ending of National Service should present a special opportunity for an enlarged recruitment of men teachers. It is clear that the additional provision of training college places is largely required to meet a temporary situation. Once the expanding teaching force has been recruited, it will not be necessary to keep so large a training machine to maintain it. This is not the difficulty that it may at first sight seem. If the expansion of the Sixth Form continues, as we think it should, it is clear that there will need to be a greater superstructure for higher education than at present exists or is planned. It is our belief that an expansion now of the training college provision, if properly sited and planned, can be diverted to this more general end when the immediate need for more teachers is past. If we do not provide sufficient places in further or higher education over the age of 18 to meet the demand, we run a real risk that the numbers staying on at school to 17 or 18 may drop instead of rise, which would, in our view, be a disaster.

243. It is, then, our considered view that the next five or six years offer an excellent opportunity to expand the supply of teachers in preparation for the equally excellent opportunity a few years later to raise the school-leaving age at a period of relatively reduced pressure on the secondary schools. This may seem to be an unexpectedly optimistic conclusion in view of the widespread anxiety of the last twelve months or so about the possibility of securing sufficient teachers barely to maintain present standards in the schools. We share this anxiety and have something to say in Chapter 37 about what can be done to remove it. Without anticipating the argument of that chapter, it is enough for our immediate purpose to say that the present situation is not in our opinion due to any falling off in the numbers of potential teachers, but to failures of anticipation in the sphere of public policy, which may have been natural in the puzzling circumstances of the last few years, but which in any case are remediable by firm and prompt government action.

244. The problem of educational advance is often represented as a difficult choice between smaller classes on the one hand and some single step forward on the other, such as raising the school-leaving age or introducing county colleges. This seems to us to be a wrong antithesis. A reduction in the size of classes is, or ought to be, a continuing process until the optimum size is reached. Whenever a major reform is introduced, there is bound to be a temporary worsening of the pupil-teacher ratio, but this deterioration should only be of short duration, provided that the supply position is carefully watched. The position changes so rapidly that anything we wrote now would almost certainly be out of date long before the leaving age was raised. For that reason we have not included in our report any tables dealing with the expected net increase of teachers, though we have carefully considered such information as could be made available to us. The sort of brief which we think should be given to those whose duty it is to secure the right supply of teachers is that the school-leaving age will be raised to 16 in a given year and that care must be taken to see that the ratio of teachers to pupils does not become worse than 1 to 19 in the year in which it is done. This implies, of course, that the ratio must be better than 1 to 19 on the eve of the reform. It is clear that some price of this kind must be paid for any major reform.

THE CHOICE OF YEAR

245. We come, then, to the choice of the time when we think the change should be made. Having considered all the elements of the problem very carefully, we are unanimous in the recommendation that the Order in Council should be issued so as to take effect from

the beginning of one of the school years 1966–67, 1967–68, and 1968–69. We are not unmindful of the fact that a tremendous effort will be necessary. Apart from all other preparations, something like 70,000 additional primary and secondary teachers will be needed in eight years from the autumn of 1959 if the change is to be made in the earliest of the three named years and with the benefit of the desirable staffing ratios in primary and secondary schools. The lowest possible estimate of additional numbers is 54,000 within ten years if the change is delayed until the last of the three named years, and carried out with the disadvantage of only barely acceptable staffing ratios. In view of what was being achieved very recently without any special measures being taken, we do not think that the higher target is an impossible one, and the lower one should be well within reach.

246. We do not make our recommendation in the form of a range of three years in order to leave a margin for flexibility. On the contrary, we attach importance to a single year being chosen and announced soon. Our reason is that, though we are unanimous in recommending that the choice of year should fall on one of the three years 1966–67 to 1968–69, there are some of us who hope that the choice will fall on the earliest of these years, while others of us would prefer that it should be the last. This difference of opinion among us does not depend on the statistical calculations—none of us would pretend that it is possible to predict these matters so closely as to make a great deal of difference between two dates well in the future but only twenty-four months apart. Nor does our difference spring from any division of opinion about the value and the requirements of the additional year itself. We are all convinced that the raising of the school-leaving age not only requires more teachers, but suitably qualified teachers, men and women with the right kind of experience and with an outlook in sympathy with 15 year-olds. We all recognise that it requires also suitable accommodation, which is at present often lacking. We all believe that it is a high educational priority to give all 15 year-olds another year's education within the next decade. We are agreed, too, that it is most important to seize the opportunities of the late 1960's for the largest possible instalment of educational reform. Where we differ is over the extent to which the value of the additional year depends on a previous general improvement in the conditions prevailing in the existing school years, which all of us agree to be in many respects unsatisfactory. The difference between us over the choice of year represents therefore essentially a difference of opinion over the order in which various improvements and reforms should be made within the same favourable quinquennium of the later 1960's.

247. Those of us who would fix the date earlier rather than later argue in the following way. The paramount consideration must be that no 15 year-old who can be given the opportunity should be allowed to miss the chance. Given the will, the extensive problems of building, of organisation and of teacher supply can be met by 1966. Much depends upon the will to do the job and the sense of urgency with which it is approached. To fix any date other than the earliest possible is to let down the boys and girls who would otherwise have had the extra year. Moreover, it is only possible to make a maximum effort for a limited period, and a maximum effort is certainly needed. If a date later than the earliest possible is fixed, the period of maximum effort will not be correspondingly lengthened, but the years of grace will be frittered away. While it is true that some temporary worsening of the pupil-teacher ratio is unavoidable when the minimum leaving age is raised, the degree of worsening will be much the same whichever of the possible years is chosen. We do not avoid trouble by making the change later rather than earlier. We merely postpone it, and with it the benefits which the change will bring. There is another reason for choosing the earliest possible date. By 1966 the "bulge" will be rapidly passing from the secondary schools, and the graph of the school population aged 15 will be entering a level phase. This phase, however, will only last until 1969 when a "new bulge" will be reaching the top of the secondary schools. Raising the school-leaving age early in this level period would give the schools the substantial advantage of a chance to settle down before the "new bulge" is upon them.

248. Some of us, however, think that it is important to leave the change as late as it can wisely be left within the relatively easy period after the "bulge". In that period, for the first time for many years, the resources available to the educational system ought to be increasing more rapidly than the demands made upon them, and it is essential that the surplus should be applied first where it will bring the greatest dividend of educational benefit. This is not to be measured merely quantitatively by the total number of pupil-hours spent in the schools but by the quality of the education provided, and from this point of view those of us who hold the delaying opinion believe that more initial benefit will be derived if the first instalment of the growing resources is applied among the age-groups below the age of 15. There are two reasons for this—first because of the great benefits in the quality of education that some relief (especially in the form of smaller classes, and particularly in the areas that are now most hard pressed) would bring in the lower age-groups themselves; and secondly because, without this improvement lower down, the additional year itself may for many young persons be largely wasted. If the extra year

is to be a success, the pre-requisite is that the overwhelming majority of boys and girls should reach the age of 15 both able and willing to profit from it. This is not true of all children today. The way to make it true is to press on as rapidly as possible with the task of bringing all the nation's schools up to the standard of the best that exist today. Those of our members who hold this point of view would prefer to postpone the raising of the leaving-age to the last of the three years, partly as a means of concentrating the first efforts where they will do most good, and partly to leave as much as possible of the 'valley' period for those improvements in quality to take effect. Urgent though the raising of the school-leaving age is, they do not believe that it is any more urgent than this.

249. There are thus, as it seems to us, strong reasons both for the earlier and the later date. But they do not lie far apart in time, nor is either of them very distant. Whichever is chosen, there is much to be done, and little enough time to do it. If the opportunities of the 1960's are not to be wasted, we would urge that a decision be taken now and that a consistent programme of action in all relevant fields be set on foot and pursued with the vigour necessary to ensure that, by the chosen date, the conditions are prepared for the extra year in school to provide its full benefit for all the nation's children.

Part Four

The Way to County Colleges

CHAPTER 16

A Majority Without Education

250. It is clear that the Education Act of 1944 did not envisage anybody's education as stopping at 15 or even at 16. It provided for the establishment of county colleges to give "young persons who are not in full-time attendance . . . such further education, including physical, practical and vocational training, as will enable them to develop their various aptitudes and capacities and will prepare them for the responsibilities of citizenship". Under the County Colleges Order, 1947, it became the duty of every local education authority to establish and maintain county colleges—some day. No date was specified. Meanwhile attention has in fact been paid in the building of new colleges of further education to seeing that there is accommodation for more than purely technical training so that they may take their place in the general pattern of county colleges for all young workers when the time comes. While attendance at county colleges is eventually to be compulsory, the Act also requires local education authorities to provide "adequate facilities for . . . leisure-time occupation, in such organised cultural training and recreative activities as are suited to their requirements, for any persons over compulsory school age who are able and willing to profit" from them. Such is the Act; what is the practice? It will be best to deal separately with these two main provisions of the Act so far as they relate to boys and girls under 19.

THE NON-PROVISION OF COUNTY COLLEGES

251. There is some confusion in usage about the term "county college". There is no doubt that the Act of 1944 provides for attendance at county colleges by all who are not receiving full-time education, but it does not prescribe in any further detail than we have just quoted what the curriculum of a county college is to be. No doubt it was intended—and rightly so—that this should be determined by the individual needs and capacities of the students. There might thus be a widely different curriculum for apprentices and for routine process workers, though both would be attending county colleges. In much common speech, however, the term "county college" has been used as if it excluded most of what now goes on in technical colleges—that is, as if it applied only to institutions designed to cater for the great number of young workers who neither need, nor could benefit from, a strictly technical education. It is this group with

which we are concerned in the present Part and in what follows the term "county college" is to be understood in this more restricted sense. The other group, which is largely confined at present to boys, and to boys in relatively few industries, is dealt with in Part Six. There we consider, among other things, how far what is now provided for them meets the broad educational objectives of the Act of 1944. Here we are concerned with those who, if this section of the Act were in force, would be getting one day a week's education, but who are not in fact now doing so. How many of them are there?

Table 21. Boys and Girls of County College Age (under 18) who are receiving neither Full-time nor Part-time Day Education, 1958 (England and Wales).

	Age			
	15	16	17	15–17
Boys—percentage	*44*	*53·4*	*62·4*	*52·9*
number (000)	136	145	173	454
Girls—percentage	*55·1*	*70·9*	*83·2*	*69·3*
number (000)	162	186	224	572
Boys and Girls—percentage	*49·4*	*61·9*	*72·6*	*60·6*
number (000)	298	331	397	1,026

The two future county college age-groups, once the school-leaving age has been raised, will be the 16 year-olds and the 17 year-olds. At these ages well over half the boys and nearly four-fifths of the girls at present get neither full-time education nor day release—a good enough indication of the length of the road still to be travelled before we can say that the 1944 Act has been brought into force. The proportions in Table 21 are, of course, proportions of the whole age-groups. If they had been calculated on that section which had been educated in modern schools the figures would have been much higher. Not only are the boys and girls in their later teens who are getting full-time education drawn overwhelmingly from the selective schools, but those who get part-time day release also come to a considerable extent from these schools.

252. There is a small but important group of students following non-vocational courses with whom we shall be much concerned in this and the following two chapters. These are the young people who are allowed by their employers to take courses of a general, mainly non-vocational, nature of the kind which will have to be provided in large number when county colleges are introduced. The experience

gained in this sort of education, both in quantity and quality, is of great importance in considering when part-time education to 18 can be made compulsory. It is exceedingly difficult to get any precise figures, because "general courses" include a great variety of types of instruction not all of which would be found in a county college. The figures in Table 22 must therefore be taken as an overstatement. Even so, it will be observed that we have here, for the first time in our report, to deal with an important section of education in which virtually no progress in the numbers attending has been made in recent years.

Table 22. Part-time Release for General Courses (Junior Level) (England and Wales).

Year	Number Released for General Courses (thousands)		Size of 15–17 Age-Group (3 Years) (thousands)		Cols. 2 and 3 as percentages of Cols. 4 and 5	
	Boys	Girls	Boys	Girls	Boys	Girls
1	2	3	4	5	6	7
1949–50	10·9	12·1	835	816	*1·3*	*1·5*
1954–55	10·2	12·0	866	842	*1·2*	*1·4*
1955–56	10·4	12·7	855	832	*1·2*	*1·5*
1956–57	10·4	11·8	839	815	*1·2*	*1·4*
1957–58	10·2	10·6	858	827	*1·2*	*1·3*

NOTE: There is no precise link between student's age and Junior courses, but there is a rough approximation to the 15–17 age-groups.

In 1957–58 the total number of all students getting day release was almost twice as great as in 1948–49, but the number following these junior general courses has not increased at all and indeed shows some decline. That the numbers attending these junior courses of a general type give a reasonable estimate of the size of non-vocational day release is borne out by the fact that among the National Service recruits to the Army covered by our enquiry the proportion who had had any part-time day release for non-vocational purposes was less about 2 per cent.

253. The same impression is gained from a glance at some of the leading institutions in this field. Eight London Day Colleges have a history going back to the Education Act, 1918. They are still only 8 in number. Rugby—which is classic ground, as the only surviving place where part-time education, under the Act of 1918, is compulsory at 15—does not in fact persuade employers to give release to

many boys and girls over that age unless there is a strong vocational purpose in mind. In York and Birmingham those employers who were already converted to the benefits of part-time education for all their young workers have remained faithful, but few new converts have been made. In York, indeed, part-time education of the kind we are concerned with in this chapter is over fifty years old, but so far only 10 per cent of an age-group benefit from it—yet this figure is probably the highest in the country, except (for the 15 year-olds) in Rugby. Two other cities, which got well ahead with their preparations for county colleges in the early days after the last war, have found it very difficult to stimulate employers to give their young workers a day off for general education. In one, the county college is clearly working to the genuine satisfaction of those large employers who use it, and also, it may be said, to that of the students who go there; but it is still working at very much less than its full capacity because other employers have not been attracted to it. In the other town the volume of purely non-vocational day release has remained constant at a low figure. The college provided for this use has grown, but it has grown by providing for the early stages in the technical education of those who will become skilled workers. The unskilled workers who provided its original students, and for whom it still does a sterling job, have been relegated, so to speak, to an annexe. The term is not used invidiously, but it is difficult to describe otherwise a separate building catering for only 9 per cent of the day release students.

254. Much of what has been accomplished is admirable. We cannot, however, base a general judgement on these experiments because of the absence of compulsion except at Rugby, where it is applied only to an age-group which we recommend should be in school and not in a county college. Many of these experiments have had advantages which it would not be easy to generalise. The colleges concerned have attracted many teachers with the devotion of pioneers. Moreover, those employers who are enlightened enough to see the value of this work are likely to be enlightened in other ways. We have, therefore, a partnership of above-average employers and teachers; good results might be expected. The failure of the scheme to grow means that we are almost as far as ever from discovering how valuable a county college education would be to the average unskilled worker, taught by the average county college teacher in an average county college, and employed by an average employer. We shall come back in Chapter 18 to consider what steps might be taken to get beyond this stage by a pilot experiment, but in this largely stock-taking chapter we can only record that in any substantial sense the part-time day education of the unskilled worker has not begun.

255. When we speak of the majority without education we naturally think mainly of those whose work calls for no particular degree of skill and whose ability is below average. They do indeed constitute the bulk of the problem, and educationally the most difficult part of it. But they are not the only part. The contrast in Table 21 between the figures for boys and girls is striking. Not much more than a handful of girls get part-time day release at any age, whether vocational or general; they do not compensate for it by a longer school life than boys. Neither the able nor the less able girls get part-time release, with certain limited and clearly defined exceptions—some occupational, such as student nursery nurses or civil servants; and some, the consequence of working for especially enlightened employers. The extent of part-time day release for girls bears no relation whatever to its value or to their ability. It is arrested in development—the numbers have less than doubled since the war, compared with the ten-fold increase for boys—because incentives have not been strong enough to attract the general run of employers; or, perhaps, rather because the relatively short working life of girls before marriage has proved too powerful a disincentive. Whatever the reason, there has been no sign up to the present of any great extension of part-time day education for girls in any sector of employment outside that of the public authorities.

EVENING CLASSES AND OTHER FORMS OF SUPPLEMENTARY PROVISION

256. Up to this point we have been concerned solely with part-time day release to institutions provided or aided by education authorities. Is it fair to leave the story at this point and conclude, as we must on this evidence, that the majority leave school long before 18 and leave formal education when they leave school? Four other forms of educational provision must be briefly considered—works schools, evening classes, private commercial colleges and correspondence courses.

257. It is the practice of some large employers to provide works training schools of their own. In some instances a broad and thorough educational job is done and the provision may fairly be regarded as the equivalent of what is normally provided through a local education authority. In other, and more frequent, instances, the provision is either limited to a brief induction period or concentrated on the acquisition of particular skills. Here it is more properly to be regarded as a useful supplement, rather than as an alternative, to public educational provision. We have tried, but without success, to form a reliable estimate of the extent to which either kind of private provision is made, but we feel justified in saying that, at any rate as

far as a broad education is concerned, the picture drawn from the public provision would not be seriously modified.

258. There are great difficulties, too, in assessing how far evening classes, the second of these other forms of provision, ought to modify our general conclusion that the majority are left without education after 15. A very thorough survey made in the winter of 1957–58 in one of the biggest industrial cities showed that of all the evening students under 18 at the beginning of the session only just over half were still attending towards the end of the course. Those students who attended both day and evening classes were excluded from the calculation. Is this experience anything like normal? The Social Survey investigation is roughly in line with this result. It shows that, among young people who had no day release but who had started evening classes, 37 per cent of the boys and 40 per cent of the girls gave up in less than six months. What addition, then, can we legitimately make to the figures for full-time education and part-time release to allow for those whose only contact after leaving school is through evening classes? The Social Survey investigation shows that 14 per cent of the boys and 21 per cent of the girls who had been educated at non-selective schools, and who had nearly all left at 15, completed at least one session of evening work. None of these had part-time release.

259. The position is complicated, especially on the girls' side, by the third factor—the extent to which girls make use of private commercial schools for the purpose of learning shorthand and typewriting, of which no account is taken in the Ministry's statistics. It is clearly considerable both in the part-time and full-time field. We do not feel it necessary to comment on private commercial schools. The point we would make is a general one, and applies wherever the time available is very short and the student's purpose strictly confined. In these conditions it is difficult to believe that what is taught can be regarded as broad enough to satisfy the general objectives laid down for part-time education in the Act of 1944. We do not wish to say anything to disparage the tenacity of the students who succeed in rising by this hard route. Indeed, they deserve better. Our purpose is simply to make it clear that private commercial colleges and evening classes for teen-agers, as they exist at present, do not seem to us an acceptable substitute for what the Act promised, and we do not see how they can be made to be.

260. Correspondence courses, the fourth of the other forms of provision, cover a wide field and for certain professions such as bankers, accountants and chartered secretaries, they represent one of the chief methods of preparation for examinations. It is to be noted that the field from which the students in these occupations are drawn

is a selected one; but even so the route is in our view arduous and progress probably slower than it need be if other methods of teaching were adopted. Some of the subjects studied have a high general educational value as well as professional relevance, but the nature of the system prevents students getting from their study what they would if there were opportunity for the free and spontaneous interplay of mind on mind.

THE YOUTH SERVICE

261. It seems clear, then, that the majority of boys, and nearly all girls, who leave school as soon as they are legally entitled to do so, are without that help in growing up which is acknowledged to be necessary. They do not get day release, nor are they enrolled within the four other forms of part-time education that we have just considered. How far does the Youth Service provide for their needs? Or does it, on the contrary, mainly attract and serve only those who also enjoy the assistance of other educational agencies? The Social Survey and the National Service enquiries, although largely devoted to other ends, do give a good deal of valuable information on this rather obscure, but very important, matter. The National Service enquiry, of course, gives us no information about girls. The Social Survey enquiry classified as "clubs" whatever the boys and girls who were interviewed regarded as a club, and this has had the result of bringing into the net many organisations, such as football supporters' clubs, which can hardly rank as educational agencies. These are serious limitations, but nevertheless it is possible to draw certain conclusions relevant to our task from the evidence. This is given in detail in Parts One and Two of Vol. II of the report.

262. The main results can be summarised under eight heads:

(*a*) It seems clear that the very great majority of boys and girls during their schooldays belong to some youth organisation which has their welfare as its objective, and which may therefore be said to be educational in purpose. This generalisation is broadly true both of boys and girls, and of pupils in selective and non-selective schools, but it has to be noted that at least one-fifth of the girls who had been pupils in modern and all-age schools said that they had never belonged to any club.

(*b*) The picture changes radically when boys and girls leave school. For boys, the National Service enquiry showed that about one-fifth of the Army recruits had belonged to some youth organisation for three years continuously after leaving school. Even when membership for a shorter period is included, the proportion rises only to little more than one-third. The figures are given in Table 23.

Table 23. Active Membership etc. in first 3 years after leaving school among 6,478 National Service Recruits who left school at 15 or 16.

Active Membership of Youth Organisations	Period after leaving school		
	Three years	Less than 3 years	Total
	percentage	percentage	percentage
Boys, exclusively	*6*	*4*	10
Mixed, exclusively	10	5	*15*
Uniformed, exclusively	*3*	*3*	6
More than one type of Organisation	2	*1*	*3*
Total	*21*	*13*	*34*
Not in Active Membership			*66*

(*c*) The sons of semi-skilled and unskilled workers take less part in youth organisations than do other boys. Only 17 per cent of them, by comparison with 22 per cent had three years' continuous active membership.

(*d*) Girls certainly have less to do with youth organisations after they leave school than have boys. Because of the unsatisfactory definition of club (from our point of view) it is impossible to give figures which are comparable to those for boys given above, but on the Social Survey data the ratio of girls' club membership to boys' is 1 to 1·5.

(*e*) After school age the uniformed organisations (e.g. Scouts, Guides, cadets of various kinds) play a smaller part and general youth clubs a larger. In the later teens, and especially from 18 on, cultural and political organisations begin to attract members. Dance clubs which have no other activities account for 23 per cent of all the clubs to which girls who had been pupils in non-selective schools belonged at the time of the Social Survey.

(*f*) Boys and girls from non-selective schools are less likely to belong to clubs after they have left school than boys and girls from selective schools. For boys interviewed by the Social Survey the ratio was 1 to 1·5; for girls the corresponding figure was 1 to 1·7. Among the National Service men the ratio was 1 to 1·3.

(*g*) Boys and girls who take no part in Further Education courses are less likely to belong to clubs than those who do. For boys in the Social Survey the ratio was 1 to 1·3; for girls it was 1 to 1·8.

(*h*) Boys continue to play team games regularly after leaving school to a considerably greater extent than they continue to belong to youth organisations. Among National Service recruits to the Army and R.A.F. 31 per cent had continued to play games at least for three years after leaving school, and 6 per cent for a shorter period. Among students in technical colleges taking National Certificate courses (the more able among apprentices) the proportion was much the same, 39 per cent.

The picture presented by these enquiries is of a Youth Service which attracts many from the abler and steadier elements in the community, but fails on the whole to retain the bottom quarter or third of the population. This is corroborated by various local surveys which have been made in a number of difficult districts in the last decade. Thus an enquiry in one inner London borough showed that, while 55 per cent of the 16 year-old boys and 30 per cent of the 16 year-old girls belonged to some youth organisation, the percentage of members among those who had been in the lowest stream in ability in modern schools dropped to 41 per cent and 22 per cent respectively. When four socially adverse factors were taken into account, it was found that a combination of two or more factors was accompanied by a drop in the proportion of club members to 29 per cent among the boys and 20 per cent among the girls. In a neighbouring borough it was found that 35 per cent of all the boys included in the survey had either a substantially below-average school record or other markedly adverse circumstances. Only one in five of these boys belonged to clubs compared with one in two of the whole population surveyed. Some brilliant work has been done in London and elsewhere in running clubs for especially difficult boys, but the total volume of work is small—even smaller, it may be guessed, in relation to the size of the problem than that of the few existing prototypes of what a county college for unskilled workers might be.

263. We set out in this chapter to discuss how far a beginning had been made with the task of providing effectively for the educational needs of those who go to work at 15. We have seen that substantial progress has been made on the educational and training side for boys in skilled jobs. It is fair to infer from the record of boys from selective schools that this holds true also of acceptable provision for leisure activities. We shall have to consider in Part Six of our report how far these two interests, at present separately provided, combine to give these individual boys and girls a rounded education. It is already clear, however, that a fund of experience and a supply of skilled teachers have been accumulated which make it possible to regard with some confidence the country's ability to provide a valuable service to all skilled young workers as soon as compulsory part-time education can be introduced. It is unfortunately just as clear that, for boys in semi-skilled and unskilled occupations, and for almost all girls, the present provision is unsatisfactory and without visible

promise of improvement. Those who most need support in the critical years of late adolescence get least. This is true both of part-time day education and of the Youth Service. The need is apparent and acknowledged, and has indeed been pressed on us by most of our witnesses.

264. We do not propose to make specific proposals on the Youth Service, since the problem of priorities in that field has been remitted by the Minister to a special committee. We would only remark that in no other field of education can the expenditure of public money accomplish so much so readily. It is only right, however, that we should record our very real sense of the devoted service that the small band of full-time youth leaders and the many thousands of voluntary workers have given to help teen-agers spend their leisure enjoyably at the time and profitably for the future. This is work in which professional and amateur will always, we hope, be associated. Both are needed. We may also, perhaps, be allowed to express something of the sorrow and personal loss which the Council felt at the death in the middle of our enquiry of Dr. Macalister Brew, who had made this field peculiarly her own. She had been a member of the Council since 1952. Her originality, imagination, shrewdness and courage did much to create a new vision of what young people need, and had helped many of them to find it.

CHAPTER 17

The Purpose of a County College

265. Does it matter that most of those who leave school at 15 rapidly lose all contact with education? What are these boys and girls of 16 and 17 missing which it is important that they should have? For most of them, these years mark the last stages in the long journey from the complete dependence of childhood to the independence of early adult life. Towards its end, there is a rapid acceleration in the speed of the transition. Going to work has a strong, maturing effect on a boy. At home and with his friends, the money he earns gives him a new financial independence. The change in his personal status is even more important. As he walks through the factory gate, he closes the door on his childhood. He has changed the security and the legally enforced attendance of the schoolboy for the contractual freedom of the man; he can now give in his notice, or be sacked. He enters a world which he may have looked forward to, but which is at first inevitably strange and intimidating. Caution as well as ambition make him take on the protective colouring of his environment. Soon he will become what he resembles. It matters greatly, then, that the last stages of adolescence should be passed in good company, since never are boys and girls more impressionable than in these years, when there is so much change in what they do and what they are. Over most of their environment the educational authorities have no control. The world is not organised for their benefit—it is part of their education to learn this—but we can at least see that some small part of their environment has as its sole concern the task of seeing that the journey is safely accomplished. This personal service is the fundamental reason why county colleges are needed.

HELP IN A NEW WORLD

266. At 16 and 17 boys and girls have, or are approaching, four new types of experience. They earn money; they have more money to spend; they are "going steady" and before long they will marry; they pay taxes and will soon be voters. They will do all these things whether we have county colleges or not. How does a county college then come in? In the first place, these experiences are new in degree, if not altogether in kind; and their freshness makes teen-agers think—there is something for a county college to get hold of. Secondly, the welfare of our society demands that they should think straight on

these things. There is here a specific task for county colleges, over and above the general aim of keeping teen-agers in touch with adults who have no other interest but to help them to mature into profitable citizens. But, put like this, county colleges are hardly likely to appeal to teen-agers. Few people particularly like having good done to them, however popular doing good to others may be. The purpose of county colleges as we have sketched it so far would be doomed to failure for unwanted benevolence. Can it be put in a way that makes sense to teen-agers as well as to their elders? Young people have a good deal of leisure, far more than their predecessors had, but still not enough to do all the things that are worth doing or enjoyable to do. They have a considerable sum of money at their command, but not enough to satisfy all their desires. They have to learn how to choose.

267. They see that it is to their advantage to choose with understanding, to know what they are doing. There is, of course, a right and a wrong use of time—they may come to discover it, if they learn to plan their own time sensibly. They are willing, and indeed, anxious to get money's worth for their spending. Help in this respect is help without the taint of "being done good to". It can take two forms. There is the kind of help which is given by what has come to be called consumer research—help in comparing the relative merits of two articles of the same kind or serving the same purpose. This carries with it rich educational possibilities as well as severely practical value. It can be a useful assistance, for example, to boys and girls who have to spend their own money on their clothes. (According to the Social Survey, 40 per cent of the boys and 49 per cent of the girls buy all their own clothes, and another 20 per cent buy some of them, presumably the more interesting.) But is buying ready-made the best way to get value for money? Sometimes it obviously is; but not always. "Do it yourself" (itself an example of an advertising slogan and as such to be treated with caution) often makes both economic and spiritual sense. The boy who really acquires skill in cabinet making, the girl who develops her talent for dressmaking, obtain satisfaction which would have been beyond their reach unless they mixed their labour with purchased materials. By this sort of approach a boy or girl may be led on to think of economics as well as of economy; but this will not, of course, be everybody's way. Some may be more interested in finding out about their wages. Curiosity may be aroused by their pay packet—by what is actually in it, and what is nominally in it. Here may be found an introduction to the welfare state, to collective bargaining and to the contrast between things which we are free to buy or not as we like, and those which we have to pay for whether or not we personally

want them or use them. There is danger to society both in the apathetic customer and the apathetic wage-earner; a healthy society presupposes men and women who think instead of accepting. Knowledge and discrimination are necessary pre-requisites of a democratic community. They can be stimulated even, and often only, by very homely means.

MORAL STANDARDS

268. Knowledge, discrimination, value—or rather values. This last is the hardest to secure, and it cannot be left to chance. In morals, bad currency drives out good, and very rapidly. There is often a critical moment at the entry into employment, when a boy or girl emerges (if he has had a good home) for the first time from a sheltered environment, in which adults have accepted a restraint on their tongues and a curb on their behaviour which perhaps they do not use as they go about their business. At school and at home he has been a member of a society which is explicitly based on moral principles, however much it may diverge from them. As he enters the outside world, he finds that much that would have been condemned at school or in the family is tolerated and accepted as natural. He discovers that many of the values he has been told he ought to live by seem to be reckoned no more valuable in purchasing power than the currency which Samuel Butler's Erewhonians drew from their Musical Banks. His first reaction may well be disgust either with the apparent cynicism of the world or with what he may now regard as the unreality of school. What will his second reaction be? It is likely to be to fall into line. But there is a chance that it may take the socially desirable form of non-conformity. That chance seems to us to depend on his meeting at this juncture men and women who can convince him that they know the world as it is, have found it not altogether to their liking, but have not let it warp their judgment or deflect their actions. Thomas Hardy spoke for our generation too when he wrote, "If a way to the better there be, it exacts a full look at the worst". The idealism that is latent in all young people can be elicited by those who are scrupulously honest and patently knowledgeable in their teaching. It is important that there should be such people on the staff of county colleges, and that no regulations should fetter the directness of their testimony. Nothing could be more fatal to their influence with the young than the reserve which prudence dictates or legislators decree. From both Christian humanist and scientific humanist young people can learn that the difference in ethics between school and work can be more of a contrast of speech than of substance. The adult public opinion in a school is nearly always on the side of the angels, though the pupils may come to doubt the practice of particular individuals. The most audible opinion

at work is often completely cynical over many important matters, and it takes a deal of finding out that many men are better, not worse, than their words. Far too many young people never discover this, or discover it too late. They need the kind of discriminating approach to human behaviour that consumer research gives to the behaviour of material things.

269. The two moralities often clash first in the world of work. Before long the conflict is experienced by teen-agers in the field of sex. They are torn in two directions by the indiscriminate pull of the blood, which grows strong in these years, and by passionate attachment to a particular person. They need a code both of morals and of behaviour, indeed of etiquette. The one can help the other; and the latter can sometimes with profit be brought down to the homely details of make-up and table manners. "How can I behave so that boys want to be with me, but will respect me? What sort of behaviour will bring me the sort of boy I want for a husband?" These are the sort of naive questions, covertly or openly put, which often emerge from a "health and beauty" session in a day release course or a youth club. They have their male equivalents. "What do you look for in a girl you're going steady with? Are you likely to find it if you're out for as good a time as she'll give you?" It sounds at best pedestrian, at worst cynical, but questions such as these have often proved the best approach to the threshold of ethics.

270. It is legitimate to ask why boys and girls cannot be fore-warned at school against these problems. Most of those who will be the students of county colleges, that is to say those who will be leaving school at 16 (or 15 today), are pretty certainly the less intellectual ones, who learn through experience. It is very difficult for them to anticipate a situation until it arises. It is essentially interpretation they need, not prophecy. Moreover, they will only be 16 or 17 when they are at a county college—their characters will not yet be formed; they are unlikely to have the poise to keep their balance without assistance in a new situation. Those who stay at school to 18, or continue full-time education to 21 or 22, are usually capable of a greater degree of introspection and abstraction; they can more successfully be prepared in advance for the world they are going to enter, and they will be more mature and able to stand on their own feet when they get there. The case for county colleges in this respect rests on the immaturity of those who enter employment at the minimum age or soon after.

THE USE OF LEISURE

271. This immaturity justifies the use of compulsion on their employers and themselves to secure their attendance. But if the

compulsion does not lead on to voluntary participation or become submerged in it, the object will have been only half attained. The county college should be a bridge to the future. It should show its students that there are many things that education can give them which they would not have thought of asking from it unless they had had this compulsory introduction. The effect of a county college should be apparent in the use its students make in the future of adult education of all kinds, and in the present of their leisure. It serves boys and girls at a time when they have almost as much freedom, and certainly as few responsibilities, as they will ever have. It is a time when many of them make a less worthwhile use of their free time than at any other period of their lives. They drop many of the things which they were beginning to do well, and which are well worth doing. Perhaps they played in the school orchestra—how many keep it up? Perhaps they painted or carved stone or made pottery—are they still doing so? Perhaps they borrowed books from the public library—have they given up membership? Almost certainly, if they were boys, they played football—how many still do so? The answer, and it was a depressing one, to these questions was given in the last chapter. To some extent the giving up of what had so recently given pleasure is caused by the lack of opportunity; to some extent by the absence of somebody to suggest going on with it. In both respects the county college in association with a strong Youth Service ought to be able to help. Neither in our judgment is likely to succeed to any large extent without the other. Both will need to use the experience of living together. In the colleges where most has been done in the way of social and personal education, great use has been made of residential week-ends or weeks of a non-vocational character. The experience of the Scandinavian Folk High Schools, often dealing with a similar age range but under very different conditions, points in the same direction.

CONTINUED EDUCATION

272. In this chapter we have so far been concerned largely with what may be called social education. What about more formal education? Few would deny that England needs a better educated democracy than it has today; but many may be inclined to doubt whether county colleges will produce one. These doubts spring from two sources—a doubt of the capacity of the boys and girls, and a doubt of the efficiency of the proposed method. The first turns on the capacity of the less intelligent half of the population to carry their formal education further than they do now. They have, it is argued, reached their ceiling at 15, if not before. This seems to us demonstrably untrue of most of them. Given the will to learn, there is reason to believe

that nearly all of them could carry their education in normal school subjects further than it has reached by 15 or 16. If this can be done, it should be done in the national interest. The second kind of doubt turns on the efficacy of part-time education. The history of English education, and experience today, show that progress can be made under far worse conditions than will prevail in county colleges. We agree, however, that the success of county colleges will be strongly influenced by the proportion of students who have first acquired a reasonable basic equipment through full-time education. That, it will be remembered, is one reason why we recommend the raising of the school-leaving age as a preliminary to the introduction of county colleges. We believe, too, that the success of county colleges depends on the actual ground to be covered during part-time education being realistically measured. If a great deal has to be accomplished within a short period, part-time education ceases to be appropriate. But, subject to these conditions, part-time education is often a satisfactory method of learning. Indeed, for some people, it is successful where full-time education has failed because their desire to learn has only been awakened by their discovery at work of new ambition or personal inadequacy.

273. The realisation of the social purpose of county colleges depends to a considerable extent on the presence in the curriculum of a substantial educational programme in the more restricted sense. It is important that the county college should not seem a soft option to work, but a part of it—work, not play. This is important, no doubt, from the point of view of the public who will pay for it. It is equally important from the point of view of the student. He may not at first like being expected to work, but he will respect the county college just as far as it makes him work. There are in our view three main reasons for using a vocational approach. First, experience both in this country and in Germany seems to show that vocational content gives students a sense of reality and purpose. Secondly, it makes clear the importance that rightly attaches to the day's work. Thirdly, by attaching the vocational content to a slightly higher rung on the employment ladder, it can often be used as an encouragement to a proper and realistic ambition. The county college should not neglect the question of what the van boy should do next. At the very bottom of the ladder, where work is almost entirely unskilled, we are likely to meet a general utilitarian need which it is just as important to meet as any technical need at the top of the ladder. The maintenance of the basic educational skills of ability to read, write and calculate correctly is for backward boys and girls a quite essential part of vocational training as well as of general education. Because they learn slowly, and think and write and read slowly, this side of their

county college training is likely to take as much of the available time as the teaching of vocational subjects to abler boys and girls.

FOUR STRANDS

274. There seem to us, then, to be four main strands out of which the curriculum of the county college should be woven. There is, first, the task of helping young workers, many of them of limited intelligence, to find their way successfully about the adult world—to spend their money sensibly, to understand the many ways in which the welfare state touches their lives and can assist them, to see how its services are paid for, and to play their part as useful citizens. Secondly, there is the more difficult job of helping them to define, in a form which makes sense to them, a standard of moral values by which they can live after they have left the sheltered world of school and find themselves in novel situations where they desperately need guidance. There is, thirdly, the easier, and infinitely rewarding, task of helping them to carry over into their working life the pursuits and activities, physical and aesthetic, which they practised at school and too often abandon. Finally, there is, as we have seen, a strictly educational task in the narrower sense. Many, perhaps most, of the county college students will have grave deficiencies in their formal school education which—now that they are out in the world and can see the handicap they have imposed on themselves—they will often be willing and anxious to put right. These, then, are the four strands. In what proportions or in what pattern they should be woven into the fabric of county college education is, we believe, as yet unknown. The methods which will prove effective are also still largely unexplored. Pioneers have done great work; but they themselves would be the first to declare that they have been too few to do enough to solve these problems of curriculum and method. That, indeed, is why experiments on a large scale are needed.

275. The social purpose behind county colleges is just as significant for apprentices and other skilled workers as it is for unskilled men and women. At present, however, their day release, if they get it, is dominated by the purely technical aspect of their studies. In future, at least equal importance should be given to these wider social purposes, though equal importance does not necessarily mean equal time. These other aims may often best be approached by incidental treatment arising out of their present studies, if the staff are alert to see the opening and trained to take it. But not all that is needed can be done in this way. Some direct teaching will have to be done in the county college day (which will, by statute, be longer than the present normal practice) and by voluntary extensions outside it, often of a residential nature. The important thing to bear in mind is

that for these students the starting point is normally vocational. They are generally of William Cobbett's opinion that "the first thing to be required of a man is, that he understand well his own calling or profession; and, be you in what state of life you may, to acquire this knowledge ought to be your first and greatest care". Unless they can be satisfied that this is being satisfactorily attended to, they will be unwilling to listen to anything else.

CHAPTER 18

The Way to County Colleges

276. When we were considering the case for raising the minimum school-leaving age in Chapter 12 we had to ask how near to the objective we could get by persuasion. We saw reason to hope that, if things continue as they are now going, half the boys and girls in the age-group might before long be voluntarily undertaking a fifth-year course. We then asked whether it was worth while using compulsion to enrol the other half, and we decided for two main reasons that it was—there were things to be done for everybody, irrespective of their ability, which could not be done in a shorter time, and there was also the certainty that without compulsion we should fail to secure for extended courses many boys and girls whose ability could ill be spared. We came to the conclusion that the experience we were now getting with ordinary 15 year-old boys and girls in schools made it possible to say with some confidence that, if it were made obligatory within a few years for all 15 year-olds to be in school, they and the country would derive great value from it. There might appear to be a certain similarity in the outlook for part-time day release. Already a quarter of all 16 year-old boys are attending classes one day a week without any legal compulsion. Are we not, then, well on the way to being able to fix a date for compulsory part-time education as well as for raising the minimum school-leaving age?

277. The analogy is misleading. Part-time day release has been developed as a partnership between employers, apprentices and the state in an area where the economic interests of all three have coincided. The content of the education has substantially been chosen for its vocational relevance. This is not, of course, to deny its general educational value; but the criterion for inclusion has been its usefulness for the job. The introduction of county colleges presupposes the same three parties, though the student element will no longer be confined to apprentices but will comprise all young workers aged 16 and 17, and the employers will no longer be volunteers drawn mainly from a few industries, but all employers of young people. It also presupposes that the field of operation will be extended for all students beyond the strictly vocational to include the developing needs of the whole man.

278. It is helpful to consider these two extensions separately—first, the enlarged body of people concerned; secondly, the enlarged field of operations. It is almost certain that an extension of the student

body without compulsion can come only as a result of the extension of the body of interested employers. We have considered the possibility of turning the privilege of one-day-a-week's release for the purpose of further education into the right of every young worker. Obviously there would be difficulties in the organisation of shop or factory if some claimed a day's release and others did not. It would be tempting for employers, and especially, perhaps, for small employers, to engage those who did not wish to make use of their legal right. In some occupations the trade unions might be strong enough and interested enough to prevent this sort of discrimination, but we fear that over too large a section of employment the "right" would be illusory. The idea is attractive because it would ensure that those who took day release really wanted it, and consequently on the educational side there would be a fair guarantee that good use would be made of the opportunities; but we must reluctantly conclude that the safeguards which would make the right effective are hard to imagine. In the near future we have to pin our hopes of expansion on increasing the number of employers who will themselves offer their employees day release.

THE EXTENSION OF VOLUNTARY RELEASE

279. There are three directions in which it is important to persuade more employers to grant day release. The first is the need to increase the volume of day release for apprentices, both by making it more nearly universal in those industries where it is already common, and by encouraging other industries to give it to their future skilled workers on as generous a scale as the engineering and building trades now do. An extension of this kind would help by reducing the numbers who will be brought in for the first time when compulsion is introduced, and by enabling a corps of teachers qualified in these new fields to be recruited in advance of the appointed day. It would not help of itself to prepare the way for a broader educational programme. The curriculum would still be vocationally determined, though the vocational content would be more varied.

280. The second direction of growth is a vertical extension to the lower levels of industry, as distinct from the horizontal extension to other industries to which we have just referred. There is no sudden division between skilled and unskilled workers, but a gradual shading of skill and ability throughout the whole range of employment. There are many occupations which, though not highly skilled, would be better filled than they now are by men who had had some serious training and education based on their trade. One of the most impressive aspects of the German system of compulsory part-time education is the fact that some form of vocational training has been devised for

the vast majority of all young workers—sometimes, perhaps, by the rather artificial invention of a "mystery", but more often by taking serious thought about a job and its requirements and ramifications. This process of vocational and quasi-vocational training has been associated in Germany with the regulation of entry to the occupations concerned. This may well not be an advantage in an age when flexibility is increasingly important. It certainly runs counter to English experience, which is that the lower the degree of skill, the more frequent the changes of job by young workers. There would be psychological as well as economic advantages and disadvantages in the setting up of specific, long-continued training programmes for a greatly increased range of less skilled jobs. This is a matter which lies outside our competence to judge, but it seems unlikely to us that extensions downwards on the German pattern will, or should, cover anything like the whole field of boys' employment.

281. The third direction, perhaps the most important and certainly the most difficult, is the need to secure a much greater release of girls. At present, as we have seen, only some 8 per cent of girls at work get part-time day education. To move suddenly from this narrow foundation to day release for all would be too formidable a venture. Today there are necessarily very few teachers with knowledge of this work to provide leadership for beginners, and there is hope of only a very gradual growth in their number unless the volume of day release for girls can be substantially increased. There is as yet little sign of any improvement. We take up the argument where it was left in paragraph 255. Although the present early age of marriage is a disincentive to employers, it should be realised that marriage no longer terminates, though child-bearing interrupts, a woman's earning life. There is a long-term advantage to employers in seeing that young entrants are properly trained, though there can rarely be any likelihood, let alone certainty, that the individual employer who provided the training will eventually get back the trained worker. The changing structure of industry and business—the replacement of the small trader by the chain store, for instance—may make it easier to overcome this difficulty. It seems to us that the way forward lies through the design of suitable courses, and through negotiations with the largest national employers for day release schemes to apply wherever really suitable facilities can be provided.

282. In the first of these possible directions of extension—horizontally, to apprentices in industries where day release is less developed than in engineering—it may be hoped that the impetus that has brought the ten-fold increase since 1937 is not yet exhausted—though, as we shall see in Part Six, the prospect is not altogether bright. In the second direction—vertically, to less skilled operatives—

there is some, but less, reason to hope for a considerable expansion as appropriate training courses are developed. The City and Guilds of London Institute is doing useful pioneering work in this field. In the third direction—to the almost untouched field of girls' employment—there is as yet little sign of progress, and small reason to expect a radical change for the better under present conditions. How then can growth be stimulated in all three directions? It is easy to imagine that some change in taxation, or even a direct subsidy to employers, would lead to a marked increase in willingness to release employees. This is not a directly educational matter; and, although it touches education closely, we do not feel competent to give it the detailed discussion that would be necessary before making recommendations.

283. The most appropriate incentive in our opinion will be a declaration that compulsory part-time education is to be introduced on a specified date. One reason why day release has not expanded to take in many semi-skilled and unskilled workers is to be found in the widespread belief that the county college clauses of the Act of 1944 are as dead as the corresponding clauses of the Act of 1918. If it were clear that county colleges, so far from being abandoned, still formed an integral part of national policy, and that they would be introduced at a time which could be stated with reasonable accuracy, we believe that this could be a stimulus to the development of voluntary schemes. We would expect this to be especially true of the semi-skilled occupations into which boys go; and expansion here would be particularly valuable because it would give the colleges experience of teaching boys of a considerably lower level of ability than most of their present students for whom different methods would be needed. We believe, too, that it would be much easier to arrange part-time release schemes for girls if discussion took place against the government's known intention to introduce compulsory day release at a certain point in time—provided it was not too remote.

A PREPARATORY PERIOD UNDER COMPULSION

284. We do not, however, believe that the voluntary growth of part-time day release, however vigorous the encouragement it receives, will carry us far enough to make it possible to proceed in one move to the nation-wide introduction of compulsory county colleges. Even a very large volume of day release would still leave unanswered many of the questions about what would happen when the system was compulsory on employers as well as on their young workers. In our view it is necessary to have a preparatory period in which there is some element of compulsion. We have considered various forms which this preparatory exercise might take, such as an initial application to one or two industries or occupations. We have, however, come to the

conclusion that such a functional approach to county colleges would not be profitable, in spite of its obvious attractions. In the first place, it is notoriously difficult to define an industry with precision—much harder, for instance, than to delimit a geographical area. Most industries, too, are widely distributed geographically, providing only in a few areas employment for anything like the great majority of those who would eventually become county college students. It would probably be necessary, therefore, to establish a large number of small county colleges, which would be difficult to fit into the ultimate pattern of provision. Moreover, one of the reasons for desiring a preparatory exercise in compulsion is to gain experience in dealing with those boys and girls who positively dislike the idea of going to a county college, and who would take evading action if they could. It is plainly much easier to avoid functional compulsion, by changing one's job, than geographical compulsion, which would usually involve changing one's home. We have, therefore, come to believe that the only satisfactory form for a preparatory exercise is by applying compulsion to one or more geographical regions.

285. Our belief in the necessity for a preparatory period under compulsion rests on three lines of argument. The first is the great uncertainty that exists about the best way of realising for semi-skilled and unskilled workers the educational aims of a county college. One school of thought holds that this could, and should, nearly always be approached through vocational interests; another strenuously denies both the desirability and the practicability of this. Which is right? Or, rather, for what proportion of unskilled workers is which right? The only way of finding out is by experiment, but this presupposes enough unskilled workers to provide the necessary experience. Besides this broad difference in principle, there are quite as important unresolved problems about actual detailed matters of curriculum, which affect the kind of building and equipment required and the type of experience that the staff will need. Only experiment can determine these matters; and, once again, experiment requires the presence of unskilled workers in adequate numbers.

286. This brings us to our second line of argument. We do not believe that day release for unskilled workers and girls can be brought by voluntary means to the point where nation-wide compulsion would be merely a rounding off, and not a substantially new undertaking. It is necessary for these groups, in our view, to have a gradual build-up, as we have already had among skilled workers. The fundamental difference is that, with skilled workers, the build-up could be done voluntarily because of the closely coinciding self-interest of employers, apprentices and the state, but with unskilled workers and girls, this is unlikely, because of the lack of any direct

and indisputable economic advantage to the employer. The greater part of the build-up must, we believe, take place under compulsion. There are no doubt difficulties with a partial and progressive application of compulsion which its universal and instantaneous introduction would avoid. They do not seem to us to be anything like as serious or damaging as the ill effects of introducing on a given day a whole generation of young unskilled workers to a body of teachers, nearly all of whom would be without experience of this work, serving under principals who had had equally little chance of discovering in practice how best to handle boys and girls without any continuing educational interest. Even in the stress of war, the call-up of recruits was tailored of necessity to the development of the training machine; the case for a similar planned and progressive application of compulsion to the education of young unskilled workers seems to us equally clear.

287. Our third line of argument for a progressive application of compulsion turns on our belief that, especially in the field of part-time education, what happens under voluntary arrangements gives little guidance in many of the most pressing problems which would arise under compulsion. If we are right in this belief, the only effective preparation for a national compulsory system is through compulsion in a limited sphere. It is worth while setting out some of these special problems. It is of the essence of the county college plan that compulsion has to be applied to two parties—on the employer to release his young worker for a day a week or its equivalent, and on the worker to attend the county college. Hitherto the employer has been entirely free from compulsion (unless his business was in Rugby). If he allowed his young workers a day off for education, it was because he thought it was worth doing and the right thing to do. By and large, day release has been taken up in those concerns which have most to gain from what vocational education can give and where the nature of the operations has made it relatively easy to adopt. The unwilling employer and the awkward work situation are problems which will arise acutely with the introduction of compulsion.

288. At present the young worker is also under no compulsion to attend a college of further education, though his freedom is often more limited than the employer's. His right not to be educated, so to speak, depends on his willingness not to be employed by firms which provide day release. Many young workers, therefore, are already by the nature of their employment under indirect compulsion; but, if they feel strongly enough about it, they are still at liberty to go elsewhere. And, on the whole, those for whom part-time day release is a condition of employment are those who are most likely to be willing to make a success of their education. Compulsion, then, will close the present escape route and bring in apathetic or even hostile students,

as well as eager ones whose employers have not up to now provided the opportunity. One of the most serious problems before the county college is to find means of arousing their interest and providing them with an incentive to take their day at the county college seriously. Nor is it the student alone whose interest needs to be aroused. He needs to feel that the man under whom he is working in industry regards his day at college as important; an uninterested or hostile foreman will soon produce unwilling and antagonistic students. Even where the heads of a firm are convinced believers in the system, a boy's immediate supervisor may not share their view. Where the firm as a whole is unfriendly there is little chance of the junior ranks of management being friendly. And yet without this encouragement there is but a poor prospect of turning a reluctant into an eager student.

289. There is still another kind of problem that compulsion will bring. Voluntary part-time day release has largely been confined to apprentices and trainees, and has, therefore, on the whole brought into the colleges a steady body of students who can be expected to remain with the same employer and continue with an ordered education. But at the other end of the scale, among unskilled workers, there is a great deal of changing of jobs. A change of employer may well mean a change of county college or a change from one day's attendance to another in such a way as to disrupt a planned programme of work in mid-course.

290. Again, there will be a need to experiment with different forms of organisation to find the type of provision best suited to the requirements of particular industries. Seasonal trades, for instance, would often be ill-served by one day a week throughout the year; agriculture and some manufacturing processes might be better suited to a form of block release (continuous release for a week or a month at a time followed by uninterrupted employment) than to the withdrawal of one-fifth of the juvenile workers each day, or of all on one day. In the distributive trades certain days might be much more readily available than others. The effective working of a system covering all kinds of employment will require a great deal of give and take, and of experiment which can hardly be undertaken on a haphazard voluntary basis.

291. On the other hand, there are some problems that compulsion will solve. Once the die is cast, many employers will become anxious to get as much as they can out of the system. Compulsion will remove the fear that the competitor who does not give his workers part-time release is at some advantage. Universal part-time education may carry with it some reconsideration of the juvenile wages structure, and it might well be that in the process one of the present psycho-

logical and economic objections to the system might disappear. It may also be that in certain types of completely unskilled employment the demand for juvenile labour might disappear with the commitment to part-time education. This need not necessarily be a bad thing.

THREE STEPS TO COUNTY COLLEGES

292. We recommend, therefore, that the introduction of county colleges should be planned in three stages. The first stage, which would take place while the Ministry and the local education authorities were heavily engaged with preparations for raising the school-leaving age, would be concerned with the development of the voluntary system, with the assistance of strong encouragement from the government. It ought to be possible during this period to secure some real progress with semi-skilled workers and girls, thus gaining some ground on which more teachers could gain experience of this kind of work. We should also expect to see some development of the education given during part-time day courses, both by adapting the courses followed by skilled workers to make them serve the broad objectives of the Act of 1944, and by introducing appropriate forms of course for the less skilled trades and the less able students. Experiments could also be undertaken to determine what incentives are most effective in eliciting the active support of those day release students who lack the spur of personal ambition. There would also be time to gain experience with methods of recruiting and training teachers for the colleges.

293. The second stage would be the introduction of compulsion in a few carefully selected areas. This should follow hard on the raising of the school-leaving age and preparations should be made for it before that event. Selective compulsion would require legislation. We have been much impressed with the evidence given to us by local authority associations in favour of the introduction of county colleges. We cannot, therefore, doubt that it would be possible to find groups of authorities, perhaps one or two adjoining counties and their associated county boroughs, which would be willing, and indeed anxious, to carry out on behalf of all a large-scale experiment embodying compulsion in order to prepare the way for the fixing of the appointed day or days. It would be essential for such an area to be as nearly self-contained as possible and to have within its boundaries a sufficient range of employment to provide a fair microcosm, in which other authorities and employers could find examples of the problems they would have to face when their turn came. The purpose of any such plan would be to provide guidance for the country as a whole, and it would therefore only be right in our opinion that the scheme should be specially financed apart from the general formula governing the

block grant. If such a proposal finds favour, we would hope that it might be possible also to take special measures to encourage the development of the Youth Service in the selected area or areas, because if a county college is doing its work well, its students will seek, and ought to be able to find, worth-while activities for their leisure. This second stage in development ought not to be undertaken in makeshift accommodation. Like the later general introduction of county colleges, it must get off to a good start in suitable buildings. We attach great importance to this experiment being initiated promptly and conducted with vigour, to give the pilot county colleges the best opportunity of showing what they can do. It is, of course, impossible to predict how long the experiment will have to be carried on to provide answers to all the essential questions. We should hope, however, that it would be possible to come to decisions within five years.

294. The third stage in the introduction of county colleges for all would be the progressive extension of compulsion to the whole country. We have in mind a phased programme spreading in successive years from region to region. How long this third stage would take would be a matter of practical ways and means more than anything else. However much preparation has been made, the recruitment and training of teachers and the provision of buildings for the whole country will inevitably take some time. But the awkwardness of having compulsory county colleges in some parts of the country and not in others is so obvious that, once the decision has been taken to proceed with this third stage, it should be made as short as possible. We think three or four years might be needed.

295. Any mention of county colleges immediately raises the failure of the day continuation schools which, under the Fisher Act of 1918, were to provide a national compulsory system of part-time education from 14 to 18. Why did they fail? Does the plan now proposed avoid the same pitfalls? Memory can be curiously selective, and it is sometimes forgotten that it was not the inadequacies of the scheme, but the sharpness of the Geddes economy axe which killed day continuation schools on a national scale. It was, however, natural that, when economies had to be made, the day continuation schools should have been selected. Undoubtedly they had started badly. The schools were to have opened only as and when they were ready; in fact they often opened before they were ready in any genuine sense, in inadequate buildings with unsuitable staff. Moreover, they were not opened in any planned national sequence, but haphazard as authorities were ready to start. In the end, six authorities, including London, took part in the scheme and the maximum number of students enrolled was 95,000 in 1920. Inevitably there developed the difficulties that might

have been expected from applying compulsion on one side only of a purely arbitrary frontier. Time no doubt would have removed some of the difficulties and reduced others, but time was not given. The suggestions we have made in the preceding paragraphs are designed to avoid the recurrence of these and similar problems. The build-up of county colleges should be gradual so that good buildings may be provided and well-trained staff secured. It should be orderly. The region or regions selected for the second or exploratory stage should have well-defined natural frontiers, running along employment watersheds so as to avoid as far as possible the administrative problems and public complaints which would arise if many people lived in an area where compulsion applied, but worked in one where it did not (and vice versa). In the third stage, that of progressive application to the whole country, it would probably not be possible to avoid halting on occasion at an arbitary frontier which did not coincide with the pattern of employment catchment areas; but we would hope that they would be kept as few as good planning can ensure, and that the halt at any one of them would be as short as possible.

AGENDA FOR THE EXPERIMENTAL PERIOD

296. We have argued that the present uncertainty about what a county college would be like, and what a county college education would provide, makes a period of experiment necessary. Of course, this means putting off the time when a national system of county colleges can be introduced, and it is already fifty years since our predecessors of the old Consultative Committee recommended a system of compulsory part-time education after school on the basis of local option, which they hoped would spread to cover the whole country*. Impatience is understandable, but in our view unwise. We have to recognise that, as far as all but young men in skilled occupations are concerned, preparation did not start in any effective way at the end of the war, but has indeed still to be begun. We think that it should begin now with the first of our three stages, and that the introduction of county colleges should be thought of as a continuous process continuing in an orderly fashion until the system is complete. But, if experiment is necessary because we do not know the answers, it is not likely to be successful unless we are clear about the questions. We confine ourselves in the following paragraphs to listing what seem to us the major educational problems and adding a few comments. We are concerned here with the agenda for the first two stages, not with a blue-print for the third, or an architect's drawing of the final system.

* Report of the Consultative Committee (1909) on Attendance, Compulsory and Otherwise, at Continuation Schools pp. 178–183.

297. The first series of problems which need investigation concern what should be taught, and methods of teaching. On the one hand, there is the difficulty of finding any time for non-vocational work by students preparing for highly skilled jobs. This is discussed in Part Six; here we will only anticipate our conclusion that developments and changes in the part-time system, which are in any event desirable, will make it possible to regard the education of these workers as satisfying the general requirements of a county college. The curricular problems of the less skilled, and completely unskilled, workers are a much more difficult matter. They were considered in Chapter 17 and the conclusions to which we there came are indeed one of the main reasons why we advocate a preparatory period under compulsion.

THE TEACHING STAFF

298. If we are right in believing that there is both a vocational and a general object to be performed, and that they often run closely together, the one often becoming the vehicle for the other, it is clear that the curriculum of the county college will need to be more differentiated than the curriculum of the secondary schools. Here is a challenge to those responsible for the training of teachers. The job is certainly very different from teaching in school. It differs, too, from teaching in a technical college if we are right in the stress we lay on guiding the personal development of the students. It will call together men and women from very varied backgrounds—one of the necessary experiments will be in recruitment. When found, they will have not only to acquire the necessary teaching techniques, but to be formed into a homogeneous body with a strong *esprit de corps*. The difficulty of finding a suitable term to describe their position is an indication that it is a new job that has to be done. Lecturer, the normal term in the technical college world, sounds quite wrong: lecturing is surely of all approaches to teaching the one most to be avoided with these students. Teacher is almost equally bad because of the suggestion it carries with it of the schoolroom. On the whole, it seems sensible to borrow the word tutor from the field of adult education because of the combination of teaching and general pastoral care which it conveys. Ability to teach, ability to understand and sympathise with the students, a knowledge of the world in which they spend all but one day a week—these are qualities which we believe all county college tutors should share. But, this said, the common ground is exhausted. Many might well be recruited, after training, from men and women who have found a career in the Youth Service or in kindred social work, which is one reason why we believe that a considerable development of the Youth Service is a desirable part of the preparation for county colleges. Many will require technical

experience in industry. Some will be drawn from the ranks of school teachers, especially perhaps from those whose entry into the profession was at a later age than the normal one. The variety of the curriculum and the variety in the staff calls for a high degree of leadership. It is clear that the principal of a county college will need a remarkably clear vision of what his college is attempting to do, and of the role of each tutor in it, if many excellent parts are not to add up to very much less than one effective whole.

299. County colleges must, then, be recognised as a new service requiring to recruit its own staff and to train them in its own ways. It is a new service, a fresh development, and not a mere projection of the present part-time day system. A regular and steady build-up of the body of tutors must be planned. How many will be needed? This is one of the points on which experiment is necessary, since estimates of desirable staffing ratios vary considerably. The more successful the college is in its wider tasks, the higher will be the ratio required. The figure of 20,000 full-time tutors, or their equivalent, may be given to provide some idea of the order of magnitude, but there is certainly a possible error of several thousands either way. The balance of full-time and part-time tutors will also need careful working out. On the face of it, county colleges should provide suitable openings for married women who only want to give one or two days' work a week, since normally each day will stand by itself with its own regular students and its own self-contained time-table. Certainly special forms of training will be required. There are similarities between county college work as we envisage it and some other forms of social work, which suggest that some university departments might be suitable and willing to undertake training. Training colleges, perhaps more like the technical teachers' training colleges than the general colleges, but with a wider brief, will be needed; and there will be a large demand for in-service training. But, whatever long-term plans may be made, there must be an initial problem during the first establishment of the service. That is one reason why we recommend a progressive introduction of county colleges. Moreover, if the sequence of reforms that we suggest is followed and the school-leaving age is raised before the introduction of county colleges, some tutors should be freed through the cessation of part-time day release for 15 year-olds, who at present account for 30 per cent of the students under 18. They will be available to help staff the new part-time day schemes which we expect to see developing once it is known that the introduction of a compulsory scheme is definitely assured and is being actively prepared. We would thus hope to see the number of teachers and the number of 16 and 17 year-old students grow side by side through the next ten years, leaving a considerably smaller balance of

both to be found on the finally appointed day than if it were to be fixed for the immediate future. In these ways it ought to be possible, as far as the provision of staff is concerned, to grow into county colleges and not to be faced with the necessity of improvising. But in the meantime there is much to be done if the ideal is not to remain a dream. It is not only the appropriate staffing ratio that will have to be determined, but a suitable salary scale and appropriate conditions of service for county colleges, which, under the Act of 1944, will have to work longer hours and have shorter holidays than either schools or technical colleges have at present. Pretty certainly there will also be evening sessions to be considered. It seems clear that a special pattern of staffing will have to be devised with great care, covering not only the conditions on the job, but conditions of entry and departure, so that a reasonably easy interchange may be developed between industry, teaching and other appropriate forms of social work.

PROBLEMS OF ORGANISATION

300. The last main educational item on which there are divergent views is the type of institution best fitted to realise the county college objectives. In pamphlet No. 8, "Further Education", published in 1947, the Ministry of Education indicated its preference for a comprehensive form of county college provision as clearly as it assumed at that date a tripartite organisation of secondary education. "Local Colleges",* it then wrote "will be required to meet a good many of the local needs for further education, whether vocational or general, full-time or part-time. Normally they will accommodate all county college activities . . . . ". The only exception envisaged was for students under 18 following either a rare trade or requiring especially expensive equipment which could be provided only in a central or regional college. Since 1947 views, based on experience, have become a good deal more fluid about secondary school organisation; and we believe that they may well become equally fluid about county colleges once it is possible to get experience of handling a whole age-group. That experience is still lacking. Nearly all the knowledge we have is of students from the upper half of the industrial and educational spectrum. Some (and those not the least successful) of the few who have had experience with day release at the other end of the spectrum are convinced that county colleges to meet the needs of the young unskilled worker should be different institutions from those dealing with craftsmen in training. There is much to be said on both sides, and we should be surprised if the final decision was so much in favour of one pattern that it could be recommended for general adoption throughout the country irrespective of local circumstances. We do

* Local Colleges are defined in paragraph 471.

not think that the presence of full-time students, side by side with one-day-a-week county college students, or of older men, can be assumed to be certainly right as a general rule. In our view it is important that, during the exploratory work of stage two of our recommendations, there should be deliberate experiment with several types of organisation and size of college. The only criteria which must be satisfied are that any institution which could be accepted as a county college must regard the education and well-being of boys and girls of 16 and 17 as the prime reason for its existence, and that its ethos must be such that no large group of county college students should feel that they are second-class members of it on the score either of their youth or their part-time status or the unskilled nature of their work. If the "county college" is to form a wing of a larger college of further education, then it seems essential for these reasons that it must either form the main concern of the Principal or at least have its own Warden free of all other commitments.

301. Since 1944 important advances have been made with educational schemes which have developed quite outside the county college concept, but which will have to be integrated with it. The experience of the Outward Bound and Brathay Hall experiments, and with the Duke of Edinburgh's Award, for instance, have shown that there are forms of training, in which physical challenge and response play a large part, which have a strong appeal to many young people. Their contribution ought to be recognised and made use of in any national system. What, too, is to be the relation between county college obligations and a residential weekend, paid for often enough by management but taking place in the worker's free time? That there is great value in introducing a periodical residential element into the rhythm of a long once-a-week programme is clear enough. How can this interplay best be developed? To what extent can the same values be realised by a system of block release without residential arrangements, e.g. continuous attendance for five days in one week instead of for one day for five weeks? There are a host of other organisational problems to which the right answers (not necessarily the same in all districts and for all industries) will need to be worked out. Where industries draw up vocational training programmes in fields at present unexplored, what criteria should be applied to determine whether they comply with the requirements of the Act? What should be the role and status of private colleges of further education provided by employers? Should there be total or partial exemption from county college obligations for those who stay another year at school; that is, should full-time education to 17 excuse part-time education between 17 and 18? Should the county college be the base for the Youth Employment Service and the Youth Service organisers? How can a continuous educational programme be

reconciled with changes of job and changes of employer? Ought county colleges to be work-based, or home-based—i.e. should the college a student attends be determined by where he lives or by where he is employed? These are only a few of the questions which need to be worked out by a process of debate and experiment and which cannot be answered in the present small and static provision described in Chapter 16. Room for manoeuvre is necessary. Provisional answers ought to be found before the introduction of general compulsion.

SUMMARY OF CONCLUSIONS

302. We sum up our recommendations and conclusions on the subjects we have been discussing in this Part of the report in the following way:

(*a*) The Minister should re-affirm his intention to implement at the earliest possible date the provision of compulsory part-time education for all young persons of 16 and 17 who are not in full-time education. It is the widespread lack of belief in this intention which, in our view, has almost stopped the growth of all part-time release other than that which is clearly essential for technical reasons.

(*b*) We are especially concerned at the loss of contact with the least skilled and least able members of the community as soon as they leave school, and with their loss of morale. In their interests (though not only for them) we regard a strong Youth Service as an essential complement to county colleges, and we recommend that steps should be taken to develop it during the interim period.

(*c*) We are also particularly concerned at the very small volume of day release for girls and at the fact that girls appear to make less use than boys of the Youth Service after they leave school.

(*d*) There are four strands that should be woven into the curriculum of county colleges: an appreciation of the adult world in which young workers suddenly find themselves; guidance for them in working out their problems of human relations and moral standards; development of their physical and aesthetic skills; and a continuance of their basic education, with a vocational bias where appropriate. There is not as yet enough experience to show in what proportions and by what methods these elements can best be combined into a satisfactory whole.

(*e*) The success of the county college will depend to a great extent on the degree to which students feel that their employers are interested in it. A careful study of incentives from the employers' side, and from the students' angle, should be undertaken.

(*f*) We attach the highest importance to the selection and training of the right kind of staff for county colleges. We are particularly anxious to avoid a sudden, unprepared introduction of county colleges with a staff which would have to be largely improvised.

(*g*) We also believe it to be essential that county colleges should not be first established in makeshift accommodation.

(*h*) A number of complicated administrative problems will arise about different ways in which the over-all obligation of attendance at county colleges might be discharged: we do not think they can be satisfactorily solved by *a priori* argument without experiment.

(*i*) We do not believe that sufficient progress can be made through voluntary persuasion with securing day release for unskilled workers and for girls to make possible the introduction of compulsory attendance for all in one move.

(*j*) The nature of compulsion—compulsion both on employers to release and on workers to attend—introduces factors which cannot be studied under the present voluntary system and which call for an exploratory period of compulsion.

(*k*) For these reasons we recommend that the introduction of county colleges should be by three stages:

(i) a period, starting now, of intensive encouragement for the extension of day release to new classes of workers by voluntary means;

(ii) an exploratory and preparatory period, starting soon after the raising of the school-leaving age, in which compulsory county college attendance would be introduced in one or more areas of considerable size. This would require legislation and special financial arrangements. The length of this stage cannot be predicted, but we should hope that it would be possible to reach decisions within five years.

(iii) The phased introduction of compulsory attendance throughout the country by a programme spreading as quickly as possible from region to region. This stage should proceed as rapidly as practical considerations permit. We think it might take three to four years.

Part Five

The Sixth Form

CHAPTER 19

The Ablest Boys and Girls

303. We were concerned in Parts Two, Three and Four with boys and girls who at the age of 11 were of average ability—some rather above average, many decidedly below. This description would still hold true of most of them at 15, but there are among them a good many who have begun by that age to develop the strength of purpose and ability of mind to fit themselves for work which requires a continued and relatively deep education. The object of policy should be to keep all doors open as long as possible. In Part Five we are concerned with those whose promise declares itself early and who at the age of 11 are abler than three-quarters of their contemporaries. This description will still hold true of most of them at 15, and the object of policy should be to see that no artificial obstacles should be placed in the way of their moving forward at their own pace, which is a quick one, towards those goals to which their abilities and their interests are most directed.

304. Some 26 per cent (157,000) of the 15 year-olds in 1958 were either in selective schools (direct grant grammar schools, maintained grammar and technical schools) or in independent schools recognised as efficient, which as a class have an intake of equal or slightly better ability.* A further 2 per cent (9,000) were in comprehensive bilateral or multilateral schools, of whom probably about one-quarter would have been in the same range of intelligence. By 17, when boys and girls are in the Sixth Form, the proportion of the whole age-group who were in selective or independent schools had fallen to 9 per cent (52,000) with a further 1,300 in comprehensive and bilateral schools. The detailed distribution for boys and girls is given in Table 24. It is at once apparent from this table that the only types of school which as yet make any appreciable numerical contribution to Sixth Form education are the maintained grammar schools, the independent schools recognised as efficient and the direct grant schools. It is with these schools, therefore, that we must be mainly concerned in this part of the report. Among them the maintained grammar schools play by far

* The distribution of ability among National Service recruits to the Army who had been educated at recognised efficient independent schools was virtually identical with that of those who had been educated at grammar schools. The independent schools had rather more in the top 10 per cent; the grammar schools had rather more in the next highest ability group. There were very few from either type of school with a lower rating. The figures are in Part Two of Vol. II.

Table 24. Number of Boys and Girls Aged 15 and 17 in Various Types of School (England and Wales, 1958).

Type of School	Boys		Girls		Total	
	At 15	At 17	At 15	At 17	At 15	At 17
	(thousands)	(thousands)	(thousands)	(thousands)	(thousands)	(thousands)
Maintained:						
Grammar	49	17	47	15	96	32
Technical	12	1	7	1	19	2
Bilateral and Multilateral	1	—	1	—	2	—
Comprehensive	3	1	4	1	7	1
Selective Central, etc.	4	—	4	—	9	—
Modern	18	—	15	—	33	—
Other	2	—	2	—	5	—
Total	89	19	80	17	171	35
Direct Grant	7	3	7	3	14	6
Independent:						
Recognised Efficient	14	7	12	3	26	11
Other	4	—	5	1	9	1
	114	29	104	24	220	53

NOTE: Owing to rounding off of figures totals do not always appear to be accurate.

the largest single part, accounting for 60 per cent of the total number of pupils. The comprehensive schools are newcomers to the field and will, even from the existing numbers of schools, no doubt figure more largely in the list once they are fully grown. There is no reason to suppose that academic courses in the Sixth Forms of comprehensive or other new types of secondary schools, when they are developed, will differ substantially from the ones we shall be describing and discussing. By a normal academic course we mean one leading to two or more subjects at the Advanced level of the General Certificate of Education. As far as we can foresee development, what is true of Sixth Forms in grammar schools will be true of the comprehensive schools, and the views we hold about the one, we should expect to hold also of the other.

305. We shall have a good deal to say in Chapters 22 and 24 about the increasing size of Sixth Forms. Here we would only note that, in spite of this, there is still only 1 pupil aged 17 at schools giving a grammar or technical education for every 3 pupils aged 15 at the same schools. Table 25 gives the detail, from which it will be seen that independent and direct grant schools represent a relatively well developed sector and that the main possibilities for expansion occur in the maintained schools section. The same point is made visually in Chart 11.

CHART NO. 11

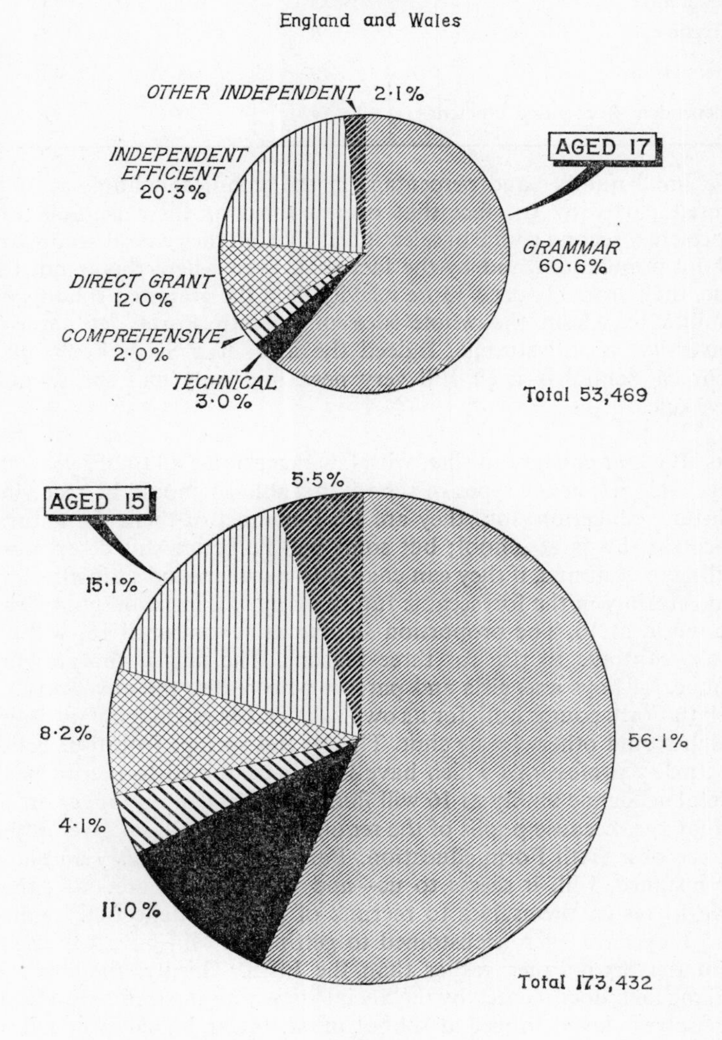
PUPILS AGED 15 AND 17 ATTENDING
CERTAIN TYPES OF SCHOOL:
1958
England and Wales
OTHER INDEPENDENT 2·1%
INDEPENDENT
EFFICIENT
20·3%
AGED 17
GRAMMAR
60·6%
DIRECT GRANT
12·0%
COMPREHENSIVE
2·0%
TECHNICAL
3·0%
Total 53,469
5·5%
AGED 15
15·1%
8·2%
56·1%
4·1%
11·0%
Total 173,432

Table 25. Pupils Aged 17 as a Percentage of those Aged 15 in Certain Types of School (England and Wales, 1958).

Type of School	Boys	Girls	Total
	percentage	percentage	percentage
Maintained:			
Grammar	35	31	33
Technical	8	9	8
Direct Grant	49	46	47
Independent Recognised Efficient	54	28	41

The small number and percentage in the technical schools at 17 is caused partly by the fact that over a third of these schools still represent a second round of selection at 13 from the general secondary school population; and by the fact that, even where this is not the case, they probably draw more heavily than the grammar schools on families to whom the whole idea of a Sixth Form, let alone a university, is still strange. Indeed the idea of a Sixth Form in a technical school is itself still very new, and only half the schools have one.

306. It is our conviction that, with few exceptions, all the 15 year-old boys and girls at the types of school in Table 25 should be receiving full-time education until they are 18. For most of them the natural place for this is at school; but some will be better suited, or more willing to continue, if they can change to another kind of institution, and certainly in the foreseeable future many will insist on going into the world at 16. The proportion staying at school until 18, will we think, continue to rise for three reasons. The first is the growing number of boys and girls and parents who realise the advantage of a Sixth Form course both for its own sake and as opening many doors which would otherwise be shut. The second springs from our belief that many professions which have been accustomed to recruit boys of real academic ability at 16 will find that they can no longer do so at that age, because pupils of the required ability will not give up the chance of a Sixth Form education. Banking, accountancy and law. for instance, will, it seems to us—and we do not regret it—either have to resign themselves to recruits of poorer intellectual quality than they have been accustomed to getting, or will have to recruit from the Sixth Form rather than the Fifth. Thirdly, there is the striking fact, documented by the Social Survey, that parents who have themselves stayed longer at school insist, in far higher proportion than other parents, on their children staying at school for the whole

course. As more and more pupils come to be of the second grammar school generation, this can be expected to have a powerful effect on the numbers staying on after 16.

307. This Part of our report, then, is concerned with those who are, or should be, Sixth Formers; and they will occupy our attention exclusively in the following chapters. Most of them in our judgement are quite capable of pursuing a normal academic course, though, as will be seen in Chapter 25, we are far from believing that the course they actually follow is always the best one for them. Some, however, who are well advised to enter the Sixth Form, should pursue a course there that is on rather different lines. Many girls at present do this; but few boys. The reason for the difference, we believe, lies in different opportunities—at school and in employment—and not in any difference of calibre between boys and girls. These Sixth Forms with a difference provide the subject of Chapter 27. At the beginning of this chapter we referred to those whose performance at 15 and after is far better than their attainments at 11 suggested that it would be. There are others whose early promise is belied by their subsequent development. This is a group to which the Council devoted considerable attention in the previous report on "Early Leaving". It will, therefore, be sufficient here to refer to three main points which were treated in detail there. There was, first, the surprisingly large size of the group (37·8 per cent of the intake) who failed to secure at least three passes at Ordinary level in the General Certificate of Education. Secondly, there was the fact that this lowest section of the grammar school output was by no means identical with the lowest third of its intake. Many who have turned out to be excellent grammar school pupils would have been excluded if it had been decided to reduce the size of the intake, perhaps with the object of drastically cutting down the proportion of failures, five years later, in the General Certificate of Education. Unless many are called, few can be chosen. There was, thirdly, the fact that in the course of grammar school education, there is a tendency for the children of non-manual workers to exceed their promise at 11 and for the children of semi-skilled and unskilled workers to make relatively less progress. Indeed, if the objective were to reduce failure rates in the G.C.E., without regard to the total yield, the easiest way to do it would apparently have been to introduce a social element into selection. The grammar school as it is in the first five years of the course is socially a pretty fair cross-section of the population. It is highly important that it should remain so; and, indeed, that the Sixth Form should take on rather more of the mixed social complexion of the main school than it has at present. This will happen as numbers grow. It is for the good of the grammar school that it should cast its net wide.

308. But is it for the good of the relative academic failure that he should be in the grammar school? This is a question that may well be asked of any school—how does it treat its least successful pupils? Even among grammar schools it happens that a boy or girl who is in the lowest stream in a highly selective school, and does badly in it, might have been in a better stream and got better results in a less highly selective school. The question of morale is all important, and morale depends very much on the attitude of the staff and the head-master. But there is more to it than morale. Many of those who disappoint come from homes which, however good in other ways—and they are often excellent—cannot give their boys and girls much assistance when they pass beyond elementary work. It may well be that some of these pupils, who fall back relatively in their progress, do so not through lack of general ability, but because some of the things they are asked to do—foreign languages, for example—are intrinsically more difficult for them than for the others for reasons arising out of their home surroundings. They have nobody there to help them to see the point of what they are doing, which must often seem remote from their interests and their parents'. Given a different curriculum, but not necessarily a less exacting one, they might have justified their early promise. What is to be done? Is it better that their course should deliberately be planned to lead to Ordinary level at 17 instead of 16? This is sometimes done with advantage in independent schools, and it would be worth trying in grammar schools if parents would agree to the longer course. Is it better that their curriculum should be modified to give more weight to such practical subjects as workshop practice or art? This is quite often done, and quite often succeeds; but, unless the school is very careful, it has the unfortunate result of labelling these subjects and these pupils as below academic par since, for better and worse, the grammar school has a single type of curriculum. In many individual instances these boys and girls would have done better in a technical school where the practical subjects have a high place in the work of the ablest as well as the least able pupils. Many would have done better in a comprehensive school with its wealth of provision. Many will do well if they can transfer at the appropriate moment from the grammar school to the kind of full-time education, discussed in Chapter 35, which has very close links with the world of industry. The important thing to realise is that these boys and girls are not stupid. They have been made to look and feel more stupid than they are by comparison with others. They are, after all, among the most intelligent quarter of the population.

309. Our concern in this Part, however, is with the Sixth Form, and these less able grammar school pupils will figure in it only to the extent that they do, in fact, stay on beyond the Ordinary level. Even

so, most of what we shall have to say about them is contained in the last chapter of this part. Chapters 21 to 26 are concerned entirely with the abler pupils who successfully surmount the hurdle of the Ordinary level and who go on to two or three years in the Sixth Form with their eyes on the university, or the college of advanced technology, on other higher education or on professional training of one sort or another. The Sixth Form, however, casts its shadow before and in Chapter 20 we must first look at what happens to these boys and girls immediately before they enter it. There follow four chapters, Chapters 21 to 24, which set out and discuss some of the salient characteristics of the Sixth Form as it exists today. Chapter 25 takes up the important question of the curriculum of the Sixth Form, on which, in one of its aspects, our terms of reference give us a special commission to report. Chapter 26 deals with the vexed issue of university entrance and its influence on the schools. Finally, Chapter 27 comes back to those Sixth Formers—relatively few today but, we hope, destined to grow in numbers—for whom the normal academic curriculum is not appropriate.

CHAPTER 20

The Approach to the Sixth Form

310. For very many years secondary schools were divided into two unequal sections by the School Certificate examination which was taken in the Fifth Form, and acted both as a leaving certificate for the great majority of those who took it and as a passport to the Sixth Form for the much smaller numbers who remained at school. When the General Certificate of Education replaced the old Higher School and School Certificate examinations in 1951, it was hoped that this division of the school would disappear. Those hopes have not been realised in the great majority of schools, and on the whole pupils still expect to be examined in a considerable number of subjects at Ordinary level at the end of their time in the Fifth Form. Only when this hurdle has been surmounted does a boy or girl pass into the Sixth Form and begin to "specialise" by devoting the greater part of his time to a few, kindred subjects. In most schools, then, the all important question for an able boy or girl is, "When can I take my 'O' levels?" On the answer to this depends the number of years available for Sixth Form study. The normal time to take Ordinary level papers is at the age of 16, that is to say at the end of five years in a grammar school, or three in a boys' independent school where the normal age of entry is 13. Since in grammar schools, whether maintained or direct grant, admission takes place only once a year in September, it is an advantage to be born in that part of the year which will secure admission to the Sixth Form when one is only just 16. This is not quite so important in the independent schools with their bye-term entries, inconvenient and disorganising though these are in other ways, but even so it has to be remembered that most schools plan their courses only with a view to the summer examinations, using the winter examination purely as a second chance for those who have failed one or more subjects in the summer.

EXPRESS ROUTES TO THE SIXTH FORM

311. It is not surprising, therefore, that efforts are made in many schools to enable the really able pupils to take the Ordinary level examinations at the age of 15 rather than 16. This can be done either by earlier transfer from the primary or preparatory school, or by telescoping a five-year course into four years (or, in an independent school, a three-year course into two years). In a few cases in indepen-

dent schools, the process is combined and exaggerated so that an able boy may take a large number of Ordinary level subjects at the end of his first year—that is at the age of about 14. This must nearly always have the effect of restricting a boy's choice of Sixth Form work to subjects which he studied at his preparatory school, which would rarely include science. There may be one or two boys for whom this is the right arrangement, but they must be very few—considerably fewer than the number of boys who take the Ordinary level at this age. We think this practice is, in general, harmful because we attach great importance to all boys having some experience of the full width of the curriculum before they choose the subjects in which they will specialise.

312. It is worth trying to find out how widespread is the use of these methods of saving time. Table 26 on the next page sets out the position as it was in 1958 as nearly as can be ascertained, though a half year separates the point at which age is reckoned in columns (*a*) and (*b*). Unfortunately it throws no light on the relative proportions of those who were transferred to secondary education at an earlier age than usual and of those who followed telescoped courses in their secondary schools. It will be seen that girls make a slighter use of "express routes" to the Sixth Form than boys—a contrast probably due to a difference in educational policy. Girls' schools on the whole attach more importance than boys' schools to a long main school course in order that reasonable time can be found throughout it for art, music and other non-academic subjects. The second point that stands out is that greater use is made of "express routes" by independent and direct grant schools than by maintained schools. It is probably true that there are a greater number of boys in these schools who are more advanced in knowledge at 13 or 14, when the decision about the length of the Ordinary level course has to be made. The reason, however, is not to be found in any differences of innate ability between boys in independent and maintained schools* but rather in differences of family background and earlier educational experience. It seems safe to assume that the parents of the great majority of pupils in independent schools recognised as efficient carried their own education beyond the minimum school-leaving age. In contrast, in the Social Survey enquiry, both parents of two-thirds of the pupils in grammar and technical schools had themselves left school at 14, and even if we limit the field to the boys and girls in these schools who followed a Sixth Form course—those who left school at 17 or 18—the proportion of the boys and girls whose fathers left school at 14 is still 63 per cent. It is not that the homes from which the grammar schools draw most of their pupils are bad

* See footnote to paragraph 304.

Table 26. G.C.E. Candidates Aged under 16 (England and Wales, 1958).

	Maintained Grammar School	Direct Grant School	Independent Efficient School	Total
Boys				
(*a*) Number aged 15 in January	49,391	7,490	13,784	70,665
(*b*) Number of G.C.E. Candidates under 16 (Summer)	8,257	2,315	5,911	16,483
(*c*) Line (*b*) as a percentage of Col. (*a*)	16·7	30·9	42·9	23·3
Girls				
(*d*) Number aged 15 in January	47,963	6,722	12,469	67,154
(*e*) Number of G.C.E. Candidates under 16 (Summer)	5,000	697	3,056	8,753
(*f*) Line (*e*) as a percentage of Col. (*d*)	10·4	10·4	24·5	13·0
Boys and Girls				
(*g*) Number aged 15 in January	97,354	14,212	26,253	137,819
(*h*) Number of G.C.E. Candidates under 16 (Summer)	13,257	3,012	8,967	25,236
(*i*) Line (*h*) as a percentage of Col. (*g*)	13·6	21·2	34·2	18·4

or careless homes—indeed they are often conspicuously the reverse—but inevitably they are often homes in which the books their children open in their later years at school have remained closed books to the parents. So far as the family is concerned, the greater part of the educational journey the children undertake must be unaccompanied. This adds greatly to the responsibility of the school and to the difficulties of the pupils. Their environment is often as unhelpful as their background. How many of them can see a play in a theatre, visit an art gallery, attend a concert? In how many of their homes are the more serious newspapers or periodicals taken? If these boys and girls are to be broadly educated, the school must undertake virtually the whole responsibility and do its best in conditions of time and space and staffing far less favourable than those which obtain in the independent schools. Free secondary education is not yet fifteen years old. It will be nearly as long again before the educational background of grammar school parents reflects this fact. In the meantime their pupils, though handicapped in these ways, must compete without any compensating allowance against boys and girls from more favoured homes and more favoured schools. Many of them nevertheless compete with success.

313. Maintained schools, then, are confronted with a problem to which there is no one right solution. On the one hand, they have a duty to give all their pupils a good general education. On the other hand, they have to equip their first-generation pupils to compete on as level terms as possible with boys and girls from a more favourable environment, and from the competitive point of view the obvious thing to do is to get as many of these bright pupils as possible into the Sixth Form as rapidly as possible so that they may have at least as long for specialisation at school as their more fortunate rivals have —for rivalry there must be while there are not enough of the most coveted university places to go round. If the present system puts too much pressure on the independent and direct grant schools (as we believe it does), it puts much more on the maintained grammar schools.

OPTIONS IN THE FOURTH AND FIFTH YEARS

314. It is important to be clear about what happens to boys and girls in the last years of their way to the Sixth Form. Some very important decisions are commonly made in the fourth and fifth years of the main school course—that is, at the ages of 14+ and 15+. It is then that routes begin to diverge through the choice of one or other "option". The most important of these options are whether or not to start a second modern language, and whether or not to take additional science. The timing of the options is shown in Table 27, which is based on 102 maintained and direct grant grammar schools inspected in 1956–57. The inspections were fairly evenly divided between boys' schools, girls' schools and co-educational schools, and together they

Table 27. Beginning of Options: 102 English Maintained and Direct Grant Grammar Schools.

Year of Course	Average age at beginning of year *	First year of— Full Science Option				Second Modern Language			
		B	Mixed	G	All	B	Mixed	G	All
5th or later	15	10	5	6	21	9	4	4	17
4th	14	18	22	25	65	6	8	12	26
3rd or earlier	13	5	10	1	16	13	13	11	37
No course available	—	—	—	—	—	5	12	5	22
Total No. of schools		33	37	32	102	33	37	32	102

* Some "express route" pupils would be one year younger.

represent 8 per cent of the total number of these schools in England. By the fourth year neither boys nor girls have become specialists; but, in practice, for four-fifths of them the decision whether they are to become science specialists or not has already been settled. Admission to the Science and Mathematics Sixth tends to be confined to those who have taken what is called a "full science option" in the middle years, usually in physics and chemistry as separate subjects at Ordinary level. Admission to a Sixth Form course in modern languages usually requires pupils to have taken two modern languages at Ordinary level. Only the English group of Sixth Form subjects makes no such special demands extending back into the main school, though in fact those who wish to go on to a university will find they need two languages by the time they attempt university entrance. The stage at which these options become available, and a choice has to be made between them, is most commonly at the beginning of the third year (age 13) for modern languages or the fourth year (age 14) for science (one year earlier for some of the pupils on an "express route"). Thus by the time he is 14 or 15, and sometimes earlier, a boy makes or has made for him a decision which strongly influences, if it does not determine, the sort of career he will be able to enter. It is true that the decision is not absolutely final; but still the assumption is that a boy will go on as he has begun. It should be noted that this early decision is enforced not necessarily because of any educational evidence that this is the right age for boys to make their choice, but in the belief that if they do not start early they will not be sufficiently prepared by 18 to meet university requirements.

315. Few first-generation grammar school boys have any firm intention of completing a Sixth Form course when they enter the school, let alone of entering a university. It is indeed the experience of most headmasters that a surprisingly high proportion even of able boys wait until they have seen their Ordinary level results before finally committing themselves to a Sixth Form course. This means that the main school curriculum is shaped to meet all eventualities in the hope—increasingly the justified hope—that boys will stay on at school and try to enter a university. Over a large field of studies no doubt these prudential considerations merely endorse the decision to include a subject which would in any event have appeared in every boy's time-table. It is doubtful, however, whether this applies to Latin. The reason why it is often taught to all the abler boys is not so much that the school considers Latin educationally right for the whole run of its pupils (though some schools would take this view), but because some knowledge of Latin is expected of candidates for admission to many universities on the Arts side, and—hitherto at least—of all candidates for admission to Oxford and Cambridge,

whatever their subject. And so Latin is often taken to Ordinary level as a precautionary measure by all able boys, whether at the time they are likely to go to a university or not, and even if they do not intend to enter the Sixth Form. The argument is that, if they do not take Latin (and if the quality of their work in their own fields later becomes so good that they have a hope of entering Oxford or Cambridge), they will have to devote a high proportion of their precious non-specialist time in the Sixth Form to elementary linguistic exercises which they have not the slightest intention of developing or employing for any other purpose than to satisfy university regulations. The high proportion of schools which either offer no second modern language, or only for a short course at the top of the school, may perhaps not be unassociated with the importance of Latin as a precaution. Secondary technical schools, having no Latin in the main school, are in particular difficulties; valuable time in the Sixth Form is unduly taken up with Ordinary level Latin. The possibility has arisen during the period of preparation of this report that Oxford and Cambridge Universities may be about to modify, or withdraw, their present requirement of Latin (or Greek) for matriculation. We welcome this willingness by the universities to re-examine their regulations, since we regard the present requirement as antiquated and serving little real purpose. However, we are not in complete agreement in our reasons for welcoming the initiative being taken in the universities, and we believe that it may be worth defining the point of difference that has arisen in our discussions; we believe it is less important than the extent of the agreement among us.

316. We are all agreed that "mastery of language" is one of the most important elements of a general education, and one where there is little ground for complacency about the effectiveness of present teaching methods. There is very widespread complaint, which we believe to be justified, about the average standards of competence in the use of language among the boys and girls who leave the schools. When we say "use of language", we mean primarily, of course, "use of their own language", which must always remain the chief objective of all language teaching. We all agree that the greatest efforts should be devoted to improving the standards attained. The abolition of compulsory Latin by itself would do nothing, and perhaps less than nothing, to achieve this. But the re-examination of the present requirements of Oxford and Cambridge provides an opportunity, which ought to be seized, for rethinking the whole basis of the teaching of linguistics in the schools. So far our view is unanimous. Most of us further believe that, in such a reorganisation of the teaching of linguistics, Latin should no longer enjoy a privileged place, enforced by compulsion from outside. The schools should be free to devise their own means of teaching mastery of language, and

if they think they can do so by revising the methods of teaching English, or by modern languages, they should be free to do so. The responsibility is theirs, and it is better that they should be free to choose the appropriate means in individual cases rather than have Latin—or, indeed, any particular number or combination of languages—forced on them by the universities as a general prescription for all. But a minority believe that the present examinations (and, to some extent, the present methods of teaching) in English and French do not offer satisfactory safeguards of linguistic teaching in the lower school, or satisfactory training in logical thought and the disciplined use of words. They believe that for the present Latin remains a valuable bulwark against facile and imprecise work and that, when there are so many external pressures on the schools for premature specialisation, some countervailing pressure from outside is necessary if the job is to be done properly. These members would therefore like to see the Latin requirement in university entrance retained, until such time as thought and experiment have clearly shown that there are other ways of "doing what Latin does".

317. There is another way in which educational routes begin to diverge long before the Ordinary level of the General Certificate of Education. This is a difference between boys and girls in the approach to mathematics and science. Elementary mathematics at Ordinary level is taken by more boys than any other subject except English language; by more than twice as many boys as take physics. It is safe to say that it is attempted by virtually every boy in a grammar school Fifth Form. The pass rate for boys in the three years 1956–1958 averaged 59·5 per cent which was 2·4 per cent above the average pass rate for all subjects combined. It is fairly safe to assume that the great majority of the boys who subsequently enter the Sixth Form secure their passes in elementary mathematics. Additional mathematics in these years was taken by 14·0 per cent of the boys who secured passes in elementary mathematics. The pass rate in additional mathematics was 71·7 per cent—higher than in almost any other subject. Among girls, on the other hand, it is not nearly so universal for mathematics to be taken at Ordinary level. Using the entries for English language as a basis for comparison, the proportion of boys taking elementary mathematics was 87 per cent and of girls 53 per cent for the period 1956–1958. Clearly mathematics is taken for examination only by the abler girls at this subject. The others do not give up the subject altogether, but in fact, a good many confine themselves to arithmetic. But in spite of this selected field, the pass rate was lower for girls than for boys by 2·3 per cent, and lower for girls in mathematics by 5·6 per cent than in all subjects combined. The number of girls taking additional mathematics is under 5·6 per cent of the number of boys.

318. The other major difference between boys and girls is in the time given to science and in the branches of science mainly taught. This is set out, as far as it is reflected in the external examinations at the end of the main school course, in Table 28.

Table 28. Average Annual Entries for Principal Science Subjects at Ordinary Level (G.C.E.) 1956–58 (England and Wales).

Subject	Boys	Girls
Physics	39,134	5,552
Chemistry	32,931	8,037
General Science and Additional General Science	1,740	691
Physics with Chemistry	9,393	5,271
General Science (1 paper)	14,735	8,895
Biology	15,354	40,298
	113,287	68,744

Physics and chemistry are the subjects most studied by boys; biology by girls. The time given to science in the main school by boys who hope to enter the Science Sixth is usually more than that given by girls, or by other boys, because they are expected to prepare for science examinations on a wider front. Passes in mathematics and in physics and chemistry as separate subjects (or in general and additional general science) are commonly asked for as a qualification for entry to the Science Sixth. On the other hand, it is as rare in girls' schools as it is common in boys' schools for such an exacting stipulation to be made about necessary qualifications for taking science in the Sixth Form. True, many girls are debarred from a full science course in the Sixth Form; but it is probably because they failed in or did not take mathematics at Ordinary level; or because they had done virtually no physics or chemistry in the main school.

OVERCROWDED TIMETABLES

319. The pressure to provide the options that look ahead to Sixth Form work, together with the parallel pressure to retain in the curriculum all those subjects in which a pass at Ordinary level may later turn out to be a necessary requirement for university entrance or for some professional qualification, inevitably leads to other things being crowded out. Table 29, which is based on the same sample of 102 schools as Table 27, shows that in the vast majority of maintained

grammar schools the practical subjects have become optional by the time at which our direct interest begins. This is true, too, of three-quarters of the schools as far as art is concerned; only music remains on the time-table for all in a majority of schools and that only in right of its secure hold on the girls' schools, where it often continues to the end. It is true that these subjects usually remain as options, but in most maintained schools few of the more academic pupils take them, or can find time to do so, in school hours. After these subjects have ceased to be compulsory, most schools make considerable efforts to provide some opportunities for art and the crafts by out-of-school activities through a school choir or orchestra, and by throwing open art and crafts rooms. But for some day schools and for many day boys the strongest will is defeated by travelling difficulties. At the best only a minority are catered for. The solution through voluntary activities can work fairly enough in a boarding school; it is no solution for the general run of pupils in day schools. A realistic appraisal of the situation must have regard not only to travelling difficulties but also to the other claims on boys' and girls' time. The Social Survey enquiry showed that over half the boys from maintained grammar and technical schools, and nearly half the Sixth Formers, had had paid jobs not in the holidays only but, for the most part, regularly every day. Less than a third of the girls had had paid employment while at school, and most of their jobs were only at the week-end, but there can be few who did not have some domestic duties at home. If we regard the development of some pride in workmanship and some aesthetic sensibility as an important part of general education, and one that is not finished by 13 or 14, we clearly cannot be content to leave it in day schools to after-school voluntary societies. Nor, if it finds a place in the time-table should the menu be *table d'hôte*. Some pupils enjoy verse, or even poetry; some hate water-colours, and some are tone-deaf.

320. The other part of the price paid for planning the curriculum from early days with an eye on university or professional requirements is less obvious, though no less heavy. It lies in the field where family background and environment count for most. The "English subjects" tend to go to the wall. After the third year, history and geography commonly become alternatives, and one or other, occasionally both, are given up. Our sample of inspection reports shows that, in 42 per cent. of the schools, history ceased to be compulsory and became an option by the fourth year (that is to say by about the age of 14), though in the girls' schools the proportion was only 31 per cent. It is curious that a subject which requires and can develop maturity of judgement should disappear so early from the curriculum of so many of the abler boys. The same comment might be made

Table 29. Last year in which Practical and Aesthetic Subjects are compulsory (102 English Maintained and Direct Grant Grammar Schools).

Year of Course	Average Age at end of year	Art				Music			
		B	Mixed	G	All	B	Mixed	G	All
5th or later	16+	3	4	—	7	8	6	24	38
4th	15	5	6	8	19	4	6	4	14
3rd	14	7	16	22	45	8	16	4	28
2nd or earlier	13—	18	11	2	31	13	8	—	21
None provided		—	—	—	—	—	—	—	—
Not clear		—	—	—	—	—	1	—	1
No. of schools		33	37	32	102	33	37	32	102

Year of Course	Average Age at end of year	Handicraft			Domestic Subjects		
		B	Mixed	All	Mixed	G	All
5th or later	16+	—	1	1	2	—	2
4th	15	2	7	9	7	1	8
3rd	14	5	15	20	14	19	33
2nd or earlier	13—	20	14	34	14	12	26
None provided		6	—	6	—	—	—
Not clear		—	—	—	—	—	—
No. of schools		33	37	70	37	32	69

about religious instruction, which is normally at this stage limited to one period a week, frequently unaccompanied by homework. The time given to English itself may be reduced, and is commonly fixed by what is considered necessary to reach a tolerable standard in the English language paper of the General Certificate of Education and to prepare the books prescribed for the English literature paper. Wider reading and original writing beyond the forms of composition externally examined have to depend on exhortation and personal encouragement. It is almost certain that more time than is given is required if boys are to be led on to the enthusiastic devouring of all the books of a favourite author, not only the one selected by an examiner, and to the sampling of a wide range of writers and writing by which individual taste is formed. This is not, of course, a problem which is confined to first-generation grammar school boys—the difference between the home in which books are read and that in which they are not is familiar to every teacher in every sort of school. As their first-generation pupils become the parents of second-generation pupils the grammar schools may justifiably look for a marked improvement in many directions; whether, as things stand, they can expect it in this crucial field of literacy in the widest sense is more doubtful.

321. How much can one get into a 35-period week? The head of a department is apt to regard his headmaster as a modern Procrustes; the head for his part may try all sorts of devices to avoid becoming the executioner of worthy subjects. Neither can avoid the implications of this question, though many methods are tried. Some schools shorten the length of periods and thus increase their number; but, do what he will, a headmaster cannot find more than about 1,400 minutes a week available for lessons. What criterion should guide his planning? Should he regard his middle school pupils primarily as potential Sixth Form specialists (in which case he will, for example, step up the time given to science by future science specialists)? Or should he give 14 year-olds what in his view they ought to have when they are 14, and hang the consequences? It is too much to hope that by some Benthamite magic the two prescriptions might turn out to be identical. There is a real element of conflict.

KEEPING THE DOORS OPEN

322. It should be noticed that the pressures that lead to this overcrowding of the Fifth Form time-table come from outside the Fifth Form itself. Some arise from the habit of finishing off with a pass in the G.C.E. all the subjects that the pupil will not be continuing in the Sixth Form—and of dealing in this way with as many subjects as any university or professional body can possibly require. Others arise from the desire to start the job of the Sixth Form in the Fifth and to ask for more periods for this purpose—or at least to meet the high entrance requirements of the Sixth Form. And that is caused by the very heavy pressure to which the Sixth Form, in its turn, is subjected by the competition that its pupils will face at 18. There can, then, be no really satisfactory solution to the problems of the Fifth Form until this external pressure is removed, until the schools are free to teach boys and girls of 15 what they think boys and girls of 15 need and not what is imposed on them, directly or indirectly, by other bodies' prescriptions and requirements. It would not, therefore, be fair in our view to blame the schools for the volume of "pre-specialisation" that is to be observed. That does not mean,

of course, that anybody should be complacent about the effects of this "pre-specialisation". In our opinion they are, on balance, bad, not only because 15 is too early for the majority even of able children to say a final farewell to education on a broad front, but mainly because the existence of "options" in these early years inevitably closes doors and freezes into permanent choices what may be no more than passing inclinations.

323. The main dividing "options", as we have seen, are the choice of a second foreign language and the choice of additional science. They need to be examined separately, not only because the major language option tends to be introduced a year earlier, but also because it raises different problems. We are agreed that the linguistic discipline implicit in the elementary as well as in the later stages of learning any foreign language is a valuable educational instrument, and has at least a reinforcing influence on acquiring a precise mastery of the mother tongue. But the elementary stages of two foreign languages do not double the intellectual value of one. Moreover, while the later stages of learning a foreign language should have a rich cultural influence, the early stages have relatively little to offer in this respect. From the standpoint of the first-generation grammar school pupil, and from the standpoint of the Fifth Form leaver, it would seem important to carry one language as quickly as possible to the stage where it provides a cultural as well as a linguistic education. We have already noted that a high proportion of schools do not in fact introduce a second modern language until a late stage. They may well be rightly advised in their circumstances. Does this mean, however, that their pupils are cut off from reading modern languages at a university? This may well be so as things now stand, but we do not think it ought to be. To insist that all boys and girls who may later want to be language specialists shall in the main school study three foreign languages (Latin and two modern languages) involves such a heavy allocation of time as to close the door to many other possibilities.

324. The main science option most frequently follows a year after the modern language option. As things stand in most schools, able boys must virtually choose by the beginning of the fourth year, when they are 14, whether they are to be arts or science specialists in the Sixth Form and thereafter. The need for making the decision at that time turns frequently enough on the difference between six and eight science periods a week for two years, that is, on whether they follow the option designed to lead on to the Science Sixth or not. It is a little absurd to ask boys aged 14 to make a decision of lifelong importance for the sake of two periods a week. It is reasonable to ask whether a revision of syllabuses, especially perhaps in chemistry, could not be devised which would enable all pupils to follow a basic course

covering sufficient ground to make Sixth Form work possible. This need not prevent the ablest pupils in science travelling faster than the majority, though on the same time allocation, provided they were separately taught.

EXPRESS ROUTES AND ABILITY SETTING

325. Our purpose in this discussion of fourth and fifth year work in languages and science has been to prevent the closing of any doors until a boy is in the Sixth Form. If, by this and other means, some of the pressure could be taken off the time-table, it would be possible to continue throughout the main school to give all pupils the opportunity to carry on those practical and aesthetic subjects which they now so generally drop, and to retain a more generous allocation of time for English subjects. Most 15 year-olds need plenty of time in school and the best teaching in order to become really literate in their own tongue: not just enough to pass easy examinations, but sufficient to give them a lively pleasure in reading, speaking and writing. They need to be introduced to the arts and given opportunity to practise them. These are not flowers, but roots of education. Fifteen year-olds need all these things, but they get a time-table designed to give them, if possible, seven or eight Ordinary level passes, and especially those which may help them to get to a university two years later. What the value is by 18 of an Ordinary level pass in a subject which has not been kept up after 16 is a question which needs asking. We are certain that the effect on the schools is to produce a congestion of the main school curriculum in the fourth and fifth years, which is detrimental to the real interests of most of their pupils, however attractive it may be from a superficial point of view to clear out of the way before the Sixth Form certain subjects which the university demands. What a particular 15 year-old boy or girl should do with his time, apart from his main line of interest, seems to us to be properly a matter for the school's clinical judgement and not for outside regulation.

326. The major solution lies, therefore, outside the schools' own powers. But meanwhile there are some things they can do to help the able pupil in his race against time to get to the university, without involving him in the evils of "pre-specialisation". We have already mentioned the practice of "express routes", by which the able boy (or, more rarely, the able girl) takes the Ordinary level at 15 and passes into the Sixth Form. This seems to us a reasonable practice, and one that could be extended to more pupils, provided that their main school curriculum was handled in the way that we have been discussing, and that really serious attention was devoted in the Sixth Form to the non-specialist part of the work. Where these conditions do not apply—and that is in far too many schools today—we agree

with the girls' schools, which in general have shown themselves reluctant to permit any curtailment of the main school course. Whether acceleration, where justified, is better made in the primary or the secondary school is a decision which falls outside the scope of our present terms of reference. There is another aspect of the case which properly belongs to a later chapter, but which may be noticed here in passing. It may often be a good thing for an individual boy to start specialising at 15, but it is a bad thing if the pressure for university entrance forces nearly all boys to follow suit.

327. Although pre-specialisation by the choice of door-closing options in the Fifth Form is to be avoided, there is another form of division which has more to be said for it. This is the kind of "setting" that is based not on a choice between subjects, but on the variation of ability in one subject. The ability to learn a foreign language varies a good deal from pupil to pupil, and often not in accordance with general ability. It is common, therefore, to re-divide all the forms in a year into ability "sets" for French. It is almost universal to do this for mathematics. Ability setting enables speed on a narrow front to be combined with steady progress on a wide one. In a three-form entry school, for example, the third of the boys who are best at mathematics will probably have been taught together for four or five consecutive years irrespective of their attainments in other subjects. No more time, however, is given by these boys to mathematics than by other boys in the same year. It is simply that they move faster because they have the ability to do so, and are given the separate teaching to enable them to do so.

328. "Ability setting" certainly works well both for able and for poor mathematicians, and the possibility of extending it to other branches of study is surely worth investigation. In its effect on syllabus and teaching it runs parallel with the method of "by-passing" Ordinary level in strong subjects which has been much advocated, but relatively little practised. It has the practical advantage that it offers something to those who are not sure whether they are going to enter a Sixth Form or not, and who, if they "by-passed" Ordinary level, would leave school with nothing to show for their strongest subject, should they leave from the Fifth Form. In the one case of mathematics, something extra is available in the form of a pass in additional mathematics as well as mathematics. This is sharply to be distinguished in its educational effects from the old credit or distinction in the School Certificate, because it provides an additional pass for work on additional subject matter, not a higher pass for more marks on the same subject matter. Of course, if all, or most, subjects were "setted", the form would disappear as a unit. Most people with day school experience would regard this with great anxiety. The form is

almost the only natural and permanent grouping to which a day school pupil belongs. To destroy it without replacement would be to atomise school life; and nobody has yet found a satisfactory replacement, although some of the experiments with continuing "tutor groups" have been encouraging. The problem, therefore, is to discover how much of the week must be spent in one's form, as opposed to sets, if the corporate life of the school is not to be destroyed. Subject to this very important proviso, we have no doubt about the educational value of "setting" in a good many subjects.

SUMMARY

329. We would summarise our conclusions about the education given to the ablest boys and girls in the years immediately before their entry to the Sixth Form in this way:

(*a*) The structure of English maintained schools is still such as to make a sharp distinction between the main school and the Sixth Form.

(*b*) The maintained grammar schools play the largest part in the education of those who remain at school until 17 or 18. Nearly two-thirds of all boys and girls at school at 17 are in maintained schools.

(*c*) In planning the curriculum it is important to consider the background from which the maintained grammar school pupils come: two-thirds of them come from families where both parents left school at 14 or before.

(*d*) The time-table of the fourth and fifth years of the grammar school course is seriously congested; and yet in most schools the practical and aesthetic subjects have ceased to be really available for the abler pupils, and the time given to English subjects has been curtailed. This is an especially serious deprivation for "first-generation grammar school" pupils.

(*e*) This congestion is caused by the increasing demands made upon the middle school time-table by those subjects in which a pupil is going to specialise in the Sixth Form. This downward pressure is more marked in boys' schools than in girls'.

(*f*) It results in a situation in which four-fifths of the boys have virtually chosen their Sixth Form course, if any, by the age of 13 or 14. We recommend that such revision of syllabuses and practice should be made as would prevent any doors being closed before a pupil enters the Sixth Form. In particular, we do not think that, save in the most exceptional circumstances, boys should be allowed to take the Ordinary level at 14.

(*g*) An effort to keep all doors open would involve particularly an examination of the position of foreign languages and science. We think that Latin and two modern foreign languages is too heavily biassed a curriculum for many "first-generation grammar school" pupils, and for those who are going to leave school at 16. We attach the greatest importance to a thorough and exacting linguistic discipline, but we do not think that this is properly or efficiently secured by the indirect pressure of those universities which are in a specially strong competitive position.

(*h*) We believe that a six-period science course could be devised which would enable every Fifth Former who had followed it successfully to undertake a normal Sixth Form course. "Setting" would enable the most promising pupils to be better prepared without giving up more time to science.

(*i*) The revision of present practice in middle school foreign language and science teaching should be carried to a point where it becomes possible to restore to pupils the opportunities for aesthetic subjects which they lose at present, and to give them more time for English studies.

(*j*) Though we condemn "pre-specialisation", we endorse the desire of schools to find ways of enabling their very ablest pupils to move faster than the general pace. We see no objection to measures designed to enable them to enter the Sixth Form at 15 instead of 16, provided that the reform of the middle school curriculum on the lines suggested above is carried out, and that far more serious attention is paid to non-specialist studies in the Sixth Form than is now the case.

(*k*) We also welcome ways by which particular ability in one direction can be encouraged, and draw attention to the practice of "setting" for mathematics with the possibility of carrying the work of the top set much further and rewarding it by a pass in additional mathematics. If this system were at all widely extended, however, it would be necessary to see that the schools did not suffer from a decay of the form system.

CHAPTER 21

The Marks of a Sixth Form

330. The Sixth Form is so important an element in our educational system that it demands thorough treatment in any discussion of education between 15 and 18. This introductory chapter deliberately attempts to sketch the Sixth Form at its best. All Sixth Form teachers, we believe, will accept the picture we have drawn as describing what they aim at; none will feel that his own form quite achieves all he desires. There never was a time, in fact, when all Sixth Forms were like this; today, as yesterday, there are some that are nearly as good.

331. Historically, the Sixth Form in the independent public schools and the old grammar schools was the stage which was actively concerned with preparation for a university. Masters and boys alike assumed that to go to a university was the natural sequel to the two or three years spent in the Sixth Form, and believed that it was important during these years to develop ways of setting about work which would be appropriate in a university. Until comparatively recent years admission to the university of one's choice was not, for most, the reward of success in a fiercely competitive struggle, as it is today. It required hard work, it required a reasonable standard; but, given these, the doors were open to all who could find the fees. This limitation cut out all but a relatively small number of pupils from the new secondary schools—and for those who needed to win a scholarship the struggle was often as competitive as it is today. But this method of selection had certain educational advantages as a by-product. It made unnecessary the competitive cramming of average pupils which mars a good deal of Sixth Form work today. In any good Sixth Form there was always, of course, a strongly competitive element—the open scholarships at Oxford and Cambridge were always difficult to win, so difficult to win that it was only the ablest pupils who thought of striving for them. For these ablest boys, it was thought that the stimulus of competition was of value; for the majority, the knowledge that there was a place waiting for them if they worked steadily and hard was thought to be the right encouragement to intellectual growth. There was room for both in the Sixth Form. Such was the theory and the practice, and in our judgement they were right. How far either theory or practice survives today will be examined in a later chapter.

332. This close link with the university is, in our opinion, one of the essential marks of a Sixth Form. But it is still true that the Sixth Form has to concern itself with a proportion of boys and girls who will not wish to go to a University or any place of higher education. It always has, and it still can. The education it gives is good in its own right, and not only as a preparation for the next stage: it is—for reasons which will be apparent from the other marks of a Sixth Form—a better last stage in education than that given in the Fifth Forms from which the majority of grammar school boys and girls still leave. The problem of the Sixth Form seems to be essentially one of proportion—how much of a Sixth Form can, without destroying its essential character, be made up of boys or girls who who will end their full-time education when they leave school?

333. If "subject-mindedness", a special devotion to a particular branch of study, is a vice of teachers—at least it is often denounced as if it were a vice—it is a virtue among pupils. It is the spring from which the disinterested pursuit of knowledge wells. It is also one mark of the good and keen Sixth Former. He has looked forward to being a science specialist, or a classic, or a historian: his mind has been set that way by inclination and by the main school mechanisms discussed in the last chapter. Now he has his opportunity. Whatever hinders specialisation is to him, at first, a waste of time. On the whole, the better his intellectual quality, the more "subject-minded" a boy is likely to be, at any rate at the beginning of his Sixth Form career. To admit this is not, of course, to deny the importance of his other studies; but the intellectual strength of the Sixth Form seems to us to be bound up with the provision it makes for a boy to develop his growing interest in a subject, and to carry it to such a depth that he encounters, and learns to overcome, the difficulties which give meaning to the old phrase "an intellectual discipline". He comes to see that difficulty is inherent in something he wants to do, not an irksome and unpleasant medicine administered by authority for his imagined good. We shall return to this whole question in a later chapter. Meanwhile it will be sufficient to recognise that specialisation is a mark of the Sixth Form, and "subject-mindedness" of the Sixth Former.

334. The third mark of the Sixth Form is independent work. It is bound up with the second mark of specialisation, without which it is hardly possible. Of course, all through their years in the main school pupils will have been accustomed to homework, and they may have been given occasional periods for private study in school. Taken together, the amount of time thus spent will have been considerable—at least the equivalent of another school day each week—but its

dispersion among a large number of subjects, its close relation to a recent or forthcoming lesson, and its detailed planning and supervision by the teachers for whom it is done, make it a different experience from that which awaits the new Sixth Former, though an indispensable preparation for it. Independent work by a pupil, as we understand it, implies a considerable amount of responsibility for the organisation of his time, and a considerable amount of time to devote to a subject, time enough anyhow to make his own discoveries, meet his own difficulties and overcome them by himself. Library and laboratory provide the setting for work which, however different in subject, is similar in the demands it makes. It is the time factor that links independent work with specialisation. It is impossible in any worthy sense without specialisation; but, of course, specialisation does not guarantee independent work. The teacher can, if he chooses, monopolise the extra time which is now available for his subject. That is why we have distinguished independent work as the third mark of Sixth Form work, separate from specialisation.

335. The fourth mark is the intimate relation between pupil and teacher which is characteristic of a good Sixth Form. There is no commonly accepted phrase to describe the situation—perhaps "intellectual discipleship" comes as near the mark as any. The position is worth analysis. It is in the Sixth Form that an intellectual life shared between pupil and teacher first becomes a possibility. The boy has time enough to devote to his subject to enable him to catch sight of some of the frontiers on which knowledge is expanding, or new literary work is being done. If he is to be taught well, he must be taught by somebody who is at home with this new work. By contrast, the Fourth Former has to learn what his teacher learned in the Fourth Form; it is hardly possible, perhaps, in some subjects to teach him anything else. The intellectual interest for the teacher must be in method rather than content. For the Sixth Form master it lies quite as much in content: there is no dichotomy between his personal intellectual life and his professional. The Sixth Former cannot but respond to the new because it is new, and no Sixth Form master who does not share this enthusiasm is likely to succeed. But the Sixth Former also responds to the best of the old as warmly as if it were still new, because it is new to him. The Sixth Form master must, therefore, if he is to succeed, practice and retain a balanced taste. He must find Shakespeare as exciting a writer as his pupils do. One factor in making this intellectual discipleship possible is specialisation, in other words the "subject-mindedness" of both teacher and pupil. Another factor is independent work. To do a great deal on one's own, to bring one's finished labours for criticism, to put up one's own ideas or observations for scrutiny and suggestion, is to

introduce a partnership both with one's contemporaries and one's teachers, and to give a voluntary colour to the compulsory relationship of the classroom. Of course, this relationship depends on the daily or frequent contact between a teacher and a small group of pupils over several years, a relation closer than that which exists in many a university. This makes it possible to deal frankly and without constraint with those ethical and metaphysical problems which confront boys and girls in their teens, and which were touched on in Chapter 11. What has for so many to be undertaken before their minds are really capable of dealing with the issues involved, can be tackled with much greater chance of success in the Sixth Form.

336. There is a fifth mark of the Sixth Form, or rather of the Sixth Former, which ought not to be passed over—social responsibility. Unlike the other four, it is not a characteristic of his work, but of the part he plays in the life of the school. Two things make it possible. The first is the mere fact of age, and the maturity which comes with it. The second is the thoughtfulness which comes from the intellectual life developed by Sixth Form work, provided that a conscious effort is made by the staff to direct this thoughtfulness to social ends. To develop a sense of responsibility for others, and to learn how to apply it sensibly and fruitfully, are important lessons, though they take place outside the classroom. It is right to regard them as a mark of the Sixth Form, because there is a close association between intellectual growth and the understanding of others which a wise Sixth Former shows.

337. A close link with the university, specialisation, independent work, intellectual discipleship and social responsibility are, then, the five marks which distinguish the Sixth Form. The sketch of the ways in which they operate given in the previous paragraphs is admittedly idealised. Yet they are found in many schools. Some, or all, of course, are absent in other schools. Which way is the tide running? Is a Sixth Form in this sense to be regarded as a luxury of the past, as a privilege which cannot extend beyond the leading schools, something which cannot of its nature be generalised? Or can we hope that the growing number and proportion of boys and girls who remain at school between 16 and 18 may receive a Sixth Form education in which all five marks are found?

CHAPTER 22

The Sixth Formers

338. One of the most striking and important features of English education since the war, and especially of the last six or seven years, has been the growth of Sixth Forms. The number of Sixth Formers is now considerably more than half as large again as it was ten years ago. We doubt very much whether the general public realises what a revolution is in progress—and still more in prospect.

THE GROWTH OF THE SIXTH FORM

339. The facts are given in Table 30. Pupils aged 17 in school will in the main be in the Sixth Form; they may certainly be used to measure changes in the size of the Sixth Form.

Table 30. Numbers of Pupils Aged 17 in All Types of School (England and Wales).*

	Boys		Girls		Boys and Girls	
	Number (thousands)	Percentage Increase over 1947	Number (thousands)	Percentage Increase over 1947	Number (thousands)	Percentage Increase over 1947
1947	18·0	—	14·0	—	32·0	—
1955	24·9	*38*	19·9	*42*	45·0	*41*
1956	26·8	*49*	22·1	*58*	49·0	*53*
1957	28·8	*60*	22·5	*61*	51·3	*60*
1958	30·2	*68*	23·0	*64*	53·2	*66*

* Excludes independent schools not recognised as efficient. These schools, for which no figures are available before 1958, contained in that year 451 boys and 651 girls of 17. Owing to the rounding off of figures, totals do not always appear to be accurate.

What is perhaps less well known is the different experience of different types of school, which is set out in Table 31 on the opposite page. In each section there were fewer Sixth Form girls than boys in each year throughout the period. In the earlier years the rate of growth of girls' Sixth Forms was greater than that of boys'. In the last two years, however, this trend has been reversed, partly because of an actual decline in the number of 17 year-olds in girls' independent schools, and partly because of a sudden great increase among boys in maintained schools.

Table 31. Relative Increase of Numbers of Pupils Aged 17 in Three Different Types of School (England and Wales).

	Maintained Grammar			Direct Grant			Independent Recognised Efficient	
	Boys	Girls	Boys and Girls	Boys	Girls	Boys and Girls	Boys	Girls
Number (Thousands) 1947	10·8	9·8	20·6	1·8	1·5	3·3	5·1	2·4
Percentage Increase over 1947								
1955	*32*	*36*	*34*	*52*	*57*	*54*	*44*	*45*
1956	*41*	*48*	*44*	*60*	*73*	*66*	*53*	*57*
1957	*53*	*52*	*52*	*66*	*79*	*72*	*54*	*54*

NOTES: (1) For reasons explained in Paragraph 341 it is misleading to aggregate the figures for boys' and girls' independent schools.
(2) figures cannot be given for 1958 owing to changes in classification of individual schools.

340. Another way of looking at the position is to compare the proportion of pupils staying on into the Sixth Form from the main school. Table 32 shows this.

Table 32. Pupils Aged 17 as a Proportion of Pupils in the Same Schools Aged 14 Three Years Earlier (England and Wales).

		Maintained Grammar		Direct Grant		Independent Recognised Efficient		The 3 types of School	
Age 14 in	Age 17 in	Boys %	Girls %	Boys %	Girls %	Boys %	Girls %	Boys %	Girls %
1947	1950	*26·5*	*24·6*	*38·8*	*34·0*	*58·6*	*36·1*	*32·8*	*27·0*
1952	1955	*29·4*	*27·6*	*44·6*	*38·4*	*55·4*	*31·2*	*36·0*	*29·1*
1953	1956	*31·2*	*30·5*	*46·3*	*40·1*	*57·0*	*31·2*	*37·8*	*31·6*
1954	1957	*33·9*	*30·1*	*48·8*	*42·0*	*58·3*	*30·6*	*40·1*	*31·3*

Perhaps the most striking feature of this table is the increasing success of the maintained and direct grant schools in retaining their pupils, which is bringing them nearer to the position of the boys' independent schools. There is no reason to suppose that the average level of intelligence in independent schools is any higher than that of the direct grant and maintained schools, with their competitive selection. It follows that there is still considerable scope for increases in the latter schools in the proportion of 15 year-olds staying on into the Sixth Form, even if the present proportion in the boys' independent schools be regarded as a satisfactory final target, which it should not be.

341. The low proportion of girls in independent schools who stay on after 16 requires explanation. Girls' independent schools are a much less homogeneous group than the boys' independent schools; almost the only common factor among the girls' schools is the fact that they have been inspected and recognised as efficient secondary schools by the Ministry. If those girls' schools which have roughly the same character as the boys' schools could be classified separately, the Sixth Form picture would almost certainly be more encouraging than it appears from the girls' independent schools as a whole, though the absolute numbers would be small. Interpretation of the figures is hazardous in the absence of detailed information, but it may be that the total of Sixth Formers in the girls' schools is further depleted by the numbers who transfer from the smaller independent schools to the Sixth Forms of grammar schools. Transfers of this kind undoubtedly occur, but we have no evidence about their volume. It is possible that the increasing difficulty girls find in securing admission to the universities—at least to Oxford, Cambridge and London—may have deterred some girls in independent schools from undertaking a course in the Sixth Form. Some, at least, are known to prefer coaching establishments because they believe this will give them a better chance of admission. It may also be that the necessity or desirability of acquiring a professional qualification is economically less apparent to girls whose parents afford the necessarily heavy fees in independent schools, and therefore that the vocational pressure towards a Sixth Form course may be less strong than in the direct grant and maintained schools. Certainly it is from the independent schools that the "finishing schools" draw their pupils, while a good many go abroad.

Table 33. Pupils Aged 17 in all schools as a Percentage of All 17 Year-olds (England and Wales).

	Boys	Girls	Boys and Girls
1947	*6·2*	*4·8*	*5·5*
1955	*8·6*	*7·0*	*7·9*
1956	*9·2*	*7·8*	*8·5*
1957	*10·0*	*8·0*	*9·0*
1958	*11·1*	*8·8*	*10·0*

342. A third aspect of the situation is given in Table 33 which sets out the size of the Sixth Form in relation to all 17 year-olds. This increase represents beyond doubt a very substantial achievement. But it is equally clear that the proportion is still much lower than is either desirable or possible.

343. One other point may properly be made. The great expansion that has taken place has been on the relatively small and fixed base of those already in selective schools. The proportion of boys and girls aged 14 who were pupils in independent, direct grant or maintained grammar schools was 21 per cent in 1947; in 1958 it was 23·5 per cent. The growth of the Sixth Form represents in the main a turnover in the selective schools from leaving at 16 to leaving at 18, a move from the Ordinary to the Advanced level of the General Certificate of Education as a school-leaving target. Among the new Sixth Formers, as we saw in paragraph 111, there are a few, but only a very few, who completed the first stage of their secondary education to the Ordinary level standard in modern schools and then transferred to a grammar school Sixth Form. But, although this group is statistically insignificant, it derives importance from the fact that it foreshadows what may be expected when a much larger proportion of boys and girls of secondary school age are in schools where there is a possibility of their taking the General Certificate of Education at Ordinary level. We have already made it clear that in our view no pupil who has the ability to do this should be denied the opportunity, whatever mechanism may be used to give him his chance. An illustration may be helpful. In the south of England there is a co-educational grammar school which each year admits at 11 about 17 per cent of the boys and girls from the primary schools in its large district—a little below the average proportion for the country as a whole. In three years it admitted direct to the Sixth Form 20 boys and girls who had failed to secure a place at 11, but had been able to take some subjects in G.C.E. at Ordinary level in their modern schools; 11 of the 20 were still at school when the information was given to the Council. Of the 9 who had left, 3 had secured county major scholarships to a university, 1 a state scholarship (this last boy had also won an open exhibition in mathematics to Cambridge), 3 had gone to teachers' training colleges, 1 had taken up nursing and 1 had been commissioned in the R.A.F. If this process grows, as it ought to do, it is clearly important that the work of Sixth Forms should be so arranged as to make transfers of this kind easy. In some areas the custom has grown up of transferring pupils from modern schools at 15. This has the advantage over the more common system of transfers at 13 of allowing for later development, and of preserving the unity of the modern school; but it necessitates special arrangements in the receiving grammar school and usually delays the

transferred pupil by one year on his route to Ordinary level which he may not be able to take until he is 17.

344. The boys and girls who are entering Sixth Forms today, but who would not have done so a few years ago, are drawn to a very large extent from the children of manual workers, and especially of skilled manual workers. In a previous report, the Council showed that nearly half the Sixth Form boys and girls in direct grant and maintained grammar schools were the children of manual workers. Three more recent enquiries give broadly similar results. The results are set out below in Table 34.

Table 34. Occupations of the Fathers of Sixth Form Pupils in Direct Grant and Maintained Grammar Schools (Percentages).

	Profess-ional and managerial	Clerical and other non-manual	Skilled Manual	Semi-skilled Manual	Un-skilled Manual	Number 100%
(1) C.A.C. Report "Early Leaving" (D.G. and Maintained Grammar Schools)	*43·7*	*12·0*	*37·0*	*5·8*	*1·5*	2,082
(2) Social Survey (Maintained Grammar and Technical Schools)	*33·4*	*24·8*	*36·0*	*5·8* (Semi-skilled and Unskilled combined)		484
(3) National Service Enquiry (D.G. and Maintained Grammar Schools) (Boys only)	*38·6*	*20·4*	*33·9*	*5·0*	*2·1*	579
(4) Yorkshire Grammar Schools enquiry (percentage)	*28·6*	*14·6*	*37·0*	*13·6*	*6·2*	1,194

NOTE: (2) and (3) are pupils aged 17 and over on leaving school, (1) and (4) are boys and girls known to be in Sixth Forms.

THE FUTURE PROSPECT

345. Thus far we have been on the firm ground of what has actually taken place. Will the expansion continue? There are factors working in both directions, though there is little doubt to which side the balance tilts. One certain fact is that the age-group reaching 16 will be bigger, and for three years very much bigger, than any we have had to educate for many years past. It seems reasonably clear that in spite of expansion both in the independent and maintained schools there will be more competition than there is now to secure places in schools providing a grammar school type of education. Those who do in fact secure places are, therefore, likely to contain a higher proportion of boys and girls who will want to stay on into the Sixth Form. This tendency will be strengthened by the fact that each year now brings a larger proportion of children into the grammar schools whose parents also had grammar school education. The full benefit of free secondary education will not be apparent until the 1970's, but the proportion of free places was rising for a good many years

before 1944, and we are already getting some of its advantages. The Social Survey enquiry showed that only 11 per cent of the fathers who had themselves stayed at school longer than the compulsory minimum period allowed their children to leave at 15; no less than 40 per cent of them insisted that their children stayed at school to 18. We should, therefore, expect to see a marked increase in the percentages given in Table 32 which compares the main school with the Sixth Form in the same schools. But there is one factor on the other side. It seems all too likely that the proportion of each age group getting into the selective schools in the "bulge" years will fall, and this could hardly fail to mean that the proportions of the whole age group who enter the Sixth Form would, at best, remain steady and might even drop—there may be no corresponding improvement in Table 33 to match Table 32. Whether this happens or not must depend on the rate of growth in the provision of G.C.E. courses in non-selective schools of all types. If this grows at a pace to keep up with the increased difficulty of getting into a selective school, the size of the Sixth Form as a percentage of the whole age-group may

Table 35. Relative Size of Sixth Form Population in different Years (1958=100) on two Assumptions. (England and Wales).

Year	Actual Size of Sixth Form	Year	Conjectural Size of Sixth Form Assumption A	Assumption B
1948	*69*	1958	*100*	*100*
1949	*67*	1959	*98*	*105*
1950	*65*	1960	*110*	*127*
1951	*62*	1961	*116*	*142*
1952	*66*	1962	*127*	*166*
1953	*73*	1963	*115*	*158*
1954	*77*	1964	*141*	*205*
1955	*81*	1965	*152*	*233*
1956	*88*	1966	*134*	*215*
1957	*94*	1967	*127*	*213*
1958	*100*	1968	*121*	*213*

NOTE: Assumption A is that the proportion of the 17 year-old age-group that is to be found in maintained schools is the same as now, and that the increase is solely caused by the high birth rate. Assumption B is that the proportion continues to rise by 0·5 per cent per annum, which is approximately the average rate of increase of the past decade.

continue to rise, since in comprehensive schools there is nothing to stop anybody entering the Sixth Form and there ought to be no difficulty in transferring at 16 from a modern school to a grammar school. But whatever happens to the proportion, this does not, of course, affect the fact that the total numbers of boys and girls in Sixth Forms will continue to rise. The only doubt in our minds is whether the rate of growth in the future will be best described as rapid or very rapid. We must expect that the Sixth Forms of 1964 and the following five years will be one-and-a-half times to twice as large as they were in 1958, when they were already well over half as large again as in 1948. What we may expect and what we have experienced is shown in detail in Table 35 on the previous page. It is both a sobering and a stimulating prospect.

346. The next ten years, therefore, seem more likely to see an acceleration of the growth of Sixth Forms than any falling off. If so, there will be a change in the shape of the grammar school. In the past, most pupils in grammar schools have had experience only of the main school, leaving from the Fifth Form at 16. Unless the proportion of grammar school places available at 11 is greatly increased, we must before long expect to approach a situation where it will be the exception rather than the rule for a boy or a girl to leave a grammar school at 16.

CHAPTER 23

The Staff of the Sixth Form

347. It is the staff that makes the Sixth Form. The secret of the intellectual excitement that characterises a good Sixth Form lies in the encounter that takes place there, in the right place and at the right time, between an awakening mind and a mature mind. Staff ratios are important, and we shall examine these a little later, but quality is even more important. The ideal Sixth Form master is a man who combines in equal measure a love of his own field of knowledge with a love for the growing minds of his pupils. Intellectually, he can hold his own with a university teacher except in the latter's speciality. It may not be lack of opportunity but a difference in ambition that has placed him in another but kindred career. He is happier as a schoolmaster because he is happiest when teaching. We attach great importance to both sides of his contribution—his personal, pastoral interest in his pupils individually, and his footing in the world of scholarship, through which his pupils gain a sense of value and a detestation of the shoddy. Both in Britain and in the countries of Western Europe the need for real intellectual distinction in teachers of the ablest boys in their later school years is recognised—the French *agrégé*, for instance, and the English schoolmaster with a first class degree are cast in the same mould. In Britain, and wherever British influence has been strong, the need for what we call the "schoolmasterly" qualities has always been accepted. Men and women with these qualities are needed more than ever today to undertake the essentially more difficult task that confronts the schools now that their Sixth Forms include many boys and girls without any family tradition of what Sixth Form work means. How are we succeeding in this task? What are our prospects?

LIVING ON CAPITAL

348. The thirties, that period of so much distress in English life, was a golden age for recruitment to grammar schools. It was a buyers' market, and headmasters and governing bodies could pick and choose between men with good honours degrees—a first class, or the upper division of the second class. The men and women recruited in those eight or nine years are now in their forties, the middle piece of a school staff, the newly appointed heads of schools and heads of departments. Not only are they men and women of good ability, but they were well taught in schools and universities

Chart No. 12

AGE DISTRIBUTION IN 1958 OF GRADUATE TEACHERS

Maintained secondary grammar schools (England and Wales)

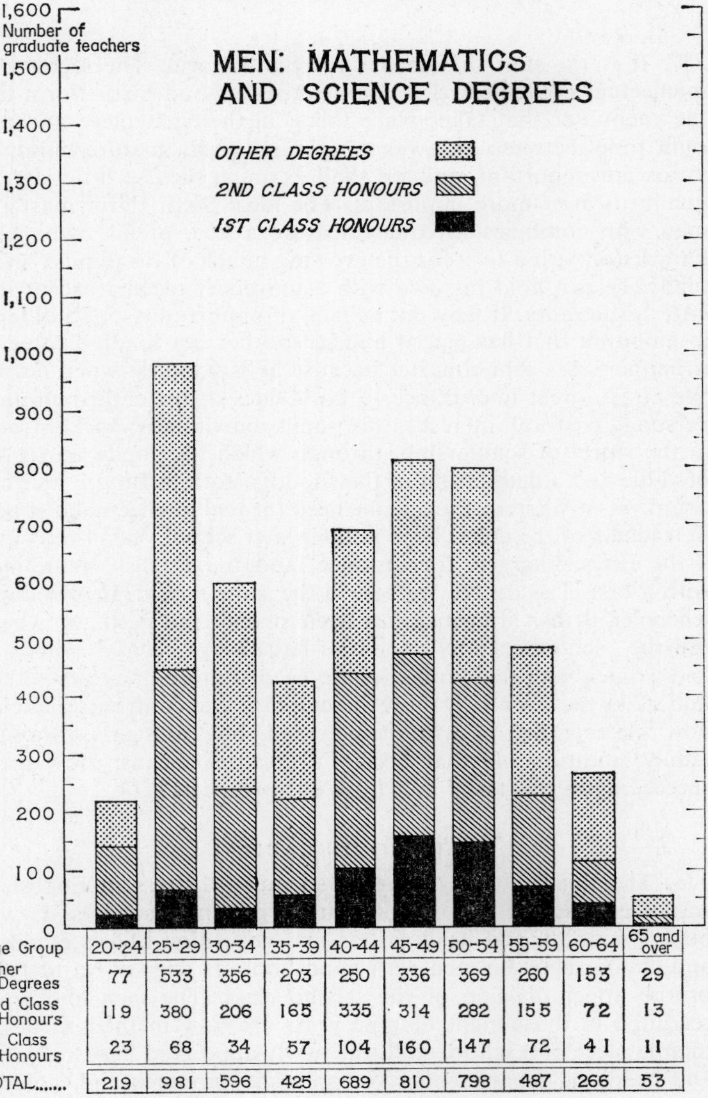

Number of graduate teachers

1,600
1,500
1,400
1,300
1,200
1,100
1,000
900
800
700
600
500
400
300
200
100
0

MEN: MATHEMATICS AND SCIENCE DEGREES

OTHER DEGREES

2ND CLASS HONOURS

1ST CLASS HONOURS

Age Group	20-24	25-29	30-34	35-39	40-44	45-49	50-54	55-59	60-64	65 and over
Other Degrees	77	533	356	203	250	336	369	260	153	29
2nd Class Honours	119	380	206	165	335	314	282	155	72	13
1st Class Honours	23	68	34	57	104	160	147	72	41	11
TOTAL.......	219	981	596	425	689	810	798	487	266	53

CHART No. 13

AGE DISTRIBUTION IN 1958 OF GRADUATE TEACHERS

Maintained secondary grammar schools (England and Wales)

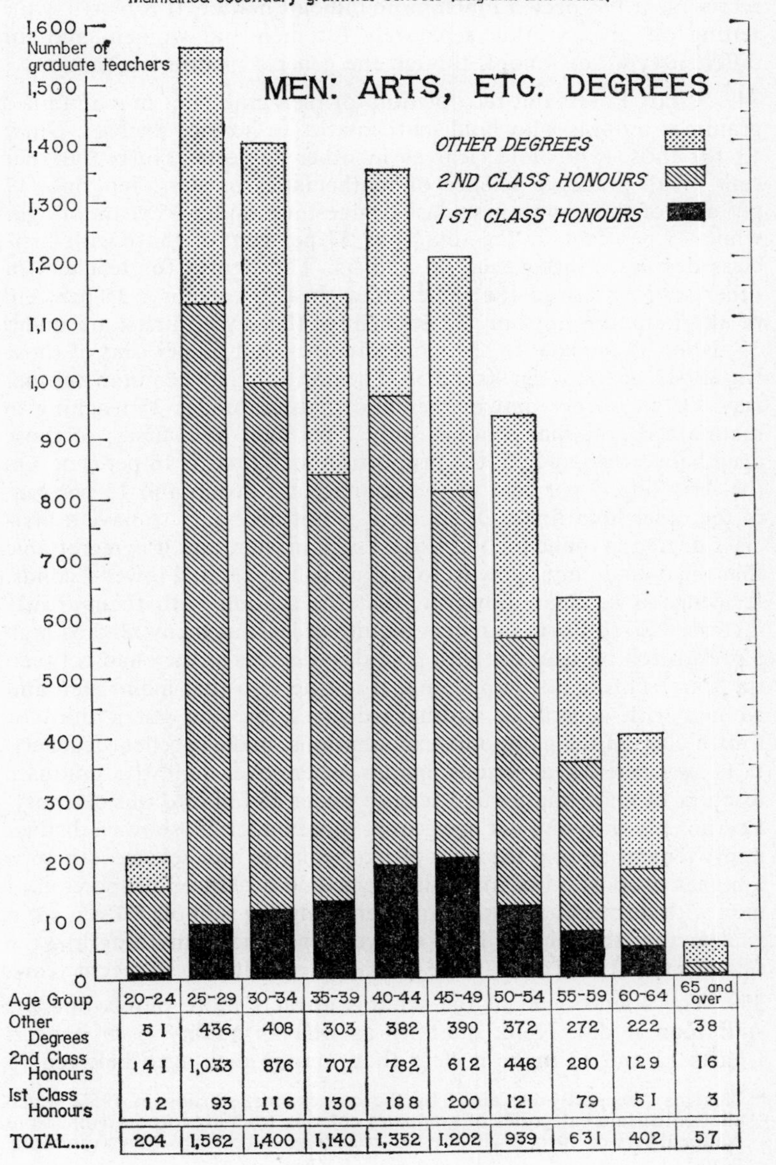

Age Group	20-24	25-29	30-34	35-39	40-44	45-49	50-54	55-59	60-64	65 and over
Other Degrees	51	436	408	303	382	390	372	272	222	38
2nd Class Honours	141	1,033	876	707	782	612	446	280	129	16
1st Class Honours	12	93	116	130	188	200	121	79	51	3
TOTAL.....	204	1,562	1,400	1,140	1,352	1,202	939	631	402	57

which were not overcrowded and understaffed. It is on their broad shoulders that the great post-war expansion of grammar schools and their Sixth Forms has taken place. During and since the war recruitment has been a much more difficult matter. It is worth while setting out the position separately for men and women, and for different types of school, though the general picture is common.

349. Chart 12 sets out the position for men graduates in maintained grammar schools who hold mathematics or science degrees; Chart 13 for those who hold degrees in other subjects. Thirty-four per cent of all graduate science or mathematics masters, but only 17 per cent of those with first-class degrees, are under 35 years of age; while 43 per cent of the total, but 57 per cent of those with first-class degrees, are between 40 and 55. The figures for teachers of other subjects are of the same order. In this category, 35 per cent of all graduates, but only 22 per cent of those with firsts, are under 35; while 39 per cent of the whole number, but 51 per cent of those with firsts, are between 40 and 55. The position may be put in another way. Of all science and mathematics masters under 35 teaching in maintained grammar schools, only 7 per cent hold firsts; of those aged between 40 and 55, the proportion with firsts is 18 per cent. On the Arts side, 7 per cent of the younger age group and 15 per cent of the older hold firsts. Of course it is not necessary to have a first-class degree to make a good Sixth Form master, and it is regrettable that the data do not allow us to distinguish upper and lower seconds. It seems to us clear, however, that the schools with their greatly increased Sixth Form numbers require at least as many, and as high a proportion of, teachers with first-class degrees as they had between the wars. This is not happening. It is true also that many men and women with general or ordinary degrees, or who got a third or fourth class in their honours examinations, make excellent teachers. It is nevertheless a serious matter when over half the graduate teachers of mathematics and science under 35 fall into this category. Fortunately the youngest age group, those under 25, shows a distinct improvement among teachers of mathematics and science—there is a higher proportion of men with firsts, and a reduced proportion of men with degrees below a second, entering the schools.* Even so, it is clear that the schools have not yet experienced anything like the full effects of the decline in the quality of recruitment in recent years.

350. The science side of the schools attracts more pupils but less staff than it did. Here, quantity as well as quality is in danger. Charts 12 and 13 make it clear that, among men aged between 35

* This may be partly explained by the concessions, starting in 1956, which allowed certain categories of graduates entering teaching to be exempt from National Service. If so, it will be a non-recurring, and perhaps even a vanishing, bonus.

and 55, the science and mathematics graduates form a decreasing percentage of all graduates in each successive five-year age-group—46 per cent of those aged 50 to 54, then 40 per cent, 34 per cent and finally 27 per cent of those aged 35 to 39. There has since been a recovery, though for the youngest completed age-group (those aged 25 to 29) they still form only 39 per cent of the whole body, and the recovery in numbers has been brought about only by recruiting men with relatively poor qualifications. Most headmasters are aged between 35 and 55, so that it is not surprising to find that those with mathematics or science degrees also form a smaller percentage of the whole for each successive five-year period—35 per cent of all headmasters aged 50 to 54 hold mathematics or science degrees; the percentage then falls to 31, 27 and finally to 16 for headmasters aged 35 to 39. While a fall in the percentage might have been expected, it is surprising to find the decline for headmasters is much sharper than for their staffs.*

351. Another approach to the same problem is to look at the kind of employment taken up by young men graduates. The most recent comprehensive information available is that contained in the thorough survey undertaken by Political and Economic Planning (P.E.P.) into "Graduate Employment" (Allen and Unwin 1956) which analysed the careers taken up by men who graduated from the Arts, Science and Technological faculties of British universities in 1950. This is nearly a decade ago, but we have no reason to suppose that the picture has altered very much since then. Indeed, enquiries we have made of the various university appointments boards and of the University Grants Committee suggest that there has been no marked change in the distribution of graduates between the various types of employment, while certain appointments boards which have details of the careers taken up by men holding first-class and second-class honours degrees confirm the picture given below. Among these various forms of employment only teachers and a proportion of university staff can be regarded as producers of graduates in the next generation. In 1950 we ploughed back into the school sector only 9 per cent of the young men who got firsts. Numerically, they were insufficient to replace in due course the schoolmasters who had taught them. And the expansion of Sixth Forms means that a mere replacement rate is not enough. It is, we believe, rare to find a schoolmaster with a first-class degree who is employed below his intellectual level. Those of us with experience of industry, the biggest single consumer of firsts, are doubtful whether this is quite as rare in industrial employment. Can it be in the national interest that only one group of occupations,

* We are indebted to the Incorporated Association of Head Masters for making for us the enquiries on which the second half of this paragraph is based.

commerce, should rank lower than teaching in the percentage of firsts among the graduates it recruited in 1950? Or that schools looking for mathematics or science masters in 1950 should have had to appoint a far higher proportion of graduates who did not get as much as a second than any other group of employers had to do? The position is set out in Table 36, which is taken from the P.E.P. Report.

Table 36. First Employment by Class of Degree (Men Graduates of 1950 United Kingdom Universities).

First Employment	No.=100%	Class of First Degree First %	Second %	Other %
Teaching (Mathematics and Science)	265	5	32	62*
Other Teaching	660	5	58	37
Civil Service and Local Government	265	11	51	38
Civil Service (Scientific)	218	25	47	28
Universities	166	53	41	6
Commerce	296	4	53	43
Industry	1,218	13	41	46
Law, the Churches, "Cultural Occupations"	397	6	52	42
Other	243	10	49	41
Total	3,728	12	47	41

*=99%

352. Charts 14 and 15 set out the position among women graduates in maintained grammar schools, of whom about a quarter are probably teaching in co-educational schools. While the general picture is roughly similar to that of the men graduates, there are a number of important differences. First, there are fewer women graduates teaching, roughly two to every three men, although there are as many girls as boys to be taught. Secondly, women graduates in mathematics or science are a smaller percentage of the whole number of graduate mistresses than are the men scientists in their group—28 per cent compared with 38 per cent. Thirdly, only 8 per cent of the graduate mistresses, compared with 12 per cent of the masters, hold first-class honours degrees. There is, however, virtually no difference between men and women in the proportion of graduates whose degree is below a second. Fourthly, whereas one master in every five is under 30, the proportion of graduate mistresses under 30 is one in three.

353. Two significant similarities should be noted. First, the general picture of a golden age of recruitment between the wars, followed by an ice age since, is just as true of women graduates as of men. Secondly, the proportion of teachers with really distinguished academic qualifications is slightly (2 per cent) higher in mathematics and science, both among men and women than in other subjects. At first sight this is surprising in view of the known difficulties in staffing science and mathematics departments, but it is explained by the fact that the better academic showing of these subjects is confined to the older men and women. This is made clear by the comparison in Table 37.

Table 37. Class of Degree and Age of Graduate in Maintained Grammar Schools, 1958 (England and Wales).

	Class of Degree									
	Men					Women				
	1st Class	2nd	Below 2nd	All		1st Class	2nd	Below 2nd	All	
	%	%	%			%	%	%		
Mathematics and Science Graduates:										
Under 35	*7*	*39*	*54*	*(1,796)*		*4*	*43*	*53*	*(1,178)*	
Aged 40–54	*18*	*41*	*41*	*(2,297)*		*15*	*42*	*43*	*(1,100)*	
Other Subjects:										
Under 35	*7*	*65*	*28*	*(3,166)*		*4*	*65*	*31*	*(3,254)*	
Aged 40–54	*15*	*52*	*33*	*(3,493)*		*11*	*57*	*32*	*(2,422)*	

It is clear that, beyond the known and already experienced difficulties, there is a serious risk of a still worse crisis in science teaching as the older men and women retire.

354. No task causes headmasters and headmistresses greater anxiety today than the filling of staff vacancies. The position is bad enough in boys' schools, but it is worse in girls' because of the quicker turnover caused by retirement through marriage as well as on pension. We are indebted to the Association of Head Mistresses (Incorporated) for figures which they collect from their members each year about their experience in filling staff vacancies. The situation has been growing steadily worse. In each subject the proportion of vacancies satisfactorily filled was lower in 1958 than in 1954. In the earlier year over 90 per cent of the vacancies in English, history and modern languages were satisfactorily filled; last year in these subjects the corresponding proportions were 73 per cent, 80 per cent and 77 per cent respectively. For the mathematics and science group of subjects the position five years ago was much more serious than in these Arts subjects and the decline since then has been no less disastrous.

CHART No. 14

AGE DISTRIBUTION IN 1958 OF GRADUATE TEACHERS

Maintained secondary grammar schools (England and Wales)

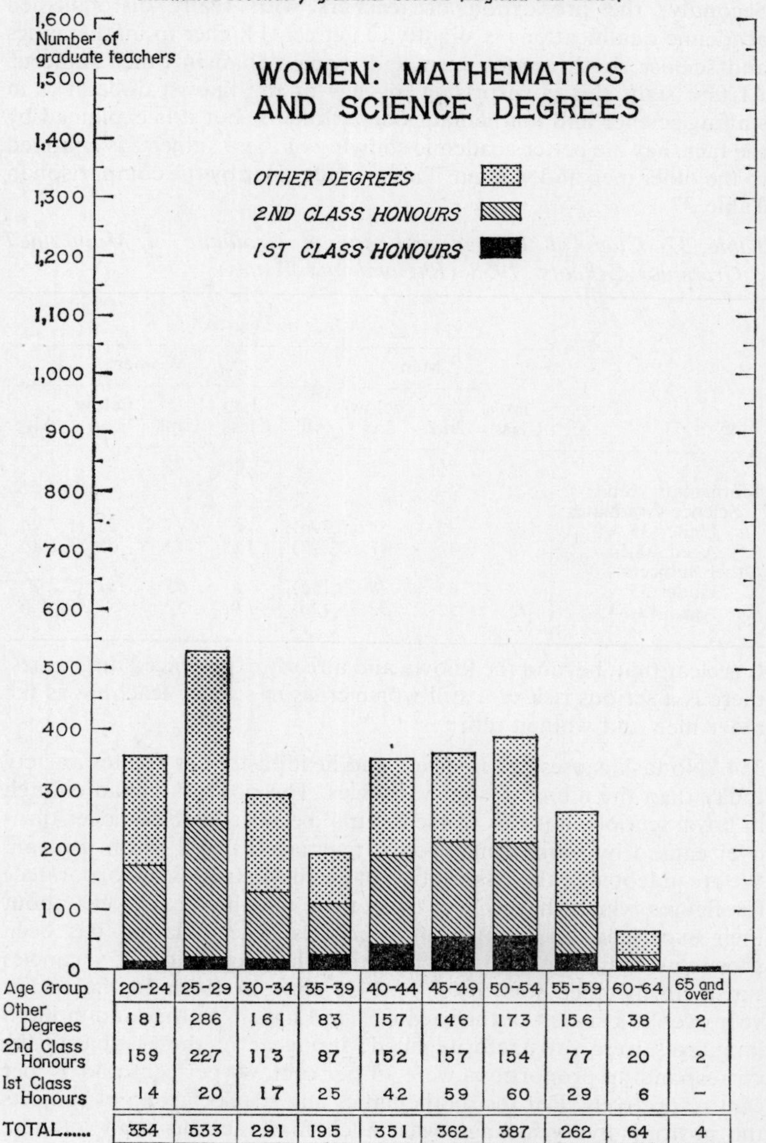

Age Group	20-24	25-29	30-34	35-39	40-44	45-49	50-54	55-59	60-64	65 and over
Other Degrees	181	286	161	83	157	146	173	156	38	2
2nd Class Honours	159	227	113	87	152	157	154	77	20	2
1st Class Honours	14	20	17	25	42	59	60	29	6	–
TOTAL......	354	533	291	195	351	362	387	262	64	4

CHART NO. 15

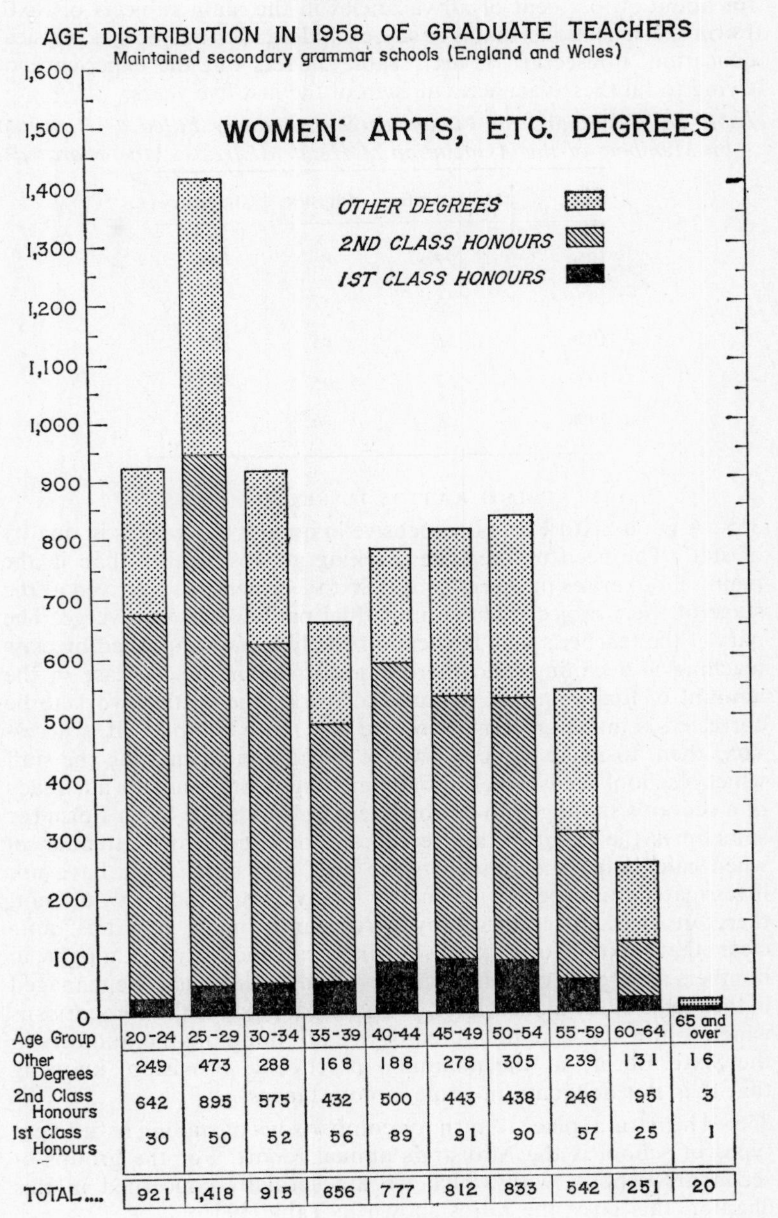

Age Group	20-24	25-29	30-34	35-39	40-44	45-49	50-54	55-59	60-64	65 and over
Other Degrees	249	473	288	168	188	278	305	239	131	16
2nd Class Honours	642	895	575	432	500	443	438	246	95	3
1st Class Honours	30	50	52	56	89	91	90	57	25	1
TOTAL....	921	1,418	915	656	777	812	833	542	251	20

Mathematics, physics and chemistry between them accounted in 1958 for about 30 per cent of all vacancies in the main subjects of Sixth Form specialisation, (that is to say, excluding such subjects as physical education, housecraft or art). Table 38 sets out the experience of trying to fill these vacancies in each of the last five years.

Table 38. Percentage of Vacancies Satisfactorily Filled as Reported by Members of the Association of Head Mistresses (Incorporated).

Year	Mathematics	Physics	Chemistry
	%	%	%
1954	77	66	66
1955	66	57	77
1956	55	45	65
1957	52	45	55
1958	48	50	52

STAFFING RATIOS IN SIXTH FORMS

355. A good Sixth Form is expensive in quantity as well as in quality of staff. The need to keep the teaching groups smaller than in the main school arises in several ways. Sixth Formers have arrived at the stage of their subjects where individual paths begin to diverge. The part of the teacher's task that can properly be accomplished by class teaching is declining, and there is a corresponding increase in the amount of time required for tutorial work. The written work to be corrected is much greater in volume and more complex. It is necessary, then, to make some allowance for this in calculating the staff which a school needs. One common method of assessing the adequacy of a school's staffing is to double the numbers in the Sixth Form (or sometimes the numbers above the age of compulsory attendance) when calculating the ratio between staff and pupils. We have not investigated this aspect of the matter in any detail; and we would not, therefore, wish to endorse any particular formula, but it is quite clear that Sixth Form pupils cannot satisfactorily be taught in numbers as large as can safely, and even advantageously, be managed in the forms of the main school. We have adopted for the comparisons which follow the time-honoured device of "doubling the numbers in the Sixth Form" as the minimum practicable provision, knowing that it is not adequate in some circumstances.

356. The natural place to turn for comparisons of staffing in different types of school is the Ministry's annual report. For the groups of secondary schools with which we are specially concerned in this chapter, this gives the ratios shown in Table 39.

Table 39. Staffing Ratios in Different Types of Secondary Schools, 1958 (England and Wales).

Maintained Grammar	Direct Grant Grammar	Independent Efficient	
		Secondary	Primary and† Secondary
1 to 18·3	1 to 18·2	1 to 13·2	1 to 16·3

† Schools covering both age ranges.

These figures, however, make no provision for the varying length of school course—the fact that boys of 11 and 12 are not found in most independent boys' secondary schools, so that the proportion of the whole school which lies below the Sixth, and which is relatively economical to staff, is consequently less than in other secondary schools. They ignore, too, the varying size of Sixth Forms, the extent of additional duties in boarding schools and any possible difference in need between boys', girls' and co-educational schools. For our purpose it is necessary to take factors such as these into consideration. Table 40 is based on the same sample of boy's maintained and direct grant grammar schools which was used for Tables 27 and 29 in Chapter 20, and on a group of 23 boys' independent schools whose headmasters are members of the Headmasters' Conference.*

Table 40. Staffing Ratios in a Sample of Different Types of Boys' Schools (England).

	Number of		Sixth Form	Crude Staffing Ratio	Staffing Ratio Doubling Sixth Form
	Schools	Pupils			
Maintained	28	12,645	1,707	1 to 19	1 to 21
Direct Grant	5	2,362	519	1 to 18	1 to 22
Independent admitting at 11+	9	5,955	1,343	1 to 16	1 to 20
Independent admitting at 13+	14	6,503	2,451	1 to 14	1 to 19

It is clear, of course, that the independent schools do have a substantial advantage in smaller classes over the maintained and direct grant schools, but it is much less than would appear at first sight from Table 39. It is clear, too, that when we are discussing the staffing of

* These independent schools may be taken as a typical group, but not as a scientifically selected sample; sixteen of them are primarily boarding schools. It should also be pointed out that Table 39 includes the full-time equivalent of any part-time teachers, while Table 40 only deals with full-time teachers. It also excludes any masters who take no part in ordinary class teaching, as is often the case with music masters, and the information about the independent and direct grant schools is drawn from a rather long period of time.

the Sixth Form in its quantitative aspects we are discussing, as far as boys are concerned, a single problem affecting all types of school, and not two separate problems, one in the maintained and the other in the independent schools. As Sixth Forms grow, maintained grammar schools necessarily become more expensive to staff. The wide differences in staffing ratios in independent schools must be remembered. In this group of 23 schools the range of the crude ratio is from 1 to 11 to 1 to 19. Among the direct grant schools it varies between 1 to 17 and 1 to 20 and among the maintained schools between 1 to 17 and 1 to 21.

357. To recognise that Sixth Form staffing is bound to be expensive in comparison with that of the main school is very different from saying that large Sixth Forms are uneconomical in comparison with with small ones. Four of the maintained and one of the direct grant schools in our sample had Sixth Forms of more than 100 pupils. The staffing ratio, after adjusting for the Sixth Form, is 1 to 22 for these schools, compared with 1 to 21 for the rest of the direct grant and maintained schools in the sample. Six of the independent schools (all with an entry at 13) had Sixth Forms of over 200. Their staffing ratio was 1 to 20, compared with 1 to 18 for the rest of the independent schools admitting at 13. The schools with the larger Sixth Forms were the more economically staffed.

358. Table 41 sets out the position for girls' schools, as Table 40 did for boys. It differs from Table 40, however, by including part-time teachers, who play a much larger part in many girls' schools than in boys'. In most instances, two half-time teachers are only nominally the equivalent of one whole-time so that the staffing ratios in all three lines of the table are not so favourable as they appear to be. It should also be noted that the independent schools usually admit at 11 or earlier and should therefore be compared with the last line but one, and not the last line, of Table 40.

Table 41. Staffing Ratios in a Sample of Different Types of Girls' Schools (England).

	Number of		Sixth Form Pupils	Crude Staffing Ratio	Ratio after Doubling Sixth Form
	Schools	Pupils			
Maintained	29	14,293	1,571	1 to 19	1 to 21
Direct Grant	7	3,020	529	1 to 17	1 to 20
Independent	18	5,271	766	1 to 13	1 to 15

Among the maintained schools there is nothing to choose between boys' and girls' schools in generosity of staffing, but the direct grant girls' schools are slightly, and the independent schools greatly, more expensive to staff than their counterparts for boys. Once again it is in general the larger Sixth Forms which are the more economical. Among the maintained schools there are seven schools with Sixth Forms of over 70. After allowing for the Sixth Form, their staffing ratio is 1 to 22; for the remaining 22 schools it is 1 to 20·5. Among the independent schools, however, the position is reversed. Seven of them have more than 50 girls in their Sixth Forms. Their adjusted staffing ratio is 1 to 14·6. For the remaining eleven it is 1 to 15·4. A similar survey has been made of co-educational grammar schools, which shows that their staffing ratios are the same as in the single sex maintained schools, the only significant difference lying in the great preponderance of men over women on the staff. This is in line with the fact, already noted, that in girls' schools much more frequent use has to be made of part-time staff than in boys' schools. Taken together, these indications suggest that any plans for developing the education of girls at the top of secondary schools must take account of the added difficulty in obtaining suitable women staff.

359. What conclusions can be drawn? Two main points seem clear. It is necessary to do more than is being done to attract men and women of the highest intellectual calibre into teaching. We cannot continue to live on our capital as we are now doing. The second point is that, since good Sixth Form teachers are scarce and likely to be scarcer, and since Sixth Forms are twice as costly to staff as Third or Fourth Forms, it is necessary to ensure that there is no unnecessary extravagance and wastefulness in the way in which teachers capable of taking the Sixth Form are employed. As between the three principal classes of secondary schools—maintained, direct grant and independent—we have seen that there is much less difference in staffing ratios than is often realised, except that the girls' independent schools employ more staff in relation to their numbers than any other class. In general, it is clear that the larger Sixth Forms are more economical than the small ones.

CHAPTER 24

The Structure of Sixth Forms

360. The quality of the work done in Sixth Forms, both by the pupils and by the teachers, will depend very greatly on the numbers in the Sixth Form as a whole, and in the various teaching groups of which it is made up. Our next subject of enquiry, therefore, is into the size of Sixth Forms.

THE SIZE OF SIXTH FORMS

361. In what sort of form is a boy likely to find himself, if he elects to stay at school beyond the Fifth Form? If he is a pupil in a boys' grammar school, he will be likely to find himself one of about 80 in the Sixth Form as a whole. Of these, half will be his own contemporaries who have just taken about 7 subjects at Ordinary level in the General Certificate of Education; the other half will be very unevenly divided between the second and third years. Only in a very few schools does the third year in the Sixth Form amount to more than a handful of boys—over the whole range of boys' grammar schools the proportion is only 12 per cent of the total Sixth Form. If the boy is a pupil in a co-educational grammar school, he will probably find himself one of a distinctly smaller Sixth Form in which there will, perhaps, be round about 60 pupils instead of nearly 80. The third year group will probably represent, too, a smaller proportion of the whole than in a boys' school. Something of this sort is what he may look forward to today; only seven years ago he would have gone into a markedly smaller Sixth Form. Then, the average size of the Sixth in a boys' grammar school was appreciably smaller than it is in a co-educational grammar school today, while the Sixth in a co-educational school was correspondingly smaller still. Twenty years ago most Sixth Forms were very small indeed.*

362. The girls' grammar schools today have, on the whole, slightly smaller Sixth Forms than the co-educational schools. They have a smaller proportion in the third year than either of the others—only 3 per cent of the whole. Taking the third year as a proportion of the second, the position is that rather over one-third remain into

* The information on which this chapter is based is derived from a comparison of the figures for the sample of grammar schools which was used in the Council's previous report on "Early Leaving" (Page 95 of that report) and the present position in the same schools as shown in their annual return to the Ministry.

the third year in the boys' schools, rather less than one-third in the co-educational schools, and one-twelfth in the girls' schools. One-fifth of the maintained grammar schools have no third-year pupils.

363. The position, so far as we have gone, can conveniently be summarised in tabular form.

Table 42. Size of Sixth Forms in a Sample of Maintained Grammar Schools 1952 and 1959 (England) —See note to para. 361.

Type of Grammar School	Year	No. of Schools	Average Size of Sixth Form	Percentage of Pupils in		
				1st	2nd	3rd year
Boys'	1952	36	52		*not known*	
	1959	36	79	*50*	*38*	*12*
Girls'	1952	38	39		*not known*	
	1959	38	56	*61*	*36*	*3*
Co-educational	1952	26	33		*not known*	
	1959	26	61	*57*	*33*	*10*
All schools	1952	100	41		*not known*	
	1959	100	65	*56*	*36*	*8*

In "Early Leaving" a warning was given about the interpretation of the figures for co-educational schools. Their relatively poor showing in 1952 was explained by the fact that they were, with one exception, either small country schools or the relatively new secondary schools established, frequently in industrial areas, since 1902. It was precisely in these kinds of school that there was most room for an expansion of the Sixth Form. It will be seen that in seven years since 1952 they have nearly doubled the average size of their Sixth Forms, and it is now the girls' grammar schools which, as a class, have the smallest Sixth Forms.

364. Up to this point we have been concerned solely with averages and with typical Sixth Forms. Table 43, printed at the top of the next page, shows the wide range in size that the averages conceal. There has been a most marked decrease in the proportion of very small Sixth Forms. Of those that are left, only one is not in a very small school. This also is in considerable contrast to the position in 1952 when, for instance, there were schools of 628 and 584 pupils with Sixth Forms of 14 and 17 respectively. In that year the sample as a whole showed that 7 of the 21 very small Sixth Forms were in schools admitting more than 100 pupils each year at the age of 11.

365. It would, of course, be wrong to suggest that a small school need have a small Sixth Form, but it is only in exceptional circum-

Table 43. Range of Size in Sixth Forms of a Sample of Maintained Grammar Schools 1952 and 1959 (England)—See note to para. 361.

Type of Grammar School	No. of schools	Year	Range in Number of Pupils	No. of Schools with Sixth Forms of	
				less than 20	20–39
Boys'	36	1952	8–137	6	4
		1959	13–178	1	3
Girls'	38	1952	5–99	8	13
		1959	12–134	2	7
Co-educational	26	1952	2–76	7	10
		1959	22–130	0	7
All Schools	100	1952	2–137	21	27
		1959	12–178	3	17

stances that we can expect to find a Sixth Form of over 70 in a school of under 300. There is only one approaching this size now or in 1952 in our sample; it is the same school in both years. In general, a small school will produce a small Sixth Form unless the entry to the school at 11 is far more selective than usual. Small schools in towns can usually be helped to grow bigger, and thus more economical in Sixth Form staffing, but small country schools are difficult to enlarge satisfactorily at the base. Four of the very small schools in our sample are country schools. Sometimes a way out can be found by combining two single-sex schools to form one moderate sized co-educational school. This has already been done in a number of instances and the practice will probably be extended, but it will not in itself eradicate uneconomically small Sixth Forms—two of the very small schools in our sample are in fact co-educational. Sometimes it may be possible for a boys' school and a girls' school either to combine their Sixth Forms as a whole, or to divide the main subjects between them, which has the great advantage of avoiding decapitating one school or the other. Another way in which this problem of sparsely populated districts is being tackled is by the conversion of grammar schools into bilateral grammar-modern schools. Another solution is to link country grammar schools with a surrounding ring of modern schools from which transfers can regularly be made either into the Fifth or Sixth Form of the grammar school. The area covered in this way may well be beyond convenient daily travelling distance. Many country grammar schools already have boarding houses—it is worth considering whether they would not be better used to give a comparatively large number of boys and girls two or three years boarding-school life in the Fifth and Sixth Forms rather than to give a smaller number a longer grammar school life starting at 11.

366. We have been considering so far only the very small Sixth Forms which are plainly uneconomic, but these are so few in number that in most instances their existence may be justified on individual grounds. Many of us with recollections of the small Sixth Forms of the past believe that they also had certain educational advantages through the intimate association of pupils following different disciplines, an association which is more difficult to reproduce today. Sixth Forms considerably larger than these very small ones would, however, still be uneconomic in the demands they would make, if they were to do their job properly, on the scarce supply of highly qualified teachers. It seems likely that the minimum economic size of a Sixth Form is not less than 40 pupils. On this basis, in spite of the progress of recent years, there is still a long way to go. A fifth of the schools in our sample still have less than 40 pupils, compared with 48 per cent in 1952. On the basis of what has been happening up to now in maintained grammar schools, it normally requires a three-form entry school to provide a Sixth Form of this size; if the proportion taking advantage of a Sixth Form course goes on rising, a two-form entry would be sufficient.

367. We have confidence that the present trend will carry many more schools into a position where the Sixth Form is economical to staff. But we recognise, too, that the trend will probably (as we hope) lead to the development of Sixth Forms in schools which have had none, or virtually none, and in which numbers at first will inevitably be small. The last thing we would wish to see is any discouragement—

Table 44. Sixth Forms in Secondary Technical Schools 1958 (*England*).

(*a*) SIZE OF FORMS

Number of Schools	Number with Sixth Forms	Range in Size of Sixth Forms	Numbers in Sixth Forms		
			under 10	50 and over	Average Size
270	133	1–167	18	15	21

(*b*) NUMBER OF PUPILS TAKING TWO ADVANCED LEVEL SUBJECTS

Type of Technical School (1)	Number of Sixth Form Pupils (2)	No. of Sixth Form Pupils working for 2 'A' Level Subjects (3)	Column (3) as percentage of Column (2) (4)
Boys'	1,649	1,151	*70*
Mixed	1,375	908	*66*
Girls'	773	336	*43*
Total	3,797	2,395	*63*

by regulations, for instance, eliminating small Sixth Forms—which stopped this natural and highly important growth. What happens in the early stages can well be illustrated from the present position of Sixth Forms in secondary technical schools, which are only at the beginning of their development. The figures are given in Table 44 printed on the previous page. Comprehensive schools, except small schools in country areas, will have no difficulty in finding sufficient over-all numbers; but—since part of their policy is to provide a great variety of courses, differing not only in subject, but in academic level—it seems clear that in the early days some of their individual Sixth Form courses will be just as immediately uneconomic to staff as those we have hitherto been considering.

368. When we turn from the maintained to the independent schools' section of secondary education we are at once faced by a great range of contrasts. The list of independent schools recognised as efficient gives us a picture of the position at the beginning of 1957 and enables us to distribute pupils aged 16 or over between schools of various sizes. This is done in Table 45. Co-educational schools are omitted from this analysis.

Table 45. Independent Schools Recognised as Efficient, showing the Number of Pupils Aged 16 or Over, 1957 (England).

Number of Pupils aged 16 or more	Boys		Girls	
	Schools	Pupils	Schools	Pupils
Under 20	28	303	151	1,693
20–39	25	695	126	3,389
40–49	7	317	26	1,154
50–99	46	3,482	46	3,178
100–149	31	3,817	3	340
150–199	21	3,631	1	194
200–249	18	4,067	—	—
250+	10	3,113	—	—
Total	186	19,425	353	9,948

Average No. of Pupils per Boys' School aged 16 or over = 104
Average No. of Pupils per Girls' School aged 16 or over = 28

While the great majority of boys in independent schools are in schools which are big enough to have properly viable Sixth Forms, the majority of girls are in schools which can hardly be said to have

Sixth Forms at all when it is remembered that many of the pupils aged 16 are still in the Fifth Form preparing for Ordinary level examinations. It is therefore worth moving in a little closer and looking at the Sixth Form position in the sample of boys' and girls' schools recently inspected—schools of more than local repute.

Table 46. Sizes of Sixth Forms in a Sample of Independent Schools Recognised as Efficient (England).

	No. of schools	Size of Sixth Form		No. of Sixth Forms with	
		Range	Average	Less than 20 pupils	20–39 pupils
Boys' Schools	23	56–303	165	—	—
Girls' Schools	18	8–79	43	4	3

While all the boys' schools in this sample have Sixth Forms which are strong enough to be economical and to offer a suitable range of courses, many of the girls' schools have Sixth Forms which must either be very extravagant in staffing or which, if they are to be financially solvent, can offer only a very limited choice of subjects.

ARTS AND SCIENCE SIXTHS

369. So far we have been concerned only with the total numbers in the Sixth Form. It is necessary, however, to look separately at the numbers taking various subjects. In boys' maintained schools (to judge by our sample) a boy on the science side is most likely to find himself in a Science Sixth (not, of course, a teaching group) of well over 40 boys; on the arts side of 30. One in 18 of the boys' schools, however, have Science Sixths of less than 20 boys, and one in 4 have fewer than 20 boys in the Arts Sixth. In only 5 per cent of the schools is the Arts Sixth now bigger than the Science Sixth, compared with 33 per cent in 1952. Altogether, in 1959, 65 per cent of the boys in the Sixth Forms of boys' schools were taking two or more mathematical or scientific subjects at Advanced level, compared with 52 per cent in 1952. (The proportion of boys taking science as specialists is even higher, as we shall see, in co-educational schools). The science side has certainly been growing faster than the arts side in most schools, though by no means in all, but there has been nothing like the withering away of the Arts Sixth that has sometimes been imagined. In rather less than one-sixth of the schools has there been an absolute decline in numbers in the Arts Sixth, and in these schools the average size of the Arts Sixth is still about 27. In one-third of the schools the Science Sixth more than doubled, in numbers from an

average of 15 boys to one of 45. Much of this information about the boys' schools is shown more systematically in Table 47.

Table 47. Sizes of Science and Arts Sixths in a Sample of Boys' Maintained Schools (England)—See note to para. 361.

No. of Schools		Science Sixths		Bigger than Arts (schools)	Arts Sixths		Bigger than Science (schools)
		Range (pupils)	Average (pupils)		Range (pupils)	Average (pupils)	
1952	36	2–71	27	22*	1–76	22	12*
1959	36	12–99	47	34	1–85	30	2

* In 2 Schools, Science and Arts Sixths were equal in size.

There is reason to be satisfied that both Arts and Science Sixths in typical schools are sound teaching units, which need make no undue demands on staffing.

370. The same kind of scrutiny shows that the typical Sixth Form in a girls' school is made up of some 31 arts specialists, 13 science specialists and 11 girls following a general course, normally a one-year course. This general course is something that is hardly found in boys' schools. It would, indeed, seem that some pupils who would follow a two-year Advanced level course, if they were boys, take instead a one-year general course (or leave at 16) because they are girls. Parents and girls seem to be content with a shorter school life; and parents, girls and employers with lower academic qualifications. Table 48 helps us to get a clearer picture of the problems of organisation that come from the division into science, arts and general courses instead of into science and arts only.

Table 48. Sizes of Science, Arts and General Sixth Forms in a Sample of Girls' Maintained Schools (England)—See note to para. 361.

Number of Schools		Science Sixths			Arts Sixths			General Sixths		
		Range	Average	Sixths with less than 5 pupils	Range	Average	Sixths with less than 5 pupils	Range	Average	Sixths with less than 5 pupils
1952	38	1–21	8·1	13	3–47	17·2	3	0–43	13·3	7*
1959	38	0–44	13·2	3	8–66	31·4	0	0–38	11·7	6*

NOTE: * In 1952 there were in addition 4 schools, in 1959, 3, which had no General Sixths.

In 1952 there were a good many Sixth Forms which on the face of it had very little right to the name or title to existence. They were weak in both arts and science. But it is never safe to judge a moving scene from a static picture. How far has the experience of the last seven years improved the position? It now appears that the majority of arts courses are probably well established and justifying the teaching power which they demand. The science courses, however, are still very weak, though progress has been made, and many of them are intolerably expensive in staffing. There has been some decline in the size of general courses—caused probably by the demand for higher qualifications by the teachers' training colleges and some other bodies which have traditionally recruited from girls who have followed a general course. It seems likely that the diversion of girls from the general courses has been more to the arts than to the science side. Nothing has happened in the last seven years to enable us to look forward with any confidence to a solution of the problem of running economic science courses in the average girls' grammar school, even after allowance for the fact that a girl who is taking biology and two arts subjects at Advanced level (which is not uncommon) is classified here as an arts specialist.

371. No doubt one reason why the problem of science in girls' schools is so intractable is the difficulty of finding suitable teachers. It is natural, therefore, to turn to the co-educational schools to see whether the position there is any better. The average Science Sixth in a maintained co-educational school is 30 strong—more than twice as large as a similar form in a girls' school. There is not the competition of a General Sixth to anything like the same extent—in 38 per cent of the schools there is none at all, and in half of them there is no girl following a general course. In spite of these factors the proportion of girls in the Science Sixth in co-educational schools is no higher than in girls' schools, while the percentage of boys is markedly higher than in boys' schools. Table 49 illustrates the point.

Table 49. Proportions in Science, Arts and General Sixths in a Sample of Single Sex and Co-educational Maintained Schools, 1959 (England).—see note to para. 361

	Science %	Arts %	General %	All %
Boys' Schools	*59*	*39*	*2*	*100*
Co-educational Schools				
Boys	*72*	*21*	*7*	*100*
Girls	*23*	*64*	*13*	*100*
Girls' Schools	*23*	*56*	*21*	*100*

Certain subjects, it would appear, are commonly thought of as girls' subjects, and certain other subjects as especially suitable for boys. A closer examination supports this view. In 6 of the 26 co-educational schools, there were altogether only 13 girls specialising in science out of 115 girls in the Sixth Forms. In 3 of the 26 co-educational schools in the sample there was no girl specialising in science, and in none were there more than 16. Conversely, in 8 of the schools there were altogether only 28 boys specialising in arts subjects out of a total of 163 boys in the Sixth Forms. In one of these 8 schools there was only one boy on the arts side, and in none of the 26 were there more than 16. In only two schools was there a reasonably even balance between boys and girls in the arts and science sections of the Sixth.

372. The considerable progress that the co-educational schools have made in numbers in the Sixth Forms between 1952 and 1959 has not been confined to one side. Both the arts and science sides are considerably stronger organisationally than they were six years ago. The progress is shown concisely in Table 50.

Table 50. Growth of Co-educational Sixth Forms (England).

	No. of Schools	Science		Arts		General	
		Range	Average	Range	Average	Range	Average
1952	26	0–36	14·1	2–40	14·5	0–20	4·3
1959	26	4–77	30·2	4–49	23·0	0–41	6·0

373. It is often implied that one of the main academic contrasts between the maintained and the independent schools is between arts and science. Like so much of the folk lore of the Sixth Form, this belief appears to be based on what was once true, but is no longer so. We have seen (para. 369) that among the maintained boys' schools the proportion of science specialists among boys in the Sixth Form has risen between 1952 and 1959 from 52 per cent to 65 per cent, leaving out of account for both years boys in a General Sixth. In

Table 51. Proportion of leavers from H.M.C. Schools entering Full-Time Courses of University Standing (1955)

	Independent Schools		Direct Grant Schools	
	Percentage of all leavers	Percentage of leavers from Sixth Form	Percentage of all leavers	Percentage of leavers from Sixth Form
Arts Specialists	*19*	*54*	*17*	*59*
Science Specialists	*28*	*83*	*27*	*83*

1956, in those independent and direct grant schools which are members of the Headmasters' Conference, the proportion of science specialists was 49 per cent in independent schools, and 54 per cent in direct grant schools, while the proportions which had gone on to full-time courses of university standing in the previous year showed an even stronger bias towards science. They are best shown in tabular form in Table 51 at the foot of the page opposite.

374. No firm information on these points is readily available for independent or direct grant girls' schools. The general impression we have, however, is that these schools approximate to the pattern of the girls' maintained schools—that is to say that the picture is for the most part an unsatisfactory one as far as science is concerned, but that there are individual schools in which the position is sound and encouraging.

375. We may sum up our impressions on the structure of Sixth Forms in this way:

(*a*) The rise in the number of Sixth Formers has raised the size of the average teaching group in the Sixth Forms of maintained boys' schools to an economic level; it has put the girls' maintained schools on a sound footing except in science, where the position is very unsatisfactory; the position of the co-educational maintained schools is much stronger than it was and should continue to improve.

(*b*) There remains the problem of the small grammar school in the country. It is clear that its Sixth Form is at present often an unsatisfactory unit both for teaching and for economy. Where it is essential to expand the base, we suggest that it is done either by merging the whole of two single-sex schools into one co-educational school, or by providing a common Sixth Form for two single-sex schools. It is desirable also to develop transfers directly into the Fifth or Sixth Form from secondary modern schools. This might imply boarding provision.

(*c*) Regarded as a whole, co-educational schools provide balanced Sixth Forms which ought not to be extravagant to staff. They are, however, seriously unbalanced in the division of boys and girls between the arts and science Sixths.

(*d*) There is a special problem about general courses in the Sixth Form. Their rarity for boys, their commonness in girls' schools, their comparative infrequency in co-educational schools, is to be explained, but not necessarily justified, by historical reasons.

(*e*) The position of the boys' independent and direct grant schools is thoroughly sound from the structural point of view. Their Sixth Forms are big enough to provide economically a wide range of courses. The position of science, contrary to general belief, is very strong.

(*f*) The position of the girls' independent schools, as a group, is less than satisfactory for advanced work. We cannot but believe that many girls who would profit from a Sixth Form education are in schools which offer little or no prospect of one. The size and organisation of many of these schools make heavy demands on the short supply of teachers.

CHAPTER 25

The Curriculum of the Sixth Form

376. The question of specialisation is particularised in our terms of reference, and we devote this chapter to a discussion of the problems it presents. Clearly allied to it are the problems created for the schools by the conditions of admission to the universities. Specialisation—the problem of the curriculum—and selection—the problem of university entrance—are indeed so closely interlocked that any separation of them is bound to be artificial. Nevertheless it seems essential for clarity to keep the two issues distinct, and we therefore reserve for discussion in the next chapter the questions arising out of the transition from school to university, to other forms of further education and to employment. The two chapters should be read in close conjunction. In this and the following chapter we exclude, unless specifically mentioned, reference to the problems of "General" Sixth Form courses which are raised in Chapter 27.

THE PREVAILING PATTERNS

377. When a pupil enters the Sixth Form, he becomes a specialist—that is to say, the subjects of his serious intellectual study are confined to two or three. They are usually interlocking, especially on the science side, and are chosen, at least for potential university candidates, with an eye on faculty requirements. It is to this concentration of the mind's attention on a limited field of study that the name specialisation is given. There are considerable and important variations in the degree of specialisation between one school and another, and between one field of specialisation and another; but the general picture is constant. Boys and girls spend up to three-quarters of their time (if private study in school hours is included) in their last two or three years at school on a range of subjects which for many of them is a little, but not much, wider than that on which they will spend the next three years as undergraduates if they go to a university. The remainder of their time, which we describe in this report as "minority time", is normally divided between a considerable number of subjects and educational activities none of which receives much time or, perhaps, the full attention of the pupils. It is out of this "minority time" that provision has to be made in most day schools for organised games and physical education.

378. Specialisation, in the sense that we have used it, is a product of the nineteenth century and a consequence of the tremendous advances

in knowledge which from that time on began to mark all branches of study. The old ideal was the polymath, the man whose education fitted him to be at home in all branches of human knowledge. It is not to be thought that the bishops who were original members of the Royal Society were laymen in scientific discussions, nor that Sir Isaac Newton was an amateur bungler in biblical studies. As late as the time when John Henry Newman was an undergraduate, the honours course at Oxford demanded proficiency in both classics and mathematics. Today an all-round education is possible only to a relatively low level; the extent of human knowledge is now so great that it is impossible for a man to be really at home in the higher reaches of more than one or two subjects. The argument is not whether specialisation is desirable or unavoidable; it is about when it should begin. In England it begins for many subjects earlier than in any other country. From the age of 15, or 16 at latest, the classical specialist in an English school will spend only a small part of his actual school time on anything but Latin, Greek and ancient history; the equivalent is true of the mathematician or scientist. In most boys' schools, however, and in almost all girls' schools, pupils on the arts side specialise to a rather smaller extent in that their main subjects do not interlock so closely, though in some schools the historians and modern linguists specialise as closely as the classics.

379. In this system of specialisation for young people while they are still at school English education is singular. Neither in Western Europe nor in North America is there anything of the sort. Even nearer to home, in Scotland, the schools insist on a much wider spread of subjects in the Sixth Form than we do in England. On the continent of Europe, there is no question of dropping altogether the study of languages or history or mathematics or science, while in some countries Latin as well is kept on the compulsory list for all pupils in the most highly selective schools. There is, it is true, the possibility in the later years of following a course with a bias towards either literary or scientific studies—the situation in this respect (though, of course, at a much higher level of attainment) is rather more like that in the Fourth or Fifth Forms of an English grammar school than in the Sixth. But admission to a university or equivalent institution depends on satisfactory performance in all subjects of the curriculum, and not only in those in the direction in which the curriculum is biassed. In the United States, similarly, the 17 year-old in High School takes a wide range of subjects. Sometimes, in our eyes, the variety is almost bizarre, though, if he hopes to enter a good college, its entrance requirements will impose a certain uniformity. He will then find himself taking a daily period of mathematics, science, a foreign language, history or political science,

and English; each of these subjects carries equal weight in fulfilling matriculation requirements.

380. But, if American and continental practices are united against the English in being non-specialist, there is one important respect in which England and the continent take the same side against America. In Western Europe, as in England, the secondary school is traditionally concerned with educating an élite, an intellectual aristocracy on whom the most stringent academic demands can be made and in whom there can be awakened a real love of learning. It treats them as adults capable of a reverence for knowledge, beginners in a lifelong quest for truth, which they can share with those who teach them. This outlook is shared equally by the *professeur* in a French *lycée* and the English Sixth Form master, widely though they differ in their actual methods of teaching. The intellectual task of an American Senior High School differs entirely from that of an English Sixth Form, because it is not dealing with, and would not wish to deal with, a segregated few. Not only is the climate of public opinion strongly against the segregation of the abler pupils into selective schools (though there are some recent signs of a willingness to consider this), but the standard pattern of an American High School does not even allow for the segregation of pupils inside the school into faster and slower streams. All are educated together, and there is an emphasis on problems of individual adjustment to a mass society which we would regard as more appropriate to the modern school than to the grammar school, whose pupils' characters, (so, rightly or wrongly, the English tradition insists), can be trained simultaneously with their minds by the "full rigour of the academic game" and the freedom of out-of-school activities. Thus while the English grammar school differs from the American High School both in its methods and in its objectives, our difference from the Europeans is chiefly one of method.

THE SPECIALIST ELEMENT IN THE ENGLISH PATTERN

381. This does not alter the fact that we are isolated at least in the method we use, and that is an important enough matter to justify asking whether isolation is worth while. Indeed the singularity of the English tradition is such that we should be very wrong not to examine it most closely. We start by stating the case against specialisation. In its essence the argument against the English Sixth Form is that it introduces specialisation too early and on too narrow a front. It is said to be too early because a decision has to be made before a boy is old enough to know his own mind. Where the decision is in fact virtually made one or two years before he enters the Sixth Form we have already endorsed the criticism, but the general argument

against specialisation goes further. Not only may specialisation begin before a boy knows his own mind, but (the argument runs) before anybody can give valid advice on what his best course is. It is easy to identify the extremes of ability and incapacity in any subject, but the great majority of gifted boys and girls could probably develop reasonably well in several directions. Early preferences are often reflections of the qualities of the teaching, or of the teacher, rather than of the pupil, and it is surely well to leave a decision, which must normally be of lifelong importance, until it can be made on more substantial grounds. Specialisation is also said to begin too early because it takes place before a boy has had time to reach in his other studies and in his own psychological development that stage at which their contribution to his education can safely be left to him to develop out of his own interests. To abandon French under the first shadow of the subjunctive is probably to condemn oneself to the tourist phrase book, to be shut out of one of the great literatures of Europe, and to sacrifice half the value of the investment already made in French lessons.

382. The other great complaint about specialisation is that it is on too narrow a front. This can mean two things. It may mean that the actual subjects selected for study are themselves too restricted and too much out of the main stream, or the complaint may be about the treatment of a subject. In either case, however, the fear is that specialisation will act as a constricting frame and not a liberating agent to the boy's mind. The more he learns, it is said, the more he will be cut off from his fellows, finding it possible to communicate freely only with those who have followed his own narrow course. His contacts with the rest of his peers will be confined to the level of gossip; for the things that matter he must retire into the private world of his own fellow specialists. A good education should aim at developing a man's intellectual interests on as wide a front as possible, even if it means postponing for a year or two the beginning, and therefore the end, of his specialised education. If he must specialise early, let us at least see that his specialist subjects have as wide a reference as possible.

383. These are telling criticisms against specialisation, as we know it, in principle. They apply to good schools as well as bad. A third type of criticism is not the less important because it applies only to below-average schools. In a good school, the argument runs, the really good teacher with the really good pupil may find the present system a grand way of encouraging a boy to think, but in an average school the average teacher with the average pupil will do little more than cram him. If this is true, the educational argument for specialisation, as a tool to sharpen the mind, has to be discarded; and the only

defence left is the utilitarian argument that it saves time in the total educational process from the infants' school to the post-graduate course. This argument, drawn from what is thought to happen in the average school, is a serious matter, and we have already referred to the shortage of highly qualified teachers, which may limit the quantity of true Sixth Form work that can properly be undertaken. It is not, however, obvious that to cram in eight subjects would be better than to cram in two or three.

384. Such are the arguments against specialisation. They are effective; but it is worth noting that the broad curriculum of Europe and America is almost equally under fire. England may stand alone in the nature of its solution to the problem of how to educate its ablest boys and girls, but it is not alone in being criticised for its solution. In America the burden of the complaint is, not that too many unrelated subjects are studied, but that they are not studied seriously enough. The spur of competition, the demand for hard work and high standards are, we are told, lacking. Certainly the American High School is under heavy criticism from the universities. On the continent, the complaints are nearly as insistent, but strikingly different. They are concerned with the pressure on pupils of a curriculum which makes serious academic demands, often of a competitive nature, over too wide a range of subjects. The strain, it is said, is altogether too great. It is tempting to say that the American and European criticisms between them destroy the case for a broad curriculum from 16 to 18. For if, as would appear, such a curriculum, taught in the average school by average teachers to average pupils, is either too superficial or too exhausting, then the field is left clear for the English recipe of specialisation. It is tempting, but it would be wrong, to conclude the argument with such a palpable debating point. Let it be said at once that there is no patent and perfect formula for the education of young minds and that all systems have their advantages and their defects.

385. For ourselves, after considering the matter most carefully, we are agreed in accepting and endorsing the English principle of specialisation, or intensive study, as it would be better described. It is the principle that we endorse. If that meant that we had to rest content with some of the practices that are to be observed in English schools at the present time, we might well reverse our view. There are undoubtedly some abuses of specialisation, which ought to be corrected. But the best line of advance, in our opinion, is to reaffirm the principle and reform its application rather than to abandon it altogether.

386. Before we set out the arguments that have led us to this view, there is one widespread misunderstanding which must be corrected.

To some people, the success or failure of a course of education is to be judged by what the student "knows" at the end of it. Now there are some things that every citizen "ought to know", and they cannot in the present age be confined to the "three R's". For example, we shall ourselves shortly be suggesting that nobody's formal education at school should be completed without some acquaintance with the fundamentals of scientific knowledge. Nevertheless, the acquisition of factual knowledge is by itself a poor test of any education, and a lamentably poor test of the education of boys and girls of 17 and 18. The process of education, as has been said, is not to be compared with that of filling up an empty pot, but rather with that of lighting a fire. The proper test of an education is whether it teaches the pupil to think, and whether it awakens his interest in applying his brain to the various problems and opportunities that life presents. If that has once been done, then factual knowledge can be assimilated. If it has not been done, then no amount of nodding acquaintance with widely varying fields of human knowledge will equip a boy or girl with an educated mind. We argue the case for intensive study, then, not primarily on the score of the information it provides, but because it awakens interest, teaches clear thinking and induces self-discipline in study.

387. The first step in the argument for specialisation is that able boys and girls are ready and eager by the time they are 16—the ablest by 15—to get down to the serious study of some one aspect of human knowledge which, with the one-sided enthusiasm of the young, they allow for a time to obscure all other fields of endeavour. "Subject mindedness", as we have already noted, is one of the marks of the Sixth Form. It is there whether we use it or not. It is sensible to direct this great emotional impetus towards intellectual effort.

388. The second step in the argument is that concentration on a limited field leads naturally to study in depth. The boy embarks on a chain of discovery; he finds that ultimately each new fact he encounters fits into the jig-saw. As he goes deeper and deeper, he acquires self-confidence in his growing mastery of the subject. He is emancipated from the textbook and goes exploring behind the stage scenery that defines the formal academic subject. No longer does he accumulate largely isolated pieces of information and separate, unrelated skills. Most of what he does has a bearing, which gradually becomes apparent to him, on the rest of his work. In a word, he begins to assume responsibility for his own education. In the course of two or three years in the Sixth Form he is bound to experience moments of frustration and periods when the material is too great to be immediately assimilated; but if he perseveres, he comes in the end into that enviable position where the picture begins to become

plain. His subject is no longer something that he must "learn"; he begins to feel himself the master of it.

389. The third step in the case for specialisation is that, through this discipline, a boy can be introduced into one or two areas which throw light on the achievement of man and the nature of the world he lives in. The honours school of *Literae Humaniores* (Greats) at Oxford is a classic example of specialisation or study in depth. With the aid of a precise linguistic discipline, it develops a knowledge of the literature, the history, the art and the thought of one of the great cultures of the world. At the schoolboy's much lower level, similar studies in depth, embracing more than one discipline, can be, and readily are, developed from starting points in half-a-dozen literary or scientific subjects. The science side has developed a unity which the arts side has lost, to the regret of many, with the decline of the classics. This is why the selection of material for specialisation at school is of great importance. We should reject certain fields, which are eminently suitable for specialisation at a later age, such as law or the technology of a particular industry, because they are not among the best means of introducing a boy to the fundamental processes of thought and the greatest achievements of the human mind. It should go without saying that a school should not offer a subject for specialisation just because it will be vocationally useful in later life. If that result follows, as it often does, it is incidental. The proper concern in the school years should be the development of the pupil's brain and character, not of his future earning capacity. This is not, of course, to deny the strong vocational interest which from the pupil's side may enter into his choice of a specialist study.

390. The fourth step in the argument is that, given the right teaching, a boy will by the end of his school days begin to come out on the further side of "subject-mindedness". He is hardly likely to do that, perhaps, much before 18; but, as he sees how the facts he has been handling in his own subject knit together, he begins to wonder how his subject fits into the whole field of knowledge. He reaches out for himself towards a wider synthesis. As he enjoys the first delights of intellectual mastery of his own subject, he observes that his fellows have the same joy in their subjects, and his interest impels him to discover what lies behind their enthusiasm. If a boy turns that intellectual corner, as he often does at the end of his Sixth Form time, we can be sure that, narrow as his education may have been during the last few years, he will take steps to widen it as well as deepen it.

391. The fifth step in the argument is that this process of intellectual growth demands a great deal of concentrated time. It virtually enforces specialisation because the time left for other subjects is bound to be small—rarely can it be more than one-third. This

intellectual ripening depends, too, on a close personal relation between pupils and teacher which can only be established if they spend many hours together in the intimacy of a small teaching group. In Chapter 21 we identified this "intellectual discipleship" as one of the marks of the Sixth Form. We must recognise that it is inconsistent with the small weekly time allocations for each subject which a wider curriculum would entail. The intellectual level of any type of Sixth Form work requires subject teaching by specialists; but, if the specialist teaching is also to be personal teaching, it is necessary that the pupils themselves should also be specialists.

WEAKNESSES INSIDE THE SPECIALIST SUBJECTS

392. But, while we accept the case for specialisation on these broad educational grounds, we reject one of the most common arguments advanced in its favour—that specialisation at school is necessary if pupils are to be brought up to the necessary standards to get university entrance. It is no part of our duty, nor is it within our competence, to consider what standards should be set for a first degree at a university, and, consequently, how long the course should be. We are, however, very much concerned to make it clear that an arbitrary fixing by the universities of the stage that a boy or girl should have reached by 18, (standards which are determined by "counting back" from the degree standard) should not be allowed to determine the nature and content of education given in pre-university years, especially (but not entirely) since less than half of the boys and girls in the Sixth Form will be going to a university. We have two main groups of complaints about things as they are. The first group concerns the specialist subjects themselves and really arises from the pressure that is put on the schools by the universities. The length of the whole course of professional training, embracing both school and university, has not been stretched to match the enormous expansion of the corpus of human knowledge, especially on the scientific side. The attempt is made to pour a quart of professional competence into the pint pot of a very few years. To take a boy from Ordinary level to graduation—as graduation is currently understood in this country—in five years is to attempt more than can be done properly in the time. Our second group of complaints is concerned with the use that is made of what we have called minority time.*

393. Our criticism of the existing syllabuses is based on two beliefs. The first is that what is taught in any subject should be taught because it is right for the pupil at that stage of his development, and not because it will be convenient for his teachers in the next stage of his education to be able to take certain knowledge for granted. The second belief is that the job of the Sixth Form is above all to

* See para. 377.

teach a boy to think and not just to memorise facts. How does the syllabus for the work of the Mathematical and Science Sixth stand in relation to these two principles? The main difficulty, and a main glory, of both mathematics and the natural sciences is the constant growth of knowledge. The syllabuses therefore naturally expand. This is not necessarily a bad thing. The capacity to assimilate new knowledge is apparently itself expanding. In time, quite ordinary people master as a matter of course what a few generations before was a mystery for the elect. Samuel Pepys was already at the Admiralty before he learned the multiplication table; today candidates of 15 to 16 are examined each year at Ordinary level in the processes of the differential calculus, which fifty years ago was known only to a few thousand Englishmen. But the expansion in the curriculum can be too rapid and cause temporary congestion. If we extend the syllabus in one direction, we should try to curtail it elsewhere. Periodical revisions of the intellectual diet are in fact necessary. The evidence given to us, and our own comparisons of Higher School Certificate with Advanced level syllabuses covering a span of thirty years, suggest that such a review is now imperative, and that it should include the specialist curriculum of the Science Sixth as a whole, and not only subject by subject. The volume of the syllabus has in general been increased—new topics have been added without compensating reductions, and the quantity of each topic, in the sense of detail rather than of penetrative thought, has been maintained. The Science Masters' Association told us that the existing syllabuses were very far from what they would wish to see, especially referring us to the accumulation of factual knowledge that is required at the expense of opportunities for developing intellectual curiosity. One division of the Incorporated Association of Head Masters, writing on the need to see specialist studies in relation to the whole field of human understanding, reports that "the science teacher's work in this direction is severely limited by the great amount of factual knowledge and practical skill demanded, not involving any depth of human understanding". The work of many science specialists in schools is in fact, we are told, far removed from the scientific spirit of enquiry. We are convinced that the disciplines proper to the Science Sixth can be a suitable instrument of a liberal education. But, until syllabuses have been revised with this purpose in mind, and are no longer regarded simply as the first stages in the vocational training of a scientific worker, it is impossible not to endorse many of the current criticisms of the ill results of over-specialisation.

394. The criticism we would make of the arts syllabuses is of a different nature. It can at least be said of the science specialists that their "majority time" is given to a closely knit group of subjects

which support one another. Alternative courses are normally provided—one in the physical sciences, and another in the biological. A third course for a few mathematicians proper exists in some, but by no means all, schools. These three courses are sufficiently related in character and approach for pupils following any one of them to feel that they are engaged in kindred work with pupils on the other courses. No such unity exists in most schools in the Arts Sixth. It is true that where there are separate classical, history and modern languages Sixth Forms each provides an integrated course which can compare in intellectual coherence with that given on the science side; but in the majority of schools there is commonly a free selection of three main subjects from a field of five or six. English, history, geography, Latin, French, a second modern language and, quite often, economics and divinity are found in many combinations. Out of these diverse elements, integrated and mutually supporting courses of study can be, and are, built, but it does not happen of itself and must be carefully contrived, not only by arranging suitable combinations of subjects, but by seeing that the teaching of one makes use of the knowledge which has been gained in others. The membership of Advanced level sets in English, history and French will, for instance, usually overlap but be far from identical—cross-fertilisation is perfectly possible and highly stimulating. Too often, however, the subjects tend to be taught in isolation, and we are in some doubt how far the virtues of intensive study apply to the work of an Arts Sixth organised in this way. Certainly specialisation has a different connotation when applied to the Arts and to the Science Sixth.

395. A boy finds when he enters the Arts Sixth that the number of teaching periods he will get in each of his three main subjects is increased by one or two, or at most by three, over what he has been accustomed to in the Fifth Form. Greater and more significant will be the increase in the time given to him to work on his own at these subjects. A rough estimate suggests that he will now have for each subject about as much time for private work at school and at home as he has of teaching, and later on even more. In the Fifth Form the ratio of teaching to private work was probably 2 to 1 or even 3 to 1. To read widely—real books, not textbooks; to reflect and argue fiercely about what he has read and heard; to write frequently, freely, critically, imaginatively, accurately—these are the ways in which the arts specialist gets his liberal education (and to some extent the science specialist as well). It is pertinent to ask how much of the time available is spent in these ways. How much goes in hearing lectures and writing up notes afterwards? How much on writing down dictated notes? How much on "getting up" from a text book selected facts and ready-made opinions? To what extent are these practices forced on schools by pressure of time and an externally

prescribed syllabus? Or by the quality of the teachers available? It is worth going back to the comparison made in the last paragraph between the practice of different schools. The contrast is not only between, so to speak, a *table d'hôte* and an *à la carte* menu, but often between two subjects at Advanced level and three. Those schools which cut down the number of Advanced level subjects have more time for study in depth. The difference is often reflected in the quantity and quality of boys' reading lists, which in schools offering three subjects are not infrequently largely restricted to set books and the larger textbooks. The schools that offer two subjects only at Advanced level are able to spend longer on the same examination syllabus, which means, for instance, that the opinions a boy expresses can be based on a more thorough examination of evidence—though of course, this does not always happen. Narrowing the examination field ought to mean deepening the quality of study; it can, however, be used merely to acquire more facts. If this is all the difference, three subjects may be better than two; but, if the teaching is good enough, the smaller field will better serve the purposes of a liberal education. We doubt whether three semi-detached arts subjects can really be studied in depth. At any rate, two is what we would prescribe for the able boy from a limited home background. In fact, it is the able boy from a favoured environment who most often gets it.

396. There are, however, schools which enter their better pupils for four Advanced level subjects. It is largely a boys' school matter and a regional one. One division of the Incorporated Association of Head Masters recently found from a survey of 48 schools that in this group the typical boys' school had 62 Sixth Form pupils only two of whom would be taking four subjects. A similar survey of 83 boys' schools in another division of the Association showed that on the arts side one-eighth of the pupils and on the science side one-third were taking four Advanced level subjects. Where four subjects are taken, a higher proportion of the whole school week is given to specialist work, but an inadequate amount of time to each of the four subjects to permit of real study in depth. This is surely a formula for getting the worst of all worlds. In the area where four subjects were commonly taken the allocation of time to specialist subjects ranged from 24 to 32 periods, with 28 as the most common allocation, out of a 35 period week. We have no hesitation in condemning this practice of taking four Advanced level subjects. It makes any idea of a balanced curriculum unrealistic, and, while increasing specialist time, adds to the difficulty of making a proper educational use of it by piling up the burden of facts to be borne in the memory. It is true that the practice is declining at present, but we fear that the increased pressure to enter universities may lead to a revival. If this happens,

we think the Secondary School Examinations Council should be asked to consider how it could best be discouraged.

LITERACY AND "NUMERACY"

397. Our second main criticism of the present practice of specialisation—and perhaps the most important—concerns the use to which the minority time, amounting usually to between one-quarter and one-third of the time-table, is put. We are strengthened in our view by the fact that it is plainly shared by many of the schools. One of the main functions of minority time should be to provide a complementary element in the curriculum; and if it is properly used, we think it will provide a remedy for some of the most serious of the justified complaints about the dangers of over-specialisation. What actually happens at present? Normally the minority time is divided between a large number of subjects none of which gets more than two periods a week, or at the very most three; a good many get only one. A typical programme for minority time in the North-East of England looks something like this:

Three Periods:	Physical Education (including games)
Two Periods Each:	English
	A Foreign Language
One Period Each:	Civics
	Music
	Religious Instruction

Other subjects and combinations would be available, but these seem to be the most widely chosen. Neither to teachers nor to pupils do they represent a major commitment or concern. Both have, in their own estimation, more important things to do. There is great pressure to use the available private study and homework time for the specialist studies—they represent commitments which must be met if a satisfactory Advanced level record is to be achieved. There is, normally speaking, no such similar incentive to devote unallocated time to the subjects taught in minority time. Some boys, it is true, have to work hard to qualify for university or professional entrance by adding Ordinary level passes in subjects which they either did not take or failed to pass a year before. They have an incentive to work, but the work is of an elementary character. The masters teaching general subjects are chary for understandable reasons of making heavy demands on their pupils outside the pittance of assigned periods. A very little reading, done only by the keenest, and perhaps one short essay a term may well be all that religious instruction involves beyond attendance at one lecture or discussion period a week. English may well involve a little more writing—perhaps five or six short pieces in a year—but much, perhaps most, of the time will be given to reading plays or poetry together in a way that provides a series of very valuable introductions without, however, leading on to developed, intensive study. The foreign language teaching is frequently of a "care and maintenance" order, "keeping up" a knowledge already gained, so that unseens may be tackled without disgrace in university or college entrance examinations. It will be noticed that all the subjects we have discussed are arts subjects. This is because only a minority of schools make any provision for mathematics and the natural sciences in the Sixth Form except as specialist subjects. It may be thought that the picture we have painted is too gloomy. For some individual schools it would be, but we doubt whether their number is growing rapidly, though there are signs of improvement. In the generality of boys' schools the practice is not unlike that which we have sketched here. In girls' schools it is probably somewhat better.

398. In schools where the conditions we have described in the last paragraph prevail, little is done to make science specialists more "literate" than they were when they left the Fifth Form and nothing to make arts specialists more "numerate", if we may coin a word to represent the mirror image of literacy. What is achieved is far nearer a successful holding operation, which prevents a relapse into illiteracy, than an advance commensurate with the growing maturity and ability of the boys. Some of the blame for this relative failure may perhaps rightly be put down to the pressure of the specialist subjects; but more, we feel, belongs to the way in which the minority time is organised. Fragmentation to the degree to which it is practised invites a lack of seriousness among the teachers and the taught. The heaviest blame, however, belongs, we believe, to a failure of determination. Schools and universities agree in theory on the need for balanced education; in practice, however, they refuse to will the means, and therefore must be held to deny the end. We attach great value to the English practice of specialisation. Equally, we attach great importance to those complementary elements in the Sixth Form curriculum which are designed to develop the literacy of science specialists and the numeracy of arts specialists.

399. What do we mean by literacy for a Sixth Former? In the first place we imply the ability to speak and write clearly and correctly at a level commensurate with his general intellectual ability, and to understand thoroughly what others write. This is much more than a simple knowledge of spelling and grammar—though accuracy in these is important. It is not something which can be acquired, at any rate by most boys, by the time they leave the Fifth Form. They are not by that time mature enough to understand the ideas and concepts—in politics or science, for instance—which they will need

to master and express as they grow older. During their Sixth Form years they will need to use language to express more difficult ideas and to develop more extended and complex arguments than they have met before. They need also to develop the skill to follow closely a chain of reasoning and to detect fallacies in it. The ability to do these things does not come to most people without teaching and practice. It is no part of our purpose to discuss teaching methods; our concern is to see that schools recognise the task and provide the time. A pass in "English language" at Ordinary level at the age of 16 does not guarantee effective communication at the level of an 18 year-old.

400. But by the literacy at which a Sixth Former should aim we mean much more than this. We mean that he should, by the time he leaves, be some distance on the way to becoming a well-read man. The teachers to whom he will say good-bye when he leaves school should have introduced him to the company of teachers to whom he need never say good-bye: great writers and thinkers whose work is a permanent enlargement of the human spirit. In history or in literature he can encounter human problems and get wisdom and understanding as he follows the interplay of the ponderable and imponderable forces which shape human destiny. By 15 he is ready for very little of this; but if he has not begun to find it by the time he is 18 or 19 he may never do so, for in the adult world he will have to find it for himself. The years in the Sixth Form are crucial years in which the foundations of a sound social and moral judgement can be laid. They are the seed-time for a lifelong harvest.

401. Literacy has long been important, and its value is as great as ever. Just as by "literacy", in this context, we mean much more than its dictionary sense of the ability to read and write, so by "numeracy" we mean more than mere ability to manipulate the rule of three. When we say that a scientist is "illiterate", we mean that he is not well enough read to be able to communicate effectively with those who have had a literary education. When we say that a historian or a linguist is "innumerate" we mean that he cannot even begin to understand what scientists and mathematicians are talking about. The aim of a good Sixth Form should be to send out into the world men and women who are both literate and numerate. It is perhaps possible to distinguish two different aspects of numeracy that should concern the Sixth Former. On the one hand is an understanding of the scientific approach to the study of phenomena—observation, hypothesis, experiment, verification. On the other hand, there is the need in the modern world to think quantitatively, to realise how far our problems are problems of degree even when they appear as problems of kind. Statistical ignorance and statistical

fallacies are quite as widespread and quite as dangerous as the logical fallacies which come under the heading of illiteracy. The man who is innumerate is cut off from understanding some of the relatively new ways in which the human mind is now most busily at work. Numeracy has come to be an indispensable tool to the understanding and mastery of all phenomena, and not only of those in the relatively close field of the traditional natural sciences. The way in which we think, marshal our evidence and formulate our arguments in every field today is influenced by techniques first applied in science. The educated man, therefore, needs to be numerate as well as literate. Side by side with this need for understanding a new and essential approach to knowledge, the educated man also requires a general acquaintance with the directions in which science is most rapidly advancing and with the nature of the new knowledge that is being acquired. Neither the understanding of scientific method nor this general scientific knowledge is possible unless a sound foundation has been laid in the main school by thorough mathematical and scientific teaching. However able a boy may be, he cannot reach a Sixth Form level of numeracy except on the foundation of a Fifth Form level; but, if his numeracy has stopped short at the usual Fifth Form level, he is in danger of relapsing into innumeracy. It is now one of the most important tasks of the Sixth Form to ensure that no boy or girl leaves school as innumerate as most have done in the past, and as far too many do even today. The boys' schools at least can no longer be criticised for providing an inadequate proportion of science specialists. The task that boys' no less than girls' schools have little more than begun is that of seeing that the Sixth Former who is not going to be a scientist or a technologist is given enough understanding of the scientific side of human knowledge to be able to hold his or her own in an increasingly scientific and technological world. By whatever means this problem is tackled in the schools, it will make heavy demands on really good teachers. But we believe that it must be done, and that the fruits will amply repay the labour

COMPLEMENTARY AND COMMON ELEMENTS

402. The literacy of the scientist and the numeracy of the arts specialist are clearly complementary needs, and it is sometimes suggested that these could be catered for by a "general studies" course in which (or in parts of which) all would find what they need. The idea is tidy and to that extent attractive. Periods could be reserved on the time-table in which the various specialist teachers might make their contributions, and pupils would, therefore, in this way obtain a general conspectus of the contributions which the different branches of the curriculum make to human culture. At a later stage, there is much to be said for such an encyclopaedic approach; but we do not

believe that it is suited to the needs of the Sixth Form. Its members have hardly yet reached the depth of knowledge in any one subject which makes introductory lectures to others profitable. The time given to any subject would necessarily be slight, and the treatment superficial. Both the science specialist and the arts specialist need for their complementary studies a syllabus which is serious enough to provide and call for real study and hard work—"something to get their teeth into". There, perhaps, the resemblance ends. The arts specialist has one over-riding deficiency which is only likely to be met in one way in any given school; the science specialist has needs which can be met in several ways and there are possibilities of various options. The two problems are, therefore, clearly distinguishable and are discussed separately in paragraphs 411 and 413 below.

403. Another proposal has been made to serve the same end. It is reasonable to leave the question of the literacy of a boy on the arts side to his specialist studies; but we cannot, as things now are, trust to his minority time to make him numerate. Similarly, the science specialist may well remain imperfectly literate. How can we enable predominantly arts men to speak and to understand, to some extent, the scientists' language? The proposal has been made that three subjects at Advanced level should remain the normal Sixth Form programme, but for the arts specialist one of these would generally be a scientific subject, and for the scientist one would be taken from the arts curriculum. Some readjustment of syllabuses at Advanced level would be necessary, and the result perhaps would be something like the continental system, but on a less broadly extended front, in order that for each Advanced level subject there might roughly remain the same quantity of class time and private study as at present. This plan would have the great advantage of simplicity, as well as that of being economical in staff. One pattern of this kind is common in girls' schools where biology at Advanced level is quite frequently taken by girls who are also offering two arts subjects. Other "bridge programmes" are, however, uncommon, and this too may be significant. If this plan were to be suitable for pupils who had a university course in mind, it would probably also involve some adjustment in university syllabuses.

404. Clearly this sort of arrangement, where it is practicable, is much better than nothing, and in a number of schools there may for some time be no other way of providing numeracy for the arts specialist. But we have, though with regret, come to the conclusion that this also does not provide an effective remedy for the monocular vision which our present system too often produces. We think that it would make specialisation less effective and valuable than it is now without providing a satisfactory way of securing numeracy for the

arts specialist and literacy for the scientist. It is best to take these objections separately.

405. First, then, what would be lost? It is basic to our thinking that what is done in "majority-time" should form a coherent whole, one subject continuously reinforcing another so that teaching and learning may be enriched by cross-references. The science side, as we have seen, nearly always provides this kind of specialisation; the arts side sometimes does and sometimes does not. A hybrid curriculum would reduce the valuable interlocking element for everybody by roughly one-third—that portion of the majority time allocated to the unrelated study. In practice the value of the two interlocking subjects would, we suspect, be reduced still further by the presence in a class of pupils who had no supporting specialist subject—the arts specialists doing their one science subject, and the scientists their arts course—and who would, therefore, be less familiar than the others with the general context of the particular work in hand.

406. It is fairly clear that a "subject-minded" pupil, as the best are at this age, is likely to resent anything that takes much of his attention from his main interests. He may well regard interlocking subjects as falling within his proper sphere, but he is pretty certain to regard the unrelated subject as a thief of his time and attention. He may put up with it because that is the way the school, or the university entrance requirements, insist on ordering things; but, although he may be an industrious worker, he will not be a satisfactory Sixth Form pupil. "I've got to get an A level in history" is, at best, an invitation to be crammed, not taught. It seems clear to us that, although this plan may command the interest of those pupils whose interests are diffuse, it would not solve the problems of most of the intellectually better Sixth Formers.

407. Our second objection is that the proposed overlapping programmes would not provide what we regard as essential because they would be bound to ignore the valid distinction between the study of a subject which is being tackled for the last time in formal education—a terminal study as it may be called—and advanced work which is designed to lead on to further study at the university or elsewhere. The latter type of course is normal for Sixth Form specialist work. The purpose of teaching history to specialists is not to store their minds with facts, but to enable them to approach a problem historically, to enter into the past and interpret it, and to begin to appreciate the nature of historical evidence. The choice of period, though important, is itself, for them, secondary; but for non-specialists it is of primary importance. Altogether different criteria are appropriate in planning a course for non-specialists whose last formal history teaching this may be. The science specialist too will

almost certainly continue his scientific education after he leaves school. The work he does at school is preparatory, and much of it must be concerned with the mastery of techniques and the acquisition of knowledge which are more relevant to his future needs than to his present understanding. But the arts specialist will in all probability receive no more science teaching after he leaves school, and the pupil from the science side will be in a corresponding position with regard to arts work. Neither, then, needs to acquire the skills and techniques required to carry their off-subject to a high level. Both require a course which will, so to speak, enable them to see what the other side is getting at. Advanced level syllabuses are not designed for this purpose; nor do we see how they could be revised to do this without spoiling them for their major purpose. This is one case where amateurs cannot be mixed with professionals.

408. But though we do not feel able to accept either of these short cuts, we are very far indeed from suggesting that there are no needs that all Sixth Formers have in common, and nothing that they cannot study with advantage together. This common ground includes religious instruction—or, rather, the very much wider field of everything that contributes to the formation of moral standards—art (also in the widest sense), and physical education. There is no reason why arts and science specialists should not be brought together for these purposes, and many reasons why they should. Music, especially in the form of appreciation, is very commonly provided; art appreciation quite often. Opportunities to paint, to carve stone or wood, or to model in clay are relatively seldom available in school time. It is our belief that the non-verbal arts have a most important contribution to make to education, and not least to the education of the ablest pupils. The education we give them is so highly and necessarily verbalised—and this applies in some measure to science as well as to the literary subjects—that it needs a counterpoise. The non-verbal arts are quite as important as physical education at this age, and we believe that opportunity for appreciation and the practice of one of them, freely chosen, should be available to the Sixth Former and that he should be actively encouraged to use them.

409. All Sixth Formers also share a common spiritual heritage. They bring to it many different attitudes. The approach, and the recoil, of the history specialist and the science specialist are likely to be different but complementary. The study of the "Christian Religion and its Philosophy", as the School Broadcasting Council now describes its series for Sixth Forms, involves ventures into scientific method and historical criticism as well as into philosophy and straight religious exposition, and this is bound to happen whether or not a school uses the broadcast talks as a basis for its teaching.

There is much to be gained from making the periods set apart for this purpose periods in which arts and science specialists can join together—provided that the members of the group know each other well enough to make discussion profitable. Each side, as we have said, has its own separate contribution to make and its characteristic viewpoint, but the reason they come together is common to both. It is the endeavour to discover and to understand the central affirmations of the Christian faith so that (whether they accept it or not) they at least may know what Christians believe.

410. In our view, then—to sum up the argument to the point it has now reached—there should be not two but three elements in a sound Sixth Form curriculum. The first and largest should be the specialist element, on which a boy will spend, say, two-thirds of his time in school and much the greater part of his homework. Secondly there should be the common element, when scientists and arts specialists should come together. And, thirdly, so to speak between the other two, there should be the complementary element, whose purposes—and in our view they must in the main be pursued separately—are to save the scientists from illiteracy and the arts specialists from innumeracy. In the next two sections we shall take up this complementary element and attempt to explain what, in our view, it should contain on either side. But first it is perhaps necessary to meet the possible objection that three distinct elements in a Sixth Form curriculum is more than can be squeezed into the time-table. We do not think this is so. Out of the conventional total of 35 periods a week, 25 or 26 (plus almost all the homework) ought to be enough for the specialist subjects, unless the pupil's programme is hopelessly overloaded (for example, by four Advanced level subjects). That leaves 9 or 10 periods for the common and complementary elements. Four or five periods for the common subjects is not a great deal, but it is probably about as much as can profitably be used. That leaves about the same for the "complementary" courses. If this amount of time is used in a purposeful and concentrated way, we believe that it could achieve a great deal. It is, in any case, doubtful whether more than a handful of schools could find staff for the sort of courses we are about to describe to an extent greater than is implied in 3 or 4 periods a week. We do not, of course, pretend that we have discovered a magical formula by which the circle can be squared and enough time be found for everything that has to be done in the Sixth Form. It is here that, for most people, the supply of time first begins to run badly short of the demands they put upon it—never, in most lives, to catch up. Our concern is only to show that, by analysing the content of a Sixth Form curriculum under three heads, we are not suggesting any net addition to the burden that the time-table has to bear.

THE LITERACY OF SCIENCE SPECIALISTS

411. There is no special difficulty in providing science specialists with the means of making themselves literate in the broad sense which we have given to this term—the establishment of moral, aesthetic and social judgement, and the development of adequate powers of verbal communication. It is something that schools are well able and well staffed to undertake. Literacy is bred in the bone of a school. To induce it is the teacher's familiar task. His pupils have the rudiments by the time they leave the Fifth Form; in the Sixth Form the task is one of development. What difficulty there is (apart from the perpetual problem of finding time) is likely to turn on the choice between the rich fields of opportunity. Some real language study is surely essential—practice in the skill of writing, and writing appropriately in different styles for different purposes; and, when it is possible, beyond that and in relation to it, some introduction to syntax and etymology as instruments of precision in thought. The art of reading for understanding and appreciation—the mastery of a complicated document, the appreciation alike of shades of meaning and beauties of expression—is something that can only be acquired by study. But, then, there is another side to literacy. No science specialist, it seems to us, should be deprived of the chance to see human society as it is now, as it has been in history, and as it should be—that world of men which is more precious, less predictable, more fragile and yet more resilient than the world of machines. The proper study of mankind can be approached in a dozen ways. Some schools will have a teacher who can stir young blood with the old issues of that French Revolution which turned the world upside down; in another there may be a classic with the gift for bringing scientists to the feet of Plato; in a third Shakespeare or T. S. Eliot may hold the needed key. Other schools and other pupils may find what they need in the study of a foreign language; but, to be worth its place as a main complementary element in the curriculum, it must be carried far enough to give the pupil some insight into the life and outlook and, if possible, the literature of the people whose language he is studying. And that implies adequate time—more than a token number of periods each week and for not less than one year. Without that, it does not seem to us worth while.

412. These two aspects of literacy—the basic one of language and communication, and the developed one which includes all that is conjured up by the term "the humanities"—can be satisfied either in conjunction in one subject or separately, and in many forms. The great danger is, of course, that of yielding to the familiar temptation of trying to do so much that nothing is well done. A properly

balanced combination is important, but the complementary subjects will weigh too little if there are too many of them, each with a derisory ration of time. The right prescription for any single school must depend on its individual circumstances (not least on the teaching strength available); but it is worth remembering that English subjects do not as a group require continuous and uninterrupted treatment. A good weekly time allocation, including provision for private study for one subject over a relatively extensive period, followed by similar arrangements for another, is a better programme, where it is possible, than shorter concurrent time allocations for each. We need to think of a rota of subjects and a curriculum planned in units of one (or at most two) complementary subjects at a time, each lasting for a term or a year. If the science specialists are numerous enough, there is no reason why there should not be alternative courses and every reason why there should.

THE NUMERACY OF ARTS SPECIALISTS

413. Schools are much further off finding a solution for the numeracy of arts specialists. The majority ignore the problem and make no provision. The minority most commonly provide a history of science, which is apt to turn into another literary subject. A few schools have made bold experiments designed to provide the kind of numeracy which we described in an earlier paragraph. They are, however, no more than pilot experiments. Standard science courses have been designed almost exclusively for the preliminary training of future scientists, and not nearly enough attention has been given to the role of science in the general education of men and women who specialise in other things. This is a matter which at the university level is profitably engaging the attention of some of the best scientific minds. It is one of the most urgent tasks that confronts the schools today.

414. The pioneers in the schools have shown that a well thought-out course can open eyes that never expected to see a scientific prospect. We assume that mathematics and science will normally have been among the subjects studied by arts specialists up to roughly Ordinary level standard. This represents probably the minimum equipment without which the kind of course we have in mind would prove impracticable. The pupils will by then have done sufficient individual laboratory work to make it reasonable (as it will certainly be necessary) to substitute demonstration for experiment over much of the Sixth Form course. On an Ordinary level foundation we could hope to accomplish something worthwhile with four periods a week, but it would be possible to make a start with three, or even with two periods, if that is all for which staff could be found. Fruitful experiments of many kinds have been made and we are indebted to the

Science Masters' Association for a clear appreciation of the problem as they now see it. Theirs is an interim report; and we are all still in the stage when we recognise the end, but are not sure we have found the means. The Science Masters' Association identify four aims. The first is to provide an introduction to "scientific method": how the scientist approaches his experiments, what sort of answer satisfies him, how his mind works. The second is to develop five or six fundamental scientific topics such as energy, living and dead matter, evolution, cosmology. The third is to illustrate the impact of science on society; and the fourth its impact on philosophy and religion. They believe that those aims could be achieved by the method of a close study of certain "case histories" or sequences of scientific discovery. Newtonian physics and Darwinian evolution are two examples that spring to mind. The study of both can be rooted in observation; used to illustrate the way in which theories are formed, tested and modified; and developed to illustrate the profound influence of science on society and on philosophy and religion. Other case histories can be found and will be needed; but the Science Masters' Association would, if we understand them rightly, lay down as a criterion for selection that no "case history" should be chosen to form part of a course in numeracy for arts specialists which does not to some degree satisfy all four aims. We agree. There are other methods which can be devised to satisfy these aims. The period of experiments is by no means finished. We would insist that the matter is one of urgency, and that concerted efforts should be made to see not only that a choice of suitable courses is planned to meet the needs of every Sixth Form, but also that sufficient staff are available to undertake them. This will involve no doubt a considerable training programme. Many qualified and successful teachers of science, as it has been taught, will require short refresher courses to make them aware of what is involved in the new task that is being put upon them. They will need in some instances a wider and clearer apprehension of what science is about than even their own training gave them, or than they are giving to the science specialists in their own Advanced level courses. It ought not to be possible to say this of future generations of science teachers; but, if they are to be free of the imputation, there will have to be a thorough reconsideration of their training both in its scientific and professional aspects.

415. Our awareness of the great additional demands these courses must make on highly qualified—and scarce—staff leads us to examine with great sympathy any suggestions for economy. Is it possible to provide the kind of interpretative course we have in mind jointly for the Arts and Science Sixths? Both need teaching which will help them to find their bearings in the world of science and its relation

to other worlds. There is nothing of this in syllabuses up to the Ordinary level, and could not be. It is essentially a Sixth Form problem. Both arts and science specialists will, we hope, in future have followed a common course in science, or at any rate a largely common course, until the end of the Fifth Form. They start from the same position. Why cannot they travel further together to the good of their own souls and with a considerable economy in staff? The argument is attractive in the same way, and for the same reasons, as the plan for a mixed specialist curriculum which we discussed in paragraphs 403 to 407. It differs from it by suggesting that the technical element in the education of science specialists, the preparatory work for the professional superstructure, should be designed for, and taken by, them alone. In this way it meets one of the principal objections to the other plan—that it would give the arts specialists what they do not want, and withhold from them what they need. But, for all that, a common course in the general aspects of science does not seem to us often likely to be practicable. It would involve the dilemma of whether or not to use scientific and mathematical symbols and language. Without them, the course would be likely to seem child's play to the scientists; if they are used freely, the arts specialists are likely to be left far behind. For the science specialist a common course with the arts men in general principles and a separate course in subject matter would cut his science course as a whole most undesirably in two. The course in the general principles of science would either have to take the form of theories isolated from evidence, or of inferences from another set of observations than those that form the staple of his Advanced level work, with which the arts specialists would not be familiar. Arts and science specialists may indeed start from the same place, but they travel at very different speeds. This is in our view the insuperable objection to a joint course in the principles of science. The science specialist should get the broader view, and a realisation of the social implications of science, within the revised curriculum of his specialist subject itself. The arts specialist should get his numeracy from a special course tailored to his needs.

HOW TO MAKE MINORITY TIME IMPORTANT

416. There is probably general agreement about the sort of things that the different groups of boys and girls in Sixth Forms ought to be taught in their minority time. There is very much less agreement about the kind of measures that are necessary if they are to be taught effectively, or even taught at all. How can we so arm these subjects that they are able to survive in a curriculum dominated by the jungle law of the survival of the fittest?

417. No artificial stimulus is necessary in a good school where the headmaster and the heads of departments are seized with the importance of the minority time and let their opinion of it be widely known among the boys. All schools will never be like this, and perhaps we shall have long to wait before even the average school could justly be described in this way. Would external examinations help the average school? In what way could they hinder it? Examinations have come to have such a high value for Englishmen that most unexamined subjects are regarded with indifference. An obvious step would be to submit the work done in minority time to external examination—not merely to examine it, but to incorporate it in examinations that the specialist has to pass, such as university entrance examinations. Nevertheless, we think there are decisive objections to any imposed external examination of complementary subjects—unless indeed, it takes a very broad form such as the "general paper" that most Oxford and Cambridge colleges include in their entrance examinations. There are two major ones: first, that it would prescribe a syllabus, and secondly, that, as scripts multiplied, marking standards would inevitably tend unduly to reward meticulous preparation which had been careful to cover the whole field. These are very serious objections. The schools are little beyond the beginnings of finding suitable science courses for arts specialists, and we believe that any externally imposed rigidity would at this stage almost destroy the possibility of doing anything useful. To some extent this is true also of the literacy courses we want to see established for the science specialists. The other objection, the depressing effect on teaching of the kind of marking which is necessary in a large-scale examination, is a very real danger.

418. Nevertheless, some sort of adventitious incentive is probably essential. Where can one be found? The most potent in our view is that those who are responsible for the next stage in a pupil's career should show as lively and informed an interest in the use he has made of his minority time as they do in his specialist work. We shall return to the selective aspect in the next chapter. Here we are concerned with how to convey the information about what he has done and how well he has done it. There are various possibilities, some of which are at present being tried out experimentally. The best known solution is the General Paper at Advanced level which is now being given a trial by the Northern Universities' Joint Matriculation Board. In its experimental run, when it was taken by only a few schools, it proved a stimulating influence on Sixth Form work. It is not yet clear whether the growth in the number of scripts to be examined will have a deadening effect, or whether, despite its sponsors' wishes, what is intended to be merely a general paper will become in effect the paper examining the work done in a

"general subject", about the value of which we expressed doubts in paragraph 402. Another possibility would be to record on the certificate given as a result of the Advanced level examination an assessment of the work done in the minority time side by side with the examination results of the specialist work. Such an assessment might, perhaps, be made internally with the help of an external assessor. Some Institutes of Education* are using analogous methods of continuous assessment instead of examinations to judge the progress of students in teacher training colleges. This method would convey both what a Sixth Former had done with his minority time and how successfully he had used it. A third method would merely record the subjects he had studied in his minority time, leaving university or employer to find out by interview, or in some other way, how well he had worked and how good he was. It is worth remembering, too, that headmasters write reports both to parents, and confidentially to employers and university authorities, which can, and do, comment on the use that a candidate has made of his minority time. They can hardly do this satisfactorily for our purpose, however, where the school, as well as the individual pupils, fails to take it seriously. There are thus a number of methods that could be used, and it should not be difficult to find which of them is the most suitable, once the essential point has been made, and school, pupil, employer and university all alike come to realise that the proper employment of a Sixth Former's minority time is nearly as important as his performance in his specialist subjects—important not only for its own sake but for the immediate purpose of being admitted to the next stage in his career.

SUMMARY

419. We summarise below our conclusions on the curriculum of those pupils following Advanced level courses in the Sixth Form.

(*a*) We endorse the principle of specialisation, or study in depth.

(*b*) We are, however, unhappy about four ways in which it is now working:

(i) The syllabuses in science make considerably heavier demands than they used to do. They need reconsidering not only subject by subject, but together as the specialist curriculum of the Science Sixth.

(ii) The combination of subjects offered by pupils in the Arts Sixth is often unsatisfactory because it does not form a coherent whole.

(iii) Some schools enter pupils for too many Advanced level

* See Glossary under Training College.

subjects. The number of pupils taking four subjects is falling, but is still too high, especially in certain areas.

(iv) Between one-quarter and one-third of the school week is given to non-specialist subjects. We refer to this as "minority time". It is often neglected or wasted. It is, however, of vital importance.

(*c*) There are two purposes for which the minority time should be used, which we distinguish as complementary and common.

(*d*) The main common elements, which should be taken by arts and science specialists together, can be summarised under three heads—religious education and all that goes to the formation of moral standards; art and music; and physical education.

(*e*) The complementary elements should be designed to ensure the literacy of science specialists and the "numeracy" of arts specialists. By literacy in this context we mean not only the ability to use the mother tongue as an adequate means of communication for adult purposes, but also the development of moral, aesthetic and social judgement. By "numeracy" we mean not only the ability to reason quantitatively but also some understanding of scientific method and some acquaintance with the achievement of science.

(*f*) We considered, and reject, proposals to make good these deficiencies either by a "General Course" or by making it normal for an arts specialist to take one science subject at Advanced level, and a science specialist one arts subject.

(*g*) The difficulty in the way of making all science specialists literate is not one of ignorance about how to do it, but of the will to see that it is done thoroughly and effectively.

(*h*) There seems to us to be no way of making the arts specialist numerate except by providing a special Sixth Form course for this purpose. Promising experimental work has been done in this field, but much remains still to be discovered about the best means to use.

(*i*) We are not unmindful of the fact that any such course would impose an extra burden on a section of the staff of Sixth Forms that is already heavily laden and—especially in girls' schools—very scarce. Furthermore, a certain amount of re-training and refresher courses would be necessary.

(*j*) There are grave dangers in the examination of work done in "minority time", but some outside influence is probably necessary if schools and pupils are to take it more seriously than at present. The most potent influence is likely to be the knowledge that prospective employers, universities and colleges of advanced technology attach importance to it.

CHAPTER 26

The Problem of University Entrance

420. No part of the ground covered by our terms of reference is more obscure and controversial than the relation between the schools and the subsequent careers of Sixth Form pupils, and especially of those who go on, or hope to go on, to universities. A close relation with the universities was one of the marks of the Sixth Form that we noted in Chapter 21. It sets the tone and maintains the intellectual standards of the work in the upper part of schools. The fact is obvious; we certainly would not have it otherwise. But it is indisputable that the close connection brings certain difficulties in its train, and we believe that those difficulties are bound to become increasingly troublesome in the next decade unless they are tackled realistically with a full understanding by the universities of the position and needs of the schools, and by the schools of the requirements of higher education. In this chapter we set out half of the story, and only one half—the position as we see it in the schools—and the general conclusions to which this survey has led the whole Council, some of whose members teach in schools, some in universities and some of whom are laymen in this whole field. It is, we think, not without significance that we are unanimous in our conclusions.

UNIVERSITY CANDIDATES AND OTHERS

421. The first point we would make is that, even if general courses are excluded, a Sixth Form has to serve the needs both of those who go on to courses of university standing and of those who do not. They have to be taught side by side and, throughout the greater part of the course at least, to follow the same curriculum. The structure of the Sixth Form, as we have analysed it in Chapter 24, makes this inevitable in many schools; it is also right for all schools. It would be altogether wrong to ask a boy to decide at 16 whether or not he wanted to go to a university when he became 18 or 19, and to hold him to his decision. It would be equally wrong to make that decision for him. This is the kind of long-range vocational guidance that cannot safely be given, and should not be attempted.

422. What is the position at the end of the Sixth Form course? It is almost impossible to be accurate because, since the war, some boys have done their National Service before and some after their university course; and, though National Service is now ending, its effect in

disrupting the orderly flow from school to university is still with us. There is another possibility of confusion. By no means all courses of university standing are in universities. The colleges of advanced technology have their courses for the Diploma in Technology which are of honours degree standard, and there are students in these and other technical colleges working for London degrees. The best answer we can give, using the wider definition of a university course, is that over half the boys and between one-quarter and one-fifth of the girls in Sixth Forms leave school with the intention of taking a university course.* The proportion in the second year of the Sixth Form who are hoping to go to a university would no doubt be higher. The conclusion is inevitable that the curriculum of the Sixth Form cannot be drawn up with the needs of only future university students in mind. It should be built up from below rather than worked back from the requirements of a degree examination which will take place five or six years after entrance to the Sixth Form. The syllabus to be followed should be designed to give the best intellectual training available to boys and girls in the late teens without reckoning on any extension or completion of it later on, though a proportion, in some instances a high proportion, will in fact enjoy longer full-time education. Any general public examination at the end of the Sixth Form course ought properly, we suggest, to be backward-looking, designed to record achievement in work done during the previous two or three years. This is in fact what the Advanced level of the General Certificate of Education is designed to do (though the scholarship papers have another purpose). On the whole, it does this fairly enough, though, as we have argued in the previous chapter, we believe that a good deal of pruning is needed in certain directions. It becomes still more important to stress that the Advanced level is a leaving, and not an entrance, examination because the great increase in Sixth Form numbers makes it clear that a smaller proportion than in the past will be using it (successfully at any rate) to secure university admission.

QUALIFICATION AND SELECTION

423. This brings us to our second main point—the difference between qualification and selection. By qualification we mean two things. The

* The basis of this estimate is the number of leavers shown in the Ministry's Annual Report for 1958 as going to universities, expressed as a percentage of pupils aged 17 at maintained or direct grant schools. This gives, for boys, 43 per cent for the maintained and 58 per cent for the direct grant schools. In 1955 the Headmasters' Conference reported that 68 per cent of the boys leaving independent schools went to courses of university standing. This information has been taken into account in making the rough estimate in the text. The figures for girls' maintained and direct grant grammar schools in 1958 were 19 and 29 per cent respectively. No figures are available for girls' independent schools.

more important is the capacity to profit by a university course and to pass the examinations which punctuate it. The less important is the possession of such certificates as the university may require before entry. In the case of Oxford and Cambridge the formal qualification is low, though, as we think, in one respect it is—or has hitherto been—unnecessarily troublesome to the schools. In other universities, where the standard qualification is two subjects at Advanced level, it is, we believe, realistically related to the nature of a university course. Qualification used virtually to ensure admission. It no longer does so. There are far too many qualified candidates for the vacancies that exist, at least in the more sought-after universities. Selection is therefore necessary. At Oxford and Cambridge the selection is made by the colleges; in the provincial universities by the faculties and departments; and in London by the departments in each college. It is necessary to labour the distinction between qualification and selection because, as entrance becomes increasingly competitive, there is a natural tendency to slide into the belief that only the finally selected candidates are really qualified for university work. This is natural enough where, as in Oxford and Cambridge colleges, the machinery of the college entrance examination, used not so long ago merely or largely to weed out the unqualified, has become a highly selective instrument. But, though natural, it is dangerous to blur the distinction, especially when the argument turns on sufficiency of provision or on standards of work.

424. Once again we must attempt to make clear the size of the problem. The position is almost unbelievably complicated. Not only are there over 20 universities, and many separate colleges within universities, all independent of one another and without any central machinery for applications, but there has been the difficulty of National Service to which we have already referred. A good deal of light on the situation as it was in 1955 has been thrown by the pioneer investigation carried out for the Committee of Vice-Chancellors by Dr. R. K. Kelsall. It showed that in the universities of the United Kingdom—though with the important (and in some matters all-important) exceptions of Oxford and Cambridge—there were in 1955 about 2,500 unfilled places, over half of them on the arts side. There were also about the same number of "qualified" candidates who failed to be "selected" for a place that year or later, but only some 37 per cent of them wanted an arts course. Moreover there was a considerable number of disappointed overseas candidates. Of the candidates for admission in 1955 we may say—very roughly—that between 80 and 85 per cent were "qualified" (at least in the university, if not always in the faculty, sense), and that some 60 per cent were "selected" that year. Another 15 per cent were "selected" in 1956 or promised a place later (usually at Oxford or Cambridge), leaving

2,000 to 2,500 candidates who, though "qualified" were never "selected". These figures are for the United Kingdom as a whole. The position for England appears to be rather worse. About three-quarters of the "selected", but 84 per cent of the "non-selected", were English. Scotland had a higher proportion of its relevant age-group admitted than the other home countries. In 1947 admissions to English universities were roughly at the rate of one for every two 17 year-olds in school; by 1955 they were at the rate of one for every two-and-a-half. In 1957, in spite of there being more university places, the rate was slightly worse. The general availability of grants to finance university courses makes it likely that the number of Sixth Formers who set their hearts on a university course will continue to grow with the numbers in the Sixth Form.

425. It follows from the excess of "qualified" over "selected" candidates that, in the absence of any central clearing house, many pupils will make application direct to more than one university or college. The 1955 investigation showed that the average candidate made more than two applications, excluding applications to Oxford and Cambridge. Moreover the candidates who had to try again in 1956, a very substantial number, probably applied to as many universities then as in 1955. Unfortunately we have no means of knowing how many candidates also applied to the separate colleges of Oxford or Cambridge. Certainly many must have applied to more than one college in both universities. These numbers, if known, ought to be added to the total of applications to other universities before averaging because—fortunately—it is impossible to separate schools into those which feed Oxford and Cambridge and those which do not. The independent schools provided 23 per cent of the "selected" candidates at London and 9 per cent at other English universities; the maintained schools 39 per cent of the "selected" candidates at Oxford and 27 per cent at Cambridge. In the last three years, 12 per cent of the pupils applying for admission to a university from the maintained grammar schools of one large city were candidates for (among other universities) Oxford or Cambridge. Another example may be given. Only 2 out of 45 maintained grammar schools in one county have sent no applications from pupils to Oxford or Cambridge during the last three years, though many were feeling that it is an increasingly useless pursuit. It is clear, therefore, that the entry problem cannot be divided into two separate halves, with Oxford, Cambridge and (to a lesser extent) London on the one hand, and the remaining universities on the other. It is a single problem for the schools, which the great prestige of Oxford and Cambridge, and the strength of the desire to gain admittance to them, do a great deal to complicate.

426. If this is the position now, what is it likely to be in ten years' time? The planned expansion of the universities will provide an increase of about one-quarter in the number of undergraduate places available for residents in England and this will not be sufficient markedly to reduce the competitive element. It is true that the increase in the number of university places is a matter of policy, whereas the increase in the number of 17 year-olds in school is only a probability. Its prospective size was discussed in Chapter 22. Given the increased size of the age-group and a continuation of the trend towards a longer school life which has been in evidence now for a long time, we should expect to see one-and-a-half times to twice as many 17 year-olds in school in the middle sixties as there are today. It is possible that the numbers wanting to go to the university may not increase in the same proportion. But it is hardly conceivable that the Sixth Forms of the country could increase by between 50 and 100 per cent. without there being an increase of much more than 25 per cent. in the number of applicants to the universities. The disparity between the increase in the size of the field and the number of available places is so great that an intensification of the fierceness of the competition to get into the universities seems virtually certain. It is natural and proper that schools should do all they can not only to prepare their pupils for the universities, but also to see that they get there. This may well have the paradoxical result that, at a time when the proportion of Sixth Formers who will in fact succeed in entering a university is dropping, the proportion of effort expended by Sixth Form masters in securing university places will be increasing. It is, then, with an uneasy eye on future developments that we approach our analysis of the effect of university requirements, and of the examinations concerned with them, on the work of the Sixth Form.

427. It is possible to group the main difficulties that arise under four heads:

- those that are caused by the multiplicity of examinations used to select candidates for admission (paragraph 428);
- those that arise from the varying qualifying passes required by different universities from students proposing to read the same subject (paragraphs 429–430);
- those that arise from the highly competitive nature of the selection (paragraphs 431–438);
- those that spring from the fact that the paymaster of most students is the local education authority (paragraphs 444–445).

THE MULTIPLICITY OF EXAMINATIONS

428. In order to understand the first group of problems it is necessary to be clear about the nature of the academic year in schools and

universities. It is customary to talk of a Sixth Form course as lasting two or three years and to think of six or nine terms as being available for work. The reality is different. A newcomer to the Sixth Form may reckon at most on four or five clear terms for new work. Early in his fifth term he may be faced by a pretty full dress rehearsal for the Advanced level papers in the General Certificate of Education. June and not July is the month chosen by all but one of the examining boards for the actual examination. If a boy or girl hopes to enter the university in the following October he or she is very likely to have other examinations to face in the spring term. Over half the girls who went to the university did so after two years in the Sixth Form, and a number of those who in the event took a third year in the Sixth Form probably tried to get admission to the university after two. The women's colleges at Oxford, Cambridge and London hold their examinations at times which limit the work of many candidates in the final year (whichever it is) to even less than one term. The scholarship examinations at Oxford and Cambridge for men's colleges are three-quarters over before the second term of the year starts, and are usually followed by the entrance examinations for commoners. The London scholarship examinations are in February. In addition to this there may be a faculty examination to be taken; and, as we have ourselves discovered, it is extremely difficult to find out in what circumstances this is done and what precisely is required. This uncertainty, together with the frequent changes, puts the schools in an impossible position in attempting to advise their pupils, whose whole future may depend on accurate information. It may very well be that if candidates took the risk of applying for only one university—but only the very good or the very unambitious are likely to do that—the pressure of examinations on teaching time would not be too bad. But in 1955 the average boy who secured a place in a British university had applied to 2·1, and the average girl to 2·5, universities excluding any applications to Oxford or Cambridge colleges. Since then the number of applications has increased by 50 per cent. No doubt this increase is caused partly by an increasing number of competitors as well as by an increase in the number of applications made by each candidate, but it is clear enough that the situation is deteriorating. It is fair to say that the systematic extension of knowledge and intellectual development is interrupted for a good many Sixth Formers by a revising and polishing-up process after the end of the fourth term. There is a place for revision and a value in polishing-up, but the relative proportions of the time spent in teaching, in revising and in examination have become distorted. We welcome, therefore, the suggestions of the Vice-Chancellors' *ad hoc* committee, which would simplify the administrative procedure and, by abolishing faculty examinations, would reduce the number of examinations to be taken. It is difficult, however, to see how the schools can settle down to a steady routine of five or eight terms' teaching, as they should, unless the problem of college entrance as well as of faculty examinations can be tackled. The *ad hoc* committee have made a useful beginning in clearing up some of the worst of the tangle, but far more remains to be done before we have a satisfactory system. The position of girls needs especial care. The cumulative competitive stress to which they are subjected, on top of the Advanced level, if they wish to go to one of the Oxford, Cambridge or London women's colleges where the competition for a small number of places is very intense, seems to us to have become so great that it should no longer be tolerated.

429. The second group of difficulties arises in the main from the varying views about supporting subjects held in different universities. By far the most serious problem is the position of Latin. We have already referred to the requirement of Latin to Ordinary level that Oxford and Cambridge impose on all their entrants; and it may be that this is in process of being modified. There are no other universities that require Latin from all candidates, but about half of them require Latin at Advanced level from candidates who hope to read modern languages, history or English. What are the schools to make of the situation? One well known school, for example, solves the problem by prescribing French, German and Latin for all its modern linguists, and history, English and French for all its historians, accepting for them the consequence that roughly half the universities will be out-of-bounds. The worst placed single subject is pretty certainly geography, because some universities regard it as an arts subject and require supporting Advanced level passes in other arts subjects, while others treat it as a science with corresponding demands. In the University of Durham there are even conflicting regulations for the two divisions of the university at Durham and Newcastle-upon-Tyne. The medical schools are among the most difficult for the schools to serve because of slight variations in what they require for exemption from 1st M.B. It is not easy for us to see why all require Advanced level passes in physics and chemistry (save Bristol, which will accept a good pass at Ordinary level or a pass at Ordinary or Advanced level in the Advanced level examination in physics) but that varying regulations apply to biology:

London only requires an Advanced level pass in zoology;

Leeds, Liverpool and Manchester require Advanced level biology or zoology;

Birmingham normally requires Advanced level biology but will in exceptional cases consider pupils who have passes in botany or zoology;

Bristol requires an Advanced level pass in biology or in zoology together with a good pass in botany at Ordinary level;

Sheffield requires an "acceptable standard" at Advanced level in biology or zoology or botany;

Newcastle requires Advanced level biology or botany *and* zoology, though in exceptional cases Ordinary level biology or botany will be accepted.

Similar lists could be compiled for other subjects. Moreover, they are constantly changing, often at short notice, and this itself adds to the schools' difficulties.

430. There is the further point that universities seem to expect, when they do not formally demand, three Advanced level passes, while state scholarships can be, and often are, awarded to candidates who have only taken two. Schools, in defence of freedom of manoeuvre for their pupils, are almost forced into choosing a heavy enough programme to satisfy the most exacting university. This does not seem to us to be necessarily in the interests of the candidates. While we hope, then, that simplification may go forward by inter-faculty agreement, we are anxious lest it should take the form of imposing the most stringent combination of conditions. The present confusion would almost be preferable to this. It must be emphasised, however, once again that in demanding such a variety of entrance qualifications the universities are doing a most serious disservice to the schools.

METHODS OF SELECTION

431. We do not for a moment want to underestimate the difficulty of the universities' task in selecting their entrants. On what rational grounds can choice be made among so many candidates who have complied with all the formal requirements for admission? From the schools' point of view, the dilemma can, we think, fairly be put in the form of five propositions:

(*a*) No satisfactory solution is possible while the situation is fiercely competitive.

(*b*) So far as can be foreseen, the competition is likely to get more severe.

(*c*) Even if there were an over-all equivalence between the number of places available and the number of applicants, there would still be strong competition to secure places in certain universities, colleges and departments.

(*d*) The methods of selection must appear, to candidates and to the public, to be fair.

(*e*) It is equally important that they should not react harmfully on the educational work of the schools.

432. In one sense selection for universities from Sixth Forms ought to be easy because all the candidates are of superior intelligence and will be guaranteed by the qualifying examination (Advanced level in the G.C.E.) to have reached a respectable order of attainment. In another sense, it is exceedingly difficult because there is often no *prima facie* reason why one candidate should be preferred to another—yet the decision must be publicly defensible. It is, of course, possible to decide which candidates know most, or answer questions best, at the moment the list is drawn up; but this is so far from making it possible to predict with precision their relative positions after three years that, for instance, only three-quarters of the state scholars who finished their awards in 1957 got first-class or second-class honours degrees. Yet state scholars are supposed to be part of the cream of the entry—they represent only about one-fifth of the admission to universities. This uncertainty of prediction does not acquit the universities of the responsibility of deciding to accept one qualified candidate and reject another. In this situation it is reasonable to ask that the methods chosen should be those which, besides being fair, do least harm to the education of the candidates while they are at school and to the other pupils in the same forms.

433. We distinguish three main types of selection procedure—those which involve a special examination; those which rely on a special mark (higher than the official pass mark) in an existing general examination; and those which rely on interview. Of course, these methods can be, and often are, used in combination. They have, however, some important things in common. For one thing, quite insufficient research work has been done on the validity of the various procedures so that it is impossible to discuss accuracy of selection. This would be a purely internal matter if all that was at stake was which university a candidate attended. It becomes a general matter when what is at stake is whether he attends a university at all. We suspect (though we are unable to prove it) that another common factor is that the great majority of successful candidates would have been selected by whichever method was used. If this is true, it is right to attach quite as much importance to what a particular method of selection does to the schools as to whom it selects.

434. The first method of selection is the setting, in addition to the university's entrance requirements, of a special entrance examination by the college, faculty or department concerned. The necessity of making multiple applications implies a certainty of being over-examined if this system became universal. And because the department is interested primarily in the candidate's specialist work, the examination tends to be a repetition of his Advanced level examination, but perhaps (since G.C.E. syllabuses vary considerably

from board to board) on a syllabus he has incompletely covered. Its advantage to the selectors, however, is great. It enables them to judge quality for themselves. Without it, they would have to rely on an examination set and corrected by somebody else, and giving no information beyond an aggregate mark, which could have been won in a number of different ways. It is not the questions, but the quality of the answers, in which the selectors are interested. We think that there may be other ways in which their legitimate curiosity could be satisfied without running the risk of over-examining, and we shall come back to this in paragraph 443.

435. In the same category as individual entrance examinations are open scholarship examinations, and especially those of the Oxford and Cambridge colleges. We know of no better way of choosing the ablest boys, though it is by no means infallible, and it is a good method of influencing in the right direction the specialist teaching they are given. But with an open scholarship examination it is even more important than with a college or faculty entrance examination that the field should be small—small enough to be individually considered without hurry and with sympathy. Small fields are rare today because the scholarship examinations are used as a means of admitting commoners (that is, non-scholars). Indeed we have been told that many maintained schools believe that their only chance of getting a candidate into an Oxford or Cambridge college is through the scholarship examination. This practice is bad for the scholarship examinations because numbers become unmanageable; and where the scholarship syllabus is effectively greater than the Advanced level syllabus, it is bad in its influence on the teaching that these pseudo-candidates receive. But the possibility of going from the ordinary grammar school Sixth Form to Oxford and Cambridge is rightly valued by the schools and should be preserved. The only way in which this can be done without causing harm to both parties is, as far as we can see, by making it abundantly clear that the scholarship examination is not in fact the means by which a college chooses all its commoners. There should be then some other method of securing admission which is known to the maintained schools and capable of being used by them. The practice of some Cambridge colleges is, we are told, to accept entries at 16 subject to a satisfactory performance at Advanced level a year or so later. This "waiting list" procedure is attractive, in that it removes pressure and anxiety. But it is of no value to the ordinary maintained school boy—it is in fact a positive disservice to him—because the idea of a Cambridge education is something that he dare not aspire to so far ahead. When he does, he finds the places earmarked. It seems to us that it could only be of benefit to the open scholarship system—and perhaps, in a few years' time, the only way

of saving it from collapsing under the pressure—if there were an alternative method of selection available at the same time and with a known proportion of vacancies reserved to be filled in this way.

436. The second main method used for selection in a competitive situation (though not by Oxford and Cambridge) is virtually to set the faculty qualifying standard above the university qualifying standard by insisting on a percentage well above the pass mark in one or all of the subjects taken at the Advanced level of the G.C.E. It seems doubtful whether this really is the effective sieve that it is intended to be. An examination designed to be taken by thousands of candidates is by its nature rather ill-designed as a selective instrument; and, when used for the purpose, it frequently has a bad influence on teaching. The need for a number of examiners to apply comparable standards is apt to lead to the kind of fore-ordained answers for which careful coaching can prepare. It sets a premium on the kind of teaching which never strays from the syllabus, which is relentless in its rejection of side issues opening up the way to deeper understanding, and which sees to it that pupils spread their time and their knowledge evenly over all parts of the syllabus. Good teaching, on the other hand, will often devote a great deal of time to some single aspect which grips a pupil and elicits from him an unusually good response. This is frequently the way in which an intellectual "break through" can be accomplished. It is, we believe, quite possible in most subjects for an experienced teacher to take his pupils through the Advanced level syllabus and still to find time for the sort of teaching we have been advocating, but only if his attention has not to be rivetted firmly to the need for securing for his pupils every attainable mark. Good marks will normally be achieved, but cannot be guaranteed in the same way as by relentless examination technique. There is one other aspect of the demand for a high fixed mark which can have unfortunate consequences. It is not infrequent for a faculty to require a boy or girl to repeat an Advanced level pass a year later in order to improve, often by quite a small amount, the number of marks first obtained. This surely ignores the fact that a percentage mark needs interpretation by what has gone before—a slightly higher mark at a second attempt may indicate stagnation or even retrogression. It is often true that a third year in the Sixth Form is intellectually important, but it seems to us extremely doubtful whether the repetition of an Advanced level syllabus* makes the best use of this time. Whether this will be a profitable way of spending a third year is much better determined by the personal judgement of the headmaster in

* The practice is fairly extensive. The Ministry's Annual Report for 1958, after allowance has been made for bias in the selection of the sample, shows that about 18 per cent of the boys from grammar schools who took Advanced level in the General Certificate of Education passed the same subject two or more times; the figure for girls was about 5 per cent.

consultation with the university than by the automatic application of a rule (whether the university's or the grant-giving Authority's) about a required number of marks.

437. A third type of selection procedure depends largely on interviews. Of course, most university departments make some use of them, though there are departments that are content to accept and reject candidates without seeing them. A few departments rely very largely for selection on an interview in combination with the candidate's school record, using the Advanced level examination purely as a qualifying measure. Interviewing, like other methods of selection, has its disadvantages. If it is to bring out qualities of personality and character in the candidate (without being biassed by the personality and character of the interviewer) it requires more skill and experience than is always realised. It also needs to be remembered that there are some born specialists who do not "interview well", but who, if given their chance, often flower in the university environment. But from the schools' point of view, selection by interview has the great merit that, from its nature, it cannot dominate the syllabuses or methods of teaching in the schools in the way that an examination does. In our view, the only sound course for a university or college to follow is to use a mixture of different methods of selection, in which not only interviews but a careful study of headmasters' reports should play a part.

THE CRISIS OF THE SIXTH FORM

438. Is the fact that more pupils are spending three years in the Sixth Form a good thing? It has long been true that admission to an Oxford or Cambridge college from a maintained grammar school has been thought to depend on a third year in the Sixth Form, and this has acted more often as a pressure to enter the Sixth Form early by an express route than as an incentive to stay longer at school. The ordinary developer—we should reject the term slow developer in this connection—has in the past had an outlet to one of the other universities after two years in the Sixth Form, at the end of his seven-year secondary course. Over half the girls who went to the universities from 25 schools for which records were available to us had only two years in the Sixth Form. The increasing pressure on all universities, however, may under existing methods of selection make three years in the Sixth seem almost necessary to secure admission to any university. As things stand, for financial reasons this will almost certainly mean a greater use of "express routes" to the Sixth Forms by boys and girls who are not really suited to them. This will, we believe, most seriously affect the first-generation grammar school pupils, and especially those from the poorer homes who are, generally speaking, most in need of five years in the main school. We shall return to this problem later.

439. The approaching crisis of the Sixth Form—and crisis is not too strong a word—is then fundamentally the insufficiency of the supply of places in universities for those qualified to take them. If a large number of boys and girls are baulked of their ambitions, there is a risk that the trend towards a longer school life may be reversed. This would, in our judgement, be deplorable both from a national and a personal stand-point. The basis of the calculations made in paragraph 426 about the pressure to be expected in the middle sixties, was the estimate that the number of 17 year-olds in school will be between one-and-a-half times and twice as large as it is now. Even at the higher figure, however, it would scarcely amount to 15 per cent of the age group, and of these hardly more than one-third would want to go to a university. A total of 5 or 6 per cent of the whole age-group constitutes, we would have thought, a select enough group to justify the belief that there ought to be a proportionate increase in the provision for higher education if they demand it. The solution of the Sixth Form crisis depends, therefore, in our view, on the provision of more places to meet the demand of boys and girls who want to carry on their studies to a degree level. Boys and girls who are not of scholarship standard, but who are well cut out by personality and intelligence to fill positions of leadership and responsibility, require and deserve education beyond the secondary school. It is true that expansion is planned for the coming years in institutions of higher education other than universities—in colleges of advanced technology, regional technical colleges and teacher training colleges. It may be that the total number of available places in all institutions catering for students of 18 and over will, by the middle sixties, bear a ratio to the total of Sixth Formers not much smaller than the present. That is, roughly, what the best available estimates show. But there are three reasons why such a forecast cannot be accepted as an excuse for complacency. First, the present situation is not so satisfactory that comfort can be derived from the thought that it will not get much worse. Secondly, even if it will not get much worse for boys, it looks like getting a great deal worse for girls. And thirdly, places in regional technical colleges and training colleges, for all their great merits, are not likely to be so acceptable as alternatives to the universities that the provision of them will divert many young people from making every effort of which they are capable to get into the university or college of their choice. The hard fact remains that the competition to get into the universities—which is what chiefly affects the schools—is going to get more severe, and perhaps much more severe, than it is today, when it is already having a serious effect. We realise that the needs of the schools are not the only considerations in determining university policy. But they should be one of the important considerations, and we therefore hope that the scale of the

university provision to be made can be reconsidered once again. If a fully qualified Sixth Former's chance of securing a place is going to shrink, we fear a disastrous reaction on the willingness to stay on at school into the Sixth Form, and a consequent loss to the nation of some of its potential supply of trained brain-power.

440. The colleges of advanced technology have a chance to exercise a healthy influence on the schools by their policy on admissions. The decision to make two Advanced level passes a sufficient qualification for admission to them—in spite of their equally resolute determination to hold the Diploma in Technology at an honours degree standard—and the stress laid on liberal studies in technological courses, should give the schools the opportunity and the incentive to experiment in the use of minority time on the lines discussed in the last section. The fact that many of the students in a college of advanced technology are selected jointly by their employers and the college, may, and we hope will, lead to attention being paid to personality factors and qualities of character as well as to academic attainments and promise. The unintentional result of the influence of the universities on the Sixth Forms of schools in industrial areas has been to put a premium not so much on "bookishness", which might be no bad thing, as on "textbookishness". Perhaps the colleges of advanced technology may redress the balance. If so, they will have to solve the problem of how factors other than success in specialist work can be fairly judged. The use that a boy from a poor home has made of his minority time should be judged in relation to where and when he started, and not absolutely. If the college of advanced technology can work out with the schools a method of assessing this—perhaps by interviews based on a school report and the knowledge of how he has spent his minority time—they will make an important contribution to the liberalising of Sixth Form studies. Some such solution is needed not only (and perhaps not even so much) for the sake of the boys who go on to universities or technical colleges—who will have three or four more years of full-time education, in which to make good their deficiencies—as for their contemporaries in the Sixth Form who go straight out to industry, commerce or the professions. There need be no conflict between general and vocational needs in the education of recruits for these occupations.

THE SCHOOLS' PLEA

441. If the schools were to be asked by the universities what principles they would like to see applied in selection procedures, we think they would be wise to reply in something like the following way. The first need is for a more uniform, more intelligible and more expeditious method of dealing with applications. To relieve the pressure on the

schools this would have to apply to all universities. No reform which leaves out the Oxford and Cambridge colleges will meet the needs of the schools. The second need is a recognition that the main purpose of the Advanced level of the General Certificate of Education is to be a school examination, and that its use for university admission should be only as a preliminary measure of matriculation requirements—that is, it should be used for qualification only, not for selection. This is not, of course, quite what is envisaged by the widely canvassed separation within the G.C.E. of Advanced level from university entrance papers, though it has the same objective. We realise, of course, that it is not intended by those who advocate the latter reform that a boy should be compelled to sit for both papers; and as things stand now, the solution might work well. But, in the much more competitive scramble to get into the university that we expect to see, it seems to us that few would be bold enough to gamble on securing admission. They would, therefore, either have to take the Advanced level papers as well as the university entrance ones in order to have something to fall back on should they fail to secure admission; or they would have to be given an Advanced level pass on their performance in the university entrance papers. Neither solution seems to us satisfactory, and we should prefer that matriculation requirements should continue to be met by Advanced level passes and that faculty qualifications should in future be expressed in the same way, though in terms of a pass, and not (as often happens) by requiring a higher percentage of marks. At all costs it is desirable to avoid selecting candidates merely or mainly by the number of marks obtained in the Advanced level examination of specialist subjects.

442. The schools' third main point should, we think, be the importance of taking carefully and fairly into account the use a candidate has made of his minority time. We have already suggested one way in which this might be done. There would also, we hope, be general agreement that, while the outstanding scholar should in all cases gain admission to a university, great attention ought to be paid in other cases to a candidate's personal qualities, both by interview and through his headmaster's report. We are aware of the difficulties of comparing reports made by individuals of unequal judgement, some of them known to the reader and some unknown; but we believe that a way must be found to overcome them. Progress depends on a much closer knowledge by the universities of the schools that habitually send them candidates. It should be realised that the least useful contact with a school from the point of view of getting to know its staff and pupils is by attending a governors' meeting or distributing prizes; but university contact with schools is often limited to these occasions. What is essential is that the actual teaching members of a university should get to know the staff of those schools who send

them pupils. This takes time and money; but it is worth the expenditure of both. If the independent public schools have sometimes seemed to have more than their share of luck in placing pupils in universities, it is partly at least not because they are more favoured but because they are better known to those who make the selection.

443. We should very much hope that the universities would be able to devise internal selection procedures of their own, which would enable them to take into account the general factors set out in previous paragraphs, while avoiding the setting of another examination which, however well designed, could hardly fail (being competitive) to react on the syllabus and methods of teaching of the schools in a restrictive and harmful manner. All candidates have taken (or will be taking) one examination in their specialist subjects in the Advanced level of the G.C.E.; it ought not to be necessary to make them do the job over again, even if it is in a slightly different manner.* This is perhaps the single way in which the universities could most help the schools, and we most earnestly ask them to consider the arguments against further formal examination. If another examination there must be, let it at least be a common one for as many universities and colleges as possible to ascertain a candidate's fitness to read for honours in his specialist subject. It is important in our view that the ground covered should not exceed the Advanced level syllabus, because of the impossibility in many schools of separating university and non-university candidates, even were it desirable to do so. The difference should be in the questions set and the answers expected; candidates should not be expected to work over the whole Advanced level field again. It would also help if any such examination could be confined to a single paper rather than a whole series of them. It is equally important, in our view, that the selection examination should be for selection only, and not be used to provide a "more advanced" certificate for general use—that is why we have doubts about the proposed G.C.E. university entrance papers. It may be that one of the reasons why the universities and colleges cling to their own examinations is that it is highly desirable for those who have to make the selection to see the actual answers as well as to know the marks. Could not this be achieved, even for multiple applications, without inflicting on the schools and candidates the menace of frequent examinations? Photography provides an easy means by which a candidate's papers could be looked at simultaneously not only by the certificate examiners but by two or three universities as well. One incidental advantage of doing away with further examinations in the process of selection—as distinct from the Advanced level as the main instrument of qualification—would be that it might open the way to

* We are not, of course, referring to open scholarship examinations, if they are restricted to their original purpose.

the selection of more entrants of the "good commoner" type, whose excellences are personal rather than academic.

FINANCIAL GRANTS

444. There remains the fourth group of difficulties that we distinguished in paragraph 427. All but a handful of candidates face not only the difficulty of getting accepted by a university, but also the difficulty of finding the money. The local education authority is the paymaster of most undergraduates. The selection procedures of authorities vary greatly, and this bears hardly as between pupils in different areas. Some, we are told, pay as much attention as any faculty to a high percentage mark in the Advanced level papers. A special committee has been appointed under the chairmanship of Sir Colin Anderson to consider the whole question of awards to university students and we have accordingly not gone deeply into the matter. There is, however, one point directly affecting the education given to potential university students with which we are concerned. Our view is that in the present competitive position there is no case for duplicate selection procedures, which add still further to the strain on candidates.

445. There is one other financial matter, however, which seems to us both more difficult and no less important. We have noticed how pressure to get into the universities has led to pressure to get into the Sixth Form young enough to have three years in it, and this has meant that a good many who would profit from five years in the main school (that is, the forms below the Sixth) have had only four. We do not for one moment believe that everybody needs five years in the main school; but, as things stand in many schools, able boys who do are not very likely to get them. There are very understandable economic reasons why poor parents are reluctant to let their boys move at a slow pace, spending five years in the main school and three in the Sixth, so that they will probably have turned 19 before they leave school. But seven terms they must have in the Sixth Form if they are to compete on an equal basis in their specialist work with boys from more favoured homes, and headmasters in consequence often allow them to follow an express route against their better judgement. It seems to us, therefore, that local education authorities might be empowered to offer substantial bursaries for a third year in the Sixth Form to suitable university candidates who have completed seven years of secondary education. For some boys and girls, as things stand, there is a compelling reason why they should have both five years in the main school and three in the Sixth, and we think that this should be made more practicable than it is at present.

SUMMARY

446. We can summarise our conclusions as follows:

(*a*) Any attempt to segregate potential university candidates from others would be wrong and, indeed, impossible during most of the Sixth Form course. About half the number of boys, and a far smaller proportion of girls, in Sixth Forms go to universities, or the equivalent.

(*b*) We believe, therefore, that—if for no other reason—the Advanced level examination for the G.C.E. should be primarily a school-leaving examination designed to test the work of the past two years.

(*c*) There is a growing difference between the number of pupils "qualified" to enter a university and those "selected" to do so. For this reason, and also because some universities or colleges and some departments are preferred to others, the process of selection is heavily competitive. It is this competition that is at the root of the troubles that afflict the schools.

(*d*) It seems to us that more places for higher education will be required than are now envisaged.

(*e*) The two or three years of the nominal Sixth Form teaching course is in fact considerably reduced by the incidence of various scholarship and college or faculty examinations.

(*f*) Considerable difficulties are caused in schools by the different entrance requirements of different universities, and of different faculties and departments within them.

(*g*) We hope that the growth of colleges of advanced technology will influence Sixth Form work for good by reducing the undue stress laid at present on obtaining the maximum number of marks in three or even four Advanced level subjects.

(*h*) While it is not within our terms of reference to advise the universities on their selection methods, we report from the point of view of the effect on the schools certain conclusions we have formed:

(i) The recommendations of the Vice-Chancellor's *ad hoc* committee have improved the position, but there is still need for a more uniform, expeditious and intelligible procedure than exists at present.

(ii) The influence of Oxford and Cambridge is so universal that no system from which their colleges are excluded will remove the pressure on the schools.

(iii) The tendency to use the Advanced level papers for selection, judging results on the basis of numerical marks, has an adverse effect on teaching in the schools. This does not, of course, apply to their use for qualification.

(iv) Preferably, selection should be done by means other than another examination in the specialist subjects. But if special examinations for selection cannot be avoided, we hope that they would be common to as many universities as possible, that they would not be used for any other purpose than selection, and that they would be confined to as few papers as possible.

(v) For this, as well as for other reasons, we hope that it will become possible for members of university staffs concerned with selection to spend much more time than they can now do in getting to know the schools.

(vi) We recognise the value of the open scholarship examinations, especially those of the Oxford and Cambridge colleges. They set a standard for the specialist Sixth Form education of the ablest pupils, and they ensure that a boy should know that he can get to the university of his choice by sheer ability and hard work. At the same time they ought not in our opinion to be used for the bulk of admissions, and the maintained schools in particular need to be reassured that there are other methods open to their boys.

(*i*) The selection procedure for financial grants from local education authorities should not duplicate the universities' selection procedures in such a way as to add to the strain on candidates.

(*j*) It seems to us that the growing pressure to get into universities is forcing more and more pupils to spend three years in the Sixth Form, and this in turn is causing some pupils who really need the ordinary five-year course to follow a truncated main school course. We think it would be worth considering whether in appropriate cases local education authorities should have the right to offer substantial bursaries for an eighth secondary school year to enable such pupils to spend five years in the main school and three in the Sixth without undue hardship. In making this suggestion we are not implying that "express routes" are wrong or that all pupils going to a university require three years in the Sixth Form.

CHAPTER 27

Sixth Forms with a Difference

447. By "Sixth Forms with a Difference" we mean Sixth Form courses which are not linked with university entrance requirements, and in which therefore two-thirds to three-quarters of the time need not be devoted to two or three Advanced level subjects. In fact these courses, which may last for one or for two years, are either designed for pupils of rather lower intellectual ability, or, on the other hand, for pupils of good intellectual ability who are preparing for careers where the further education involved (there is usually some) does not consist mainly in a straight-line continuation of subjects studied at school. Schools have in consequence a much freer hand to plan the course to suit the individual requirements of the pupils—there is time to give good measure to such non-academic subjects as art or music; or to subjects with a new vocational interest and value such as dress-making or commercial subjects. Sometimes none of the work is externally examined; sometimes part of it. Sometimes the members of the general course are a separate body; sometimes they take a good many of their subjects with pupils who are engaged on Advanced level courses. There is no one end in view—and, therefore, there is no one pattern or type of course. It is possible to generalise fairly enough about the Arts Sixth or the Science Sixth; it is quite impossible to generalise about a General Sixth—that is why we have given this chapter a plural heading—Sixth Forms with a Difference.

A PROVISION FOR GIRLS

448. This chapter is largely about girls' schools. The reason for this is clear. There were until very recently few careers open to a boy who left school at 18—or at least very few which offered any advantage to a boy who ended his full-time education at 18 instead of at 16. From a practical point of view it was 16 or 21. Consequently a boy who stayed at school until 18 pretty certainly had his eye on a career which involved higher education, full-time or part-time. Even today the boy who enters an apprenticeship in industry at 18 is a boy who will disappoint his employer and himself if he does not eventually obtain a qualification which can roughly be equated with a degree. It is, therefore, natural and proper that a university preparatory type of course should have provided the education of nearly all boys in Sixth Forms. But girls have long had available to them a

large number of openings in careers which accept entrants at 18, but not before, and which entail further education, but not to a university standard. It is, therefore, natural that there should be much more variety in the pattern of Sixth Form courses for girls than for boys.

449. If we look to the future, it seems that on educational grounds we shall need a much greater elasticity in the shape of Sixth Form courses. The "trend" towards a longer school life is steadily bringing into the Sixth Form girls (and, for that matter, boys) who would not have entered one a few years ago. They come into the grammar schools not only at 11 but by transfer from modern schools at various ages. They are found in increasing numbers in comprehensive schools. Some of these new Sixth Formers prove to be of the highest academic calibre, but more are of somewhat lower academic capacity than Sixth Forms have recruited in the past. We are quite sure that they are right to continue their full-time education, but we are a good deal less certain that they will find what they educationally need in the ordinary Sixth Forms of grammar schools. They might more easily find it in the Sixth Form of a technical or comprehensive school. What they need and what they are looking for is not necessarily the same thing. There is a magnetic force in the Advanced level of the G.C.E. In the same way, we are sure that employers are right to recruit girls who have been at school until they are 18; but, once again, we are a good deal less certain that employers are willing for them to have had the most suitable kind of education between 16 and 18. It is employers who magnetise the Advanced level of the G.C.E.

450. How far does this magnetism of the Advanced level divert these new Sixth Formers from their true course? If they expect, and are expected, to get the same number, and the same sort of combination, of subjects as more academic pupils, their education will go seriously astray. But there are Advanced level syllabuses in art and music; in domestic subjects as well as in Latin, physics and history. Provided that this new type of Sixth Former is not expected to get a particular number or combination of subjects, and provided that she has two years to give to Sixth Form work, there is no reason why a suitable course should not be devised for her which would include in many instances some Advanced level work. But for some there is no question of a two-year course. Besides those for whom a one-year course is a deliberate choice, there will be others for whom a late start (at 17 rather than 16), or early restlessness, or the desire for training of a kind the school cannot give, may confine their Sixth Form course to one year. It cannot then be an Advanced level course. Fortunately there are many good examples of courses designed to serve those who have only one year to spend in the Sixth Form.

PREPARATION FOR TEACHING

451. The outstanding example of a career which has normally demanded some Sixth Form education, but not necessarily the standard pattern of two or three Advanced level subjects, is teaching in primary and non-selective secondary schools. It is worth considering experience in this field with some care, not only for its own sake but for the light it throws on the general problem. In actual numbers the teachers' training colleges are nearly twice as important an outlet for girls as are the universities. For boys, the universities are nearly five times as important numerically as the training colleges. The minimum academic qualification for admission to a training college is five passes at Ordinary level in the G.C.E., a qualification which can be obtained without entering a Sixth Form. The minimum age qualification is 18, so that a girl can have one or two years in the Sixth Form without the necessity of working for a formal examination. For a good many years five Ordinary level passes have also in fact been enough to secure a place in a training college. In the last five or six years, however, more candidates have been coming forward and an increasing number of training colleges have been able to recruit a high proportion of students who have secured at least one or two Advanced level passes. This has been possible because more girls have been willing to spend two years in the Sixth Form. It is well known that colleges have hoped that the introduction of three-year training will enable them substantially to increase the proportion of students with Advanced level qualifications. It is fair to say that, as the selective power of the colleges has improved, it has been used to favour candidates who have followed a more academic type of programme in the schools, and it is now possible to distinguish two patterns of general Sixth Form course specially designed for potential training college students as well as the full academic course which some have always followed.

452. The earlier pattern often took the form of one or two years in a general Sixth Form course, according to the age of the girl on entry. That course might well have to include work for one or two additional Ordinary level passes to bring the candidate up to the required number of five. It would also include a selection of subjects studied, not necessarily for examination, but because they appealed to the pupil and were often likely to prove useful in training college work and, at one remove, in teaching. Music and art, crafts and English subjects figured prominently in the curriculum. Mathematics unfortunately did not, although three-quarters of the women teachers in the country are employed in primary schools, and all primary

school teachers normally teach arithmetic. The kind of course described above was felt by the schools to be well suited to the girls who took it. The girls themselves seemed likely in time to make sound teachers in primary schools. There are still many girls of this type preparing in Sixth Forms to enter training colleges, and we hope that room will always be found for those who have personality and a real gift of knowing and teaching children, even if their own academic attainments by the age of 18 are no more than moderate. Specialisation in the sense in which we have used it in Chapter 25—that is to say, concentration on two or three academic subjects at Advanced level—is almost certainly beyond their reach or unsuitable in content. They should not be asked to tackle a large number of subjects—there should certainly be some reduction from the number studied in the Fifth Form—and we would attach great importance to their work being directed in such a way as to develop for them too the power of self-reliance and independent study. In their strongest subjects, there should always be adequate time for library or laboratory work as the case may be. We should expect their curriculum normally to combine elements from both the science and the arts sides. Some mathematical work is essential. If teachers are ever to give young children a delight and a confidence in the handling of figures, they must themselves see clearly and move certainly in this world. It needs a gifted teacher (and they are desperately hard to come by), to give Sixth Form pupils this confidence in a subject which they often wish to give up out of fear and dislike. But it is here that the vicious circle can best be broken.

453. More recently a new pattern of Sixth Form work for training college candidates has been crystallising as a result of the increasing stress laid on the possession of Advanced level passes. The first effect has been to make a full two-year course much more common than it used to be, and this we think is all to the good, since it gives girls another year in which to develop before they enter a profession in which maturity is very important. The newer type of course is, moreover, not only longer but of a different composition. The older pattern tended to give roughly equal attention to a fairly wide range of subjects. The newer pattern gives especial prominence to one or two subjects which attract more time and more attention because of the relatively extensive syllabus and difficult examination involved. At present this type of course is closely tied to work for one or two subjects at Advanced level. While we think this is generally practicable and right, we should be sorry to think admission to a training college should turn on the possession of Advanced level passes, or that work for an Advanced level is the only valuable form of specialisation. The close relation that exists between schools and

training colleges should make it possible to retain in the future the valuable flexibility which has prevailed in the past. Some specialisation, however, should mark the education of these girls, but there should be less of it than in the full academic course, and so more time will be available for supporting subjects. This fits in better with the range of work which they will be expected to follow at training college and as general practitioners in primary schools and with the younger pupils of secondary schools.

454. A course of this type seems to us appropriate for the great run of ordinary candidates for training college places, including most of the academically weaker ones who in the past have followed the earlier pattern. The only rider necessary to safeguard their interests is that, while it may be appropriate for them to take an Advanced level course in one or two subjects, we do not think they should be automatically excluded from a training college if they have not done so or if they fail to secure a pass, provided that their claims on grounds of personality are really strong and that the nature and quality of their Sixth Form study has gone well beyond the Ordinary level syllabus.

455. Side by side with this pattern of preparation, there will no doubt continue to be a considerable number of recruits to training colleges from the academic Sixth Form courses—either girls who have hoped or thought of going to a university, or those who, though of comparable ability, are quite sure that their vocation is to a form of teaching for which a university degree is not the best form of preparation. At school, however, they can, and should, benefit from the most exacting intellectual training the school can give.

NURSING AND COMMERCE

456. There are two other groups of careers which recruit largely from girls in the Sixth Forms of grammar schools and which exercise a considerable influence over the curriculum. The first is nursing and the various medical auxiliary services. Nursing makes no preliminary academic demands which cannot be satisfied below the Sixth Form level, and indeed it recruits many girls who have never been to a grammar school, but it does impose a minimum age of entry of 18 (though various pre-training courses take girls earlier), and this fits in well with a two-year Sixth Form course. It is a definite advantage for some girls to have done this. There seems little doubt, moreover, that the considerable amount of training that student nurses have to undertake makes it desirable that many entrants should have had full-time education until 18. A Sixth Form course with at least one or two Advanced level subjects is desirable for most of the medical auxiliary services. Nursing and teaching are alike in both requiring

a reasonable standard of education and certain personal qualities which often, though not always, go with a felt vocation to that particular work and no other. There is plenty of room in both occupations for girls who have real intellectual ability, side by side with many more who do not rise above a reasonable competence. Both therefore recruit to some extent from the full academic Sixth, and to some extent from girls who have followed a less exacting course. We believe, moreover, that the kind of general course, incorporating an element of specialisation, which we have already noted as coming into vogue for potential teachers, is the best preparation also for this other group of careers. Future nurses and teachers may well work together for many subjects and be all the better for so doing.

457. The other group of careers which influence the Sixth Form considerably can be classified as business and secretarial. The majority of girls who take up this sort of work leave school at 16 or before, but a good many schools have commercial courses in the Sixth Form and there is no doubt that a longer general education is a great asset to girls who have the ability and the ambition to occupy a position which corresponds roughly to a technician's, as distinct from a skilled craftsman's, among careers for boys. Many are realising this. It is the general education that counts in the end; it is the vocational skills that attract at the start. Shorthand, typewriting and, in some schools, accounts are the core round which secretarial courses are developed. It may be argued that these skills could be better and more quickly acquired in a full-time commerce course, and this is true. But they can be begun in the Sixth Form, and may persuade many who would otherwise leave to stay on for that general education which a really good secretary needs. It is important to remember that all professions and occupations need secretaries: the only specific common factor is the possession of the clerical skills. Beyond that, there is room in this field of employment for the most diverse interests and knowledge to find a satisfying and useful place. It is this characteristic of the secretarial career which makes a Sixth Form course an appropriate preparation. It is true that at present a course of this kind for girls usually lasts one year, but there is no doubt in our mind that a two-year course, including one Advanced level subject, would be a better basis on which to build. Really able girls—and business needs them as much as nursing or teaching—should be encouraged to follow a full academic course. They would later have to add the office skills, which are not a suitable use for minority time.

458. Ten years ago it was common to divide the Sixth Form of a girls' grammar school into two mutually exclusive sections—an

academic course in preparation for the Higher School Certificate and requiring therefore two years, and a general course for girls who would only stay one year. There are, as we have seen, slightly fewer General Sixth Forms today than there were, and they are rather smaller; there are certainly fewer one-year courses. In their place a new pattern of curriculum is appearing which has some of the characteristics of the academic Sixth and some of the old one-year type of course. A pattern of this kind suits, we believe, the needs of a large number of girls, and gives a good preparation for several important careers. Sometimes the girls taking such a course are grouped together in a special form called a General Sixth. Sometimes there is no separate organisation. What is important is the pattern of course they follow, and the emerging pattern seems to us sensible—considerably better than most general courses were ten years ago. It must be recognised, however, that the demand for Advanced level certificates has killed some excellent non-examination courses, which gave the right kind of teacher the scope she needed to make the education fit the girl. It would be a great pity if these courses disappeared.

GENERAL COURSES FOR BOYS?

459. If a curriculum of this kind is good for many girls, would it not also be good for boys of similar ability? We are quite sure that it would. And we are certain that boys of this level of ability are now entering Sixth Forms, but receiving a far less suitable education, because there are too few large bodies of employers of boys who welcome a two-year course of this less academic type. At present the boy whose Sixth Form course had this sort of pattern would probably be at a disadvantage in his career, though he might be better educated than if he had just scraped two or three Advanced level passes. Will things change? It seems probable that, as more and more boys stay on into the Sixth Form, those occupations and professions, such as banking, accountancy and the law, which have normally recruited at 16, will increasingly turn towards 18 year-old entrants. Some, but not all, will be suitable for a full academic course. Industry too, may find that it needs boys better educated than the entrants it now gets at 16, but who are yet unsuited for the full curriculum of two or three Advanced level subjects of an academic kind. If there are developments of this kind on the employment side, we do not doubt that the kind of curriculum we have been considering in this section will prove to be as suitable for boys as it is for girls. There are already Advanced level syllabuses in a number of practical subjects which are linked with boys' occupations as well as with those normally entered by girls. The introduction of general courses for boys on a large scale, however, requires two conditions to be fulfilled. The

number of Sixth Form boys who know from the beginning that they are not potential university candidates must be large enough to support courses of this kind. Employers on their side must realise that it is better to recruit boys who have had a course made to their slighter intellectual measure than boys who have taken the ready-made university entrance course but found it does not fit.

460. General courses seem to us certainly to have an assured future, although at present they are confined almost entirely to girls' schools and even there have not shown any sign of growth in recent years. They have an assured future because of the increasing demand for longer full-time education by able boys and girls who do not aspire to the university. At present, these boys and, to a less extent, girls are often diverted to an exclusively academic course which is not really suitable to their needs. But, although we believe that general courses have a future, it is certainly not clear whether that future will be in schools or in other institutions. This is a matter which will be discussed in Chapter 35. All we would say here, generalising from the experience of those schools which have general courses, is that their members are well able to make a valuable contribution to the life of their schools. A general course in the Sixth Form is a strength, not a weakness, to a school.

Part Six

Technical Challenge and Educational Response

CHAPTER 28

Neglected Educational Territory

461. In the previous parts of this report we have been dealing with fairly well defined groups of young people and the educational problems they present. In Parts Two, Three and Four we were concerned with those boys and girls whose education ceases when, or within a few months after, the law removes its compulsion. As a very rough approximation, they can be regarded as about half the total of young people in this country. Part Five dealt with the older boys and girls in the grammar and technical schools and the selective streams of comprehensive schools. At the age of 15, they represent just a little less than a quarter of the total. Most of them will stay at school for at least one more year, and a fair proportion of them for longer.

462. Between these two groups there lies the remaining quarter of our young people. These are the boys and girls whose full-time schooldays end at 15 or 16—in any case, long before they are 18—but who continue to spend a significant part of their time in further education, training or instruction, either full-time in an institution other than a school or—overwhelmingly in numbers—by part-time study. It is to this remaining quarter* that we address ourselves in this part. The largest single block of them are the technical apprentices and trainees, working in various industries and following a variety of part-time courses at the Technical Colleges. Just because they are the largest block, and because the remainder are scattered across a great number of different courses and programmes, whose variety defies generalisation, there is a temptation to concentrate attention upon these technical students. But these are not by any means the only young people who fall into this area of education; nor are they the only concern of this part. There is a great deal of further education to be found in non-technological industries, in service trades and in commerce. There are a good many thousand girls taking courses—often full-time, though of short duration—in the office skills. There are courses to meet the special needs of agriculture, the merchant navy and art. There are some courses for young people who wish to continue their general education (though these are usually for the

* These fractions must not be read too precisely. Even at the starting point—the school leaving age—they are far from accurate, and there are many transfers thereafter. Thus there are large numbers of boys (and some girls) who are to be counted in the grammar school quarter at 15, but who leave school a year later and follow some part-time course of further education

purpose of obtaining some particular qualification needed for a vocational reason) and among them there are a substantial number of foreign students. There is a great variety of provision made for young people of a part-educational, part-welfare kind coming under the general heading of the Service of Youth. All these come within the general educational territory with which this part of our report is concerned.

463. It must not be thought that these young people are all, or even mostly, of markedly inferior intelligence to those who are to be found in the Sixth Forms of grammar schools. That is by no means the case. For one thing, selection at 11, even if it were wholly fair and accurate at that age, would still be an inadequate way of classifying what the potentialities will be at the age of 16. Thus, the National Service surveys showed that a substantial minority of the ablest 18 year-old recruits had left school at 15. There are many boys and girls coming up through other streams who, by the time they have reached the age with which we are concerned, can fully hold their own in intelligence with the Sixth Former. Some of them, indeed, transfer into the Sixth Form and do well there. But a greater number pursue their further education by means with which we shall be dealing in this Part. Furthermore, as we shall see, there are many students in further education who came to it from the Sixth Form, and as the facilities it has to offer are further developed, we expect there will be many more. It is not (in its higher ranges at least) an inferior level of education to the Sixth Form that is here in question, but a different type. It is not a second route to the common goal (as it is often described) so much as an alternative route.

464. There is, as we have seen, much diversity in the modern schools with which we were concerned in Parts Two and Three, and in the grammar schools which were the topic in Part Five. But both of these seem almost monolithic compared to the infinite variety of the field on which we now enter. To our sorrow, there is hardly a single generalisation that can be made about further education in England that does not require an array of reservations and exceptions before it is accurate. In part, this is because of the inevitable variety in the needs that have to be met. In the main, however, it is due to the fact that further education has grown up empirically, in response to one special need or demand after another, with the arrangements for each segment devised *ad hoc* and without those periodic attempts at a synoptic review that have been made in the sphere of school education. Yet, after the recommendations that we have made in the earlier parts of this report have been carried out, this will, we believe, be the next great battleground of English education. The metaphor is accurate if it conjures up the need for great effort and for the deploy-

ment of large resources and the possibility, at the end, of striking advances. It is misleading if it carries the implication of strong opposing forces. Fortunately, the two great challenges that impinge on this sector of English education are not in opposition to each other. Though they are not identical, they are convergent and overlapping. It is these two challenges that we must now identify.

465. The first is the challenge of the technological age. We had something to say about this in Chapter 5, and many of our recommendations in Part Five were concerned with its impact on the Sixth Form. But the challenge of the age cannot be met by the grammar schools alone. For one thing, the numbers of trained men and women that will be needed are far beyond what can be expected to flow from so relatively small a section of the total population as is represented by the grammar schools. We shall have to mobilise far more of our human potentialities if there are to be not only enough pure scientists and technologists, but the whole army of technicians and craftsmen that will be needed for industry and agriculture. The White Paper on Technical Education (1956) suggested that five or six technicians are needed for every technologist. Moreover, the sort of education that many in this army will need is significantly different in several respects from the grammar school tradition. This is not only a matter of what is needed, it is also a question of what will evoke a response from the young people themselves. We believe—there is evidence for it on every side—that there are many thousands of boys, and not a few girls, whose brains can be quickened by the excitement of applied science and technology. Moved by this incentive, their further development can often be best pursued by a combination of class room study and of work in the realistic surroundings of actual industry. Even if they continue full-time in some educational institution, they still need a significantly different curriculum. We need hardly say that nothing written here should be taken to imply that the grammar school has not an important part to play in applied science and technology, as well as in pure science. As we shall see, it plays a larger part now than is often realised, and is still only at the beginning of what will be a great expansion. But it needs powerful reinforcement from what we have called "the alternative route" if the requirements of the future are to be successfully met.

466. The other great challenge that impinges on this educational territory is that of numbers. One of the starkest statistics in the whole of English education is that only 1 out of every 8 young people in the three years 16 to 18 are still engaged in full-time education. True, the proportion is growing; but the rate of growth is slow, and it will take many years, as things are now going, for the proportion to be doubled. We do not believe that the nation can be content with this. There are

other countries, sharing much the same culture and traditions as ourselves, which openly aim at 100 per cent and are a long way on the road to this goal. There is hardly one among the advanced English speaking countries which would profess itself content with so small a trickle as one in eight continuing in full-time education into the later teens. Whether it be looked at as a matter of relative national efficiency, or as part of the duty that a progressive community owes to its citizens, we do not think that England can afford to be content with any aim lower than that of having, within twenty years or so from now, half its young people continuing in education until they are 18. They need not all be full-time in school; many of them, as we have just argued, will be serving their own development better if they divide their time. But we do not think that any of them should be counted (for this purpose) as "continuing in education" unless that is the major object to which their time is devoted, other activities being subordinated to it. Thus we would regard a properly organised sandwich course as "continuing in education", but we could not regard attendance at a county college by itself as meeting this particular requirement.

467. This is an ambitious objective; but in our opinion a necessary one—no more ambitious, and no less necessary, than those other great steps embodied in the Education Acts of 1870, of 1902, of 1918 and of 1944 were in their own day and age. If it is accepted, there will be a need to make provision for an enormous increase in the facilities available for full-time and not-less-than-half-time education for young people between 16 and 18. This is where the answer to the second challenge converges with the first. Not all of these thousands of young men and women whom we hope to keep in education will be technicians. Many of them, perhaps the majority, will want courses of a different kind; and the experience of those countries that keep a high proportion of their young people in education testifies to the benefits that accrue in every walk of life from having large numbers of people in the middle grades of ability and attainment, who stand in the same relationship to the fully-qualified professional as the technician stands to the technologist. We hope to see a great expansion of all kinds of education in the years from 16 to 18, some of it by continued growth in the Sixth Forms of grammar schools, some of it by expansion of the existing kinds of technical education, some of it of kinds hardly yet developed at all. This we discuss in greater detail in Chapter 36. By no means all of it will be technical. But clearly the two needs—for more teen-age education in general, and for a greater supply of technologists and technicians—overlap, and the one can be satisfied in the course of providing for the other.

468. It is, then, with these two challenges in mind that we have

approached the task of surveying this area of English education. We are not presenting a blueprint for its development. We have, indeed, been able, thanks to the very willing help we have received from principals and staffs of technical colleges, to throw a good deal of light on some very obscure corners of the present provision.* But in our treatment of this part of our task our aim has been much more general and much less detailed than in the other parts. We have attempted no more than to examine how further education (in the widest sense of that term) can best be fitted into English education of the future.

469. Even within this more modest objective, we are conscious of leaving many loose ends. We say very little, for example, of further education in agriculture, and less about commerce or art; the first two of these have been the subject of recent reports, while for the third a new National Advisory Council has just been appointed. We are conscious of the fact that we have made no contribution to the problem of extending the opportunities for vocational and professional education among girls. Our enquiries, in fact, have led us to the view that this is not, at present, an educational problem so much as an economic and social one. If there were more real opportunities for skilled work and professional careers for girls, there would be no lack of demand for the training required. The educational system can hardly be blamed for failing to provide courses which could not, in present circumstances, be profitably used. We have not, therefore, attempted in the following chapters to be complete. This part of our report, in fact, should be regarded as an attempt to set up a few bench marks and signposts in a territory as yet largely unmapped, where there are a number of settlers (and not a few squatters). It is a territory which, we believe, offers rich rewards for careful cultivation.

* See Vol. II, Part Three.

CHAPTER 29

The System of Further Education

470. The purpose of this chapter is to attempt a broad description of the present provision of further education for young people and to define some of the terms that are familiar within it. In Chapter 30 we shall pick out some of its features that seem to us to deserve particular notice, and in Chapters 31 and 32 we shall present evidence on the degree of success with which further education is attaining some of its objectives, and attempt some general conclusions on the system as it is today. Perhaps the first of the terms that requires definition is "further education" itself. As used in official documents and statistics, it is something of a term of art. It is defined by types of institution rather than by types of instruction given; the institutions are those, conducted mainly by local education authorities, which come under the Further Education Regulations of the Ministry of Education. This is, for our present purposes, an imperfect definition. It excludes public institutions for which another Government department is responsible (such as, until recently, the Farm Institutes, though responsibility for these was transferred to the Ministry of Education on the 1st April, 1959). It also excludes the universities and all private institutions, including works schools, private commercial and correspondence colleges and a great variety of other such institutions. On the other hand, it includes students of all ages, with the result that the greater part of the corpus of further education lies outside the range of years with which we are concerned. In 1957–58, out of a gross total of 2,548,462 students enrolled in further education courses, 1,443,321, or 57 per cent, were aged 19 or over.

THE INSTITUTIONS AND THE STUDENTS

471. Nevertheless, for statistical purposes, the official definition of further education has to be accepted since there is none other. The institutions falling within the definition are divided into "major establishments" and "evening institutes", the former category being further sub-divided into eight sub-categories. These are as follows:

Colleges of Advanced Technology. These form the apex of the new structure of technical education and are devoted to training technologists and scientists. Their work is to be national as well as regional in character, and comprise courses of undergraduate and postgraduate standard and research. Nine colleges have been designated so far. Their students are almost all over 18 years of age, with entry qualifications at the G.C.E. (Advanced Level) or the Ordinary National Certificate* level in the relevant subjects.

Regional Colleges, of which there are 22, gather students from a wide region. A substantial proportion of their work is at undergraduate level and much of it takes the form of sandwich and full-time courses. Courses may be held for London University degrees, for the Diploma in Technology and for the Higher National Diploma. Research work is also done. These colleges train senior technicians and craftsmen as well as technologists.

Area Colleges, some 160 in number, provide courses for technicians and craftsmen, mainly part-time, up to Higher National Certificate* and City and Guilds Final† examinations for students in industry. Many are developing sandwich courses leading to the Higher National Diploma, together with block release courses at technician level. There may also be courses in general education, art and commerce. About half their students are aged 15 to 18, attending mainly part-time courses.

Local Colleges, of which there are about 300, are very varied in their work, and in their names—such as college of further education, technical institute and technical college. Their courses reach Ordinary National Certificate standard, the Intermediate Examination of the City and Guilds† and perhaps in a few cases the Final standard. Courses may be held for G.C.E., and for intermediate professional examinations. Most of their students are aged 15–18, and few of them attend full-time courses.

Colleges of Commerce, of which there are 23, are separate establishments in addition to the departments of commerce in other colleges. They vary considerably in the nature and standard of their work. A few of them provide courses only up to the level of the Ordinary National Certificate in commerce. A number of them, however, are concerned with professional courses up to the level of final examinations. Courses are offered in most of them in the secretarial and office arts and in G.C.E. subjects. Most of the students attend part-time, especially in the evenings.

Colleges, Schools and Departments of Art. There are 177 art establishments some of which are separate colleges or schools and some of which are departments of technical colleges. The subjects which may be taught include Fine Arts, Commercial Design, Dress Design, Industrial Design, Architecture, Photography and all kinds of handicrafts. About 100 art schools are approved for courses leading to the National Diploma in Design. The proportion of students of 18 years and under varies from

* For a definition of this term, see paragraph 480.

† Defined in Appendix B to this Chapter.

college to college, but in most the proportion of full-time work is much greater than in local and area technical colleges.

National Colleges, of which there are 8, have been established to meet the needs of important but widely dispersed industries. Practically all their students are aged 19 or over.

Miscellaneous: this is a very diverse group of 57 institutions which include such institutions as Nursery Training Centres (24), National Sea Training Schools (12) and Works Schools (10) which are established for the young employees of a particular firm, but are run by the local education authority.

In all these "major establishments" there were, in 1957–58, 728,861 students enrolled aged 18 and under. In the following paragraphs, we shall be mainly concerned with the area colleges and the local colleges, where most of these younger students are to be found.

472. An "evening institute" is an establishment which has no day work, and which therefore is usually accommodated in the premises of a school or some other institution—and largely staffed, it may be added, by men and women who teach in school by day. The number of evening institutes varies from year to year according to the demand for courses; in 1957–58 there were 8,299 institutes. Most of their students are over 18, but the numbers who are 18 and under are by no means negligible: there were 198,789 boys and 177,491 girls in 1957–58. The total of young students, however, is likely to decline as more pupils stay on at school or pass directly into vocational or preparatory courses in major establishments (all of which, of course, provide evening as well as day courses). Though the evening institutes have in the past played a useful part in bridging what was once a two-year gap between school and further education, their future seems increasingly to lie in the field of non-vocational activities for adults, where they can and do provide an invaluable service.

473. Apart from this classification by the type of institution attended, another way of classifying further education is by the time of day at which courses are given. The figures of enrolments among young people of 18 and under in 1957–58 were as follows:

	No.	Percentage
Full-time Day	58,028	*5·3*
Part-time Day (overwhelmingly one day a week)	306,281	*27·7*
Evening—Major Establishments	364,552	*33·0*
Evening Institutes	376,280	*34·0*
Total	1,105,141	*100·0*

These figures involve some double counting, since some students attend both part-time day and evening classes. In Table 52, however, this duplication has been eliminated as far as possible. This table shows the figures as percentages of each age-group, with the school percentage for comparison.

Table 52. Percentage of Population at certain Ages in Schools and Further Education in 1957-58 (England and Wales).

Age	Number in Age-Group	Percentage in school	Percentage in Further Education (excluding Universities)		
			Full-time	Part-Time Day	Evening* Enrolments
Boys					
15	309,000	*37·4*	*2·4*	*16·2*	*24·5*
16	272,000	*20·0*	*2·1*	*24·5*	*25·3*
17	277,000	*11·1*	*1·9*	*24·6*	*23·8*
18	289,000	*4·5*	*1·9*	*18·1*	*17·8*
19	299,000	*0·7*	*1·6*	*13·6*	*13·0*
20	291,000	—	*1·4*	*9·4*	*9·8*
Girls					
15	295,000	*35·7*	*4·0*	*5·2*	*23·1*
16	263,000	*18·5*	*3·5*	*7·1*	*23·7*
17	269,000	*8·8*	*2·0*	*6·0*	*20·3*
18	283,000	*2·3*	*1·1*	*2·2*	*14·9*
19	287,000	*0·4*	*0·6*	*1·2*	*11·2*
20	285,000	—	*0·4*	*0·7*	*9·5*

* The figures for enrolment at evening classes only are given for the sake of completeness but they are not strictly comparable. They are the numbers in attendance three weeks after the beginning of the course, but the enrolment in evening classes is very much higher than the attendance by the end of the course. This decline is not paralleled in the other types of provision.

FULL-TIME AND PART-TIME COURSES

474. The number of full-time students in further education is steadily growing (it has increased by 70 per cent in five years), but it is still small relatively to the population. Of the total of about 58,000 aged 18 and under in 1957–58, 25,000 were boys and 33,000 girls. Table 53, on the next page, gives a general idea of the main courses they take.

Table 53. Principal Courses Taken by Full-time Students aged 18 and under, in Further Education, 1957–58 (England and Wales).

	Boys	Girls
General Certificate of Education (O and A levels)	9,000	4,000
Intermediate degree	1,100	—
Ordinary National Diplomas*	1,900	—
Other diplomas in engineering, building, etc.; including pre-technical courses	4,000	—
Nautical	1,000	—
Other industrial—clothing, textiles, catering	1,000	500
Art	3,800	5,000
Commerce (including "pre-commercial" courses)	2,000	16,000
Nursing, etc. (preliminary)	—	2,000
Domestic Science	—	1,000

* For definition see paragraph 480.

Most of these students have one thing in common: they have their eyes firmly fixed on a particular career and are anxious to achieve the necessary qualifications in the shortest possible time. Many of them are in full-time further education either because they have not done very well in school (which applies to a good number of the G.C.E. students) or because the subjects they are studying were not taught at all (for example, commerce), or were taught badly, in their particular school.

475. The great area of growth since before the war has been in part-time day courses. There has been a ten-fold increase in the number of students to 485,000, of whom 435,000 have day release. Of the total, 306,000 are under 19 years of age, virtually all of them having day release. Over three-quarters of them are boys. This great growth has been primarily due to the fact that the new apprenticeship schemes drawn up in a number of industries just after the war provided for apprentices to receive one day off from work each week for the purpose of attending courses. This type of provision is therefore usually referred to as part-time day release (PDR). Attendance at the classes is normally made a condition of the release, and the students are often also required to attend on one or two evenings a week in their own time. Something has already been said in Chapter 16 about

the post-war growth in part-time day release, and we have also there expressed our apprehension lest the continuous expansion of the post-war years may now be coming to an end.

476. A rough division of the total of part-time day students according to the type of course they take is as follows:

Table 54. Principal Courses Taken by Part-time Day Students Aged 18 and Under, in Further Education, 1957–58 (England and Wales).

	Boys	Girls
General Certificate of Education (A and O Levels)	* 10,000	* 5,000
Industrial Courses including pre-technical courses	210,000	4,000
Art (mainly industrial or commercial)	12,000	2,500
Commerce including pre-commercial courses	10,000	16,000
Nursing, etc. (preliminary courses)	—	9,000
Distributive Trades	3,000	4,500
Domestic Science	—	5,000
General Courses	12,000	12,000

* Figures include some double counting.

It will be noticed that some of these categories are simply repetitions of those that were to be found among the full-time students, and many of the comments that were made in paragraph 474 apply equally here. The two exceptions to this are the general courses and the industrial courses. We have already referred to "general courses" in Chapter 16. They cater for the young employees of a number of large firms and government departments which make a practice of releasing all their employees under the age of 18 for one day a week, whether or not they are training for skilled jobs. The courses vary a good deal, and the number of students is difficult to determine with any accuracy, but the total is certainly small. These general courses are the prototypes (on a minimal scale) of the county colleges with which we were concerned in Chapters 16 to 18.

477. The largest single category of part-time day courses, and the one that has come to be regarded as the standard variety, consists of the industrial courses being followed by 210,000 boys and 4,000 girls, or about 9 per cent of the four age-groups 15 to 18 inclusive. It must not be thought that all industries give day release to their apprentices and trainees. For the under 18's the pattern is very spotty, as can be seen

from Table 55 (Appendix C to this chapter). Several relatively small industries show a high percentage of release. But the largest aggregate numbers come from two sources, from the engineering industry in its different ramifications (including motor vehicles), with 71,844 boys and 4,894 girls, and from the building and contracting industry with 30,732 boys and 241 girls. We return to these industrial courses in paragraph 479.

478. It remains to identify briefly the third category, the three-quarters of a million boys and girls aged 18 and under in evening classes. Twenty years ago evening students dominated the further education field. They still do so in numbers, but—mainly owing to the dramatic increase in part-time day release—not to anything like the same extent. It is hard to analyse the total at all accurately. Nearly half of it comes from the evening institutes, where the statistical returns do not enable direct deductions to be drawn about the courses being taken by the younger students. Most of the evening students in the major establishments are probably taking classes closely connected with their jobs. Perhaps half the boys are also taking part-time day courses and most of the other half are taking very much the same sort of courses, though wholly in the evenings.

TECHNICIANS AND CRAFTSMEN

479. We return, then, to the industrial courses in the major establishments. These occupy 210,000 boys of 18 or less in day courses and well over half as many again (after eliminating duplication) in evening courses. This, in fact, is the central core of further education as it now exists and it requires closer analysis. It must not be thought that all these boys are of the same level of ability. They are all travelling together on the same road of further education, but they joined it at different points, they are moving at different speeds and they have different destinations. The White Paper on Technical Education published in February, 1956 contained some definitions of the main grades in industry, under the titles of *technologist*, *technician* and *craftsman*. These definitions are given in Appendix A to this chapter together with a suggested definition of a fourth grade, that of the *operative*. In most of what follows, we shall be mainly concerned with the grades of technicians and craftsmen. Until recently, the majority of the country's technologists—the highest grade—have come up by the part-time route. But before the age of 19 the path taken by the future technologist does not greatly diverge from that of at least the higher technician; it is what he does after 18 that makes him a technologist. At the other end of the range, although vocational courses intended for operatives are not unknown, and are showing some tendency to grow, they are still exceptional. The two intermediate grades, those of *technician* and *craftsman*, both have

well established special courses and their own recognised examinations and qualifications.

480. The ladder up which the technician climbs is that of the *National Certificate*.* National Certificates are given in 15 Faculties, listed in Table 56 (Appendix D to this chapter). Most of these are awarded at two levels, Ordinary and Higher, but four of the certificates are given only at the Higher level. As the Ordinary level is not normally taken until at least 18, it is only with the 11 Ordinary National Certificates that we need concern ourselves. It will be seen that the engineering certificates account for over three-quarters of the entrants and nearly the same proportion of the successful candidates. An Ordinary National Diploma is given for success in a course similar to the Ordinary National Certificate but of a full-time nature; the numbers given are small.

481. Each National Certificate is administered by a Joint Committee representative of the industrial, professional and educational interests concerned; and these Joint Committees determine the syllabus and standards of the examination. The part played by the major professional bodies is especially important, because the possession of a Higher National Certificate with endorsements for one to three years' further study in certain subjects is one of the most widely used routes to membership of such professional institutions as the Institutions of Mechanical and Electrical Engineers. All the schemes have a number of points in common. The course for the Ordinary National Certificate is based upon a standard of three years, known as S.1, S.2 and S.3. Some students, however, can gain exemption from S.1 by virtue of passes gained at the Ordinary level of the General Certificate of Education, while two passes at Advanced level may exempt from both S.1 and S.2. Contrariwise, students who are not thought to be adequately prepared for the course are required to take a preparatory course before entering S.1. Thus the candidate sitting the final examination for the Ordinary National Certificate may have taken courses designed to represent one, two, three or four years' work in further education preparing for it. These courses are not merely a matter of time spent. One of the features of the National Certificate system is that an examination is set each year, and that a candidate is normally required to pass in all subjects in one year before he is admitted to the next. There is consequently a great deal of repeating courses. Another feature of the system is that certain standards of attendance and performance at classes during the year, as well as the

* This identification of the National Certificate with the technician is an example of the fact that no generalisation in further education is accurate without qualification. Some National Certificate courses are of such a level that they are unlikely to attract any candidate who does not at least have the ability to become a technologist. Some attract many who do not in fact rise to a higher status than that of craftsman.

required standard of performance in the examination at the end of the year, are necessary to pass.

482. If the National Certificate system is designed for the technician, the craftsman's needs are mainly met by the system of examinations administered by the City and Guilds of London Institute, and the various regional examining unions—though the identification is even less exact than it is between the National Certificate and the technician. The variety of these courses is very great, and the range of ability catered for much wider than in the relatively homogeneous National Certificate schemes. Indeed, it is increasingly possible to make a distinction between higher and lower craftsmen—or at least between the courses provided for them. The higher courses have a considerable scientific element and the examinations are largely of the familiar written kind. The lower courses with which the Institute has been experimenting in recent years are much more practical in nature. Further details of the City and Guilds courses are given in Appendix B to this chapter. In the commercial field the examinations conducted by such bodies as the Royal Society of Arts are especially important.

483. One further technical term requires to be defined. This is the "sandwich course". The term is not in every way appropriate, but it has come into general use, and we employ it for lack of a better. A sandwich course is one in which the student alternates between periods of full-time study in a technical college (totalling not less than 19 weeks in the year) and periods of full-time employment. Sandwich courses have hitherto been largely confined to the higher ranges of ability and to ages above 18. They are now, however, beginning to make their appearance lower down both scales. In the statistics, sandwich courses are counted as "full-time study". In this respect, a sandwich course is to be differentiated from "block release" which is simply a total time normally equivalent to one day a week or a little more, but concentrated into, say, eight continuous weeks at a technical college, with day release for the rest of the year.

484. The one and only generalisation about further education that is true of all students under 20 with hardly any exception is that the courses they attend are strongly vocational in motive and character. This is reflected in the attitude of the students and the atmosphere of the colleges. Students enter for further education courses because they want specific qualifications in connection with their employment. Even the G.C.E. courses in technical colleges are often restricted to the G.C.E. subjects required as a qualification. The eyes of the students—and of the staff—are fixed on success in examinations and the students tend to be impatient of any irrelevant subjects or restrictions which smack of the school environment they have left behind.

Against this strongly vocational background it is perhaps not surprising that general education has not hitherto found much of a place in further education for the 15–18 age-group, and that it tends to be regarded, at least by the students, as an unwelcome intrusion. This is not to say that nothing is done. Apart altogether from general classes and lectures, of which there are an increasing number, there has been an effort in recent years in a number of colleges to devise a broader treatment of the technical subjects themselves. But to all these efforts there is one over-riding limitation—which provides the appropriate note on which this brief survey can end. The greatest enemy of the whole further education system is shortage of time.

Appendices to Chapter 29

A. LEVELS OF QUALIFICATION IN INDUSTRY

The White Paper on Technical Education (Command 9701) contained definitions of the terms technologist, technician and craftsman. A fourth category, "operative", is here added for convenience, and the list could of course be further elaborated.

The *Technologist* is competent by virtue of his fundamental education and training to apply scientific method to the analysis and solution of technological problems. He should be capable of closely and continuously following progress in his branch of engineering science by consulting and assimilating newly published information and applying it independently. He should thus be able to make contributions on his own account to the advancement of technology. His work is predominantly intellectual and varied, requires the exercise of original thought and judgement, and involves both personal responsibility for design, research, development, construction, etc., and also supervision of the technical and administrative work of others.

The *Technician* is one who is qualified by specialist technical education and practical training to apply in a responsible manner proven techniques which are commonly understood by those who are expert in a branch of engineering, or new techniques prescribed by a professional technologist. His work involves the supervision of skilled craftsmen, and his education and training must be such that he can understand the reasons for and the purpose of the operations for which he is responsible. Not all industries acknowledge technicians as such. The job, however described, may involve:

the design of plant and equipment under the direction of a technologist;

supervising the erection and construction and maintenance of plant;

testing and surveying;

inspection etc.

A *Craftsman* is a man equipped with the necessary skill to make components under the supervision of a technician or technologist, using established techniques; or to follow established practice in erecting, maintaining or servicing engineering machinery. He must be capable of understanding technical descriptions and following an engineering drawing.

The *Operative* is a man who after a period of training which may vary from a few weeks full-time or part-time up to two or three years part-time, is capable of carrying out specific operations involving the use of machinery and plant which do not call for traditional craft skills. As the latter become more highly developed and specialised, there is the greater need for a generalised basic training which will enable the operative to become quickly familiar with changing methods and techniques.

In some industries where craftsmen have no specific place, e.g. the chemical industry, the operative works under the supervision of a technologist or technician, or may attain junior supervisory status.

B. CRAFT COURSES

The City and Guilds of London Institute examines in over 200 subjects, drawn up by expert advisory committees on which industry, the professional institutions, associations of the teachers in technical colleges, the Ministry of Education, and other bodies are represented. The examinations are set by the Institute in local centres in the United Kingdom and overseas, and the scripts are marked by examiners appointed by the Institute.

The syllabuses differ greatly in respect of length of course, number of years and grades of examination, academic standard on entry, the inclusion or otherwise of practical work and so on. Broadly speaking they are intended to help an industry to develop schemes of further education as an integral part of apprenticeship training arrangements. Most of the syllabuses provide for an examination after two or three years of part-time study, usually called the "Intermediate" examination, and a "Final" examination which may be taken after a further two years of study. Some schemes also provide for a "Full" technological certificate to be awarded after further study in managerial, administrative, scientific or more advanced technical subjects.

The published syllabuses fall into three broad (and overlapping) categories:

Courses for Plant Operatives: these are generally of limited duration, related to processes such as boiler plant operation, iron and steel plant operation, metal finishing, flour milling. The academic content is generally, though not in every case, less than in the other courses mentioned below, and more attention is paid to detailed knowledge of specialised plant and machinery.

Courses for Craft Apprentices: the object of such courses is to provide the further education needed by the general body of craft apprentices in an industry, for whose training in the purely craft skills the industry itself is responsible.

Courses for Higher Grade Craft Apprentices or Technicians: Courses of this type, intended for ambitious and intelligent workers in industry were the earliest City and Guilds courses to be established. A number of new schemes for technicians' courses have also been developed since the war, especially in the field of electrical engineering.

It is characteristic of many of the City and Guilds schemes that the Intermediate and Final stages span different levels. In the scheme for Electrical Installation Work, for example, and also in Machine Shop Engineering, the Intermediate examination is pitched at craftsman level, while the Final is at technician level. Revised schemes which are being prepared in Building Crafts provide for a succession of courses which may be taken "end-on", each leading to a more advanced level. In other subjects, parallel schemes exist, as in Mechanical Engineering, where the Craft Practice syllabus reaches in four years at Final stage roughly the level of the Intermediate examination in the Machine Shop Engineering course. Some of the more advanced courses in the Institute's programme approach the technologist level.

In general the demand for a new course arises directly from the industry, and the introduction of new schemes and the revision of old ones has been a continuing feature of the Institute's activities since the war. In 1958, some 130,000 candidates from home and overseas were examined in over 200 subjects and 77,121 passes were secured.

C. STATISTICS OF DAY-RELEASE

Table 55. Students (Aged 17 and Under) Released for Part-time Day Education by Industry, 1957–58 (England and Wales).

Students released by their employers to attend courses for part-time education shown as a percentage of the estimated number, aged under 18 years, who are insured under the National Insurance Acts.

Industry	Boys			Girls		
	(1) Estimated Numbers insured at end of May 1958	(2) Numbers released by their Employers during the year	(3) Column (2) as percentage of Column (1)	(4) Estimated Numbers insured at end of May 1958	(5) Numbers released by their Employers during the year	(6) Column (5) as percentage of Column (4)
Agriculture, Forestry and Fishing	38,530	1,201	*3·1*	7,310	119	*1·6*
Mining and Quarrying	31,430	20,032	*63·7*	1,490	116	*7·8*
Treatment of Non-metalliferous Mining Products other than Coal	10,000	1,029	*10·3*	6,660	246	*3·7*
Chemical and Allied Trades	8,560	4,585	*53·6*	13,390	3,058	*22·8*
Metal Manufacture	15,140	7,524	*49·7*	5,030	969	*19·3*
Engineering, Shipbuilding and Electrical Goods	73,030	53,966	*73·9*	34,620	3,781	*10·9*
Vehicles	47,330	17,878	*37·8*	14,440	1,113	*7·7*
Metal Goods not elsewhere specified	17,620	2,603	*14·8*	13,610	592	*4·3*
Precision Instruments, Jewelry, etc.	4,790	1,424	*29·7*	4,520	212	*4·7*
Textiles	14,990	2,309	*15·4*	39,640	1,366	*3·4*
Leather, Leather Goods and Fur	2,000	88	*4·4*	2,160	25	*1·2*
Clothing	11,800	1,862	*15·8*	57,280	1,872	*3·3*
Food, Drink and Tobacco	21,630	2,629	*12·2*	33,110	2,573	*7·8*
Manufacture of Wood and Cork	17,050	2,082	*12·2*	5,320	39	*0·7*
Paper and Printing	19,820	7,275	*36·7*	24,930	427	*1·7*
Other Manuf. Industries	5,960	1,610	*27·0*	9,870	951	*9·6*
Building and Contracting	61,030	30,732	*50·4*	5,120	241	*4·7*
Gas, Electricity and Water Supply	6,490	5,202	*80·2*	2,660	663	*24·9*
Transport and Communication	31,850	8,750	*27·5*	12,550	3,680	*29·3*
Distributive Trades	87,470	5,950	*6·8*	168,650	5,602	*3·3*
Insurance, Banking and Finance	7,520	106	*1·4*	24,500	310	*1·3*
Public Administration and Defence	10,090	8,422	*83·5*	11,260	8,257	*73·3*
Professional Services	12,300	3,223	*26·2*	34,720	11,507	*33·1*
Miscellaneous Services	21,570	1,407	*6·5*	52,160	2,917	*5·6*
	578,000	191,889	*33·2*	585,000	50,636	*8·7*

NOTES: (*a*) Cols. (1) and (4) show the number of insured people who were under the age of 18 on 31st May, 1958.

(*b*) Cols. (2) and (5) show the number of boys and girls released during the academic year 1957–58 who were under the age of 18 on 1st August, 1957. Many of these would become 18 during the year.

(*c*) The total number of people aged 15–17 inclusive, estimated by the Registrar General at 31st December, 1957 was—Boys 858,000, Girls 827,000.

(*d*) This table concerns release by industries, not by occupations. This means, e.g. that an engineering apprentice in the transport industry is shown under the latter heading.

D. NATIONAL CERTIFICATES AND DIPLOMAS

Table 56. Examination Results of National Certificates and Diplomas, 1958 (England and Wales).

National Certificates	Ordinary		Higher	
	Entrants	Successful Candidates	Entrants	Successful Candidates
Building	2,476	1,597	1,118	929
Chemistry	2,466	1,437	1,231	852
Chemistry, Applied	43	22	38	30
Commerce	711	380	8	7
Engineering, Chemical	—	—	70	61
Engineering, Civil	—	—	413	278
Engineering, Electrical	8,006	4,271	3,190	2,165
Engineering, Mechanical	18,778	8,599	6,012	3,926
Engineering, Production	—	—	647	542
Metallurgy	728	373	341	269
Mining	1,378	715	275	205
Mining Surveying	—	—	163	118
Naval Architecture	175	100	56	47
Physics, Applied	618	405	233	169
Textiles	193	129	59	49
Total	35,572	18,028	13,854	9,647
National Diplomas				
Building	129	77	100	77
Engineering, Electrical	16	11	126	110
Engineering, Mechanical	526	290	308	246
Engineering, Production	—	—	5	5
Mining	—	—	172	135
Total	671	378	711	573
National Certificates and Diplomas	36,243	18,406	14,565	10,220

CHAPTER 30

Characteristics of Further Education

485. After the previous chapter's attempt at a systematic description of the present provision in further education, the purpose of this chapter is to pick out some of its salient characteristics which seem to us to need closer attention. We identify a round dozen of these. Some of them are inevitably by implication criticisms of the existing system. It is therefore the more important for us, by way of prelude, to emphasise that we are fully alive to its merits, which are many and great. Thousands of young people every year find in further education a path to the development of their individual personalities and to the realisation of their ambitions. If it did not exist, both they and the country would be spiritually and materially poorer. Many of them, no doubt, could have done as well, and even better, had they stayed at school. But this is not by any means true of all. In particular, the association of work and study is for many a most valuable educational method, which can sometimes produce results where nothing else could.

EMPLOYMENT AND EDUCATION

486. The *first* observation to be made about the present state of further education is that it is only in a minority of industries, of which only two or three can be classed as large, and even there only for boys, that the "standard pattern" of apprenticeship* plus part-time day release has emerged. So much of the discussion of further education inevitably concentrates on this standard pattern that we are apt to forget that, outside these industries, the picture is still chaotic and the provision very varied. There are still some industries, and some that insist on a relatively high standard of intelligence among their employees, which do not give any day release at all. In banking and insurance, for example, the proportion is as low as 1 per cent.

487. *Secondly,* it is important to bear in mind that the further education institutions are not dealing with a single level of intellectual ability. On the contrary, the range from, say, the National Certificate in chemistry to some of the City and Guilds operatives' courses is enormous. We have attempted, somewhat arbitrarily, to identify three

* Throughout this part, we use the term "apprenticeship" to cover a wide variety of organised schemes of training at work, not confining it to the narrow legal meaning.

educational levels—appropriate to our age range—the technician (who is sometimes a future technologist); the lower technician or craftsman; and the operative, who is sometimes no more than semi-skilled—although a certain amount of overlap may be possible in the early stage. However hard they may be to define, we have no doubt that these three levels exist, and that a course designed for one will be of little use to another. Somewhere in further education, courses can be found that cater for all these levels of ability. But only in the engineering industry can each of the three levels be identified, and even there it could hardly be claimed that there is country-wide provision for each level. Even if a boy has been fortunate enough to find an employer who will give him day release, he still needs to find, within reasonable travelling distance, a course exactly suited to his requirements.

488. These things arise, *thirdly*, from the fact that further education has grown up as the handmaiden of employment. For the overwhelming majority of boys and girls in further education, the choice of job (or at least the choice of type of employment) comes first, and the entry into further education courses follows as a consequence, either as a condition of employment (as with most part-time day release) or as a means of obtaining the qualifications for a specific employment (as with the girls' full-time commercial courses) or as a means of obtaining promotion in employment. English further education cannot be understood without realising that virtually everything that exists in it has come into existence as the conscious answer to a demand arising from industry or from individual workers. Where something does not exist, it is because no effective demand for it has been expressed.

489. This dependence of further education upon employment is very clearly illustrated by the close association of part-time day release, the great growth of which is the most encouraging feature of recent years, with apprenticeship. Of the total number of boys entering upon apprenticeships in the year 1957–58, 57 per cent went into the engineering, shipbuilding, vehicle and building industries; and of the total number of employees under the age of 18 who, in the same year, were granted day release for education, 53 per cent were to be found in the same industries. The only industry that provides a substantial amount of day release without contributing significantly to the total of apprenticeships is mining. On the other hand, in building the proportion of day release, though absolutely high, is lower than the proportion of apprenticeship. Two-thirds (65 per cent) of the intake are apprentices; half of the men under 18 get day release. And this occurs in an industry whose apprenticeship scheme (which, however, applies only to firms which meet the conditions of the National

Joint Apprenticeship Board) makes day release obligatory. In engineering on the other hand, where apprenticeship schemes only recommend day release, 74 per cent of men under 18 get it, although the proportion of apprentices in the intake is only 63 per cent. There could be no clearer indication of the basis on which the day release system stands. The structure of industry and the attitude of employers determine the issue. It is not only employers' organisations which are concerned; the attitude of individual employers can be just as important, as the example of the building industry shows. Technical colleges can only do their job by day if the employers send their young workers. The college can invite and advise; it cannot compel. The individual worker may desire release (though by no means all do), but he cannot demand it. The employer alone has the power to give or to withhold.

490. But though there would be little part-time day release without apprenticeship, the nature and structure of the two systems differ radically. This is the *fourth* point to which we draw attention. Since the Statute of Apprentices was repealed in 1814, there has been no legal regulation of craft apprenticeship in this country. From the point of view of a boy's upbringing it can mean much or little according to the individual employer, the trade in which he is engaged and the nature of the apprenticeship scheme (if any) that has been adopted by the trade. Generally speaking, no test of competence is required either to enter apprenticeship or to graduate from it to the status of skilled worker, or whatever other term the trade may use. Many trades set a maximum age for completing apprenticeship (usually 21) and there is nearly always a minimum duration, very frequently five years, but that is all. This has several consequences. One is that there can be, and often is, a far wider range of intellectual ability among the apprentices in a single workshop than can be accommodated within a single course at the technical college. Two young men, who spend four days a week doing the same work side by side, may be doing very different things on their one day a week at the technical college.

491. Another consequence is that the boys with whom we are mainly concerned are climbing two ladders simultaneously. One is the apprenticeship ladder, in which the training is practical and (usually, though not invariably) untested by any authority other than the employer. (In this, English practice is markedly different from that of most of the continental countries). Apprenticeship leads to adult status and wage rates at 21 without any formality other than the passage of the prescribed time. Four-fifths of a boy's working time is normally spent on this ladder, with which we are not directly concerned except in so far as it is usually a necessary concomitant

to the educational ladder; what he does on it is no concern of the educational system. There are, however, obvious disadvantages in too strict a separation between education and industrial training, which ought to be closely related. The educational ladder takes much less of a boy's week, but is a great deal steeper. It is marked by annual examinations which must be passed in due succession—there is no going forward to the next stage before the immediate one is cleared. But success in these examinations is not necessary for the successful completion of an apprenticeship, nor is time (which is nowadays the essence of apprenticeship) relevant to the educational ladder. A man can be in the late twenties and still be climbing the educational ladder. The privilege of paid day release may depend on success in passing the annual examination, but passing examinations has hitherto rarely been a condition of a particular status in employment until well above the skilled craftsman's level. We do not, of course, mean to imply that status in an industry ought to depend upon the passing of examinations solely, or in some cases at all; that would be an absurd contention. We are concerned for the moment merely to point out the very different nature of the two ladders that an ambitious boy will set himself to climb.

THE TRANSITION FROM SCHOOL

492. The *fifth* characteristic we pick out is one that also flows quite naturally from the basis of the system in employment. This is that it makes little or no provision for a smooth transition from full-time education at school to part-time further education. The normal age of entering apprenticeship is 16. But this does not mean that apprentices normally stay at school until they are 16. No doubt they ought to; we shall present evidence in the next chapter that shows what an advantage it would be to them on the technical education ladder if they did. But in fact four-fifths of them do not, and their record is not nearly as good as that of boys entering clerical employment, less than half of whom left school at 15. There are several reasons for this. To stay a full extra year at school would carry a boy beyond his 16th birthday, while he must normally enter apprenticeship before that day if he is to complete it before he is 21. Again, though success on the educational ladder might be assisted by staying on at school, success in securing an apprenticeship (which is often a necessary condition for getting day release) may depend, or at least may be thought to depend, on getting established with a good firm well before the crucial age. There is, therefore, often a conflict between educational and employment considerations. On the other hand, there is a clearly marked tendency in such branches of the engineering industry as aeronautical engineering, where the importance of a good

education is most widely felt, to expect apprentices to have secured some passes at the Ordinary level of the General Certificate of Education before they are taken on. No doubt this tendency is growing, but it has not yet become general; and it would be unrealistic to suppose that, until the school-leaving age is raised, any educational policy for future skilled workers of all grades could neglect the gap which occurs between the end of the term in which a boy becomes 15 and the September or October following his 16th birthday, when he becomes eligible to start one of the main technical college courses. He may have a year to wait.

493. What happens to him during this period? The Social Survey found that of the former modern school boys who had originally started work in skilled manual occupations, about 10 per cent had moved to a second job in a semi-skilled or unskilled occupation by the time they were interviewed; but there was a rather more than compensating movement from semi-skilled and unskilled jobs to skilled ones. There was a good deal more changing of jobs within the same level of skill—nearly a quarter (23 per cent) of those who had originally started work in a skilled manual job had moved to a second job of the same type. Nearly all this changing of jobs inside the skilled workers category and into it must have taken place within the first twelve or fifteen months after leaving school. It is difficult to believe that any system of vocational guidance would be so perfect that nobody would feel the need to change their first job until their period of training was finished. From the educational standpoint, then, we shall always have to expect that a minority (though smaller, we hope, than at present) will make a delayed start with their serious vocational studies. Whether this means that the maximum age for entering an apprenticeship should always be a year or more later than the minimum age for leaving school is an industrial rather than an educational matter. For the educational ladder, however, it would clearly be a mistake to prescribe any maximum age for beginning a course, and thus rule out the possibility of recovery from a false start. But the important thing is that half of the former modern school boys in the Survey (virtually all of whom left school at 15) were originally in skilled manual jobs, and that nearly two-thirds of these were still in their original jobs two years later. What happened to them educationally during the gap between 15 and 16? Some were given part-time day release from the start, but more of them probably had to wait for it until they were 16. It is unfortunate not to be able to be precise about what is, after all, an important matter, but this is one of the gaps in information which we have not been able to fill. Certainly, as Table 52 shows, 15 is very nearly the peak age of attendance at evening classes (most of them probably taking pre-

technical courses) while the proportion of 15 year-olds receiving day release is markedly lower than that of 16 year-olds or 17 year-olds.

494. Our *sixth* point concerns the educational and social antecedents of the boys who get chosen for apprenticeship. Unfortunately, it is only about those who are following National Certificate courses, the highest grade in intellectual ability, that we have precise information. Three tables, drawn from our National Certificate enquiry, are printed as an Appendix to this chapter. Table 59 is concerned with the socio-economic group from which the students come, as defined by the occupation of the father. The largest group at all stages consists of the sons of foremen and skilled workers, but whereas this group shows some tendency to bulk less large among students in the later stages of the course, that consisting of the sons of administrative and professional men is doubled between the first year (S1) and the last (A2). This is no doubt largely explained by the fact that those with a firmer educational background are excused the first two stages of the course. This is confirmed by Table 60 which shows how high a proportion of students on National Certificate courses come from the grammar schools. The second highest group comes from the technical schools; indeed, in relation to the numbers of boys to be found in these schools, it is much the largest of all. But though it is right to lay emphasis on the advantages even for this purely technical ladder of a good grounding in general education, it would be wholly wrong to imply that the further education ladder is not available to the modern school boy, or that our present system puts an exclusive premium on being selected at the age of 11. Quite on the contrary, one of the strongest points of the further education system in England —and one that has frequently been admired by visitors from other countries—is that it never closes the door or refuses a second chance to anyone who has the persistence to continue and the ability to succeed. The third table (Table 61) gives the age at which students on these courses left school. At once one contrast is clear. Less than half the National Certificate students left school at 15, the age at which over three-quarters of all boys, including, we believe, the great majority of students on craft courses, left. That, no doubt, is what one would expect to find: it is none the less important. But even more important, perhaps, is the fact that, in spite of all the so-called "creaming" for grammar schools, there are still so many who eventually come to the front in spite of a truncated education in schools which were often not equipped to provide the basic scientific education they need. They have a double handicap to overcome—they left school early, and they have more hazards to face in their further education than their more fortunate fellow apprentices.

495. The *seventh* comment we wish to make is to draw attention to one marked contrast between the technical examination system and

the system in schools. A schoolboy is examined each year in each subject he is taught, but he is not disqualified from going on to the next year's work because he did rather badly the previous year—it takes exceptionally bad work to hold a boy back a year. But in the technical field we are now considering, each annual examination must be passed in all subjects* before work for any subject for the next stage can begin. This is reinforced by the requirement (in the National Certificate courses, and to some extent also in the City and Guilds courses) that a certain standard of attendance, and of performance in class work, is necessary, as well as a pass mark in the sessional examination, for graduation from one stage to the next. It is not surprising, therefore, that there is a very marked difference between the theoretical length of a further education course and the actual time taken to complete it. Theoretically we ought to find 18 year-old boys in the third year (S3) of one course or the other just as we find 17 year-old boys in the second year of the Sixth Form. In practice, however, relatively few have got as far. It is also necessary to make allowance for the various educational short cuts (which are not, however, short cuts to the end of craft apprenticeships) open to those who stay longer at school and secure exemption from one or more stages of a course. The effects of these arrangements are shown in Chapter 31.

THE PROVISION FOR GIRLS

496. The *eighth* characteristic of the present system is the great inequality of the provision made for boys and girls. The figures were given in Table 52 in para. 473, and it is easy to see from them in what part of the system the discrepancy arises. The numbers of boys and girls in evening classes are not greatly different, and there are actually more girls than boys in full-time courses in the earlier years, owing largely to the number of full-time commercial courses. The big difference is in part-time day courses. About as many girls as boys enter employment every year; and the proportions starting work at 15 (roughly four-fifths), at 16 (about 15 per cent) and at 17 (about 5 per cent) are very much the same for both sexes. But only 8 per cent of the girls get day release compared with about one-third of the boys; about 36 per cent of the boys get apprenticeships, but only 6 per cent of the girls. This is not, of course, the result of a deliberate decision on anybody's part that girls require, or deserve, less education than boys. It is partly an accidental consequence of the fact that the great concentration of apprenticeships and day release is in two industries, engineering and building, which are from their nature boys' industries rather than girls'. But it is mainly due to the funda-

* There are certain alleviating exceptions to this general rule, but in the main it holds good.

mental difficulty of girls' employment which we discussed in paragraph 255. A girl has a much shorter expectation of uninterrupted working life than a boy. It is this fact, rather than the nature of the work she does or any deliberate sex discrimination, that explains how unlikely she is to get part-time day release. It underlines once again the fact that release, paid for by the employer, is in most instances not primarily given for the sake of the young person's education but in order to increase his vocational competence.

497. The largest single form of employment entered by girls is clerical work, which about 33 per cent of all girls enter on leaving school. There are several things that make clerical work (especially for girls) different from almost all other kinds of employment. The best vocational training for it—to a higher extent than elsewhere—is a sound general education. But it also requires (especially where shorthand and typewriting are involved) certain mechanical skills, and though those mechanical skills are less important in the long run than intelligence and education, there is a tendency, because competence in them is necessary and can be defined, to give them the greater importance at the time of seeking the first job—to the detriment, all too often, of general education. These skills, however, (unlike almost all others) cannot be learned on the job (or can be learned there only with pain and grief to the employer). This ought to make them peculiarly suitable for teaching in school. We have, however, already expressed the opinion in Chapter 27 that their educational content is too small, and the concentration of time necessary to secure proficiency too great, for them to be suitable subjects for inclusion in the curriculum before the compulsory school-leaving age. The obvious answer to which all these elements lead is a short, full-time course after leaving school but before seeking employment, and there is considerable provision of such courses both in public and private institutions. We have no quarrel with these arrangements in principle. They do, however, tend to obscure the fact that the real preparation for clerical work is to be found in general education. There is pressure on girls to leave school as soon as they can in order to take rather narrow courses in shorthand and typing; there is pressure on the schools to take time away from other subjects to teach these office skills. In either event, the real preparation is neglected, and girls enter clerical jobs ill equipped. Nearly two-thirds of the girls entering clerical employment do so at 15. In the distributive trades, engineering, textiles and clothing, which between them account for over half the total number of girls employed, the proportion of female clerical workers recruited at 15 is about three-quarters. At the other end of the scale are the professional services (accountancy, law, medicine, etc.), insurance and banking,

and central and local government which respectively recruit only 52, 40 and 38 per cent of their young clerical workers at 15.

498. As far as industrial groups are concerned, by far the biggest source of employment for girls (in clerical and other jobs) is the distributive trades, which take on 29 per cent of all girls entering employment under 18. (No industry group takes so many boys, for whom the biggest employer is engineering with 14 per cent). The two biggest manufacturing industries from the point of view of girls' employment are clothing (14 per cent of all girls employed under 18) and textiles (7 per cent). In clothing the percentage recruited at 15 is 95 and in textiles it is 94. Clothing provides the largest proportion of apprenticeship openings (28 per cent of the small total)—93 per cent of them are taken up at 15. In all these trades—distributive, clothing, and textiles—the amount of day release is almost negligible; 3·3 per cent, 3·3 per cent and 3·4 per cent respectively. Of all the day release given to girls, 39 per cent is accounted for by public administration and the professional services, which provide less than 9 per cent of the total employment, and in which incidentally only 43 per cent of the girls are recruited at 15 compared with over 80 per cent in all forms of employment. It is impossible to escape the conclusion that the country has hardly as yet made a beginning with the continuing education of girls after they leave school.

EVENING CLASSES

499. The *ninth* point relates to those young people whose contact with further education is confined to evening classes. A rough calculation suggests that there are some 580,000 students (300,000 boys and 280,000 girls) under 19 who attend evening classes, but who have no day release. (Some of these are also pupils in schools, because it is not uncommon for boys and girls to be allowed to start evening classes shortly before they leave school in the hope that they will continue afterwards—a hope by no means always realised). It is impossible to make any firm statement about the subjects studied by students under 19 or about the regularity or length of their attendance; the figures given above are the numbers of boys and girls whose names are entered on a permanent class register—that is, of those who survive for three weeks. But, while accuracy is impossible, approximation is practicable. Table 57 shows the average number of hours attended by students taking different courses.

500. The Ministry's annual report, from which this table is drawn, does not enable us to distinguish the age or sex of the students or whether they are also receiving part-time day education. All we have been able to do is to pick out the subjects that are likely to be taken by students in the age-group with which we are concerned. The last

Table 57. Average Number of Hours' Attendance by Registered Students at Evening Classes in 1957–58 (England and Wales).

Subject or Group of Subjects	Number of Names Registered	Total Student Hours	Average number of hours per Student*
Clerical subjects	335,131	8,350,000	24·9
Professional Subjects (e.g. Accountancy)	64,248	1,735,000	27·0
Mathematics	301,261	9,631,000	32·2
Subjects Relating to Manufacturing Industry	358,711	14,506,000	40·4

* A student who attended all the meetings of a class throughout a session would receive between 70 and 75 hours of instruction.

two entries refer to courses which are much more likely to be associated with day release than the first two, and where attendance at an evening course is a condition of apprenticeship and of day release it is much more likely to be regular than where it is left to the student's discretion. As far as purely evening students are concerned, it seems safe to infer either that their attendance is highly irregular or that a very high proportion of those who start a course do not finish it. There are doubtless still many young people who doggedly and successfully make their way upwards in life by study in evening classes alone—the original form of all further education. In no circumstances would it be right to prevent those who have no other means of continued education from doing so—though whether anybody should be expected to do so is a different matter. In general, we doubt very much whether evenings-only study should be considered an appropriate form of education for boys and girls under 18.

FULL-TIME AND SANDWICH COURSES

501. The next, *tenth*, point concerns the small number of boys and girls who are taking full-time courses in establishments of further education. How few they are can be seen from Table 58 overleaf. It is clear from these very small proportions that those boys and girls who want full-time education still overwhelmingly find it in schools. There are, of course, a number of private colleges which provide full-time courses for young people. We have no precise information about the numbers of students they enrol. But we do not think that they would greatly change the statistical picture. Full-time students represent only 5 per cent of the total number of students who use the "major establishments" in a year, and only 14 per cent of those

Table 58. Full-time Students Aged 15 to 18 Inclusive, in Colleges of Further Education, 1957–58 (England and Wales).

	Age 15	16	17	18
BOYS:				
Number in Colleges of Further Education	7,273	5,624	5,234	5,423
Percentage of age-group in Colleges of Further Education	*2·4*	*2·1*	*1·9*	*1·9*
Percentage of age-group at school	*37·4*	*20·0*	*11·1*	*4·5*
GIRLS:				
Number in Colleges of Further Education	11,849	9,330	5,406	3,014
Percentage of age-group in Colleges of Further Education	*4·0*	*3·5*	*2·0*	*1·1*
Percentage of age-group at school	*35·7*	*18·5*	*8·8*	*2·3*

who use them by day. As things stand, they can rarely, if ever, form the major concern of the Principal.

502. What courses do these young full-time students follow? The rough classification given in Table 53, in para. 474, permits two tentative generalisations to be made. Among the boys, there is a large group taking one or two subjects in the General Certificate of Education. These full-time courses at technical colleges act to a large extent as a retrieving mechanism for work that is normally done at school. On the girls' side, the commercial courses occupy a dominant position. Some, but relatively few, will last more than one year. We do not wish, of course, to deprecate the necessity or desirability either of commercial courses for girls or of "retrieving" courses for boys or girls. But the realisation that so much of the small full-time provision for boys and girls under 19 falls under these two heads serves to show how very little there is at present in colleges of further education on which it would be possible to build an alternative national system of balanced full-time education of a different kind from the traditional.

503. For our *eleventh* comment, however, we can strike a more cheerful note. During the time that we have been preparing this report, a most significant change has begun to affect the higher levels of technical education. This is the growth of "sandwich courses", which were defined in paragraph 483. There are many variants of sandwich courses, but they all have two things in common. One is that the ratio of study to work at the bench is much larger than the ratio of one to four that is implicit in part-time day release

(without further evening classes). The student gets more time for study, and he has to do less of it at night. The other characteristic is that the study time is concentrated in periods of full-time attendance. The educational advantages of this are obvious; but there is evidence that employers also find it to be to their advantage. It is true that most of the sandwich courses are for students over the age of 18, and therefore lie outside our age range. But they are beginning to appear at the lower ages. And even if they did not, their existence would still have a beneficial effect in the years 16 to 18. They make it a much more attractive and practicable procedure for a boy to stay at school, taking subjects at the Advanced level of the G.C.E., and then, at the age of 18, either to find an employer who will accept him as an engineering or student apprentice (various terms are used) on a sandwich course, or to apply to a technical college to be enrolled as a college-based student. We shall have much more to say about sandwich courses in Chapter 34.

THE STAFF

504. The *twelfth* and last point we wish to make is that the teaching force engaged in further education differs in a number of important respects from that employed in schools. It is, to begin with, made up to a much larger extent of part-time teachers. When the Willis Jackson Report was issued in 1956 there were four part-time teachers to every full-time teacher. Secondly, it is to an overwhelming extent composed of men—there are seven full-time men teachers for every woman. Thirdly, it recruits largely men with technical or scientific qualifications. The technical colleges employ 14 per cent of the total of men graduate teachers in the public sector of education as a whole, but they employ 20 per cent of the 12,000 mathematics and science graduates and 75 per cent of the 2,000 technological graduates in teaching. Fourthly, the teaching force in further education is composed to a much greater extent of teachers without specific training for teaching. Only one-quarter of the graduates teaching in maintained and assisted schools are untrained and virtually none of the non-graduates. About three-quarters of the annual intake of 2,400 full-time teachers to further education are without training. Rather over half of those who are trained were students at one of the three technical teachers' training colleges.

Appendix to Chapter 30

THE NATIONAL CERTIFICATE STUDENTS

Table 59. The Occupations of the Fathers of a Sample of Students in National Certificate Courses (England).

Socio-Economic Group	Stage of Course			
	S.1 (First Stage)	S.3 (Last Stage of O.N.C.)	A.2 (Last Stage of H.N.C.)	Distrib. of Socio-Economic Groups (1951 Census)
	%	%	%	%
Administrative and Professional	*10·6*	*17·5*	*20·3*	*14·8*
Shopkeepers, Shop Assistants, Clerical Workers	*13·1*	*15·3*	*15·4*	*13·5*
Foremen	*11·7*	*11·8*	*11·0*	*4·0*
Skilled Workers	*31·5*	*27·1*	*25·4*	*34·8*
Semi-skilled workers	*18·0*	*16·1*	*13·0*	*10·9*
Unskilled Workers	*7·9*	*7·1*	*7·1*	*11·0*
Other Categories	*7·2*	*5·1*	*7·8*	*11·0*
Total=100%	1,731	1,573	717	—
No. unclassified	424	350	154	—

Table 60. National Certificate Students Analysed by The Type of School Last Attended (England).

Course	All-age %	Modern %	Tech-nical %	Gram-mar %	Other* %	No.= 100%
Electrical Engineering	*11*	*24*	*22*	*36*	*7*	2,035
Mechanical Engineering	*8*	*25*	*28*	*33*	*6*	4,100
Other National Certificates	*5*	*16*	*23*	*52*	*4*	2,323
All National Certificates	*8*	*22*	*25*	*40*	*5*	8,458
All Boys aged 14	*7*	*57*	*6*	*17*	*13*	

* "Other" includes independent schools.

Table 61. The Age at Which a Sample of Students in National Certificate Courses Left School (England).

National Certificate	Age on leaving School					
	15 or under %	16 %	17 %	18 %	19 or over %	No.= 100%
Electrical Engineering	*51*	*35*	*9*	*4*	*1*	2,029
Mechanical Engineering	*48*	*41*	*8*	*2*	*1*	4,097
Building	*46*	*41*	*9*	*4*	*Tce**	580
Applied Science (Chemistry, Metallurgy, Applied Physics)	*18*	*57*	*14*	*8*	*3*	692
Other National Certificates	*43*	*43*	*9*	*4*	*1*	1,048
All National Certificates	*46*	*41*	*9*	*3*	*1*	8,446
Incomplete answers						12
Total						8,458

* Tce=trace

CHAPTER 31

The Effectiveness of Part-Time Courses

505. No section of the educational field is in a state of such rapid change as further education. Nowhere can it be so confidently said that what is true today may be irrelevant tomorrow. Nevertheless, nowhere is stock-taking more necessary. Can we count on change in the directions in which it is now taking place, and proceeding at its present pace, to provide us with an effective educational instrument to secure that technological mastery on which our future depends? Will it, at the same time, bring forth men to match the machines, men who are fit to control instruments of power and potential destruction with which no previous generation could safely have been entrusted? The second of these questions does not permit of any exact answer, but it has to be asked. To the first we can be more precise. Some part of our answer has already been given in earlier chapters. We have noticed and welcomed the movement by which more boys and girls are staying at school until 16, but we have calculated that we shall not achieve enough in this foundation task unless we raise the school-leaving age for all to 16. We have discussed trends in the development of the Sixth Form which seem to us satisfactory in point of numbers, but disquieting as far as the sufficiency of suitably qualified teachers is concerned. We have recommended that more thought and attention need to be given to the twin problems of the numeracy of arts specialists and the literacy of science specialists. In this chapter we are concerned with what is happening, and not happening, in that combination of part-time day release with technical courses which, though not characteristic of the whole of further education, is the heart of it as it exists today.

THE CONTINGENT NATURE OF DAY RELEASE

506. The main instrument of further education in pre-war days was evening classes. Day release by employers was in its infancy. There were in 1938 only 41,539 workers who got education in this way compared with 435,000 today. A ten-fold increase in twenty years is a considerable achievement, and we can say that the system of one day a week's education, usually supplemented by some evening classes, is now the leading form of English technical education for students under the age of 19. But this ten-fold increase stops far short of what is needed. If all employed young people within our

terms of reference (the four age-groups from 15 to 18) are to get day release we need a further six-fold increase; but the curve of growth is already flattening out for the younger ages. It is the rather older workers who account for the greater part of the recent increases in the numbers released. Since 1948–9 the over-all increase in the numbers of boys and men released has been 106 per cent, but the increase in the number of 15 year-olds has been less—88 per cent and in 16 year-olds, 65 per cent. This aspect is so easily ignored that it is worth looking carefully at the changing age-structure of day release. This is shown visually in Chart 16 and the figures are given in Table 62.

Table 62. Number of Males of Certain Ages Released by Their Employers for each year from 1948 to 1957 (Thousands, England and Wales).

Age	1948–1949	1949–1950	1950–1951	1951–1952	1952–1953	1953–1954	1954–1955	1955–1956	1956–1957	1957–1958
15 or under	32	33	37	47	52	52	55	56	58	59
16	40	42	47	53	57	60	65	69	71	66
17	39	40	43	47	51	54	59	63	68	67
18+	71	80	87	90	97	106	120	137	158	178
All	182	195	214	237	257	272	299	325	355	370

NOTE: The years are reckoned from the 1st August and a boy is entered according to his age on that day.

507. Of course, the chart simplifies by showing separately each of the first three years after the end of compulsory school attendance but putting all the subsequent years together. This inevitably distorts the picture; and it is necessary, therefore, to look a little more closely into the changing balance of the age structure. This is done in Table 63, which shows the percentages released at the ages with which we are concerned for the last six years. It is clear that employers are increasingly willing to give educational facilities to their employees in their late teens and early twenties. This is no doubt largely a reflection of their greater willingness to recruit student apprentices who have carried their education at school on to the end of the Sixth Form course and to prolong it beyond 18 for apprentices who have been making good progress.

508. We have not so far considered the relation of day release to the varying size of age-groups. In the ten years under review in Table 62 it is unlikely that this will have been an important factor. There was not very much variation from year to year in the number of 15 year-olds; and there were not, relatively speaking, many of them.

CHART NO. 16

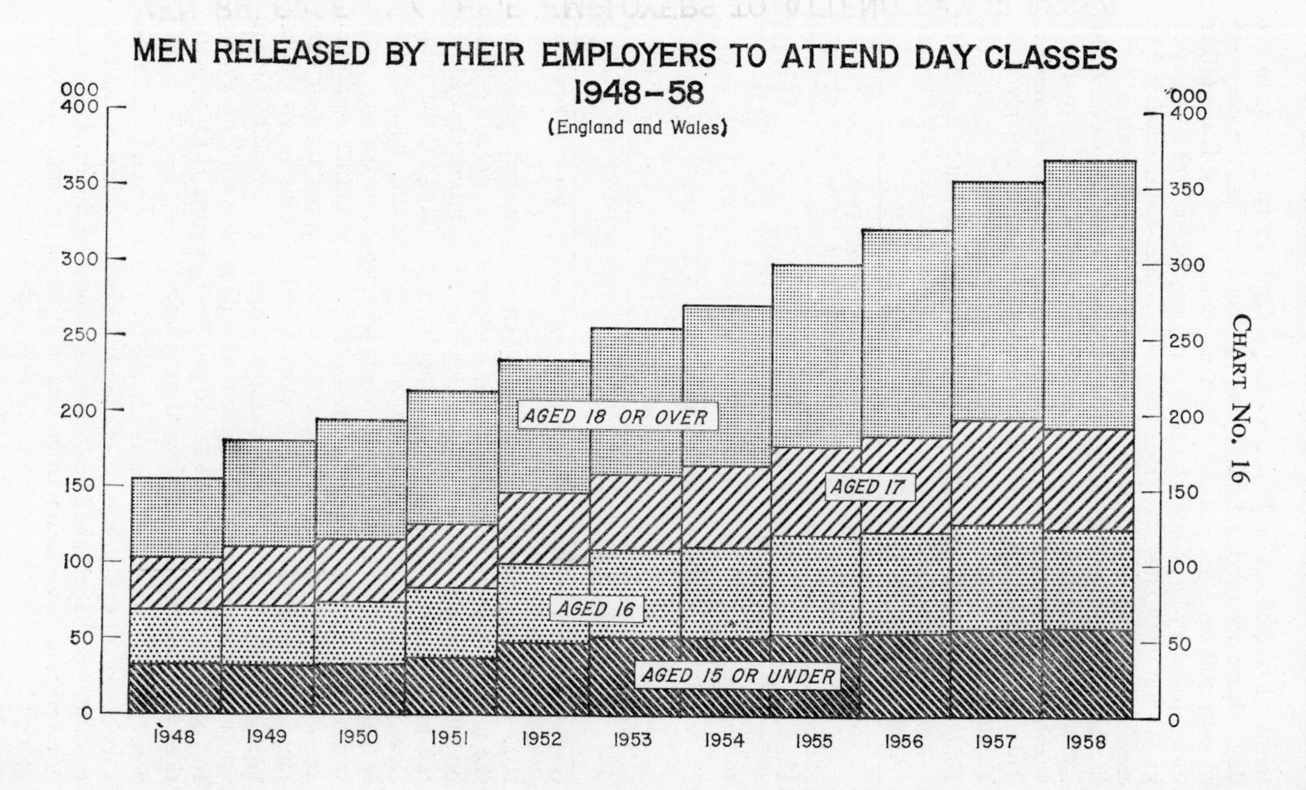
MEN RELEASED BY THEIR EMPLOYERS TO ATTEND DAY CLASSES
1948–58
(England and Wales)
000
400
350
300
250
200
150
100
50
0
AGED 18 OR OVER
AGED 17
AGED 16
AGED 15 OR UNDER
1948
1949
1950
1951
1952
1953
1954
1955
1956
1957
1958

Table 63. Males Released by Their Employers at Different Ages (Total Number Released=100%) (England and Wales).

Age	1952–53	1953–54	1954–55	1955–56	1956–57	1957–58
	%	%	%	%	%	%
15 or under	*20*	*19*	*19*	*17*	*16*	*16*
16	*22*	*22*	*21*	*21*	20	*18*
17	*20*	*20*	*20*	*20*	*19*	*18*
18	*11*	*12*	*12*	*13*	*13*	*14*
19	*8*	*8*	*9*	*9*	*10*	*11*
20	*6*	*6*	*6*	*6*	*7*	*7*
21+	*13*	*13*	*13*	*14*	*15*	*16*
	100	*100*	*100*	*100*	*100*	*100*

The average number of 15 year-olds was 561,000, the largest number was 604,000 in 1957–58 and the smallest 532,000 in 1948–49; a range of variation of 13 per cent. Employers on the whole were looking for apprentices. In the succeeding ten years the number of 15 year-olds will fluctuate widely from year to year; and there will be many more of them. The average number will be 692,000, the highest number will be 829,000 in 1962–63, the lowest 628,000 in 1960–61—a range of variation of 32 per cent. Potential apprentices will be seeking employers. Charts 17 and 18 overleaf show the actual rate of increase of release for 16 year-old boys from 1948 to the present—an average of about 2,900 additional workers released each year and an increase from 15 per cent to 31 per cent in the percentage of the age-group (other than those in full-time education) released. The charts* also estimate the future volume of day release in the years up to 1964 calculated on three different assumptions. The first (A) is that the average annual increase in the number of 16 year-old boys released is maintained but not increased. The larger age-groups concerned in this event would result in each individual boy having a smaller chance than today of getting day release—28 per cent instead of 31 per cent of the age-group not in full-time education would get it. In terms of the percentage of 16 year-olds getting day release the clock would by 1964 have been put back to 1956. The second assumption (B) is that the percentage of boys released would be maintained at its present figure of 31 per cent. This would entail an increase of nearly 28,000 by 1964—an increase comparable to that achieved in the 10 years from 1948. The third assumption (C) is that the numbers released can be increased

* The charts deal only with boys; for girls the present and future pictures are far less encouraging.

CHART No. 17

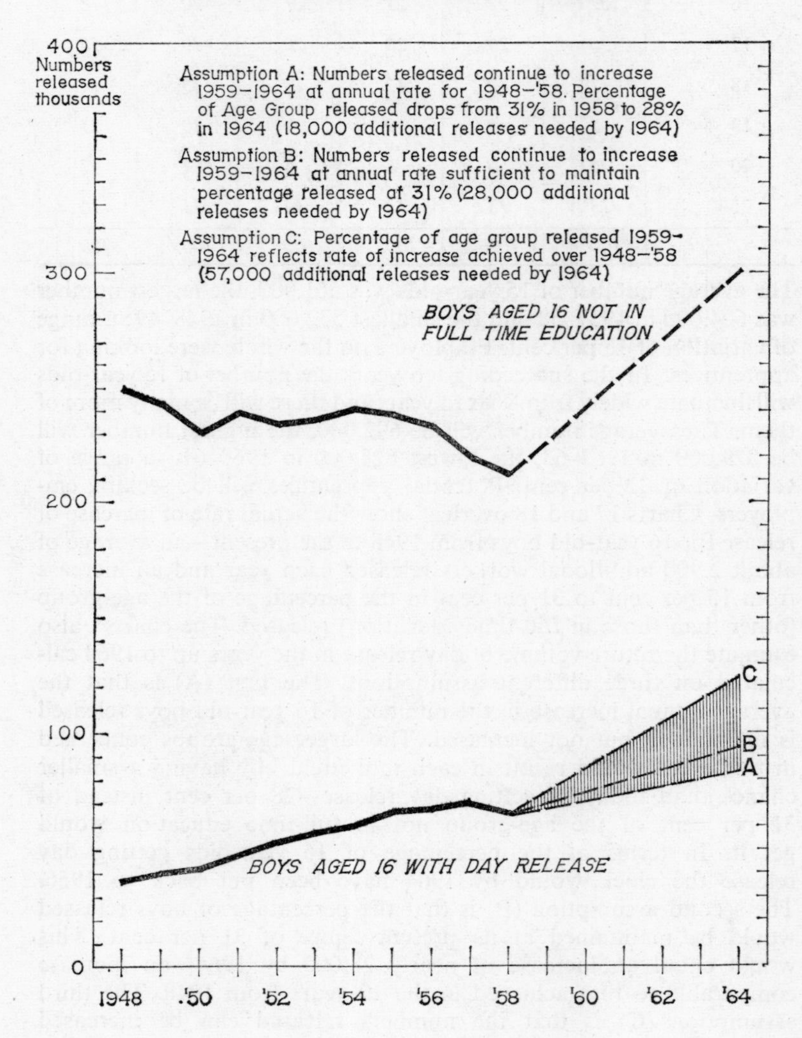
DAY RELEASE (16 YEAR OLDS)
1948 – 1958 AND 1959 – 1964 ON
DIFFERENT ASSUMPTIONS
400
Numbers released thousands
Assumption A: Numbers released continue to increase 1959–1964 at annual rate for 1948–'58. Percentage of Age Group released drops from 31% in 1958 to 28% in 1964 (18,000 additional releases needed by 1964)
Assumption B: Numbers released continue to increase 1959–1964 at annual rate sufficient to maintain percentage released at 31% (28,000 additional releases needed by 1964)
Assumption C: Percentage of age group released 1959–1964 reflects rate of increase achieved over 1948–'58 (57,000 additional releases needed by 1964)
300
BOYS AGED 16 NOT IN FULL TIME EDUCATION
200
C
100
B
A
BOYS AGED 16 WITH DAY RELEASE
0
1948
'50
'52
'54
'56
'58
'60
'62
'64

CHART NO. 18

INFORMATION ON PREVIOUS CHART EXPRESSED AS PERCENTAGE OF ALL THOSE AGED 16 NOT IN FULL TIME EDUCATION

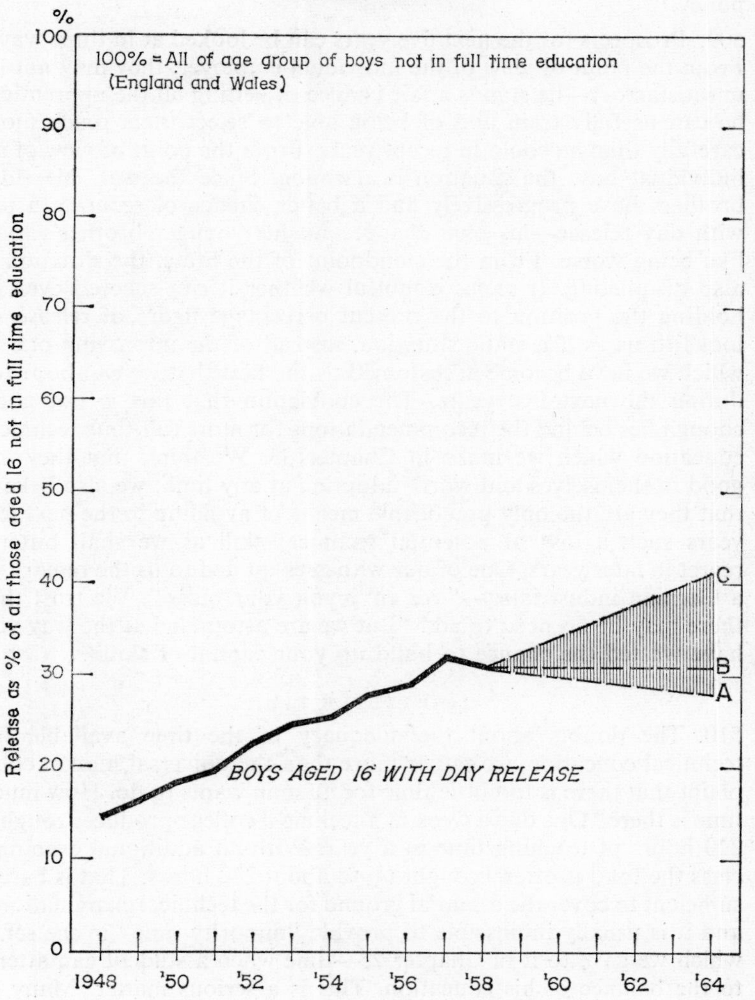

sufficiently to maintain the post-war rate of percentage growth so that by 1964 nearly a third of all 16 year-old boys not in full-time education would get day release. To do this we should have nearly to double the number getting day release by 1964. The two latter assumptions seem highly improbable: indeed we shall be hard put to it to realise the first. The educational system can play only a contingent role in the English day release system. The presence or absence of students depends on employment and not on educational policy.

509. Prospects for the next five years can be looked at in three ways. From the point of view of the individual employer, they may not be unsatisfactory—he stands a fair chance of getting all the apprentices he can usefully train and of being able to select them much more carefully than he could in recent years. From the point of view of an individual boy, the situation is alarming. Since the war, his elder brothers have progressively had a better chance of securing a job with day release—his own chance and his younger brother's look like being worse. From the standpoint of the State, the situation is also disquieting. It seems doubtful whether it can succeed even in holding the position to the present percentage figure of release. It looks to us as if a static situation, instead of the improving one to which we have become accustomed, is the best that we can hope for during the next five years. The conviction that this is not good enough lies behind the recommendations for more full-time technical education which we make in Chapter 35. We think that they are good in themselves and worth adopting at any time; we also believe that they are the only practicable means of avoiding in the next few years such a loss of potential technical skill as we shall bitterly regret in later years. One of our witnesses quoted to us the remark of a German industrialist—"We envy you your bulge". We trust that there may be no need to add "But we are astounded at the way you have wasted the chance to build up your capital of skill".

TOO LITTLE TIME

510. The doubts about the adequacy of the time available for technical education are rather more than the universal human complaint that there is too little time for all man wants to do. How much time is there? One day a week at a technical college produces roughly 220 hours of teaching time in a year. With an additional evening's class the total is often brought up to about 270 hours. That is barely sufficient to cover the essential ground for the technical examinations, and it is usually impossible to provide "minority time" in the sense which we gave to it in Chapter 25—time when a student can attend to the balance of his education. This is a serious matter. Many of the day release students have the intellectual ability of Sixth Formers,

but more than the school science specialist's difficulties in matters of literacy, both in the narrow and in the broader significance of that term. Of course, the technical college is not the only educational influence to which they are exposed. There is the maturing influence of wage-earning. There is the free play of those cultural (and anti-cultural) forces which permeate the modern world through newspapers, books, cinemas, wireless and television. But none of these is directed to the special needs of a particular young man attending a technical college in the same way as good Sixth Form teaching is directed to the individual condition of the pupils. Indeed the bewildering and bludgeoning nature of the impact made by the mass media of communication is one of the reasons why we cannot be content that so many intelligent young people should be left without a guide through the maze. In this matter, technical education in the form of day release (and still more of evening classes) can do virtually nothing for the abler students who already have too much ground to cover, though it can do something for the less able whose technical studies hardly fill the whole time available. Here, then, in the importance of finding "minority time", is another reason which lies behind the recommendations we make in Chapter 35 for more full-time education for technicians and technologists.

511. There is too little time also for the proper development of what in the Sixth Form context we called "majority or specialist time". It is true that a student who enters a technical college with an exemption from the first year of the National Certificate course has the same number of years as he would have had in the Sixth Form at school in which to reach a similar standard in mathematics and science. He will, however, have a far smaller number of hours of teaching in those subjects, and far less opportunity for private study. The teaching given him must be strictly relevant to the examination syllabus, and is often confined to it, necessarily avoiding that discursiveness and exploration in depth which is apt to set minds on fire. If we are dissatisfied with a good deal of what goes on in the specialist teaching in Sixth Forms, we must be even more dissatisfied with the nature of the approach that is forced on technical colleges by the shortness of the available time.

512. Need the time be quite so short as it is? When compulsory part-time day education to 18 is introduced, it will have to be longer. Instead of the present technical college teaching year of about 36 weeks, the Education Act of 1944 specifies a working year of 44 weeks for county colleges. An increase in time of this magnitude would make a good deal possible that is now out of the question. Need it wait for the implementation of this section of the Act of 1944? We come back to this question in Chapter 33.

SUCCESS AND FAILURE IN TECHNICAL COURSES

513. There has long been great uncertainty about the rates of success and failure in technical courses—not, of course, in the sense of how many candidates sit a particular examination and how many pass it, but in the more important sense of how many of the students who begin a particular course of study are able to carry it through successfully to the end. Latterly there has been much anxiety as well as uncertainty, and we have regarded it as a most important part of our task to ascertain the facts. We were fortunate in securing the co-operation of the principals of 114 colleges, selected so as to give a true cross-section of all the students in technical colleges working for National Certificates and for six City and Guilds courses. In this way we have obtained a national picture to set beside the local studies carried out in recent years by, among others, Professor Lady Williams, Dr. Ethel C. Venables, the National Institute of Industrial Psychology and the Chemistry sub-panel of H.M. Inspectorate. The results obtained in our national survey correspond closely enough, allowing for expected local variations, with those earlier findings, and it is possible to feel confidence that the picture given in the following paragraphs is a true account of what is happening to students who take this route to technical qualifications. Full details are given in Part Three of Volume II of this report, for which we are indebted to Mr. G. F. Peaker, H.M.I.

514. There are some important differences between the various National Certificates in the demands made on students and in their prospects of success. These are shown separately in Volume II. They are not, however, inconsistent with the broad general picture with which this chapter is concerned so that, since engineering accounts for 80 per cent of all National Certificate students, we confine ourselves here in the main to the figures for the 5,857 students in the sample who were taking engineering courses. The six City and Guilds courses selected for survey were Electrical Installation, Machine Shop Engineering, Motor Vehicle Mechanics, Carpentry and Joinery, Plumbing, Brickwork. Once again there are important differences; but, for the most part, we have left these for detailed study to Volume II and contented ourselves here with general statements about the 4,558 City and Guilds students as a whole.

515. The first question to ask is "*how many succeed*?" This appears to be answered by the fact that in 1958 over half the candidates sitting for the final examination for Ordinary National Certificates and 70 per cent of those sitting for the Higher National Certificate were successful. This statement, though true, is highly misleading. It should be compared with the number of students who originally

started the course. Unfortunately, we can only account satisfactorily for students from the time they achieve admission to a National Certificate or City and Guilds course. Many of them had to do a preliminary pre-technical course at an evening institute, and they are the survivors of a much more numerous group who started but did not finish such a pre-technical course. In the absence of any national statistics on the extent of such failures even before the beginning of the course proper we must fall back on a study by H.M. Inspectors of one large industrial city, where the position for 1956–57 is given below.

Table 64. Enrolments, Attendance and Examination Results of the Introductory Technical Course in one City, 1956–57.

Enrolments			Number still attending towards end of course	Number who sat the examination	Number who passed the examination
Boys	Girls	Total			
1,004	12	1,016	510 (*50%*)	391 (*38%*)	252 (*25%*)

Success in this examination, which comprises papers in English, mathematics, technical drawing and science, is required in this city of all who left school at 15 and wish to enter a National Certificate or Craft course. We have no means of knowing how far this situation is typical of the country as a whole, but there is no reason to think that it is exceptionally bad. The state of affairs appears to be such as to demand either a national sample investigation on the lines of our technical courses enquiry or such an alteration in the system of collecting statistics for the Ministry as to throw adequate light on what seems to be a dark patch of the educational system, not only in the sense that it is largely unknown territory, but also that it is an area made dark by unnecessary educational casualties.

516. Fortunately, we can now give a pretty full account of what happens to students once they have joined a National Certificate or City and Guilds course. Table 65, which is printed on the following page, gives the numbers of students who start and the percentage who eventually complete National Certificate and selected City and Guilds courses (whether in the standard time or longer). The method used to produce these figures is fully explained in Part Three of Volume II. It appears that in the five-stage courses rather more than a quarter of the original students get either an Ordinary National Certificate or a City and Guilds Intermediate Certificate, and 10 per cent or less a Higher or Final. In four-stage courses over half get an O.N.C. or Intermediate and between one-fifth and one-quarter a H.N.C. or Final. The marked similarity between the general pattern of National Certificate and City and Guilds rates is odd and striking. Not only are the courses very different in difficulty; but, while the basis for

Table 65. Success and Wastage Rates in Some Technical Courses (National Certificate 1956, City and Guilds 1958) (England).

(This table shows the number of students for whom information was collected in the Technical Courses Survey entering National Certificate and certain City and Guilds courses and the percentage of them who received certificates.)

Course	Five Stage Courses			Four Stage Courses		
	(Students without Exemption)			(Students Exempt S.1)		
A. National Certificates	Nos. enrolled	Percentage obtaining O.N.C.	Percentage obtaining H.N.C.	Nos. enrolled	Percentage obtaining O.N.C.	Percentage obtaining H.N.C.
Engineering	4,757	*25*	*9*	1,100	*49*	*25*
Building	429	*30*	*17*	102	*54*	*34*
Science	329	*39*	*27*	219	*70*	*33*
Commerce	53	*21*	—	62	*35*	—
Others	218	*42*	*27*	102	*55*	*37*
All	5,786	*26*	*10*	1,585	*51*	*26*
	(Colleges with 3 Stages to Inter; 2 to Final)			(Colleges with 2 Stages to Inter; 2 to Final)		
B. City and Guilds		Percentage passing Inter.	Percentage passing Final		Percentage passing Inter.	Percentage passing Final
Electrical Installation	510	*21*	*2*	—	—	—
Machine Shop Engineering	1,207	*28*	*6*	294	*39*	*7*
Motor Vehicle Mechanics	701	*27*	*8*	—	—	—
Carpentry and Joinery	272	*39*	*5*	622	*60*	*27*
Plumbing	134	*42*	*7*	345	*59*	*29*
Brickwork	153	*17*	*5*	320	*49*	*13*
All	2,977	*28*	*6*	1,581	*53*	*20*

NOTE: It should be stressed that both Ordinary National Certificates and City and Guilds Intermediate Certificates are complete in themselves, and correspond to certain levels of industrial employment. Failure to proceed to H.N.C. or a City and Guilds Final cannot be accounted failure except in the sense of not going on to promotion to a different and higher level. This is made explicit in the Motor Vehicle certificates where the Intermediate has the word "Mechanics" and the Final "Technicians" in the title.

exemption from S.1 in National Certificate courses is the student's knowledge at the beginning of the course, the distinction between two-stage and three-stage courses to City and Guilds Intermediate standard is a difference between colleges, and not between students. It certainly looks as if the actual length of the course has some bearing on success.

517. It ought not, however, to be assumed that all students who do not receive a certificate get no benefit from their education. We can break down the position a good deal further and find the number of stages successfully completed by candidates who do not achieve the qualification which they set out to obtain. This is shown in Table 66.

Table 66. Percentages of Students Covered by Table 65 successfully completing Different Stages in National Certificate and City and Guilds Courses (England).

	Five Stage Courses: Percentage of Students successfully completing following stages				
Course	1st	2nd	3rd	4th	5th
National Certificate	*68*	*44*	(*O.N.C.*) *26*	*14*	(*H.N.C.*) *10*
City and Guilds	*66*	*46*	(*Inter.*) *28*	*12*	(*Final*) *6*

NOTE: Stages 1–3 are labelled S1, S2, S3 and lead to O.N.C. or C. and G. Inter.: Stages 4 and 5 are labelled A1, A2 and lead to H.N.C. or C. and G. Final.

	Four Stage Courses: Percentage of Students successfully completing following stages			
Course	1st	2nd	3rd	4th
National Certificate	*77*	(*O.N.C.*) *51*	*34*	(*H.N.C.*) *26*
City and Guilds	*74*	(*Inter.*) *53*	*36*	(*Final*) *20*

NOTE: Stages 1 and 2 are labelled S2 and S3 in the National Certificate courses—4 Stage courses are for students exempt from S1. Stages 1 and 2 in C. and G. courses are labelled S1, S2 and are in colleges which provide only two stages to Inter. Stages 3 and 4 are labelled A1, A2 and lead to H.N.C. or C. and G. Final.

Charts 19 and 20, on the two following pages, show the flow of students through the various stages. They also separate those who gave up the course after successfully completing a stage from those who gave up after failing to complete it successfully. Of the National Certificate students 33* per cent left at a point where they had just successfully passed an examination—nearly half of them, however, at a stage in the course for which no certificate is awarded. Very similar

* 5 stage courses.

CHART No. 19

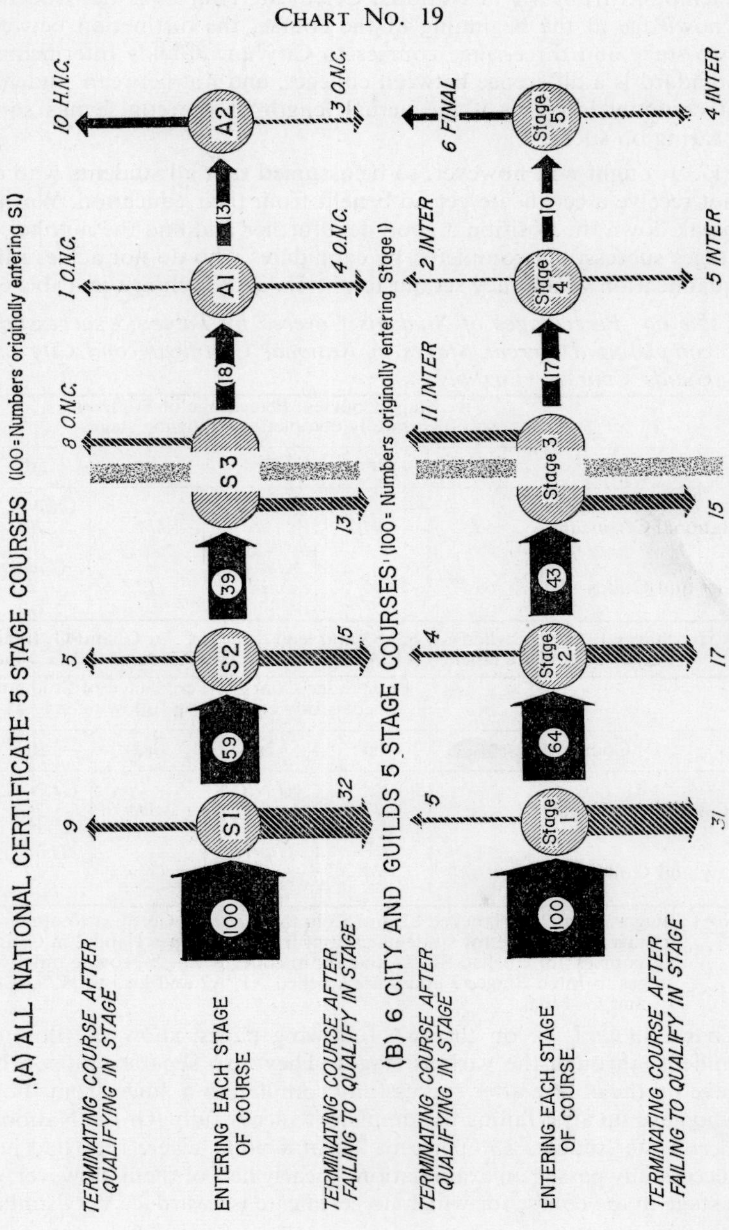
(A) ALL NATIONAL CERTIFICATE 5 STAGE COURSES (100 = Numbers originally entering S1)
TERMINATING COURSE AFTER QUALIFYING IN STAGE
ENTERING EACH STAGE OF COURSE
TERMINATING COURSE AFTER FAILING TO QUALIFY IN STAGE
100
S1
9
32
59
S2
5
15
39
S3
8 O.N.C.
13
18
A1
1 O.N.C.
4 O.N.C.
13
A2
10 H.N.C.
3 O.N.C.
(B) 6 CITY AND GUILDS 5 STAGE COURSES (100 = Numbers originally entering Stage 1)
TERMINATING COURSE AFTER QUALIFYING IN STAGE
ENTERING EACH STAGE OF COURSE
TERMINATING COURSE AFTER FAILING TO QUALIFY IN STAGE
100
Stage 1
5
31
64
Stage 2
4
17
43
Stage 3
11 INTER
15
17
Stage 4
2 INTER
5 INTER
10
Stage 5
6 FINAL
4 INTER

CHART No. 20

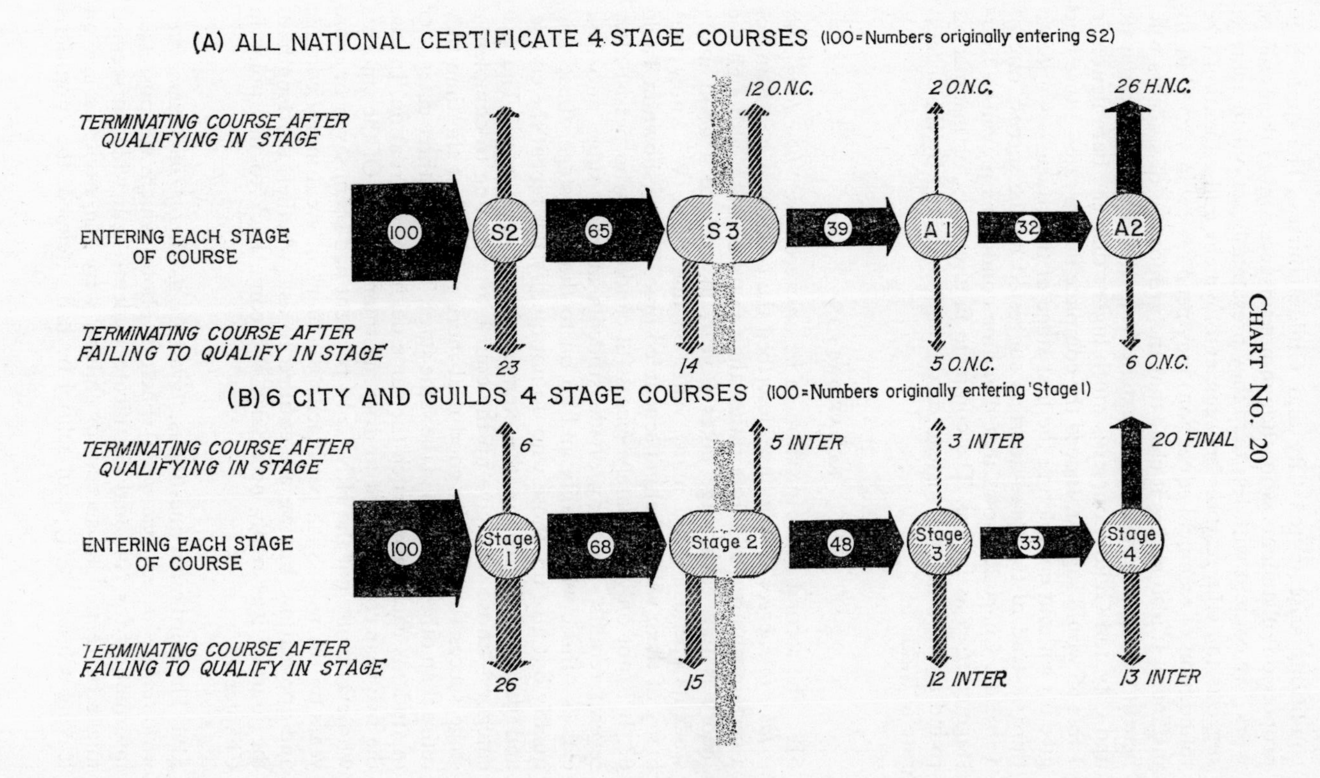
(A) ALL NATIONAL CERTIFICATE 4 STAGE COURSES (100=Numbers originally entering S2)
TERMINATING COURSE AFTER QUALIFYING IN STAGE
ENTERING EACH STAGE OF COURSE
TERMINATING COURSE AFTER FAILING TO QUALIFY IN STAGE
100
S2
65
S3
39
A1
32
A2
12 O.N.C.
2 O.N.C.
26 H.N.C.
23
14
5 O.N.C.
6 O.N.C.
(B) 6 CITY AND GUILDS 4 STAGE COURSES (100=Numbers originally entering 'Stage 1')
TERMINATING COURSE AFTER QUALIFYING IN STAGE
ENTERING EACH STAGE OF COURSE
TERMINATING COURSE AFTER FAILING TO QUALIFY IN STAGE
100
Stage 1
68
Stage 2
48
Stage 3
33
Stage 4
6
5 INTER
3 INTER
20 FINAL
26
15
12 INTER
13 INTER

conditions arise in the City and Guilds courses. The quite high proportion of students who, though not unsuccessful in their college work, are content with less than they presumably set out to achieve, suggests that the relation between employment and education (the foundation of technical education) may need review in a good many instances. It also makes it clear that the proportion of students who benefit educationally to some extent from the National Certificate and City and Guilds courses is much higher than the bare figures in Table 65 would suggest. Indeed the complete failure rate—those who give up without completing the first stage of the course—is under a third instead of the three-quarters suggested by the success rate of Table 65. Chart 20 shows that the same conditions prevail in four-stage courses as in five. The complete failure rate, for instance, is round about a quarter instead of the half suggested by the success rate in Table 65.

RETARDATION

518. The second main question to be answered, is, "*how long does it take to succeed*?" We have described the courses as consisting of a certain number of stages rather than years because, although the theory is that each stage takes a year, in practice a good many students spend a good many years on one stage. We know that many of them will be behind scheduled time. This is shown in Table 67. It is not only ultimately successful candidates who persist after several rebuffs. We may divide students at each stage into four classes—those who qualify and go on to the next stage, those who qualify but give up, those who do not qualify but repeat the course, and those who give up the course without qualifying. The last category—those who give up the course after failing to complete a stage successfully—are a good deal more retarded at the time they retire than other students in the same stage. The other three categories of students each show much the same degree of retardation. Indeed the five-year course is apt to drag out interminably. Of the students who eventually got the H.N.C. 19 per cent had spent seven or more years on the way. Such pertinacity is a mark of great moral courage and application, but we are entitled to ask whether the length of the journey was really necessary. We come back to this point in Chapter 33.

519. The third main question is, "*what are the factors most associated with failure or retardation*?" Factors about which we possessed information for National Certificate students, and which it seemed might be related to success or failure, were the student's age on leaving school, the type of school he had attended, the conditions

Table 67. Percentages of Students gaining National Certificates in Engineering or passing the Intermediate Stage of certain City and Guilds Examinations and the Length of Time Taken to do so, as shown by the Technical Courses Survey (England).

Students without exemption		Students exempt S.1	
A (i). Percentage gaining O.N.C.		(ii). Percentage gaining O.N.C.	
in 3 years (standard time)	*11*	in 2 years (standard time)	*33*
in 4 years	*8*	in 3 years	*11*
in 5 years	*4*	in 4 years	*3*
in 6 or more years	*2*	in 5 or more years	*2*
Altogether	*25*	Altogether	*49*

Students without exemption		Students exempt S.1	
B (i). Percentage gaining H.N.C.		(ii). Percentage gaining H.N.C.	
in 5 years (standard time)	*3·3*	in 4 years (standard time)	*12*
in 6 years	*3·0*	in 5 years	*7*
in 7 years	*1·4*	in 6 years	*4*
in 8 or more years	*1·3*	in 7 or more years	*2*
Altogether	*9·0*	Altogether	*25*

C (i). Percentage gaining City and Guilds Intermediate Certificates. 3 Stage Courses

	Electrical Installation	Machine Shop Engineering	Motor Vehicle Mechanics
In 3 years	*4*	*5*	*5*
In 4 years	*12*	*16*	*17*
In 5 years or more	*5*	*7*	*5*
Altogether	*21*	*28*	*27*

(ii). Percentage gaining City and Guilds Intermediate Certificates. 2 Stage Courses

	Carpentry and Joinery	Plumbing	Brickwork
In 2 years	*47*	*46*	*39*
In 3 years	*12*	*10*	*8*
In 4 years or more	*1*	*3*	*2*
Altogether	*60*	*59*	*49*

under which he had taken the course (day classes, day and evening classes, evening classes), the nature of his home background as shown by his father's occupation, his general vigour as shown by his participation in organised games, and the difficulty he found in certain subjects in the course. It was found that the percentage gaining Ordinary and Higher National Certificates was somewhat below average among students who had left school at 15, who had attended all-age or modern schools, whose fathers were in unskilled occupations or who took no part in playing games. Details are given in Part Three of Volume II. On two further counts, however, the differences in yield were so marked that we give them here in Table 68.

Table 68. Percentage of Engineering Students gaining National Certificates, A. by Type of Technical College Attendance and B. by Subject Difficulty, as shown by the Technical Courses Survey.

Category of Student	No Exemptions. Percentage gaining		Exempt One Year. Percentage gaining	
	O.N.C.	H.N.C.	O.N.C.	H.N.C.
A. Part-time Day and Evening Attendance	*29*	*11*	*52*	*29*
Part-time Day	*25*	*12*	*50*	*34*
Evening Only	*19*	*6*	*43*	*15*
B. Students with no specially difficult subject	*38*	*14*	*60*	*32*
Mathematics specially difficult	*10*	*3*	*23*	*11*
All Students	*25*	*9*	*49*	*25*

The disadvantage suffered by students who attempt these courses solely by evening study emerges very clearly. The biggest single handicap, however, is a weakness in mathematics (while an earlier analysis showed that the possession of an Ordinary level pass in mathematics in G.C.E. was the surest predictor of success). It seems probable that at least one of the reasons for the below-average showing of students who had attended modern or all-age schools and of students who left school at 15 is precisely that they may be expected to have less mathematical knowledge at the outset of the course. It may also very well be that mathematics as a subject requires more time with a teacher and more individual help in understanding and overcoming difficulties than most subjects. It may, therefore, suffer more than the rest of the curriculum from the compression of the technical college curriculum and the gaps that necessarily occur between lessons. In schools, mathematics is one of the subjects for which the regularity of daily periods is thought to be almost essential. Whatever the reasons may be for the failure of so many National Certificate students to succeed in this subject, it is of the utmost importance that no reforms in the conditions of technical education should be ruled out as too great if they would be likely to improve the situation in this respect. Not only does the country need all the technicians and technologists it can get, but most technicians and technologists now require an appropriate mastery of mathematics.

520. A fourth main question is, "*what is the relation between students who are granted exemption from S.1 in National Certificate courses and those who are not?*" There are various ways by which exemption can be obtained and students were asked to record the way in which they secured it. Table 69 records the result.

Table 69. Methods of Securing Exemption From S.1 and Results Obtained by Students in National Certificate Courses in Engineering as Shown by the Technical Courses Survey (England).

Basis of Exemption	No. of Students	Percentage gaining O.N.C.	Percentage gaining H.N.C.
G.C.E.	589	*60*	*30*
Technical School Record and Interview	208	*30*	*15*
Transfers from C. and G. Courses	87	*46*	*27*
Special Waiver	42	*32*	*20*
Not recorded	147	*43*	*17*
All Exempt Students	1,073	*49*	*25*
Students without Exemption	4,757	*25*	*9*

The relatively poor showing by the second method—technical school record and interview—needs consideration. It does not, of course, include all students who attended technical schools and secured exemption; indeed it only accounts for about one-third of them. Technical school students exempt from S.1 show as a class a yield of 44 per cent at O.N.C. and 25 per cent at H.N.C. The explanation of the divergence probably lies in the fact that technical school pupils who can obtain the necessary G.C.E. passes do so, and their exemption is classified under that heading. There can be no doubt that (with the possible exception of exemptions granted on technical school record alone) the high yield from these four-stage courses reflects a better preparedness for the academic work. It is, of course, arguable that the eventual yield from the exempt category might have been higher still if some of its members had in fact started at the bottom—that is something we cannot know. By contrast, the yield from those students who start without any exemptions is disappointingly low. Even so, they account for 63 per cent of all the Ordinary National Certificates awarded each year. Indeed 33 per cent of all O.N.C.'s are obtained by students who left school at 15. But a straightforward comparison is not in this instance a fair one. We should really compare the record of those students in S.2 who entered it by exemption from S.1 with that of those who came to it through S.1. On this basis the percentage of students with no exemption who gained a H.N.C. is 15 per cent (instead of 9) compared with 25 per cent for direct entries into S.2.

521. Technical examinations are not by any means the only ones over which a great deal of uncertainty persists. There are many other professional examinations in which the yield is unknown, if it is defined, as we think it should be, in terms of those starting a course of preparation and those finally qualifying. It is often, too, extremely difficult to say how great is the degree of retardation which candidates must expect to encounter. This applies with much the same force to examinations for such occupations as accountancy and law as to the technical examinations we have been considering. Even school examinations are not as well documented as they should be. It is impossible to tell, for instance, from the published figures whether the position with regard to the General Certificate of Education has changed since our report "Early Leaving" was issued. We know the numbers entering the examination and passing. We do not know for a more recent date than 1953 the numbers starting a course and completing it or the degree of success they achieve. But information of this kind seems to us to be essential for the proper planning of education and examinations, which ought not to be carried on in mutual ignorance. Certainly we should not have felt justified in proposing the changes we do in technical education if we had not first cleared the ground by the enquiry whose results we have just been describing. We close this chapter, then, with a plea for a more systematic and regular study of what is happening in other courses of training and education and in the examinations to which they lead.

CHAPTER 32

Principles of Expansion

522. The greater part of the existing structure of further education in England came into existence, as we have seen, to serve vocational purposes, to provide for the needs of young people striving to qualify themselves for the jobs they wanted, or (more usually) for promotion in the jobs they already held. This is still its major aim, recognised as such by staff and students alike. The strong link between the more closely organised courses and the system of industrial apprenticeship, powerfully reinforced since the war by the growth of part-time day release, serves only to underline the dependence of further education on employment. We have not thought it right to concern ourselves with the industrial aspects of this double relationship. But there is little doubt that, in its general outline, the present structure meets with the approval of both sides of industry, as expressed most recently in the Report of the Carr Committee.* Those who approach the system from the side of education and, with that preoccupation, wish to suggest some changes in it, should take particular care lest in so doing they diminish its value to industry—if for no other reason than because a voluntary system of further education that had no appeal to industry could not rely, as it does today, on part-time day release for so many of its students.

523. We do not, however, think this means (as is sometimes implied) that educational considerations should always be subordinate to employment considerations. Further education is in the nature of a partnership, and if industry bears some of the cost by releasing some of its young workers with pay, the rest of the cost is met almost entirely by the taxpayer's and the ratepayer's money, provided on educational votes. We do not believe that public opinion nowadays regards this money as being mainly provided to help industry to train its workers, or even to help the young people to improve their vocational status. It is provided as part of the national system of education, to serve broad educational ends. It is from this point of view that we have looked at further education. We have tried to find out what its contribution is to the education (in the broadest sense of the term) of the many thousands of boys and girls who pass through it.

524. There can be no doubt that the contribution is great. It would be a mistake, in our view, to draw too sharp a distinction between

* "Training for Skill." Report of a Sub-Committee of the Minister of Labour's National Joint Advisory Council.

"vocational studies" and "education". Often, they are the same thing. Sometimes, it is true, they are not, and the vocational training is no more than the acquisition of one or two manual skills which contribute little to the development of the student's mind or personality. But these are the exceptions, and the greater part of the work done in institutions of further education would fit into any definition of what education should be. Indeed, in many cases, as we have emphasised, this (or something very much like it) is the only way of stimulating the further intellectual growth of a boy or girl. Not only for industrial reasons, but on sound educational grounds too, we should beware lest any proposals for change should be so sudden and so drastic as to disrupt the good work that is being done before anything better could be substituted.

525. Nevertheless, we have come to the conclusion that the system has several serious defects from the educational point of view and that, if it is to play its proper part in a coherent and progressive national structure of education, thought should be given to the means of removing them. We have not attempted to carry out a detailed enquiry into the present state of affairs. Similarly, we have no intention of presenting any complete or precise proposals. Here is a fruitful field for further research and enquiry. Our purposes are more general. It does not, however, require a comprehensive enquiry to be able to point to three major defects in the present arrangements.

526. The first defect—chronologically the first, not the most important—is the lack of integration between the education that students receive in the technical colleges and the education they have received at school. Historically, there was in most cases a long gap between leaving school at 14 and entering further education two years later. Not unnaturally, this was usually regarded as a fresh start, for a different purpose, in wholly novel surroundings. School and college were two different worlds, and rarely did the twain meet. The gap is now shorter, but the old habits remain. Here and there examples can be found of close co-operation between the schools of an area and the local college of further education, but we have the impression that in general it is sporadic and not very effectual. We do not believe that the fault lies more on one side than on the other. If in the schools there is insufficient attempt to prepare boys for what they will find in the technical colleges, there is insufficient trouble taken in the colleges to adjust what is taught the students to what they have learnt before. The course in which a boy finds himself is all too likely to depend upon accidents of his employment or his unguided choice than upon any deliberate assessment of what he is qualified to profit by. We believe that the boy coming from a school into a technical college is entitled to have his transition from the one institution to the other as

carefully thought out and watched over as the transition of the Sixth Former to the university should be. This is needed not only in the boy's own interest; it would also help, as we saw in the previous chapter, to increase the efficiency of the system.

THE NEED FOR TIME

527. The second defect of the system as it is today is the very high proportion of effort put into it that is wasted, or at least attains goals far short of what was originally aimed at. Only one student in 11 succeeds in climbing the National Certificate ladder from bottom to top, and only one in 30 does so in the time for which the course was designed.* Against the background of the nation's present and future needs for trained manpower, these wastage rates are shocking. Differences are, of course, to be expected between a part-time system, where the major interests lie elsewhere, and a full-time one, and it must always be expected that many more will fall by the wayside in the former than in the latter. But this does not, in our view, explain or excuse the facts that were set out in the previous chapter. There is no escaping from the fact that the ladder of further education is at present too steep for most of those who are attempting to climb it. Something could be done by better methods of selection: many of those who now enter upon courses have not the ability to succeed in them; it should be possible to identify them and steer them towards other courses where their chances will be better. But this is not the only, nor even the main explanation, as is shown by the painfully large proportion of those who eventually pass the various examinations but who take extra years to reach the goal. Even for those with the ability to climb, the ascent is too steep. Very many of those who do succeed, do so only at the cost of giving up to their studies, over many years, the whole of their spare time. Nowhere else in our educational system do we expect such sacrifices for success. Not only does the present system bear very hardly on the young people who are working their way through it, it also deprives the country every year of thousands of potential technicians. No one would advocate any lowering of the standards of the qualifications. Indeed, the expanding universe of technology is constantly raising them. If the ladder cannot thus be made less steep, the only alternative is to provide more help for the climbers.

528. For this, the prescription is more time. If we were confined to one comment and one recommendation about English further education, it would be this. At every stage, and on every level, the need is

* Some students, of course, do not aim at, and could not reach, anything beyond the Ordinary National Certificate. Even so, only one in four who start at the bottom reach this stage, and only one in nine in the standard time.

for more time, for less pressure on both staff and students. Even a little more time would, in our opinion, much more than proportionately raise the educational yield. Some courses, as we shall argue in Chapter 34, cannot be done properly in less than half the student's time and all of them could be made much more rewarding if every minute did not have to be so jealously preserved for the immediate task of covering the syllabus for a set examination.

529. There is one aspect of the need for time on which we wish to make a special comment. We are unhappy about the reliance that is still placed on evening classes for this age-group. The growth of part-time day release since the end of the war has brought a great improvement in this respect—but only to some young people (mainly boys) in some industries. Even in the National Certificate courses and those craft courses covered by our survey, 29 per cent of the students were attending evening classes *only* and a further 55 per cent were combining day and evening classes. Only 16 per cent were able to do all their classwork (not, of course, their homework and reading) by day. Moreover, part-time day release often does not begin until 16; over one-fifth of the students enrolled in evening institutes are under 16.

530. The possibility of rising in the world by evening study has historically been one of the great safety-valves of English society. The lives of eminent men provide plenty of examples of the value of what can be done despite all the difficulties. That value still exists, and where a boy who has no other means of progress is driven by his own ambition, by energy or by curiosity into attending evening classes, we would not put any further obstacles in his way. But in many instances today, evening classes are compulsory—compulsory not by law but by circumstances that are fully as compelling. Attendance at evening classes may be made a condition of day release. There are occupations where the acquisition of qualifications is required (or at least desirable) for promotion, but there is no day release. This is not good enough for the present age. The state long ago accepted the responsibility for seeing that the hours of employment for juveniles were not excessive, and we think the same concern should now be directed to the pressure that is put upon them by their studies. It should not be forgotten that many young people who are pursuing courses of further education (though, to be fair, not all) have homework and serious reading to do in the evenings. We do not think it is possible (even if it were desirable, which is arguable) to ban all evening classes. But we are glad to observe that much less reliance is placed on them than was the case twenty years ago and we should like to see this progress continued. With this object in view, we make three recommendations. The first is that no boy or girl under the age of 18

should be expected to follow a course of further education that relies entirely upon evening classes; those industries and professions that do now expect this of their young employees should be invited to reconsider their practices. Secondly, we think that any course that requires more than one evening of classes a week of a boy or girl under 18, in addition to part-time day classes, is too heavy and should be rearranged; and even one evening a week may be too heavy if there is a considerable burden of homework or reading. Thirdly, when the county college provisions of the Act of 1944 are enforced (or come into operation by prior voluntary agreement) and the standard year goes up to 330 hours of daytime teaching, we should hope that even the one evening a week would prove to be unnecessary.

THE NEED FOR BREADTH

531. We do not urge the necessity of providing more time simply as a matter of justice to these young students, but also because it would make possible a great improvement in the quality of the education they receive. This brings us to the third of the major points we want to make. The education provided in the colleges today is far too narrowly concentrated on the immediate vocational target. Some of it is perilously close to the line that separates education from mere instruction. Even where this is not so, the syllabuses are so heavy (inevitably so) and the time so short that the students are unable to lift their eyes from the immediate objectives even to glance at the surrounding intellectual country. More time is an essential condition for any remedy; but more time will not achieve anything by itself. There is need for a great deal of thought about what can be done to make these courses, while still serving their vocational purposes, come closer to the ideal of what a balanced education should be for young people of above average intelligence. We do not think this should be done only, or even perhaps mainly, by the addition of courses in the humanities—though there should be some movement in that direction. We think as much could be done by broadening out the syllabuses in some of the technical subjects themselves. We understand that there have recently been some discussions with a view to seeing whether it would not be possible to devise a common basis for some of the courses in the engineering industry that are now quite separate. With more time available, it should be easier to arrange something of the sort, which from the educational point of view could hardly help but be beneficial.

532. Such a broadening out would also serve another of the educational purposes that we have in mind. We do not want to deprive further education courses of their vocational value. But the

more it becomes possible to detach them from their narrow dependence on the employment of the students, the more possible it becomes to make them attractive to other young people who have not yet chosen their employment. This is the only way in which the numbers can be increased as rapidly as we believe to be necessary. There have been some signs in the last year or two that the numbers of young workers who will be brought into further education because it is directly useful to their employers are nearing their peak. The expansion we hope to see will have to be based on the principle of providing both for those who have a direct vocational interest (because they are in a job that requires it) and, on a full-time basis, for those who have not. There should be provision for those who have already decided upon their employment and for those who have still to make the choice and therefore have a wider interest. This involves a great growth of "college-based" practical education to set alongside the "work-based" courses that now exist. The purpose should not be to reduce what is vocationally useful, but to add courses whose main purpose is to provide a broad education. This is, in particular, the only way in which the numbers of girls in further education will be greatly increased.

533. These, then, are the three principles that we propound. The first is that there should be a greater degree of integration between the schools and further education, so that the transition can be made from one to the other smoothly and without any loss of educational momentum. The second is that, in all phases of further education, more time should be provided for the job to be done properly and without strain. The third is that an effort should be made, in the decades to come, to transform what is now basically a varied collection of plans for vocational training into a coherent national system of practical education. In the remaining chapters of this part, we make some suggestions about how these principles could be implemented.

CHAPTER 33

Beginning Further Education

534. The purpose of this chapter is to consider the transition between school and further education. This can, as we have seen, take place at various ages—15, 16 and 18 are the most common. It may be a direct exchange of one form of education for another after no greater gap than the length of a summer holiday, or the entry into further education may be delayed for one or more years after leaving school. The first point for consideration, then, is the guidance available to help parents and pupils make a wise decision about when to leave school and what to do afterwards.

LEAVING SCHOOL

535. The decision whether a particular pupil is to leave school at 15 or to enter an extended course is probably made at the age of 13 or 14. A year later there is a similar choice, especially for grammar school pupils, between leaving school or entering the Sixth Form. The decision is often associated with the choice of a career (at least in general terms) but not necessarily with engagement by a particular employer. The school and the youth employment service are the two bodies which are in a position to advise pupils and parents at this stage. It is clearly necessary that this advice should be based on a realistic assessment of what the boy or girl is capable of achieving, and of what it is best for him to do. In many areas there is increasingly close contact between schools, technical colleges and employers, but this is by no means universal. Even where there are very good personal relations, however, it does not always follow that the school has the intimate knowledge of what is involved in a particular career, and the course of study related to it, to be able to advise its pupils effectively. The staff of a grammar school is often called on to advise about the possibilities of a university career. They are usually able to do so with some confidence because they are themselves graduates and have probably kept in close contact with recent developments in universities. Relatively few schools are in such a strong position where technical colleges are concerned. There are certainly not many teachers in schools who are themselves the products of technical colleges; and, although a large number teach in evening institutes and some in technical colleges, probably not many of them have an adequate knowledge of further education courses as a whole, and especially in their later stages. Two types of knowledge are required.

The first may be described as general knowledge. It ought to cover the length and gradient of the various courses and the nature of the syllabuses, at least in outline. It should include an acquaintance with the relative difficulty of various courses and of the odds in favour of or against success by various groups of students—all those matters with which Chapter 31 was concerned and which are more fully set out in Part Three of Volume II. The second type of knowledge is not general, but local or particular. It is the power to form a reasonably reliable estimate about the chances of success of a particular pupil. It is gained by experience of what has happened in the past to others from the same school with whom the present pupil can be fairly accurately compared. It is necessary for this purpose not only to know that one candidate failed and another succeeded in his technical college course, but why (as far as can be found out) this should have happened.

536. The question of when to leave school and what to do at school is a matter for the school rather than the technical college; but it requires a sound knowledge of possibilities which can only be acquired through the technical college. On the other hand, the question about what further education course should be followed is a concern of the technical college and not of the school; but to answer it correctly requires a thorough knowledge of the student's capacity which, initially at least, the school has and the technical college has not. The results of external examinations, local certificates and school reports can be helpful. But the technical college also needs a good general knowledge of the school system as well as a particular knowledge of the individual student. Those who use out-of-date time-tables may catch more trains than they miss, but they make some bad mistakes. To judge the schools and examinations of today by what one remembers from one's own schooldays is even more misleading. Anybody called on to interpret school records needs up-to-date information. There is, then, a great need for schools and technical colleges to know something of each other's business and of the fortunes of individuals who pass through both. Without such a basis of case law good advice is impossible.

THE PROCESS OF ENROLMENT

537. One of the major difficulties in the way of the satisfactory placing of students in courses is the rush with which the technical college year begins. The programme of work to be got through in the session of 36 weeks (or 39 at the outside, including examinations) is so heavy that it is necessary to get straight on with teaching on the first whole day's attendance—in itself a good and businesslike thing to do. In this way the year gets off to a good start—a good start, that

is to say, from the point of view of those students, certainly the majority, who are correctly placed in the right course for their intellectual capacity, but a bad start for the substantial minority who are enrolled in a course which proves to be too stiff for them. How did they come to get into the wrong course? Sometimes it springs from lack of advice (itself the consequence of lack of time), but sometimes also from one of the strongest, and one of the most valuable, of the traditions of further education—that it stands ready to provide whatever is asked for. Fundamentally it thinks of itself as a service for adults, capable of knowing what they want. The onus is on them to choose wisely; on the college to supply their wants. The position is in a sense akin to that of a public library—it issues the book a borrower wants, whether or not he is capable of understanding it. This is, of course, a gross overstatement of the situation, but it is important to put the case strongly because in this respect the further education tradition runs counter to that which controls schools. The principal modification which must be made to the oversimplified statement of students' choice is that most technical college courses are designed to lead up to an external examination, and that in the most important of them, it is necessary to pass one stage successfully before going on to the next. The tradition of students' choice, therefore, applies principally at the beginning of a course.

538. Most of the part-time day students with whom we are concerned, however, attend technical colleges wholly or mainly in their employer's time. To some degree we can, therefore, substitute employer's choice for student's choice. What should an employer say to a young apprentice who is anxious to start a National Certificate course but who in his opinion is much more likely to make a success of a craft course? And what does he say? Some deliberately take the line that the apprentice should find his own level for himself. If he is prevented by authority from trying his hand at the more difficult course (in which success increases the prospects of promotion), he may well harbour a grudge. He will blame his employer, and not his own lack of ability, for his failure to realise his ambitions. If, however, he is allowed to try the more difficult course and himself "chucks his hand in", he will realise his own limitations and feel that he has had a fair deal. Where this attitude is adopted—and it is a good deal commoner than might be expected—employer's choice virtually becomes student's choice. It is difficult, too, even for those employers who possess an organised education and training department to be sure of a new apprentice's capacity to do relatively advanced educational work. One of the marks of the industrial side of the system is that technical education is commonly related to a stage above the student's present employment. As a manager watches a new apprentice at work and talks to him, he may form a reliable opinion of his

character and personality, but this will give little to guide him, for instance, in assessing his competence in mathematics, that major cause of failure to climb from craftsman to technician status. Once again, employer's choice may become student's choice—and this may be exercised in ignorance of what the chosen course of study really involves and the probability of the student being able successfully to tackle it.

539. It is not so much the tradition of student's choice that is wrong—indeed, as we have said, we attach great importance to it—as the condition of ignorance in which it is often exercised. We have already referred to the possibility of more realistic counselling at school. We must now turn to the technical college to see whether it is possible for more to be done there than is commonly attempted to steer new students into the best course for them.* The same rush at the beginning of the year, which dictates a prompt start to teaching, dominates the process of registration and enrolment. Each September, newspapers find an impressive subject for photographs in the queues that form outside technical colleges. In one sense this is a fine advertisement for the popularity of technical education. In another sense it is a condemnation of the system of enrolment, because it means that it is often impossible to spend adequate time in considering each student's needs.

540. It is possible, as a number of colleges have shown, to adapt the system so as to avoid some of the present difficulties. Most of the returning students are straightforward re-enrolments. There is a minority, however, who need careful advice, and time must be set aside to deal with their problems. One method that has been found successful is to separate the new students from those in their second or subsequent years, and to assign different enrolment days or times to the two groups. Where this plan is adopted, more time can be set aside for first-year students. It should be long enough to allow for testing borderline students. Most of the advisory work will inevitably have to be done in the enrolment period; but some of it can be more satisfactorily carried out rather earlier if a member of the college staff is made available for this purpose. After all, a good many boys secure employment well before the technical college year begins.

A FULL-TIME INDUCTION PERIOD

541. Individual colleges have shown that minor changes in procedure of the kind we have been discussing can make a considerable contribution to efficiency. They stop far short, however, of what we should like to see attempted. It is widely recognised in industry today that

* A very recent validation study of "Tests for Engineering Apprentices" by the National Institute of Industrial Psychology, shows how valuable they can be.

an induction period has great value. It gives the boy or girl straight from school time to take his bearings in the factory, to see something of the purpose of the whole and, therefore, the purpose of the part he is to play. It offers an opportunity to meet some of the major figures of the concern. It provides for careful briefing about such important matters as pay packets, welfare, safety precautions and the many things that are soon second nature, but which to begin with are bewildering and confusing. A similar induction period to the technical college would be of great value. If the college is to be more to the student than just a series of classes, it is necessary for him to be properly introduced to it, to get to know it as a society, and a society with a purpose, in the same way that he knows the works in which he is employed. This takes time; and it is time which is missing under the present conditions of part-time study. These conditions are not, however, immutable, and we think they should be changed.

542. We have carefully considered one proposal which has been made to us for a full-time induction period. Briefly, the proposal is that day release should be prefaced by a continuous period of one month's attendance at a technical college during the autumn term of each year. It would take the place for first-year students of the one day a week which they would otherwise have had from September to December. Two classes of part-time students would be difficult to fit into this scheme: there does not seem to be any way to give evening students the opportunity to get a month's continuous education; and it would be difficult, but not impossible, to bring in side by side with the great mass of new students those who had secured exemption from the work of the first stage. With such exceptions as prove to be unavoidable, however, we think it ought to apply to all students, irrespective both of their ability and of the industry in which they are employed. We recommend that a pilot experiment should be undertaken in a number of colleges in different parts of the country.

543. The first thing we hope to achieve by this full-time introductory period is a much better assessment of a student's capacity than would be possible without it, even in those colleges where improved enrolment methods are in use, and where there is really close contact with schools. These will never be sufficient to cover all new entrants for two reasons. First, in thickly populated districts, colleges deal with many schools, and schools with several colleges. Secondly, as we saw in Chapter 30, there is a good deal of changing jobs within the first year or so of leaving school so that a substantial minority will not come straight from school to college. Two illustrations may be given of the assessment problems which could be tackled in an induction period and of the use to which the knowledge gained ought to be put. The first concerns the different ways in which intellectual ability may

show itself. As between two persons of equal basic intelligence, one may be much more adept than another at those forms of expression that involve the use of words. The traditional academic route, which lies through the grammar schools to the universities, relies very heavily (and for scientists almost as much as for non-scientists) on verbal methods. The intelligence tests designed for use on this route equally have a verbal bias. In her "Placement Problems in Technical College Day Release Courses", a study based on a group of Lancashire colleges, Dr. Ethel C. Venables compared the intelligence ratings of groups of students taking both National Certificate and craft courses with the performance of the top 75 per cent of university students (omitting the "tail" of the universities so as to keep the standard of comparison high). She found that when verbal intelligence tests were used, very few (8 per cent) of the National Certificate students and hardly any (1·5 per cent) of those taking craft courses came up to the university standard. But when non-verbal tests were used, 40 per cent of the National Certificate students and even as many as 12 per cent of the craft students showed themselves to be the equal in intelligence of the university students. Much depends, of course, in this sort of comparison on the precise nature of the tests employed. But it is hardly possible to deny that there is a great deal of native intelligence that will run to waste if it is treated only in the conventional way. The problem of counselling is thus a delicate one. There is little doubt that there will be a good many students of comparable basic capacity who will need a quite different teaching approach. Some will respond well to a traditional academic approach; others will find a great obstacle in the extent to which this depends on verbalisation, at least until something has been done to improve their own powers of communication. This ought to be tackled both as part of the students' general education and because poor verbal ability is a serious handicap in the last two stages of the course leading to the Higher National Certificate.

544. The second illustration concerns mathematics. It is clear from the Technical Courses Survey that mathematics, the most abstract of the subjects in technical courses, presents more serious difficulties than any other. We saw in Chapter 31 that only 10 per cent of those students who find mathematics very difficult eventually secure a National Certificate (compared with 25 per cent of all students).* There is nothing surprising in this; but that does not mean that nothing can be done about it. It has long been recognised in schools that, whatever may be done in other subjects, it is important to divide pupils for mathematics into teaching groups of equal mathematical

* The figures are for students with no exemptions; for students with one exemption the comparable figures are 23 per cent and 49 per cent.

ability—"setting" as it is called. Given this, pupils without a mathematical bent, who would have failed in mixed company, succeed in mastering the necessary subject matter. "Setting" is rarely arranged for day release students, not because it is not considered desirable, but simply because it is hardly practicable in present circumstances. It would involve a considerable amount of negotiation with employers to ensure that day by day there was available a sufficient number of students of comparable mathematical ability to provide teaching sets of suitable sizes. But, given the time in which to do it, this is something that could be arranged. The college would first of all have to satisfy itself that it knew where each new student stood, and then arrange appropriate teaching and day release programmes with the contributory firms. This might exceptionally be possible with improved enrolment arrangements, but it would require a disproportionate effort. We do not think that it could generally be done without an induction period of the kind we are now discussing.

545. There is another aspect of placing which is highly important. It is the choice of the right kind of course for a particular student. The problem may present itself in the light of a choice between three levels of course distinguished in difficulty by differences in intellectual content and in suitability by the level of employment to which it is hoped that the apprentice will in time rise. An example may be given in terms of engineering. The National Certificate course is appropriate for the boy who will rise to technician or even technologist status. There are also two City and Guilds courses, which we may distinguish as upper and lower craft courses, called respectively Machine Shop Engineering and Mechanical Engineering Craft Practice. There is, we think, no doubt that this particular division into three levels makes sense both in terms of the range of ability to be found among students, and also of the structure of the industry. Sometimes it may be possible to devise a common first stage of a course which would delay a definitive placing until the students have settled down and shown what they are capable of doing, but in the nature of things this common element could not cover more than the initial work, which the abler students would quickly finish. It is, perhaps, doubtful if it could profitably be extended beyond the full-time induction period we have in mind, which would provide rather more than half the teaching time normally available in the first year of day release. Certainly in the light of the experience gained during that period it ought to be possible to avoid a good many of the misplacings that occur at present. Even so, it will always be necessary to provide for students to transfer from one course to another, whether up or down, according to their progress; but transfer schemes never seem to bring in all those students who would benefit from them. They can only be a supplement to, and not a substitute for, great care in the original placing.

546. The second main benefit we should expect to spring from a full-time induction period is a much better start with the work of the course. Continuous periods of study are nearly always more effective than isolated days. This is especially true at the beginning of a course, when new teachers and teaching methods have to be met and new subject matter introduced. The gain in work done should be more than the simple proportionate gain from the additional days of attendance in the first term. A good beginning should also be reflected in faster progress in the subsequent terms when the one-day-a-week procedure was being followed.

547. We have put first these tangible benefits of an induction period. Not less important are the more personal benefits it would provide. It would give the college an opportunity to show the new students the relation between the courses they will be following and their employment. This is the more necessary where, as we have seen is frequently the case, there is no immediately apparent connection between the work done in the workshop and much of that done in the college. It would also give students the opportunity to get the feel of the college as a college—something which they do not just attend but to which they belong. Most important of all, it could mark the beginning of a continuing personal relationship between students and members of staff. If there were sufficient teachers available it would be possible to give a good start to a tutorial system which would continue to operate through the years of day release following the induction period. In the course of the study mentioned in paragraph 543, lack of interest was classed high as a reason for failure by the students who were interviewed. A student's lack of interest in technical college work is often a reflection of his feeling that nobody on the college staff is interested in him, and that nobody at work is really interested in what he does at college. The remedy for the latter condition is a matter for industry; the former could be put right by a sound tutorial system. By "sound" we mean a system which did not so overburden the tutors that they had no time to get to know their students well. A tutorial system is, of course, possible without a full-time induction period, but an introductory course of the kind we have been discussing would give it a better start and a better chance of success.

548. It remains to add a word on how such a full-time induction period can best be fitted into the technical college year and the pattern of employment. We should for many reasons have liked to advocate a complete term of full-time education, but we have come to the conclusion that at present this would be to ask too much. We envisage, then, that the autumn term would be filled with three successive one-month courses and that there would be no single day release for first-year students that term. It has been put to us that a

boy should settle down with his employer before he is asked to settle down in the technical college, and we accept this as being normally the right order. The first of the three courses would, therefore, be made up of Easter and Christmas school leavers (though we hope before long to see Christmas leaving abolished). The succeeding two courses would be composed of summer leavers. All first-year students would then be able to start together on a normal routine in January. The cost to an employer in terms of additional release would be eight days per student. In return we are quite satisfied that employers as well as students would get far better results from the day release that followed, while the additional days involved would come at a time when the boys had not yet become a productive asset. From the point of view of the technical college, these induction courses would produce a peak load for three months of the year, but we believe that local colleges in new buildings would have sufficient accommodation to meet the demand. Staffing ratios would have to be carefully reviewed.

SUMMARY OF RECOMMENDATIONS

549. The recommendations made in this chapter can be summarised as follows:

(*a*) Active measures should be taken not only to extend and improve the contacts between the schools in an area and the further education institutions, but also to increase the knowledge that school teachers possess of what further education has to offer, and that technical colleges have of recent developments in secondary education.

(*b*) In the process of enrolment, colleges should separate new students from those who are returning for continued courses, in order that more time and attention can be given to advising the former on the best courses for them to take.

(*c*) Experiments should be undertaken with a full-time induction period, lasting one month in the autumn term, for all students who start at the beginning of the normal three-year or five-year courses.

(*d*) Efforts should be made to develop a continuing personal relationship between the students and the staff of further education institutions by means of a tutorial system.

CHAPTER 34

The Problem of Time

550. We look for considerable improvements when a full-time introductory period is provided, but we do not think that they will amount to a satisfactory solution of the problems associated with the further education of boys and girls aged between 16 and 18. Ultimately the success of an induction period must depend on whether the arrangements to which it is an introduction are themselves satisfactory. In our view they are at present unsatisfactory because the amount of time available and the length of time required are both wrong. Most of the problems presented by craft courses and technicians' courses are essentially different and must be treated separately, but there is one matter which is common to both. It seems to us clear that the solution for a crowded programme does not lie in a course spread over a still greater number of years. One of the most striking results of the Technical Courses Survey was the substantial number of students who give up both National Certificate and craft courses after successfully completing one of the three stages (S.1, S.2 and A.1) which do not result in the issue of a certificate. There are no doubt a number of contributory reasons; one of them seems to us to be reluctance to continue a course which has already occupied a large number of years—possibly as many as eight or nine years of part-time study since leaving school. Any extension of the minimum time required to complete a course would seem to us likely to lead to a still greater retirement of undefeated candidates. Part-time study usually begins before a young man thinks seriously of marriage; new adverse factors arise if it has to be carried on through the early years of marriage. We do not therefore believe that the solution to the overcrowded programme can be found by extending the duration of the course. On the contrary, we believe that every effort must be made to enable more of the students who in the end successfully complete the course to do so at the rate of one stage a year. What is at present a minimum duration for a course should become more nearly the normal duration.

551. By way of preface to a discussion of the problem of time in further education, it may be of service to set out how many teaching hours per annum are involved in the different sorts of courses that now exist (not all colleges have exactly the same practices). This is shown in Table 70.

Table 70. Teaching Hours per Annum on various Types of Course (including Examination Periods).

Course	Hours per annum
DAY RELEASE	
(*a*) (1 day)	220
(*b*) (1 day+evening)	270
County College (Standard prescribed by Act of 1944)	330
BLOCK RELEASE	
(*a*) 8 weeks full-time + 1 evening in remainder of year	296
(*b*) 3 months full-time+1 evening in remainder of year	408
SANDWICH COURSES	
(*a*) Minimum: 19 weeks attendance at college	570
(*b*) Normal: 24 weeks attendance	720
FULL-TIME	
1 academic year (36 weeks)	1,080

MORE TIME FOR CRAFT COURSES

552. There seem to us to be two ways in which more time can be achieved for craft courses. One of them will become obligatory as soon as compulsory part-time education is introduced. It is the extension of the present working day and working year in technical colleges to the minimum figure of 44 weeks or 330 hours laid down in the Act of 1944 for county colleges. Present practice differs a good deal from one technical college to another, but it is probable that the introduction of the county college day and year would in general increase the amount of time available by at least one-fifth. It seems to us abundantly clear that such an extension would appreciably increase the number of successful candidates at each stage. At present it could, of course, only be introduced by arrangement between technical colleges and employers. We may hope that the advantages would be sufficiently obvious to employers for them to welcome the change. Before it would be possible to introduce it, however, there would have to be a reconsideration of the staffing of technical colleges. We recommend that consideration should be given to introducing the "county college" day and year, as laid down in the Act of 1944, in the immediate future, wherever it is possible to secure agreement to do so.

553. We are, however, by no means sure that the present pattern of release for one day a week is necessarily the best way of organising the available time. It has served well; and may, in a good many circumstances, still be the most appropriate form of release. Its discontinuous form of study may, however, be a contributing factor to high failure and retardation rates, even at craftsman level. There is in our view a clear case for a great many more experiments in "block release" than have yet taken place. By block release we mean

a system by which roughly the equivalent number of days which would have been available under the normal arrangements are taken on end in units of a week, a month or three months at a time followed by roughly three or four times as long an unbroken period at work. Where evening classes are also attended, these are usually continued throughout the period at work so that the student does not lose touch with the technical college.

554. An example of what may be achieved by block release at craftsman level can be given by way of illustration. It comes from a firm which is experimenting with a block release system of three months a year for four years leading to the City and Guilds Machine Shop Engineering Final Certificate. The examination results at the end of the first year's work at the technical college showed a 90 per cent pass rate, with 40 per cent placed in the first class. The corresponding result for day release students over two years was a pass rate of 39 per cent. It is still early days with such schemes, and it would not do to count on exceptionally good results like this as a regular occurrence; but at least they show that schemes of this sort are well worth considering.

555. How much extra does a block release scheme of this kind cost the employer? This particular scheme is scheduled to reach City and Guilds Final standard in four years compared with five years on day release. Out of the four years the block release student is allowed 230 working days at the technical college; out of five years the day release student is allowed 180 days. The block release student, therefore, gets an additional 50 days, but none in the last year of his apprenticeship when his work is presumably of greatest value to his employer. On the other hand, the block release system allows for full-time manning of each machine; the day release system means (in this particular plant) that each machine worked by boys is idle for 36 days in the year. The student on block release is also expected to attend 35 hours of evening classes per year for four years compared with the day release student's 50 hours per year for five years.

556. Block release may very often be a better form of part-time attendance than one day a week, but we doubt whether it could itself be a complete answer for one of the most striking problems of the part-time system. This is the great prevalence of retardation even among students who finally succeed. Looked at in one way, the retardation rate shows remarkable persistence by the student. In another way, it suggests inefficiency in the system or its organisation. Some students take eight or more years to complete a course scheduled to last five. Success in five years might well always have been beyond them, but with a differently organised course they might have been successful in less than eight or nine years. The present system is

based on annual assignments which are the same for students of every level of ability. Those who fail to complete the whole assignment successfully in a year repeat it the following year, and again and again, if necessary, until they succeed. Normally they must repeat all the subjects of the course although they may have failed in only one. This repetition of work already successfully accomplished has in our view little to commend it, and we should like to see a system whereby colleges were empowered on their own authority to allow a student to proceed to the next stage of the course provided that his failure was limited to one subject. Of course, work which has not been mastered cannot be put on one side. The ground has to be covered, and the success with which this is done must be tested. But need it wait another twelve months? If there is a case for winter as well as summer examinations for the General Certificate of Education might there not be similar provision in the field of further education? We recommend that this should be tried at least for those three stages (S.1, S.2 and A.1) which do not lead to the issue of certificates. If every schoolboy had to pass an annual examination in every subject before being promoted to the next form, it would take many of them as long to reach G.C.E. as it does many apprentices to complete a craft course.

557. The suggestions we have made would, we hope, save time by avoiding vain repetition, increase time by adding to the college day and the college year, and ensure a more fruitful use of time by concentrating it in block release periods. Is this sufficient? In our view, provided that students are placed in a suitable course, these changes should give far more of them time enough to complete their course within the official allowance and yet leave something over for their general education. But it would still not be a generous time allowance. The county college provisions were presumably inserted in the Act of 1944 in the belief that all boys and girls up to the age of 18 deserved, and could benefit from, one day's worth in each week of general education, or at least of education a great deal of which would not be directly related to their employment. If the craft apprentices are to have only one day's release, and if their technical courses are not to be skimped, can their need of general education be fairly met?

558. We have therefore considered whether we should recommend that the period of release for young people who are taking vocational courses should be one and a half or even two days a week. Wherever employers are willing to concede so much release, they should of course be encouraged to do so. But there seems to us to be no possibility of enforcing by law more than the standard amount of release, and in these circumstances to insist that any time spent on

the craft courses must be in addition to a full day in "general education" would merely result in a disastrous fall in the numbers entering them. We must rest content, so far as these future craftsmen are concerned, with what can be done in the one day a week. With "county college hours" a great deal can be done, both through broader syllabuses and a rather different kind of teaching in the technical subjects, and also by the addition of more general studies.

MORE TIME FOR TECHNICIANS

559. When we turn to the technicians, however, we cannot be equally content. We do not believe that the part-time system can be made a satisfactory one for these key men in the community. Their need for more time is too great—more time for their ever more complex special subjects, and more time for their general intellectual development. We do indeed feel confident that changes of the kind suggested for the craft courses in the preceding six paragraphs would, if they were applied to the technicians' courses, result in more candidates qualifying in a shorter time. That would be pure gain, and we cannot reasonably expect changes of the kind we have been discussing to produce any more. But it is not enough. A variation on the present part-time plan would certainly leave insufficient opportunity now, or in the conceivable future, for study in fields outside the main line of examination work or for sufficient depth of basic studies in the natural sciences. It would still involve a strictly utilitarian approach to the main task in hand—the shortness of time would forbid the exploration of byways or the introduction of scientific subject matter which is not strictly essential to the examination syllabus. There would still be many potential technicians (though fewer than at present) who would fail to reach that status because there was too much to do in too short a time. To expect to educate a technician in less than one-fifth of his working time is already to expect too much. Educational demands will rise still further in the years to come. The technician of today already needs a far better grasp of fundamental science and a stronger mathematical equipment than the technician of yesterday. To-morrow the need will be greater still. If the part-time day release system is working wastefully now, we do not believe that it can be adjusted to meet to-morrow's needs.

560. There is a need both for more time in total and for more continuous time, but without complete separation from industrial training. These needs are being increasingly recognised in the higher stages, which are taken by men slightly older than those with whom we are especially concerned. There are now some 9,000 students in sandwich courses of all kinds; five years ago there were under 1,500. Most of these are over 18, and there are still very few such courses for

boys of 16 or 17; but a beginning has been made; and, where the practice has been adopted, the results are encouraging. We give one illustration from what is technically a block release course (i.e. in the number of weeks of full-time study it falls just short of the sandwich course minimum), but, in the calibre of the students and in the total time spent in study, is effectively a sandwich course for technicians and technologists. Day release and block release courses have for several years been run side by side in the college in question. The day release students as well as the block release students are a much above-average group. The block release students have, of course, a very great deal more time for study, but they have also a great deal more work to do—they work simultaneously for two Ordinary National Certificates (in mechanical and electrical engineering) compared with the one taken by the day release students. The pass rate for day release students has averaged 41 per cent at O.N.C.; for block release students it has been 95 per cent. It will no doubt be a long time before we shall be able to abandon the part-time day release route without endangering the supply of technicians—after all, the excessively wasteful evening course route is still being extensively used. But we are convinced that a maximum effort should be made to popularise the sandwich course route. Its development depends, we believe, on making clear to employers, to boys leaving school and to their parents how arduous and how uncertain is the day release route, and still more reliance on evening classes alone. Once the facts which we have set out in Chapter 31 are widely known, we believe that there will be an irresistible demand for courses which are continuous enough to be far less of a gamble, and which will have the advantage of providing much better education.

"COLLEGE-BASED" SANDWICH COURSES

561. What are we advocating when we talk of sandwich courses at this stage? The student we have in mind is a boy who has stayed at school until he is 16 and has reached roughly the equivalent of an Ordinary level pass in the General Certificate of Education in mathematics and in a science subject and has also had a good general education. We think of him as then embarking on a two-year course leading to an Ordinary National Diploma or an equivalent City and Guilds course. Half his time would be spent in the classrooms and laboratories of the technical college and half in industrial training. He would do six months of one followed by six months of the other. At the end of his course, if he were successful, he would have had a thorough introductory training in general engineering, for it is part of our proposal that the educational work should be more broadly based than it is at present—for example that one of his spells of

industrial training should have been in mechanical engineering and the other in electrical. What would his status in college be during industrial training? At present virtually every student on a sandwich course for the Ordinary National Diploma is "work-based"—that is to say, he is primarily an employee of a particular firm and is normally paid wages by his employer while he is at college as well as while he is at work. We envisage that an increasing number of the students will be "college-based", that is to say the student would earn wages only while he was at work, and would be eligible to be financed at college by a grant from a local education authority. This is a matter on which there is already agreement between the Ministry of Education and the Federation of British Industries. This initial independence from one individual employer might make it easier to secure the width of course and the work experience of the different branches of engineering which we have in mind. It might also in the years of the "bulge", when apprenticeships may be hard to come by, help to make it easier to secure training for all who can profit by it and desire it.

562. There is, however, one over-riding condition without which college-based students ought not to be enrolled. No student should be accepted for whom suitable industrial training cannot be guaranteed. The training arrangements need quite as thorough preparation as the educational—both must be already defined and assured before a course is started. The guarantee ought to apply to the quality as well as to the quantity of training. A large firm with a well established apprentice workshop and training scheme of its own presents no difficulties, but small employers can often give only a very limited training which is not really adequate to produce an all-round, adaptable man. It seems to us that, in addition to the various group apprenticeship schemes which are being developed, there is a part to be played by the workshops of the college itself. It is possible to imagine a course, college-based or work-based as the case might be, in which the periods of industrial training were spent either in the apprentice workshops of a big firm or in the workshops of the colleges which would act as the agents for one or more smaller employers. It is not always realised how numerous small manufacturing firms are and how considerable a number of workpeople they employ. Table 71 shows that three-quarters of the country's manufacturing firms employ less than 100 workers each, and that one-fifth of all the country's workers in manufacturing industry are employed by firms of this size. It seems clear that far more firms need to employ technicians than are able to provide suitable works training for them.

563. We have been describing two-year sandwich courses for Ordinary National Diplomas enrolling students who would have to

Table 71. Number of Employees in Manufacturing Firms of Various Sizes, April, 1959 (Great Britain).

	Firms grouped by Number of Employees					
	11–24	25–99	100–499	500–999	1,000 and above	Total
Firms Nos.	14,874	26,145	12,052	1,524	1,144	55,739
Percent	*26·6*	*46·9*	*21·6*	*2·7*	*2·2*	*100*
Employees Nos.	258,000	1,326,000	2,492,000	1,048,000	2,611,000	7,735,000
Percent	*3·3*	*17·1*	*32·2*	*13·6*	*33·8*	*100*

be at least 16 years old and suitably qualified. If our recommendations in Part Three are accepted, there will in less than ten years' time be no 15 year-old workers to be considered. For the next few years, however, the majority of boys will continue to leave school at 15; and, at least in certain parts of the country, there will continue to be among them a substantial proportion of boys who want to enter industry and who have the capacity to become technicians, or, some of them, technologists. These next few years will be the years of maximum difficulty in getting apprenticeships, because they are the years when the young people of the "bulge" leave school and look for work. If skill, which we shall need for the future, is not to be lost through temporary superfluity, it will be necessary in certain districts at least to take emergency steps. One of them, in our view, should be the development of one-year full-time courses in local colleges designed to give a general introductory training, mainly in craft skill, which could also be used to distinguish those who have the makings of a technician from those who are better fitted to remain craftsmen. Such a course—of which there are one or two interesting examples—would usefully serve for those who need it as an introductory year to the kind of sandwich course we have been discussing.

564. We feel the time is propitious for developments of the kind we have been considering. The instrument is there, ready and indeed waiting with some impatience to be given a distinctive and distinguished role in the new advance of technical education. The instrument is the local technical college. The recent stratification of technical colleges into colleges of advanced technology at the apex, with regional and area colleges as the middle piece and local colleges at the foundation level has, perhaps inevitably but certainly unjustly, left the local colleges with a feeling of frustration. Their daytime work

is now almost entirely confined to boys under the age of 19, or to men who, through examination failures, are still at a stage of the course designed for boys of 17 or 18. Very little of their work is with full-time or sandwich course students; most of it is with boys who come to the college only once or twice a week. It is valuable, indispensable work, but confined by lack of time in a strait jacket. It could be as interesting and worthwhile as any kind of education if only there were more time to get to know the students better, to help them individually in their intellectual problems and to assist their personal development. This is the justifiable complaint of many a technical college teacher. Here is the chance to give the colleges the opportunity they are waiting for; and to develop in the process what would be essentially a new form of educational institution, centred on a considerable body of whole-time students in the later teens, but reaching out to incorporate a larger number whose attendance could only be occasional. Of course both elements are already there, and what we are proposing is in the direct line of evolution of the college. But the change in the proportion of full-time and part-time work would, we believe, lead the students to look on the college less as an educational facility which they use and more as a corporate body to which they belong.

565. The partnership of colleges and industry is an essential part of the structure of technical education. It has, we believe, consequences for organisation which have not yet been fully realised but which are becoming increasingly apparent with the development of sandwich courses. If the normal composition of a sandwich course is equal periods of study and training, it is clear that it will be a great deal easier to organise and to provide opportunities for industrial training if the college year and the factory year follow substantially the same pattern. At present the college year, because of its origin, follows the general pattern of school and university years, with a long summer vacation. Technological needs now suggest (so it seems to us) an approximation to the modern industrial year if an equal interchange of students is to be affected; and, indeed, if a great deal of extremely expensive equipment is not to be left unused for three months in the year. If such a reorganisation were to take place—and it would, we agree, be a revolutionary change—it would necessarily carry with it a reconsideration of the staffing arrangements. When this was being done, it would be easy, and in our view important, to see that adequate provision was made for a full tutorial system for both sandwich and part-time students. We should in particular like to see that the tutor of a student on a sandwich course had opportunities to see him during that half of the course when he was getting his industrial training. Technical college staffs are already familiar with

a teaching load which is divided between the day and the evening. We suggest that it should now be adjusted to spread over what has been regarded as vacation or holiday as well as term. We do not suggest that there should be any increase in the amount of teaching that any one member of staff would be expected to do. An appropriate increase in staff would, therefore, be necessary.

566. We do not believe that anything less than a sandwich course from 16 to 18 will be adequate to provide the technicians of the future with a deep enough and broad enough education. The technician needs more time for education in specialist studies than the craftsman or the operative, and he is better able to profit from depth and breadth in his studies. The sandwich course is increasingly being accepted as the appropriate education for those recruited to industry at 18 or older. It is not yet appreciated that the need of boys of similar ability recruited at 16 is at least as great. We recommend that every effort should be made to see that sandwich courses leading to the Ordinary National Diploma replace day release courses leading to the Ordinary National Certificate as the normal method of educating boys who join industry at 16 and have the makings of technicians or technologists.

SUMMARY OF RECOMMENDATIONS

567. The main recommendations contained in this chapter are as follows:

(*a*) Consideration should be given to introducing for day release students, wherever it is possible to secure agreement to do so, the length of year laid down by the Act of 1944 for county colleges (namely, 44 weeks or 330 hours).

(*b*) "Block release" should wherever possible be substituted for release on one day a week.

(*c*) Colleges should be empowered to allow students who have failed in only one subject of a sessional examination to proceed to the next stage of a course, with subsidiary examinations in the winter for the purpose of repeating individual subjects.

(*d*) For technicians, sandwich courses should in future be regarded as the standard, and the only satisfactory, method for young men of 16 to 18. Part-time courses should not be prevented, but every effort should be made to secure their progressive replacement.

(*e*) There should also be expanded provision for "college-based" sandwich courses for young people aged 16 to 18, always provided that satisfactory arrangements can be made for training in industry.

(*f*) Special arrangements are necessary for sandwich courses for the employees of firms which are too small to make adequate provision for the industrial component of the course. This could be done by an extension of the existing group apprenticeship schemes or alternatively by making the college workshops agents for a group of smaller firms.

(*g*) For the next few years of the "bulge" before the school-leaving age is raised to 16, special steps will be necessary to assist boys who leave school at 15 and who have difficulty in finding apprenticeships giving them day release. Among these emergency measures should be one-year full-time introductory courses in local colleges.

CHAPTER 35

The Alternative Road

568. An observer of English education can hardly fail to be disturbed by the large number of able boys and girls who lose their intellectual curiosity before they have exhausted their capacity to learn. There are, of course, dull patches in every subject, but the distaste to which we refer goes much deeper than this temporary boredom. It is more akin to *accidie*, that deep-seated apathy which theologians class as one of the seven deadly sins. They may go on working; but it will be more for what they can get out of it than for what they can find in it. Is this inevitable? Where so many patently lose interest in developing powers they undoubtedly possess, and in which they used to delight, it seems to us that the fault must, in part at least, lie in the kind of education they are offered. We cannot afford to do without their talent. The country's interest requires that all who can profit from a full-time education up to 18 should have one; and the boys and girls to whom we are referring fall into that category. How can we restore their willingness and eagerness to learn?

WHAT IS A PRACTICAL APPROACH?

569. The answer, we think, lies in an alternative approach to knowledge to that which has traditionally dominated European education. We are very far from decrying the academic tradition which inspires and is embodied in our grammar schools and universities. We could not have written of it in the terms we used in Part Five if we did not believe that there is no finer intellectual discipline and none more fitting to certain types of mind. It is not, however, the only road by which good minds can travel. If the country is to benefit fully from the intelligence of all its able boys and girls, it will be necessary to rehabilitate the word "practical" in educational circles—it is often used in a pejorative sense—and to define it more clearly. How in fact is it commonly used? There is a tendency today to say that science and mathematics are practical and that the traditional subjects of the arts side are not. There is another usage which classifies woodwork and cookery as practical, as opposed to science or French, which on this reckoning are both academic. Clearly, then, "practical" is an ambiguous and emotionally charged word. What does a boy mean when he demands a more practical education? He may perhaps just be complaining that he cannot see the point of what he is asked to do. He demands that the purpose of what he is taught

should be clear, and that it should commend itself to him as worth while.

570. Practical may have quite another meaning. This is especially true of the arts, where a boy or girl may be asking that he should be taught to do as well as to appreciate what others have done. He wants, perhaps, to play in an orchestra, and not merely to listen to one; to paint and not only to receive lessons in art appreciation. He stands in a tradition many thousands of years old, an educational tradition, though not historically a school or university tradition. It is a task of importance to make this other tradition of artistic or creative education (historically a matter of professional or technical training) as much a respectable part of the general educational system as the largely analytical tradition of the schools. It is right to add that some of the most encouraging educational achievements of our time have been precisely in this sphere.

571. A boy may, however, have something still different in mind when he speaks of a practical education. He may want to use his hands and his mind not so much to create as to invent. The boy with whom we are concerned is one who has pride in his skill of hand and a desire to use that skill to discover how things work, to make them work and to make them work better. The tradition to which he aspires to belong is the modern one of the mechanical man whose fingers are the questioning instruments of thought and exploration. He would readily understand and respond to the impulse which side-tracked Lord Kelvin for five years between the first and the second of a promised series of articles on the Mariner's Compass for the Victorian periodical *Good Words* because, once his attention had been directed towards the compass, he could not stop until he had revolutionised its design. There is always a risk that the practical approach may be written down as a second-best method for rather less able boys. We quote Lord Kelvin's example to show that this should not be done. The motor car engine and the radio set are to a boy of this kind an irresistible invitation to discovery. He will not be content with understanding one of them, but will want to explore both, and more machines as well of different kinds. His is not a narrow vocational interest, but a broad scientific curiosity. Fortunately this breadth of appetite is in line with the new demand for technical adaptability, and we can encourage his discursiveness. So strong is this mechanical inquisitiveness that today it drives many to educate themselves who yesterday could hardly be compelled to be educated. So new is it that it has not yet been able thoroughly to permeate the educational system. It is normally accompanied by a manual competence which, it is true, is not a common possession of all men; and which, even in those who have it, needs to be developed

by patient teaching. Sometimes the process may be reversed, and mechanical inquisitiveness may lead a boy on to acquiring skill of hand. But in whichever order it comes, the boy who sets out on this sort of exploration soon requires to add considerable theoretical knowledge, which he will undertake with determination because he now sees the need for it. It is clear that what we have been describing is not every boy's road to knowledge, let alone every girl's. It is not even every scientifically minded boy's, let alone every mathematician's. But for some it is the only way, and for many the most congenial.

572. The illustrations we have just given are drawn from engineering, and indeed it is the most obvious field in which to find examples. But the principle of a practical approach to theoretical knowledge is not by any means limited to this field. It is of wide application. We confine ourselves to two further illustrations. The first may be made by a quotation from the recent report of Lord De La Warr's Committee on Agricultural Education. In the last thirty years, the report states, "new varieties of almost every type of crop including grass have been bred to give heavier yields, and there are new methods of combating pests and diseases. New and more elaborate machinery has been produced, and British agriculture is now one of the most highly mechanised in the world. More scientific breeding and management of livestock is practised . . . . There is no longer a place for the unskilled worker". The second illustration is from the field of commerce. Here too, the scientific revolution is being experienced. Machines are replacing men and women and changing the kinds of skill that are in demand. Problems which used to be insoluble can now be solved by calculating machines, provided that the right questions are put to them. To do this does not involve a mechanical or electrical knowledge of how the machine works, but it does involve a real familiarity with what it can do. There is room for a new type of office worker, roughly in the technician range, who has an ingenuity in turning to the best advantage the power of the new machinery. On the other hand, there is a growing number of office workers who require less skill than their predecessors. This may be illustrated by the decline in the number of students taking shorthand in evening classes at a time when the number taking typewriting is still growing, and by the halving within six years of the numbers taking book-keeping.

573. There is still another way in which the need for a different kind of education can be seen. It is not simply a matter of the things that are taught or of the uses to which they are to be put when the pupil goes out into the world; it is often as much a matter of the way in which subjects—often the old familiar subjects—are taught. Different

kinds of minds must be approached in different ways. There is one type of mind which is readily attuned to abstract thinking and can comprehend the meaning of a generalisation. For these minds, the teacher can best proceed by first expounding the principle and then illustrating it, by teaching the rule and its exceptions, and then setting the class to work on examples. This is (in the main) the academic approach. But there are other minds which cannot grasp the general except by way of the particular, which cannot understand what is meant by the rule until they have observed the examples. Some minds are analytical; others can only build up. There is also the distinction between the mind that takes easily to verbal methods of expression and the mind that moves more easily by other means. We referred to this distinction in paragraph 543, where we quoted Dr. Ethel C. Venables' demonstration that the non-verbal mind, when its basic intelligence is assessed by a test appropriate to it and not by tests designed for verbal minds, is not so inferior to the academic mind as is sometimes supposed. It may be that a similar demonstration could be made of some of the other types of mind that we have been attempting to distinguish. Whether this is so or not, we feel confident that the "yield" of the whole educational system could be much increased if there were available a wider variety of forms of education and a wider choice of sequence in learning, so that every young person could find one that was designed to develop his potentialities in the most suitable way.

574. Hitherto in this country, there have been for most boys and girls at the age of 15 or 16 only two alternatives—the full-time academic route, for which they may not be suitable and which may not attract them; and the part-time route, which, for all its merits, has the disadvantages of requiring a prior entry into the labour market, of being rather narrowly vocational, of being very arduous, and of not being available at all to many boys and most girls. We think it should be accepted as one of the major tasks before English education to construct a new system of education for the years between 15 or 16 and 18 which would neither suffer from these defects of the part-time route nor be academic in the old conventional sense. This is what we have attempted to characterise as a "practical" education, recognising as we do how imperfect is the word. We are not here concerned (though we shall be in the next chapter) with the institutions in which this "practical" education should be provided. Our present purpose is to try to define the sort of education that is needed if a large part of the native intelligence of our people is not to continue to run to waste.

575. It is an essential part of our thinking that this alternative system of education should not be regarded as wholly, or even mainly, technical and still less as confined to the special needs of a narrow

range of occupations. On the contrary, we think of it as providing the widest range of instruction for young people who will be proceeding into a great variety of different employments; one of its incidental purposes would be to enable them to postpone their final choice of occupation until two or three years later than now, when they will be much better able to choose. At the same time, it is no less essential that the progressive expansion of full-time "practical" education for young people up to the age of 18 should not be conceived of as something that has to be done in isolation from, or even in rivalry with, the existing patterns of further education. On the contrary, the obvious need is for a converging movement. As technical education gradually moves (as we believe it must) towards a full-time basis, it should, so to speak, meet half way the growth of a new form of full-time "practical" education in which it can take its natural place. This is, indeed, the way in which we would attempt to implement the third of the principles that were laid down in Chapter 32—the transformation of a varied collection of plans for vocational training into a coherent system of practical education. Our aim, in talking of an alternative route, is not to widen the gap between the grammar school Sixth Forms and the technical colleges by inserting still a third rival type of education between them, but rather to knit them together in a comprehensive system of alternative provision for the many different varieties of human nature and individual ambition.

ALTERNATIVE ROUTES

576. An educational approach of the kind we have described as "practical" can be made either in school or in further education. Circumstances will determine where in any individual instance it is best made. Practical courses may be full-time in the sense that all the work, both practical and theoretical, takes place in an educational institution; they may be part-time in the sense that the practical experience (or most of it) is provided in employment. But we would insist that all courses designed for able boys and girls—those, let us say, who will rise at least to technician level or its equivalent in other occupations—ought to be full-time in the special sense that the whole of the student's time up to the age of 18 should be devoted to gaining relevant educational experience. If he goes out to work, it should be for the educational benefit that he derives from it, and not to play a part as a producer. We do not want to rule out productive work (indeed it can have very great value), but we would stress that the reason for undertaking it should be educational and not economic.

577. At the age of 15 or 16, then, there ought to be an effectively free choice for every young person of ability between two different routes

of proceeding, the one that we have labelled "academic", the other "practical". It may be that the "academic" route would normally proceed through the grammar school to the university or the college of advanced technology, while the "practical" route would normally go through a college of further education. But this need not always be so; there is an increasing number of schools—grammar, grammar-technical, technical or comprehensive—which can offer the two routes within the one institution, and equally there is no reason why "academic" courses should not be offered by colleges of further education, as indeed they are. We are not arguing for one sort of institution as against another—though we repeat here our previously expressed opinion that part-time day release courses are no longer to be recommended as a proper method for the higher grades of technician, or evening classes for any form of sustained education for young people. These two systems ought no longer to be recommended because, as we have seen, they are wasteful and precarious and the education given must be narrowly confined by examination requirements. Nevertheless there will certainly be some who take them, even when they need not, for psychological reasons. In our view the way ought to be wide open for them to return at any point to the sandwich or full-time route where they should provide a group of students marked by especially strong purposefulness in their studies.

578. It is idle to pretend that an effectively free choice between alternative routes is at present universally available, or even generally so, for young people of 16 to 18. How many schools provide it? Many of the abler boys and girls who would benefit from a practical approach are in grammar schools. The curriculum of the grammar school below the Sixth Form was discussed in Chapter 20. The mere possession of a craft room or the provision of teaching time for craft subjects is, of course, very far from constituting a practical approach, but it is at least a necessary prerequisite. It may be sufficient then, to say here that, while science and mathematics are generously represented on the time-table of the grammar school, craft after the second or third year usually becomes an optional subject taken only by the weaker boys academically. Many of these schools provide only for woodwork; in only a small minority is technical drawing taught. In three out of twenty-one boys' or co-educational grammar schools on which full inspection reports were written in 1958 there was no provision for craft work; in one school only 15 boys, and in another less than 20, did any craft work after the second year. It is, we think, true to say that rarely in such schools is craft teaching the starting point for a technical education which reaches out into science and mathematics. To put things this way round would be contrary to the inherited grammar school tradition. On the whole then, the practical approach as we have described it cannot start for boys in these

schools until they transfer to further education. But it must be added that many grammar schools are changing their approach.

579. The position in modern schools is very different. There must be few boys who do not follow a craft course right up to their last week in school and usually with an increasing allocation of time towards the end. A beginning is often made with technical drawing and in a good many schools there is an approach to science through the study of machines. There is nothing in the short history of the modern school to stand in the way of its providing just this kind of educational approach and much to encourage it. The education that an enlightened modern school gives to its ablest boys may in fact be better fitted for many of the less able boys in a grammar school than the education they are getting there. After all, they are often very much the same boys, sent to different types of school by the hazard of an examination or by the chance of the district in which they happen to live. But, at present, the route through modern schools virtually stops at 16 and pupils must then either transfer to the Sixth Form of some other school or to further education.

580. If we want to see whether the kind of approach we have in mind is capable of providing a severe enough intellectual challenge for the Sixth Form, we shall have to turn to the secondary technical schools —soon to be reinforced by the technical Sixth Forms of the comprehensive schools. It seems to us that the technical schools have shown that it can be done. A practical approach need not fizzle out in acquiring the skill to carry out simple or complicated processes. An illustration may make the point clear. In one school at the present time a new electrically driven saw-bench is being designed and made. It is the job of the fourth-year boys to do the work, of the fifth-year boys to make the detailed drawings from which the fourth-year work, and of the Sixth Form to design the equipment and provide the sketches from which the detailed drawings are made. Here is an illustration of what we mean by a practical education making progressively exacting intellectual demands.

581. Those who follow a parallel road cannot hope to do all the things that are done on the older road (nor would they always wish to do so.) The practical approach, taken seriously, is a time-consuming one. Something of the traditional education will have to go. What should it be? No doubt different schools will decide differently, and we hope that all schools will allow as much latitude as possible to their pupils in selecting some at least of the elements of their curriculum. But we doubt very much, for instance, whether many schools using the parallel road will be able to spare the time for their pupils to learn two foreign languages. We would, however, feel that it is essential

that some time and care should be devoted to aspects of education other than the technical. In Chapter 25 we gave a good deal of attention to what we have called the "minority time" of the Sixth Form specialist. What we have in mind here is a special case of the same principle, and it is not necessary to develop the argument in detail twice over. One particular point, however, must be made. Boys and girls for whom this parallel route is the natural and appropriate one are often, as we saw in Chapter 33, those who find it relatively difficult to express themselves adequately in words. It is, indeed, one reason why they are at a disadvantage when they are asked to follow a traditional grammar school curriculum, and why we suggest a different starting point for them. It is, however, highly important that their education should not neglect the importance of words, or they will be at a disadvantage all their lives. They need quite as much English teaching as their bookish contemporaries.

582. Schools provide education that is full-time and not linked to the requirements of any occupation; but very little of it in the years after 16, is as yet "practical". In technical colleges, on the other hand, there is plenty of "practical" education but very little of it, in these years, is full-time or divorced from occupational requirements. There are, as we have seen, as yet hardly any sandwich courses for these ages. Day release courses are available; but, as we have also seen, they cannot be made broad and deep enough to provide a satisfactory education for able boys and girls of this age. In some directions, however, there is a good deal of full-time education which merits consideration. This is particularly true of engineering, building and nautical courses for boys, and in commerce, catering and pre-nursing courses mainly for girls. Some of these courses undoubtedly make comparable intellectual demands to those made by schools.

THE NEED FOR ENQUIRY

583. It is apparent, then, that we are advocating something that is as yet only in the early stages of development when we recommend full-time practical courses for able pupils from 16 to 18. There is fairly good provision before that age and there is getting to be good provision in many directions at a later age; but between 16 and 18 there is a gap where the only choices available to many boys and girls are the wasteful expedient of part-time education, or a full-time academic course which is not suitable for them. We wish to see this gap in the practical approach closed both in schools and in further education. Clearly the provision would take different forms in these two very different settings, but we believe the educational problems to be similar, and we should like to see them jointly examined. One of the tasks of such an enquiry might well be to examine the solutions

that have been found for similar problems in other countries, perhaps notably in France and Holland. Several of our members, at our request, visited some of these countries, and a note by Mr. H. A. Warren on the results of their enquiries is printed as Appendix III to this report.

584. We give two illustrations of the kind of problems which we think are unsolved. First, how is the programme of practical work to be designed so that the intellectual stimulus and the theoretical knowledge arise out of it? We suspect that too often, even when both elements are present, they remain separate. Secondly, how can the practical work and the intellectual value deriving from it best be assessed? Any education in England which aims at equipping its pupils for a professional status has to conform to an examination system designed in relation to an educational curriculum of which both the main subjects and the approach to them are academic. It will be apparent that it is not always easy to reconcile this parallel road with traditional examinations. Sometimes it can only be done with undesirable distortion. Some of the most valuable aspects of the education it can give would, we suggest, more naturally be tested by a scrutiny of work done during the course and by an oral examination upon it. We do not forget the recent development of examinations of practical subjects within the framework of the General Certificate of Education, but we do not believe that these provide a wholly satisfactory answer. New thought will indeed be necessary about the best way of appraising the standards of work done in this different approach.

585. We have not had sufficient time to carry out the detailed study which these problems urgently need and which we hope will be the subject of a separate enquiry. This study should not be confined to a professional approach from the point of view of the occupations which students are hoping to enter or to make their careers. It is true that professional requirements are important and relevant, but they are not the only matter of concern, nor in the final analysis are they at this stage the main consideration. Students of 16 and 17 are still boys and girls in need of a general education and, whether they are at school or in a full-time technical college course or at work, it is broad educational considerations which should be applied. They are in a stage of transition from school to work. We have devoted a large section of our report to the difficult problems that arise of necessity in the transition from school to university. We do not expect that the problems will be any easier, or ought to be, in the field with which we have been concerned in this part.

APPENDIX TO PART SIX

Note on Agriculture

586. Flexibility must be a characteristic of any educational system which attempts efficiently to serve the needs of a wide variety of occupations, each with its own different economic structure. Most of this part of our report has been concerned with what happens in manufacturing and constructional industry; this note is designed by way of contrast and supplement to identify some of the common tasks and different conditions which exist in agriculture. We are informed that the Minister has under consideration the recommendations made in December, 1958 by Lord De La Warr's Committee on "Further Education for Agriculture Provided by Local Education Authorities", and that a series of practical proposals based on these recommendations are being discussed with a special sub-committee of the National Advisory Council on Education for Industry and Commerce under the chairmanship of Mr. B. G. Lampard-Vachell, a member of our Council. This would, therefore, be an inappropriate moment for us to attempt the kind of detailed discussion which gives rise to recommendations; but it is perhaps an appropriate one to draw attention to certain considerations of a broad nature which have arisen in the course of our discussions. There is no doubt that agriculture is as much in the middle of a technological revolution as any part of the economic structure. Some instances may be given. The improvement of both crops and stock receives a concentrated attention from research workers and from practical farmers which would have delighted the pioneers of scientific agriculture in the eighteenth century. Mechanisation has been extensively introduced, and the internal combustion engine is now used everywhere. The coming of electricity to the farm has changed out of recognition the conditions of life and of work. The labour force is contracting; the output is rising. The need for skill of a mechanical kind and for knowledge of a scientific character increases. Technical education is as necessary in agriculture as in engineering.

587. But it is not as generally provided. There are many reasons. One of the most intractable is the small size of many holdings and the small number of workers they employ. Half the agricultural workers in 1957 are estimated to have been employed on farms where there were less than 5 workers, and a further quarter on farms with not more than 10. Half the agricultural holdings employ no full-time paid workers. The smallness of the units not only makes release for technical education difficult, it also makes technical education in breadth more necessary. Virtually all regular workers in agriculture

need to be skilled; few can be specialised; most need, in the words of the De La Warr report, to be "masters of a variety of jobs requiring such diverse skills as the care of different types of animals, the maintenance and use of several machines, the handling of different soils under varying conditions, the use of fertilizers and so on". It is necessary to remember too that, although agriculture may be one industry, it differs widely from one part of the country to another in what it does, how it does it and how it is organised. No one educational pattern is likely to meet all the varying circumstances.

588. The De La Warr Committee recommended universal part-time day release for all young workers in agriculture. At present, however, agriculture (as may be seen from Table 55 in Chapter 29) provides release for only 3 per cent of the boys it employs, a lower percentage than in any other industrial group except insurance, banking and finance. Day release will therefore have to start almost from the beginning. Part-time education for all young workers is recommended because all who work on farms need skill. A period of full-time education after practical farm experience is recommended from the age of about 18 for many more than now get it, because of the very high proportion in the industry (over one-third) who have some managerial or supervisory function. Remarkably enough, the proportion of those entering the industry who go to a farm institute as full-time students is as high as 10 per cent. In Part Four of our report we were concerned with the difficult problem of the large number of boys and girls for whom there was no obvious vocational need for education—agriculture is an occupation in which this class of employee seems not to exist, and one in which the proportion who require to carry their technical education to a relatively high level is unusually high. From the point of view of educational possibilities it ranks high, even if at the moment it ranks low in the provision of educational opportunities. The difficulties in the way of educational advance are administrative and economic, neither educational nor intrinsic.

589. These considerations point unmistakeably in our view to the desirability of a longer school life than the minimum for those who wish to enter agriculture. We hope that before long the minimum school-leaving age will be raised to 16, but we believe that even before this is done it is important that there should be a great development of extended courses with a rural bias but with a continued emphasis on the basic subjects, so that recruitment to agriculture may normally take place at 16 and not at 15 as at present. The need for education in agriculture is indeed a striking example of the case for raising the school-leaving age as a form of that national capital investment to which we devoted Chapter 12.

590. The drift from the country to the towns is an old complaint. Some compensating movement is desirable but difficult to set in motion. For this reason we attach importance to a real development of the farm apprenticeship scheme, whose progress so far has been disappointingly slow. In 1953 the industry established an Agricultural Apprenticeship Scheme with a normal age of entry at 15 providing a three-year period of practical training on a farm or horticultural holding, combined with day or block release courses for the first two years totalling 80 days. The total number of apprentices on farms in 1954 was 303, and in the four succeeding years 522, 609, 540 and 567 respectively. The majority were concentrated in a few counties, and one county in the south of England at present accounts for 205. Two major factors that inhibit the development of the apprenticeship scheme are, first, the organisation of the industry itself, and secondly the fact that there is at present no distinctive recognition either in status or official wage rate for a worker who has passed through an apprenticeship. Subsidiary but important factors that also apply include the difficulty of releasing young workers from the smaller farm units to attend classes, the problem of arranging viable class groups in scattered rural areas without making abnormal demands on time for travelling to them, and the problem of arranging for living accommodation near the place of employment.

591. One other important human factor must be borne in mind. The boy who enters farming is often going to be a lonely person. He may well come into contact at work with only one adult and seldom meet boys of his own age either at work or during his leisure time. His need to rub shoulders with his peers is very real. For this reason we believe that consideration should be given to the development of various kinds of provision for block release. This might often be centred appropriately at the farm institute, where additional boarding accommodation might be provided to meet the need. Block release would have the added advantage of eliminating wasteful travelling time and of making it possible to fit release into the seasonal demands of the industry. Block release involving a continuous period of boarding could not, however, provide more than a proportion of the facilities needed. In some cases the solution might be found by the local education authority providing day classes, either through the development of an extra-mural department of the farm institute, or by a centrally organised staff. The work could be done in collaboration with technical colleges and "village colleges" where these exist, and also possibly at large farms which could offer facilities for practical work and demonstration "on the job". The first-class herdsman cannot learn his craft away from the animals he tends.

592. The isolation of so many farm workers during working hours makes it more necessary than in other occupations to provide for communal pursuits to be available at leisure periods. Imaginative provision for leisure-time educational and recreational facilities is particularly important. It so happens that in agriculture, as in few other industries, there has been developed a youth organisation with strong educational activities. The Young Farmers' Clubs have developed effective informal methods of education which we believe ought to be still more widely used and copied. We do not, however, believe that all the education of young agricultural workers should take place in separation from their fellows. The isolation of so many workers on the land should be broken down as far as possible by joint activities in which they continue to meet after school years those boys and girls who were their friends at school but who have gone into other jobs. There are plenty of villagers who are not farm workers, and a village college ought to be representative of the whole community and not of one section of it alone.

Part Seven

Institutions and Teachers

CHAPTER 36

Changing Patterns in Organisation

593. In Chapter 2 we looked at the pattern of secondary education as it is today and at some of the new forms of school organisation that are beginning to appear. From the point of view of our terms of reference the most striking fact that emerged was, perhaps, that it is a system in which the centre of gravity is so much more than half-way down. There are so many more pupils under 15 than between 15 and 18 that they are bound to dominate the present structure. The essence of our enquiry has been to discover how rapidly this situation is changing, and to suggest means by which it can be made to change more rapidly. While it is clear that the educational system as a whole must be logically planned from the bottom up, there is need also to look at it from the top downwards. Is it constructed in such a way that it is likely to attract many more young people to stay longer in full-time education? Or do we need as fresh an experimental approach to the institutions which set out to cater for the older teen-agers as we already have to the schools which receive them at 11?

A FOUR-FOLD EXPANSION

594. The nation is committed to the task of providing some education for all up to the age of 18, and full-time education for all up to 16. The proportion of boys and girls who will continue full-time education between 16 and 18 is an open question not settled by legislation. How many should they be? At present only 12 per cent of the 17 year-old age-group (taking this as the middle of the range) get full-time education; we think that by 1980 half should. But, if anything like this is to be achieved, it will be necessary to make a great deal of progress in persuading more young people to prolong their education not only in grammar schools but in other types of schools. Sixth Forms have been growing at the rate of roughly 6 per cent per annum for a number of years and now attract nearly half those in the forms below. All the evidence suggests that they have not yet reached their natural limit of growth—there are still many boys and girls capable of following with profit a normal academic Advanced level course who do not get, or do not take, the chance. Some of them are already in schools with Sixth Forms—for them it is a matter of persuasion; some of them are not—for them it is a matter not only of persuasion, but also of provision.

595. But the hardest, and the most exciting, part of the task ahead lies with those who would benefit by full-time education to the end of the year in which they reach 18 but who are not academically minded. Some of them are in grammar schools; more are not. If our target of half the age-group is to be reached by 1980 we shall need to retain in full-time education up to 18 (including sandwich courses) not merely virtually all those who go to selective schools (including those who now leave at 16) but about one-third of those who at present go to non-selective schools. It is with these that we start very nearly from the beginning. There are full-time courses and sandwich courses for young people up to 18 in technical colleges,* but apart from sandwich courses, of which there are very few, much of the full-time work is on the same lines as in grammar schools and often serves little purpose beyond that of retrieving a previous examination omission or failure. There is virtually no provision beyond 16 in modern schools. In this situation, there is not, and could not be, in any section of the community a tradition of full-time education to 18 of a more practical nature for the non-academically minded. When a boy or girl reaches 15, every family has to make up its mind between employment and education, or a combination of the two. There are usually many forms of employment, but there may often be only one form of full-time education effectively open to a 16 year-old boy or girl. It may be, for instance, that there is in his neighbourhood (as far as he knows) only one place, the local grammar school, where there is any full-time education after 15 or 16 and only an academic Sixth Form course available there. If he attends some other school, or is clearly not an academically minded person, the family therefore concludes that the choice between education and employment is really Hobson's choice. The boy looks for a job. Effectively his choice lies at best between a job with day release and one without. Of course, the actual educational possibilities may be a good deal wider and better than a family realises, but boys and girls cannot choose something they have never heard of, and are hardly likely to choose something of which they are only dimly conscious. Unless the educational provision for boys and girls of 16 and 17 is both varied in its nature and well-known, the choice between education and employment, though theoretically open to all, will in practice be limited to those who went to certain sorts of school at 11 and who liked the subjects taught there.

596. The increase in numbers has to be achieved by persuasion without compulsion. This makes the task more difficult, but also more stimulating. The form of the institutions available and the kind of education they can offer will have a decisive influence on success. There is certainly nothing impossible in the target we have suggested.

* As well, of course, as the provision for older students.

Other countries have achieved as much in about the same time. In the United States, for instance, the legal compulsion to attend school (which usually begins a year later than in this country) ends in most states on the 16th birthday, but two-thirds of the boys and girls are in fact at school eighteen months later. Roughly speaking, the stage of the journey that lies immediately ahead of us was accomplished in America in the twenty years between 1920 and 1940, during which the proportion of 17 year-olds who stayed at school and successfully completed the high school course rose from 17 per cent to 51 per cent.

597. Why is it worth while making the effort? There seem to us to be three main reasons. One is the country's need to make the fullest use of the native supply of talent of all kinds. Nobody seriously doubts that we must complete the Sixth Forms of the future by bringing into them all those who can profit from a full academic course. We can call them the old Sixth Formers for short. But the need does not stop there. We saw in Part Six how great is the deficiency of intelligent, educated technicians and their equivalent grades in commerce and business and how many defects there are in the present part-time methods of producing them. There is plenty of scope for sound and solid education of a different kind from the customary Sixth Form courses, if boys and girls can be persuaded to go on with their full-time studies. It is just this practical kind of work which is likely to persuade them to stay. We can call them for short the new Sixth Formers. There is, we believe, a sufficiently close approximation between what they want to do and what the country needs.

598. Another reason for seeking a four-fold increase in the number of young people continuing full-time education up to the age of 18 is to give a larger number of boys and girls a sound and healthy environment in which to grow up, where they will be in daily contact with sympathetic and enlightened adults who have a care and responsibility for their upbringing. We have no doubt that those who are willing to remain longer in full-time education benefit from it immensely as people: they develop internal resources which will make them, when the time comes, much better citizens and parents.

599. The third purpose is allied to the second: it is the need to secure that society itself is healthy. The social purpose of education is to see that boys and girls from every sort of social background, going to many different kinds and levels of jobs, learn to like and respect and be at ease with one another irrespective of class or race or creed. This is something that can be helped or hindered by the way we plan the upper stages of education. Personality changes so much in these later teen-age years that it is important to see that as many

people as possible have experience of living in a mixed society at this age as well as when they are younger. Good conditions for it are more easily found in education than at work.

600. It is, then, in the national interest that many more young people of 16 to 18 should receive full-time education. How can we persuade them to do so? At least two conditions have to be satisfied. One concerns what is taught; the other, the society in which they learn. A teen-ager will leave school unless he is satisfied that he is learning something worth knowing, which interests him and which will be useful to him. He is also not likely to stay at school, if he can help it, unless the conditions of life there are congenial to him. The two conditions are fairly closely related to one another, but they are certainly not identical. Both require a considerable amount of variety in the education that is provided. What interests one is dull to another; what one can do defeats another; the kind of life that one enjoys is distasteful to another. We certainly do not suggest that the 16 or 17 year-old should have everything his own momentary way—a degree of discipline in work and of conformity with regulations made for the general good is normally acceptable, and is certainly an essential part of education. But we believe that unless school (or its equivalent) can meet him over the way in which it provides what he needs, it will not have the opportunity of providing him with anything at all.

601. There is no sudden or magical change in educational needs that occurs when the compulsory school attendance age is passed. All that is different is the pupil's legal status—he and his parents are now able to give effect to what they already feel. If their reasons for deciding on longer full-time education go beyond a simple yielding to the pressure of social custom, it will be more because they are satisfied with what they have already had than because of anything they are promised for the future. In fact, once the school-leaving age is raised to 16, the last year or two of compulsory school life will in some ways have more in common educationally with what comes after than with the first two years at the secondary school. We have drawn attention to the earlier physical maturity of boys and girls, and to those other powerful forces which produce earlier social development. The near approach of the time when they can leave school and earn their living gives both the possibility of a new interest in school work and also a touchstone by which in any event it will be judged. Workaday relevance becomes for the first time a criterion consciously applied by pupils. It is most unlikely that many of those who at 14 find school lessons pointless and school life restrictive will extend their period of full-time education. It follows that the competition between education and employment starts, and

the issue is often decided, well before there is any actual possibility of taking a job. In planning the pattern of educational provision above the minimum school-leaving age, it is important not to forget the needs of boys and girls aged 14 to 16.

PATTERNS OF ORGANISATION

602. The institutions that boys and girls attend for full-time education between the ages of 16 and 18 are organised in a good many different ways, although they may be teaching essentially the same things. We pick out for discussion four ways in which the different environment they provide may have a significant bearing on their power to attract and retain different groups of young people. One general point may, perhaps, be made first, which would indeed be trivial if it were not often felt to be important by teen-agers. It is the question of names. A 17 year-old boy may attend a school or a college—the former may sound childish to him, the latter a trifle high falutin' to us. A 17 year-old girl may be known officially by her Christian name or as Miss Smith or Miss Jones. Schools have pupils; colleges have students. Does it matter? To some, clearly, these distinctions are important. For the sake of simplicity we refer in this chapter to schools and pupils (without prejudging the issue) except where in a particular context we are clearly referring only to a technical college and its students, and we use the phrase "a 17 year-old" as a short way of describing a boy or girl who is over compulsory school-age but under 18.

603. The first of the points of organisation is the *age-range*. This can be 11 to 15 or 16; 11 to 18; 13 or 14 to 18; 16 to 18 and beyond. The characteristic pattern of grammar, technical and comprehensive schools is from 11 to 18. Most of the independent boys' public schools have an age-range from 13 or 14 to 18, and this is the pattern adopted for the Leicestershire experimental grammar schools which are open to all who at 14 promise to undertake at least a two-year course in them. Technical colleges and a number of private colleges of various types start at 15 or 16. Modern schools (and they are two-thirds of all secondary schools) cater for pupils from 11 to 15 or 16. For the overwhelming majority of modern school pupils the only way beyond 16 in full-time education is by moving elsewhere. Schools with an 11 to 18 age-range involve nearly twice as long in the same institution as in any other stage of the educational system (unless the infants and the juniors are run together, as is now uncommon). The presence of quite young boys and girls involves a paternalism in discipline which often spreads upwards to those who do not need it. Schools with a wide age-range, covering very different stages of growth, need to make a conscious effort to see that each

stage gets its appropriate environment. It can be done, and where it is, pupils who persevere find satisfaction and valuable experience in the responsibilities which come to them. As they come up the school, they live very much in the present with their contemporaries; but, when they reach the top, they are brought into contact with the whole age-range of pupils and they meet the staff on a new footing. They have to learn how to get on with boys and girls of all ages and how to get the best out of them; and in the process they get a valuable insight into the development of character and personality. Schools with the restricted age-range of 13 or 14 to 18 recruit at an age when boys and girls are still young enough to need a paternalistic discipline but it brings them into a society whose centre of gravity is at a much higher age than in the ordinary secondary school type. The shorter span of school life or, to put it another way, a second wind at a time when personality changes rapidly and boredom often sets in, may make such a school an acceptable place up to 18 for some who would never complete that long seven-year journey from 11. A fresh start at 16 in a technical college or some similar quasi-adult institution has a strong appeal to those who are anxious to get on to the next stage or to demonstrate, as much to themselves as to others, that they have outgrown childish things. For them, the custom of being treated as an adult in the conventions of speech and administration may be the best way of eliciting genuinely mature behaviour in place of the rebelliousness which so easily springs up in resentment at any fancied affront to their still insecure sense of adult dignity.

604. Almost as important as the age-range of the society to which a boy or girl belongs is its *size*, the second of our four points of organisation. There are certainly some who can flourish easily in either a big or a small school; there are others who find a stimulus in the larger society, with its wider choice of opportunities, which they would never have got from a small community. There are others who need the intimate close-knit unity of a small school where everybody must play as many parts as he can manage. There is no reason to suppose that the size of school which is right for a boy at the age of 12 is right for the very different person that he will be at 17 (though of course it may be). Indeed only a large school may be able to provide the variety of courses that older boys and girls need. With many individual exceptions, it is probably true to say that the older the pupil, the larger the school can be.

605. The third of our aspects of organisation is the choice between a *single sex* or a *co-educational* school. This is a matter on which parents and public opinion differ about what is desirable, as much as pupils do in what they prefer. Nor is there any stability in their attitudes. What is right for a boy at 12, and what he wants then,

may be quite wrong at 16 or 17. But, as with the size of school, so with the type of organisation—where he goes at 11 normally determines where he will be at 17 if he is still at school. Roughly half the modern schools, and well over half the comprehensive schools, are co-educational; but two-thirds of the maintained grammar schools and nine-tenths of independent and direct grant grammar schools are single sex.

606. The fourth way in which different forms of organisation provide differences in environment is the contrast between the self-contained world of the school and the semi-detached world of the technical college. Is there room for *part-timers* as well as *full-timers* in the same institution? The overwhelming majority of boys and girls who are receiving full-time education at 17 are in schools where there are no part-timers. Those who go to technical colleges, however, form part of a mixed community. The contact with the world in which they are going to spend their working lives is much closer. Some will happily continue in full-time education in this way who would have been restless and dissatisfied at school. Others may find it disturbing. There is another consideration. We normally think of full-time education as a continuous process which goes unbrokenly on until it is finally given up. And so it is in most cases. But adolescence is at best an unsettled time and mistakes are bound to be made. Few boys and girls who have gone out to work are likely cheerfully to return to school, although they may before long agree that they made a mistake in leaving. They can, however, easily return to full-time education in a technical college, and a good many do so. No difficult change of status is involved. They have taken the decisive step in leaving school and moving into the adult world, and nobody is going to ask them to reverse it.

ORGANISATION AND THE NATURE OF THE CURRICULUM

607. The possibility of leaving school at 15 raises the question of the desirability of staying on. What is the purpose to be served? This is a question that all families must face and, to some extent at least, the answer must be given in terms of the kind of life that the boy or girl is planning to lead. Translated into educational terms, it involves a decision about curriculum. There is the possibility of an academic course either on the science or the arts side on the lines we discussed in Chapter 25 or of a cognate but intellectually less exacting nature described in Chapter 27. There is also the possibility of a course, which again could be either at a high or an intermediate level, following the practical approach we were concerned with in Chapter 35. Where are these various kinds of course best provided? How are pupils to get admission to them?

608. Academic courses are provided for the most part in the Sixth Forms of schools, though there are similar courses also in some technical colleges. The greater part of the work is a straight-line continuation of subjects studied throughout their secondary school course. There is a strong case for continuity of teaching. The pupils know their teachers and are known individually by them. Arrangements can be, and often are, made for them to go as fast and as far as they can in their strong subjects without waiting for their weaker subjects to be brought up to the level (usually Ordinary level in the G.C.E.) at which they can be put on one side. Practical courses for pupils over 16 are at present provided mainly in technical colleges, though they can be—and to some extent are—also provided in schools. One of the ways in which they differ from academic courses is that they introduce a wide range of subjects which are either completely new or not so firmly rooted in the main school curriculum as the traditional subjects of the Sixth Form. This does not, of course, mean that the traditional subjects as a whole disappear, but that those which remain bulk less largely in the minds and in the timetables of the pupils and that the methods of teaching them may be significantly different. The new subjects in the main have a close connection with the world outside the school, and are rather more loosely linked to the curriculum that has been followed in earlier years. Schools (like technical colleges) might well develop courses which, though full-time education, involved a good deal of practical work experience. Teachers would need to have close connections with the world of work in the same way that Sixth Form masters keep in touch with the universities. There is no educational reason why this sort of work should not be done in school—after all, as we have said, a good part of every course would be school work in the strict sense—but there would not be the same sort of presumption as there is in the academic courses, that school is the best or only place for it.

609. It is apparent that there is no one simple institutional solution to the problem of full-time education for boys and girls over 16. Indeed for a thoroughly satisfactory solution it is essential that every boy or girl should be conscious of having both a choice of course—which ought to be possible everywhere—and also a choice of the institution in which it is to be taken, which may not be possible in all country districts. It will not be possible to achieve the desired four-fold increase in full-time education over 16 simply by persuading everybody to stay on longer in the schools in which they happen to be. For one thing, some pupils will positively want to move—and will move out of full-time education if they cannot move inside it. This may be irresponsible behaviour, but it has to be reckoned with.

For another thing, there is the problem of the size of institution necessary to support one or more courses for pupils over 16. In only a relatively small number of modern schools can there be much hope of providing academic courses for them, both because of the small numbers who will want to take them and because of the absence of suitably qualified staff. Transfer to a school with an academic Sixth (or to a technical college) will usually be unavoidable even if some potential candidates are lost in the process—it is not everybody who wants to transfer—and others are delayed by the difficulty of getting used to new ways of teaching and a new way of life. On the whole, however, it should not be difficult to provide a choice of academic courses over most of the country.

610. A more difficult decision is where to provide new style courses for pupils who, as they approach the end of compulsory attendance, are in grammar or modern schools. The practical approach is the right one for the great majority of modern school pupils; it is the one their schools already use. The difficulty about providing continuing courses in their own schools is solely one of numbers. A small modern school with under 300 on roll would reach its target for full-time education for 17 year-olds if it persuaded 20 to 25 of its pupils each year to stay on beyond 16. This is not a large enough number to provide much in the way of variety of courses—and some variety is essential if we are to secure the numbers. If the school were a co-educational one, the difficulty in securing sufficient variety would be greatly increased and perhaps almost doubled. There is the same problem about numbers in the grammar schools as in the modern schools. Many grammar schools are small—one-seventh of them have less than 300 pupils. If we assume that even one-third of their pupils (and the proportion would certainly not be higher) need continuing courses of a non-academic kind, we are left with the same problem of inadequate numbers for practical courses as in the smaller modern schools.

611. There is a further difficulty about new-style courses in grammar schools. While an advanced course along practical lines is a natural development from the work of earlier years in modern schools, it would be in contrast to the traditional grammar school approach, which has abundantly justified itself as a stimulus and discipline for certain valuable types of mind. It is in this field that grammar schools can be regarded as specialised or pace-setting institutions. A new-style course, then would have to be a "Sixth Form with a difference" —and with a different difference from that of the General Sixth described in Chapter 27. In the larger schools there would be room for it. But would there be a welcome for it? And would it be done

as well as it could be done elsewhere? We conclude that more grammar schools than now do so could run good courses of the kind we have in mind, but that this would be by no means true of all.

612. The technical schools may be regarded in one sense as specialists in providing the kind of education which is most likely to attract, inspire and develop the new Sixth Formers, just as the grammar schools are specialists in catering for the old Sixth Formers. Specialised schools have the double job of showing what true excellence in their own speciality can mean, and in influencing other less specialised schools which have the same job to do for at least some of their pupils. It is a continuing job which is not finished when other schools have been shown the way. Technical schools have not finished their mission because they and the influences that have brought them into being have profoundly affected what many grammar and modern schools do. It is, in our view, important that there should be a sufficient number of them so distributed throughout the country as to enable their influence to pervade all the schools. Really high standards are much more likely to be set, and the maximum possible benefit to be derived from this particular approach if there is in each district one school to show what really able (and less able boys as well) can achieve when taught in this way by men who passionately believe in it. There is also a special role that the Sixth Form of a technical school can play—it is in a peculiarly favourable position to receive transfers from other sorts of schools. We have argued in Chapter 35 that the special approach of the technical school to learning is the right approach for many at all levels of ability. There are able grammar school boys who by 16 are so decided in their ambitions and so clear in their knowledge of how they will set about attaining them that it is plain that they would do best in a Technical Sixth Form. There are also boys in modern schools who have shown that they have the ability to go on to a Sixth Form, but who are more likely to find just what they want in a technical college or a technical school rather than in a grammar school. We do not believe that most of either group could have been identified at 11, and the right way to meet their needs seems to us to be to see that technical schools are so planned as to have disproportionately large Sixth Forms for their main school base.

THE PROBLEM OF THE RURAL AREAS

613. About one-fifth of the population live in rural districts. Country boys and girls have the same diverse needs and aspirations as those who live in towns; but they can only be satisfied by different means. Density of population and ease of travel vary greatly from district to district, but one or two common points emerge. If there is to be

a variety of courses available, there must be more teachers and equipment than the same number of pupils would justify in a town. Sometimes, as in the Cambridgeshire village colleges, it is possible to make the additional provision economically by combining secondary and further education; and thus incidentally doing a good deal to make school a place with more adult associations and, to that extent, a more acceptable place to teen-agers. But a complete rural educational service cannot be provided by taking teachers to pupils; it is often necessary to bring the pupils to the teachers. One reason why we have larger secondary schools than primary schools is because it is reasonable to ask an 11 year-old to travel further than a 5 year-old. It is just as reasonable to ask a 17 year-old to travel further than an 11 year-old. Larger catchment areas for full-time education after the end of compulsory school life are practicable and necessary if a full range of options is to be provided. This means that if the courses for "new Sixth Formers" are provided in a secondary school, it will sometimes be a school whose top will contain a large number of pupils who were not there at the beginning. The centre of gravity of this school, then, would be in the upper and not the lower ages. It may well be that boarding accommodation would be necessary, especially for the older boys and girls, and this would be true whether the provision is at the top of a school or in a college of further education. The fact that a country boy, unlike a town boy, cannot be free to choose where he learns as well as what he learns places a special responsibility on the schools to see that they do not treat their older pupils as children. And because a boy must be free to choose his course (even though he cannot choose where he does it), the school or college will have to develop at least for its older pupils a more comprehensive curriculum.

THE COMPREHENSIVE SCHOOL

614. Is transfer on the scale we have in mind inevitable if we are to achieve our aim? Granted that over the greater part of the country for a good long time to come this may be the only way forward, need it always be the only way? At this point we take up the question of the comprehensive school where we left it in Chapter 2.* Comprehensive schools have two specialised functions. The first is educational—to show how many of the failures of the educational system can be avoided by finding the right kind of course for each particular pupil. In this respect their special role is to play Theseus to the Procrustes of the tripartite system. One of their great strengths is that it is much easier to change forms than to change schools. It is possible

* Much of what we say in the following paragraphs of the comprehensive school applies equally to the bilateral school. Indeed, there is often difficulty in deciding to which category an individual school belongs.

to adjust the curriculum which a particular pupil is following as the need arises. There should, therefore, be considerably less waste of time or talent through pupils following for four or five years courses for which they are unsuitable, either as a result of a mistaken diagnosis of their attainments at 11 or because their progress in subsequent years has been faster or slower or in another direction than could then have been foreseen. A further great strength lies in the range of options that a large organisation can offer to 15 year-olds. There is, or ought to be, something for nearly everybody. Find it (as the comprehensive school ought to be able to do) by 14 and there will be no need to transfer at 16 and, very likely, much less desire to leave then. The comprehensive school's second specialised role is social. If it is placed in a suitable neighbourhood, it ought to act as a socially unifying force drawing pupils together at an age when they otherwise begin to draw apart. In a comprehensive school, the different social backgrounds from which the pupils come, and the different kinds and levels of employment to which they are going more closely correspond to the national pattern than in other schools. This width of experience within a common life is surely of great value. When a comprehensive school really commands the loyalty and affection of its members, it acts as an effective sign of that unity in society which our age covets. Comprehensive schools have the same double job as other specialised schools. They exist to set a standard of excellence in their own field; and, to the extent that they attain it, they influence other schools.

615. The fears that a good many people concerned with education have about comprehensive schools turn really on the related questions of size and the maintenance of standards. To achieve its social purpose, a comprehensive school need not be large. There are American high schools bigger than any English comprehensive school, but the typical one is no bigger than the average English secondary school. Size is necessary in order to provide older pupils, who are spread over the whole range of ability, with the curriculum best suited to their individual needs, and to enable them to go as far and as fast in it as they would be able to do in any other sort of school. Neither educational opinion nor the country's economic interests would allow any lower standard to be set for an English comprehensive school. The price that has to be paid is size. To achieve our target in full-time education at 17 it would generally be reckoned that a comprehensive school would have to be somewhere between 1,200 and 2,000 strong. Some would argue that this is too many anyhow. Some would say that, since no school is better than its headmaster, we stake the future of too many boys and girls on one man's strength. Others, while admitting the danger of a loss of

personal contact would claim that forethought, imagination and determination can overcome it.

616. But need these risks be run? There are two matters of organisation which do not affect the basic demands of a comprehensive system, but which do directly influence the size necessary to guarantee width and depth of curriculum. The first is the choice between co-educational and single sex schools. A co-educational school will need to be larger than a single sex school because it will need to offer a greater choice of courses, especially at the top of the school. More important, perhaps, is the common assumption that all comprehensive secondary schools must cover all the years from 11 to 18. Need they? Where it is possible to divide these years between two schools, the total numbers on the roll of any one school could be reduced by two or three age-groups (between 500 and 700 for an 8 form-entry school, and between 700 and 1,100 for a 12 form-entry school); or, alternatively, the size of each age-group could be increased within the same total roll, thus throwing up larger Sixth Forms. A great deal of thought is being given at present by many local education authorities and individuals to the best forms of school organisation between 11 and 18. It can no longer be assumed that the pattern to which we have been accustomed, by which a boy attends only one school between these ages, will necessarily continue. It does not seem to us, however, that the time has yet come (if indeed it ought ever to come) when a single national pattern can be prescribed. Whatever the local pattern may be, not even a comprehensive school is likely to be able to satisfy all the varied demands which may properly be made by 17 year-old boys and girls. Nor, if it could, is it in our opinion wise to have only one place in which a 17 year-old can get full-time education. Freedom to choose the institution as well as freedom to choose a course is important to teen-agers and their parents. We welcome comprehensive schools, not as being the right place for all 17 year-olds, but as pace-setters both in persuading boys and girls to stay longer at school and in showing how education, though it must divide us intellectually, can still unite us socially.

617. Any judgement of English comprehensive schools at this stage must be made in faith rather than knowledge. It is to everybody's interest that in this experimental period they should have the benefit of good conditions. They need, and get, an enthusiastic staff—the time has hardly come when they must rely on teachers who hold no special brief for or against them. They need, but do not always get, new buildings thoughtfully designed for their particular needs. Makeshift accommodation is at best a nuisance; with a new venture inevitably creating complicated administrative problems it is a

menace. At present, then, the only sensible attitude to comprehensive schools seems to us to be a non-dogmatic one that neither condemns them unheard nor regards them as a prescription for universal application. Clearly there are many situations in which a comprehensive school is a sensible way, sometimes perhaps the only sensible way, of meeting local needs. One example is a densely populated area where a variety of schools can be made accessible. Another is a new area—a large housing estate or a new town perhaps—in which the existing provision is clearly insufficient in relation to present needs, and where it is especially important to develop a united community. Others are thinly populated country districts and small self-contained industrial townships where one good all-purpose secondary school may be the only viable alternative to two poorly equipped, and inadequately staffed, separate institutions. Often enough the road forward may be through the expansion of an old, but very small grammar school. On the other hand, a decaying area in the centre of a large city seems to us a place to be avoided for initial experiments.

618. Most comprehensive schools will have to be introduced into what may be called settled educational territory. But there are degrees of density of settlement. The most fertile soil seems to us to be in those areas where the existing provision in grammar and technical schools is clearly inadequate either because it is well below the national average or because the nature of the population requires above-average provision. There are enough areas of these various kinds to provide a long building programme. Over-all figures for local education authorities are apt to be very misleading in this respect—figures for individual wards or electoral divisions would be much more indicative—but it is worth remembering that there are 6 English counties and 10 county boroughs where in 1958 less than one-fifth of the children aged 13 were in any sort of selective school. In settled educational territory a comprehensive school is bound to be a close neighbour of well-established schools which have built up a spiritual capital in their traditions, in the loyalty of their staff, in the standard of their work and in the goodwill of former pupils, parents and local public opinion. There is in many districts no reason why one school should harm the other, and indeed they may gain from being neighbours. But there are other situations where a comprehensive school could only be established by doing harm to existing schools which are doing a very good job. We cannot afford to lose any good school, whatever its classification.

NOT IN SCHOOL

619. We do not see either the comprehensive school or any kind of school as a sufficient provision for the needs of all boys and girls

between 16 and 18 for full-time education. This is no reflection on the schools. It is simply that the problem is not wholly soluble in terms of school. There will always be boys and girls who want to leave school at 16, but who are yet willing to continue their full-time education. There will also be things that 16 and 17 year-olds want to learn, which provide a perfectly sound education, but which need to be learnt in a closer relation to the adult world than is normally practicable in schools. These two needs are met at present in a local technical college. Its characteristic note, as we have seen, is purposefulness in relation to the things it teaches. The subjects of its curriculum are vocational; the outlook of its staff is vocational; the aspirations of its students are vocational. They are none the worse for that. It would be quite wrong, however, for the objectives of any educational institution for this age-group to be wholly vocational. We have indicated in Chapter 35 how such a college may in the future develop both the quality and the quantity of its full-time work; but technical colleges, even as they are now, play a vital part in educating 17 year-olds who want to feel more out in the world than they could at school.

620. There are a number of aspects of a local college which make it quite unlike the other institutions with which we have been dealing. It is largely but by no means exclusively a teen-age institution. Its work is determined by content and level rather than by age—it provides, for instance, Ordinary National Certificate but not Higher National Certificate courses—and, as we have seen, the road to a further educational qualification is lined with men whose journey is taking longer than they expected. It is an institution housing a variety of *ad hoc* courses of varying lengths, each adapted to the precise amount of ground to be covered. (A school, on the other hand, sets out to provide an education for a given number of years and its courses are, by and large, determined by the amount of ground that can be covered in the time.) The day students in a technical college comprise some full-time students and a much more numerous group of part-time students. The full-time students themselves are of two kinds. There are those who are as much students and nothing else as if they attended a university or a school. There are others (those on sandwich courses) who may put in as many weeks of term as an Oxford or Cambridge undergraduate, but who have a full-time job for the other half of the year. They have a stake in two worlds—and this is just what some people need. The full-time students may be, or may become, the core of the college; they cannot be the college as the pupils are the school. Lastly, the college has a very considerable body of evening work. These four aspects of its organisation combine to make the technical college a more impersonal

institution than a school; on the other hand, it does not make demands on a student for loyalty, which he may (especially if he is in a temporarily rebellious mood) resent as irrelevant and impertinent. There are boys and girls for whom the atmosphere of a technical college is right at this stage of development and not least so because of its self-organised student activities. Its place in the educational provision for 16 and 17 year-olds is bound up with the fact that it is different from school. We would not have it otherwise.

621. It seems to us, then, that local technical colleges are really bridge institutions—they belong to the worlds both of school and of adult education because the adolescents whom they serve have one foot in the world of childhood and one in adult life. Administratively, they belong wholly to the world of further education. This ought not to matter, but it does apparently act as a barrier to those whose knowledge is of schools. The world of further education is often to them a foreign country, whose language is incomprehensible and for which they feel a visa is probably necessary. It seems at least probable that a good many boys and girls who would have welcomed a full-time course at a technical college leave school without ever having realised that it was a possibility. In our view it is important not only that there should be close co-operation between institutions on both sides of the line, but also that the education authorities, the heads of schools and the principals of colleges should all regard all forms of education catering for boys and girls of these ages, and especially those which provide full-time education, as being parts of one service, planned as such and deliberately setting out to feed one another.

622. Have we all the elements that are needed to make a suitable provision for the full-time educational needs of 16 and 17 year-olds? Or is there a missing piece? Have we in particular provided sufficiently for the very numerous group (especially numerous among girls) who are so very sure that they are neither children nor schoolgirls, but who yet are at a stage (or so it seems to us) when their social life is marked by extreme gregariousness? Is there a case for a Junior College which would be essentially a full-time institution without part-time students? What we have in mind is an institution with the adult atmosphere of a technical college but with a much wider range of curriculum and with terms of reference nearer to those of a school, in that equal weight would be attached by the staff to the subjects taught and to the personal development of the students. We do not think of an institution of this kind as starting before the end of compulsory attendance or thereabouts, nor as continuing beyond, say, the age of 19. As we see it, there would be a wide range of practical courses—commerce, pre-nursing and catering, for instance, all lend themselves to full-time courses of two to three years duration

—and also of academic courses roughly parallel to those that are found in the Sixth Forms of schools. There would also, we hope, be room for courses that were not tied to examinations and regulations, but existed just because they provided a good education. It is courses of this kind which bring the best out of an experimentally minded staff—and a Junior College would hardly be worth trying if it were not staffed by men and women with the spirit of pioneers. There would, we hope, be access from the Junior College to further education of all kinds as well as to employment, for it would be our hope that a very wide range of ability and interests would be found among its students. We do not, then, think of a Junior College as replacing Sixth Forms, but as standing side by side with them, providing an alternative form of education for those who had got incurably tired of school and for those whose schools had no Sixth Forms. There might well be scope for such a Junior College in widely contrasted circumstances. It is difficult to believe that the conurbations which house two-fifths of the country's population would not each throw up sufficient students for such a venture. It is easy also to see that a Junior College might be of value in areas where the nature of the population and the pattern of secondary school organisation make it likely that a good many secondary schools will each produce only a handful of pupils wanting to continue their full-time education after 16. We are not, of course, sure that there is room for such an institution in the English educational system—it would be impossible to be sure without a trial—but we have an impression that, various though the present available forms may be, there is a gap which ought to be filled. We would welcome experiments.

623. Even when the four-fold expansion of full-time education up to 18 at which we are aiming has been accomplished, half the boys and girls will continue to leave school at 16 and go to work. They will not, of course, have done with education, once county colleges have been introduced, but the end of compulsory school attendance will mark a much more decisive stage in their education than in that of those with whom we have hitherto been concerned in this chapter. Throughout the preparation of our report we have been conscious of an anxiety lest schools, in doing more and more for those who will stay longer in them, should do less for those who will leave as soon as they are allowed to. We have had a good deal to say about their interests in Chapters 8 and 9. They must not be left out of consideration in this chapter. School to 16 and a county college to 18 can, we are sure, provide a satisfactory education for those who are likely to choose it, provided that both the schools and the county colleges are convinced that the work they are engaged on for their pupils is second to none in importance. Those who

leave school at 16 must not be looked on as premature leavers. They need courses specially designed to reach a satisfactory stopping point at the end of their school career, and they need quite as good teaching as anybody else. We have no doubt that some of these pupils will be found in all the types of schools we have been discussing in this chapter. No doubt, too, all these schools can provide an effective education for their 16 year-old leavers. But schools which have to concentrate on pupils who leave at 16, because they have few others, are obviously in the most favourable position to develop appropriate techniques for serving their interests. They are likely to be pace-setters in this field. If there were no such schools, it would, we believe, be necessary to invent them, lest the interests of those who go to work at 16 should be overlooked.

SUMMARY OF CONCLUSIONS

624. We summarise our conclusions in this way :

(*a*) If by 1980 (or thereabouts) about half the boys and girls in the country are to continue in full-time education (including sandwich courses) until they are 18 a four-fold increase will be needed.

(*b*) This increase in the years above the limit of compulsory attendance can only be achieved through persuasion. Needs and wishes differ widely so that, wherever possible, there should be freedom to choose not only what to study but the sort of institution to attend.

(*c*) Existing institutions can be differentiated by the age-range they serve, by whether or not they are co-educational, by their size and by whether or not they enrol part-time as well as full-time students. In all these respects choice, wherever possible, should be open to boys and girls.

(*d*) The situation in rural areas, where choice will often not be practicable, imposes special obligations on authorities and on staff to cater for the varying needs and wishes of older teen-agers.

(*e*) A four-fold expansion of full-time education which we envisage requires that all (or nearly all) those who attend selective schools should remain in full-time education until 18 and that about one-third of the remainder should do so. This will involve not only an expansion of Sixth Forms of the types described in Part Five, but the development of sandwich courses in further education and of practical courses of the types described in Chapter 35.

(*f*) The presumption is that Sixth Form courses of the customary academic kind are best provided in schools because of the advantage of continuity of teaching. Parallel provision of academic courses in institutions other than schools is, however, also required.

(*g*) There is no similar presumption about where practical courses are best provided, but there is nothing against their being developed in schools. They could be provided either in schools or in other institutions.

(*h*) The size of school necessary to support practical courses suggests that many grammar and modern schools will be unable to produce the numbers necessary to make such courses economic beyond the age of 16.

(*i*) We hope to see the development of more secondary technical schools, commonly with provision for Sixth Forms disproportionately large in relation to the main school, in order to allow of transfers from other types of school.

(*j*) Comprehensive schools have a specialised role in two respects —to make it easier to provide without delay or friction appropriate courses for the varied needs of boys and girls of all levels of ability, and to serve as a socially unifying force in the community.

(*k*) The first purpose involves relatively large numbers if each comprehensive school is to contain pupils of all ages from 11 to 18. The necessary numbers could be reduced if this age range were divided between two schools.

(*l*) Typical situations in which comprehensive schools can suitably be introduced are:

(i) in densely populated areas where a variety of schools can be made accessible;

(ii) in areas where the selective provision is unsatisfactorily low;

(iii) in newly developing areas where existing secondary provision is clearly inadequate, and where it is especially important to develop a united community;

(iv) in thinly populated country districts and small self-contained industrial townships, where one good all-purpose secondary school may be the only viable alternative to two poorly equipped and inadequately staffed separate institutions.

(*m*) The difficulties which confront all new institutions ought not to be aggravated by introducing comprehensive schools in makeshift accommodation.

(*n*) Comprehensive and other schools may gain from being neighbours. But there are situations where a comprehensive school could only be established by doing harm to existing schools which are doing a very good job. We cannot afford to lose any good school, whatever its classification.

(*o*) Local technical colleges have a special part to play because of their more adult atmosphere (facilitated by the absence of boys and girls under 15) and of their close connection with the outside world (made apparent by the presence of part-time students).

(*p*) There may be room for a special Junior College parallel with, but not in place of, Sixth Forms, enrolling only full-time students, offering a wide variety of courses both academic and practical. Experiments should be invited and encouraged.

(*q*) We expect that half the boys and girls in the country will still be leaving school at 16 in 1980. Their interests must not be neglected. Schools where most pupils give up full-time education at 16 are especially well placed to look after their interests and to develop the best kind of courses for them.

CHAPTER 37

The Teachers

625. This report has been concerned with a programme of educational advance. Everything in education depends ultimately on the teacher, and everything in educational progress depends upon there being teachers with the right qualities, and in the right numbers, to carry it out. More teachers will be needed because with a school-leaving age of 16, there will be more pupils to be taught. More teachers will also be needed to do more effectively what is already being done, since most teachers at present have too many pupils to teach. The additional number required to meet the first of these demands is, on a teacher/pupil ratio of 1 : 17, much smaller than the number needed to meet the second. Moreover, if we can satisfy the first demand, we shall find it a good deal easier, at one remove, to satisfy the second. Longer staying on at school means a bigger field from which to recruit teachers. Recently one in three of all 17 year-olds at school have gone on to become teachers; and among girls the proportion was two in three. With rising demands from so many other occupations for a greater number of recruits from Sixth Forms, there cannot be an adequate improvement in the supply of teachers from the present numbers. We saw in Chapter 1 that 9 per cent of all army recruits in the top group of ability, and 65 per cent of the next group, had left school at 15. Thus there is evidence that the field of recruitment for teachers can be enlarged if a longer school life can be achieved. So far then from the two kinds of demand for additional teachers being in competition, we regard meeting the smaller demand (more teachers for new work) as being to some extent a condition for being able to satisfy the larger demand (more teachers for existing pupils). Similarly, whatever we can do to reduce the size of classes in primary and secondary schools will result in more boys and girls reaching the end of compulsory school life with a good knowledge for their age and an interest in their school work. More of them will want to go on with their education, thus increasing the first kind of demand and, incidentally, the field from which future teachers can be found. The problem of teacher supply is essentially one of pump-priming.

QUANTITY AND QUALITY

626. Not only do we want enough teachers; we want enough good teachers. Are these two demands inconsistent? The question is openly asked and must be treated seriously. Behind it often lies the politely

suppressed question—are enough of the existing teachers good enough? When a parent asks this question, he usually means "is the teacher's discipline good?"; or, "do the children get their 11 plus (or G.C.E.)?" The first question is in any event fundamental; the second no less so if it is interpreted to cover the necessity for developing every child's latent ability. Teachers themselves would wish to add further items for self-examination. They would, for instance, want to know how much a teacher knows of the background and progress of every boy or girl in the class, and not only of the bright or troublesome ones. Teachers need this individual knowledge to be able to teach effectively; they need it still more to be able to help boys and girls to grow up into the strengths they have in them and to circumvent and finally to discard the weaknesses that lie beside those strengths within the human personality. This knowledge cannot be gained, or this help given, if a teacher sees his pupils during lessons only. He must get to know them also when they are relaxed and should not be expected to be on their best behaviour. It takes all sorts to make a good staff. Let us take two extreme types. At the one end, there is the slightly aloof, rather astringent man or woman who never plays to the gallery, rarely unbends, is never content to accept shoddy work and, it is implicit in the character, is scrupulously just. Blame from such a teacher is accepted as deserved; praise is treasured as worth having. The standards set in such a teacher's classroom are not easily forgotten. At the other end of the scale are the teachers whose presence is welcomed on many occasions out of school hours. Without them, societies and games would not flourish, plays would not be produced nor music made. It is with them that boys and girls learn the self-discipline and pleasure that come from the voluntary completion of a self-appointed task. It is they who seem to their pupils to understand what boys and girls are really like. It would be a poor staff which did not contain teachers with whom their pupils like to be, even when they need not be.

627. Both types, and all the intervening kinds, of good teachers have this in common—an integrity and a humility in their work which clearly puts their pupils' interests before their own. Whatever reasons may have brought them to teaching—and they are surprisingly various—they will before long find their chief satisfaction in what happens to their pupils. It would be a mistake to suppose that the pupils have no sense of this. At school it may mainly take the disconcerting negative form of quickness in detecting sentiments that do not ring true, but in later years it is surprising to find how many men and women (and often still more surprising to find which men and women) realise that it was these men of little showing who " . . . . . with toil of their Today Bought for us Tomorrow". A good teacher

needs, too, another form of integrity—an intellectual integrity that neither the dilettante nor the cynic possesses, but which marks the man who has honestly fought his way through to a philosophy of life which he would like his pupils to share, but which he is determined they must not accept on his authority or for any other reason than a genuine conviction of its worth after considering all that can be said against it.

628. But integrity and humility are not enough. There must also be maturity and strength. Maturity—a good teacher must be a grown man, not an arrested adolescent. He must have a life of his own as well as the life he shares with his pupils. Strength—first of all, that curious combination of qualities which makes a group of boys and girls obedient (as they will enjoy being) instead of disobedient (which they will try to be). And the good teacher needs another kind of strength. He needs competence in what he teaches. If he is not master of his subject, his pupils will not feel any confidence that he could, had he wanted, have held just as good a position in the world outside the school as in it. And that feeling of confidence is a matter of importance to boys and girls as they get near the stage when they are ready to leave school, which was once their world, and begin to fix their eyes on the world of employment to which they are going. Auburn's children no doubt felt an added respect for their schoolmaster because "the village all declared how much he knew".

629. It is an exacting picture we have drawn of the qualities required of a good teacher. Are we asking too much? Can we really expect the 300,000th teacher to have all these qualities? Of course not. Let it be granted that the best teachers are born teachers who would not be happy doing anything else. They are, and will always be, few in number. We are more concerned with good teachers, of whom we may hope to secure enough, for good teachers can be made. Two things are necessary. There must be a supply of men and women of the right level of education and type of personality, and their introduction to teaching must take place under favourable conditions both while they are training and in their first year of teaching. As far as personality is concerned, there is no need to complain about the young people now coming forward—the only justifiable criticism (and it is one that time cures) is that they are too young. On the score of their own educational standards, there has been more room for doubt. The recruitment of graduates in recent years has been disappointing in quality. The students in training colleges have often had too low a standard of general education both when they entered and when they left. The three-year course should help here. A more widely justified complaint, however, has been about the conditions in their first jobs. The schools which are most difficult to teach in are generally the

schools which have most vacancies for teachers. They are the schools to which too many new teachers go. It can be a kill-or-cure initiation. The pupils are unsettled; and neither the head nor anyone else on the staff has any opportunity to train the newcomer properly. Two at least of the reasons why some schools are difficult to teach in are large classes and a heavy turn-over of staff. Both are associated with the general shortage of teachers. An increase in the quantity of teachers would mean an increase in the quality of new teachers, since they could be better trained.

630. An increase in the quantity of teachers would also mean a decrease in the number of pupils who today are badly taught even by good, even by first-rate, teachers. We shall never make the best of the country's talent as long as it is possible for a child to sit quietly unobserved in the middle of a large class attracting neither much praise nor much blame. The larger the class, the more certain it is that there will be some such. In many schools, the most profitable way to an improvement in the quality of teaching lies through an increase in the size of the staff. There is another way, too, in which the quality of education in some schools today is defective through lack of sufficient teachers. Whole subjects may be omitted, or aspects of them cut out, because there is nobody competent to teach them. The housecraft room or workshop may be empty; the gymnastic apparatus unused; physics and chemistry untaught because, although there may be enough teachers in the school, and even enough good teachers, there is none qualified in these subjects. There are, too, the really backward children, who, in a good many schools, must tail along at the bottom of a class for lack of enough teachers to take them separately or—what is quite as important—enough teachers with the right experience and skill for this particular work. We make no apology, then, for the fact that our approach to the problem of teachers must necessarily be a quantitative one.

631. But, if the quality of education in a good many secondary schools suffers from the lack of teachers with specialist qualifications, it is also true that the diversification of the curriculum as boys and girls grow older, and the contrast between the work of teachers at different stages of education, gives us ground for hope. We come back to the 300,000th teacher. Out of each annual intake of 15,000 or 16,000 teachers will there not be such a tail that it would be better to be content with fewer teachers and a shorter educational programme? We should be tempted to agree if all teachers were doing the same job and had to have the same sort of qualifications, but that is not the case. What good teachers have in common—and it is quite an essential quality—is a real personal interest in the boys and girls they teach and in their progress towards maturity. But the jobs they do differ

greatly and require very different other qualities and interests. For this reason it is more realistic (and also more encouraging) to talk about the 900th new housecraft teacher, or the 3,000th new infant teacher, or the 100th new classical graduate than about the 16,000th new teacher. We really have to think in terms of recruiting a few large and many small groups of differently qualified people. This has always been true. It will, we hope, be true in an even more important sense in future. The extensions to the educational system that we recommend are extensions at its upper end where the curriculum is already more diversified than in earlier years, and must become even more so. More teachers will be needed with really professional skills and with active interests in a wide variety of the occupations to which their pupils will go. There is no reason to suppose that people with these practical skills are any less interested in young people than others whose interests have been in line with the normal school curriculum. There just has not in the past been sufficient opportunity to teach the things that interest them, and so they have not become teachers.

NUMBERS AND RATIOS

632. What are the facts about the present position? The number of full-time teachers in England and Wales in 1958 was 319,000, about 100,000 more than in 1947. This total excludes teachers in universities. It includes not only maintained schools but independent schools (whether recognised as efficient or not) and also the staffs of training colleges and establishments of further education. Out of the 258,000 in maintained schools nearly 6,000 (2·3 per cent) were not qualified teachers. The distribution of the teachers among these various institutions is shown in Table 72 on the following page; the same data are also presented visually in Chart 21 on page 433. Half the teachers are employed in primary schools, where there is rightly a preponderance of women because of the young age of the children. It is this which accounts for the fact that in the schools as a whole there are three women teachers for every two men, so that teaching appears to be predominantly a women's profession. In those parts of it, however, with which we have been principally concerned in this report—the secondary schools and establishments of further education—the proportions are reversed. There are roughly three men to every two women teachers; while, in further education by itself, 85 per cent of the full-time teachers are men. We quote these proportions not because we think they necessarily represent a satisfactory state of affairs, but because it is important to realise what the present position is.

633. About 22 per cent of all teachers are graduates or have equivalent qualifications. The total of 69,000 graduates is some 25,000

Table 72. Distribution of Full-time Teachers by the Type of Institution in which they teach, 1958 (England and Wales).

Type of Institution	Numbers of Teachers (000)		
	Graduate*	Non-Graduate	Total
Primary	6	143	149
Secondary—			
Modern	11	51	62
Grammar	29	8	37
Technical	2	3	5
Other	2	3	5
Independent Efficient†	10	9	19
Other Independent†	—	— 13**	13
Further Education	6	9	15
Training Colleges	1	1	2
Miscellaneous	2	10	12
Total	69	237 13	319

* There are about 4,500 teachers who, though not holding a university degree, are classified as graduates for salary purposes on the strength of their professional qualifications. In the Table they are counted as non-graduates.
† These schools include pupils of both primary and secondary age.
** Division between graduates and non-graduates not known.

more than it was in 1947. About half the graduates are in secondary grammar schools or in independent schools giving the same kind of education. There are three men graduates to every two women, but it is important to remember that a much higher proportion of women graduates than of men become teachers, since only about a quarter of the students entering the universities each year are women.

634. It is clear that 319,000 teachers—great though that figure is—are not now sufficient to provide tolerable conditions in all districts and in all subjects. For this reason we insisted in Chapter 15 that, when the school-leaving age is raised to 16, there must be enough teachers to prevent the staffing ratio in secondary schools from deteriorating beyond 1 to 17 or 1 to 19 (the present figure is 1 to 21). There are wide variations in staffing ratios from school to school. For instance 900,000 out of the 2·3 million pupils in maintained secondary schools pupils are already in schools with staffing ratios of this magnitude. But 500,000 of these pupils were in grammar schools, and grammar schools owe their relatively good staffing ratios to the number of older pupils doing advanced work for whom smaller

CHART No. 21

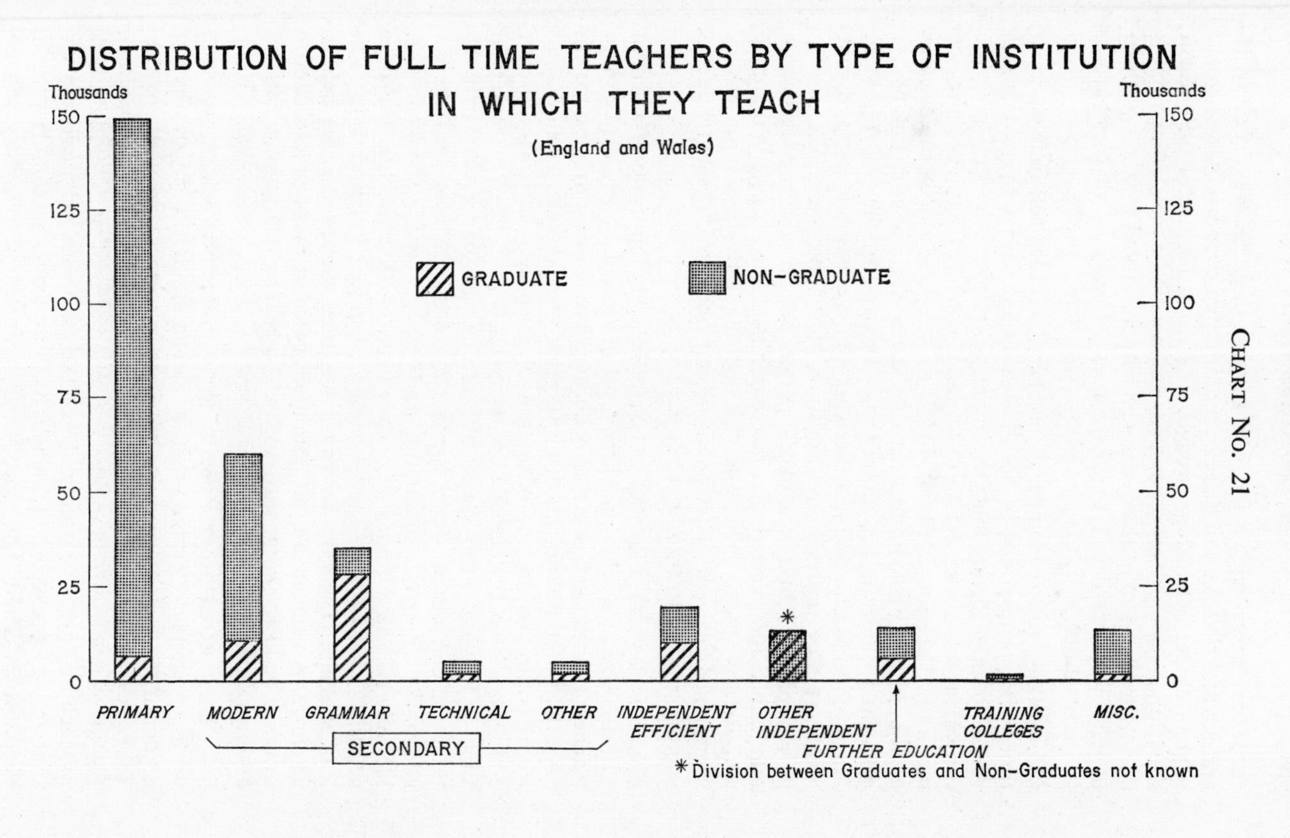
DISTRIBUTION OF FULL TIME TEACHERS BY TYPE OF INSTITUTION IN WHICH THEY TEACH
(England and Wales)
GRADUATE
NON-GRADUATE
Thousands
150
125
100
75
50
25
0
PRIMARY
MODERN
GRAMMAR
TECHNICAL
OTHER
SECONDARY
INDEPENDENT EFFICIENT
OTHER INDEPENDENT
FURTHER EDUCATION
TRAINING COLLEGES
MISC.
*
* Division between Graduates and Non-Graduates not known

classes are necessary. As the total number of pupils staying on to 16 and beyond rises, so will there be a more than proportionate increase in the number of teachers needed. The worst feature of the present situation is the number of pupils in schools where the staffing ratio is decidedly worse than the average. There are about 130,000 of them in schools where it is 1 to 26 or worse. Nearly all of these are in modern schools.

635. Staffing ratios include all teachers, whether full-time or part-time, whether qualified or not. The use made of part-time teachers varies greatly throughout the country. Altogether they give the equivalent of about 6,500 full-time teachers. The figure for the maintained schools is about 4,000. In the three northern divisions of the Ministry of Education they represent an addition of 1·7 per cent to the number of full-time teachers; in the Metropolitan, Eastern and Midland Divisions (where most use is made of part-time teachers) they represent an addition of 3·5 per cent. We saw in paragraph 632 that a little over 2 per cent of all full-time teachers in maintained and assisted schools are unqualified. Once again there are considerable local variations. In one big industrial county they represent 4 per cent of the total—about one-third of them students waiting to get into training colleges.

636. It is easy for a layman to confuse the staffing ratio of a school with the size of its classes. There must in secondary schools be more teachers than classes, principally because smaller teaching groups are essential for some subjects at all stages of the secondary school, and for all subjects at the top of the school. Any secondary class of over 30 pupils is officially classified as oversize. On this basis there were in 1958 in England over 38,000 oversize classes—more than half the total number. Let us accept the fact that some of these are only just above the approved maximum and apply a more stringent test. Nobody will deny that a secondary class of 36 is too big. But over a fifth (21 per cent) of the secondary classes in England were of at least that size. The story as regards regional variations is depicted in Table 73. A teacher in the Midlands is twice as likely as a teacher in London or in the south-east to find himself in charge of a class of 36 boys or girls.

637. There is one other aspect of the shortage of teachers, to which we have already referred. We have had something to say in Chapter 23 about the lack of graduate teachers in science and mathematics. There is quite as acute a shortage in many of the practical subjects. Enquiries made in 1958 showed 400 school workshops closed for lack of teachers. In 1955 a survey of 3,500 schools with girl pupils showed that only 11 per cent had teachers with a recognised qualification in needlework. There are some 4,000 maintained secondary schools

Table 73. Percentages of Secondary School Classes with 36 or more Pupils, by Ministry of Education Divisions (England), 1958.

Division	Percentage of Secondary classes with 36 or more pupils
Northern	*18*
East and West Ridings	*21*
North Midland	*18*
Eastern	*21*
Metropolitan (London and Middlesex)	*13*
South-Eastern	*14*
Southern	*18*
South-Western	*16*
Midland	*28*
North-Western	*15*

which are either girls' schools or co-educational, but there are only 1,600 to 1,700 women teachers who are fully qualified for physical education. And so we could go on. There is no doubt that regional variations would be as marked in this field as in the over-all picture. We have a long way to go before we can claim to be giving everywhere a full secondary education. We look to the introduction of three-year teacher training as a means of seeing that some of these specialist gaps are filled. What could not be done with two years is in many fields perfectly possible in three, provided that the opportunity is taken (as it surely should be) to recruit selectively for appropriate courses.

SOURCES OF SUPPLY: 1. THE TRAINING COLLEGES

638. We have sketched a gloomy picture. It was necessary to do so, for the facts in many places are grim. But how long need it remain a dark one? We turn from demand to supply. There are two main sources of supply of teachers, the training colleges and the universities. Both draw their students mainly from the grammar schools. Recruitment of teachers who have spent part at least of their secondary education in other types of school is, however, growing, and we should like to see it further developed. It is usually clear enough in a Sixth Form which pupils are possible university candidates and which ought to aim at a training college. There is, however, some overlapping. A number of candidates who eventually go to training colleges were serious applicants for university places and some of equal calibre always intended to go to a training college. The education of future training college students while they are still at school is discussed in Chapter 27.

639. There is also a good deal of overlapping—and with three-year training we hope there will be more—in the kind of schools in which they take up teaching. The primary schools are, as Table 72 showed, staffed almost entirely by teachers educated in training colleges, and

this no doubt will substantially continue. In the secondary field, virtually all physical education specialists, housecraft and handicraft teachers are college-trained (as distinct from university-trained). With these exceptions, the grammar schools have been almost entirely staffed by graduates (or teachers with equivalent status e.g. in music or art), and the modern schools substantially by college-trained teachers. The modern schools need more graduates and are beginning to attract them straight from the universities. The grammar schools could pretty certainly do with some college-trained general teachers, provided that the three-year course does in fact produce teachers with a sufficient competence in one or two subjects to be able to lay sound foundations for more advanced work. Recent developments in science courses in training colleges have been encouraging in this respect.

640. Nevertheless, in spite of this developing tendency to an overlap both in their recruitment and in the employment they find, the problems presented by the two sources of supply are different. In the training colleges at present the general picture is that the demand for places exceeds the supply. There are exceptions (especially in the housecraft colleges), but it is fair to say that the present trouble is lack of opportunity for training. The Association of Teachers in Colleges and Departments of Education maintains a Clearing House which deals with applications for all training colleges (with the exception of the Roman Catholic colleges for women and specialist colleges for women for such subjects as physical education and housecraft). The registrations for the academic year 1959–60 showed 6,420 applications from men for 4,417 places—a surplus of 2,003 candidates—and 12,176 applications for women for 8,799 places—a surplus of 3,377. It would be tempting to add the two surplus figures together and say that the country could have had 5,000 more teachers in 1961 if there had been that number more places available in training colleges in the autumn of 1959. It would, however, be wrong to do this because a good many applications are from unqualified or unsuitable persons, while others are withdrawn for various reasons, among them the fact that some applicants have succeeded in obtaining a university place. But, even when allowance is made for all this, it still seems certain that the number of applications would have justified rather more places than were in fact available.

641. What are the prospects for the future? It is difficult as yet to assess the effect of the extension of two-year training to three years. Will Sixth Form pupils see it as an advantage (which we are quite sure they will find it) or as a disincentive which will make them turn to other careers with less exacting training? Although some potential candidates may be discouraged, we feel fairly confident that the number (as distinct from the proportion) of Sixth Formers who come

forward for training as teachers will continue to rise. Teaching is a satisfying career and, for women who do not go to a university, is at present an attractive one in pay as compared with others. We saw in Chapter 27 that Sixth Form general courses contain many pupils of roughly equal ability who are considering nursing, secretarial work and teaching as possible careers. Teaching is certainly not the least attractive among them from an economic standpoint. The position is more doubtful for men, but we are still inclined to think that the numbers needed can be obtained.

642. The main reason for temperate optimism is that a policy of expanding the number of places in training colleges would be working with natural forces and not against them. After a considerable period when they have been working steadily against the schools we are now in sight of a favourable conjunction. It is not always realised how big a difference ten years can make in the task of the schools. This is illustrated in Table 74, which sets out the number of boys and girls of what is now compulsory school age (5–15) who were alive in 1938, 1947 and 1958. The actual staffing ratio for 1958 in maintained primary and secondary schools combined was 1 to 26·1. Using this ratio as a basis, the table shows, first, the number of teachers who would have been required in each year to teach all the children aged 5 to 15 (and not only those in maintained schools); and, secondly, the staffing ratio which would have resulted if the number of teachers required for 1958 had been available for this purpose in 1938 and 1947.

Table 74. Number of Boys and Girls aged 5 to 15 in 1938, 1947 and 1958 and the hypothetical Number of Teachers and Staffing Ratios for the earlier Years on the Basis of the 1958 Figures. (England and Wales).

Year	Number of Boys and Girls aged 5 to 15 (000)	Number of Teachers Required to teach them on ratio of 1 to 26·1 (1958 ratio for maintained schools) (000)	Staffing Ratio if 262,000 Teachers had been available in 1938 and 1947
1938	6,054	232	1 : 23·1
1947	5,594	214	1 : 21·3
1958	6,839	262	1 : 26·1

We have been passing through a period when conditions for educational advance have been singularly unfavourable—rising aggregate numbers, headed by relatively small 18 year-old age-groups. The candidates for training college places this year and the next two years come from small age-groups, but in 1961 we enter a period of rapidly rising numbers of 18 year-olds. If we have been able throughout the lean period not only to maintain but slightly to increase the number of students entering training colleges, it seems clear that the number could be maintained, and pretty certain that it could be increased, in the years from 1961 onwards—always provided the places are there. We have been glad to observe the decisions, based upon the advice of the National Advisory Council on the Training and Supply of Teachers, to increase the number of places in training colleges. But these steps were not designed to make provision for any further advances in the educational system such as we propose in this report—notably the raising of the school-leaving age. We therefore recommend that the National Advisory Council should now be invited to consider as a matter of urgency the further steps that will be necessary. We are approaching a period when recruiting conditions ought to be favourable, which will be followed by a period when the aggregate number of children of school age will be lower—a favourable period for raising the school age. "We must take the current when it serves, or lose our ventures".

SOURCES OF SUPPLY: 2. THE UNIVERSITIES

643. Our main anxiety about the supply of teachers through the training colleges is the possible lack of opportunity for training. Our main anxiety about the supply of graduates is the lack of desire to enter the profession. The position is difficult in all subjects (especially where women are concerned) and particularly so in mathematics and science. We do not want men and women who become teachers because they could not get any other job. Teaching now compares well in pay with other careers open to boys and girls of 18 who are not going to the university, but it does not now rank anything like so highly among the openings available to graduates. They need a good deal of convincing before they consider taking it up. It is the only career, after all, which they have seen stripped of its glamour. They know the difficulties a teacher experiences—they have helped to create them. As yet, the satisfactions that teaching can give must be unknown. It is, apparently, nobody's business to put the positive case for teaching before students in their university years. Those of our number who are concerned with recruiting at the university for industry report that they have to meet heavy and organised competition from almost every alternative calling, except teaching. We are not aware of any campaign to persuade young men and women to take up teaching that is as assiduous and effective as the efforts made to recruit, for example, engineers. A recruiting campaign should not be confused with a jeremiad—complaints of lack of teachers and of poor teachers are audible enough, but they serve to repel rather than to attract recruits. There is a clear need for a national campaign under

the highest auspices to convince young people of the challenge and opportunities which teaching offers, and of its place as one of the most important agents of social and individual progress. It is not only the young people who need convincing. It is essential that teaching should be as highly regarded in society as any of the professions—it cannot give this standing to itself.

644. What would a recruiting campaign for teachers, particularly as directed to university students, have to offer? A good teacher is interested in learning. He is a man or woman who is still interested in developing his own knowledge of his subject after his formal education in it stops. He is the sort of man who will not be content to put it on one side, keeping it only as a leisure time interest (if that) as he turns to real work. He is determined that it shall be his work. The historian, the classic, the French scholar with a true passion for his subject, is more likely to be able to satisfy it by becoming a teacher than in any other way. This has not been true in recent years of mathematicians and scientists. Teaching has not presented itself to them in any great numbers as the obvious thing for them to do. They have to be shown (and can be shown) that it is at least one obvious thing to do, and one which has many advantages if their interest in their subject is on a broad front. This explanation is important, and we are by no means sure that it is being sufficiently given at present. Scientists and mathematicians need to be satisfied that the conditions under which they will live and work in a school, though very different from those which prevail in other types of employment open to them, are more satisfactory in some ways and for some purposes.

645. Besides the born teachers whom no one can keep out, we need those men and women who are brought into teaching because they are interested in their subjects. Does teaching offer all the inducements it could, and should, to men and women with this desire? We repeat what we said in an earlier chapter. Opportunities for private study, for writing, for contact through professional associations with others whose interests lie in the same field, for travel and for acquiring such tools of one's trade as books or scientific apparatus—these are attractions which teaching can offer to the men and women it seeks to recruit and in which it can, and should, compete with other possible employers. We doubt if it does so at present in sufficient measure; and we are by no means sure that individual teachers and individual schools are left that freedom from tiresome minor restrictions that professional men in other occupations expect. It is no good having a recruiting campaign for highly qualified teachers based on false promises.

646. Nor can any recruiting campaign, however well organised and energetically pressed, be expected to achieve much success if the

material rewards of teaching for a graduate are noticeably lower, all things considered, than those of other careers that are equally open to him. The great difference between the university graduate and the student leaving a training college is that there is severe competition from many quarters to secure the services of the former, and that it is therefore necessary to offer much more pay to get him into teaching.

EMERGENCY MEASURES

647. In the long run the schools will not be able to get the graduates they need without an expansion of the universities. But the crisis in the schools is here and now. For years past, the passage through the schools of the very large number of children born just after the end of the last war has obsessed administrators, exhausted teachers and penalised each individual pupil. In a few years, what has been education's biggest handicap will become education's biggest opportunity. Each year from now on will, however, also see an increasing pressure on those whose job it is to teach those older boys and girls who will themselves become teachers. If the job is to be well done, there will have to be a marked increase in the number of graduate teachers with good honours degrees. We saw in Chapter 23 how distorted is the age structure of the teaching profession as far as men and women with first-class honours degrees are concerned. At a time when there are more Sixth Formers with more varied interests than ever before to teach, there is a serious risk that there will be fewer teachers really qualified to teach them. What can be done to reduce the risk? Three steps seem possible.

648. The first step immediately open seems to us to be in the universities. The number of university places in the years immediately ahead is already determined—the problem is to recruit a greater proportion of teachers from among the undergraduates who entered the universities this year, last year, and the year before. There may well be a temporary opportunity of a kind which we had forgotten could exist. There are some indications, we are told, that in a number of industries the demand for scientifically trained recruits has passed for the time being from the stage when new developments were having to be staffed from the beginning to the stage when little more than normal wastage has to be met. However this may be, there has undoubtedly been a small increase recently in the number of men with first-class honours degrees in science and mathematics who are becoming teachers. It seems to us extremely doubtful whether this favourable moment will last; this makes it necessary not to delay the recruiting campaign we recommend. Now is the time to launch it, with real force behind it.

649. The second possible step is to encourage short-service recruitment of various types. It would make all the difference in the world to the girls' schools and to the co-educational schools with Sixth Forms if it were possible to bring back to their staffs a good many of the married women who have left them in recent years, and to bring in men and women from other occupations. There is both a long-term and a short-term aspect of this problem. Women teachers as a group will always have a shorter expectation of teaching life than men because of the claims of marriage and bringing up a family; but, of all the professions open to women, teaching is the easiest to reconcile with these needs. It is important that the internal organisation of the schools and the conditions of service (full-time and part-time) should be carefully scrutinised to make sure that full advantage is taken of the possibilities. The short-term problem is to secure the return for a period of five to ten years of sufficient graduate specialists to make sure that we do not lose through lack of teachers the promise of the immediate future. The armed forces have short-service commissions for young men to meet some of their special needs; might not education have a financially attractive short-service scheme to meet the present great need and surpassing opportunity in Sixth Forms? The main untapped resources are no doubt of women teachers, but we believe that there are also men who might be available. There are already some very late entrants to the profession whose work has enabled them to keep their specialist knowledge fresh. More might be brought in for a limited period of years if the financial conditions were suitable and the possibility brought to their notice. Teaching has also always recruited a fair number of young men who never intend to make it their life work, but who want to teach for a limited period of time. May there not be room for expansion here?

650. There is a third immediate step that could be taken. There is no possible, or at least tolerable, delegation of the tiresome, routine, yet exacting task of correcting exercises and essays. Unless the teacher knows the individual mistakes that particular pupils make, unless (at the top of the school) he can study the whole "form" of his pupils, he cannot teach well. Teacher's assistants are not really a possibility. But there is no reason why teachers should not be freed of a good deal of clerical and routine work that could be better done by others. It is a wrong use of a teacher's time to employ him on secretarial work—there has been a considerable increase in the amount of secretarial help available to headmasters, but we doubt if any serious study has been made of the extent to which it could lighten the load of all teachers. Teachers of those subjects which use a great deal of apparatus and materials can be helped in other more direct ways. There is a well-recognised case for laboratory technicians; there is a strong

case for non-teaching assistants in craft shops, school gardens, art rooms and libraries. A realistic study of possible ancillary services of all kinds to save the teacher's scarcer skill would be well worth while.

651. The immediate steps we have been listing are not only, of course, applicable to grammar schools and their Sixth Forms but to all schools. The crisis is not only one of the Sixth Forms—though in its bearing on the supply of future teachers it is most acute there. In all other respects it is at least as serious in modern schools.

652. The conditions which govern the supply of teachers for technical colleges differ in a good many respects from those which affect schools, and in some ways they make the problem more difficult. There is, for instance, no regular school-college-school sequence, because a fair amount of industrial, professional or research experience is expected of candidates for teaching posts in technical colleges. There are obvious personal disadvantages in the fact that so many teachers in schools have no experience of anything else but education, but it does at least simplify the problem of recruitment. There are obvious advantages in the technical college teacher's wider experience (provided that it was reasonably successful experience), but there is always the risk that the more successful in industry are the less willing to come out of it. The greater age of entry also brings its own problems of recognition of previous experience for pension and salary purposes. There are special features, too, of the technical college teacher's life which distinguish it from the schoolmaster's. His actual teaching hours are spread over a much longer period of time each week, and may well in future be spread also over a larger portion of the year. It is every bit as important for him to know his students personally, but it is a good deal more difficult because so much of his work lies with students who attend only one day a week. This infrequency of contact is experienced in schools only by specialist teachers of subjects which have a minimum time allocation, and it is recognised by their colleagues as one of the greatest possible handicaps. In technical colleges, however, it is not the exception but the rule, and the rarity of contact in teaching cannot be supplemented or corrected by more frequent "out-of-school" meetings. If further education is to develop in the way we would desire for those aged between 15 and 18, it will be necessary to contrive a staffing policy which will confront and overcome these difficulties.

CHANGING TASKS AND THEIR CONSEQUENCES

653. Technical colleges, county colleges, Youth Service—each of these aspects of teaching has its own special problems of recruitment and training, but they also share in the difficulties and opportunities of

the general situation as we have sketched it. In our view there is also a good deal of room for overlapping functions. As school education extends upwards for more and more boys and girls, it will develop new subjects and require a higher proportion of more specialised teachers than formerly. It will, we believe, be necessary to review with great care the whole procedure for training teachers, including the role of the university departments of education. We shall almost certainly need new types of training colleges, considerably more overlap than there is at present between training for those who are going to teach in schools and in further education, and a considerably wider age-range of recruitment, especially for certain types of teachers. In addition to the residential college, often in a country area, which will always have a place in the system, there is room for more day training colleges like those in Manchester and Leeds which appeal to people with family commitments.

654. Since teachers are not freely interchangeable, but are effective only over a relatively narrow range of subjects, or able to teach well children of a comparatively restricted age range, it is likely that not only their training, but their conditions of employment should be varied and less uniform than at present. We think, as we have already said, that the technical colleges may have to diverge from the traditional academic year just as their teaching "day" is already spread over a greater number of hours than the schoolmaster's. We have suggested that the pattern of attendance and teaching that suits the young child, or the grammar school pupil with a stiff homework assignment, may need more modification than we have yet given it when 15 year-old boys and girls of a non-academic kind are concerned. This will involve a reconsideration of the teacher's conditions of work. There will be other instances. Similarly it will, we believe, be necessary to look not only at the terms of employment of one type of teacher in relation to other types of teacher, but of one kind of specialist—a craftsman or a scientist for instance—when employed in teaching and in industry. None of this re-assessment is easy, but we believe it to be necessary.

655. In the last resort we shall get the teachers we deserve. If ordinary people have a high regard for teachers and for what they stand for, they will be willing to encourage their children to take up this work. If, on the other hand, teaching is not ranked high, it will not attract recruits of good quality. Our present large teaching force is, in part at least, still the product of a situation when teaching represented an easy, and to a girl often the only, way out of what was then the precarious and lowly regarded status of the weekly wage-earner. That, fortunately, is no longer true. Teachers have by their own efforts helped to create the conditions in which teaching has to compete hard

for recruits. Never before has there been such a widespread interest in and demand for education. Public opinion is in favour of it. It has moved to the centre of politics. But the teacher is probably less highly regarded in large sections of society than he was. We must try to find out why this has come about and how it can be corrected. Part at least of the remedy must lie in the schools themselves. If our emphasis in education is unduly placed on its economic advantages, it betrays its own cause. The teacher should be a lover of learning for its own sake and of people in and for themselves. He usually is. He must see to it that he commends the goods he deals in for their inherent worth and not merely for their cash value. And this is just as true of science and of technology as of the humanities.

656. We have spoken of the bad areas in which inadequate staffing is endemic. There are perhaps not many areas where the conditions are really bad. But where they are, the results are disastrous. These areas —and that means the children of these areas—pay much more than their fair share of the price for a shortage of teachers. They suffer badly even when the shortage, in the country as a whole, is a small one. One way to solve the numerical problem of finding teachers for the schools in these bad areas would doubtless be to train more and more teachers until men and women were driven to these areas to find employment. The present quota system is intended to operate in a similar manner. We do not like relying, as a matter of policy, on the compulsion of unemployment. Nor can it ever provide any solution to the qualitative problems of the bad areas. We think their necessities will have to be tackled more directly. It would be of help to find out, by experiment, whether the unattractiveness (in teachers' eyes) of these areas could be got over by financial inducements, the provision of housing and the like. If this were once established, it would be reasonable to ask whether empowering the authorities concerned to offer such inducements was really as contrary to public policy as is today commonly believed. In any case, we suggest that any teachers recruited by the emergency measures outlined above, especially by the short-service engagements suggested in paragraph 649, should be enrolled first for service in the areas where they are wanted most.

657. We cannot close this chapter, or our report, without reiterating our belief that the nation's welfare depends now more than ever on the quality of its teachers. We need our children to be brought up by men and women who are good people, good teachers and good at the things they teach. It is as simple as that, and as difficult. Those of us who have had the good fortune to be taught by such people know that it is worth any sacrifice to secure it for our children.

SUMMARY OF CONCLUSIONS

658. The conclusions of this chapter can be summarised as follows:—

(*a*) An increased supply of teachers will be needed both because of the additional duties that are to be put on the schools, by the raising of the school-leaving age and otherwise, and also because of the necessity to improve the quality of the work that is already being done by the schools (especially by reducing the size of classes). These two demands are not in competition with each other, as a longer average school life will produce more candidates for training as teachers.

(*b*) The good teacher needs a range of qualities that are not easily come by. But the problem of quality should properly be analysed into its parts, since what appears as a global demand is in fact the aggregation of a number of particular demands for different kinds of teachers.

(*c*) Staffing ratios are still a long way from what is desirable, and there are too many overlarge classes. There is also considerable variation between different parts of the country.

(*d*) There are two principal sources of supply of teachers—the training colleges and the universities. Although there is considerable overlapping between them, both as to the candidates they recruit and the varieties of posts taken up in the schools, the problems of the two sources of supply are largely distinct.

(*e*) In the case of the supply of the college-trained teachers, the main difficulty is the number of places in the training colleges. There is little doubt that the number of qualified entrants could be increased, especially in the years just ahead, when the "bulge" will reach the age of 18. We recommend that the National Advisory Council on the Training and Supply of Teachers should be asked to advise on the additional number of teachers that will be required to raise the school-leaving age, and on the further measures—additional to those that have been announced in recent months—that will be necessary to supply the number of college-trained teachers required. Special attention might be paid to seeing that training arrangements are sufficiently flexible to meet the needs of older men and women who are attracted to teaching as a career.

(*f*) In the case of graduates, the chief difficulty in increasing the supply is the inadequate numbers, especially of the graduates with higher qualifications, who evince any desire to enter the profession of teaching. There should be an energetic campaign to explain the attractions to a university graduate of a teaching career. This is the more necessary because of the recruitment campaigns set on foot by a wide range of other callings. No campaign, however, will succeed unless the material rewards of teaching compare favourably with those of other professions open to the graduate.

(*g*) Married women not only now play a large part in teaching of all kinds, but have a specific contribution of their own to make. Attention should be paid to seeing that the terms and conditions of their employment are such as to attract the large numbers needed.

(*h*) Emergency measures to be considered, apart from a prompt start with the recruitment campaign, should be the institution of short-service engagements, and a sustained effort to economise teaching capacity by relieving teachers of clerical and routine tasks.

(*i*) There are special difficulties which affect both the recruitment and the effective use of teachers in technical colleges. Among them are the need for prior industrial or other non-educational experience, and the infrequency with which a teacher sees each of the very large number of students he teaches.

(*j*) There should be more variety of conditions of employment for teachers. They are not a homogeneous body and will become less so with the growth in the upper forms of schools, which have a wide range of specialist requirements. This tendency will be increased with the advent of county colleges and other specialist institutions.

(*k*) The bad areas, which pay much more than their fair share of the price for a shortage of teachers, need a direct attack upon their problem. There should be an attempt to discover by experiment whether financial incentives to teachers to serve in difficult areas would be effective.

CHAPTER 38

Summary of Principal Conclusions and Recommendations

659. Several of the more important of the foregoing chapters have concluded with summaries of the recommendations for action contained in them. In this chapter we repeat these, adding some summary of the argument of the other chapters.

PART ONE. EDUCATION IN A CHANGING WORLD

660. *Chapter 1. Sixty Years of Growth*

(*a*) In 1894 it is probable that 4 per cent of all boys and girls aged 14 or 15 were in school and only 1 per cent of those aged 16 and 17. It was not until 1918 that full-time education until 14 became binding on everybody. By 1938 there were roughly six times as many pupils over the age of 14 as in 1894.

(*b*) About two-fifths of all boys and girls aged 15 to 17 inclusive get education either full-time or for one day a week. The proportions of boys and of girls getting full-time education are about the same, but only 6 per cent of the girls (compared with 22 per cent of the boys) get day release.

(*c*) Part-time education by day did not begin to develop on a large scale until the end of the last war.

661. *Chapter 2. The Pattern of Secondary Education*

(*a*) There are over 2,550,000 boys and girls in maintained secondary schools; only 320,000 of them are aged 15 or over.

(*b*) Most pupils of secondary school age are in modern schools, the successors to the old senior elementary schools. The course that most pupils take is now between three and four years in duration instead of between two and three as it was until 1947.

(*c*) About half the modern schools and under 30 per cent of the grammar schools are co-educational. A varied national provision, however, does not ensure varied local opportunities.

(*d*) Fee-paying in maintained grammar schools was abolished by the Education Act of 1944 which rounded off a process already well advanced. By 1938 the majority of pupils admitted to secondary schools paid no fees.

(*e*) Secondary Technical Schools have been created since 1944 out of the old, more restricted, Junior Technical schools, but over 40 per cent of the local education authorities have no technical schools. In much of England the "tripartite" system of grammar, technical and modern schools has never come into existence.

(*f*) New types of secondary schools are being developed in many districts to provide within the same institution for pupils of the whole range of ability. In 1956 they provided for some 2 per cent of the pupils in maintained secondary schools; in 1959 for 6 per cent; the Association of Chief Education Officers estimate that by 1965 they may well contain 11 per cent.

662. *Chapter 3. Population Changes and their Educational Consequences*

(*a*) It seems clear that most families can now support their children throughout a longer school education than would formerly have been practicable. This is a consequence of earlier marriage, earlier child-bearing within marriage, smaller families, longer expectation of life and more opportunities of paid employment for married women.

(*b*) But there is evidence that children in unusually large families are less likely to get a long education than other children.

(*c*) Child-bearing and child-care now represent a break in employment for married women rather than an end to it. This has important consequences for teaching as well as other careers. It points to the need for an education which encourages girls to qualify before marriage for careers and to develop interests which they can resume in later life.

(*d*) The early age of marriage points to a radically different concept of how girls of this age should be treated and educated. Over 4 per cent of the girls with whom this report is concerned are married women.

663. *Chapter 4. Changing Social Needs*

(*a*) If the family is to be as secure in the future as it has been in the past (and we can be content with nothing less), there will have to be a conscious effort to prepare the way for it through the educational system on a much greater scale than has yet been envisaged.

(*b*) The problem of sexual ethics is wider than marriage. Young people enjoy a freedom of unsupervised association which is quite new and brings both gain and loss. At the same time there is much public indecision over what is right and wrong. Disaster often results for the young.

(*c*) Juvenile delinquency and other social problems are especially marked in certain areas in which, more even than elsewhere, the teacher has to be a social worker. A quick turnover of teachers is to be especially avoided in these areas, but is commonly to be found in them.

(*d*) The fact that the peak age for juvenile delinquency is the last year at school suggests that more thought ought to be given to the conditions of boys' and girls' life, both in and out of school, during the last year or so before they reach the leaving age.

(*e*) Teen-agers are especially exposed to the influence of the "mass media" of communication. The duty to see that this power is used responsibly is one for the whole community, but there is a specific educational responsibility to see that the young learn how to approach the mass media with discrimination.

664. *Chapter 5. The Pressure of Economic Change*

(*a*) The community is about one-third richer in material wealth than it was in 1938.

(*b*) The larger part of the rise in the national standard of consumption has been in the lower income groups—those who knew the schools twenty years ago can see the revolution in the faces of the children.

(*c*) The earnings of young people have risen faster in proportion than those of adults. Those who stay at school have to resist the lure of a high immediate wage and to reconcile themselves to a lower earning capacity, until they are over 20 years of age, than that enjoyed by those who leave at 15. But it is evident that they do then catch up and go well ahead. On balance, the effects of prosperity have been beneficial to education.

(*d*) There is a growing stress on the need for special qualifications and for a good general education to secure entry into an increasing number of occupations. This tendency may be reinforced by the fact that the proportion of young people to the whole population of working age is going to rise again after a long period of decline.

(*e*) The rapidity of technological change presents an exciting challenge for those who can qualify themselves as scientists, technologists and technicians. The numbers of these produced by the schools have risen rapidly and will continue to do so. But they will remain a minority of the working population. For the remainder, the advent of a technological age creates different needs—to be able to comprehend something of the language of science and technology; to be at home in a world of machines; and to be able to adjust to a rapidly changing environment. There may be less need in the future of "skill" in the old fashioned sense of the word; what will be needed in ever-growing volume will be the quality that can perhaps be described as "general mechanical intelligence".

665. *Chapter 6. Burdens and Benefits*

(*a*) Education can be regarded in two ways—either as a duty that the state owes to its citizens, and therefore as part of the "welfare state"; or as a means of increasing the economic efficiency of the whole community, and therefore as a form of productive national capital investment. The cost of education must therefore be compared both with the other forms of welfare expenditure and with other forms of capital investment. We have not attempted to disentangle these two purposes.

(*b*) So far as can be ascertained, expenditure on the central purposes of education in schools (as distinct from school health and nutrition programmes on the one hand and from expenditure on university and other forms of higher education on the other) has in the last twenty years been doing little more than keep up with the general expansion of the national income.

(*c*) The cost of our recommendations would not be very large when set against such other items of national capital investment as expenditure on dwellings or plant and machinery, or alternatively against such items of consumption expenditure as drink and tobacco.

PART TWO. THE DEVELOPMENT OF THE MODERN SCHOOL

666. *Chapter 7. The Demand for a Longer School Life*

(*a*) Extended courses should be made available for all modern school pupils. By 1965 we think it possible that extended courses will be needed for half the 15 year-olds, averaged over the country as a whole. This is therefore the target at which, in the absence of special circumstances, local authorities should aim.

(*b*) Wherever possible, these extended courses should be in the schools that the pupils have attended since they were 11. But special provision for transfers will have to be made for children in all-age schools and in unusually small secondary modern schools.

667. *Chapter 8. The Nature of Extended Courses and the Place of External Examinations*

(*a*) Many, probably more than half, of the pupils of the modern schools would have their education deflected from its proper lines by being prepared for an external examination. It is important that attention to the needs of the minority of abler pupils should not be allowed to lead to neglect of the interests of these boys and girls, who are and will remain by far the largest single group in the modern schools. All our other recommendations in Chapter 8 are subject to this.

(*b*) In the examinable minority, two groups can be distinguished. One of these consists of those boys and girls who have the ability to attempt some of the subjects in the G.C.E. at Ordinary level. It is important that none of them should be denied the opportunity to do so.

(*c*) There remains another group—consisting of about one-third or rather more of the pupils in modern schools over the age of 15—for whom external examinations below the level of the G.C.E. may serve a useful purpose, and official policy should be modified to recognise this.

(*d*) We are, however, impressed with the dangers of large-scale external examinations, which a national system could not avoid. External examinations should therefore develop on a regional, or preferably a local, basis. Experiments on these lines should continue for a period of about five years, and a further enquiry should be held into their results, before any decision is taken concerning the creation of a national system.

(*e*) There is also need for further experience and enquiry before a judgement can be expressed on the relative advantages of subject examinations and group examinations.

(*f*) Some of the purposes served by an external examination can also be met by a formal assessment by the school, at the time of leaving, of a pupil's performance and attainments during his whole time at the school. Irrespective of the growth of external examinations, we recommend that thought should be given to the development of a system of leaving certificates on these lines. This also, in our view, can best be organised locally or regionally, not nationally.

(*g*) There is no case, except as a temporary measure in a few localities, for an external examination at the end of the fourth year—that is, at the age of 15. Where such examinations exist, they should be purely local.

(*h*) Examinations designed for part-time students should not be taken in secondary schools.

668. *Chapter 9. The Consequences of Extended Courses for the Modern School*

(*a*) The development of extended courses means that many modern schools have at the top a group of older pupils who are there as a result of a deliberate, personal decision. Their influence in setting relatively mature and responsible standards of behaviour and of work is apparent throughout the school.

(*b*) A due proportion of special responsibility allowances should be assigned to those teachers whose work is with below-average pupils.

Authorities and governing bodies should not judge their modern schools by public examination results.

(*c*) Special arrangements are necessary for extended courses for boys and girls of below-average ability who are too immature to go out into the world at 15.

(*d*) The success of extended courses has taken place in spite of a static, and in some respects slightly worsening, staff position in modern schools as a whole.

(*e*) Nearly a third of the modern schools have an annual intake of 75 pupils or less, which will be too small to provide adequate extended courses for their older pupils. In districts where sparse population prevents bigger schools, staff must be provided on a more generous scale than normal.

(*f*) Modern schools are liable to have fewer able pupils than their predecessors because of freer access to selective schools, but (because of economic changes) they have to produce more boys and girls capable of doing jobs which require a sound basic education of an academic kind. Their success in doing so is encouraging.

PART THREE. "SECONDARY EDUCATION FOR ALL"

669. *Chapter 10. The Act of 1944*

Both the unfulfilled provisions of the Education Act of 1944 affecting older children—the raising of the school-leaving age to 16, and the creation of county colleges for compulsory part-time day education to 18—should be re-affirmed as objectives of national policy.

670. *Chapter 11. Why the School-Leaving Age should be Raised: (1) The Benefit to the Individual*

(*a*) Throughout the period, not only of physical puberty, but of emotional and social adolescence, the welfare of the individual ought to come before any marginal contribution that he or she can make to the national income.

(*b*) Many of the things that the schools can do for boys and girls can be carried much nearer completion by 16 than by 15. The secondary education for all promised in the Education Act of 1944 cannot be effectively provided unless it is continued for all to 16.

(*c*) The additional year should offer new and challenging courses and not be simply a continuation of what has gone before. These should be so devised that they satisfy the adolescent's intensified interest in the real world and recognise his rapidly growing need for independence.

671. *Chapter 12. Why the School-Leaving Age should be Raised: (2) The National Interest*

(*a*) The country is a long way from tapping all the available supply of talent by present methods—half the National Service recruits to the Army who were rated in the two highest ability groups had left school at 15.

(*b*) It is most unlikely that this waste of talent can be remedied within a reasonable period without compulsion, because leaving at 15 is so deeply embedded in certain parts of the social structure. Among National Service recruits to the Army coming from families of manual workers, two-thirds of those rated in the two highest ability groups had left school at 15.

(*c*) The part-time route, even with day release, is not an efficient substitute for longer full-time education.

(*d*) While the number staying on at school voluntarily is increasing, this trend provides only a precarious basis for a national system, and may depend to a considerable extent on the continuation of general prosperity and, in particular, a plentiful supply of good jobs for young workers.

(*e*) The demand both for more educated workers and for more deeply educated workers is growing at almost all levels in industry—raising the school-leaving age to 16 would give those near the bottom a better foundation, and would be reflected in larger numbers receiving full-time education to 18 or beyond.

(*f*) The strongest part of the case is the general need for secondary education for all to 16 extending through the difficult and important period of adolescence.

672. *Chapter 13. The Duration of Secondary School Life*

(*a*) The present system of three leaving dates in the year has unfortunate consequences for the schools.

(*b*) Educationally, the ideal would be to have only one leaving date at the end of the school year. But there are objections to fixing the operative age for a single date either at 15, or at 15½ or at 16.

(*c*) Moreover, a single leaving date is likely to create difficulties in finding employment for school leavers, especially for those most in need of help.

(*d*) We therefore recommend that there should be two dates, with those pupils whose birthdays fall in the months September to January inclusive being free to leave school at the following Easter, and the remainder in July.

(*e*) Amending legislation to fix two leaving dates should be introduced now to come into effect as soon as possible—that is, with the present leaving age of 15. It does not seem to us that this reform need wait for the passing of the "bulge" through the secondary schools.

673. *Chapter 14. School-Leaving Age or County College: The Problem of Priority*

(*a*) To provide compulsory part-time day education to 18 before the school-leaving age is raised to 16 would involve *either* providing county colleges for three years *or* confining their scope temporarily to the 16th and 17th years, whereas their eventual concern will be with the 17th and 18th years. The former course would be wasteful, the latter educationally mistaken.

(*b*) While an extra year of full-time schooling can do much to make subsequent part-time education more fruitful, the converse is not true.

(*c*) Considerably more building would be necessary for county colleges than for an extra year at school.

(*d*) We therefore recommend that the raising of the school-leaving age should have priority in time over the introduction of compulsory county colleges.

674. *Chapter 15. When the School-Leaving Age should be Raised*

(*a*) The most favourable period in sight for raising the school-leaving age is from 1965 to 1969, which lies in the valley between two peaks of numbers in the schools.

(*b*) The most important consideration (out of many) is the relationship between the numbers of additional teachers required and the prospective supply. The additional numbers required depend not only on the year chosen for raising the school-leaving age but also on the pupil-teacher ratio deemed to be acceptable. It should not be allowed to become worse than 1 to 19 in the year the leaving-age is raised.

(*c*) We recommend that the year to be chosen should be one of the three years 1966–67, 1967–68, 1968–69. Some of us would prefer the earliest of the three, some the latest.

(*d*) The year should be chosen and announced now and a programme of action set on foot to ensure that the necessary conditions are prepared.

PART FOUR. THE WAY TO COUNTY COLLEGES

675. *Chapter 16. A Majority Without Education*
Chapter 17. The Purpose of a County College
Chapter 18. The Way to County Colleges

(*a*) The Minister should re-affirm his intention to implement at the earliest possible date the provision of compulsory part-time education for all young persons of 16 and 17 who are not in full-time education. It is the widespread lack of belief in this intention which, in our view, has almost stopped the growth of all part-time release other than that which is clearly essential for technical reasons.

(*b*) We are especially concerned at the loss of contact with the least skilled and least able members of the community as soon as they leave school, and with their loss of morale. In their interests (though not only for them) we regard a strong Youth Service as an essential complement to county colleges, and we recommend that steps should be taken to develop it during the interim period.

(*c*) We are also particularly concerned at the very small volume of day release for girls and at the fact that girls appear to make less use than boys of the Youth Service after they leave school.

(*d*) There are four strands that should be woven into the curriculum of county colleges: an appreciation of the adult world in which young workers suddenly find themselves; guidance for them in working out their problems of human relations and moral standards; development of their physical and aesthetic skills; and a continuance of their basic education, with a vocational bias where appropriate. There is not as yet enough experience to show in what proportions and by what methods these elements can best be combined into a satisfactory whole.

(*e*) The success of the county college will depend to a great extent on the degree to which students feel that their employers are interested in it. A careful study of incentives from the employer's side, and from the student's angle, should be undertaken.

(*f*) We attach the highest importance to the selection and training of the right kind of staff for county colleges. We are particularly anxious to avoid a sudden, unprepared, introduction of county colleges with a staff which would have to be largely improvised.

(*g*) We also believe it to be essential that the county colleges should not be first established in makeshift accommodation.

(*h*) A number of complicated administrative problems will arise about different ways in which the over-all obligation of attendance at county colleges might be discharged: we do not think they can be satisfactorily solved by *a priori* argument without experiment.

(*i*) We do not believe that sufficient progress can be made through voluntary persuasion with securing day release for unskilled workers and for girls to make possible the introduction of compulsory attendance for all in one move.

(*j*) The nature of compulsion—compulsion both on employers to release and on workers to attend—introduces factors which cannot be studied under the present voluntary system and which call for an exploratory period of compulsion.

(*k*) For these reasons we recommend that the introduction of county colleges should be by three stages:

(i) a period starting now of intensive encouragement for the extension of day release to new classes of workers by voluntary means;

(ii) an exploratory and preparatory period, starting soon after the raising of the school-leaving age, in which compulsory county college attendance would be introduced in one or more areas of considerable size. This would require legislation and special financial arrangements. The length of this stage cannot be predicted but we should hope that it would be possible to reach decisions within five years.

(iii) The phased introduction of compulsory attendance throughout the country by a programme spreading as quickly as possible from region to region. This stage should proceed as rapidly as practical considerations permit. We think it might take three to four years.

PART FIVE. THE SIXTH FORM

676. *Chapter 19. The Ablest Boys and Girls*

(*a*) By the age of 17, only 10 per cent of the age-group is still at school. Maintained grammar schools, direct grant schools and independent schools recognised as efficient are the only types of school which at present make any appreciable numerical contribution to the total of Sixth Forms. (There will be a growing contribution in future years from the secondary technical, comprehensive and other new types of school).

(*b*) The proportion of pupils in these types of school staying on into the Sixth Form has risen sharply in recent years and will, we think, continue to rise.

(*c*) There is, however, still considerable waste of talent through early leaving from the grammar school. More boys and girls would stay on—or at least remain in full-time education through transfer to other institutions—if there were a greater variety of curriculum open to them.

677. *Chapter 20. The Approach to the Sixth Form*

(*a*) The structure of English maintained schools is still such as to make a sharp distinction between the main school and the Sixth Form.

(*b*) The maintained grammar schools play the largest part in the education of those who remain at school until 17 or 18. Nearly two-thirds of all boys and girls at school at 17 are in maintained schools.

(*c*) In planning the curriculum it is important to consider the background from which the maintained grammar school pupils come: two-thirds of them come from families where both parents left school at 14 or before.

(*d*) The time-table of the fourth and fifth years of the grammar school course is seriously congested; and yet in most schools the practical and aesthetic subjects have ceased to be really available for the abler pupils, and the time given to English subjects has been curtailed. This is an especially serious deprivation for "first generation grammar school" pupils.

(*e*) This congestion is caused by the increasing demands made upon the middle school time-table by those subjects in which a pupil is going to specialise in the Sixth Form. This downward pressure is more marked in boys' schools than in girls'.

(*f*) It results in a situation in which four-fifths of the boys have virtually chosen their Sixth Form course, if any, by the age of 13 or 14. We recommend that such revision of syllabuses and practice should be made as would prevent any doors being closed before a pupil enters the Sixth Form. In particular, we do not think that, save in the most exceptional circumstances, boys should be allowed to take the Ordinary level examination for the G.C.E. at 14.

(*g*) An effort to keep all doors open would involve particularly an examination of the position of foreign languages and science. We think that Latin and two modern foreign languages are too heavily biased a curriculum for many "first generation grammar school" pupils, and for those who are going to leave school at 16. We attach the greatest importance to a thorough and exacting linguistic discipline, but we do not think that this is properly or efficiently secured by the indirect pressure of those universities which are in a specially strong competitive position.

(*h*) We believe that a six-period science course could be devised which would enable every Fifth Former who had followed it successfully to undertake a normal Sixth Form course. "Setting" would enable the most promising pupils to go ahead more rapidly without giving up more time to science.

(*i*) The revision of present practice in middle school foreign language and science teaching should be carried to a point where it becomes possible to restore to pupils the opportunities for aesthetic subjects which they lose at present, and to give them more time for English studies.

(*j*) Though we condemn "pre-specialisation", we endorse the desire of schools to find ways of enabling their very ablest pupils to move faster than the general pace. We see no objection to measures designed to enable them to enter the Sixth Form at 15 instead of 16, provided that the reform of the middle school curriculum on the lines suggested above is carried out, and that far more serious attention is paid to non-specialist studies in the Sixth Form than is now the case.

(*k*) We also welcome ways by which particular ability in one direction can be encouraged, and draw attention to the practice of "setting" for mathematics with the possibility of carrying the work of the top set much further, and rewarding it by a pass in additional mathematics. If this system were at all widely extended, however, it would be necessary to see that the schools did not suffer from a decay of the form system.

678. *Chapter 21. The Marks of a Sixth Form*

Ideally, there are five marks that distinguish the Sixth Form or the Sixth Former. These are:—

(*a*) A close link with the university, even though not all the Sixth Formers are going there;

(*b*) Concentration on the study in depth of a relatively restricted range of subjects;

(*c*) Provision for a greatly increased amount of independent work;

(*d*) An intimate relationship between pupil and teacher, best described as "intellectual discipleship";

(*e*) The growth of social responsibility.

679. *Chapter 22. The Sixth Formers*

(*a*) The total number of boys and girls in Sixth Forms in 1958 was about 66 per cent larger than in 1947. The proportionate increase has been slightly larger among boys than girls.

(*b*) The over-all percentage of 14 year-olds in selective schools who are still there three years later has risen to about 37 per cent. It is highest in the boys' independent schools.

(*c*) The increasing numbers of Sixth Formers have been almost entirely drawn from those boys and girls who have attended selective schools for several years before the age of 15. There is, however, a small number who have transferred from modern schools, and this may be expected to grow.

(*d*) It is clear that the absolute numbers in the Sixth Forms will continue to grow and that the total in the years 1965–70 will be between 50 per cent and 100 per cent more than in 1958. Whether the proportion of the age-group will continue to rise through the "bulge" years as rapidly as hitherto is more doubtful.

680. *Chapter 23. The Staff of the Sixth Form*

(*a*) The quality of men graduate recruits to the teaching profession (as measured by the class of degree they took) has been considerably lower in the last two decades than it was in the thirties. The proportion of men with first-class degrees falls steadily as one descends the age scale, though there has been some recovery in the last few years. This means that the schools are not maintaining their intellectual capital.

(*b*) This position is worse among mathematics and science graduates than in other subjects.

(*c*) The facts about women graduates are broadly similar to those about men though in general less satisfactory—there are fewer graduates teaching, fewer with good degrees and a sharper decline in quality. The outstanding difference between men and women graduate teachers is that the average age of the women is much less.

(*d*) Sixth Forms require higher staffing ratios than lower forms. If the familiar device of doubling the numbers in the Sixth Form before working out staff ratios is used, there is not much difference to be observed among the different types of boys' schools. Among girls' schools it would appear that independent schools are particularly expensive to staff. In all types of school, the large Sixth Form is somewhat more economical to staff than the small Sixth Form.

(*e*) It is necessary to do more than is being done to attract men and women of the highest intellectual calibre into teaching.

(*f*) It is necessary to ensure that there is no unnecessary waste or extravagance in the way in which teachers capable of teaching the Sixth Form are employed.

681. *Chapter 24. The Structure of Sixth Forms*

(*a*) The rise in the number of Sixth Formers has raised the size of the average teaching group in the Sixth Forms of maintained boys' schools to an economic level; it has put the girls' maintained schools on a sound footing except in science, where the position is very unsatisfactory; the position of the co-educational maintained schools is much stronger than it was and should continue to improve.

(*b*) There remains the problem of the small grammar school in the country. It is clear that its Sixth Form is at present often an unsatisfactory unit both for teaching and for economy. Where it is essential to expand the base, we suggest that it is done either by merging the whole of two single-sex schools into one co-educational school, or by providing a common Sixth Form for two single-sex schools.

It is desirable also to develop transfers directly into the Fifth or Sixth Form from secondary modern schools. This might imply boarding provision.

(*c*) Regarded as a whole, co-educational schools provide balanced Sixth Forms which ought not to be extravagant to staff. They are, however, seriously unbalanced in the division of boys and girls between the Arts and Science Sixths.

(*d*) There is a special problem about general courses in the Sixth Form. Their rarity for boys, their commonness in girls' schools, their comparative infrequency in co-educational schools, is to be explained, but not necessarily justified, by historical reasons.

(*e*) The position of the boys' independent and direct grant schools is thoroughly sound from the structural point of view. Their Sixth Forms are big enough to provide economically a wide range of courses. The position of science, contrary to general belief, is very strong.

(*f*) The position of the girls' independent schools, as a group, is less than satisfactory for advanced work. We cannot but believe that many girls who would profit from a Sixth Form education are in schools which offer little or no prospect of one. The size and organisation of many of these schools make heavy demands on the short supply of teachers.

682. *Chapter 25. The Curriculum of the Sixth Form*

(*a*) We endorse the principle of specialisation, or study in depth.

(*b*) We are, however, unhappy about four ways in which it is now working:

(i) The syllabuses in science make considerably heavier demands than they used to do. They need reconsidering not only subject by subject, but together as the specialist curriculum of the Science Sixth.

(ii) The combination of subjects offered by pupils in the Arts Sixth is often unsatisfactory because it does not form a coherent whole.

(iii) Some schools enter pupils for too many Advanced level subjects. The number of pupils taking 4 subjects is falling, but is still too high especially in certain areas.

(iv) Between one-quarter and one-third of the school week is given to non-specialist subjects. We refer to this as "minority-time". It is often neglected or wasted. It is, however, of vital importance.

(*c*) There are two purposes for which the minority-time should be used, which we distinguish as complementary and common.

(*d*) The main common elements, which should be taken by arts and science specialists together, can be summarised under three heads—religious education and all that goes to the formation of moral standards; art and music; and physical education.

(*e*) The complementary elements should be designed to ensure the literacy of science specialists and the "numeracy" of arts specialists. By literacy in this context we mean not only the ability to use the mother tongue as an adequate means of communication for adult purposes, but also the development of moral, aesthetic and social judgement. By "numeracy" we mean not only the ability to reason quantitatively but also some understanding of scientific method and some acquaintance with the achievement of science.

(*f*) We considered, and reject, proposals to make good these deficiencies either by a "general course" or by making it normal for an arts specialist to take one science subject at Advanced level, and a science specialist one arts subject.

(*g*) The difficulty in the way of making all science specialists literate is not one of ignorance about how to do it, but of the will to see that it is done thoroughly and effectively.

(*h*) There seems to us to be no way of making the arts specialist numerate except by providing a special Sixth Form Course for this purpose. Promising experimental work has been done in this field, but much remains still to be discovered about the best means to use.

(*i*) We are not unmindful of the fact that any such course would impose an extra burden on a section of the staff that is already heavily laden and—especially in girls' schools—very scarce. Furthermore, a certain amount of re-training and refresher courses would be necessary.

(*j*) There are grave dangers in the examination of work done in "minority time", but some outside influence is probably necessary if schools and pupils are to take it more seriously than at present. The most potent influence is likely to be the knowledge that prospective employers, universities and colleges of advanced technology attach importance to it.

683. *Chapter 26. The Problem of University Entrance*

(*a*) About half the number of boys, and a far smaller proportion of girls, in Sixth Forms go to universities or the equivalent.

(*b*) Any attempt to segregate potential university candidates from others would be wrong and, indeed, impossible during most of the Sixth Form course. We believe, therefore, that—if for no other reason—the Advanced level examination for the G.C.E. should be regarded primarily as a school leaving examination designed to test the work of the past two years.

(*c*) There is a growing difference between the number of pupils "qualified" to enter a university and those "selected" to do so. For this reason, and also because some universities and some departments are preferred to others, the process of selection is heavily competitive. It is this competition that is at the root of the troubles that afflict the schools.

(*d*) It seems to us that more places for higher education will be required than are now envisaged.

(*e*) The two-year or three-year length of the nominal Sixth Form teaching course is in fact considerably reduced by the incidence of various scholarship and college or faculty examinations.

(*f*) Considerable difficulties are caused in schools by the different entrance requirements of different universities, and of different faculties and departments within them.

(*g*) We hope that the growth of colleges of advanced technology will influence Sixth Form work for good by reducing the undue stress laid at present on obtaining the maximum number of marks in three or even four Advanced level subjects.

(*h*) While it is not within our terms of reference to advise the universities on their selection methods, we report from the point of view of the effect on the schools certain conclusions we have formed:

(i) The recommendations of the Vice-Chancellors' *ad hoc* committee have improved the position, but there is still need for a more uniform, expeditious and intelligible procedure than exists at present.

(ii) The influence of Oxford and Cambridge is so universal that no system from which their colleges are excluded will remove the pressure on the schools.

(iii) The tendency to use the Advanced level papers for selection, by judging results on the basis of numerical marks, has an adverse effect on teaching in the schools. This does not, of course, apply to the use of the Advanced level for qualification.

(iv) Preferably, selection should be done by means other than another examination in the specialist subjects. But if special examinations for selection cannot be avoided, we hope that they would be common to as many universities as possible, that they would not be used for any other purpose than selection, and that they would be confined to as few papers as possible.

(v) For this, as well as for other reasons, we hope that it will become possible for members of university staffs concerned with selection to spend much more time than they can now do in getting to know the schools.

(vi) We recognise the value of the open scholarship examinations, especially those of the Oxford and Cambridge colleges. They set a standard for the specialist Sixth Form education of the ablest pupils, and they ensure that a boy should know that he can get to the university of his choice by sheer ability and hard work. At the same time they ought not in our opinion to be used for the bulk of admissions, and the maintained schools in particular need to be reassured that there are other methods open to their boys.

(*i*) The selection procedure for financial grants from local education authorities should not duplicate the universities' selection procedure in such a way as to add to the strain on candidates.

(*j*) It seems to us that the growing pressure to get into universities is forcing more and more pupils to spend three years in the Sixth Form, and this in turn is causing some pupils to follow a truncated main school course who really need the ordinary five-year course. We think it would be worth considering whether in appropriate cases local education authorities should have the right to offer substantial bursaries for an eighth secondary school year to enable such pupils to spend five years in the main school and three in the Sixth without undue hardship. In making this suggestion we are not implying that "express routes" are wrong or that all pupils going to a university require three years in the Sixth Form.

684. *Chapter 27. Sixth Forms with a Difference*

(*a*) There is a considerably greater provision of general courses (i.e. courses in the Sixth Form which do not aim at two or more Advanced level passes and which are therefore less specialised) for girls than for boys. This is because of the existence of several well recognised professions for girls which recruit at 18 but without (hitherto) requiring Advanced level passes or the equivalent.

(*b*) In the past, many girls intending to enter teacher training colleges spent one or two years in the Sixth on truly general courses, including little or nothing for examination beyond Ordinary level. In recent years there has been a tendency for the training colleges to look for one or more Advanced level passes and the nature of the general course is therefore changing.

(*c*) This new tendency is satisfactory, provided that too much emphasis is not placed on the Advanced level work.

(*d*) A similar general course is suitable for girls intending to enter nursing.

(*e*) Courses in shorthand and typewriting are permissible (after 16) if they are the means of persuading girls to stay on and continue their general education.

(*f*) There may be a growing demand in the future for similar general courses for boys as some of the occupations which now recruit at 16 (e.g. banking, insurance and the law) begin to recruit at 18.

PART SIX. TECHNICAL CHALLENGE AND EDUCATIONAL RESPONSE

685. *Chapter 28. Neglected Educational Territory*

(*a*) Parts Two, Three and Four were concerned with those boys and girls—roughly half of the total—whose education ceases at or soon after the compulsory leaving age. Part Five was concerned with the boys and girls in grammar schools and other selective schools and streams, who at 15 are roughly a quarter of the whole. This Part deals with the remaining quarter of the total—those who leave schools at 15 but continue in some form of further education.

(*b*) There are two reasons for desiring a great advance in this field. The first is the need to produce far greater numbers of technicians and craftsmen (as distinct from technologists) and of persons with equivalent qualifications in other callings.

(*c*) The other reason for advance is the need to raise the proportion of the whole population that continues in education after the age of 16. The proportion of young people in the three years 16–18 in full-time education is now only a little over 1 in 8. We recommend that the objective of policy should be to raise it to 50 per cent within twenty years from now.

686. *Chapter 29. The System of Further Education*
Chapter 30. Characteristics of Further Education

Twelve characteristics of the present system of further education for young people up to 18 are picked out as being significant:

(*a*) The "standard pattern" of one-day-a-week release has emerged only in a few industries, of which only two or three can be classed as large, and even there only for boys.

(*b*) The further education institutions deal with a very wide range of ability. Three grades can often be distinguished in the years from 15 to 18—technician, craftsman and operative—but there is no consistency of provision for these three grades.

(*c*) Further education has grown up entirely as the handmaiden of employment. In particular, day release is closely dependent upon apprenticeship.

(*d*) In spite of this close dependence, however, there is little resemblance in the organisation and nature of apprenticeship and further education. A boy therefore finds himself climbing two very different ladders simultaneously.

(*e*) There is inadequate provision for a smooth transition from full-time school to part-time further education.

(*f*) The largest groups of boys entering further education courses are the sons of foremen and skilled workers and boys who left school at 15. But at the higher stages the proportion of boys from more favourable backgrounds or with longer full-time education steadily grows.

(*g*) It is a feature of the system that a student must pass in all the subjects of one stage before he can enter the next. In consequence, there is a great deal of retardation.

(*h*) There is very little day release for girls. This is a consequence of the different nature of girls' employment.

(*i*) So far as can be told from the scanty evidence available, the attendance of students who go to evening classes only is very irregular and a high proportion of those who start courses fail to finish them.

(*j*) Full-time courses in further education are preponderantly either commercial courses of short duration for girls or courses designed to repair particular deficiencies in G.C.E. qualifications.

(*k*) Sandwich courses, which have great educational advantages, are beginning to spread into the 15–18 age-range.

(*l*) The teaching staff in further education differs in several respects from that in schools. It has a heavy participation of part-timers; it includes few women; it recruits a higher proportion of men with technical and scientific qualifications; and relatively few of its members have been trained as teachers.

687. *Chapter 31. The Effectiveness of Part-Time Courses*

(*a*) Day release has recently been increasing less rapidly in the lower ages than above 18.

(*b*) With the "bulge" moving into the 15–18 age range, it is very probable that the proportion of boys getting day release will fall even though the absolute numbers may continue to rise.

(*c*) The shortage of time in part-time courses makes it difficult for them to serve any broader educational purposes beyond the immediate vocational object in view.

(*d*) There appears to be a heavy failure rate among those boys who take a preliminary course before entering a technical course proper.

(*e*) Of all students entering a National Certificate course without exemptions, 26 per cent eventually obtain an O.N.C. and 10 per cent an H.N.C. The figures for students who are exempt from the first year are 51 per cent and 26 per cent respectively. Of those entering the six City and Guilds five-year courses selected for survey, 28 per cent pass the intermediate examination and 6 per cent the final. For four-year courses the figures are 53 per cent and 20 per cent respectively.

(*f*) Many of the successful students, however, take extra time on the course. For example, only 11 per cent of students entering Engineering courses without exemptions obtain an O.N.C. in the standard time of three years, and only 3·3 per cent obtain an H.N.C. in the standard time of five years.

(*g*) Of the various causes of failure or retardation, the two most important are having to rely on evening classes only, and, even more, lack of an adequate standard in mathematics.

(*h*) Of the various methods of securing exemption from the first year, the most effective (judged by subsequent performance) is exemption by the required number of passes at the Ordinary level of the G.C.E.

(*i*) There are other professional examinations of which little or nothing is known about "yield" or "retardation", as defined in this chapter. Similar investigations should be made.

688. *Chapter 32. Principles of Expansion*

We propound three principles for the development of further education. These are:

(*a*) A greater degree of integration between schools and further education.

(*b*) The provision of more time for all courses, in order to reduce the failure rate and to enable further education courses better to serve the purposes of general education. We recommend that less reliance should be placed on evening classes for students of 18 and under. No young person should be expected to follow a course by evening classes only. More than one evening a week should be considered excessive; and when the day time hours are increased to the standard set by the Act of 1944, even one evening a week should become unnecessary.

(*c*) The long-term aim should be to transform what is now a varied collection of plans for vocational training into a coherent national system of practical education.

689. *Chapter 33. Beginning Further Education*

(*a*) Steps should be taken not only to extend and improve the contacts between the schools in an area and the further education institutions, but also to increase the knowledge that school teachers possess of what further education has to offer, and likewise to assist technical colleges to be aware of recent developments in secondary education.

(*b*) In the process of enrolment, colleges should separate new students from those who are returning for continued courses, in order that more time and attention can be given to advising the former on the best courses for them to take.

(*c*) Experiments should be undertaken with a full-time induction period, lasting one month in the autumn term, for all students who start at the beginning of the normal three-year or five-year courses.

(*d*) Efforts should be made to develop a continuing personal relationship between the students and the staff of further education institutions by means of a tutorial system.

690. *Chapter 34. The Problem of Time*

(*a*) Consideration should be given to introducing for day release students, wherever it is possible to secure agreement to do so, the length of year laid down by the Act of 1944 for county colleges (namely, 44 weeks or 330 hours) in advance of the implementation of the Act.

(*b*) "Block release" should wherever possible be substituted for release on one day a week.

(*c*) Colleges should be empowered to allow students who have failed in only one subject at one stage to proceed to the next stage of a course, with subsidiary examinations in the winter for the purpose of repeating individual subjects.

(*d*) For technicians, sandwich courses should in future be regarded as the standard, and the only satisfactory, method for boys of 16 to 18. Part-time courses should not, of course, be prevented, but every effort should be made to secure their progressive replacement.

(*e*) There should also be expanded provision for "college based" sandwich courses for young people aged 16 to 18, always provided that satisfactory arrangements can be made for training in industry.

(*f*) Special arrangements are necessary for sandwich courses for the employees of firms which are too small to make adequate provision for the industrial component of the course. This could be done by an extension of the existing group apprenticeship schemes or alternatively by making the college workshops agents for a group of smaller firms.

(*g*) For the next few years of the "bulge" before the school-leaving age is raised to 16, special steps will be necessary to assist boys who leave school at 15 and who have difficulty in finding apprenticeships giving them day release. Among these emergency measures should be one-year full-time introductory courses in local colleges.

691. *Chapter 35. The Alternative Road*

(*a*) Many boys and girls, of considerable innate ability, who fail to make progress with ordinary academic education, could develop their powers to the full by a more "practical" approach. Minds that move more easily from the practice to the theory, or that reason better in non-verbal ways, are not necessarily inferior. If there is not to be waste of talent there should be more provision for them.

(*b*) At present for most boys and girls at the age of 15 or 16 there are only two alternatives—the full-time academic route for which they may not be suitable, and the arduous and often wasteful part-time route. It should be regarded as one of the major tasks before English education to construct a new form of education which would suffer from the defects neither of the part-time route nor of the academic in the old conventional sense. This would not be confined to technical subjects.

(*c*) The new form of full-time "practical" education could be provided either in schools or in further education, though there is little at present in either to build on, except in the Sixth Forms of technical schools.

(*d*) We recommend further enquiry into the possibilities of such a development, which should take into account what is being done in other countries.

PART SEVEN. INSTITUTIONS AND TEACHERS

692. *Chapter 36. Changing Patterns in Organisation (Full-Time Education)*

(*a*) If by 1980 (or thereabouts) about half the boys and girls in the country are to continue in full-time education (including sandwich courses) until they are 18, a four-fold increase will be needed.

(*b*) This increase, in the years above the limit of compulsory attendance, can only be achieved through persuasion. Needs and wishes differ widely so that, wherever possible, there should be freedom to choose not only what to study but the sort of institution to attend.

(*c*) Existing institutions can be differentiated by the age-range they serve, by whether or not they are co-educational, by their size and by whether or not they enrol part-time as well as full-time students. In all these respects choice, wherever possible, should be open to boys and girls.

(*d*) The situation in rural areas, where choice will often not be practicable, imposes special obligations on authorities and on staff to cater for the varying needs and wishes of older teen-agers.

(*e*) A four-fold expansion of full-time education which we envisage requires that all (or nearly all) those who attend selective schools should remain in full-time education until 18 and that about one-third of the remainder should do so. This will involve not only an expansion of Sixth Forms of the types described in Part Five, but the development of practical courses of the types described in Chapter 35, and of sandwich courses for these ages.

(*f*) The presumption is that Sixth Form courses of the customary academic kind are best provided in schools because of the advantage of continuity of teaching. Parallel provision of academic courses in institutions other than schools is, however, also required.

(*g*) There is no similar presumption about where practical courses are best provided, though there is nothing against their being developed in schools. They could be provided either in schools or in other institutions.

(*h*) The size of school necessary to support practical courses suggests that many grammar and modern schools will be unable to produce the numbers necessary to make such courses economic beyond the age of 16.

(*i*) We hope to see the development of more secondary technical schools, commonly with provision for Sixth Forms disproportionately large in relation to the main school, in order to allow for transfers from other types of school.

(*j*) Comprehensive schools have a specialised role in two respects—to make it easier to provide without delay or friction appropriate courses for the varied needs of boys and girls of all levels of ability, and to serve as a socially unifying force in the community.

(*k*) The first purpose involves relatively large numbers if each comprehensive school is to contain pupils of all ages from 11 to 18. The necessary numbers could be reduced if this age range were divided between two schools.

(*l*) Typical situations in which comprehensive schools can suitably be introduced are:

(i) in densely populated areas where a variety of schools can be made accessible;

(ii) in areas where the selective provision is unsatisfactorily low;

(iii) in newly developing areas where existing secondary provision is clearly inadequate and where it is especially important to develop a united community;

(iv) in thinly populated country districts and small self-contained industrial townships, where one good all-purpose secondary school may be the only viable alternative to two poorly equipped and inadequately staffed separate institutions.

(*m*) The difficulties which confront all new institutions ought not to be aggravated by introducing comprehensive schools in makeshift accommodation.

(*n*) Comprehensive and other schools may gain from being neighbours. But there are situations where a comprehensive school could only be established by doing harm to existing schools which are doing a very good job. We cannot afford to lose any good school, whatever its classification.

(*o*) Local technical colleges have a special part to play because of their more adult atmosphere (facilitated by the absence of boys and girls under 15) and of their close connection with the outside world (made apparent by the presence of part-time students).

(*p*) There may be room for a special Junior College parallel with, but not in place of, Sixth Forms, enrolling only full-time students, and offering a wide variety of courses both academic and practical. Experiments should be invited and encouraged.

(*q*) We expect that half the boys and girls in the country will still be leaving school at 16 in 1980. Their interests must not be neglected. Schools where most pupils give up full-time education at 16 are especially well placed to look after their interests and to develop the best kind of courses for them.

693. *Chapter 37. The Teachers*

(*a*) An increased supply of teachers will be needed both because of the additional duties that are to be put on the schools, by the raising of the school-leaving age and otherwise, and also because of the necessity to improve the quality of the work that is already being done by the schools (especially by reducing the size of classes). These two demands are not in competition with each other, as a longer average school life will produce more candidates for training as teachers.

(*b*) The good teacher needs a range of qualities that are not easily come by. But the problem of quality should properly be analysed into its parts, since what appears as a global demand is in fact the aggregation of a number of particular demands for different kinds of teachers.

(*c*) Staffing ratios are still a long way from what is desirable, and there are too many over-large classes. There is also considerable variation between different parts of the country.

(*d*) There are two principal sources of supply of teachers—the training colleges and the universities. Although there is considerable overlapping between them both as to the candidates they recruit and the variety of posts taken up in the schools, the problems of the two sources of supply are largely distinct.

(*e*) In the case of the supply of college-trained teachers, the main difficulty is the number of places in the training colleges. There is little doubt that the number of qualified entrants could be increased, especially in the years just ahead, when the "bulge" will reach the age of 18. We recommend that the National Advisory Council on the Training and Supply of Teachers should be asked to advise on the additional number of teachers that will be required to raise the school-leaving age, and on the further measures—additional to those that have been announced in recent months—that will be necessary to supply the number of college-trained teachers required. Special attention might be paid to seeing that training arrangements are sufficiently flexible to meet the needs of older men and women who are attracted to teaching as a career.

(*f*) In the case of graduates, the chief difficulty in increasing the supply is the inadequate numbers, especially of the graduates with high academic qualifications, who evince any desire to enter the profession of teaching. There should be an energetic campaign to explain the attractions to a university graduate of a teaching career. This is the more necessary because of the recruitment campaigns set on foot by a wide range of other callings. No campaign, however, will succeed unless the material rewards of teaching compare favourably with those of other professions open to the graduate.

(*g*) Married women not only now play a large part in teaching of all kinds, but have a specific contribution of their own to make. Attention should be paid to seeing that the terms and conditions of their employment are such as to attract the large numbers needed.

(*h*) Emergency measures to be considered, apart from a prompt start with the recruitment campaign, should be the institution of short-service engagements, and a sustained effort to economise teaching capacity by relieving teachers of clerical and routine tasks.

(*i*) There are special difficulties which affect both the recruitment and the effective use of teachers in technical colleges. Among them are the need for prior industrial or other non-educational experience, and the infrequency with which a teacher sees each of the very large number of students he teaches.

(*j*) There should be more variety of conditions of employment for teachers, who are not a homogeneous body and will become less so with the growth in the upper forms of schools, which have a wide range of specialist requirements. This tendency will be increased with the advent of county colleges and other specialist institutions.

(*k*) The bad areas, which pay much more than their fair share of the price for a shortage of teachers, need a direct attack upon their problem. There should be an attempt to discover by experiment whether financial incentives to teachers to serve in difficult areas would be effective.

CONCLUSION

694. This is a formidable list of recommendations. There are, of course, degrees of urgency among them. But we have attempted to bear in mind the inter-relationship of the various proposals we have put forward, and we present them for consideration as a consistent programme for the development, during the next twenty years or so, of English education for young people between 15 and 18. We cannot in conscience advise that anything less is necessary if the national educational system is to meet the requirements of this tumultuous and dynamic century. Already there is some danger, we think, of English education lagging behind the times. Even in the education of our brightest children—which is what the English system does best—there is still a grave waste of talent through too early an abandonment of formal education. We do not think that the figure of about 12 per cent of the age-group still in full-time education at the age of 17, and of 6 per cent at 20, is nearly good enough. The education that is provided for the great mass of children is inadequate both in its quality and in its duration. In the middle, between the brightest quarter and the great mass of ordinary children, the deficiencies, relatively to the need, are greatest of all, for it is in this "second quartile" that the richest vein of untapped human resources lies, which will have to be exploited if this country is to keep a place among the nations that are in the van of spiritual and material progress.

695. There is thus a very great deal to do. The penalty for not doing it, as for allowing any other form of necessary development to lag behind, is to be forced to make an even greater effort to catch up later on. Yet when one sets the list of our recommendations against the customary pace of educational progress, it is difficult not to quail. So much needs to be done. Is there any hope of its being accomplished? Any attempt to answer this question lies outside our present terms of reference. But the Act imposes on the Council the duty of advising the Minister on "such matters connected with educational theory and practice as they think fit", and we therefore add one or two comments on the means, as distinct from the substance, of educational progress.

696. We do not believe that there is any hope of carrying out the measures we have outlined—or any other list of proposals adequate to the needs—unless they are worked out and adopted as a coherent, properly phased development programme, extending by timed and calculated steps a long way into the future. Nothing of this sort has ever hitherto been possible in English education. There has been no lack of aspiration, or of definition of objectives; but the attainment of them has been left to the mercies of the parliamentary time-table

and of financial exigencies. Nothing more than this has been possible because there has not been support in public opinion for anything more. We believe this situation may be changing. Public interest in educational policies is steadily rising, and we think it should not be difficult to convince the public that there is as much need for a twenty-year programme of educational development as there is for similar programmes of railway modernisation or of atomic generation of electric power.

697. For any such programme the primary need is a public determination to will it. But when this is forthcoming, attention will have to be paid to the inadequacy of the tools that lie to the hand of the educational planner in this country. There are the most extraordinary gaps in our knowledge of what goes on in the schools and technical colleges we have today, let alone in the minds of their pupils. The Ministry's statisticians are constantly in the position of being asked to make bricks without straw. Other countries are wrestling with the same problems as ourselves and, some of them, finding interesting solutions to them; but our knowledge of what they are doing rests far too much on the subjective basis of returning travellers' tales. When one moves from what is to what might be—the proper field of research—the absence of information is even greater. In view of the very large sums of money that are spent on education every year, the expenditure on educational research can only be regarded as pitiable. If there is to be a consistent programme of educational development, almost the first step should be to review the provision for statistics and research.

698. We plead, then, for a forward plan for education. Just as with similar plans for transport or for power, there need be nothing immutable; the money will have to be voted every year, and the details can be subject to constant modification. But if the objectives are to be attained, there will have to be a programme, with dates fixed in the future for the execution of its various component parts. Education, after all, should be peculiarly susceptible to forward planning. Teachers, once trained, practise their profession for up to forty years. The processes of institutional change, of educational fashion and practice, are necessarily slow-moving. And though the children, the objects and beneficiaries of the whole apparatus, flash through the schools in a few brief years, we know, within close limits, how many of them there will be, at least in the secondary schools, for a long way ahead. The problem is to make sure that an instrument requiring many years to prepare will be ready for opportunities that must be seized at once or they are gone for ever. Only by the most careful planning can we make sure that most of them are taken.

ACKNOWLEDGEMENTS

699. We have heavy obligations of gratitude to acknowledge. A list of the individuals and organisations who presented evidence to us is given in Appendix I. In many cases, they gave us the benefit of oral evidence as well as of written memoranda. The total volume of time and trouble taken must have been considerable, and the resulting opinions were of the greatest assistance to us.

700. The staff of the Ministry of Education and several of Her Majesty's Inspectors have been very generous with their time and experience, for our benefit. We would particularly wish to mention the assistance we have had from Mr. G. F. Peaker, H.M.I., with our statistical enquiries, especially in the construction of their sampling designs, and indeed in the whole of the technical courses survey, which he has described in Part Three of Volume II, and from Mr. D. S. S. Hutton, the Ministry's chief statistician. We have had great help over many months from Major L. Tolmie of the War Office, and from officers and officials of the Air Ministry in connection with the National Service surveys. We are also much indebted to Mr. A. J. Curtis of the Combined Tabulating Installation for carrying through the statistical tabulations on our surveys.

701. Our thanks are also due to the authorities, principals and staffs of schools and institutions of further education both in London and the provinces visited by our members. These visits provided a valuable supplement to the written and oral evidence we received. We would also like to thank the authorities of Berufsschulen in Baden-Wuerttemberg and North Rhine Westphalia (Germany), and technical schools in Holland for their hospitality to our members. Particular thanks are due to Dr. Max H. Schneebeli, Chief Executive of Georg Fischer A. G. of Schaffhausen, Switzerland, by whose generous hospitality our drafting committee were enabled to accomplish the most difficult part of their task at Klostergut Paradies on the banks of the Rhine. The Chairman and the Assessor undertook a number of visits and enquiries in the United States of America in January, 1958 and would like to acknowledge the great help received from the United States Office of Education and from various education authorities and institutions in the States visited.

702. Since we began the consideration of the terms of reference that have led to this report, the Council and its committees have sat on no less than 133 days, including 21 days out of London, chiefly at weekends. It will readily be understood what a burden this has thrown on a small staff. Mr. J. A. Humphreys, our Secretary, has made himself responsible for a formidable volume of organisation with cheerful and imperturbable efficiency. He has also done most of the work involved in preparing Volume II. Our debt of gratitude

to him is very great, as it is to Mr. F. G. Ward, who assisted us with the chapters on Further Education, and to our successive Assistant Secretaries, Mr. R. Burgess and Mr. A. H. Prosser, and their staff. Miss M. L. Smith has acted as Clerk to the Council throughout the period of our enquiries and the preparation of our report. The sheer task of handling the material involved in so long a document would have daunted a less willing person. We have also had the benefit of much time and effort given to the preparation of the report by three persons not in the Ministry's employment—Miss P. M. Wilson, Miss M. Deane and Mr. H. R. Natkiel.

703. Our greatest debt, however, is to our Assessor, Mr. D. G. O. Ayerst, H.M.I. In the earlier stages of our work, his wide knowledge of the educational system, his sympathy with the problems of the schools, and his judicial mind were of the greatest assistance in clarifying the issues before us. At a later stage, Mr. Ayerst undertook the immense task of acting as our chief draftsman. We could not, in the time, have produced a report on such a wide range of difficult topics were it not for his willingness to take so much of the burden on to his own shoulders, and for his ability to carry it so lightly. Our obligation to him is beyond any possibility of verbal discharge.

(*Signed*)

GEOFFREY CROWTHER (*Chairman*)
G. S. BOSWORTH
M. H. BROWN
MICHAEL H. CADBURY
S. M. CAFFYN
A. B. CLEGG
H. FRAZER
T. F. GILBERT
B. ANNE GODWIN
M. G. GREEN
V. M. GRUBB
R. HOLROYD
E. M. HUXSTEP
JAMES OF RUSHOLME
A. P. JEPHCOTT
A. V. JUDGES
B. G. LAMPARD-VACHELL
PATRICK LINSTEAD
N. F. MOTT
WALTER OAKESHOTT
S. H. PORTER
S. G. RAYBOULD
MARJORIE REEVES
T. S. SIMEY
G. H. SYLVESTER
P. F. R. VENABLES
HUGH A. WARREN
E. M. WEDEKIND
J. V. C. WRAY
B. W. M. YOUNG

J. A. HUMPHREYS (*Secretary*)
D. G. O. AYERST H.M.I. (*Assessor*)

APPENDIX I

A. List of Witnesses who gave Oral (and in most cases Written) Evidence (in addition to those from Government Departments)

(i) ASSOCIATIONS OF LOCAL EDUCATION AUTHORITIES AND OF EDUCATION COMMITTEES

Association of Education Committees

Alderman R. S. Butterfield, O.B.E., M.C., President of the Association; Chairman of the North Riding Education Committee.

Alderman P. H. Edwards, Past-President of the Association; Member of the Newcastle-upon-Tyne Education Committee.

Mr. Stanley Hirst, Director of Education, Middlesbrough.

Alderman W. S. Howard, M.B.E., D.L., J.P., Chairman of the Warwickshire County Council.

Sir Wilfrid Martineau, M.C., T.D., Past-President of the Association; Member of the Birmingham Education Committee.

Lady Prior-Palmer, O.B.E., Vice-Chairman of the West Sussex Education Committee.

Dr. F. Lincoln Ralphs, Chief Education Officer, Norfolk.

Dr. Elfed Thomas, Director of Education, Leicester.

Councillor Mrs. E. M. Wormald, J.P., Vice-President of the Association; Chairman of the Liverpool Education Committee.

Dr. W. P. Alexander, Secretary of the Association.

Association of Municipal Corporations

Alderman T. J. Brennan, Vice-Chairman of the Education Committee of the Association.

Mr. S. R. Hutton, Chief Education Officer, Southport.

Alderman Mrs. E. V. Smith, J.P., Chairman of the Education Committee of the Association.

Mr. K. P. Poole, Assistant Secretary of the Association.

County Councils Association

Mr. R. Beloe, Chief Education Officer, Surrey.

Mr. G. S. Bessey, Director of Education, Cumberland.

Mr. J. Haynes, County Education Officer, Dorset.

Mrs. M. H. Hichens, C.B.E., Member of the Education Committee of the Association; Alderman, Oxfordshire County Council.

Dr. B. E. Lawrence, C.B.E., Chief Education Officer, Essex.

Mr. A. Lubbock, Chairman of the Education Advisory Sub-Committee of the Association; Chairman, Hampshire County Council.

Mr. H. R. Thomas, C.B.E., Vice-Chairman of the Education Advisory Sub-Committee of the Association; Alderman, Flintshire County Council.

Captain Sir Offley Wakeman, BT., C.B.E., J.P., Chairman of the Education Committee of the Association; Chairman, Salop County Council.

Mr. J. R. Sampson, County Treasurer, Hampshire.

Mr. R. R. Meyric Hughes, Deputy Secretary.

London County Council

Mr. Harold C. Shearman, Chairman of the Education Committee.

Mr. W. F. Houghton, Education Officer.

(ii) ASSOCIATION OF CHIEF EDUCATION OFFICERS

Mr. F. J. Birkbeck, Vice-President of the Association; Director of Education, Lindsey, Lincolnshire.

Dr. B. E. Lawrence, C.B.E., Past-President of the Association; Chief Education Officer, Essex.

Mr. George Taylor, President of the Association; Chief Education Officer, Leeds.

(iii) ORGANISATIONS REPRESENTING TEACHERS

Association of Assistant Masters

Mr. S. J. Berry, Chairman of the Education Sub-Committee of the Association; King Edward VI School, Southampton.

Mr. H. W. T. Jago, Chairman of the Association; The Grammar School, Hampton.

Mr. C. Watters, Vice-Chairman of the Association; St. George Grammar School, Bristol.

Association of Assistant Mistresses

Mrs. P. Kelvin, Tottenham County School, London, N.15.

Miss K. E. Parks, North London Collegiate School, Middlesex.

Miss E. R. Walker, President of the Association; Cambridgeshire High School.

Association of Head Mistresses (Incorporated)

Miss A. M. Bozman, President of the Association; High School for Girls, Manchester.

Miss A. F. Bull, Chairman of the Executive Committee of the Association; Wallington County School for Girls, Carshalton.

Miss E. G. Harold, Chairman of the Education Committee of the Association; Haberdashers' Aske's School, West Acton.

Miss M. C. Sharp, Treasurer of the Association; County School for Girls, Enfield.

Association of Principals of Technical Institutions

Mr. A. W. Gibson, O.B.E., J.P., Hon. Secretary of the Association; Principal, Dudley and Staffordshire Technical College.

Dr. E. C. Smith, President of the Association; Principal, Wigan and District Mining and Technical College.

Association of Teachers in Technical Institutions

Mr. E. G. Godfrey, President of the Association; Lecturer at the Borough Polytechnic, London.

Mr. W. Hatton, Vice-President of the Association; Head of Department, College of Building, Liverpool.

Mr. D. N. Bates, Member of the Executive Committee of the Association; Principal, Hereford Technical College.

Dr. E. A. Seeley, Secretary of the Association.

Association of Technical Institutions

Dr. J. E. Richardson, Hon. Secretary of the Association; Director, Education, The Polytechnic, Regent Street, London.

Incorporated Association of Head Masters

Mr. H. J. H. Dyer, J.P., President of the Association; Queen Elizabeth's Grammar School, Alford.

Mr. E. H. Goddard, Chairman of the Examinations Committee of the Association; Haberdashers' Aske's Hatcham Boys' School.

Mr. R. R. Hancock, J.P., Vice-President of the Association; Northern Grammar School, Portsmouth.

Mr. A. W. Humphreys, Deputy Secretary of the Association.

National Union of Teachers

Mr. E. L. Britton, Past-President of the Union.

Miss A. M. Crawley, Secretary of the Association of Teachers of Domestic Subjects.

Mr. S. W. Exworthy, J.P., Vice-Chairman of the Education Committee of the Union.

Sir Ronald Gould, General Secretary of the Union.

Mr. W. Griffith, Secretary of the Education Committees.

Mr. R. G. K. Hickman, Assistant Secretary, Education Department.

Mr. J. V. A. Long, Chairman, Technical Committee.

Miss O. Morris, Assistant Secretary, Education Department.

Dr. E. A. Seeley, Secretary to the Technical Committee.

Science Masters' Association

Dr. H. F. Boulind, Department of Education, University of Cambridge.

Mr. H. F. Broad, The Cedars School, Leighton Buzzard.

Mr. E. H. Coulson, Braintree County High School, Essex.
Mr. W. D. Dowdeswell, Winchester College.
Mr. C. Holt, Harrow Weald County School.
Mr. I. G. Jones, Doncaster Grammar School.
Mr. E. W. Moore, Kings Norton Grammar School, Birmingham.
Mr. H. P. Ramage, Gresham's School, Holt.

(iv) OTHER INSTITUTIONS AND ORGANISATIONS

City and Guilds of London Institute

Major General C. Lloyd, C.B., C.B.E., Director of the Institute.
Mr. B. C. Lucia, Deputy Director.
Mr. D. E. Wheatley, Deputy Director (Development).

Federation of British Industries

Mr. A. G. Grant, Chairman of the Education Committee of the F.B.I.; Managing Director, Whessoe Ltd.
Mr. L. S. Newton, Member of the Education Committee of the F.B.I.; Group Education Officer, Pilkington Bros., Ltd., St. Helens, Lancashire.
Mr. W. H. Taylor, Member of the Education Committee of the F.B.I.; Controller, Education and Personnel Services, General Electric Company Ltd.
Mr. P. J. C. Perry, Secretary of the Education Committee of the F.B.I.; Head of Education Section, Technical Department, F.B.I.

Institute of Bankers

Mr. Maurice Megrah, Secretary.

Institution of Civil Engineers

Dr. W. K. Wallace, C.B.E., President.
Mr. A. McDonald, Secretary.

The Institute of Chartered Accountants in England and Wales

Mr. W. G. Campbell, Member of the Council and Chairman of the Examination Committee of the Institute.
Mr. A. S. MacIver, M.C., Secretary.
Mr. C. H. S. Loveday, Assistant Secretary.

Institution of Chemical Engineers

Mr. G. U. Hopton, Vice-President and Chairman of the Board of Examiners of the Institution; Senior Research Chemist, North Thames Gas Board.
Mr. A. S. White, Vice-President and Chairman of the Education Committee of the Institution; Head of the Chemical Engineering Division, Atomic Energy Research Establishment, Harwell.

Institution of Electrical Engineers

Mr. S. E. Goodall, Vice-President of the Institution; Chief Engineer, W. T. Henley's Telegraph Works Company Ltd.

Mr. N. C. Stamford, Education Officer of the Institution.

Institution of Mechanical Engineers

Mr. F. H. Reid, Education Officer of the Institution.

Royal Institute of British Architects

Mr. T. E. Scott, C.B.E., Vice-President of the Institute; Head of Department of Architecture, Surveying and Building, Northern Polytechnic, London.

Standing Conference of National Voluntary Youth Organisations

Mr. J. F. Colquhoun, O.B.E., Vice-Chairman; Headquarters Commissioner for Relationships, Boy Scouts Association.

Professor N. Haycocks, Chairman; Professor of Education, University of Nottingham.

Miss M. Shipp, Liaison Officer, National Association of Mixed Clubs and Girls' Clubs.

Mr. J. G. Turvey, Senior Field Secretary, National Association of Boys' Clubs.

Mr. R. W. J. Keeble, Secretary.

Trades Union Congress

Mr. W. B. Beard, O.B.E., Member of General Council; Chairman of the Education Committee.

Mr. A. Hallworth, Member of General Council and Education Committee.

Mr. J. O'Hagan, O.B.E., Member of General Council and Education Committee.

Mr. L. Poole, Member of General Council and Education Committee.

Mr. D. Winnard, Secretary of the Education Committee.

Workers' Educational Association

Professor Asa Briggs, President of the Association; Professor of Modern History in the University of Leeds.

Miss E. McCullough, Deputy President of the Association; National Woman Officer of the Transport and General Workers' Union.

Miss M. Marsh, Education Officer of the Association.

Mr. Harold C. Shearman, Vice-President of the Association; Academic Adviser on Tutorial Classes in the University of London.

The Lady Simon of Wythenshawe, Vice-President of the Association.

Mr. Harry Nutt, General Secretary of the Association.

(V) INDIVIDUAL WITNESSES

Mr. H. Brooks, M.C., Vice-Chairman, International Correspondence Schools Ltd.
Mr. J. Cawley, M.C., Managing Director, Jones Brothers, Holloway.
Mr. M. V. Crehan, Principal, Pitman's College.
Mr. E. S. Dreblow, Production Manager, Hilger and Watts, Ltd., London.
Miss M. M. Edwards, M.V.O., Director, King Edward's Hospital Fund for London.
Mr. J. H. Evernden, M.B.E., Principal Youth Employment Officer, Croydon.
Miss E. L. Gibbs, Manager, Staff Training Department, Selfridges Ltd.
Mr. E. H. Goddard, Headmaster, Haberdashers' Aske's Hatcham Boys' School.
Professor D. W. Harding, Professor of Psychology, Bedford College, University of London.
Professor G. R. Hargreaves, O.B.E., Professor of Psychiatry, University of Leeds.
Mr. E. M. Hutchinson, Secretary, National Institute of Adult Education.
Mr. E. J. Larkin, Director of Work Study, British Transport Commission.
Mr. H. D. P. Lee, Head Master, Winchester College.
Miss K. M. Lloyd, Principal Youth Employment Officer, Leicester.
Mr. John Marsh, Director, Industrial Welfare Society (Incorporated).
Mr. L. S. Newton, Group Education Officer, Pilkington Bros., Ltd., St. Helens, Lancs.
Dr. A. J. McIntosh, Director, City of London College.
Professor R. A. C. Oliver, Director, Department of Education, University of Manchester.
Dr. R. Pedley, Senior Lecturer, Department of Education, University of Leicester.
Mr. E. Pennell, Head of Vocational Training Department, John Lewis Partnership.
Miss E. M. Pepperell, Industrial Welfare Society (Incorporated).
Mr. I. J. Pitman, M.P.
Mr. J. A. Ratcliffe, O.B.E., Reader in Physics, University of Cambridge.
Miss E. L. Sewell, General Secretary, National Association of Mixed Clubs and Girls' Clubs.
Mr. E. G. Sterland, Principal, Apprentices' School, Bristol Aeroplane Company Ltd.
Dr. J. M. Tanner, Institute of Child Health, University of London.

Dr. Ethel C. Venables, Nuffield Research Fellow, University of Birmingham.

Professor F. A. Vick, O.B.E., Department of Physics, University College of North Staffordshire, Keele.

Mr. P. V. N. Warner, Principal, North London Day College (for Further Education).

Dr. W. Warren, Bethlem Royal Hospital and Maudsley Hospital, London.

Miss C. Watson, Assistant Education Officer, East Suffolk Local Education Authority.

Mr. G. H. Webb, Technical Training Officer, Michelin Tyre Company, Ltd.

Dr. Stephen Wiseman, Director, School of Education, University of Manchester.

Professor Sir Solly Zuckerman, C.B., F.R.S.

B. List of other Organisations and Persons who wrote Memoranda and submitted Statistics or other Data

Professor John H. Argyris, Professor of Aeronautical Structures, Imperial College of Science and Technology, London.

Association of Education Officers.

Association of Heads of Secondary Technical Schools.

Association of Teachers in Colleges and Departments of Education.

British Association for Commercial and Industrial Education.

British Council of Churches.

British Employers' Confederation.

British Federation of University Women.

Miss Joan M. Camp, Deputy Head, Langley Grammar School.

Catholic Education Council.

College of Preceptors.

Communist Party.

Mr. W. Flemming, Lecturer in Education, University of Leicester.

Professor F. T. H. Fletcher, James Barrow Professor of French, University of Liverpool.

Dr. Dennis Gabor, F.R.S., Reader in Electronics, Imperial College of Science and Technology, London.

Garnett College, London.

Geographical Association.

Professor W. K. Hayman, F.R.S., Professor of Pure Mathematics, Imperial College of Science and Technology, London.

Headmasters' Conference.

Dr. J. Henderson, Academic Registrar, University of London.

Institute of Christian Education at Home and Overseas.

King George's Jubilee Trust.

Library Association.
National Association for Education for Commerce.
National Association of Head Teachers.
National Association of Local Education Authority Youth Service Officers.
National Association of Principal Agricultural Education Officers.
National Association of Schoolmasters.
National Association of Youth Employment Officers.
National Association of Youth Leaders and Organisers.
National Farmers' Union.
National Federation of Women's Institutes.
National Institute of Adult Education.
National Institute of Industrial Psychology.
National Union of Townswomen's Guilds.
National Union of Women Teachers.
Outward Bound Trust.
Royal Society of Arts.
Union of Educational Institutes.
Union of Lancashire and Cheshire Institutes.
University Appointments Boards in England, Wales and Scotland.
Dr. W. D. Wall, Director, National Foundation for Educational Research in England and Wales.
Women's Employment Federation.

APPENDIX II

Minor Examinations.

Correspondence between the Minister of Education and the Chairman of the Council relating to minor examinations.

1st July, 1957.

Dear Geoffrey,

About two years ago my predecessor, Sir David Eccles, issued a Circular (No. 289) in which he set out his provisional views about the part that external examinations should play in the work of the secondary schools, in particular of the secondary modern schools, and invited comments on them. Last summer he referred all the comments he had received to the Secondary School Examinations Council, and asked for their advice on the issues raised. So far as concerned questions connected with secondary school examinations other than the General Certificate of Education, the Council did not feel that they were fully qualified to advise me, and suggested that I might appoint an *ad hoc* body "to consider whether any, and if so, what arrangements should be made for the examination of those secondary school pupils for whom the General Certificate of Education was recognised to be inappropriate".

Since taking office, I have been studying this problem very fully, particularly as it affects the secondary modern schools. While I am entirely persuaded by the Examinations Council that it would not be wise to reach any final decisions on this aspect of examinations policy until it has been studied further, I feel that it cannot be usefully studied in isolation, but only as part of the much wider set of problems that your own Council are now considering. I think you will agree from your side that it would be difficult for your Council to do full justice to their remit if they did not give at least some consideration to the place of external examinations in the education of young people between the ages of 15 and 18. These considerations have led me to the conclusion that rather than set up a new body to make a separate study of this topic, I ought to ask you if you will accept it as part of your Council's present terms of reference. I am not, of course, asking you to duplicate the main work of the Secondary School Examinations Council, and I do not wish to suggest either that your Council should devote to this issue more of their time than they feel its importance deserves, or that they should give it priority of treatment over the many other important topics that they are considering. I am therefore happy to leave it to your Council to decide how and when their advice should be tendered on it.

I enclose an advance copy of the Circular in which I have made known my decision, and I have given instructions that the Secretary of your Council is to be supplied with copies as soon as it is issued, and with all the comments that have been received on this issue.

Yours sincerely,

HAILSHAM.

15th July, 1957.

Dear Minister,

Thank you for your letter of the 1st conveying your decision not to set up an *ad hoc* body to consider the question of external examinations below the level of the G.C.E. You are right in your assumption that the Central Advisory Council will be covering this subject in the course of the report that it will submit to you in due course on its general remit. In view of your wishes I will take particular care to see that the subject is adequately dealt with. I am, however, grateful to you for saying that you will not require us to make a special report on the subject as that would involve rather wrenching it out of the context in which it naturally belongs.

Yours sincerely,

GEOFFREY CROWTHER.

APPENDIX III

Technical Education and Vocational Training in Western Europe

Hugh A. Warren

INTRODUCTION

For many centuries Western Europe has held a pre-eminent place in the intellectual affairs of the world. Only in very recent years has its academic supremacy been challenged. European schools and universities are second to none elsewhere, and so far have not failed to adapt themselves to changing patterns of thought, philosophy and science.

It is as yet too early to attempt a similar appraisal in respect of technical and technological education in Europe, for little more than a century has elapsed since the foundation of any general or organised educational system for that purpose. Certainly Europe had the lead in this work until the beginning of the 20th century. So far as quality is concerned the facilities for technical education now offered in such countries as Holland and Switzerland are superb and provide the very basis of their economies.

The Council had no mission to provide a comprehensive review of such facilities in Europe. Rather was its interest restricted to the more limited task of gleaning from those countries information which might stimulate its deliberations in the education of the teen-ager in England. Recent changes and developments—such as the French "centre d'apprentissage", or the German "second way" (der zweite Bildungsweg), or the Dutch intermediate technical school (uitgebreid technische school)—were thus of greater interest than stable time-honoured and well-known institutions such as the German Technische Hochschule, or the École Polytechnique of France.

The Council sent out two parties simultaneously (2–13 June, 1958):

1. To Baden-Wurttemberg and the Ruhr district.
2. To Holland and the Ruhr district.

The first party comprised Mr. Wray, Mr. C. W. Harvey, H.M.I. and the Secretary, Mr. Humphreys, and tended to specialise on curricula, methods, human relations, etc. The latter party included Dr. Frazer, Mr. A. G. Gooch, H.M.I. and the writer and had more especially in mind the institutional framework and system of each country. The two parties came together for a few days in Dusseldorf.

In addition the Council had amongst its members several who had had previous experience of this branch of education in France or Germany or who had attended recent inter-European conferences on vocational training, apprenticeship, etc. From the earliest days of its deliberations therefore the Council was kept informed of recent developments in our neighbouring countries.

PREFACE

The general educational systems—school and university—in Western European countries were founded in those centuries when, despite differences of creed, race and tradition there existed an academic unity making it possible and at times normal for both teachers and students to migrate from country to country, from university to university, in the pursuit of learning. This happy state of affairs brought about a certain degree of uniformity in the general educational systems of the different countries of Europe.

The growth of technical and technological education has however occurred more recently. It has evolved during the years in which national consciousness, economic competition, and military rivalry based on technical armaments, obstructed the same free interchange of knowledge as had been possible, if not general, in the older educational system. Moreover, the common inheritance from Greek and Roman sources and the former use of Latin as an international medium of thought-exchange had little significance in this new field of study.

It is not surprising therefore that there is no uniformity in the framework of technical education as between, say, Holland and Italy, France and England. Whereas an English G.C.E., a French Baccalauréat and a German Abitur are at least comparable and possess a measure of equivalence which has even been the subject of European protocol (Council of Europe, 1953) no such equivalence even on an approximate basis can be stated as between, say, an English Higher National Certificate and a Dutch H.T.S. Diplom. They are different in kind and represent a different approach and a varying sequence in the pattern of education and training. At the sub-professional and technician levels the system in use in each country is much influenced by apprenticeship customs. These in turn are affected greatly by history e.g. the influence of the Guilds; by modern social organisation e.g. the trade unions; the general importance attached to efficient industrial training e.g. the German system; by educational philosophy and practice e.g. the school-leaving age or the reaction against vocational studies in schools; and by taxation measures e.g. the French taxe d'apprentissage.

The following lines, ascribed to Ekkehard the monk of St. Gallen, remain therefore as true for present day technical education in Europe as when used over 1,000 years ago to describe a pastoral Europe yet in its formative years. (Historia Waltarii A.D. 930: trans. from Latin and pub. as "Ekkehard" J. V. Scheffel, 1826–86)

"Der dritte Erdteil, Brüder, Europa wird genannt
Viel Völker mannigfaltig bewohnen dieses Land
Durch Sitte, Sprache, Glaube, verschieden und getrennt"

The third continent, Brothers, is called Europe
Many and various races inhabit this land
Through custom language and faith, separate and distinct.

It is inevitable by reason of such diversity that this account should now separate into national divisions, each providing a very brief but factual account of the system of general education, technical education, apprenticeship and vocational training in the country concerned. The countries selected for this study—France, Germany and Holland—do not of course form the whole of Western Europe, but are sufficiently representative to include all important developments. The Council were not unmindful of the excellence of Swiss technical education, culminating in the Federal Technical University (Eidgenössische Technische Hochschule) at Zürich; nor of the high esteem in which Belgian technical institutions are held, especially in the sister countries of Benelux; nor of the post-war developments in Italy, the expansion of the "Istituti Professionali" and the "Istituti Tecnici" conforming to the needs of a growing industrial economy; nor of the achievements of the Spanish syndical organisations in combining craft training with the moral welfare of the apprentice both during and after training; nor of the development of apprentice-training methods in the Scandinavian countries; but limitations of time and space precluded a detailed account being submitted in this Appendix.

FRANCE

(Note: The Educational Reform measures which became law on 6th January, 1959, are described at the end of this section. The following account is in terms of the existing institutions and their nomenclature).

School attendance is compulsory between the ages of 6 and 14 years commencing in the école primaire. At or about 11 years a child may secure, usually by selective test, a place in a grammar school (lycée or collège) or in a technical school (école nationale professionnelle, or collège technique) or may, still within the école primaire, commence a special 3–4 year course (cours complémentaire) up to age 15–16, which sometimes has a technical or commercial component.

Failing any of these possibilities—which will be touched on later—he will leave school at 14+ with or without the primary leaving certificate, "le certificat d'études primaires".

It is compulsory for all young people up to 17 years seeking employment to possess and to show a certificate provided by the vocational guidance service (Orientation Professionnelle) which sets out aptitudes, suggests suitable and notes any unsuitable occupations. This certificate is advisory only and is not legally binding.

Apprenticeship in industry, whose normal duration is three years, is administratively of two kinds, suited respectively to large-scale production and to small owner-craftsman trades respectively. In the former class the apprentice should, by Loi Astier, 1919, attend part-time classes (cours professionnel) and may after three years or more sit for an examination comprising tests both of practical skill and of elementary theory to gain the qualification "Certificat d'aptitude professionnelle" i.e. C.A.P. After a further two years he may elect to sit for a higher qualification—the Brevet professionnel.

All industries pay a tax, taxe d'apprentissage, amounting to 0·4 per cent of their wages bill, this being one of the provisions of Loi Astier, 1919. This tax is paid irrespective of whether the firm engages apprentices or not. If an apprentice school is maintained certain defined costs can legally be offset against this tax, or alternatively if the apprentices are released during working hours to attend classes their wages for this time may be counted for deduction.

The second kind of apprenticeship, apprentissage artisanal, in small-scale crafts is controlled by a statutory body known as the Chambre de Métiers. This body, with the help of advisers from the Department of Technical Education sets the examination, l'examen fin d'apprentissage (E.F.A.), at the end of the period of apprenticeship, regulates the contract signed, assists in the tuition of the apprentice and maintains an advisory service for all relevant matters. The executive organisation is to be found in each département but there is a national council—Assemblée des Présidents des Chambres de Métiers—in Paris.

There is a proposal to unify the two examinations set at the termination of these two kinds of apprenticeship but both systems of training are now regarded as less satisfactory than the post-war development of the specially created apprentice-training centre, the centre d'apprentissage. In these centres, which may be publicly organised under the technical branch of the Ministry of Education, or privately founded by trade bodies e.g. Metal industries, Building federations, or by Chambers of Commerce or municipalities, the student-apprentice receives *both* the theoretical *and* the practical instruction necessary for full apprenticeship requirements, as well as continued general and civic education. The instructors are pedagogically trained in special training colleges, Écoles normales nationales d'apprentissage (E.N.N.A.), which deal with the needs of the adolescent as distinct from the child of school years.

The weekly curriculum varies of course according to the trade being taught but the general pattern is approximately as follows:—

	Hours		
Civics and Literary Subjects ..	6		
Mathematics and Scientific Subjects	5		
Drawing and Design	4		
Physical Education	4	19	General
Technology and Workshop ..	23	23	Vocational
	42	42	Total

It will be noted that the general subjects and the vocational subjects occupy some 45 per cent and 55 per cent of the time respectively. Productive work—often making articles such as furniture and machine-tools for the educational service—is undertaken. Public service may be provided in occupations such as clothes-pressing and dyeing, hair cutting, catering, etc. The qualifying examination taken is the same as that taken by apprentices in industry—the C.A.P.—and the pass rate is higher in these centres than for candidates who have followed the part-time route. The placement figures for the leavers show that 85 per cent do in fact enter the kind of work for which they have been trained. The total numbers enrolled include an almost equal number of boys and girls.

This is almost entirely a post-1940 development and the numbers are still growing. In 1955–56, 129,814 boys and 131,732 girls—being approximately one-third of all apprentices in France—were following this new system of apprenticeship education and training. It has happily coincided with the "bulge" years in France and has had a perceptible influence on the efficiency of that country's industry.

If there be justifiable criticism it is that the C.A.P.—unlike the British National Certificate—tends to be a terminal qualification and is not very suitable as a lead-in to more advanced studies. Some attempts are now being made to rectify this—cours de promotion du travail.

Reverting to the technical schools—the école nationale professionnelle and the collège technique—these provide a five and four years course respectively leading to examinations, Diplôme d'Élève Breveté and Brevet Industriel respectively, which correspond in technical level to our Ordinary National Certificate but also connote a general education comparable to "O" level G.C.E. work with concurrent craft training of City and Guilds Intermediate standard. The student may then leave to take up employment in industry or he may, in many of these schools, continue in further study for a higher qualification such as the Baccalauréat Technique, or the Brevet de Technicien, the former of which will give entry to technical institutions, grandes écoles, of University level or alternatively to the technical teacher training college in Paris. In the former he will then secure after four years' study the "diplôme d'ingénieur" in one or other of the many specialities available. The Universities proper are restricted to the five traditional faculties of Law, Medicine, Science, Letters, and Pharmacy but are often closely connected with an associated "Institut", which may grant the "diplôme d'ingénieur" qualification, or even provide technician courses as well, as in the newly opened, October, 1958, "Institut National des Sciences Appliqués" at Lyons.

Despite these facilities and the fact that no institution under the Department of Technical Education charges any tuition fees, France is still faced with an acute shortage of qualified engineers and technicians. For that reason and also from motives of social justice, fresh impetus has been given to part-time courses suitable for ex-apprentices of exceptional ability and also for intelligent workers of more advanced age.

The Conservatoire des Arts et Métiers, founded in Paris in 1794 on the proposals of Abbé Grégoire, advised by the great scientist Lavoisier and supported by the republican National Convention, was the first determined effort to provide evening classes in scientific and technical studies. It is possible, but extremely arduous, to gain over a period of at least 5 years the diplôme d'ingénieur. Only 66 out of a total enrolment of 21,975 did so in 1956. In recent years associated provincial centres have been opened at Lille (1952), Lyons (1953), Mulhouse (1956), Bordeaux, Rheims, Clermont Ferrand (1957–58) and there are proposals for shortening the course by conversion to full-time study.

Other university colleges, e.g. at Grenoble, are seeking to recruit through part-time preparatory courses, cours de promotion supérieure du travail, without reference to previous educational attainment. Some 20 per cent of the entries succeed in gaining entry to the main course.

Whilst such measures may be justifiable in the present emergency they are not the final solution. On 6th January, 1959, the French Council of Ministers approved the educational reform measures which had been prepared, debated and revised for some 13 years. In this reform technical education becomes an integral part of the national system and has its roots well down into the schools. An ample and controllable supply is thus assured for later technological qualification. No one who aspires to full professional status will normally leave school before 18 years: all will stay until 16 years.

Under the new provisions the compulsory range is 6–16 years. This will be binding upon all who enter school in September, 1959. It will thus begin to take effect in 1967 and be complete in 1969. Five years in primary school, followed by 2 years, 11–13 in the "cycle d'observation" and then selection—on the basis of class reports, tests, etc.—for one of the following five educational roads:

(1) "L'enseignement terminal"—3 years terminating in employment in an unskilled or semi-skilled capacity.

(2) "L'enseignement technique court"—3 years in a centre d'apprentissage to be re-named "collège d'enseignement technique" leading to employment in a skilled capacity.

(3) "L'enseignement général court"—3–4 years in the 'cours complémentaire' to be re-named "collège d'enseignement général" leading to: either positions in the middle but non-technical levels of industry: or entry to a training college for primary school teachers.

(4) "L'enseignement technique long"—providing 4, 5 or more years in a "lycée technique" being the new name for the present technical schools—E.N.P. and C.T. Pupils will be prepared for entry to promising careers in industry and commerce, or for further study in a University or technical institution of equivalent rank; or for entry to a technical teacher training college. The Baccalauréat technique and various other technical qualifications may be obtained.

(5) "L'enseignement général long"—in the traditional lycée following courses which include scientific, modern or classical options and lead to the Baccalauréat.

The detailed organisation of these reforms will take at least ten years, during which time the present emergency measures involving part-time courses will no doubt persist.

The importance attached in France not only to technical education itself but to the need for its liberalisation—the synthesis between technics, art and the humanities—led the late M. André Siegfried, diplomat, scholar and educational adviser to write: (Encyclopédie Générale de L'Éducation Vol. III).

"Maintenir la France à l'avant garde du progrès industriel, c'est le souci principal des responsables de notre enseignement technique, mais il ressort également de leur oeuvre qu'ils ne conçoivent pas ce programme comme pouvant se dissocier du maintien de ces valeurs individuelles, c'est à dire de culture, qui sont et doivent rester la source véritable de notre génie.

WEST GERMAN FEDERAL REPUBLIC

Strictly speaking, no general account can be given of education in the federal republic as a whole since its constituent states (Länder) are autonomous in this field and have diverged in recent years in their various educational measures. The account that follows is based in the main upon the educational system in the state of Nordrhein-Westfalen which, including as it does the industrial region of the Ruhr, has given particular attention to technical education.

GENERAL EDUCATION

Schooling legally begins at 6 in the Volkschule. After 4 years or more (Grundschule)—that is, at or about 10 years of age—transfer to one of two varieties of secondary school is possible.

The Realschule, or Mittelschule, provides a 6 years' secondary education terminating in the qualification Mittlere Reife, and sometimes has an extension course beyond this.

The Gymnasium offers the full 9-year grammar school course leading to the qualification "Abitur" and thus gives entrance to the University proper or to the Technische Hochschule, which in Germany is of equal rank and deals with all technological studies leading to "Diplom Ingenieur" status.

Failing selection for either of these secondary schools—or the ability to pay the fees—the pupil will remain in the Volkschule for a further 4 years (Oberstufe). Some regions have a 9th school year to 15; in some places this is compulsory, in others voluntary. When the leaving age is universally 15 the age of transfer will probably be 12 in place of 10.

APPRENTICESHIP

Leaving the Volkschule at age 14–15 the pupil with any measure of ambition or intelligence will seek a position as an apprentice (Lehrling), or as a trainee (Anlernling). In this aim approximately 65 per cent of those who leave Volkschule are successful (Boys 85 per cent, Girls 45 per cent) in finding either apprenticeship in a fully skilled trade, Lehrberuf, or an organised training in a semi-skilled occupation, Anlernberuf. This extraordinarily high percentage is due to the consistent and meticulous care with which apprenticeship has been fostered in Germany for over half a century. As long ago as 1908 an Executive Committee, Deutscher Ausschuss für Technisches Schulwesen, was founded with powers to advise the relevant Ministries on technical education and vocational training. For some years, as in France also, the technical schools were controlled by the Ministry of Commerce and Industry and only in 1934 did they finally revert to the Ministry of Education.

From the end of the 19th century continuative part-time general education was commenced in the Fortbildungschulen (still popularly known under that name in Austria). These failed in their purpose until, after the first world war, they were transformed into the present Berufsschulen which also provide for continued general education but are firmly based on the student's vocational needs and interests.

These Berufsschulen provide the educational background to the practical and sometimes theoretical instruction received by the student in the Works in the course of apprenticeship training. Preparation for the examination taken at the end of apprenticeship is, however, not primarily the responsibility of the Berufsschule but of the employer, through his apprentice training master, Ausbilder. Herein lies a fundamental difference in comparison with an English technical college and its responsibility in preparation for (say) City and Guilds' examinations.

Apprenticeship in present-day Germany is under the general aegis of the Federal Ministry of Economics, but its powers are in practice delegated to two executive bodies.

(1) The Industrie- und Handelskammer, Chamber of Industry and Commerce, and

(2) the Handwerkskammer, Chamber of Crafts

both of which work in co-operation with the trade unions, with the Ministry of Labour and, Handwerkskammer, with the Guilds, Innungen. These bodies regulate apprenticeship conditions in (1) large scale industry and (2) small scale crafts, respectively. It is also these bodies, sometimes in co-operation with technical teachers, who set the examination standard and finally judge results.

A full apprenticeship in a skilled trade lasts 3 to 3½ years; the trainee period in a semi-skilled trade is usually 2 years. At the end of full apprenticeship the qualification (1) Facharbeiterbrief (Certificate of a skilled worker) or (2) Gesellenbrief (Journeyman's ticket), respectively, are obtainable on the results of examinations both practical and theoretical. Only two attempts are permitted but approximately 90 per cent of those who enter do in fact succeed. Without such qualification the ex-apprentice cannot practice a skilled trade and certainly cannot become a master-craftsman. After five years further practice in the trade the apprentice, of either type, may submit himself for the qualification of Master, Meisterbrief.

BERUFSSCHULE

The course given in the one-day-per-week Berufsschule includes approximately 40 per cent general and 60 per cent vocational study. Amongst the former may be mentioned civics, German, science, arithmetic, religious instruction, letter writing, and for girls: domestic economy, cookery, art and crafts, baby care. Amongst the vocational subjects are craft theory, knowledge of materials, technical drawing, industrial practice, trade calculations.

Such courses are sufficiently general to permit of several trades being grouped together—the necessary differentiation takes place in the works apprenticeship not in the college.

On the other hand the degree of specialisation in apprenticeship training and qualification is very great. For each recognisable occupation a specification, Berufsbild, is drawn up and published by a Federal office, Arbeitstelle für betriebliche Berufsausbildung, at Bonn. In industry alone (1953) there were over 368 skilled trades, plus commerce 26 and crafts 125. At the same time 176 semi-skilled occupations were recognised. Since then the tendency has been to increase the number of skilled and decrease the semi-skilled occupations but the total remains at over 600 occupational varieties. Through the schools and in the vocational guidance centres of the Labour Office, attractive pamphlets are available setting out in simple language the kind of life a boy or girl will lead in any particular occupation.

In 1956 there were, in thousands, 2,191 in attendance at Berufsschulen, of whom 1,566 were either in full apprenticeship or in recognised trainee occupations—a proportion of 71·5 per cent. Of the 1,566 in such training 1,040 (67 per cent) were boys and 526 (33 per cent) were girls. Of this same 1,566, 575 were registered under the Handwerkskammer, 788 under the Industrie- und Handelskammer and the small remainder under other authorities (e.g. Agriculture). Of the 788 under the I.H.K. 301 were in industrial and 487 in commercial occupations. Of this same 788, 438 were boys and 350 girls.

There is a slight discrepancy in these figures taken from official Berufsschule sources as compared with Ministry of Labour statistics.

The above analysis however gives the true picture from the Berufs-schule point of view, namely the large proportion of its students undergoing systematic occupational training, and the high percentage of girls included in apprenticeship and similar schemes.

All the above refers to the Volkschule leaver. What of those from the Realschule—the 6 year secondary school? They may secure worthwhile employment and if having a taste for further study and qualification, may spend 2 years in industry as a "Praktikant". They may then enter by selective examination an "Ingenieurschule" (or Technicum, or Höhere Facschule) giving a course of 5 or 6 semesters, i.e. 2½–3 years, for the qualification "Ingenieur"—not to be confused with "Diplom Ingenieur" which certifies a much higher level. Such a course has an academic level comparable to our Higher National Certificate but covers a wider spread of technical subjects and also includes a few general or at least non-technical studies, e.g. German Language, industrial economy, sociology, appreciation of art, civics, history of technology or a foreign language.

Those who receive their education in the 9 year Gymnasium course and succeed in obtaining Abitur may, amongst other careers of course, elect to enter a Technische Hochschule and do so often after ½ to 1 year's practical experience. After some 5 years or more study they may obtain the "Diplom Ingenieur" the normal professional qualification in Technology.

The need of rapidly developing industry for more and more technicians has brought it about that West Germany like its neighbours is facing a shortage of both "Diplom Ingenieur" and "Ingenieur" qualified men. At the same time the claims of social change and of democratic ideals have favoured the development of a second way, der zweite Bildungsweg, by which an intelligent apprentice can, albeit by long and arduous study, attain Ingenieur or even Diplom Ingenieur qualification.

THE SECOND WAY

In the second or third year of apprenticeship and for one or two years afterwards, an ambitious apprentice may attend an additional evening course, known as "Berufsaufbauschule". This lasts 7 semesters, involves attendance for 12 hours per week, and is usually spread over four evenings or the equivalent in the week-end. Beginning with such general subjects as German, English, Algebra, Geometry, Physics and Chemistry in the first four semesters, the course later includes technology and technical drawing. The object is twofold—extension of general education and foundation for later technical study. The technical level reached at the end approximates to S.2 of our National Certificate.

The apprentice must also, after success in his "Facharbeiterbrief" qualification at the end of his time, serve an extra term of apprenticeship, giving a training extended over related crafts, for 6 months or more.

There are thus in all four conditions to be observed:

(*a*) Successful completion of Berufsschule
(*b*) Successful completion of Berufsaufbauschule
(*c*) Completion of apprenticeship and qualification
(*d*) Extended practical training in related crafts.

These four components are brought together on one document (Fachschulereifevermerk) and duly certified. The student then has a right to apply for entry to an Ingenieurschule, or similar institution in a course corresponding to his training. He is thus given the same chance as those coming from a Realschule. Some Ingenieurschulen now have more than half of their entries coming in by this "second way", but in general the proportion is less.

At the end of the 5/6 semester course in the Ingenieurschule, the brilliant candidate can secure a further passport—the Hochschulereife—giving him a restricted right of candidature for entry to a Technische Hochschule—restricted to a relevant faculty and sometimes to one Tech. Hochschule. It does not, like the Abitur of a Gymnasium, give him a nominally unrestricted right of entry to any University or T.H. faculty. On the other hand his previous studies at the Ingenieurschule may lessen his work especially in technical subjects in the early years of the T.H. courses.

The way is thus pioneered from Volkschule to Hochschule, without passing through a Gymnasium.

VARIATIONS ON THE SECOND WAY

(*a*) *Berufsfachschule*. This is a one or two year full-time pre-apprenticeship course, counting at half-rate for remission of the duration of the latter. Preliminary workshop training, continued general education and the science underlying the future technology make up the curriculum. Such students can be excused up to 4 semesters of the later Berufsaufbauschule. The "second way" is thus greatly eased.

(*b*) *The Oberhausener Institut*. The apprentice who has, as described earlier, secured a Fachschulereife after apprenticeship may, instead of going on to an Ingenieurschule, apply for entry to this Institut. It gives a 2 year full-time residential course and prepares for Abitur. Following success in that qualification the student may then proceed to a University or T.H. or enter a technical teacher training college, thus re-gaining the same possibilities as if he had been to a Gymnasium. Other such Institutes are planned to open in the near future. The "second way" has other variations for girls' education and for commercial occupations. The educational significance is that this second way tends to build theory on to practice rather than follow the usual academic sequence of theory first and practical experience later. The social significance, for Continental countries, is that the horizontal stratification so long engendered by their rigid and mainly full-time system of technical education has been pierced by this "second way". Numerically, however, it is still barely significant, for less than 10 per cent of Technische Hochschule students have as yet come up by this new route.

HOLLAND

Holland is a small country (32,450 sq. km.) but it is thickly populated (10,888,000) having a higher density (336) than any other European territory except the Saar (390). Both the population, and the land area, are still increasing—the latter by reason of land reclamation works. It has a higher precentage of children under 15 than any other country in Western Europe and the highest birth-rate.

Within living memory the emphasis has changed from an agrarian to an industrial economy—electronics, shipbuilding, aviation, oil, textile-fibres, steel, etc., are now becoming the main sources of national wealth. The index of industrial production has risen by 51 per cent between 1950 and 1957, compared with 23 per cent for this country. "Technology is the modern millstone for our daily bread" said Queen Juliana in opening the new University College of Technology at Eindhoven in 1957.

A small country seeking foreign markets and in free competition with her partners in Benelux and the European Economic Community must therefore train not only technicians and technologists but see to it that these are also "men of the world" able in several languages, having an understanding of economics and of commerce as well as of technical developments. These requirements are reflected in the curricula of the various technical institutions in Holland.

EDUCATION

The following abbreviations are in common use:

G.L.O. = gewoon lager onderwijs
U.L.O. = uitgebreid lager onderwijs
L.T.S. = lagere technische school
U.T.S. = uitgebreid technische school
H.T.S. = hogere technische school
H.B.S. = hogere burgerschool

Attendance legally need not begin until seven but in practice commences at six years. Eight completed years in the elementary school, G.L.O., is the compulsory minimum. After 6 years, transfer to one of several types of grammar school, Gymnasium, Lyceum, H.B.S., etc., is possible or to an advanced elementary school U.L.O., or to a junior technical school L.T.S.

The L.T.S. is undergoing a transition. The older type gave a 2 year, 13–15 years full-time pre-apprenticeship course; the newer type provides a 3 or 4 year course from 12 years upwards. The proportion of children leaving G.L.O. coming into this form of education in 1953 was 35 per cent. The curriculum for the main course occupies 36 periods of 50 minutes each, averaging approximately:

> Workshop 16, Drawing 6, Maths and Science 3, Dutch 3, Modern language 2, Social and Civic studies 4, Physical education 2, periods.

The preparatory year, in a 3–4 year school, provides for Mathematics and Science 6, General subjects 10, Crafts 14, Physical Training 2.

The workshop practice, after the preparatory year of basic non-trade instruction, then specialises in one or two trades. The subsequent period of apprenticeship is shortened by one year for ex-L.T.S. pupils.

In 1955 there were 202 such schools having 60,238 pupils. Only 16 of these schools were provided publicly, 75 having been established by religious denominations and 113 by secular bodies. In all these types 100 per cent grant is, or can be, paid from public funds. The more successful pupils may, if they desire, proceed further in full-time education.

The U.T.S. provides the next higher level of technical education. This provides a 3 year full-time course, 2 years in college and one in industry, preceded by a one year preparatory course if necessary. The technical level reached approximates to Ordinary National Certificate but comprises a much wider curriculum. This occupies 40 periods per week, each of 50 minutes and is divided approximately as follows:

> Languages, Civics and P.E. 8; Maths and Science 3; Technology, theory 12; Drawing 10; Workshop and Laboratory 7.

Admission may be given after,

(*a*) 2 years grammar school (H.B.S. etc.) or
(*b*) 3 years U.L.O., or
(*c*) L.T.S. but into the preparatory class.

The final diploma is not awarded until after the 1 year probationary period in industry has been satisfactorily served.

The occupational purpose of such schools, which are mainly a post-war development, is to train for the middle levels of industry. This education also has value for future technical teachers.

The able student may, if he so elects, proceed further to the higher technical school (H.T.S.). Such transfer, however, usually takes place from the preparatory class of the U.T.S. direct to the preparatory class of the higher school.

The H.T.S. has as object the education and training of the upper level of technicians. The course lasts, overall, four years of which the whole of the third year is spent in approved experience in industry, sometimes abroad. There is a preparatory year for those who need it.

Approximately 45 per cent of admission comes from grammar schools, 30 per cent from the U.L.O. type school and 25 per cent from the U.T.S. Of the latter some may have had their origin in the L.T.S. The age of entry is normally in the region 16–18 and subsequent qualification is therefore around 20–22 years of age.

The curriculum during the first two years is of course inclined towards the vocational necessities of the third year which is to be spent in industry. After return from this year, however, there is a swing towards general education and languages, partly for its own sake, partly no doubt with an eye to markets, customers and commerce. The following 3 year summary serves as a general indication of the curriculum:

	Periods of 50 m.		
	1st year	2nd year	4th year
General Education, Economics, Languages	5	8	12
Science, Mathematics	15	11	3
Technology	7	8	14
Workshop and Design Practice	12	12	11
	39	39	40

The technical standard of the final examination approximates to Higher National Certificate, but the scope of subjects is much wider. Every candidate will be competent in three languages—Dutch, English, German—will have a good knowledge of accounts, costing, company law, factory organisation, civics and social studies in addition to his technology, design ability and the included 3rd year of industrial experience.

There are now 24 such establishments providing for 9,500 full-time students and dispensing 2,000 diplomas per year. Some of these have parallel evening provision; attendance being for four evenings per week, each evening including 4 periods of 50 minutes each. The course may last 5, 6 or 7 years according to the standard of entry. The cost of evening attendance, including materials, books etc., is estimated at f.300 (£30) per year.

After H.T.S. qualification the student normally takes up responsible employment in industry, but he may, under certain conditions, present himself as a candidate for admission to one of the Technical Universities—Delft or Eindhoven. This privilege was granted by a decree of 30th July, 1952. During the five years 1952–56, 69 per cent of such applications were successful in gaining (by examination) their right of entry. The proportion of such candidates to the whole student body of the Technical University is about 10 per cent—the remainder coming from the traditional grammar school sources.

Thus a second road all the way from apprentice level to "Diplom Ingenieur" at Delft has been pioneered. The number following through from end to end is negligible. That, however, is less serious than it sounds. For between the old ladder of primary school, secondary school, university and the new ladder of L.T.S., U.T.S., H.T.S., Technical University there are many horizontal transfer gangways and the flow along them is invariably from the older to the newer system. At the same time the importance and the quality of grammar school education—for the select 14 per cent who succeed in finding a place there—is in no way being diminished. The 86 per cent however need not suffer lifelong disability through having missed that chance; the "second way" is wide open to anyone with ability.

APPRENTICESHIP

Apprenticeship in Holland, although regulated by a law of 1919, has developed mainly in post-1945 years, as the following figures show:

1938— 2,600
1946— 8,400
1950—19,000
1954—30,000
1955—37,000

The period of contract is usually 3 to 4 years but is reduced by one year for ex-L.T.S. pupils. In some trades no less than 80 per cent come from that source, the average over all trades is 55 per cent. This shows the extent to which such pre-apprenticeship work in school is valued. The responsibility for apprenticeship is undertaken by industrial association, Stichtingen, representing both employers and employees. There are some 27 national and 4 regional organisations of this kind. One of the largest and most well-known is Bemetel. (Metal and Electrical Trades).

In addition to practical and sometimes theoretical instruction in the works the apprentice takes evening or day-release classes. In 1955, approximately 16,000 students, including non-apprentices, were so attending. There are 290 establishments providing these courses for 40 or more different trades. The 4 evenings per week, or two half days, include instruction in Civics, Dutch, Mathematics, Science, Technology and (possibly) Workshop Practice. Efforts are being made to increase the proportion of day-release attendance.

The Ministry of Education has wide responsibilities for the supervision of apprenticeship training and for the end-examination, this being standardised nationally for any one trade. Such examination generally comprises a practical test of 8 days' duration (48 hours), and a theory paper on technology. The certificate gained is a national one, valid throughout Holland.

No account of educational conditions in Holland can conclude without reference to the major part played by religious denominations in the foundation and government of schools, both general and technical. In primary education 70 per cent of the total attendance is in schools that have been "privately" founded, either by the Protestant or Catholic Churches or by secular organisations. This may sometimes cause, especially for technical schools, a dispersion of local facilities into small units, which if coalesced would provide a more economic size.

Educational reforms are pending which would reorganise secondary education under two distinct aspects, namely pre-university and pre-employment (or technical training) and would raise the school-leaving age to 15 or 16.

CONCLUSION

Certain general comparisons with English practice can be made without difficulty.

(1) Continental technical education is largely on a full-time basis, only humble levels being normally attainable by part-time study. This is in part accounted for by thinner population density (France) making it difficult to form satisfactory evening classes. Where population density is higher (Paris, Lille, Marseilles) part-time classes can—but rarely do—lead to full professional status. Holland is rapidly developing evening classes of Higher National Certificate standard. Sandwich courses are rare, except as vacation experience or as whole years of supervised industrial training.

(2) European institutions, more frequently than English, are monotechnic and often restricted to one sex. There is nothing comparable to the "mixed bag" of an English provincial Technical College where all faculties, all levels, all ages, both sexes and all attires produce a

kaleidoscopic student pattern unknown in serious academic circles abroad.

(3) The student Hostel or the equivalent in approved student lodgings is generally regarded as a normal and indispensable part of the school or college. In France even the technical *schools* (collegès techniques, écoles nationales professionnelles) provide in this way for non-local boys and girls. This makes possible the establishment of regional or national colleges for specialised studies and avoids the dissipation of equipment and staff so commonly associated with part-time classes.

(4) The hours of attendance for pupils are substantially higher than in this country. A figure between 35 and 42 hours per week is common in both France and Germany. On top of this there may be homework or design exercises. This heavy load is sometimes imposed on boys and girls as young as 14 years. It does however enable the curriculum to be spread over a wider range of subjects including non-technical fields, such as languages.

(5) In those countries which have developed extensive industrial economies, the need has become urgent to train large numbers of sub-professional technicians. Both by pressure of numbers and for educational reasons these cannot come entirely or even mainly from the grammar schools. They must therefore have their origin in the elementary (secondary modern) school and for their further education a new route—the second way—is being opened up. This in part adopts a sequence of education, perceptibly different from the traditional. It puts practice first and, out of work with the hands, develops trains of thought which then successfully face the underlying theories; the protractor first, Euclid afterwards.

(6) The problem of "liberal education in a technical age" is being faced in all these countries. Many and various are the solutions. It would seem that it is not so much a matter of not knowing the answer but of finding difficulty in formulating the underlying question. In one country art, in another letters, in another citizenship, in another sport, yet again religious instruction are variously offered as correctives to the alleged "narrowness" of technical instruction. Yet on the question of *why* a technical education should be less enlightening than one based on, say, law, no one has a very clear philosophy. The serious decline of the religious attitude to and explanation of life has left a vacuum. That vacuum has yet to be satisfactorily filled and Europe still seeks to formulate its own distinctive ideals.*

* For further discussion on this point see "Technical Education" published by World Council of Y.M.C.A.s, International Institute, Mainau, Constance. Obtainable from London Central Y.M.C.A., Tottenham Court Road, W.C.1. price 8/-. English Edition.

(7) Apprenticeship is generally shorter than in England, the average being 3 years in duration with variations down to 2 or up to 4 years. It commences most frequently between the ages 14–15. The form of training given is thorough but sometimes narrower and often for a specific occupation e.g. lathe-turning rather than machine shop practice in general. Both in Germany and in Holland national end-of-apprenticeship tests are customary and in the former country compulsory. In France, national systems of certification (certificat d'aptitude professionnelle, and examen fin d'apprentissage) are available and commonly used but are not always legally compulsory for further employment.

The short continental apprenticeship, so frequently lauded by critics of the English system has, however, its disadvantages. Only 3 years part-time education above the age of 14 years cannot carry the student very far. In England, 5 years part-time education above 16 can lead to a Higher National Certificate. Moreover apprentice wages in England do not differ greatly from full employment scales for youths of 18–21 in Continental countries. Those apprentices in Western Europe who would climb higher must usually return to a full-time institution, e.g. in Germany the Ingenieurschule, leading to higher technician level.

(8) What lessons can be learnt, what features selected as of particular interest or relevance to England?

(*a*) The French "centre d'apprentissage" providing at once both a trade apprenticeship and further education, under one direction and one roof, is attractive. The nearest equivalent in England is the works school. The centre d'apprentissage has undoubtedly made a great contribution to the commercial and industrial efficiency of France and has happily coincided with the rejuvenation years in that country. Its continued existence is assured under the 1959 reform of education, as part of the general system.

(*b*) The Dutch chain of 3 technical schools from age 12–13 to 21–22 or higher is noteworthy. From age 12 a child may follow an educational sequence radically different from that which has been traditional and yet finish up at University level. It provides an alternative educational road, based on practice first, advanced theory later.

(*c*) The German Ingenieurschule (or Höhere Fachschule or Technicum) providing 2–3 years of full-time education *after* apprenticeship, up to a level comparable with Higher National Certificate but on a broader curriculum, including economics and liberal subjects, is worthy of consideration. An approximate equivalent now exists in this country through the sandwich courses in Colleges of Technology.

(*d*) The compulsory part-time day release, existing in Germany in present form since 1919 is clearly a feature of relevance in connection with the Education Act, 1944. But even the German law has yet to be fully implemented in all districts to the full number of hours. It has been successful only since it became firmly tied up with vocational interest. Where vocational interest is lacking, as with the unskilled worker, the Berufsschule has not yet made much headway. Perhaps for that reason many occupations in Germany have been somewhat arbitrarily coded as worthy of full apprenticeship (Lehrberufe) which in England are not always so regarded. In addition there are the learnerships or minor training schemes (Anlernberufe) usually of 2 years' duration. All these through systematic training provide at least an incentive towards education and certification.

In France by contrast, Loi Astier, also of 1919 and providing for part-time day release of apprentices, has never been satisfactorily implemented. It is for practical purposes a dead letter and full-time training in a centre d'apprentissage is now the recognised means whereby one-third of France's apprentices are trained and educated. Many may feel that there should be scope in a wide and flexible apprenticeship system for both these systems to operate as alternatives. Some skills are best learned on the job in the factory or the shop; others (e.g. typewriting, cookery, librarianship) may be more suitably learned wholly or partly in full-time pre-employment courses.

(*e*) The six nations of the European Economic Community (France, Germany, Italy, Belgium, Holland, Luxembourg), now aim at the free exchange of men, money and materials within their own area—the Common Market. It is inevitable, therefore, that a professional man qualified in one country will sooner or later practise in one of the others. Some standardisation of the various qualifications current and some assimilation of the respective systems of education is therefore bound to take place. Preliminary conversations on this point have already been held.

Britain, although outside the Six, will certainly have to assure herself that the quality and quantity of her technical education is at least the equal of that offered in European countries, different as her system of training may be, and may remain. This necessity applies as much to apprenticeship training as to graduate or technician levels, a correct adjustment and orientation in the years 15–18 is the key to future attainment.

GLOSSARY

[Many terms of art are inevitably used in this report. Definitions in the sense in which we have used them in this report are given below. We have aimed at providing definitions that will be illuminating to the non-expert reader. They are therefore not to be regarded as precise official definitions nor as the only possible ones. Where there is a conflict of usage we have usually pointed this out.]

ALL-AGE SCHOOL
A school containing children throughout the statutory age-range from 5 to 15.

APPRENTICESHIP
A term used in this report to cover a wide variety of organised schemes of training at work, extending over a number of years (usually three to five); we have not confined it to the narrow legal meaning of the term, i.e. indentured apprenticeship. It may or may not carry with it any educational obligations or facilities.

BILATERAL SCHOOL
A secondary school providing, in two clearly defined sides, different courses for children of differing grades of intelligence. It is, however, often difficult to distinguish in practice between bilateral and other schools catering for the whole range of ability (e.g. comprehensive schools q.v.).

BLOCK RELEASE
A form of day-time education in working hours by which employers free students (with pay) to attend technical colleges for an unbroken period, followed by an unbroken period of work. The amount of time available for study is often only a little more than that provided under part-time day release (q.v.) arrangements, but in some cases it may fall only a little short of that provided on a sandwich course (q.v.). Evening classes are normally used to bridge the period between spells of block release.

"BULGE", The
The term commonly applied to the exceptionally high age-groups moving through the schools as a result of the sharp rise in the birth-rate in the years 1946, 1947 and 1948.

BUTLER ACT
The Education Act of 1944. Mr. R. A. Butler was President of the Board of Education at the time.

BYE-TERM LEAVING
The school year conventionally begins in September and ends in July. Pupils who leave at Christmas or Easter may be described as "bye-term" leavers.

CITY AND GUILDS (see also Regional Examining Unions)
"The City and Guilds of London Institute for the Advancement of Technical Education"; the largest of the examining bodies in technical education, formed in 1878. It holds examinations and gives guidance in relation to a wide variety of courses for craftsmen and technicians. Intermediate, Final and Full Technological Certificates are awarded. (See page 328).

COLLEGE-BASED STUDENTS
Students following sandwich courses (q.v.) who are not primarily employees of any particular employer (though they temporarily become employees during their periods of experience in industry). In other words, the college is their main base; they earn wages only while employed, and for the rest of the year are eligible for grant from public funds. See paragraph 561.

COLLEGE OF FURTHER EDUCATION—Defined in paragraph 471 under "Local colleges".

COMMONERS
Students at Oxford and Cambridge who have not won an open scholarship (q.v.) or exhibition (although they may well hold a State Scholarship).

COMPREHENSIVE SCHOOL
This term was first used in England to describe a secondary school intended to cater for the secondary education of all the pupils over 11 in a given area, organised as a unified whole and not in clearly defined grammar, modern and technical sides. By contrast, the term "multi-lateral" was used to describe a secondary school with similar spread of ability but organised in three clearly defined sides and "bilateral" for a school with two of these sides. In practice the word "comprehensive" is being increasingly applied to all publicly provided schools which are directed to the needs of the full range of aptitudes and abilities of pupils between the ages of 11 and 19. Except where otherwise stated it is in this latter sense that we use it in this report.

CONSULTATIVE COMMITTEE (See also Hadow and Spens Reports)
The statutory body appointed under the Act of 1899 and continuing until 1944 to advise the Board of Education on educational matters referred to it.

COUNTY COLLEGE
An institution to be provided by an L.E.A. (q.v.) under the 1944 Act and attended part-time on a compulsory basis by young people under 18 not in full-time attendance at a school or other educational institution. The term is sometimes used to cover any institution which might be attended by young people receiving compulsory part-time education, and sometimes to refer only to an institution designed to provide for those whose education at this stage will not be mainly vocational. Except where otherwise stated we use the term in the more restricted sense.

CRAFTSMAN—Defined on page 328

DAY RELEASE (See Part-Time Day Release)

Day Continuation School
An institution providing education by day for young workers released by their employers.

Direct Grant Grammar Schools
Direct grant grammar schools receive grant direct from the Ministry of Education (as distinct from the local education authority—q.v.) and charge fees which in the case of day pupils (but not boarders) are graduated according to income. Grant at present is at the rate of £39 per year per pupil below the Sixth Form and £105 in the Sixth Form. A main condition governing the admission of pupils is that the school should provide free places to the extent of 25 per cent of its intake to pupils who have spent at least two years in a maintained (q.v.) primary school; they may be offered either directly by, or at the expense of the school, or, through the agency, or at the expense of the local education authority, which also has the right to require additional places. A few nursery and technical schools also receive direct grant.

"Eleven (11) Plus"
The conventional term used to cover the various techniques (e.g. examination, intelligence tests) which a local education authority (q.v.) may use to allocate pupils leaving primary schools at or about the age of 11 to the appropriate type of secondary education.

Evening Institute—Defined in paragraph 472

Extended Course
Any extended course in this report refers to a fifth-year course in a secondary modern school (i.e. a school from which at present most pupils leave during, or at the end of, their fourth year). See paragraph 96.

External Examination
An examination set by some body outside the school attended by the candidates. Most commonly used of the examinations for the General Certificate of Education (q.v.).

Fisher Act
The Education Act, 1918, passed when Mr. H. A. L. Fisher was President of the Board of Education.

Form Entry
A method of describing the size and organisation of a secondary school by the number of forms which are admitted each year, e.g. 2-form entry, 3-form entry. By this conventional reckoning a form should consist of 30 pupils; in practice it is often 35.

Forster Act
The Elementary Education Act of 1870, introduced by Mr. W. E. Forster, the Vice-President of the Committee of the Privy Council on Education.

Further Education—See Chapter 29
Vocational and non-vocational education provided for young people who are over the school-leaving age, and for adults. Many of the students are of secondary school age, i.e. under 19. The official term does not include the universities.

General Certificate of Education (G.C.E.)
A certificate awarded as a result of a national examination, set by any one of nine examining boards. The first examinations for the G.C.E. were held in 1951. The G.C.E., for which candidates are examined at Ordinary and Advanced levels, is the successor to the School Certificate and Higher School Certificate. It differs from them in being a subject examination, which means that a candidate may offer any number of subjects at a sitting (from one subject upwards), whereas the regulations for the School and Higher School Certificates required the candidate to sit a given number of subjects, chosen from prescribed groups, at one and the same examination. The Ordinary level is customarily taken at the age of 16 or (more rarely) at 15 or 14, and though it may be taken in one subject alone, grammar school (q.v.) pupils usually take from four or five to eight or nine subjects. The Advanced level is taken at 18 or thereabouts, and usually in two to four closely related subjects.

Graduate Teacher
A teacher holding a university degree. Teachers holding certain other professional qualifications are recognised for salary purposes as "graduate equivalent". Graduate teachers may or may not have received a year's professional training, for which they receive a Diploma or Certificate in Education.

Grammar School
Type of Secondary School providing an academic course from 11 to 16 or 18. It provides the main route of access to the universities and professions. The term is used to cover 3 types of school.

(*a*) maintained grammar schools, in which no fees are charged;
(*b*) direct grant grammar schools (q.v.);
(*c*) some independent schools (q.v.).

We have sometimes used the term to cover the first type only—more often to cover all three types.

Group Examination
An examination in which candidates are required to take a given number of subjects of which some are compulsory and others are selected in a set proportion from prescribed groups of subjects. All of the required subjects must be taken at one and the same time.

Hadow Report
Report of the Consultative Committee (q.v.), under the chairmanship of Sir Henry Hadow, on "The Education of the Adolescent", published in 1926. It recommended *inter alia*, the provision of separate senior schools for children over 11 years of age.

Higher Education
Systematic education beyond the level of G.C.E.(A) leading to a University degree or to qualifications of equivalent standard in a College of Advanced Technology or a Technical College.

Independent Schools
Schools which do not receive money from public funds and therefore depend on fees and (in some instances) on private endowments. Two types are to be distinguished:

(*a*) independent schools recognised as efficient after inspection by the Ministry;
(*b*) other independent schools (with which, unless otherwise stated, this report is not concerned.)

JUNIOR SCHOOL (JUNIOR DEPARTMENT)
Primary school (or department) for pupils of about 7 to 11 years of age, maintained by a local education authority.

"LITERACY"—The special sense in which we have used this word is defined in paragraph 399 and 400.

LOCAL EDUCATION AUTHORITY (L.E.A.)
Local Authority (county council or county borough council) responsible for providing and administering all stages of education in its area. There are 129 local education authorities in England. The local education authority exercises its functions through an Education Committee. The main executive officer is called the Chief Education Officer or, sometimes, the Director of Education, the Education Officer or the Secretary for Education.

MAIN SCHOOL
The forms in a grammar school (q.v.) below the Sixth Form (q.v.).

MAINTAINED SCHOOL
The largest category of schools in England. It includes all those schools for which the costs are wholly met out of rates and taxes by the local education authority (q.v.) and also the categories of "aided and special agreement" schools, in which a small part of the costs are met by the Managers or Governors of the school. (Most aided schools are associated with the Church of England or the Roman Catholic Church.)

"MINORITY TIME"
The time available to the Sixth Former for the study of subjects other than those in which he is specialising. See Chapter 25.

MODERN SCHOOL
A maintained secondary school providing education for those children not selected at 11 years of age for grammar or technical schools.
The percentage of such selected children varies from area to area and in consequence the range of ability and the courses found in modern schools also vary. On the average of the whole country, however, the modern schools contain a clear majority of all pupils of secondary school age.
Schools of this type provide a general education with a practical bias, and an increasing number offer extended courses (q.v.), some based on vocational interests, others leading to external examinations including G.C.E. (q.v.) at "O" level.

NATIONAL CERTIFICATES AND DIPLOMAS
Certificates and Diplomas at Ordinary and Higher levels awarded jointly by the Ministry of Education and various Professional Institutions (q.v.) concerned. The Ordinary level is broadly equivalent on a subject for subject basis to G.C.E. at Advanced level (q.v.) and the Higher level is, on the limited range of subjects taken, broadly equivalent to ordinary degree

standard. Certificates are obtained by part-time study, and Diplomas by full-time courses including sandwich courses. See paragraph 481 and page 331.

NATIONAL SERVICE SURVEY
Survey of a random sample of men beginning their National Service; conducted for the Council between 1956 and 1958 with the agreement of the War Office and the Air Ministry. (See Volume II, Part Two).

"NUMERACY"
Defined in paragraph 401.

OPEN SCHOLARSHIP
A scholarship to a university or college awarded by the university or college after a competitive examination open to candidates within certain specified age limits.

OPERATIVE—Defined on page 328.

PART-TIME DAY RELEASE (P.D.R.)
The system by which employers allow certain employees time off from work without loss of pay for the purpose of obtaining further education. Part-time day release courses are arranged by technical colleges in association with local industry and provide part-time education, usually for one day, sometimes more days, per week. Most of the students are apprentices since day release is a feature of most agreed training schemes in industry. Some firms give day release to other employees also.

PRIMARY EDUCATION
Primary education covers the nursery, infant and junior stages up to about the age of 11.

PROFESSIONAL INSTITUTIONS
Organisations of the professions concerned whose objects are to advance their own branches of specialised knowledge by the exchange of information and views amongst members and to secure and maintain proper standards in preparation for and in the practice of their professions. A few examples are the Institutions of Civil, Electrical and Mechanical Engineers, the Royal Institute of Chemistry, and the Royal Institute of British Architects.

REGIONAL EXAMINING UNIONS
Bodies which conduct examinations of work done mainly in further education. Each has its own defined territory and they work in association with the City and Guilds of London Institute (q.v.).

SANDWICH COURSES
Courses consisting of alternate periods, usually 5–6 months but not less than 19 weeks, of full-time study in a technical college and of supervised experience in industry, extending over a number of years. See paragraph 561.

SECONDARY SCHOOL
A school providing full-time education starting at the age of 11 and extending to 15 and upwards.

SELECTIVE SCHOOL
Schools (grammar and technical) to which admission is confined to pupils whose performance, as measured by the local education authority's selection procedure, indicates ability to benefit from a more academic kind of education. Direct grant (q.v.) and independent efficient (q.v.) schools may in wider usage also be reckoned as selective schools.

SETTING
Re-division of forms in a given year into "sets" of pupils of roughly equal ability in a particular subject e.g. mathematics or modern languages.

SIXTH FORM
The upper part of a grammar or technical school, entered ordinarily at 15 or 16 after taking some subjects at the Ordinary level of the G.C.E. examination (q.v.). A full Sixth Form course lasts two to three years. See Part Five.

SOCIAL SURVEY
A survey carried out for the Council in 1957 by the Central Office of Information of boys and girls who had left maintained secondary schools (grammar, technical and modern) in 1954 and 1955. See Volume II, Part One.

SPECIAL SCHOOL
A school for handicapped children suffering from a disability of mind or body.

SPECIALISATION
The practice in English Sixth Forms by which pupils concentrate the major portion of their studies on two, three or, in rarer instances four, subjects with a view to taking them at Advanced level in the G.C.E. examination (q.v.) and in many cases to studying them further at a university. See Chapter 25.

SPECIALIST TEACHING—SPECIALIST TEACHER
Teaching by a master or mistress who teaches virtually only the one subject in which he has gained his main qualification.

SPENS REPORT
Report of the Consultative Committee (q.v.) in 1938, of which the Chairman was Sir Will Spens, on "Secondary Education, with special Reference to Grammar Schools and Technical High Schools".

STATE SCHOLARSHIPS
Scholarships awarded by the Ministry of Education, for the purpose of attending a university, usually on the results of the examination for the General Certificate of Education or of the open scholarship (q.v.) examinations of the universities and colleges.

STATE SCHOLARSHIPS (MATURE STUDENTS)
The purpose of these scholarships is to provide an opportunity for university education to men and women over 25 years of age who were unable to take a university course at the normal age but who have pursued some form of continued study since leaving school.

STREAMING
The division of the pupils [in a year] into forms based on their general ability. The top form is always "A". The "C" stream is conventionally used

to describe the lowest third in ability, although in a particular school the lowest may be the "D" or "E" stream, according to numbers.

SUBJECT EXAMINATION
An examination such as that for the G.C.E. in which a candidate may be examined in one or more subjects of his choice. To be contrasted with a group examination (q.v.).

"SWING" The
The relatively recent, yet pronounced, tendency among the pupils of the Sixth Form to specialise in science.

TECHNICAL COLLEGE (area, regional and local)
See paragraph 471.

TECHNICAL SCHOOL
A selective (q.v.) secondary school, providing an integrated academic and technical course from 11 (or, commonly in the past, 13) to 16 or 18 with a vocational flavour, and leading to the universities and colleges of advanced technology, as well as directly into industry, commerce and the professions.

TECHNICIAN—Defined on page 327.

TECHNOLOGIST—Defined on page 327.

TRAINING COLLEGE
College for training teachers, mostly non-graduates starting at the age of 18 or above. Hitherto, the course in nearly all colleges other than specialist colleges (e.g. for physical education) has lasted for two years. Starting in 1960, this is to be extended to three years. Institutes of Education (which, in all but one case, are part of a university) exercise supervision over, approve courses and conduct examinations for, training colleges.

"TREND" The
The tendency to stay at school beyond 15, e.g. in modern schools by taking an extended course (q.v.) or in grammar schools by taking a Sixth Form course (q.v.).

TRIPARTITE SYSTEM
The division of secondary education into separate grammar, technical and modern schools. See Chapter 2.

WORK-BASED STUDENTS
The "work-based" student is an employee, released by his employer for his periods of study at a college during a sandwich course (q.v.) and normally in receipt of wages from the employer for the whole year.

YOUTH EMPLOYMENT SERVICE
The Youth Employment Service helps young persons in the transition from school to work. It is available to help and advise all young persons up to the age of 18 or until they leave school. It is provided in most areas by the local education authorities or occasionally by the Ministry of Labour and National Service. The Minister of Labour and National Service is responsible to Parliament for the whole Service.

Index

Contents of Volume II

Reference has been made from time to time throughout this Report to three surveys sponsored by the Council and referred to as the "Social Survey", the "National Service Survey" and the "Technical Courses Survey".

Brief particulars are as follows:—

Description	Undertaken through	When undertaken	Numbers involved	Ages of those in the Survey
Social Survey	Central Office of Information	Spring–Summer, 1957	3,960	16–19 years (boys and girls)
National Service Survey	(i) Army War Office	1956–1957	6,850	18–26 years (men)
	(ii) R.A.F. Air Ministry	1957–1958	2,000	18–26 years (men)
Technical Courses				
(i) National Certificate	117 Technical Colleges	Dec. 1956 (follow-up) 1958	9,000	mainly 16–26 years
(ii) City and Guilds of London Institute	114 Technical Colleges	Summer, 1958	7,000	,,

The findings of these surveys extended beyond the length of a normal appendix and it has therefore seemed best to publish them separately in Volume II to this report. The contents are:—

Printed in England under the Authority of Her Majesty's Stationery Office
by McCorquodale, London S.E.

Wt. 3265 K200 12/59